BLUES RECORDS

January, 1943 to December, 1966

© 1968 Mike Leadbitter & Neil Slaven

Published by
HANOVER BOOKS LTD.,
4 Mill Street,
London, W.1.,
England.

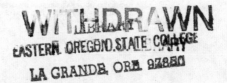

Sole Selling Agents for the U.S.A. and Canada
OAK PUBLICATIONS
33 West 60th Street,
New York, NY 10023

Library of Congress Catalog No. 68-57795

PRINTED IN GREAT BRITAIN BY OFFSET LITHOGRAPHY BY
BILLING AND SONS LTD., GUILDFORD AND LONDON

BLUES RECORDS : 1943-1966

INTRODUCTION:

Neil and I began the long task of assembling this Discography in late 1965 with the idea of providing a much needed companion volume for "Blues & Gospel Records : 1902–1942" by Godrich & Dixon. However the sheer volume of Gospel recordings issued since 1943 caused us to drop the idea of their inclusion, and thus this volume covers Blues only. We began by amalgamating all the published artist discographies we knew of with those in my personal files and then compiled our own on any artist not yet covered with the help of our co-workers. When the first draft was ready we checked every item when possible and the scores of corrections that resulted from this forced us to produce a second draft. Though several last minute corrections and additions had to be inserted, this draft was the one used by the Publisher.

This discography includes the work of many well known Researchers and full acknowledgement is given to them. Most of the more obscure data listed is published for the first time and has been collected over the last two years by myself and several friends with the aim of making this Book as complete as possible. We have tried to include every artist who is of interest to Blues collectors. Several artists who made good Blues recordings had to be excluded due to space, while only the initial recordings of others are included for the same reason. To cover the work of these and other artists who recorded under the various headings of "Rock 'N Roll", "Rhythm & Blues", "Jazz Blues" or "City Blues" a second Discography is being planned.

We both hope that this book will be enjoyed by Collector and Discographer alike and that it will provide a solid foundation for further research and field-work. It took an awful lot of work, love and time to get it finished, but we feel it was worth it, and hope that everyone who buys it will too.

Mike Leadbitter (May 1968)

Blues Records : 1943-66

By Mike Leadbitter & Neil Slaven

THE AUTHORS

Mike Leadbitter is 26 years old and married. He has lived most of his life in Sussex, and became interested in Blues at the age of 14. Leaving school at 16 he began collecting records in earnest and corresponding with other collectors. In 1961 he started a "Blues Appreciation Society" with Simon Napier another local enthusiast and soon after the results of his early research appeared in specialist magazines like "Jazz Statistics" or "Blues Research". In 1963 he and Simon decided to start producing their own magazine, and the result was the now well known "Blues Unlimited", which continues to be published monthly and has an international reputation. Mike continued to write for other Blues or R & B publications and it was through a request for help from one of these, "R & B Monthly", that he met the co-editor Neil Slaven. Though Neil's home was in Surrey, their ages and interests were in common and friendship resulted. In 1965 they decided to produce this book between them, but it only began to reach the completion stage after Mike toured the Deep South of the U.S.A. in 1967 collecting much of the badly needed data.

Today Mike continues to co-edit "Blues Unlimited" and is well known on both sides of the Atlantic to buyers and producers of Blues recordings. A civil-servant by day, all his work on Blues has to be done in the evening or at week-ends. Neil too is associated with "Blues Unlimited" and works for Decca Records in London. He is best known for his writing through "R & B Monthly" and as one of the original partners in the now very successful "Blue Horizon" Record Company.

EXPLANATORY NOTES

1) THE DISCOGRAPHY
None of the individual discographies have been copied out in parrot fashion from previously published ones. All have been carefully prepared, checked and revised. Some, like those of Brownie McGhee, Sonny Terry or Sleepy John Estes are a little "weak" due to lack of help with or interest in their recordings. Where material arrived too late for inclusion in the main work, it has been included in a special section at the end.

2) EUROPEAN RELEASES
Unless European releases cover material recorded and only issued in Europe, then they are excluded. This decision was made to enable us to provide a discography that is as easy as possible to follow. European Blues releases are however thoroughly documented in Standard Jazz reference works.

3) THE ARTISTS
These are all listed in strict alphabetical order. Where an artist has recorded under his own name, then all his material is listed under that name. (e.g. Professor Longhair. See under Roy Byrd). If an artist is only known by a pseudonym, then he is listed under this. (e.g. Carolina Slim is under C). Where a part pseudonym is used or a nick-name, then the artist will be listed under his surname. (e.g. Shy Guy Douglas is under D). Where identities behind pseudonyms are known then full cross references are provided.

4) MATRIX NUMBERS
All matrix numbers where known are given for completeness sake, even though they may only be the issue number with A or B suffixes or numbers allocated by pressing plants.

5) LOCATIONS AND DATES
These have all been carefully checked and are as accurate as possible. Where there is doubt concerning a location or date then the information is followed by a question mark.

6) ABBREVIATIONS
a) Record Labels: All label names are given in full except for: —
RIH = Recorded in Hollywood   SIW = Sittin' In With   ABC = ABC—Paramount

b) Instruments: The abbreviations used to denote instruments are: —

Accdn	—	Accordian	Hca	—	Harmonica
Alt	—	Alto saxophone	Mdln	—	Mandolin
Bari	—	Baritone saxophone	Org	—	Organ
Bjo	—	Banjo	Pno	—	Piano
Bs	—	String bass	Tbn	—	Trombone
Bs—gtr	—	Guitar played as a bass	Ten	—	Tenor saxophone
Clt	—	Clarinet	Tpt	—	Trumpet
Dms	—	Drums	Vcl (s)	—	Vocal (s)
El	—	Electric bass	Vcl grp	—	Vocal group
Flt	—	Flute	Vln	—	Violin
Gtr	—	Acoustic or Electric guitar	Wbd	—	Washboard

7) ACKNOWLEDGEMENTS

The following publications have been extensively used: —

Blues Research	— Anthony Rotante & Paul Sheatsley	Jazz Records Jazz Report	— Jorgen G. Jepson — Paul Affeldt
Blues Unlimited	— Simon Napier & Mike Leadbitter	Jazz Statistics Record Research	— Otto Fluckiger — Len Kunstadt
Jazz Directory	— Albert J. McCarthy	R & B Monthly	— Neil Slaven & Mike Vernon

Plus the variously published works of Anthony Rotante, Derek Coller, Marcel Chauvard, Jacques Demetre, Paul Oliver, Chris Strachwitz and Mack McCormick.

Unfortunately the scores of collectors who sent in data to us are just too numerous to mention individually, but we would like to thank them all for their help and support. This was invaluable and deeply appreciated.

Several names must be mentioned though for the extensive help they provided by actual field-research or through loaning us their files. These are: —
John Holt, who was responsible for the Lightnin' Hopkins discography,
Dave Sax, who was responsible for the John Lee Hooker discography,
Wolfie Baum, John Broven, Neil Paterson, Chris Strachwitz, Simon Napier, Kerry Kudlacek, Mike Rowe, Bruce Bastin, Bruce Bromberg, Larry Skoog, Fred L. Davis, Rick Milne, Don Kent, Bob Koester, Peter Welding, Gary Paulsen, Henry Vestine, Frank Scott, Darryl Stolper, Pete Lowry, Kurt Mohr, Karl Knudsen, Eddie Shuler, Bill Holford, Jay Miller, Steve La Vere, and Paul Sheatsley.

J. T. ADAMS

Real name John Tyler Adams. Born in Morganfield, Kentucky on February 17, 1911.
See under Shirley Griffiths.

WOODROW ADAMS

Born Tchula, Mississippi in 1917.

WOODROW ADAMS & THE THREE B's
Vcl/gtr. with Sylvester?, hca; Joe Martin, dms.   Memphis, 1952
C 1030   Pretty Baby Blues   Checker 757
C 1031   She's Done Come And Gone   -

WOODROW ADAMS & THE BOOGIE BLUES BLASTERS
Vcl/hca/gtr. with pno; Joe Hill Louis, lead gtr; Joe Martin, dms.
                                                                 Memphis 1955
MR 5032   Wine Head Woman   Meteor 5018
MR 5033   Baby You Just Don't Know   -

WOODROW ADAMS
Vcl/hca. with Dacy Williams, Curtis Allen, gtrs; Joe Martin, dms.
                                                                 Memphis, 1961
HB 2523   Something on My Mind   Home of the Blues 109
HB 2524   Sad and Blue   -

Note: Robinsonville, Mississippi Artist.

ALABAMA SLIM

See under Ralph Willis.

LITTLE DAVID ALEXANDER

Vcl. with Hammie Nixon, hca; Booker T. Washington, pno. Chicago ?
            Sweet Patootie   Ebony 1005
            Dupree Blues   -

Note: these may be edited pre-1942 sides.

DUDLEY ALEXANDER

Vcl/accdn. with Alex Robert, vln; Vincent Frank, wbd.   Houston April, 1959
            Baby Please Don't Go   "77" LA 12/3

TEXAS ALEXANDER (the late)

WITH BENTON'S BUSY BEES
Alger Alexander, vcl/gtr, with Buster Pickens, pno; Leon Benton, gtr.
                                                    Quinn Studio, Houston, 1950
1604   Bottom's Blues   Freedon 1538
1605   Crossroads   -   , Blues Classics 16

BIG CLYDE ALLEN

AND THE MOVIN' MASTERS BAND
Vcl. with ten; pno (-I); gtrs; dms.   Los Angeles, 1966
MR-100-12-A   Stranger At My Door   Movin' 100-12
MR-100-12-B   My Baby's Coming Home -I   -

GEORGE ALLEN

See under George Smith

RICH AMERSON

Vcl.
                                                    Livingstone, Ala., Jan/Feb, 1950.
            Black Woman   Folkways FE 4417, P 417
            Railroad   Folkways FE 4471, P 417

8

John Henry
Add Earthy Anne Coleman, vcl:
                     Jonah   Folkways FE 4418, P 418

Note: Folk tales and the like by this artist are not included.

IRA AMOS

Born Houma, Louisiana?
Vcl. with   Los Angeles, 1950
MM 1525   What Have You Been Doing To Me   Modern 20-817
MM 1526
MM 1527   Blue And Disgusted   Modern 20-817
Vcl. with Jesse Belvin, pno; Charles "Chuck" Norris, gtr.   Los Angeles, 1951
OCT-23-19 I'm Lonesome   Octive 23-20-I
OCT-20-19 Raining The Blues   Octive 23-20-2

NEW ORLEANS SLIM
Same, but add 2nd gtr; dms.
OCT-23-20 All Night Long   Octive 23-20-5
           (rev. by Les Mozart)

CURTIS AMY

Hubert Robinson, vcl. with William Smith, tpt; Curtis Amy, alt; Phillip Williams, ten;
Oma Galloway, pno; Joyce McQuarn, gtr; Nat White, bs.   Houston, 1947
618A   Realization Blues   Gold Star 618
618B   Sleeping Blues   -

Note: This record included only out of interest. Hubert Robinson also recorded under his
own name, q.v.

JIMMY ANDERSON

Jimmy Anderson & His Joy Jumpers
Vcl/hca. with Al Foreman, Bobby McBride, gtrs; Austin Broussard, dms.
                                                              Crowley La. 1962
Z-7494   I Wanna Boogie   Zynn 1014, Dot 16341
Z-7495   Angel Please   -   -
JIMMY ANDERSON
Same: Crowley, La. 1962/63
A   Naggin'   Excello 2220
B   Nothing In This World   -
A   Going Through The Park   Excello 2227
B   I'm A King Bee   -
Same: Crowley, La. 1964.
A   Love Me Babe   Excello 2257
B   Going Crazy Over T.V.   -

Note: Crowley, La. artist.

PINK ANDERSON

Vcl/gtr. with Jumbo Lewis, wbd (-1).   Charlottesville, La. May 29, 1950
           John Henry   Riverside RLP 12-611, RLP 148
           Every Day In The Week -1   -   -
           The Ship Titanic   -   -
           Greasy Greens   -   -
           Wreck Of The Old 97   -   -
           I've Got Mine   -   -
           He's In The Jailhouse Now   -   -
Vcl/gtr.   New York City, prob. 1960
           Baby Please Don't Go   Bluesville BVLP 1308
           My Baby Left Me This Morning   -
           Mama Where Did You Stay Last Night   -

9

Big House Blues	-
Meet Me In The Bottom	-
Weeping Willow Blues	-
Baby I'm Going Away	-
Thousand Women Blues	-
I Had My Fun	-
Everyday In The Week	-
Try Some Of That	Bluesville BVLP 1055

Vcl/gtr.

New York City, 1961

I Got Mine	Bluesville BVLP 1051
Greasy Greens	-
I Got A Woman 'Way Cross Town	-
Travelin' Man	-
Ain't Nobody Home But Me	-
That's No Way To Do	-
In The Jailhouse Now	-
South Forest Boogie	-
Chicken	-
Walk Through The Streets Of The City	-

Vcl/gtr.

New York City ? 1962

The Titanic	Bluesville BVLP 1071
Boweevil	-
John Henry	-
Betty And Dupree	-
Sugar Baby	-
The Wreck Of The Old 97	-
I Will Fly Away	-
The Kaiser	-
In The Evening	-

ARCHIBALD

Real name Leon T. Gross.
Vcl/pno. with Dave Bartholomew's Band: Tpt; saxes; gtr; bs; dms;

New Orleans, March 23, 1950

IM 164	Stack-A-Lee Pt. 2	Imperial 5068, 5358, 5563
IM 165	Stack-A-Lee Pt. 1	- -
IM 166	Shake Baby Shake	Imperial 5082
IM 167	Ballin' With Archie	-
IM 173	Frantic Chick	Imperial 5089

Note: An alternative take of IM 167 was issued on French Polydor 27.721 and credited
to T-Bone Walker. Reverse 5089 by Dave Bartholomew.

Similar:

New Orleans, 1950

IM 202	My Gal	Imperial 5101
IM 203	Little Miss Muffett	Colony 105
IM 204	Crescent City Bounce	-
IM 205	She's Scattered Everywhere	Imperial 5101

Similar:

New Orleans, 1952

IM 481	Early Morning Blues	Imperial 5212
IM 482	House Party Blues	unissued
IM 483	Great Big Eyes	Imperial 5212
IM 484	Those Little Reds	unissued

Notes: New Orleans artist. Though previously listed as having been recorded in Los
Angeles, these sides are definite New Orleans recordings. The Band present is definitely
Bartholomew's.

ALPHONSE ARDOIN

Vcl (-1)/accdn. with Canray Fontenot, Vcl (-2)/vln; Reven Reed or Isom, Reed, triangle.

Falls Church, Va., July 24, 1966.

Les Blues Du Voyageur -1	Melodeon 7330
Jolie Bassette -2	

Quo' Faire	1	-
Bon Soir Moreau	-2	-
La Robe Baree	-1	-
Le Chicot A Bois-Sec	-1	-
'Tit Monde		-
Valse A Canray	-1	-
La Valse De La Prison	-2	-
La Valse A Oberlin	-1	-
Les Haricots		-
Fait Pas Ca!	-1	-
Duralde Ramble	-1	-
'Tit Galop	-1	-
Allez-Vous En	-1	-

BILLY BOY ARNOLD

Real name William Arnold. Born Chicago, Illinois on September 16, 1935

BILLY (BOY) ARNOLD
Vcl/hca. with Bob Carter's Orch: Ten; pno; gtr; bs; dms.   Chicago, 1953

| E3CB-4064 | I Ain't Got No Money | Cool 103 |
| E3CB-4065 | Hello Stranger | - |

BILLY BOY
Vcl/hca. with Henry Gray, pno; Jody Williams, gtr; Milton Rector, el-bs; Earl Phillips, dms.
                                                                 Chicago, Spring 1955

| 55-262 | I Was Fooled | Vee Jay 146 |
| 55-263 | I Wish You Would | -   , LP1020, Vivid 109 |

Quinn Wilson, el-bs. replaces Rector   Chicago, 1955

55-344	Don't Stay Out All Night	Vee Jay 171
55-345	I Ain't Got You	-
55-346	Here's My Picture	Vee Jay 192
55-347	You've Got Me Wrong	-

Vcl/hca. with Henry Grey, pno; Sylvester Thompson, Odell Campbell, gtrs; Fred Below, dms.
                                                                 Chicago, November 1956

56-575	My Heart Is Crying	Vee Jay 238
56-576	How Come You Leave Heaven	unissued
56-577	Heartache And Trouble	unissued
56-578	Kissing At Midnight	Vee Jay 238

Vcl/hca. With Sunnyland Slim, pno; Sylvester & Mack Thompson, gtrs; Reynolds
Howard, dms.   Chicago, September 1957

57-749	Prisoner's Plea	Vee Jay 260, Vivid 109
57-750	No, No, No, No. No	unissued
57-751	Rockinitis	Vee Jay 260
57-752	Every Day, Every Night	unissued

BILLY BOY ARNOLD
Vcl/hca. with Lafayette Leake, pno; Mighty Joe Young, gtr; Lee Jackson, bs-gtr; Junior
Blackman, dms.   Chicago, January 7, 1964

A	You're My Girl	Bluesville 827, Prestige 7389
B	School Time	- ' -
	Goin' By The River	Prestige 7389
	You Don't Love Me No More	-
	Oh Baby	-
	Evaleena	-
	I Love Only You	-
	Two Drinks of Wine	-
	I'll Forget About You	-
	Billy Boy's Blues	-
	You Better Cut That Out	-
	Get Out of Here	-

VIRGIL ASBURY

Lead vcl. with Morgan White, Floyd James, Henry Landers, John Bell, John Gibson, Lemon

Jefferson, vcls.   Retrieve Farm, Texas, Fall, 1951
         Forty-Four Hammers   Elektra EKL-296

NETTIE DADY AVERY

NETTIE DADY AVERY w. FLORIDA GATORS
Vcl. with unk. group incl. wbd.
         Realty Blues   Asco 1009
         Got Nobody   -

B

BABY FACE
See under Leroy Foster

BABY FACE LEROY
See under Leroy Foster

BACK PORCH BOYS
See under Alec Seward.

HOUSTON BAINES
See under Houston Boines

C. B. BAKER
No details: Houston, 1951
         Unknown titles   SIW 623
2392   Skin to Skin   SIW 625
2393   Goin' Back Home   -

SAM BAKER
Vcl. with saxes: gtr: bs: dm s.   Nashville, 1964
A   Sweet Little Angel   Athens 212
B   Tossin' and Turnin'   -

Note: Later recordings not included.

WILLIE BAKER
Vcl. with ten (-1); gtr; bs; dms.   1953
GR-15109-1 Before She Leaves Town -1   Rockin' 527, DeLuxe 6023
GR-15110-1 Goin' Back Home Today   —   -

Note: This is not the same man as the artist who recorded pre-1942

JAMES BANISTER & HIS COMBO

Vcl. with hca; gtr; bs; dms.   Chicago 1954
1468 Gold Digger   States 141
1469 Blues And Trouble   -

JOHN HENRY BARBEE

Real name William George Tucker. Born in Hennings, Tennessee on November 14, 1905
Died Chicago November 1965.
Vcl/gtr. with Homesick James Williamson, gtr; Washbeard Sam, wbd.
            Chicago, March 26, 1964
   Early In The Morning   Spivey LP 1003
   No Pickin', No Pullin'   -

Vcl/gtr.   Copenhagen, October 8, 1964
   Dust My Broom   Storyville SLP 171
   Hey Baby   -
   That's Alright   -
   Early Morning Blues (Early In The Morning) -   , 188
   I Heard My Baby   -
   I Ain't Gonna Pick No More Cotton -
   Worried Life Blues   -
   Miss Nellie Gray   -
   Miss Nellie Gray   unissued
   Tell Me Baby   Storyville SLP 171
   John Henry   -
   Your Friend   Storyville SLP 166
   Backwater Blues   -

Vcl/gtr.   Hamburg, October 9, 1964
   Cotton' Pickin' Blues   Fontana 681.522TL

JUKE BOY BARNER

See under Juke Boy Benner

BARRELHOUSE BUCK

Real name Buck McFarland
Vcl(-1)/pno.   Alton, Illinois, May 12, 1961
   Lieutenant Blues -1   Folkways FG 3554
   Alton Blues   -
   Four O'Clock Blues   -
   20th Street Blues -1   -
   Mercy Blues   -
   So Long Buck   -
   I'm Going To Write You A Letter -1 -
   Mary Ain't I Been One Good Man To You -1 -
   Reminiscences -1   -
   Make Me A Soldier Of The Cross -1 -
   Nina Blues   -
   Taylor Avenue Blues   -

BARRELHOUSE SAMMY

See under Blind Willie McTell

JOSEPH VON BATTLE

Vcl. with Robert Richard, Walter Mitchell, hcas; Boogie Woogie Red, pno; bs.
            Detroit, 1948
DE-3 Looking For My Woman JVB 75828
   (rev. by Robert Richard)

ALLEN BAUM

See under Allen Bunn

13

ANNIE LEE BAXTER

Vcl. with Leo Baxter & another, saxes; Irving Williams, pno; dms.

Houston, c. 1949

| C 2 | Fine Little Fella
(rev. by Leo Baxter) | Vee Jay C 2 |

JOHNNY BECK (The Blind Boy)

Vcl/gtr.

Houston, 1950

| 2029 | Locked In Jail Blues | SIW 531 |
| 2030 | You've Gotta Lay Down Mama | - |

BROTHER BELL

Vcl/ten; with Ernest Lane, pno; gtr; bs; dms

Clarksdale, Miss. 1951

| MM 1792 | If You Feel Froggish | Blues & Rhythm 7002 |
| MM 1793 | Whole Heap of Mamma | - |

ANDY BELVIN

vcl. with hca; vibes(-1); pno; bs-gtr; dms.

Los Angeles c. 1963

| FB-2002A | Travelin' Mood | Vault 908 |
| FB-2002B | Flip Flip -1 | - |

BOBBY (GUITAR) BENNET

BOBBY GUITAR
Vcl./gtr. with saxes; pno; bs; dms.

New York City? 1965

| ZTSP 96476 | When Girls Do It | World Artists 1035 |
| ZTSP 96477 | She's So Fine | - |

BOBBY (GUITAR) BENNETT
Same:

| | Goin' Home | Junior 1005 |
| | Lawdy Miss Clawdy | - |

HENRY BENSON

Vcl/hca (-1). with Little Brother Montgomery, pno; Walter Vinson, gtr; Pops Foster, bs;
Earl Watkins, dms.

Chicago, September S, 1961

| 394 | Jelly Jelly | Riverside RLP 403, 9403 |
| 395 | I'm A Jelly Roll Baker -1 | - - |

BROOKS BERRY

Born in Sturgis, Kentucky in March 1915.
Vcl. with Scrapper Blackwell, gtr/pno (-1)

Indianapolis, 1962/3

	Cold Blooded Murder	Bluesville 1074
	My Man Is Studyin' Evil	
	Blues And Trouble -1	-
	Sweetest Apple	-
	Sun Burnt All My Cotton	
	'Bama Bound	-
	Can't Sleep	
	Life Ain't Worth Living	-
	Blues Is A Feeling -1	-
	Ive Had My Fun	-
	How Long	

BIG AMOS

Real name Amos Patton
Vcl/hca. with pno; gtr; bs-gtr; dms.

Memphis, 1966

| HI-2444 | He Won't Bite Me Twice | Hi 2108 |
| HI-2445 | Move With Me Baby | - |

14

BIG BILL

See under Big Bill Broonzy

BIG CHIEF

See under Wilbert Ellis.

BIG ED & HIS COMBO

See under Eddie Burns

BIG JOE

Real name Joe McCoy

BIG JOE AND HIS RHYTHM
Vcl/gtr. with Edgard Sancier, alt; Charles McCoy, mdln; Little Brother Montgomery, pno;
Ransom Knowling, bs.   Chicago, December, 15, 1944
D4-AB-332   Your Money Can't Buy Me   Bluebird 34-0723
D4-AB-333
D4-AB-334   I'm Alright Now   Bluebird 34-0723

BIG MAC

Vcl. with pno; gtr; bs-gtr; dms.   1966
TM 2037   Rough Dried Woman Part 1   Ronn 8
TM 2038   Rough Dried Woman Part 2   -

BIG MACEO

Real name Maceo Merriweather. Born Texas on March 30, 1905 Died Chicago, Illinois
on February 26, 1953.
Vcl/pno. with Tampa Red, gtr; Melvin Draper, dms.   Chicago, February 26, 1945
D5-AB-317   Kid Man Blues   Bluebird 34-0735, Victor 20-2687
D5-AB-318   I'm So Worried   Victor 20-2505
D5-AB-319   Things Have Changed   Bluebird 34-0735
D5-AB-320   My Own Troubles   Victor 20-2353
Vcl/pno. with Tampa Red, gtr; Tyrell "Little T" Dixon, dms.
                                                             Chicago, July 5, 1945
D5-AB-350   Maceo's 32-20   Victor 20-2028
D5-AB-351   Come On Home   Victor 20-2173
D5-AB-352   Texas Stomp   Victor 20-2028
D5-AB-353   Detroit Jump   Victor 20-2173
Vcl/pno. with Tampa Red, gtr; Charles Saunders, dms.   Chicago, October 15, 1945
D5-AB-1204   Winter Time Blues   Bluebird 34-0743
D5-AB-1205   Won't Be A Fool No More   Victor 20-1870
D5-AB-1206   Big Road Blues
D5-AB-1207   Chicago Breakdown   Bluebird 34-0743, Victor 20-2910,
                                                             42/47-0003, Greeve 5001,
                                                             Camden CAL 740

Vcl. with Eddie Boyd, pno; Tampa Red, gtr; Ernest Crawford, bs; Charles Saunders, dms.
                                                             Chicago, February 27, 1947
D7-VB-338   Broke And Hungry Blues   Victor 20-2687
D7-VB-339   If You Ever Change Your Ways   Victor 20-2910
D7-VB-340   It's All Over Now   Victor 20-2505
D7-VB-341   I lost My Woman   Victor 20-2353
Vcl/pno. With Tampa Red, gtr; Ernest Crawford, bs.   Chicago, 1949
320A   Do You Remeber   Specialty 320
320B   Big City Blues   -   , Blues Classics
                                                             BC-12
346A   One Sunday Morning   Specialty 346
346B   Just Tell Me Baby   -

Vcl/pno. with Johb Brim, gtr; Alonze Tucker, bs.   Detroit, 1952
137A   Leavin' Blues   Fortune 137, LP 3002
137B   Have You Heard About It   -   -
805A   Worried Life Blues No. 2   Fortune 805,   -
805B   Strange To Me Blues   -   -
              Without My Baby Life Don't Mcan A Thing   -   -

BIC MEMPHIS MA RAINEY

Real name Lillian Glover.

WITH THE ONZIE HORNE COMBO
Vcl. with vibes (-1); gtr; bs; dms.   Memphis, 1953
U-71   Call Me Anything, But Call Me -1   Sun 184
U-72   Baby, No, No.   -

BIG WALTER

On States Records. See under Walter Horton.

BIG WILLIE

See under Willie Mabon.

BILLY BOY

See under Billy Boy Arnold.

BINGHAMPTON BLUES BOYS

Unk. vcl with pno; 2 gtrs. dms.   Memphis, 1964
XL-10   Cross Cut Saw   XL 901, Ford
XL-11   Slim's Twist   -   -

BIRM INGHAM SAM

See under John Lee Hooker.

BLACK ACE

Real name Babe Kyre Lemon Turner. Born Hughes Springs, Texas in 1905
Vcl/gtr.   Fort Worth, August 14, 1960
              I'm The Black Ace   Arhoolie F 1003
              Bad Times Stomp   -
              Drink On Little Girl   -
              Santa Fe Blues   -
              New Triflin' Woman   -
              Farther Along   -
              Evil Woman   -
              'Fore Day Creep   -
              Little Angie   -
              Your Leg's Too Little   -
              No Good Woman   -
              Santa Claus Blues   -
              Golden Slipper   -
              Hitch-Hiking Woman   Arhoolie F 1006

BLACK COFFEE

Vcl/gtr.   Bluestown
              Unknown sides

BLACK DIAMOND

Real name James Butler.
Vcl./gtr.   Oakland, 1948
JB-4-848   T. P. Railer   Jaxyson 50A
JB-7-848   Lonesome Blues   -   B, 6
              Note: Reverse of Jaxyson 6 is by Goldrush, q.v. Butler also was accompanist
              on Gospel issues by Charles White & Sis. Matthews on Jaxyson.

16

SON BLACK

Vcl/gtr.

> Reputed to have recorded for Stomper Time Records in Memphis.

SCRAPPER BLACKWELL

Real name Francis Blackwell. Born Indianapolis? Died Indianapolis on Saturday, October 6, 1962.

Vcl/gtr.		Indianapolis,
	Little Girl Blues	Collector JEN 7
	Life of a Millionaire	–
	Little Boy Blue	–
	Blues	–
Vcl/pno.		Indianapolis, September, 1959
	How Long Blues	"77" LA 12/4
Vcl/gtr.		Indianapolis, March 31, 1960
	Blues Before Sunrise	"7" LA 12/4
	Sally-In-The-Alley Blues	–
	Shady Lane Blues	–
	E Blues	–
	Goin' To Jail About Her	–
Same. Add Bud White, whistling (−1):		Indianapolis, April 14, 1960
	Soft Blues	"77" LA 12/4
	No Good Woman Blues	–
	Leaving You Blues	–
	Blue 'n' Whistling −1	–
	Back Stop Blues	–
Vcl/gtr/pno (−1)		Indianapolis, July 1961
	"A" Blues	Bluesville BVLP 1047
	Going Where The Moon Crosses The Yellow Dog	–
	Nobody Knows You When You're Down And Out	–
	Little Girl Blues	–
	George Street Blues	–
	Blues Before Sunrise	–
	Little Boy Blues	–
	"E" Blues	–
	Shady Lane −1	–
	Penal Farm Blues	–

SUNNY BLAIR

Vcl/hca. with Baby Face Turner, gtr; Junior Brooks, gtr; Bill Russell, dms.

		North Little Rock, Ark. 1952
MM 1811	Five Foot Three Blues	RPM 354
MM 1812	Glad To Be Back Home	–
Add unk. ten (−1); Ike Turner, pno.		North Little Rock, Ark. May 6, 1952
MM 1870	Please Send My Baby Back	Meteor 5006
	My Baby's Gone	unissued
	Send My Baby Back (no hca) −1	unissued

> Note: Reverse of Meteor 5006 is by Baby Face Turner, q.v.

BILLY BLAND

Vcl. with pno; gtrs; dms.		New York City? 1955
OT 825	Chicken In The Basket	Old Town 1016, Tip Top 708
OT 826	The Fat Man	–
Add Sonny Terry, hca:		
OT 837	Oh You For Me	Old Town 1022
OT 838	Chicken Hop	– , Tip Top 708

> Note: Later recordings by this artist are of no interest.

SAMMY BLANN

Vcl. with hca; bs–gtr; dms.　　　　　　　　　　　　　　　　　　　　　　　　c. 1964
M 1003　　Lovie's Love Groove　　　　　　　　　　Progress 206
M 1004　　Crying Won't Make Me Stay　　　　　　　　–
　　　　　Note: Credits to J. Anderson.

BLIND WILLIE

See under Blind Willie McTell.

THE BLONDE BOMBER

No details:　　　　　　　　　　　　　　　　　　　　New York City, 1961
　　　　　　Strollie Bun　　　　　　　　　　　　　Hull 737
　　　　　　Am I To Blame　　　　　　　　　　　　Hull 737
　　　　　Note: Possibly Little Red Walter, q.v.

BLUE CHARLIE

Charlie Morris, vcl/gtr. with pno; gtr; dms.　　　　　Crowley, La. 1957
A　　　　　I'm Gonna Kill That Hen　　　　　　　Nasco 6002
B　　　　　Don't Bring No Friend　　　　　　　　–
　　　　　Note: Florida artist.

BLUE SMITTY & HIS STRING MEN

Real name Clarence Smith. Born Chicago on December 25, 1937.
Vcl/gtr. with pno; gtr; bs; dms.　　　　　　　　　Chicago, July 11, 1952
U–1128　　Crying　　　　　　　　　　　　　　Chess 1522
U–1129　　Sad Story　　　　　　　　　　　　　–
C-1030　　Elgin Movement　　　　　　　　　　unissued
C-1031　　Date Bait　　　　　　　　　　　　　unissued

BLUES IN THE MISSISSIPPI NIGHT

Talking, singing and playing by "Sib", "Leroy" and "Natchez", alias Sonny Boy Williamson, Memphis Slim and Big Bill Broonzy respectively, with comments from Alan Lomax.
Recorded Chicago, c. 1951.　　　　　　　　　　　United Artists 4027

THE BLUES BOY

See under Alec Seward.

BLUESBOY BILL

Vcl/gtr.　　　　　　　　　　　　　　　　　　　　　　　　　c. 1953
　　　　　　Come On Baby　　　　　　　　　　　Bluesman 101
　　　　　　Little Boy Blue　　　　　　　　　　–

THE BLUES BOYS

See under Alec Seward.

THE BLUES KING

See under Alec Seward.

THE BLUES ROCKERS

Unknown vcl. with pno; gtr; bs; dms.　　　　　　　Chicago, 1950
U 7218　　Trouble In My Home　　　　　　　　Aristocrat 407
U 7219　　Times Are Getting Hard　　　　　　　–
U 7239　　When Times Are Getting Better　　　　Aristocrat 413
U 7240　　Blues Rocker's Bop　　　　　　　　　–

18

| U 7241 | Little Boy, Little Boy | Chess 1483 |
| U 7242 | My Mama's Baby Child | – |

Lazy Bill Lucas, Vcl/pno; with hca; Earl Dranes & another, gtrs; dms.

		Chicago, 1955
A	Calling All Cows	Excello 2062, 2268
B	Johnnie Mae	–

Note: Reverse of Excello 2268 is by Jerry McCain, q.v.

BLUES SLIM

See under Gus Jenkins.

HILARY BLUNT

Vcl/gtr.

| | | Mississippi, 1959/60 |
| | A Thousand Miles From Nowhere | Storyville SLP 129 |

BO DIDDLEY

Real name Ellas McDaniel. Born McComb, Mississippi on December 30, 1928.
Vcl/gtr. with Lester Davenport, hca (−1); Otis Spann, pno (−1); Jerome Green, mrcs;
Frank Kirkland, dms.

		Chicago, June 1955
7787	I'm A Man −1	Checker 814, 997, LP 1431, 1525, Argo 4027
7788	Bo Diddley	Checker 814, 997, LP 1431, 1525, 2973, 2982

Vcl/gtr. with Billy Boy Arnold, hca; Henry Grey, pno; Jerome Green, mrcs; Frank Kirkland, dms.

		Chicago, 1955
	You Don't Love Me	Checker LP 1436
	Little Girl	–

Grey out – add Moonglows, vcl. grp (−1).

| 7836 | Diddley Daddy −1 | Checker 819, LP 1431 |
| 7837 | She's Fine, She's Mine | – |

Same – Jerome Green, vcl (−2).

7877	Pretty Thing	Checker 827, LP 1431
7878		
7879	Bring It To Jerome −2	Checker 827, LP 1431

Vcl/gtr. with Little Willie Smith, hca (−1); Jody Williams, gtr (−2); Willie Dixon, bs; Jerome Green, mrcs; Frank Kirkland, dms; Moonglows, vcl. grp (−1).

| 7946 | Diddy Wah Diddy −1 | Checker 832, LP 1431 |
| 7947 | I'm Looking For A Woman −2 | – , LP 2982 |

Vcl/gtr. with unk. gtr; Jerome Green, mrcs; Frank Kirkland, dms.

		Chicago, 1956
8122	I'm Bad	Checker 842
8123	Who Do You Love	– , LP 1431, 2982

add Otis Spann, pno; Willie Dixon, bs.

| 8272 | Cops And Robbers | Checker 850, LP 2974 |
| 8273 | Down Home Train (no pno) | |

Vcl/gtr. with Otis Spann, pno; Jody Williams, gtr; Willie Dixon, bs; Jerome Green, mrcs; Frank Kirkland, dms; vcl. grp (−1).

		Chicago, 1957
8441	Hey Bo Diddley −1	Checker 860, LP 1431, 2982
8442	Mona (I Need You Baby)	– , LP 2974

Spann out.

| 8556 | Say Boss Man −1 | Checker 878, LP 1431 |
| 8557 | Before You Accuse Me | |

Vcl/gtr/vln (−1). with Lafayette Leake, pno; Jerome Green, vcl (−2)/mrcs; Frank Kirkland, dms.

		Chicago, 1958
8748	Say Man −2	Checker 931, LP 1436
8749	Hush Your Mouth	Checker 896, LP 1431
8750		
8751	The Clock Strikes Twelve −1	Checker 931, LP 1436

19

| 8752 | Dearest Darling | Checker 896, LP 1431, 1436 |

Note: Later records not included.

HOUSTON BOINES

HOUSTON BAINES
Vcl/hca. with unk. pno; Charley Booker, gtr; Cleveland Love, dms.

Clarksdale, Miss., 1951

MM 1790	Going Home	Blues & Rhythm 7001
MM 1791	Relation Blues	– , Blues
		Classics 15

HOUSTON BOINES
Same:

	G Man Blues	unissued
MM 1853	Monkey Motion	RPM 364
MM 1854	Superintendent Blues	–
	Operator Blues	unissued

ZU ZU BOLLIN

Vcl/gtr. with Bobby Simmons, tpt; David Newman, alt; Leroy Cooper, bari; Charles Morgan, pno; Arthur Blake, bs; Sylvester Morton, dms.

Dallas, 1952

6910A	Why Don't You Eat Where You Slept Last Night	Torch 6910
6910B	Headlight Blues	–
2002	Cry, Cry, Cry	Torch 6912
2012	Stavin' Chain	–

JUKE BOY BONNER

Real name Wheldon Bonner. Born Belleville, Texas on March 22, 1932.

JUKE BOY BARNER
Vcl/hca/gtr. with Lafayette Thomas, gtr.

Oakland, 1957

IIIX	Well Baby	Irma 111
IIIXX	Rock With Me Baby	–
no mx	It's A Dirty Deal	Irma dub
no mx	I'm Hep To It	–

JUKE BOY BONNER – THE ONE MAN TRIO
Vcl/hca/gtr. with Katie Webster, pno; Lightnin' Mitchell, dms.

Lake Charles, La. 1960

	Let's Boogie	Storyville SLP 177
	My Time To Go	–
	Going Crazy Over You	–
	Just Got To Take A Ride	–
	Blue River Rising	–

Vcl/hca/gtr. with Guitar Joe, gtr; Little Brother Griffin, dms.

	Call Me Juke Boy	Goldband 1102, Storyville SLP 177
	Can't Hardly Keep From Crying	–
	I'm Not Jiving	Storyville SLP 177
	True Love Waiting	unissued
	Life Is A Dirty Deal	Jan & Dil EP 451

LOUIS BONNER

Hca.

Nr. Tunica, La. c. 1950

| | Old Country Horn Hunt | Folkways FA 2659 |

BOOGIE JAKE

M. Jacobs, vcl/pno. with gtrs. dms.

New Orleans, 1959

K80W–8703/SO:660
| | Bad Luck And Trouble | Minit 601, Chess 1746 |

        Early Morning Blues   Minit 602,   –

    Note: This artist is a resident of Baton Rouge, La.

THE BOOGIE MAN

See under John Lee Hooker.

BOOGIE WOOGIE RED

Real name Vernon Harrison. Born Louisiana in 1926.
Vcl/pno.

		Detroit, July 7, 1960
	So Much Good Feeling	Decca LK 4664

CHARLEY BOOKER

Vcl/gtr. with Houston Boines, hca; pno (–1); Cleveland Love, dms.

		Clarksdale, Miss. 1951
MM 1794	Rabbit Blues –1	Blues & Rhythm 7003
MM 1795	Moonrise Blues	Modern 878
MM 1796	No Ridin' Blues	Blues & Rhythm 7003
MM 1852	Charley's Boogie Woogie –1	Modern 878

CONNIE MACK BOOKER

See under Connie McBooker.

JOHN LEE BOOKER

See under John Lee Hooker.

(WEA) BEA BOOZE

Vcl. with Jack Dupree or Sam Price, pno; gtr; bs; dms.

		New York City, March 19, 1942
70543	If I'm A Fool	Decca 8619
70544	I Love To Georgia Brown So Slow	Decca 8629
70545	Uncle Sam Came And Got Him	Decca 8619
70546	If I Didn't Love You	Decca 8629
Similar:		New York City, March 26, 1942
70570	See See Rider Blues	Decca 8633, 48055
70571	Let's Be Friends	Decca 8621
		New York City, March 27, 1942
70580	Catchin' As Catch Can	Decca 8633, 48055
70581	War Rationing Papa	Decca 8621
Vcl. with		New York City, February 4, 1944
71738	Mr. Freddie Blues	rejected
71739	Gulf Coast Blues	rejected
71740	Uncle Sam Took A Darn Good Man	rejected
71741	These Young Men Blues	rejected
Vcl. with Sam Price, pno; Abe Bolar, bs; Hal West, dms.		New York City, March 9, 1944
71844	Mr. Freddie Blues	Decca 48033
71845	Uncle Sam Took A Darned Good Man	unissued
71846	Gulf Coast Blues	Decca 48033
71847	These Young Men Blues	Decca 8658
71848		
71849		
71850	Achin' Hearted Blues	unissued
71851	So Good	Decca 8658
Vcl. with		
	See See Rider	20th Century 20–48
	I Love You After All	–

Vcl. with Larry Johnson's Band: George Kelly, ten; Larry Johnson, pno; Chris Powell, bs;
Panama Francis, dms.

		New York City, May 15, 1950
R 1416	I Gonna Put You Down	Apollo 419
R 1417	Don't Tell Me Nothing About My Man	–
	Easy Rider Blues	Apollo 424
	Just Ain't Feeling Right	–

Vcl. with Sammy Price, pno. New York City, 1962
       Good Time Poppa Stardust
       What Else Ain't-Cha Got –

MEMPHIS WILLIE BORUM

Vcl/gtr/hca (−1). Memphis, 12 August, 1961
       Brownsville Blues Bluesville BVLP 1034
       Country Girl Blues −1 –
       Highway 61 –
       Bad Girl Blues –
       The Stuff Is Here −1 –
       Overseas Blues –
       Stop Crying Blues –
       Worried Man Blues –
       Mailman Blues −1 –
       Everyday I Have The Blues –
       Mattie Mae −1 –
       Grief Will Kill You –
       Car Machine Blues Bluesville BVLP 1048, 1055
       Lonesome Home Blues –
       L & N Blues –
       Hardworking Man Blues –
       Dying Mother Blues –
       Honey Maker Blues –
       P 38 Blues –
       Funny Caper Blues –
       Good Potatoes –
       I Have Found Somebody New –
       Uncle Sam Blues –
       Wine Drinking Woman –

CALVIN BOSTICK & HIS TRIO

Vcl/pno. with Chicago, 1950
U7281   All Of My Life Chess 1444
U7282   People Will Talk About You –

          Chicago, 1951
U7300   I'm In Love With You Chess 1451
U7301   Fleetwood Blues –

Vcl/pno. with bs; dms. Chicago, 1952
7440   Four Eleven Boogie Chess 1530, 1571
7440A   Bang, Bang Blues Chess 1571

          Chicago, 1953
7492   Christmas Won't Be Christmas Without You Chess 1530

BOTTLENECK SAM

Vcl/gtr.
       unknown titles Bluestown

BOY BLUE

Real name Roland Hayes.
Vcl/hca (−1). with Willie Jones, gtr; Joe Lee, dms. Arkansas, 1959
       Boogie Children Atlantic LP 1352
       Joe Lee's Rock −1 –

EDDIE BOYD

Born Clarksdale, Mississippi on November 25, 1914.

LITTLE EDDIE BOYD
Vcl. with J. T. Brown's Boogie Band: Howard Dixon, alt; J. T. Brown, ten; James Clark, pno;
Lonnie Graham, gtr; Willie Dixon, bs. Chicago, April 3, 1947
D7−VB−389 I Had To Let Her Go Victor 20−2311
D7−VB−390 Kilroy Won't Come Back –

LITTLE EDDIE BOYD AND HIS BOOGIE BAND
Vcl/pno. with Oett "Sax" Mallard, alt; Bill Casimir, ten; E. L. Liggett, bs; Booker T.
Washington, dms.   Chicago, September 16, 1947
D7–VB–1021
       You Got To Love That Gal   Victor 20–2555
D7–VB–1022
       Rosa Lee Swing   Victor 20–2703
D7–VB–1023
       Unfair Lovers   Victor 20–2555
D7–VB–1024
       Blue Monday Blues   Victor 20–2703
Same: Chicago, October 28, 1947
D7–VB–1109
       Why Did She Leave Me   Victor 20–3058
D7–VB–1110
       Playmate Shuffle   Victor 20–2920
D7–VB–1111
       Mr. Highway Man   Victor 20–3058
D7–VB–1112
       Getting My Divorce   Victor 20–2920
Vcl/pno. with Willie Lacey, gtr; Ransom Knowling, bs; Judge Riley, dms.
                                                             Chicago, December 24, 1948
D8–VB–3260
       What Makes These Things Happen To Me   Victor 50–0006, 22–0022
D8–VB–3261
       Baby What's Wrong With You   Victor 22–0002
D8–VB–3262
       Chicago Is Just That Way   Victor 50–0006, 22–0022
D8–VB–3263
       Eddie's Blues   Victor 22–0002
Vcl/pno. with Sam Casimir, gtr; Ransom Knowling, bs.   Chicago, June 29, 1949
D9–VB–1097
       Baby Come Back To Me   Victor unissued
D9–VB–1098
       I Can Trust My Baby   –
D9–VB–1099
       Down Beat Rhythm   –
D9–VB–1100
       Something Good Will Come To Me   –
       Note: Eddie Boyd claims to have recorded four titles for Aristocrat in late 1947/
       early 1948, accompanied by Lonnie Graham, gtr; Henry McCall, bs. and an
       unknown drummer.

ERNIE BOYD
Vcl/pno. with Sam Casimir, gtr; Alfred Elkins, bs; Judge Riley, dms.
                                                             Chicago, 1950
1326   Why Don't You Be Wise Baby   Regal 3305
1327   I Gotta Find My Baby   –

EDDIE BOYD
Vcl/pno. with Ernest Cotton, ten; L. C. McKinley, gtr; Alfred Elkins, bs; Percy Walker, dms.
                                                             Chicago, 1952
50–181   Five Long Years   J.O.B. 1007
50–182   Blue Coat Man   –
Vcl/pno. with Lee Cooper, gtr; Alfred Elkins, bs; Percy Walker, dms.
1005AA   It's Miserable To Be Alone   J.O.B. 1005, 1009
1005BB   I'm Pleading   –   –

EDDIE BOYD & HIS CHESS MEN
Vcl/pno. with Little Sax Crowder, ten; Robert Lockwood, Jr., gtr; Alfred Elkins, bs;
Percy Walker, dms.   Chicago, late 1952
C 4311   Cool Kind Treatment   Chess 1523

| C 4312 | untitled | unissued |
| C 4313 | Rosalee Swing | Chess 1523 |

Same, but Willie Dixon, bs. replaces Elkins.   Chicago, early 1953

U 7486	24 Hours	Chess 1533, LP 1446
U 7487	Hard Time Getting Started	unissued
U 7488	Best I Could	unissued
U 7489	The Tickler	Chess 1533

Vcl/pno. with Little Sax Crowder, ten; Lee Cooper, gtr; Alfred Elkins, bs; Percy Walker, dms.
         Chicago, 1953

U 4373	That's When I Miss You So	Chess 1552
U 4374	Third Degree	Chess 1541, LP 1446
		Argo LP 4042
U 4375	Four Leaf Clover	Chess 1634
U 4376	Back Beat	Chess 1541

Same, but Robert Lockwood Jr., gtr. replaces Cooper (−1).
         Chicago, 1954

U 7558	Tortured Soul	Chess 1552
U 7559	Rattin' And Runnin' Around	Chess 1576
U 7560	Just A Fool	Chess 1634
U 7561	Hush Baby Don't You Cry −1	Chess 1573

Same, but Ellis Hunter, gtr. replaces Cooper.   Chicago, 1955

U 7576	Came Home This Morning	Chess 1573
U 7577	Picture In The Frame	Chess 1561
U 7578	Nothing But Trouble	−

Vcl/pno. with Percy Brockenburg, ten; Lee Cooper, gtr; Alfred Elkins, bs; Percy Walker, dms.

U 7665	The Nightmare Is Over	Chess 1595
U 7666	I Got The Blues	Chess 1674
U 7667	Driftin'	Chess 1576

Same:

7735	The Story Of Bill	Chess 1582
7736		
7737	Please Help Me	Chess 1582

Prob. as last:

| 7808 | Real Good Feeling | Chess 1595 |

Vcl/pno. with Percy Mayfield's Band: tpt; alt; ten; Ellis Hunter, gtr; bs; dms.
         Chicago, 1956

7894	I'm A Prisoner	Chess 1606
7895	I've Been Deceived	−
8022	Don't	Chess 1621
8023	Life Gets To Be A Burden	−

Vcl/pno. with Percy Brockenberg, ten; Lee Cooper, gtr; Alfred Elkins, bs; Percy Walker, dms.

| 8472 | I Got A Woman | Chess 1660 |
| 8473 | Hotel Blues | |

Vcl/pno. with Robert Lockwood Jr., gtr; Alfred Elkins, bs; Billie Stepney, dms.
         Chicago, early 1957

| 8553 | She's The One | Chess 1674 |

Vcl/pno. with Willie Cobbs, hca; Eddie King Milton, gtr; Willie? Jones, bs; Chink Evans, dms.
         Chicago, 1958

JO9W−1339	Five Long Years	Oriole 1316, Blues
		Classics BC−8
JO9W−1340	24 Hours of Fear	Oriole 1317

Cobbs, out. Add vcl. grp.

| U 5172 | I Love You | J.O.B. 1114 |
| U 5173 | Save Her Doctor | − |

Vcl/pno. with Ronald Wilson, ten; Robert Lockwood, Jr., gtr; Bob Carter, bs; Sonny Allen, dms.
Christine Kittrell & The Daylighters dubbed on*.   Chicago, 1959

101−A	I'm Comin' Home	Bea & Baby 101
101−B	Thank You Baby	−
107−A	Blue Monday Blues	Bea & Baby 107
107−B	The Blues Is Here To Stay	−

108–A	Come Home	Bea & Baby 108, Keyhole 107*
108–B	You've Got To Reap What You Sow	– –
114–A	All The Way	Keyhole 114*
114–B	Where You Belong	– *

Note: All the above titles were recorded at one session.

EDDIE BOYD BLUES COMBO
Vcl/pno. with Eugene Pierson, gtr; Robert Lockwood Jr., bs–gtr; Jump Jackson, dms.
Chicago, October 15, 1960

	Nothing But Trouble	Esquire EP 247
	Her Picture In The Frame	–
	Five Long Years	–
	Stroller	–
	La Salle Street Breakdown	unissued
	Lonely Man	unissued

EDDIE BOYD
Vcl/pno. with saxes; gtr; bs; Jump Jackson, dms.　Chicago, 1961

| A 117 | Vacation From The Blues | La Salle 503 |
| D 120 | I Cry | – |

Vcl/pno. with Bobby Geddins Jr.'s Band: tpt; alt; ten; bari; Geddins, org; gtr; bs–gtr; dms.
Oakland, 1962

832X	I'm Comin' Home	Art–Tone832
832XX	Operator	–
A	Ten-To-One	Push 1050
B	Come On	–

Vcl/pno. with The Strojers: alt; 2 tens; gtr; bs; dms.　Big Spring, Texas, Sept. 1963
| 3220 | Empty Arms | Palos 1206 |

Vcl/pno. with ten; gtr; bs; dms.　Chicago, 1964
| 3219 | Early Grave | Palos 1206 |

Vcl/pno. with Buddy Guy, gtr; Jack Meyers, bs–gtr; Clifton James, dms.
Chicago, August 1965

| | Where You Belong | Decca LK 4748 |
| | All The Way | – |

Vcl/org. with Buddy Guy, gtr; Jimmy Lee Robinson, bs–gtr; Fred Below, dms.
Hamburg, October 7, 1965

| | Five Long Years | Fontana 885.422TY |
| | The Big Question | – |

Vcl/pno/org (–1). with Buddy Guy, gtr; Jimmy Lee Robinson, bs–gtr. Fred Below, dms.
London, October 20, 1965

	Five Long Years	Fontana 883.905TY
	Hello Stranger –1	–
	Where You Belong	–
	I'm Coming Home	–
	My Idea	–
	The Big Question –1	–
	Come On Home	–
	Blue Monday Blues	–
	Eddie's Blues –1	–
	All The Way	–
	24 Hours Of Fear	–
	Rock The Rock	–

| | It's Too Bad | Mojo 2167 |
| | Vacation From The Blues | – |

ERNIE BOYD
See under Eddie Boyd.

ROBERT BOYD
See under Roy Byrd.

BLIND JAMES BREWER

Born Brookhaven, Mississippi on October 3, 1921. Vcl/gtr.

		Chicago, July 11, 1960
	I'm So Glad Good Whiskey's Back	Heritage HLP 1004

Vcl/gtr. with Fannie Brewer, vcl (−1)/gtr.

		Chicago, 1964
	I Want To Know Why (duet)	Testament S-01
	Why Did He Have To Go	−
	When We Got The Message −1	−

Vcl/gtr.

	Big Road Blues	Storyville SLP 180
	Pea Vine Whistle	Milestone LP 3002

BIG CHARLEY BRADIX

Vcl/pno. with gtr; bs.

		Dallas, 1948
BB153A	Boogie Like You Wanna	Blue Bonnet 153, Colonial 108
BB153B	Dollar Diggin' Woman	−
450	Numbered Days	Aristocrat 418
451		
452	Wee Wee Hours	Aristocrat 418

Note: Credits on Aristocrat to Bob Thomas & James Collier.

AVERY BRADY

Born Clarksdale, Mississippi in 1903.

Vcl/gtr.

		Chicago, 1964
	Poor Kennedy	Testament S-01

Vcl/gtr.

		Chicago, 1965
	Bad Weather	Testament T-2209
	Let Me Drive Your Ford	−
	I Don't Want You No More	Storyville SLP 180
	Gonna Let You Down	Storyville SLP 181

GRACE BRIM

MRS. JOHN BRIM

Vcl. with Roosevelt Sykes, pno; John Brim, gtr.

		Chicago, 1951
G−103	Going Down The Line	Random 202
G−104	Leaving Blues	−

GRACE BRIM

Vcl. with Sunnyland Slim, pno; John Brim, gtr; bs.

		Chicago, 1952
51921	Man Around My Door	J.O.B. 117
51922	Hospitality Blues	−

Note: Wife of John Brim, q.v.

JOHN BRIM

Born Hopkinsville, Kentucky in 1922.

JOHN BRIM & HIS COMBO

Grace Brim, vcl/hca; James Watkins, Big Maceo, pnos; John Brim, gtr.

		Detroit, 1950
A	Strange Man	Fortune 801
B	Mean Man Blues	−

JOHN BRIM

Vcl/gtr. with Roosevelt Sykes, pno.

		Chicago, 1951
G−101	Dark Clouds	Random 201
G−102	Lonesome Man Blues	−

JOHN BRIM TRIO

Vcl/gtr. with Sunnyland Slim, pno; bs.

		Chicago, 1952
JB−41533	Trouble In The Morning	J.O.B. 110
JB−41534	Humming Blues	−

JOHN BRIM & HIS STOMPERS

Vcl/gtr. with hca; Eddie Taylor, gtr; Grace Brim, dms.

		Chicago, 1953
P53−194	Tough Times	Parrot 799
P53−195	Gary Stomp	−

JOHN BRIM & HIS GARY KINGS
Vcl/gtr. with Little Walter, hca; Robert Lockwood Jr., gtr; Fred Below, dms.

4350	Rattlesnake	Checker 769
4351	It Was A Dream	–

JOHN BRIM TRIO (as for J.O.B. 110)   Chicago, 1954
S–1924   Drinking Woman   J.O.B. 1011
           (rev. by Sunnyland Slim)

JOHN BRIM & HIS GARY KINGS
Vcl/gtr. with James Dalton, hca; W. C. Dalton, bs–gtr; Grace Brim, dms.
                                       Chicago, 1955

	Lifetime Baby	unissued
	Ice Cream Man	unissued
7766	Go Away	Chess 1588
7767	That Ain't Right	

Vcl/gtr. with Little Walter, hca; Robert Lockwood, Jr., gtr; Willie Dixon, bs; Fred Below, dms.
                                        Chicago, 1956

8080	I Would Hate To See You Go	Chess 1624
8081	You've Got Me Where You Want Me	–

MRS. JOHN BRIM

See under Grace Brim.

JUNIOR BROOKS

Vcl/gtr. with Elmon Mickle, hca (–1); Baby Face Turner, gtr; Bill Russell, dms.
                                   North Little Rock 1951

MM 1737	Lone Town Blues	RPM 343
MM 1738	She's The Little Girl For Me –1	– , Blues Classics 15

BIG BILL BROONZY

Real name William Lee Conley Broonzy. Died Chicago on 14 August, 1958.

LITTLE SAM
Vcl/gtr. with Don Byas, ten; Kenny Watts, pno; John Levy, bs; Slick Jones, dms.
                                   New York City, early 1945

Hu 418	Please Believe Me	Hub 3003
Hu 419	Why Did You Do That	–
Hu 420	You Got To Play Your Hand	Hub 3023
Hu 421		
Hu 422	Just A Dream	Hub 3023

            Note: Records issued as by Don Byas.

BIG BILL
Vcl/gtr. with Buster Bennett, alt; Big Maceo, pno; Tyrell Dixon, dms.
                                   Chicago, February 19, 1945

C 4380	Doing The Best I Can	unissued
C 4381	Partnership Woman	Columbia 30143
C 4382	Where The Blues Began	unissued
C 4383	Humble Blues	Columbia 36879, 30002
C 4384	Oh Baby	Okeh 6739, Columbia 37454, 30021
C 4385	Cell No. 13 Blues	Columbia 37164, 30009
C 4386	Believe Me What I Say	unissued
C 4387	1944 Blues	unissued

Omit Bennett: Chicago, February 24, 1945

C 4414	When I Get To Thinkin'	Okeh 6739, Columbia 37454, 30021
C 4415	Roll Dem Bones	Columbia 36879, 30002
C 4416	Letter To Tojo	unissued
C 4417	You Got The Best Go	Columbia 37164, 30009

27

BIG BILL AND HIS RHYTHM BAND
Vcl/gtr. with John Norton, tpt; Oett "Sax" Mallard, alt; Bill Casimir, ten; Charles Belcher, pno;
Ransom Knowling, bs; Judge Riley, dms.

		Chicago, December 4, 1946
CCO 4686	I Can Fix It	Columbia 37502, 30051
CCO 4687	Old Man Blues	— —
CCO 4688	I Can't Write	unissued
CCO 4689	What Can I Do	Columbia 37314, 30016

BIG BILL
Vcl/gtr. with Memphis Slim, pno; Ransom Knowling, bs; Tyrell Dixon, dms.

		Chicago, January 28, 1947
CCO 4711	San Antonio Blues	Columbia 38070, 30109
CCO 4712	Saturday Evening Blues	Columbia 37314, 30016
CCO 4713	Martha Blues	unissued
CCO 4714	Texas Tornado Blues	unissued

Vcl/gtr. with Oett "Sax" Mallard, alt; Bill Casimir, ten; Bob Call, pno; bs; Judge Riley, dms.

		Chicago, September 29, 1947
CCO 4848	Big Bill's Boogie	Columbia 37965, 30101
CCO 4849	Just Rocking	Columbia 38070, 30109
CCO 4850	Shoo Shoo Blues	Columbia 37965, 30101

Add Johnny Morton, tpt; Ransom Knowling, bs.

		Chicago, December 19, 1947
CCO 4950	Stop Lying Woman	Columbia 30143
CCO 4951	Rambling Bill	Columbia 38180, 30118
CCO 4952	Summertime Blues	— —
CCO 4953	Bad Luck Man	Columbia 30143

BIG BILL BROONZY AND HIS FAT FOUR
Vcl/gtr. with Antonio Casey, alt; Carl Sharp, pno; Ransom Knowling, bs; Alfred Wallace, dms.

		Chicago, January 4, 1949
2176	I Love My Whiskey	Mercury 8122
2177	You've Been Mistreating Me	Mercury 8160
2178	I Stay Blue All The Time	—
2179	Water Coast Blues	Mercury 8122

BIG BILL BROONZY
Vcl/gtr. with Alfred Wallace, dms.

		Chicago, February 4, 1949
2497	Five Feet Seven	Mercury 8126
2498	I Wonder	—
2499	Keep Your Hands Off Her	Mercury 8139
2500	Mindin' My Own Business	—

Vcl/gtr.

		Paris, September 20, 1951
51V4095	House Rent Stomp	Vogue 131, LDM 30037
51V4096	In The Evening	Vogue 138, LDO 30, LDM 30037
51V4097	The Moppin' Blues	Vogue 142, — , LD 524
51V4098	Hey Hey Baby	Vogue 148, LDM 30037
51V 4099	Willie Mae Blues	— —
51V 4100	Black Brown And White	Vogue 125, LDO 30, LDM 30037, LD 605
51V4102	Low Down Blues −1	Vogue 138, LDO 30, LDM 30037, LD 524
51V4103	Feelin' Low Down −1	Vogue 142, LDM 30037
51V4104	What I Used To Do	Vogue 125
51V4105	Make My Getaway	Vogue 118, LDO 30
	Hollerin' And Cryin' −1	Vogue LDO 30, LDM 30037, LD 605

Note: −1 Different takes issued of these matrices.

Same:

		Paris, September 21, 1951
51V4106	Blues in 1890 −1	Vogue 131, LDO 30, LDM 30037
51V4107	Big Bill Blues	Vogue 134
51V4108	Lonesome Road Blues −1	Vogue EPL 7138, LDM 30037, LD 524
51V4109	When Did You Leave Heaven	Vogue EPL 7138 —
51V4110	John Henry	Vogue 118, LDM 30037, LD 524

CHICAGO BILL
Vcl/gtr.   London, September 24, 1951
MEL 467   Keep Your Hands Off   Melodisc 1191, EPM 7–65
MEL 468   Stump Blues   –   –
MEL 469   Five Foot Seven   Melodisc 1203,   –
MEL 470   Plough Hand Blues   –   –

BIG BILL BROONZY
Vcl/gtr.   Paris, October, 1951
          Make Me A Pallet   Jazz Society LP–6
          Take Me Back   –
          Frankie And John   –
          Hard Headed Woman   –
          St. James Infirmary   –
          Dyeing Day Blues   –
          Friendless Funeral Blues   –
          Crowded Graveyard   –

Vcl/gtr. with Ransom Knowling, bs.   Chicago, November 8, 1951
4521   Hey Hey   Mercury 8271, 71352, EmArcy
                                            MG 36137
4522   Stump Blues   Mercury MG 20822, EmArcy
                                            MG 36137
4523   Get Back   –   –
4524   Willie Mae   Mercury 8261, MG 20822,
                                            EmArcy MG 36137
4525   Walkin' That Lonesome Road   Mercury 8271, EmArcy MG
                                            36137
4526   Mopper's Blues   Mercury 8284,   –
4527   I Know She Will   –   –
4528   Hollerin' Blues –1   Mercury 8261,   –
          Note: –1 Add Bob Call, pno.
Add Oett "Sax" Mallard, alt; Bill Casimir, ten; Bob Call, pno; Judge Riley, dms.
                                            Chicago, November 9, 1951
4529   Leavin' Day   Mercury 70039, EmArcy MG
                                            36137
4530   South Bound Train   –   , MG 20822,
                                            EmArcy MG 36137
4531   Tomorrow   Mercury 71352, MG 20822,
                                            EmArcy MG 36137
4532   You Changed   EmArcy MG 36137
Vcl/gtr. with prob. Big Crawford, bs.   Chicago, December 10, 1951
4649   John Henry   Mercury MG 20822, EmArcy
                                            MG 26034
4650   Crawdad   EmArcy MG 26034
4651   Bill Bailey   Mercury MG 20822, EmArcy
                                            MG 26034
4652   Make My Get Away   EmArcy MG 26034
4653   Blue Tail Fly   Mercury MG 20822, EmArcy
                                            MG 26034
4654   Backwater Blues   EmArcy MG 26034
4655   In The Evenin'   Mercury MG 20822, EmArcy
                                            MG 26034
4656   Trouble In Mind   –   –
          Note: All titles, except 4650 & 4652, also on EmArcy MG 36052.
Vcl/gtr. with Blind John Davis, pno.   Paris, February 5, 1952
          It's Your Time Now   Vogue LD 605
          Nobody Knows The Trouble I've Seen –
          Guitar Shuffle   –
          Feelin' Low Down   –
          How Long Blues   –

Vcl/gtr.   Paris, March 19, 1952
          Coal Black Curly Hair   Vogue LD 524
          Letter To My Baby   Vogue LD 072, 524, POP
                                            SPO 17002

29

	Hey Bud Blues	–	–	, 605
	Baby Please Don't Go	–	–	
	Do Right Blues	–	–	
	Kind Hearted Blues	–	–	
	Louise Louise	–	–	
	Down By The Riverside	–	–	
	Stand Your Test In Judgement	–	–	
	Guitar Shuffle	Vogue EPL 7138, LDM 30037		

Vcl/gtr. with Lee Cooper, gtr; Big Crawford, bs; Washboard Sam, wbd.

Chicago, 1955

U 7508	Little City Woman	Chess 1546, LP 1468
U 7509	Lonesome	– –
	Jacqueline	–
	Romance Without Finance	–

Vcl/gtr. with Memphis Slim, pno; Big Crawford, bs; Washboard Sam, wbd.

	All By Myself	Chess LP 1468

Vcl/gtr. with Leslie Hutchinson, tpt; Bruce Turner, alt; Kenny Graham, ten; Benny Green, bari; Dill Jones, pno; Jack Fallon, bs; Phil Seamen, dms.   London, October 26, 1955

	It Feels So Good	Nixa NJ 2016, NJE 1005, NJL 16
	Southbound Train	– , NJE 1015, –
	Trouble In Mind	rejected
	Whiskey Head Man	rejected

Vcl/gtr.   London, October 26, 1955

	Southern Saga	Nixa NJE 1047, NJL 16
	When The Sun Goes Down	– –
	Going Down The Road Feeling Bad	– –

Note: Above recorded at a private party.

Vcl/gtr.   London, October 27, 1955

	Saturday Evening	Nixa NJE 1005, NJL 16
	Glory of Love	
	St. Louis Blues	– –
	Mindin' My Own Business	Nixa NJE 1015, –
	When Do I Get To Be Called A Man	– –
	Partnership Woman	– –

Vcl/gtr. with Kansas Fields, dms.   Paris, February 10, 1956

	Rock Me Baby	Columbia ESDF 1162, FP 1080
	Careless Love	–
	Somebody's Got To Go	–
	Water Coast	Columbia ESDF 1121, –
	Big Bill's Guitar Blues	–
	Take This Ole Hammer	–
	Diggin' My Potatoes	–

Vcl/gtr.   Bearn, Holland, February 17, 1956

	Bossie Woman	Philips BOS.012L
	Texas Tornado	
	Trouble In Mind	– , B681.555L
	Martha	–
	Key To The Highway	–
	Goodbye Baby Blues	–
	See See Rider	– , 430.714BE
	Tell Me What Kind Of Man	– –
	When I've Been Drinkin'	– –
	Swing Low Sweet Chariot	– –

Vcl/gtr.   Copenhagen, May 4, 1956

DGF 33	Going Down The Road	Storyville SEP 316, SLP 114
DGF 34	Ananias	unissued
DGF 35	In The Evening	Storyville SLP 154
DGF 36	This Train	Storyville SEP 316, SLP 114
DGF 37	I Love You So Much	Storyville SLP 143
DGF 38	Diggin' My Potatoes	Storyville SEP 383
DGF 39	Willie Mae Blues	– , SLP 154

30

DGF 40	Bill Bailey	Storyville SEP 316, SLP 114
DGF 41	Take This Hammer	unissued
DGF 42	John Henry	Storyville SEP 383
DGF 43	Glory Of Love	unissued
DGF 44	The Crawdad Song	Storyville SLP 114
DGF 45	Blue Tail Fly	—
DGF 46	Black Brown And White	— , A 45053
DGF 46A	Guitar Blues	—
DGF 47	Hey Bud	—
DGF 48	Irene	—
DGF 49	Sixteen Tons	Storyville SEP 383, SLP 143
DGF 50	Pennies From Heaven	unissued
DGF 51	Shanty In Old Shanty Town	Storyville SEP 316, SLP 114

Vcl/gtr.   Copenhagen, May 5/6, 1956

	Swanee River	Storyville SLP 154
	Swing Low Sweet Chariot	—
	Big Bill Talks	unissued
	Take This Hammer	Storyville SLP 143
	When Things Go Wrong	Storyville SLP 154
	Barrelhouse Shuffle (Guitar Rag)	—
	Down By The Riverside	—
	See See Rider	Storyville SLP 143
	John Henry	Storyville SLP 154
	Diggin' My Potatoes	Storyville SLP 143
	Bill Bailey	unissued
	Just A Dream	Storyville SLP 154
	Careless Love	Storyville SLP 143
	Ananias	Storyville SLP 154
	Midnight Special	Storyville SLP 143, A 45053
	Keep Your Hands Off Her	—
	I Got A Girl	—
	You Better Mind	—
	Hey Bud	unissued
	John Henry	unissued
	Glory of Love	Storyville SLP 143
	I Get The Blues When It Rains	Storyville SLP 154
	My name Is William Lee Conley Broonzy	Storyville SLP 143
	Big Bill Talks	Storyville SLP 154
	Louisiana Blues	—

Vcl/gtr. with Pete Seeger, vcl/bjo (−1).   Concert, Chicago 1956

	Midnight Special −1	Verve VL 9008
	Green Corn −1	—
	Backwater Blues	—
	This Train Is Bound For Glory	—
	Crawdad	—
	Glory Of Love	—
	Willie Mae	—
	Bill Bailey	—

Same: Chicago, 1956

	The Midnight Special −1	Folkways FP 86/4, FS 3864,
	You Got To Stand Your Test In Judgement −1	— —
	That Lonesome Valley −1	— —
	Alberta	— — , FA 2328
	In The Evening	— — , FA 2326
	I Wonder Why	— —
	Makin' My Get Away	— —
	Love You Baby	— —
	Crawdad Hole	— —
	John Henry	— —
	Trouble In Mind	Folkways FA 2326
	When Things Go Wrong	—
	Diggin' My Potatoes	—
	Poor Bill Blues	—

I Wonder When I'll Get To Be Called A Man	–
Louise Louise	–
Frankie and Johnny	–
Southbound Train	–
Joe Turner No. 2	–
Hey Hey Baby	–
Saturday Evening Blues	–
This Train –1	Folkways FA 2328
Goin' Down The Road –1	–
John Henry –1	–
Backwater Blues	–
Bill Bailey	–
I Don't Want No Woman	–
Martha	–
Tell Me Who	–
Tell Me What Kind Of Man Jesus Is	–
Glory Of Love	–

Vcl/gtr.   Milan, June, 1956

St. Louis Blues	Ricordi DRF 3
In The Evening	–
See See Rider	–
Sixteen Tons	–

Vcl/gtr. and talking with Studs Terkel.   Chicago, November 14, 1956

Plough Hand Blues	Folkways FG 3586
See See Rider	–
Bill Bailey	–
Willie Mae Blues	–
This Train	–
Mule Ridin'	–
Key To The Highway	–
Black Brown And White	–
Joe Turner Blues No. 1	–
Talkin' Blues	–

Vcl/gtr. (–1). with Sonny Terry, vcl/hca (–2); Brownie McGhee, vcl/gtr (–3). Interviewed by Studs Terkel.   Chicago, May 7, 1957

Keys To The Highway –1, 2, 3	Folkways FS 3817
Interview	–
Red River Blues –3	–
Crow Jane –2	–
Willie Mae –1	–
Daisy –3	–
Louise –2	–
Shuffle Rag –1	–
Blues –1, 2, 3	–
Beautiful City –2	–
I'm Going To Tell God –3	–
Hush Somebody Is Calling Me –1	–
When The Saints Go Marching In –1, 2, 3	–

Vcl/gtr. and talking with Bill Randle.   Chicago, July 12/13, 1957

Key To The Highway	Verve MGV 3000/5, MGV 3001		
Mindin' My Own Business	–	–	
Saturday Evening Blues	–	–	
Southbound Train	–	–	
Tell Me What Kind Of Man Jesus Is	–	–	
Swing Low Sweet Chariot	–	–	
Ploughhand Blues	Verve MGV 3000/5, MGV 3001		
Joe Turner Blues	–	–	
Boogie Woogie	–	–	
I Ain't Gon' Be Treated This Way	–	–	
Makin' My Getaway	–	–	
Hollerin' Blues	–	–	
See See Rider	–	–	, 8505
Outskirts Of Town	–	–	

This Train	–	, MGV 3002
Hush Hush	–	–
The Flood	–	–
Blues	–	–
It Hurts Me So	–	–
Kansas City Blues	–	–
When The Sun Goes Down	–	–
Worried Life	–	–
Trouble In Mind	–	–
Take This Hammer	–	–
The Glory Of Love	–	–
Willie Mae Blues	–	, MGV 3003
Louise Blues	–	, MGV 3002
Alberta	–	, MGV 3003
Old Folks At Home	–	–
Crawdad Hole	–	–
John Henry	–	–
Just A Dream	–	–
Frankie And Johnnie	–	–
Bill Bailey	–	–
Slow Blues (Lookin' For That Woman)	–	–

Note: the remaining part of the five record set MGV 3000/5 is talking between Broonzy and Randle.

BROTHER BLUES

See under Jack Dupree.

B. BROWN

See under Buster Brown.

BUSTER BROWN

Vcl/hca. with saxes; pno; Jimmy Spruill, gtr; bs; dms.　　New York City, 1959

FM 114	Fannie Mae	Fire 1008, FLP 102, Roullette LP 25242
FM 115	Lost In A Dream	Fire 1008, FLP 102

B. BROWN & HIS ROCKIN' McVOOTS

As above, omit saxes (–1):　　New York City, 1960

DR 2001	My Baby Left Me –1	Vest 827
DR 2002	Hardworking Man –1	–
DR 2008	Candied Yams	Vest 830
DR 2007	Fannie Mae Is Back	–

BUSTER BROWN

Same:

FM 141	John Henry (no saxes)	Fire 1020, FLP 102
FM 142	The Madison Shuffle	– –
FM 147	Don't Dog Your Woman	Fire 1023, FLP 102, Oldies 111
FM 148	Is You Is Or Is You Ain't My Baby	– –
FM 167	Doctor Brown	Fire 1032, FLP 102
FM 168	Sincerely	– –
FM 183	I Got The Blues When It Rains	Fire 1040
FM 184	Good News	

Same:　　New York City, 1961

FM 199	Sugar Babe	Fire 507
FM 200	I'm Going But I'll Be Back	– , FLP 102
FM 223	Raise A Ruckus Tonight	Fire 516
FM 224	Gonna Love My Baby	–

Probably from above sessions:

	St. Louis Blues	Fire FLP 102
	When Things Go Wrong	–
	Blueberry Hill	–

Same:
| 2005A | My Blue Heaven | Serock 2005 |
| 2005B | Two Women | – |

Vcl/hca. with pno; gtr; bs–gtr; dms.   Chicago, 1962
| no mx | Slow Drag Blues Pt. 1 | Gwenn 600 |
| no mx | Slow Drag Blues Pt. 2 | – |

Note: "recorded 'live' in Old Sam Jones' Basement".

Add saxes:
| A | Trying To Learn How To Love You | Gwenn 601 |
| B | Broadway On Fire | – |

Vcl/hca. with Shakey Horton, hca; Lafayette Leake, pno; Buddy Guy, gtr; Matt Murphy, gtr;
Reggie Boyd, bs–gtr; Clifton James, dms.   Chicago, April 14, 1965
13886	I Love My Baby	Checker unissued
13887	Hoodoo Doctor	–
13888	No More	–
13889	What Do You Want Me To Do	–

No details:
| | Crawling King Snake | Checker 1099 |
| | In The Presence Of You | – |

DUSTY BROWN

Vcl/hca. with pno; gtr; dms..   Chicago, 1955
| P55–273 | Yes, She's Gone | Parrot 820 |
| P55–274 | He Don't Love You | – |

Vcl/hca. with 2 gtrs; dms.   Chicago, 1958
Ba 7844, 4544
| | Please Don't Go | Bandera 2503 |
Ba 7845, 4545
| | Well, You Know | – |

ENOCH BROWN

Vcl.   Livingstone, Ala? Jan/Feb., 1950
| | Complaint Call | Folkways FE 4417, P 417 |

GABRIEL BROWN

Vcl/gtr.   New York City, 1945/46
A	I Get Evil When My Love Comes Down	Joe Davis 5003, Gennett 5003
B	You Ain't No Good	–
A	Black Jack Blues	Joe Davis 5004, Beacon 5004, Gennett 5004, Blues Classics BC–14
B	Going My Way	Joe Davis 5004, Beacon 5004, Gennett 5004
A	Down In The Bottom	Joe Davis 5006
B	Bad Love	–
A	I've Got To Stop Drinkin'	Joe Davis 5008
B	Cold Love	–
A	Not Now, I'll Tell You When	Joe Davis 5015
B	I'm Gonna	–
A	I Don't Feel So Good	Joe Davis 5016
B	Stop Jivin' Me	–
A	Stick With Me	Joe Davis 5017
B	I've Done Stopped Gambling	–
A	It's Getting Soft	Joe Davis 5020
B	Don't Worry About Me	–
A	Boogie Woogie Guitar	Joe Davis 5021, Beacon 5021
B	Hold That Train	– –
A	Wrap Me Up Tight	Joe Davis 5025
B	I Want A Little Fun	–

34

A	I'll Be Seeing You	Joe Davis 5026
B	It's Time To Move	–
A	You Have Got To Be Different	Joe Davis 5027
B	The Jinx Is On Me	–
A	Pleading	Joe Davis 5028
B	Mean Old Blues	–
Vcl/gtr.		New York City, 1949
A	Cold Mama	MGM 11407
B	I'm Just Crazy	–
75291A	I Can't Last Long	Coral 65019
75292A	Suffer	–

Note: The MGM and Coral sides are from Davis sessions. MGM issued around 1953.

CLARENCE "GATEMOUTH" BROWN

Born Vinton, Louisiana in 1924. Vcl/gtr. with Maxwell Davis Orch: Maxwell Davis & others, saxes; pno; bs; dms.   Los Angeles, August 21, 1947

AL 230	Gatemouth Boogie	Aladdin 198
231 L	Guitar In My Hands	Aladdin 199
AL 232	After Sunset	Aladdin 198
AL 233	Without Me Baby	Aladdin 199

Vcl/gtr. with Jack McVea's Orch: Houston, January, 1949

	Mercy On Me	Peacock 1500, 1501
	Didn't Reach My Goal	–
	Ditch Diggin' Daddy	Peacock 1501
A	My Time's Expensive	Peacock 1504
B	Mary Is Fine	–

Vcl/gtr. with George Alexander, tpt; Wilmer Shakesliner, alt/ten; Clarence Green, pno; Harold Easton, dms. unk. saxes; bs.   Houston, late 1949

ACA 1350	I Live My Life	Peacock 1568
ACA 1351	Two O'Clock In The Morning	Peacock 1505
ACA 1352	Boogie Rambler	–
ACA 1353	I've Been Mistreated	Peacock 1508
ACA 1354	It Can Never Be That Way	–
ACA 1355	Stop Your Teasing	unissued
ACA 1356	Justice Blues	Peacock 1568
ACA 1357	Just Got Lucky	Peacock 1600

Vcl/gtr. with   Houston, 1951

ACA 1785	She Walks Right In	Peacock 1561
ACA 1786	Win With Me Baby	–
ACA 1787	Too Late Baby	Peacock 1586
ACA 1788	Taking My Chance	–

Vcl/gtr. with   Houston, 1952

ACA 1934	Bop Me With The Boogie	unissued
ACA 1935	Baby Take It Easy	Peacock 1600
ACA 1936	Sure Is A Serious Business Baby	unissued
ACA 1937	The Best You Ever Seen	unissued

Vcl/gtr. with

ACA 1970	She Winked Her Eye	Peacock 1576
ACA 1971	Sad Hour	–
ACA 1972	Blues Is A Combination Baby	unissued
ACA 1973	I Can't Believe It Baby	unissued

Vcl/gtr. with

ACA 1989	Pale Dry Boogie Part 1	Peacock 1575
ACA 1990	Pale Dry Boogie Part 2	–

Vcl/gtr. with saxes; Jimmy McCracklin, pno; bs; dms.   Houston, 1953

ACA 2229	Echo Blues	unissued
ACA 2230	untitled instrumental	unissued
ACA 2231	Dirty Work At The Crossroads	Peacock 1607
ACA 2232	You Got Money	–

Vcl/gtr. with Al Grey, tbn; Joe Scott, tpt; Johnny Board, ten; Bob Little, bari; Paul Monday, pno; Ray Johnson, bs; Ellis Bartee, dms.

ACA 2348	September Song	Peacock 1662

ACA 2349	Boogie Uproar	Peacock 1617
ACA 2500	Gate Walks To Board	Peacock 1619
ACA 2501	Hurry Back Good News	Peacock 1617
ACA 2502	Please Tell Me Baby	Peacock 1619

Vcl/gtr. with similar: Houston, 1954
ACA 2740	Midnight Hour	Peacock 1633
ACA 2741	Good Looking Woman	unissued
ACA 2742	For Now So Long	Peacock 1633
ACA 2743	That's Your Daddy Yaddy Yo	unissued

Vcl/gtr. with Pluma Davis, tbn; tpt; saxes; pno; bs; dms.
ACA 2850	Okie Dokie Stomp	Peacock 1637
ACA 2851	Sally In The Alley	unissued
ACA 2852	Depression Blues	Peacock 1637
ACA 2853	Radio Gal	unissued

Vcl/gtr. with Henry Boozier, tpt; Pluma Davis, tbn; Bill Harvey, ten; Allen Clark, bari;
Carl Owens, pno; Nat Douglas, gtr; Carl Lott, bs; Emile Russell, dms.

Houston, July 3, 1956
ACA 3062	Gate's Salty Blues −1	Peacock 1653
ACA 3063	Without A Woman	unissued
ACA 3064, HHA 22702		
	Ain't That Dandy	Peacock 1662
ACA 3065	Rock My Blues Away	Peacock 1653
	−1 Gatemouth plays harmonica.	

Vcl/gtr/vln (−1). with brass; pno; bs; dms.   Houston, 1960
ACA 3936	Just Before Dawn −1	Peacock 1692, Duke DLP 74
ACA 3937	Swingin' The Gate	−
FR 1058	Slop Time −1	Peacock 1696, Duke DLP 74
FR 1059	Gate's Tune	−

Vcl/gtr. with saxes; pno; bs; dms.   Houston, 1964
| 1050−1 | Summertime | Cue 1050 |
| 1050−2 | Left Over Blues | − |

Same: Nashville, 1965
ZTSB 101969
| | May The Bird Of Paradise Fly Up Your Nose | Hermitage 869 |
ZTSB 101970
| | A Long Way Home | − |

ELIJAH BROWN

Vcl/gtr.   East St. Louis, 1965
	Won't Be Troubled Long	Testament T−2209
	Pearline	−
	Windin' Ball	−
	Cryin' Won't Make Me Stay	Milestone LP 3002

HENRY BROWN

Born in Troy, Tennessee in 1906.
Vcl/pno.   St. Louis, August 25, 1960
	Deep Morgan Blues	unissued
	Henry Brown Blues	"77" LA 12/5
	Blues In St. Louis	unissued

Vcl/pno.   St. Louis, August 28, 1960
	O'Fallon Blues	"77" LA 12/5
	Bottled In Bond	−
	Papa Slick Head	−
	Henry Brown Boogie	−
	Handyman Blues	−
	My Blues Is In The Bottle	−
	Got It And Cain't Quit It	−
	Scufflin' Boogie	−
	Blues For Charlie O'Brien	−

36

	Blues For Charlie O'Brien	unissued
	Deep Morgan Is Delmar Now	"77" LA 12/5
Vcl/pno.		
	21st Street Stomp	Euphonic 1204
Vcl/pno.		St. Louis, March 13, 1965
	Deep Morgan Blues	Storyville SLP 188
	New Eastern Chimes	Storyville SLP 183
	Becky Thatcher Blues	Storyville SLP 183
	St. Louis Sweet Patootie	—

JAMES "WIDEMOUTH" BROWN – HIS GUITAR & ORCH.

Vcl/gtr. with Henry Hayes, alt; Ed Wiley, ten; Willie Johnson, pno; Donald Cooks, bs; Ben Turner, dms.　　　　　　　　　　　　　　　　　　　　Houston, 1951

4026–JA	A Weary Silent Night	Jax 306
4027–JA	Boogie Woogie Night Hawk	—
	Note: Brother of Gatemouth Brown q.v.	

JIMMY BROWN

Born Jackson, Mississippi in 1910
Vcl/vln.　　　　　　　　　　　　　　　　　　1964

	He Was Loved By All The People	Testament S-01

Vcl/vln with Big Joe Williams, gtr; Willie Lee Harris, hca　　1965?

	I Can See My Baby In My Dreams	Storyville SLP 180

Note: See also Big Joe W illiams.

JOE BROWN

Hca.　　　　　　　　　　　　　　　　　Livingstone, Ala? Jan/Feb. 1950

	Mama Don't Tear My Clothes	Folkways FE 4417, P 417
	Southern Pacific	—　　　　　　—

TEXAS JOHNNY BROWN

Vcl/gtr. with　　　　　　　　　　　　　　Houston 1949

A 223	The Blues Rock	Atlantic 876
A 224		
A 225	There Go The Blues	Atlantic 876

Vcl/gtr. with ? Brown, gtr.　　　　　　　　Houston 1951

ACA 1668	Christmas Time	ARC unissued
ACA 1669	You Won't Let Me In	—
ACA 1670	Streamlined Baby	—

Note: Later recordings not included.

LEE BROWN "THE HEARTBREAKER"

Vcl/pno. with ten: bs: dms.　　　　　　　　Chicago, 1946

C-11	My Little Girl Blue	Chicago 104
C-12	Bobby Town Boogie	—　　　, 20th Century 20-46

LEE BROWN & HIS BARBETON BOOGIE WOOGIE CATS
Vcl/pno. with ten; Leroy Foster, gtr; Big Crawford, bs.

K-5160	New Little Girl	Queen 4157, King 4157
K-5161	Brownie's Boogie	—　　　—

RAYFIELD BROWN

Vcl/hca. with gtr: bs: dms.　　　　　　　　c. 1964

	Snatching Back	Dumas 1207
	I'm So Glad Baby	—

LITTLE WILLIE BROWN

Vcl/hca. with ten: gtr: dms.   Houston, 1956
1111   Going Back To The Country   Suntan 1112
1112   Just Like This   –

LITTLE WILLIE BROWN & THE CAMEOS

Vcl/hca. with ten: pno: gtr: bs; dms; vcl. grp (-1)   Nashville, 1961
F-794   Cut It Out   Do-Ra-Me 1404
F-795   Gonna Make It On Back -1

Vcl/hca. with pno; gtr; bs-gtr; dms.   Nashville, January 1962
            Tell Me Why Love Don't Last   Do-Ra-Me unissued
            Do It Like That   –
            Together   –
            Your Good Loving   –

Note: There is also a Willie Brown who recorded jump blues for Decca who
has no connection with this artist.

W. B. "PIANO BILL" BRYSON

Vcl/pno   Chicago, 1964
            Sometimes I Rate   Storyville SLP 181
            Mean Old Train   Milestone LP 3002

BUDDY BOY

See under Buddy Guy.

MOJO BUFORD

Real name George Buford. Born Memphis, Tennessee on November 10, 1929.

LITTLE MOJO

Vcl/hca. with Little Sonny Rogers, gtr; Little Joe Williams (Jody Williams), el-bs; Francey
Clay, dm s.   Minneapolis, 1961/2
            Paula   Norman 505
            You Ain't The One   –
076   Something On My Mind   Indigo 139
077   Mojo Theme   –

MOJO & CHI 4

Same: Minneapolis, 1963
            Mojo Woman   Vernon VS 19
            Steal My Chickens   –
            Standing On The Corner   –
            Somebody Knockin'   –
            Tell Me Watcha Gonna Do   –
            Twin City Blues   –
            Chicago Four Blues   –
            Mojo Woman No. 2   –

MOJO /MUDDY WATERS Jr.

Add pno; saxes.
            Knocking On My Door   Folk-Art FLRP 101
            Shake For Me   –
            Flying Easy   –
            Come Home Easy   –
            Slim And Trim Mama   –
            Have You Ever Been Mistreated   –
            Blues For Slim   –
            Mojo's Woman   –
            The Morning Before Day   –
            Mojo Cha-Cha-Blues   –
            Shake It Baby   –
            Mojo Ride   –

38

MOJO
Similar   Minneapolis, 1964
                  It Was Early One Morning   Adell
                  Mojo Woman   –

MOJO BUFORD
Same, but org. replaces pno.
KB 4414A   Whole Lotta Woman   Bangar 00622
KB 4415B   Messin' With The Kid   –

JOHN BULLARD

JOHN BULLARD QUARTET
Vcl/pno. with gtr; bs; dms.   Miami, c. 1950
A   Don't Talk Dem Trash   Index 300
B   Callin' The Blues   –

JOHN BULLARD
Same, but Bobby Sands, vcl (-1)   Miami, 1952
GR 15139-1 Wester Union Blues –1   Deluxe 6019
GR 15140-1 Spoiled Hambone Blues   –
GR 15141-1 Mary Lou   Deluxe 6035
GR 15142-1 Help Me Find My Right Mind   –

BUMBLE BEE SLIM

See under Amos Easton.

ALLEN BUNN

Born North Carolina c. 1932
Vcl/gtr; with Sonny Terry, hca (-1); Wilbert Ellis, pno.   New York City, 1952
AP 3410   She'll Be Sorry -1   Apollo 436
AP 3411   The Guy With The "45" -1   –
AP 3412   Discouraged   Apollo 439
AP 3413   I Got You Covered   –
Add ten: bs: dms:
AP 3421   Wine   Apollo 442
Ap 3422   My Flight   Apollo 447
AP 3423   Baby I'm Going To Throw You Out   Apollo 442
AP 3424   Two Time Loser   Apollo 442

ALLEN BAUM
Vcl/gtr. with pno: bs; dms; vcl. grp (-1)   New York City, 1953
R 3043   My Kinda Woman -1   Red Robin 124
R 3044   Too Much Competition   –

TARHEEL SLIM
Vcl/gtr. with pno(-1); bs; dms.   New York City, 1958/59
FM 100   It's Too Late   Fire 1000
FM 101   Don't Ever Leave Me -1   –
            Much Too Late   Fire 1009
            Lock Me In Your Arms   –
Vcl/gtr. with pno; Jimmy Spruill, gtr; bs; dms.   New York City, 1959
F 1031   Wildcat Tamer   Fury 1016
F 1032   No. 9 Train   –

        Note: Later records by this artist are too commercial for inclusion in this
        discography.

DAN BURLEY

Born in Kentucky
Vcl(-1)/pno. with Brownie & Sticks McGhee, Gtrs; Pops Foster, bs.
                                                           New York City, June 11, 1946
NY-13-A   Big Cat, Little Cat -1   Circle 1021
NY-14-A   Shotgun House Rag   Circle 1022
NY-15-A   Lake Front Blues -1   –
NY-16   Fishtail Blues   unissued

39

NY-17-A	Three Flights Up	Circle 1021
NY-18	Hersal's Rats	unissued
NY-19	Dusty Bottom(no gtrs)	Circle 1020
NY-20	31st Street Blues	unissued
NY-21	Landlady's Night	unissued
NY-22	South Side Shake	Circle 1020

DAN BURLEY & HIS SKIFFLE BOYS

Vcl/pno. with James Archey, tbn; John Hardee, ten; Danny Barker, Herman Mitchell, gtrs; Pops Foster, bs. New York City, October, 1947

| DB 100 | Chicken Shack Shuffle | Arkay 1001, Exclusive 77 |
| DB 101 | Skiffle Blues | – |

EDDIE BURNS

Born Belzoni, Mississippi on February 8, 1928

SLIM PICKENS

Vcl/hca. with John T. Smith, gtr. Detroit, 1948

| 5353 B | Papa's Boogie | Holiday 202 |
| 5354 B | Bad Woman Blues | – |

Note: Originally recorded for Sensation as "Swing Brother".

EDDIE BURNS

Vcl/hca. with Chuck Smith, pno; Percy Lee Brown, gtr; Washboard Willie, wbd.

Detroit, 1952

| C-2-126 | Hello Miss Jessie Lee | Deluxe 6024 |
| C-2-127 | Dealing With The Devil | – |

BIG ED & HIS COMBO

Vcl/hca. with pno; gtr; bs; dms. Detroit 1954

| U 4409 | Superstition (vcl. duet) | Checker 790 |
| U 4410 | Biscuit Baking Mama | – |

EDDIE BURNS

Vcl/gtr. with pno: bs; dms. Detroit, 1957

| 82A | Treat Me Like I Treat You | JVS 82, Chess 1672 |
| 82B | Don't'Cha Leave Me Baby | – |

Vcl/gtr/hca (-1). with tpt; 2 tens; pno; bs; dms. Detroit, 1961

MO8W 2469 -1	Orange Driver	Harvey 111
MO8W 2470 -1	Hard Hearted Woman	–, 118
MO8W 4918	The Thing To Do -1	Harvey 115
MO8W 4919	Mean And Evil (Baby)	–
G-580-H	Messin' With My Bread	Harvey 118

Vcl/gtr. with pno; dms. Detroit, c. 1965

| 709A | You Say That You're Leaving | Von 709 |
| 709B | Wig Wearing Woman | – |

Vcl/hca/gtr (-1); with pno; gtr; dms Detroit, c. 1954

	She Keeps Me Guessing	Modern unissued
	Sitting Here Wondering	–
	I Love To Jump The Boogie	–
	Tavern Lounge Boogie -1	–

Note: FL 129/30 in wax on above tests, indicating recorded for Flair release

HAROLD BURTON

Vcl. with group vcl. Ramsey State Farm, Texas, March 17, 1951

Yellow Gal 77 LA 12/2

JOHNNY BUSBY

No details: 1960
        Cadillac Mama   Talent 108
        When The Blues Get You   —

JESSE BUTCHER

Vcl/hca. with Guitar Welch, gtr.   Angola, 1959/60
        They'll Miss Me When I'm Gone   Storyville SLP 125

GEORGE (WILD CHILD) BUTLER

Born Autaugaville, Alabama on October 1, 1936.
No details
        Down In The Chili   Shaw
        Aching All Over   —

Vcl/hca. with Shakey Horton, hca; Johnny Twist, gtr; Jack Meyers, bs-gtr; Vince Chappel,
dms; Willie Dixon, 2nd. vcl (-1).   Chicago, 1966

TM 1723	Do Something Baby	Jewel 769
TM 1724	Hold Me Baby -1	—
TM 2002	Open Up Baby -1	Jewel 780
TM 2003	Big Momma, Little Momm a	—
	Axe In The Wind	Jewel unissued
	You Treat Me Like I Treat You	—
	Moaning In The Morning	—
	You Must Have Another Man	—
	Rent Money	—
	Gone Again	—

ROLAND BYRD

See under Roy Byrd.

ROY BYRD

PROFESSOR LONGHAIR & HIS SHUFFLING HUNGARIANS
Vcl/pno. with saxes (-1): bs; dms.   New Orleans, 1949

280	She Ain't Got No Hair	Talen 809
281	Bye Bye Baby -1	—

ROY BYRD & HIS BLUES JUMPERS
Vcl/pno. with Robert Parker, alt; bs; John Woodrow, dms.   New Orleans, 1949

7804-3	Her Mind Is Gone	Mercury 8184
7805-1	Bald Head	Mercury 8175
7806-1	Hey Now Baby	—
7807-1	Oh Well	Mercury 8184
7820	Hadacol Bounce	Mercury 8184

      Note: Mercury 8184 issues with alternate reverses.
      The Mercury sides may precede the Talent issue.

ROY 'BALD HEAD' BYRD -1

ROLAND BYRD -2
As last   New Orleans, early 1950

A 336	Mardi Gras In New Orleans	Atlantic 897 -1
A 337	She Walks Right In	—
A 338	Hey Little Girl	Atlantic 947 -2
A 339	Willie Mae	—
A 340		

PROFESSOR LONGHAIR & HIS BLUES SCHOLARS
As last, but add ten:

A 341	Walk Your Blues Away	Atlantic 906
A 342	Professor Longhair Blues	—

ROY BYRD
Vcl/pno. with Charles Burban, ten; Walter Nelson, gtr; Willie Suregal, bs; Charles
Joseph Otis, dms.   New Orleans, December 4, 1951
F 208   K. C. Blues   Federal 12061

F 209	Curly Haired Baby	–
F 210	Rockin' With Fes	Federal 12073
F 211	Gone So Long	– , King LP 875

ROBERT BOYD
Vcl/pno. with gtr; dms.   Memphis?
| 5 | East St. Louis Baby | Wasco 201 |
| 6 | Boyd's Bounce | – |

PROFESSOR LONGHAIR & HIS BLUE SCHOLARS
Vcl/pno. with Robert Parker, ten; bs; dms.   New Orleans, 1954
| A 1173 | In The Night | Atlantic 1020 |
| A 1174 | Tipitina | – |

PROFESSOR LONGHAIR
Vcl/pno. with saxes. bs; dm s.   New Orleans, 1957
14551	Cry Pretty Baby	Ebb 101
14558	No Buts, No Maybes	–
106	Misery	Ebb 106
106X	Look What You're Doing To Me	–
17897	Looka No Hair	Ebb 121
17898	Baby Let Me Hold Your Hand	–

Same: New Orleans, 1959
R 113	Cuttin' Out	Ron 326
R 114	If I Only Knew	–
R 119	Go To The Mardi Gras	Ron 329
R 120	Every Day, Every Night	–

Note: Recent records by this artist not included.

C

WILLIE C.
See under Willie Cobbs.

ROBERT CAFFERY
No details: Chicago, 1951
| U 7339 | Ida Bee | Chess 1470 |
| U 7340 | Blodie's Blues | – |

BUTCH CAGE & WILLIE THOMAS
James Cage, born Franklin County, Mississippi on M arch 16, 1894. Willie Thomas, born
Lobdell, Louisiana on May 25, 1912.
Cage, vcl/ vln. with Thomas, Vcl/gtr; Martha Thomas, tom-tom(-1).

Zachary, La. 1959/60
44 Blues   Folk-Lyric FL-111

Who Broke The Lock		–
Jelly Roll		–
Brown Skin Wom an -1		–
It's The Sign Of The Judgement		–
Bugle Call Blues		Storyville SLP 129
If I Could Hear My Mother Pray Again		Storyville SLP 135
When I See The Blood		–
Jesus On The Mainline		–

same.   Newport, R.I. July 1959

I'm A Stranger Here		Folkways FA 2431
44 Blues		–

Cage, vcl/gtr.   Zachary, LA. August, 7, 1960

'Tween Midnight And Day		Decca LK 4664

add Thomas Vcl/gtr. Cage plays vln.

Kill That Nigger Dead		Decca LK 4664
One Thin Dime		Arhoolie F 1006
Forty Four Blues		Arhoolie F 1005
Butch's Blues		–

PERRY CAIN

Born in New Waverley, Texas in 1929
Vcl. with Buster Pickens, pno; Skippy Brown, bs.   Houston, 1948

A	All The Way From Texas	Gold Star 632
B	Cry, Cry	–

Vcl. with Ed Wiley, ten; Nathaniel Haskins, ten; Walter Green, tpt; Buster Pickens, pno;
unk. gtr; bs; Ben Turner, dms.   Houston, 1949

	My Heart Belongs To You	Freedom ?
	Big Timing Grandma	–

See also Henry Hayes.

BOB CALL

Vcl/pno. with   1949

	Talkin' Baby Blues	Coral 65009
	Call's Jump	–

BOB CAMP

BOB CAMP & HIS BUDDIES
Vcl/gtr. with pno; bs; dms.   New York City, 1945

C-1	Lonely	Southern 130
C-2	Gonna Pitch A Boogie Woogie	Southern 121
C-3	Blues Mixture	
C-4	Without Your Love	Souther 130

BOB CAM P & HIS BUDDIES
Vcl/gtr. with Lil Armstrong, pno; Brownie McGhee, gtr; Billy Taylor Sr., bs; Herb
Cowans, dms.   New York City, July 13, 1949

75061-3A	Reading Blues	Decca 48112
75062-4A	When You Surrender To Me	Decca 48118
75063-3A	Between You and Me (gtrs. out)	–
75064-1A	My Little Rose	Decca 48112

THE NIGHTHAWKS
Bob Camp & another, gtrs; bs; traps.   New York City, 1952

NH-1	Out Cattin'	Essex 714

BOB CAMP & THE NIGHTHAWKS
Add Camp, vcl.; pno; ensemble vcl;

NH-2	Pitch A Boogie	Essex 714

Note: The Bob Camp sides on Ebony are of no interest.

CARL CAMPBELL

Vcl. with		Houston, 1949
1196	Between Midnight And Dawn	Freedom 1521
1197	Ooh Wee Baby	–

CARL CAMPBELL WITH HENRY HAYES 4 KINGS
Vcl. with Henry Hayes, alt; ten; Elmore Nixon, pno; gtr; bs; dms;

		Houston, 1950
ACA 1552	Traveling On	Peacock 1538
ACA 1553	Early Morning Blues	

Vcl. with		Houston, 1958
ACA 3634	I Love You Baby	Magic
ACA 3635	Paree	–

BLIND JAMES CAMPBELL

Vcl/gtr. with Beauford Clay, Vcl/vln; Bell Ray, vcl/gtr; George Bell, tpt; Ralph Robinson, tuba, (collective personnel).

	Nashville, October, 25-26, 1962 Or April 14, 1963.
Sittin' Here Drinkin'	Arhoolie F 1012
Have I Stayed Away Too Long	Arhoolie F 1015
I'm Crazy About You Baby	–
Buffalo Girl	–
Will The Circle Be Unbroken	–
The Moon May Rise In Blood	–
John Henry	–
Baby Please Don't Go	–
Jimmy's Blues	–
Monkey Man Blues	–
This Little Light Of Mine	–
Detroit Blues	–
Beauford's Breakdown	–

LOUIS CAMPBELL

THE LEAPFROGS
Vcl (-1). with Jimmy Johnson, hca; Arthur & Al Gunter, gtrs; bs; dms.

		Nashville, 1954
A	Dirty Britches	Excello 2014
B	Things Gonna Change -1	–

LOUIS CAMPBELL
Vcl. with Jimmy Johnson, hca; Skippy Brooks, pno; gtr; bs; dms.

A	Gotta Love You Baby	Excello 2035
B	The Natural Facts	

GUS CANNON

Born Red Bank, Mississippi c. 1887
Vcl/bjo (-1)

	Memphis, December 5, 1956
Interview	Folkways FA 2610
Old John Booker -1	–
Kansas City Blues -1	–

Vcl/bjo. with Will Shade, jug; unk. wbd.

	Memphis, 1963
Narration	Stax 702
Kill It	–
Walk Right In	–
Salty Dog	–
Going Around The Mountain	–
Ol' Hen	–
Gonna Raise A Ruckus Tonight	–
Ain't Gonna Rain No More	–
Boll-Weevil	–
Come On Down To My House	–
Make Me A Pallet On Your Floor	–
Get Up In The Morning Soon	–
Crawdad Hole	–

CAROLINA SLIM (The Late)

Real name Ed Harris.
Vcl/gtr. with gtr. (-1)   1951
US 11640   Mama's Boogie -1   Acorn 3015
US 11641   Come Back Baby   Acorn 319
US 11642
US 11643   Black Chariot Blues   Acorn 3015
US 11644   Pleading Blues   Acorn 319

COUNTRY PAUL
Vcl/gtr.   early 1952
8212-1   Mother Dear Mother   King 4573
8213-1   Side Walk Boogie
8214-1   I'll Never Walk In Your Door   King 4560
8215-1   Black Cat Trail   —

LAZY SLIM JIM
Vcl/gtr. with dms. (on -1)   Atlanta? 1952
AC 3654   Georgia Woman   Savoy 854
AC 3655   Money Blues
ALT 3656   Wine Head Baby -1   Savoy 887, Sharp 2002
ALT 3657   One More Drink   —   —

CAROLINA SLIM -1

JAMMIN' JIM -2

LAZY SLIM JIM -3
Vcl./gtr. with dms.*
AS 23002   Shake Boogie -2*   Savoy 1106, Sharp 2002
AS 23003
AS 23004   Slo Freight Blues -3*   Savoy 868, Sharp 2002
AS 23005   Rag Mama -1*   Acorn 324,   —
AS 23006   Sugaree -3   Savoy 868,   —
              Carolina Boogie -1* (duet)   —

CAROLINA SLIM -1

JAMMIN' JIM -2
Vcl/gtr.
CS 496   Jivin' Woman -2   Savoy 1106
CS 497NI   I'll Get By Somehow -1   Acorn 324, Sharp 2002
CS 498NI   Blues Knocking At My Door -1   Acorn 323,   —
CS 499NI   Worry You Off My Mind -1   —   —

CAROLINA SLIM
Vcl/gtr.
              Blues Go Away From Me   Sharp 2002
              Worrying Blues   —

        Note: See also Country Paul.

GUNTER LEE CARR

See Under Cecil Gant.

CARROLL COUNTY BOYS

No interest but see Pee Wee Crayton

BIG BLUES CARSON

Vcl. with ten; pno; gtr; dms.   Detroit, c. 1963
F 297   The Night You Left   Fortune 860
F 298   Why Did You Leave   —

NELSON CARSON

See under Nelson Carter.

CARTER BROTHERS

Born Garland, Alabama?
Roman Carter, vcl/gtr; Jerry Carter, vcl/pno; Al Carter, Gtr; with saxes; el-bs; dms.

		Los Angeles? 1964
	Consider Yourself	Coleman 1925
	Do The Watusi	–
Same:		Los Angeles? 1965/66
745-1	Do The Flo Show	Jewel 745
745-2	Southern Country Boy	–
TM 1426	Booze In The Bottle	Jewel 754, A-Bet LP 401
TM 1427	Stop Talking In Your Sleep	–
TM 1516	I've Been Mistreated	Jewel 760
TM 1517	I Don't Care	–
TM 1656	Booby Trap Baby	Jewel 766
TM 1657	So Glad She's Mine	–

Note: San Fernando Valley Based group. Records produced by Earl Coleman.

GOREE CARTER (OR GOREY/GORY CARTER)

Vcl/gtr. with		Houston, 1949
ACA 1045	Sweet Ole Woman's Blues	Freedom 1502
	(rev. by Little Willie Littlefield)	

GOREE CARTER & HIS HEPCATS

Vcl/ gtr. with Nelson Mills, tpt; Conrad Johnson, alt; Sam Williams, ten; Lonnie Lyons, pno; Louis "Nunu" Pitts, bs; Allison Tucker, dms.

F 1055	Back Home Blues	Freedom 1506
F 1056	Rock Awhile	–
ACA 1068	I'll Send You	Freedom 1511
ACA 1069	How Can You Love Me	–
ACA 1078	My Love Is Coming Down	Freedom 1525
ACA 1079	Hoy, Hoy	Freedom 1516
ACA 1080	I'll Make It All Right	unissued
ACA 1081	Where Shall I Be	unissued
ACA 1097	I Just Thought Of You	Freedom 1516

GOREE CARTER WITH HIS GUITAR & ROCKIN' RHYTHM ORCH.

As last:

SMK 1164	She's Just Old Fashioned	Freedom 1518
ACA 1165	Workin' With My Baby	Freedom 1525
SMK 1178	Is It True	Freedom 1518
1225	What A Friend Will Do	Freedom 1522
1226	She's My Best Bet	–

GOREE CARTER

As last:

ACA 1279	Serenade	Freedom 1536
ACA 1280	Rhumba Blues	unissued
ACA 1281	Getting High	unissued
As last:		Houston, 1950
ACA 1496	Come on Let's Boogie	Freedom 1536

From above sessions and possibly retitled:

FK 12	Drunk Or Sober (rev. by Clarence Samuels)	Bayou 010
IM 327	You're My Everything	Imperial 5152
IM 328	Every Dog Has His Day	–

Vcl/gtr. with Henry Hayes, alt; Ed Wiley, ten; Willie Johnson, pno; Donald Cooks, bs; Ben Turner, dms.

		Houston, 1950
2058	Jumpin' At Jeff's -1	SIW 572
2088	Everybody's Love Crazy	SIW 556
2091	Let's Rock	–
2092	True Love is Hard To Find	SIW 572

-1 This does not feature Goree, though credited to him.

Possibly from last session: –
8150   I've Got News For You   Coral 65058
8151   I'm Your Boogie Man   Coral 65064
8152   Please Say You're Mine
8153   Tell Me Is There Still A Chance   Coral 65058

AS ROCKY THOMPSON (JADE) OR GORY CARTER (MODERN)
As last: Houston, 1951
2267   Bull Corn Blues   Jade 207
2268   My Wish   –
MM 1536   Seven Days   Modern 20-819
MM 1537   When Night Falls   –
No details: Houston, 1954
ACA 2962   Let's Make Love   Peacock unissued
ACA 2963   My Love Comes Down To You   unissued
ACA 2964   Let Me Be Your Fellow   unissued
ACA 2965   All Exhausted   unissued

See also Joe Turner in Vol. 2

NELSON CARTER & HIS GUITAR

Vcl/gtr. with Henry Hayes, alt; Ed Wiley, ten; Willie Johnson, pno; Donald Cooks, bs;
Ben Turner, dms.   Houston, 1950
2094   My Baby Left Me   SIW 557
2098   Crazy About My Baby

Note: This is a probable pseudonym for Goree Carter, or may be a relative.

CASANOVA JR.

No details: 1957
              Sally Mae   Port 7001
              They Call Me Casanova   –

CAT-IRON

Vcl/gtr.   Buckner's Alley, Miss.,1958
              Poor Boy, A Long Long Way From Home   Folkways FA 2389
              Don't Your House Look Lonesome   –
              Tell Me, You didn't Mean Me No Good   –
              Jimmy Bell   –
              I'm Goin' To Walk Your Log   –
              Got A Girl In Farriday, One In Greenwood Town   –

Note: Other Side of this LP is devoted to Gospel songs.

ANDREW CAUTHEN

Vcl/hca with Jesse Jones, hca; Big Joe Williams, gtr.   East St. Louis,1965
              Canary Bird   Testament T-2209

GODAR CHALVIN

Vcl/accdn.   Abbeville, La.,1959
              Annons Au Bal Colinda   Louisiana Folk Soc. A-1
              Settin' Side Dat Road   –

CHAMBERS BROTHERS

Joe & Willie Chambers, vcl/gtrs; Lester Chambers, vcl/hca; George Chambers; vcl/bs-gtr;
Mike Konnic, dms.   Los Angeles & Boston 1966
              Yes, Yes, Yes   Vault LP 9003
              Tore Up   –
              Reconsider Baby   –
              You've Got Me Running   –
              People Get Ready   –

47

Money (That's What I Want)		–
You Can Run (But You Can't Hide)		–
Hooka Tooka		–
Call Me		–
Summertime		–
Your Old Lady		–
It's All Over Now		–
Seventeen		Vault 920
Call Me		–

CLISTON CHANIER

See under Clifton Chenier.

ROOSEVELT CHARLES

Vcl/gtr.   New York City, c.1964
     Bye Bye Baby Blues   Storyville SLP180
     unknown titles   Vanguard VRS 9136

SAM CHATMAN

Born Bolton, Mississippi in 1899
Vcl/gtr.   Hollandale, Miss., July 25, 1960
     I Have To Paint My Face   Arhoolie F 1005
     Nigger Be A Nigger   –
     Sat And Wondered   –
     God Don't Like Ugly   Arhoolie F 1006

BOOZOO CHAVIS

Real name Wilson Chavis. Born Lake Charles, La. on October, 23, 1930.
Vcl/accdn. with ten; Classie Ballou, gtr; Sid Lawrence, bs; Wilson Semien, dms.

                                           Lake Charles, 1954

6096 IM957	Boozoo Stomp	Folk Star 1197, Imperial 5374
6097 IM956	Paper In My Shoe	–
A	Forty One Days	Folk Star 1201
B	Bye Bye Catin	–

Vcl. (-1)/accdn. with gtr; Little Brother Griffin, vcl(-2)/dms. Lake Charles, 1964

SO:4534	Hamburgers And Popcorn -2	Goldband 1161
SO:4535	Tee Black -1	–

BIG CHENIER

Real name Morris Chenier. Born Opelousas, La. in 1929

BIG CHENIER & THE R. B. ORCH
Vcl/gtr. with Robert Jackson, pno; Guitar Joe, gtr; Ice Water, bs; Joe Payne, dms.

                                           Lake Charles, La.,1957

A	Let Me Hold Your Hand	Goldband 1051
B	Please Try To Realise	–
	The Dog And His Puppies	Storyville SLP 177
	Going To The City	–

BIG CHENIER & HIS NIGHT OWLS
Vcl/gtr. with Eddie Williams org.   Lake Charles, Nov. 14, 1960

A	The Dog And His Puppies	Goldband 1131
B	Let Me Hold Your Hand	–

CLIFTON CHENIER

Born Opelousas, Louisiana on June 25, 1925

CLISTON CHANIER ON -1 OR CLIFTON CHENIER ON -2
Vcl/accdn. with Big Chenier, gtr; Robert Pete, dms.   Lake Charles, La., 1954
226,920B   Louisiana Stomp -1   Elko 920, Imperial 5352,
                                           Arhoolie LP 1009

227, 920A	Cliston Blues -1	issues as previous page
IM 870N	Tell Me -2	Post 2016
IM 871	Country Bred -2	Post 2010
IM 935	Rockin' The Bop -2	–
IM 935N	Rockin' Hop -2	Post 2016
	Just A Lonely Boy	unissued

CLIFTON CHENIER

Vcl/accdn. with James Jones, pno; Philip Walker, gtr; "Candy", bs; unk. dms.

Los Angeles, 1955

SP 552,3943	Boppin' The Rock	Specialty 552
XSP 552	Ay-Tete-Fee	

Vcl/accdn. With James Jones, pno; Lonesome Sundown, gtr; "Candy", bs; Little Brother Griffin, dms.

SP 556	Think It Over	Specialty 556
XSP 556	The Things I Did For You	–
SP 568	The Cat's Dreaming	Specialty 568
XSP 568	Squeeze Box Boogie	–

Vcl/accdn. with Lionel Prevo, B. G. Jones, saxes; James Jones, pno; Philip Walker, gtr; "Candy", bs; Wilson Semien, dms.

Los Angeles, 1956

8331	Where Can My Baby Be (Standing On The Corner)	Argo 5262
8332		
8333	The Big Wheel (omit saxes)	Argo 5262

Same:

Chicago, 1957

8568	Bayou Drive	Checker 939
8569	My Soul	

Same:

Crowley, La.,1961

Z-7452	It Happened So Fast	Zynn 506
Z-7453	Goodbye Baby	–
Z-7476	Worried Life Blues	Zynn 1004
Z-7477	Hey Mama	
Z-7488	Night And Day My Love	Zynn 1011
Z-7489	Rockin' Accordian	–

Vcl/accdn. with Elmore Nixon, pno; Bob Murphy, dms. Houston, February 8, 1964
506A, LH 2676

	Ay Ai Ai	Arhoolie 506, F 1031, Bayou 704
506B	Why Did You Go Last Night	– F 1018

Vcl/accdn/hca (–1). with Elmore Nixon, pno; Cleveland Keyes, gtr; Fulton Antoine, bs; Robert St. Judy, dms. Houston, May 11, 1965

	Accordian Boogie	Arhoolie F 1024
	Hot Rod	Arhoolie 509, F 1024, Bayou 701
	Banana Man	Arhoolie F 1024
	Hey Tete Fee	
F 2595	It's Hard –1	Arhoolie 518, F 1024
	I Can't Stand –1	Arhoolie F 1024

Vcl/accdn. with Cleveland Chenier, wbd; Madison Guidry, dms.

	Clifton Waltz (no dms)	Arhoolie F 1024
511A	(Zydeco) Haricots Et Pas Sale	– , 511, Bayou 702
LH 2519	Lafayette Waltz	– , Bayou 703
	Louisiana Two Step	–
	Louisiana Blues	– , 509, Bayou 701
511B	I Can Look Down On Your Woman	– , 511, Bayou 702

Vcl/accdn. with Francey Clay, dms. Berkeley, Calif.,April 15, 1966

	Louisiana Rock	Arhoolie F 1030
	Clifton's After Hours	–
	Pinetop's Boogie Woogie	–

Vcl/accdn. with Big Chenier, vln; unk. dms.   Passadena, Texas, May 10, 1966
LH 2675   Oh Negresse   Arhoolie F 1031, Bayou 704
             Black Gal   —
LH 3049   Baby Please Don't Go   —   , Bayou 705
Vcl/accdn. with Elmore Nixon, pno; Cleveland Keyes, gtr; unk. bs–gtr; dms.
                                                               same date
LH 2518   Bon Ton Roulet   Arhoolie F 1031, Bayou 703
F 2596   Keep On Scratchin'   —   , 518
LH 3048   Frog Legs   —   , Bayou 705
             If I Ever Get Lucky   —
             Long Toes   —
             Sweet Little Doll   —
             Jolè Blonde   —
             Can't Stop Loving You   —
Vcl/accdn. with bs–gtr; dms; pno.   Pasadena, late 1966
CC 1   Say Too Koreck   Crazy Cajun 520
CC 2   La Coeur De La Louisianna   —

ROSCO CHENIER

No details.   Opelousas, La., 1963
A   I Broke The Yo Yo   Reynaud 1018
B   Born For Bad Luck   —

CHICAGO BILL

See under Big Bill Broonzy.

CHICAGO SUNNY BOY

Vcl/hca. with pno; gtr; bs; dms.   Chicago, 1953
MR 5012 Re Jack Pot   Meteor 5004
MR 5015   Western Union Man   —
             Note: Probably Forect City Joe, q.v.

BUDDY CHILES

Vcl/gtr.   Houston, 1949
660A   Mistreated Blues   Gold Star 660, Blues Classics 16
660B   Jet Black Woman   —

CHARLES CLARK

Vcl. with Willie Dixon Band: Sonny Boy Williamson, hca; Harold Burrage, pno; Otis Rush,
Louis Miles, gtrs; Willie Dixon, bs; Billie Stepney, dms.   Chicago, 1958
C-1040   Row Your Boat   Artistic 1500
C-1041   Hidden Charms   —

JAMES "BEALE STREET" CLARKE

Vcl. with clt; pno; dms.   Chicago, October 22, 1945
CCO 4461   Who But You   unissued
CCO 4462   I'll Never Be Good No More   unissued
CCO 4463   Love Me Or Let Me Be   Columbia 36948, 30005
CCO 4464   Get Ready To Meet Your Man   —   , —

MEMPHIS JIMMY
Vcl. with Leonard Caston, pno; Ollie Crawford, gtr; Alfred Elkins, bs.
                                                               Chicago, February 22, 1946
D6-AB-1838 Drifting   Victor 20-1887, Bluebird
                                                               34-0748

JAMES "BEALE STREET" CLARKE
Vcl. with   Chicago, February 24, 1946
CCO 4492   Since We Been Together   Columbia unissued
CCO 4493   Bad About Them Things   —
CCO 4494   We Are Going Down Together   —
CCO 4495   Country Woman Blues   —

Vcl. with   Chicago, September 27, 1946
CCO 4655   Come To Me Baby   Columbia 37391, 30020
CCO 4656   You Can't Make The Grade   –   –

MEMPHIS JIMMY
Vcl/pno. with J. T. Brown's Boogie Band: Howard Dixon, alt; J. T. Brown, ten; Lonnie
Graham, gtr; Willie Dixon, bs.   Chicago, April 3, 1947
D7-VB 0387 Where Shall I Go   Victor 20-2278
D7-VB-0388 Jimmie's Jump   –

DOCTOR CLAYTON

Name variously given as Peter J. Clayton or Cleighton. Died Chicago in 1946.
Vcl. with Leonard Caston, pno; Ollie Crawford, gtr; Alfred Elkins, bs.
                                             Chicago, February 22, 1946
D6-AB-1834 Root Doctor Blues   unissued
D6-AB-1835 Midnight Rambler   unissued
D6-AB-1836 Angels In Harlem   unissued
D6-AB-1837 Chain Eagle Blues   unissued

Vcl. with Blind John Davis, pno; Willie Lacey, gtr; Ransom Knowling, bs.
                                             Chicago, August 7, 1946
D6-VB-1921 I Need My Baby   Victor 20-1995
D6-VB-1922 Ain't Gonna Drink No More   Victor 20-2153
D6-VB-1923 Angels In Harlem   –
D6-VB-1924 Root Doctor Blues   Victor 20-2323
D6-VB-1925 Copper Colored Mama   –
D6-VB-1926 Hold That Train Conductor   Victor 20-1995, Groove 4G-
                                             5006

   Note: The two titles remade from February 22, 1946 session on August 7 are
   assumed to be those chosen for release.

HENRY CLEMENT

Vcl/gtr. with gtr; bs–gtr; dms.   Crowley, La., 1961
LH 1922   Late Hour Blues   Spot 1000
LH 1923, Z-7480
            Trojan Walla   –   , Zynn 1006
Z-7481   I'll Be Waiting   Zynn 1006

PAUL CLIFTON

Vcl. with ten; hca; pno; gtr; bs; dms.   Los Angeles, 1957
127A   Are You Alright   Flash 127
127B   Ain't I Cried Enough   –

WILLIE COBBS

Vcl/gtr. with saxes; pno; bs; dm.   Memphis, 1961
M-18,16872 You Don't Love Me   Mojo 2168, Home Of The Blues
                                             231, Vee Jay 441, Boot Heel
                                             182
M-19   You're So Hard To Please   Mojo 2168, Home of The Blues
                                             231, Vee Jay 441

Vcl/gtr. with saxes; org; bs; dm.   Memphis, 1962
3000   Don't Say Goodbye   C & F 300/1, Ascot ?
3001   Five Long Years
   Note: 3000 reissued as "Hoppin' Bird" (S-2980) with vcl. grp. dubbed on Ruler
   1131 and Rice Belt 1131.

Vcl/gtr. with bs–gtr; dms.   Memphis, 1963
S-2981   Slowdown   Ruler 1131, Rice Belt 1131

WILLIE C.
Vcl/gtr. with pno; bs; dm; vcl. grp.
S 241   We'll All Be There (duet)   Ruler 5000
JB 242   Slow Down Baby   –

WILLIE COBBS

Vcl/gtr/hca (−1) with saxes; tpt; pno; bs; dm.   Chicago, 1963
| 2003 | Too Sad −1 | JOB 1127 |
| 2004 | Come On Home | − |

Vcl/gtr. with tpt; saxes; org; bs; dm.   Memphis, 1964/65
PG-504	Lonely Boy	Pure Gold 302
PG-505	Here Is My Heart	−
PG-518	Big Boss Man	Pure Gold 309
PG-519	Kissa Me One More Time	−
PG-526	Come On Home	Pure Gold 313
PG-527	Too Sad	−

Vcl/gtr. with tpt (−1); org; dm.   Memphis, late 1965
W-11765A	My Little Girl −1	Whirl-A-Way 1065
W-11765B, 16871		
	Mistreated Blues	− , Boot Heel 182

J. C. COLE

Vcl/gtr.   Memphis, c. 1953
	No Right Blues	Sun unissued
	Southside Blues	−
	Ida Mae Blues	−
	Move Me No More	−

GEORGE COLEMAN

Vcl/pno.   Galveston, Texas, 1958
| | After Hours Improvisation | "77" LA 12/2 |
| | This World Is In A Terrible Condition | "77" LA 12/3 |

HONEY COLEMAN

Vcl. with pno; gtr; dms.   Los Angeles, c. 1952
| JP 3 A | Talk About A Girl Child Being Down | Combo 3 |
| JP 3 B | Daddy Why Did You Leave Me | − |

BIG TOM COLLINS

See under Brownie McGhee.

CONFINERS

Hca (−1) or ten (−2). with pno; gtr; dms.   Miss. State Prison, 1961
| SJW 3648 | Harmonica Boogie −1 | Electro 261 |
| SJW 3648 | The Toss Bounce −2 | − |

CONNIE'S COMBO

See under L. C. Williams and Conrad Johnson.

ASHTON CONROY

See under Katie Webster.

JOHN LEE COOKER

See under John Lee Hooker.

DONALD COOKS

SILVER COOKS WITH THE GONDOLIERS

Vcl/hca. with Papa Lightfoot, hca; unk. pno; Edgar Blanchard, gtr; unk. dms.   Houston, 1949
ACA 1314	Mr. Ticket Agent	Peacock 1510
ACA 1315	Coming Back Home	−
ACA 1316	Sailboat On The Ocean	unissued
ACA 1317	Even Though	unissued

52

DONALD COOKS & HIS BAND
Vcl/bs. with Henry Hayes, alt; Ed Wiley, ten; Willie Johnson, pno; Ben Turner, dms.

		Houston, 1951
2210	Dolphin Street Stomp	Jade 202
2235	Trouble Making Woman	–

SILVER COOKS

See under Donald Cooks.

COOL CATS

Robert Young, vcl. with Arthur Williams, ten; Edward Davenport, alt; Robert Milton, Philip Amour, Fred Hollingsworth, gtrs; Junior Jones, dms.   Angola, 1959
Goin' Home To My Old Used To Be   Storyville SLP 125

LITTLE COOPER

LITTLE COOPER & THE DRIFTERS
Probably Little Sonny Cooper, vcl/hca. with 2 gtrs; dms.   Granite, Ill., 1959

377	Evening Train	Stevens 105
378	Moving Slow	–

LITTLE SONNY COOPER

Vcl/hca. with Freddie King, Willie Wine, gtrs; Jimmy Robinson, dms.

	Chicago, 1953
unissued titles	Parrot

Vcl/hca. with Eugene Williams, gtr; Hayes Winkfield, dms.   Chicago,
unissued titles   Chess

RATTLESNAKE COOPER

Vcl/gtr. with Sonny Boy Davis, pno.   Dallas?, 1949

180	Rattlesnake Blues	Talent 804
181	Lost Woman	–
	See also Sonny Boy Davis.	

JOHN COPELAND

See under Mississippi String Band.

JAMES COTTON

Born Tunica, Mississippi on July 1, 1925.
Vcl. with Raymond Hill, ten; Albert Joiner, pno; Pat Hare, gtr; John Bowers, dms.

		Memphis, 1954
U 98	My Baby	Sun 199
U 99	Straighten Up Baby	–

Vcl. with Pat Hare, Willie Johnson, gtrs; John Bowers, dms.

U 120	Cotton Crop Blues	Sun 206, Blues Classics 15
U 121	Hold Me In Your Arms	–

Vcl/hca. with Pat Hare, Luther Tucker, gtrs; Willie Smith, dms.

		Chicago,
	I Want To Boogie	Abb unissued
	A Panic	–

Note: Above titles subsequently sold to Chess Records.

Vcl/hca. with Keith Scott, pno (–1); Alexis Korner, gtr; Chris Barber, gtr (–2)/bs (–3)/
tbn (–4).   London, August, 1961

	Dealing With The Devil –1, 3	Columbia SEG 8141	
	Standing Around Crying –2	–	
	Slow And Easy –2	–	
	Rock Me Mama –1, 4	–	, SEG 8226

	Jimmy's Jump −1, 3	Columbia SEG 8189
	Decoration Day Blues −2	−
	Polly Put The Kettle On −1, 3	−
	Goin' Down Slow −2	−

Vcl/hca. with Otis Spann, pno; James Madison, gtr; S. P. Leary, dms.

Chicago, 1965

	Cotton Crop Blues	Vanguard VRS 9217
	The Blues Keep Falling	−
	Love Me Or Leave Me	−
	Rocket 88	−
	West Helena Blues	−

Vcl/hca. with pno; Sammy Lawhorn, gtr; gtr; bs; Sammy Lay, dms.

Chicago, 1966

| JX 70101 | Complete The Order | Loma 2042 |
| JX 70102 | Laying In The Weeds | − |

SYLVESTER COTTON

Vcl/gtr.   Detroit, 1949

7024	Ugly Woman Blues	Sensation 7000, Modern 20-655
MM 1927	I Tried	Modern 893
7032	Sak-Relation Blues	Sensation 7000, Modern 20-655

Note: Modern 893 issued as by John Lee Hooker.

LITTLE WILLIE COTTON

with Al Prince Orch.
Vcl/gtr. with pno; bs; dms.   Los Angeles, 1952

| ST 319A | Gonna Shake It Up And Go | Swing Time 319 |
| ST 319A+ | A Dream | − |

Note: See also Al Prince.

COUNT ROCKIN' SYDNEY

See under Rockin' Sydney.

COUNTRY JIM

Real name James Bledsoe.
Vcl/gtr. with bs.   New Orleans?, 1949

IM 144	Old River Blues	Imperial 5073
IM 145	I'll Take You Back Baby	−
IM 146	Rainy Morning Blues	Imperial 5062
IM 147	Avenue Breakdown	−

add dms.   New Orleans?, 1950

IM 186	Sad And Lonely Blues	Imperial 5095
IM 187	Good Looking Mama	Imperial 5091
IM 188	Phillipine Blues	Imperial 5095
IM 189	Plantation Blues	Imperial 5091

HOT ROD HAPPY
Vcl/gtr. with el−bs; dms.   Shreveport, early '50's

| HB 1014A | Hot Rod Boogie | Pacemaker 1014 |
| HB 1014B | Worried Blues | − |

COUNTRY PAUL

Vcl/gtr.   late 1951

K 8146-1	Since I Seen Your Smiling Face	King 4532
K 8147	Your Picture Done Faded	King 4517
K 8148	Ain't It A Shame	−
K 8149-1	One More Time	King 4532

Note: Credits to P. Howard. Other Country Paul issues are by Carolina Slim. This may also be the same artist.

Vcl/gtr. with Buddy Floyd, ten; David Lee Johnson, pno; Bill Davis, bs; Candy Johnson, dms. & others.

COUNTRY SLIM/MISS COUNTRY SLIM
See under Ernest Lewis.

COUSIN LEROY
Real name Leroy Rozier.
Vcl/gtr. with unk. hca (−1); Jack Dupree, pno; Larry Dale, lead gtr; Sid Wallace, bs;

Gene Brooks, dms.		New York City, July 1, 1955
F5-JB-5145	Lonesome Bedroom	unissued
F5-JB-5146	41 Highway	unissued
F5-JB-5147	Goin' Back Home (no pno) −1	Groove 4G-0123
F5-JB-5148	Catfish	−

Wallace out:		New York City, August, 1957
E-2132	Will A Matchbox Hold My Clothes	Ember 1016
E-2134	I'm Lonesome −1	Ember 1023
E-2135	Highway 41	Ember 1016
E-2136/39		
E-2140	Up The River −1	Ember 1023

Same: probably at same session.		
H-1458	Waiting At The Station	Herald 546
H-1459	Crossroads	−

PEE WEE CRAYTON
Real name Connie Curtis Crayton. Born Austin, Texas on December 18, 1914.

Vcl/gtr. with		Los Angeles, 1947
3091	After Hours Boogie	Four Star 1304
3092	Why Did You Go	

Vcl/gtr. with saxes; pno; bs; dms.		Los Angeles, 1949
MM 866	Bounce Pee Wee	Modern 20-719
MM 867−1	Blues After Hours	Modern 20-624, Crown CLP 5175, Kent 5027
MM 868		
MM 869−1	I'm Still In Love With You	Modern 20-624, LP 2005
MM 870		
MM 871		
MM 872-1	Rock Island Blues	Modern 20-658, Crown CLP 5175
MM 924 (FL 224)		
	Texas Hop (Dizzy)	Modern 20-643, Flair 1061
MM 925-3	Central Avenue Blues	−
MM 926	I Love You So	Modern 20-675
MM 927-2	When Darkness Falls	−
MM 1074-1	The Bop Hop	Modern 20-658
MM 1147-3	Brand New Woman	Modern 20-707
MM 1148		
MM 1149-4	Tired Of Travelin'	Modern 20-796, Crown CLP 5175
MM 1162AS	Long After Hours	Modern 20-707
MM 1224-3	Old Fashioned Baby	Modern 20-719, Crown CLP 5175

Vcl/gtr. with Harry Edison's Orchestra:		
MM 1294-1	Please Come Back	Modern 20-732
MM 1295-1	Louella Brown	Modern 20-763
MM 1296		
MM 1297-3	Rockin' The Blues	Modern 20-732

No details:		
MM 1332-5	Some Rainy Day	Modern 20-742
MM 1333-3	Change Your Way Of Lovin'	Modern 20-796
MM 1334		
MM 1335-3	Huckle Boogie	Modern 20-742

Note: "Dizzy" on Flair 1061 credited to The Carroll Country Boys.

Vcl/gtr. with saxes; pno; bs; dms.   Los Angeles, 1950
MM 1351-4   Good Little Woman   Modern 20-774
MM 1352-5   Dedicating The Blues   –

                                Los Angeles, October, 1951
MM 1542-3   Poppa Stoppa   Modern 20-816
MM 1543-4   Thinking Of You   –
MM 1922   Cool Evening   Modern 892
MM 1923   Have You Lost Your Love For Me

From unknown sessions:
                Blues In My Heart   Crown CLP 5175
                Phone Call From My Baby   –
                California Woman   –
                Blues For My Baby   –
                My Everything   –
                Pee Wee's Boogie   –

WITH MAXWELL DAVIS ORCH:
Vcl/gtr. with Maxwell Davis, ten;   Los Angeles, November 5, 1951
RR 1792   Pee Wee's Blues   unissued
RR 1793   When It Rains It Pours   Aladdin 3112
RR 1794   Daybreak   –
RR 1795   Blues Before Dawn   unissued

WITH RED CALLENDER SEXTET:
Vcl/gtr. with Bumps Meyers, ten; Red Callender, bs; Chico Hamilton, dms; & others.
                                  Los Angeles, 1954
A   Pappy's Blues   RIH 408
AA   Crying And Walking   –
A   Baby Pat The Floor   RIH 426
AA   I'm Your Prisoner   –
                Steppin' Out   Hollywood 1055
                Hey Little Dreamboat   –

       Note: Hollywood 1055 issued as by Homer The Great.

Vcl/gtr. with saxes; pno; bs; dms. (Probably Dave Bartholomew's Band).
                                  New Orleans?, 1954
IM 722   Win-O (no saxes)   Imperial 5297
IM 723   Do Unto Others   Imperial 5288
IM 724   Every Dog Has His Day   –
IM 725   Hurry, Hurry   Imperial 5297

Same:
IM 775   Eyes Full Of Tears   Imperial 5345
IM 776   I Need Your Love   Imperial 5321, LP 9099
IM 777   You Know-Yeah   –
IM 778   Runnin' Wild   Imperial 5345

Same: New Orleans? January, 1955
IM 839   Baby Don't You Cry   unissued
IM 837   My Idea About You   Imperial 5338
IM 838   I Got News For You   –
IM 840   Don't Break My Heart   unissued

Same: Add vcl. grp (–1).   New Orleans?, 1955
IM 858   Wondering Why   unissued
IM 859   Yours Truly –1   Imperial 5353
IM 860   I Must Go On   Post 2007
IM 861   Be Faithful   Imperial 5353
IM 903   Don't Go   Post 2007
IM 902   Blues Before Dawn   unissued

Vcl/gtr. with Red Holloway, ten; McKinley Easton, bari; Horace Palm pno; Lefty Bates, gtr;
Quinn Wilson, bs; Paul Gussmann, dms.   Chicago, September 7, 1956
56-519   Tie It Down   unissued
56-520   Fiddle De Dee   Vee Jay 266
56-521   A Frosty Night   Vee Jay 214
56-522   The Telephone Is Ringing   –

Al Duncan, dms. replaces Gussmann.		Chicago, February 5, 1957
57-607	I Found My Peace Of Mind	Vee Jay 252
57-608	You Don't Love Me Any More	unissued
57-609	I Don't Care	Vee Jay 252
57-610	Blues Daze	unissued
Same:		Chicago, August 2, 1957
57-725	Is This The Price I Pay	Vee Jay 266
57-726	Second Hand Love	unissued
57-727	I Love Her Still	unissued
57-728	Blues After Hours	unissued
No details:		1961
	'Tain't Nobody's Business	Jamie 1190
	Little Bitty Thing	–
G-PWC-1	I'm Still In Love With You	Guyden 2048
G-PWC-2	Time On My Hands	–
with R. A. Blackwell Orchestra:		1962
23867	Git To Gittin'	Smash 1774
23868	Hillbilly Blues	–

G. DAVY CROCKETT

See under G. L. Crockett.

G. L. CROCKETT

G. DAVY CROCKETT
Vcl. with saxes (–1); pno; gtr; bs; dms.   Chicago, 1957

25-121	Look Out Mabel (or Mable)	Chief 7010, USA 816, Checker 1121
25-122	Did You Ever Love Somebody –1	– – –

Note: 25-121 on Checker 1121 is a different take.

G. L. CROCKETT
Vcl. with saxes (–1); pno; gtr; bs–gtr; dms.   Chicago, 1965
ZTSC-10485, 003
    It's A Man Down There   Four Brothers 445
ZTSC-10486, 004
    Every Hour, Every Day –1   –
ZTSC-107003, 015-4
    Every Goodbye Ain't Gone   Four Brothers 448
ZTSC-107004, 016
    Watch My 32 –1   –

BIG BOY CRUDUP

Real name Arthur Crudup. Born Forest, Mississippi in 1905.
Vcl/gtr. with Melvin Draper, dms.   Chicago, December 15, 1944
D4-AB-340-1 Cool Disposition   Bluebird 34-0738, Victor 20-2978

D4-AB-341-1 Who's Been Foolin' You   Bluebird 34-0725
D4-AB-342-1 Rock Me Mama   –   , Victor 20-2978

D4-AB-343-1 Keep Your Arms Around Me   Bluebird 34-0738
Vcl/gtr. with Charles "Chick" Saunders, dms.   Chicago, October 22, 1945
D5-AB-1208-1
    Dirt Road Blues   Victor 20-2757
D5-AB-1209-1
    I'm In The Mood   Bluebird 34-0746, Victor 20-2659
D5-AB-1210-1
    That's Your Red Wagon   Victor 20-2387
D5-AB-1211-1
    She's Gone   Bluebird 34-0746

Vcl/gtr. with Armand "Jump" Jackson, dms.		Chicago, February 22, 1946
D6-AB-1830-1	Ethel Mae	Victor 20-1949
D6-AB-1831-1	So Glad You're Mine	— , Camden LP 740
D6-AB-1832-	Boy Friend Blues	Victor 20-2989, 50-0001
D6-AB-1833-1	No More Lovers	Victor 20-2565
Vcl/gtr. with Ransom Knowling, bs; Judge Riley, dms.		Chicago, September 6, 1946
D6-VB-1939-	You Got To Reap What You Sow	Victor 20-2105
D6-VB-1940-1	Chicago Blues	Victor 20-3261
D6-VB-1941-1	Crudup's After Hours	Victor 20-2205, 50-0000
D6-VB-1942-	I Want My Lovin'	Victor 20-2105
D6-VB-1943-	That's All Right	Victor 20-2205, 50-0000
D6-VB-1944-	I Don't Know It	Victor 20-2387
As Last:		Chicago, April 9, 1947
D7-VB-0391-1	Cry Your Blues Away	Victor 20-2757
D7-VB-0392-1	Crudup's Vicksburg Blues	Victor 22-0029, 50-0013
D7-VB-0393-1	Gonna Be Some Changes Made	Victor 22-0007
D7-VB-0394-1	Train Fare Blues	Victor 20-2565
As last:		Chicago, October 7, 1947
D7-VB-1060-1	Katie May	Victor 20-2989, 50-0001
D7-VB-1061-1	Hey Mama, Everything's All Right	Victor 20-3261
D7-VB-1062-1	Hoodoo Lady Blues	Victor 22-0048, 50-0032
D7-VB-1063-1	Lonesome World To Me	Victor 22/50-0100
D7-VB-1064-1	Roberta Blues	Victor 22/50-0126
D7-VB-1065-1	Just Like A Spider	Victor 20-3140
D7-VB-1066-1	Someday	Victor 22-0007
D7-VB-1067-1	That's Why I'm Lonesome	Victor 20-3140
As last:		Chicago, March 10, 1949
D9-VB-0418	Tired Of Worry	Victor 22-0048, 50-0032
D9-VB-0419	Dust My Broom	Victor 50-0074
D9-VB-0420	Hand Me Down My Walking Cane	Victor 22/50-0100
D9-VB-0421	Shout Sister Shout	Victor 22-0029, 50-0013, Camden CAL 371
As last:		Chicago, March 11, 1949
D9-VB-0422	Come Back Baby	Victor 22-0061, 50-0046
D9-VB-0423	You Know That I Love You	Victor 50-0074
D9-VB-0424	Mercy Blues	Victor 22-0061, 50-0046
D9-VB-0425	She's Just Like Caldonia	Victor 22/50-0105
As last:		Chicago, March 23, 1950
EO-VB-3428	Mean Old Santa Fe	Victor 22/50-0092
EO-VB-3429	Behind Closed Doors	Victor 22/50-0126

58

EO-VB-3430	She Ain't Nothin' But Trouble	Camden CAL 371
EO-VB-3431	Oo-Wee Darling (Love Me With A Thrill)	Camden CAL 371
As last:		Chicago, November 8, 1950
EO-VB-4574	Anytime Is The Right Time	RCA 130.284
EO-VB-4575	My Baby Left Me	–
EO-VB-4576	Nobody Wants Me	Victor 22/50-0117
EO-VB-4577	Star Bootlegger	–
As last:		Chicago, April 24, 1951
E1-VB-1535	Too Much Competition	Victor 22/50-0141
E1-VB-1536	Second Man Blues	Victor 20-4933
E1-VB-1537	Pearly Lee	Victor 20/47-5070
E1-VB-1538	Love Me Mama	Victor 20-4367
E1-VB-1539	Never No More	unissued
E1-VB-1540	Where Did You Stay Last Night	Victor 20-4367
E1-VB-1541	I'm Gonna Dig Myself A Hole	Victor 22/50-0141
Vcl/gtr. with J. Sheffield, bs; N. Butler, dms.		Atlanta, January 15, 1952
E2-VB-5049	Goin' Back To Georgia	Victor 20-4572 Camden CAL 371
E2-VB-5050	Mr. So And So	–
E2-VB-5051	Do It If You Want To	Victor 20-4933
E2-VB-5052	Keep On Drinkin'	Victor 20/47-5167
E2-VB-5053	Worried About You Baby	Victor 20-4753
E2-VB-5054	Late In The Evening	–
E2-VB-5055	Lookin' For My Baby	Victor 20/47-5070
E2-VB-5056	Nelvina	Victor 20/47-5167

ELMER JAMES
Vcl/gtr. with hca. bs.   Jackson, Miss. late 1952

DRC128: ACA 2280		
	Gonna Find My Baby	Trumpet 186, Jewel 764
DRC129: ACA 2279		
	Make A Little Love With Me	– , Jewel 783

Note: Jewel 764 issued as by Elmo James. Aurally the harmonica player does not sound like Sonny Boy Williamson. Both Crudup and the bass player refer to him as "Sam"

PERCY LEE CRUDUP
Vcl/gtr. with hca; bs; dms.   Jackson, 1952

C 1022	Open Your Book (Daddy Wants To Read With You)	Checker 754
C 1023	Tears In My Eyes	
	Recorded in the McMurray Studio.	

BIG BOY CRUDUP
Vcl/gtr. with Robert ?, hca; pno; bs; dms.   Jackson, 1953

ACA 2371	I Wonder	Ace 503
ACA 2372	My Baby Boogies All The Time	–

ARTHUR "BIG BOY" CRUDUP
Vcl/gtr. with J. J. Jones, ten; Edward Lumpkin, pno; Charles Holloway, bs; Lafayette
Lawson, dms.   Atlanta, November 9, 1953

E3-VB-2612	I Love My Baby	Groove 4G-0011
E3-VB-2613	My Wife And Women	Victor 20/47-5563
E3-VB-2614	The War Is Over	–
E3-VB-2615	Fall On Your Knees And Pray	Groove 4G-0011

Vcl/gtr. with Robert Fulton, gtr/poss. hca; Thomas Patten, pno; Joe Thomas, bs;
Willie Willis, dms.   Atlanta, April 8, 1954

E4-VB-3938	If You Have Ever Been To Georgia	Groove 4G-0026
E4-VB-3939	Help Me Bear This Heavy Load	RCA RCX-7161
E4-VB-3940	I Love You	unissued
E4-VB-3941	She's Got No Hair	Groove 4G-0026

Vcl/gtr. with bs; dms.   c. 1959

FM-205, 42568		
	Katie Mae	Fire 1502, LP 103
FM-206, 42568X		
	Dig Myself A Hole	– –

FM-207	Rock Me Mama	Fire 1503,	–
FM-208	Mean Old Frisco	–	–
	That's Alright	Fire LP 103	
	Too Much Competition	–	
	Coal Black Mare	–	
	Look On Yonder Wall	–	
	Ethel Mae	–	
	Standing At My Window	–	
	Greyhound Bus	–	
	So Glad You're Mine	–	

Note: Doctor Ross stated that the above sides were recorded in Nashville with Elvis Presley putting up the money. They were then issued on a Fireball label and leased to Fire.

PERCY LEE CRUDUP

See under Big Boy Crudup.

JAMES CRUTCHFIELD

Vcl/pno.

| | How Long Blues | Euphonic 1204 |

JAMES "KING" CURRY

Vcl. with   Los Angeles, 1956

| | My Promise | Flash 110 |
| | Please Baby | |

Vcl. with Movin' Masters Band: brass, pno; gtr; bs; dms.   Los Angeles, 1965

| A | My Memories | Movin' 127 |
| B | You Left Me | – |

D

DADDY STOVEPIPE

Real name Johnny Watson. Born Mobile Alabama in 1870. Died Chicago in 1963.
Vcl/gtr/hca.   Chicago, 1960

	Tennessee Waltz	Heritage HLP 1004
	South Of The Border	–
	Old Time Religion	–
	Monkey And The Baboon	–

LEROY DALLAS

Vcl/gtr. with Wilbert Ellis, pno (−1); Brownie McGhee, gtr.   New York City, 1949
C2000	I'm Down Now, But I Won't Be Always −1	S.I.W. 522, Blues Classics BC-14
C2001	Jump Little Children	− −
C2002	Good Morning Blues −1	S.I.W. 526, −
C2003	I'm Going Away −1	− −
4112	Your Sweet Man's Blues −1	S.I.W. 537, Jade 707
4113		
4114	Baby Please Don't Go Back To New Orleans	S.I.W. 537, Jade 707

Vcl/gtr.   New York City, January, 1962

Sweet Man Blues   Storyville SLP 181
She Caught The M & O   Milestone LP 3002

DANNY BOY & HIS BLUE GUITAR

Real name Danny Thomas.
Vcl/gtr. with hca; gtr; dms.   Tifton, Ga., 1961
10101:M90W-3366
     Wild Women   Tifco 824
10102:M90W-3367
     Kokomo Me Baby   −

COW COW DAVENPORT

Born ? Died Chicago on 2 December, 1955
Vcl/pno.   Chicago, 1945

     Jump Little Jitterbug   Comet C-1
     Gotta Girl For Every Day Of The Week   −
     Jeep Boogie   Comet C-2
     Chimin' Away   −
     Hobron City Stomp   Comet C-3
     Run Into Me   −
     Cow Cow's Stomp   Comet C-4
     Gin Mill Stomp   −

Vcl. with Peggy Montez, vcl. acc. Montana Taylor, pno.   Chicago, April 18, 1946
C 25	Hang Crepe Upon My Door	Circle unissued
C 26	Patrol Wagon Blues	−
C 27	Rabbit Blues	−
C 28	Come Home Blues	−
C 29	Casey Jones Blues	−
C 30	One More Gal For Me	−

REVEREND GARY DAVIS

Born South Carolina in 1896.
Vcl/gtr/banjo/hca.   New York City, 1960

     Maple Leaf Rag   Prestige 14033
     Slow Drag   −
     The Boy Was Kissing The Girl   −
     Candy Man   −
     United States March   −
     Devil's Dream   −
     The Coon Hunt   −
     Mister Jim   −
     Please Baby   −
     Fast Fox Trot   −
     Can't Be Satisfied   −

New York City, June, 1957

     Mountain Jack   Folk Lyric 125
     Right Now   −
     Hesitation   −
     Buck Dance   −
     Devil's Dream   −
     Coco Blues   −

                         Candy Man   –
                         Bad Company   –
                    Note: Gospel sides not included.

BLIND JOHN DAVIS

Born Chicago on 7 December, 1913.

BLIND JOHNNY DAVIS TRIO
Vcl/pno. with gtr; bs.   Chicago, 1949
UB9-1134   No Mail Today   MGM 10574
UB9-1135   Walkin' And Talkin'   –
Same: Chicago, 1950
UB50-327   My Love   MGM 10738
UB50-328   Honey Babe   MGM 10919
UB50-329   Telegram To My Baby   –
UB50-330   Your Love Belongs To Me   MGM 10738
Vcl/pno. with George Barnes, gtr; Ransom Knowling, bs. Chicago, March 1951
no mx   The Day Will Come   MGM 10976
no mx   Magic Carpet   –
            Don't Cheat Boogie   MGM (E) 463
            Hurry Home Blues   –
Pno.   Paris, February 5, 1952
52V 4192   Paris Boogie   Vogue V 3100
52V 4193   O Sole Mio   –
52V 4216   Sunrise Boogie   Vogue V 3146, LDO 66
52V 4217   Rockin' In Boogie   –
            Everybody Got The Blues   Vogue EPL 7139
            How Long Blues   –
            Paris Bounce   unissued
            After Hours   unissued
            Home Town Blues   Vogue EPL 7139
            Davis Boogie   –
Vcl/pno. with Joe Benjamin, bs; Bill Clark, dms.   Paris, April 9, 1952
            Coquette   Vogue LDO 78
            Jim Town Blues   –
            Just A Little Blues   –
            Lady Be Good   –
            What Is This Thing Called Love   –
            If I Could Be With You   –
            In The Shade Of The Old Apple Tree   –
            West End Blues   –

KING DAVIS

Vcl/hca. with pno; gtr; bs; dms.   Los Angeles, 1954
422A   Someday You'll Understand   Hollywood 422
422AA   Waggin' Your Tail   –

LARRY DAVIS

Vcl/gtr. with David Dean, ten; pno; Fention Robinson, gtr; el–bs; dms.
                                                       Houston, 1958
FR-3075-1   I Tried   Duke 192
FR-3076-1   Texas Flood   –
Vcl/gtr. with ten; Booker T., pno; Fention Robinson, gtr; el–bs; dms.
                                                       Houston, 1959
FR 7018   Angels In Houston (no ten)   Duke 313
FR 7019   (My) Little Girl   –
            Will She Come Home   Duke 328
            Come Home   –
        Note: Memphis artist.

MAXWELL STREET JIMMY DAVIS

Real Name Charles Thomas.
Vcl/gtr.

		Chicago, 1964/65
	Crying Won't Make Me Stay	Testament T-2203
	Hanging Around My Door	–
		Chicago, early 1965
	What More Can A Good Man Do	Elektra EKL-303
	Two Trains Running	–
	Long Haired Darlin'	–
	My Baby Done Changed The Lock On My Door	–
	Driftin' From Door To Door	–
	I Got My Eyes On You	–
	Me And My Telephone	–
	Dust My Broom	–
	She's My Babe	–
	Alberta	–
	Babt Please Don't Go	–
	Drifting Blues	–

LITTLE SAM DAVIS

Vcl/hca. with gtr; dms.

		Memphis? 1952
GR 15077-1	Goin' Home To Mother	Rockin' 512
GR 15078-1	1958 Blues	–
GR 15079-1	She's So Good To Me	Rockin' 519, DeLuxe 6025
GR 15080-1	Goin' To New Orleans	–

SONNY BOY DAVIS

Vcl/pno. with Rattlesnake Cooper, gtr.

		Dallas?, 1949
178	Rhythm Blues	Talent 802
179	I Don't Live Here No More	–
	See also Rattlesnake Cooper.	

WALTER DAVIS

Born Granada, Mississippi on March 1, 1912. Died St. Louis, Missouri 1964.
Vcl/pno. with Armand "Jump" Jackson, dms.

		Chicago, February 12, 1946
D6-AB-1808	My Friends Don't Know Me	Victor 20-2156
D6-AB-1809	New B & O Blues	Victor 20-1999
D6-AB-1810	When You Need My Help	Victor 20-2156
D6-AB-1811	Please Remember Me	Victor 20-1999

Note: Victor files give drummer's name as Arnold Jackson.

Vcl/pno. with Leonard Caston, gtr; Charles Saunders, dms.

		Chicago, February 5, 1947
D7-VB-304	Things Ain't What They Used To Be	Victor 20-2335
D7-VB-305	Oh! Me! Oh! My! Blues	Victor 20-1999
D7-VB-306	Just One More Time	Victor 20-2335
D7-VB-307	It's Been So Long	Victor 20-2487

Vcl/pno. with gtr; bs.

		Chicago, 1949/50
	Move Back To The Woods	Bullet 305
	You've Got To Reap What You Sow	–
	Wonder What I'm Doing Wrong	Bullet 311
	I Would Hate To Hate You	–
	Santa Claus Blues	Bullet 321
	Got To See Her Every Night	–
	Stop That Train In Harlem	Bullet 326
	So Long Baby	–
	I Just Can't Help It	Bullet 341
	You Are The One I Love	

Vcl/pno. with John Moore, sax; Henry Townsend, gtr.

		Chicago, July 27, 1952
E2-VB-6864	You Make My World So Bright	Victor 20-5012
E2-VB-6865	Tears Came Rolling Down	–

63

| E2-VB-6866 | So Long Baby | Victor 20-5168 |
| E2-VB-6867 | What May Your Trouble Be | – |

DAVID DEAN'S COMBO

See under Fention Robinson.

JIMMY DE BERRY

JIMMY & WALTER
Jimmy De Berry, vcl (–1)/gtr. with Walter Horton, hca (–2); Willie Nix, dms.

Memphis, early 1953

| U 61 | Easy –2 | Sun 180 |
| U 62 | Before Long –1 | – |

JIMMY DE BERRY
Vcl/gtr. with pno (–1); dms.

Memphis, Summer 1953

| U 73 | Take A Little Chance | Sun 185 |
| U 74 | Time Has Made A Change –1 | – |

DELTA JOE

See under Sunnyland Slim.

DELTA JOHN

See under John Lee Hooker.

DETROIT COUNT

Vcl/pno.

Detroit, 1948

| | Hastings Street Opera Pt. 1 | JVB 75830, King 4264, Blues Classics BC–12 |
| | Hastings Street Opera Pt. 2 | JVB 75830, King 4264, Blues Classics BC–12 |

Add Saxes; bs; dms.

K 5584-2	I'm Crazy About You	JVB 75831, King 4265
K 5585	Hastings St. Woogie Man	– –
K 5614	Little Tillie Willie	King 4279
K 5615	My Last Call	–
	Note: Credits to "White".	

DETROIT JR.

Real name Emery Williams Jr.
Vcl/pno. with Eddie King Milton, Bobby Dean Anderson, gtrs; Robert Whitehead, dms.

Chicago, February 18, 1960

| A | Money Tree | Bea & Baby 111 |
| B | So Unhappy | – |

Vcl/pno. with saxes; gtr; bs; dms; vcl. grp.

Chicago, 1961

| 1565 | This Time For Christmas | Foxy 002 |
| 1566 | Christmas Day | – |

Vcl/pno. with saxes; gtr; bs; dms; The Delrays, vcl. grp.

Chicago, 1964

A	Zig Zag	C. J. 636
B	I'm Gonna Find Me Another Girl	–
A	Can't Take It	C. J. 637
B	Mother-In-Law	–

Vcl/pno. with saxes; gtr; bs; dms.

Chicago, 1965

| S3KM6754-1 | Talk Fast | USA 807 |
| S3KM6755-1 | It's Bad To Make A Woman Mad | – |

Vcl/pno. with Ike Perkins, gtr (–1).

| M 4000 | Call My Job | USA 814 |
| M 4001 | The Way I Feel | – |

DETROIT SLIM

Vcl/gtr. with hca.   Detroit,
     Nelly Mae   JVB unissued, Arhoolie F 1018

GROVER DICKSON

Vcl. with group vcl.   Retrieve Farm, Texas, March 12,
                                                  1951
     Grizzly Bear   "77" LA 12/2

DIRTY RED

Real name Nelson Wilborn. Born Sumner, Mississippi on August 31, 1907.
Vcl. with pno; gtr; bs.   Chicago, June 2, 1947

4016	Hotel Boogie	Aladdin 207
4017	Mother Fuyer	Aladdin 194
4018	You Done Me Wrong	Aladdin 207
4019-2	Home Last Night	Aladdin 194
4014	Let's Have A Nice Time	unissued
4015	End of 1946	unissued

        Note: musicians on above session are almost definitely Lonnie Johnson, gtr. and Blind
        John Davis, pno.

DIXIE BLUES BOYS

Dee Dee, vcl/hca. with hca; gtr; dms.   Memphis?, 1955

FL 242	Monte Carlo	Flair 1072
FL 243	My Baby Left Town	–

FLOYD DIXON

Vcl/pno. with Tiny Webb, gtr; Eddie Williams, bs; Ellis Walsh, dms.

		Los Angeles, 1947
SU 190	Houston Jump	Supreme 1528, Swing Time 261
SU 191	You Need Me Now	Supreme 1546, Swing Time 287
SU 218	Broken Hearted	Supreme 1535, Swing Time 261
SU 220	Worries	Supreme 1547, Swing Time 287

FLOYD DIXON TRIO

Vcl/pno. with Tiny Webb, gtr; Bill Davis, bs.

		Los Angeles, 1949
MM 978	Dallas Blues	Modern 20-653
MM 979	Helen	
MM 996-4	Drafting Blues	Modern 20-700
MM 997		
MM 998-5	That'll Get It	Modern 20-664
MM 1019	Till I Grow Old	Modern 20-664
Same:		Los Angeles, May 1949
MM 1132-2	Mississippi Blues	Modern 20-700
Same:		
MM 1245-2	Precious Lord	Modern 20-724
MM 1246-3	Milky White Way	–
MM 1247		
MM 1248		
MM 1249-2	You Made A Fool Out Of Me	Modern 20-797
MM 1250-3	Doin' The Town	–
MM 1251-1	Cow Town	Modern 20-725
MM 1252-1	Forever And Ever	–
MM 1270-1	It's Getting Foggy	Modern 20-761
MM 1271-1	Gloomy Baby	Modern 20-727
MM 1272		
MM 1273-6	Roamin' Around	Modern 20-727
MM 1327-2	I'll Be Lonely	Modern 20-761
	People Like Me	Modern 20-744
	Shuffle Blues	–

	Playboy Blues	Modern 20-776
	Baby Come Home	–

Vcl/pno. with ten; gtr; bs; dms.   Houston, 1949

ACA 1358, RR-1596		
	Rockin' At Home	Aladdin 3083
ACA 1359, RR-1593		
	She's Understanding	Aladdin 3073, Peacock 1544
ACA 1360	I'm So Unhappy	unissued
ACA 1361, RR-1598		
	Don't Cry Now Baby	Aladdin 3084
ACA 1362, RR-1595		
	Let's Dance	Aladdin 3078, Peacock 1528
ACA 1363, RR-1599		
	I'm So Worried	Aladdin 3084
ACA 1364, RR-1597		
	We'll Be Together	Aladdin 3078, Peacock 1528
ACA 1365, RR-1592		
	Pleasure Days	Aladdin 3083

Same: Houston, 1950

ACA 1634, RR-1594		
	Sad Journey Blues	Aladdin 3073, Peacock 1544
ACA 1635	Train	unissued
ACA 1636	Short Session	unissued

Note: Peacock 1528 issued as by J. Riggins Jr.

FLOYD DIXON WITH JOHNNY MOORE'S THREE BLAZERS
Vcl/pno. with Johnny Moore, Oscar Moore, gtrs; Johnny Miller, bs; dms. Mari Jones, vcl (–1).

Los Angeles, September, 1950

RR-1570	Married Woman	Aladdin 3196
RR-1571	Wine Blues	unissued
RR-1572	Empty Stocking Blues	Aladdin 3074
RR-1573	Walkin' And Talkin' The Blues	Aladdin 3069
RR-1574	Girl Fifteen	–

Same: Los Angeles, October 26, 1950

RR-1585	Bad Neighbourhood	Aladdin 3121
RR-1586	You Played Me For A Fool	Aladdin 3166
RR-1587	Real Lovin' Mama –1	Aladdin 3075
RR-1588	Unlucky Girl –1	Aladdin 3082
RR-1589	Evil Lover Blues	unissued
RR-1590	Four Years –1	Aladdin 3082
RR-1591	Telephone Blues	Aladdin 3075
RR-1584	Long Distance Telephone Blues	unissued

Same: Add ten (–1):   Los Angeles, December 15, 1950

RR-1608	Blues For Cuba	Aladdin 3121
RR-1609	Time And Place	Aladdin 3101
RR-1610	You Need Me Now	Aladdin 3230
RR-1611	Broken Hearted Traveller –1	Aladdin 3166
RR-1612	Do I Love You	Aladdin 3101
RR-1613	A Long Time Ago	Aladdin 3230
RR-1614	Lovin'	Aladdin 3196

FLOYD DIXON AT FRANK BULL & GENE NORMAN'S BLUES JUBILEE
Vcl/pno. with Maxwell Davis (?), ten; gtr; bs; dms.   Los Angeles, July, 1951

RR-1748	Too Much Jelly Roll	Aladdin 3111
RR-1749	Baby Let's Go Down To The Woods	–

FLOYD DIXON
Vcl/pno. with Roy Hayes, gtr; Eddie Williams, bs; Nat 'Monk' McFay, dms.

Los Angeles, May 12, 1952

RR-1928	Tired Broke And Busted	Aladdin 3151, Imperial LP 9210
RR-1929	Come Back Baby	–
RR-1930	Call Operator 210	Aladdin 3135, Imperial LP 9210
RR-1931	Wine, Wine, Wine!	–

FLOYD DIXON & HIS BAND
Vcl/pno. with flt (−1); gtr; bs.   Los Angeles, July 18, 1952
RR-1959   The River −1   Aladdin 3144
RR-1960   I Don't Know Any Better   unissued
RR-1961   Red Cherries   Aladdin 3144
RR-1962   The River   unissued

FLOYD DIXON
Vcl/pno. with saxes: gtr; bs; dms.   Los Angeles 1953
XSP 468   Hard Living Alone   Specialty 468
SP 468   Please Don't Go   −
XSP 477   Hole In The Wall   Specialty 477
SP 477   Old Memories   −
XSP 486   Ooh-Eee Ooh-Ee   Specialty 486
SP 486   Nose Trouble   −

FLOYD DIXON & HIS BAND
Vcl/pno. with 2-3 saxes; gtr; bs; dms.   1954
C-1270   Moonshine   Cat 106
C-1271   Roll Baby Roll   −
             Is It True   Cat 114
             Hey Bartender   −

FLOYD DIXON
No details:
             For Mother   Pearl 25
             Mother's Day   −
No details: Los Angeles, 1957
             Oh Baby   Cash 1057
             Never Can Tell   −
Vcl/pno. with saxes; gtr; bs; dms.
15823   What Is Life Without A Home   Ebb 105
15824   Ooh Little Girl   −
No details, but may be reissues with changed titles from Modern:
                                       Los Angeles, 1958
             Change Your Mind   Kent 311
             Dance The Thing   −

FLOYD DIXON
Vcl/pno. with saxes; Robert Lockwood Jr., gtr; Willie Dixon, bs; Fred Below, dms.
                                       Chicago, 1958
8217   Alarm Clock Blues   Checker 857
8218
8219
8220   Shamed of Myself   Checker 857

FLOYD DIXON & BAND
No details   1960
HH-6024: E-6946   Tight Skirts   Swingin' 626
HH-6025:E-6947   Wake Up And Live   −

FLOYD DIXON
Vcl/pno. with ten: gtr; bs; dms.
ACA 4438   Daisy   Houston, 1961
ACA 4439   Opportunity Blues   Dodge 807
No details: 1962
             Late Freight Twist   Club Long Island ?
             Tell Me, Tell Me   Chatta-Hoo-Chie 652
             There Goes My Heart   −
             Don't Leave Me Baby   Chatta-Hoo-Chie 697
             Me Quieres   −

Note: Add to Aladdin session of September, 1950:-

RR-1575	Hard Road Blues	unissued
RR-1576	Blues In My Heart	unissued
RR-1577	San Francisco Blues	Aladdin 3074

WILLIE DIXON

Born Vicksburg, Mississippi in 1915

WILLIE DIXON & THE ALL-STARS
Vcl/bs. with Harold Ashby, ten; ten; Lafayette Leake, pno; Fred Below, dms.

		Chicago 1955
U 7842	If You're Mine	Checker 822
U 7843	Walkin' The Blues (no tens)	– , LP 2173, Argo LP 4034
U 7942	Crazy For My Baby	Checker 828
U 7943	I Am The Lover Man	–
U 7944	The Pain In My Heart	Checker 851
		Chicago, 1956
8190	29 Ways	Checker 851

Vcl/bs. with Harold Ashby, ten (-1); Memphis Slim, pno; Wally Richardson, gtr; (-2); Gus Johnson, dms.

		Englewood Cliffs, late 1959
	Nervous -2	Bluesville BVLP 1003
	Good Understanding -1	–
	That's My Baby -2	–
	Slim's Thing	–
	That's All I Want Baby -1	–
	Don't Tell Nobody	–
	Youth To You -2	–
	Sittin' And Cryin' The Blues -1,2	–
	Built For Comfort -1,2	–
	I Got A Razor	–
	Go Easy	–
	Move Me -1	–

Vcl/bs. with Memphis Slim, pno; Matt Murphy, gtr; Biklie Stepney, dms.

		Bremen, October, 13, 1963
	Sittin' And Cryin' The Blues	Fontana TL 5204
	Crazy For My Baby	–

Vcl/tamb. with Homesick James, Evans Spencer, John Henry Barbee, gtrs; Washboard Sam, wbd.

		Chicago, March 26, 1964
200	So Long!	Spivey LP 1003
Vcl/gtr.		Chicago, April, 4 1964
211	Weak Brain! Narrow Mind!	Spivey LP 1003

Vcl/bs. with Sunnyland Slim, pno; Hubert Sumlin, gtr; Clifton James, dms.

		Berlin, November 1, 1964
	Blues Anytime	Amiga 8 50 043
	My Baby	–
Vcl/gtr.		
	Big Legged Woman	Amiga 8 50 043

DOCTOR CLAYTON'S BUDDY

See under Sunnyland Slim.

DOCTOR FEELGOOD

Pseudonym for Piano Red, q.v., but records issued under this name are not included.

BIG BILL DOTSON & HIS GUITAR

Vcl/gtr.		1950
MM 1799	Dark Old World	Blues & Rhythm 7004
MM 1800	Thinking Life Over	–, Crown CLP 5224, 5369

Note:Crown LP issued as by Lightnin' Hopkins.

JIMMY DOTSON

Vcl/gtr. with Katie Webster, pno; Bobby McBride, bs-gtr; Warren Storm, dms.

		Crowley, La.,1960
R 7030	Oh Baby	Rocko 516
R 7031	I Need Your Love	–

JIMMY DOTSON & THE BLUES BOYS

Vcl/gtr. with Jimmy Anderson, hca; Bobby McBride, bs-gtr; Warren Storm, dms.

		Crowley, La.,1962
Z-7462	I Wanna Know	Zynn 511
Z-7463	Looking For My Baby	–

DR. HEP CAT

See under L. Durst.

SALLY DOTSON

See under Smoky Babe.

K. C. DOUGLAS

Born Canton, Mississippi on 21 November, 1913
Vcl (-1)/gtr; with Sidney Maiden, vcl (-2)/hca; Ford Chaney, gtr; Otis Cherry, dms.

		Oakland, 1948
DT 2004	Mercury Boogie -1	Down Town 2004, Gilt Edge 5043
DT 2005	Eclipse Of The Sun -2	–
Vcl/gtr.		Oakland, 1954
	Lonely Blues	Rhythm 1780, Hollywood 1040
	K. C. Boogie	–
Vcl/gtr.		Oakland 1956
	Canned Heat	Cook LP 5002
	Catfish	–
	Big Road Blues	–
	Kansas City	–
	I Got The Key To The Highway	–
	Casey Jones	–
	Mercury Blues	–
	I Met The Blues This Morning	–
	I Have My Women	–
	Had I Money	–
Vcl/gtr.		1961
	Broken Heart	Bluesville BVLP 1023
	Hen House Blues	–
	Wake Up, Workin' Woman	–
	Rootin' Ground Hog	–
	Meanest Woman	–
	Born In The Country	–
	Love Me All Night Long	–
	Tell Me	–
	Cryin'	–
	K. C.'s Doctor Blues	–
	You Got A Good Thing Now	–
	Watch Dog Blues	–
	Big Road Blues	Bluesville BVLP 1050
	Howling Blues	–
	Move To Kansas City	–
	Buck Dance	–
	Tore Your Playhouse Down	–
	Bottle Up And Go	–
	Whiskey Headed Woman	–
	Catfish Blues	–
	Canned Heat	–

69

	K. C. Blues	–
	Key To The Highway	–

Vcl/gtr. with C. V. Hook, 2nd vcl; George Hurst, pno; Jimmy Raney, dms.

Berkeley, Calif.,August 19, 1963

504A	I Know You Didn't Want Me	Arhoolie 504, LP F 1018
504B	I'm Gonna Build Me A Web	–

SHY GUY DOUGLAS

Real name Thomas Douglas.

Vcl. with alt; pno; gtr; bs; dm.

Nashville,1953

A	Detroit Arrow	Excellow 2008
B	New Memphis Blues	–

Vcl/hca. with pno; gtr; dms.

Nashville 1954

A	I'm Your Country Man	Excello 2024
B	Wasted Time	–

Omit hca.

A	No Place Like Home	Excello 2032
B	She's My Kinda Girl	–

Vcl. with brass; pno; gtr; bs; dm.

A	Yankee Doodle	Chane 517
B	Harvest Moon	–

Vcl. with pno; gtrs; el-bs; dms.

Nashville,1966

A	No Point In Cryin'	Excello 2279
B	Long Gone	–

Vcl/hca. with gtrs; dms.

PC 10070	What's This I Hear	Todd 1092
PC 10071	Monkey Doin' Woman	–

DOWN TOWN TRIO

Lee Hamilton, vcl/pno; Ulysses James, gtr; Floyd Montgomery, bs.

Oakland, 1948

DT 20017A	Make Love To Me Baby	Down Town 2017
DT 20017B	Down Town Shuffle	–

DRIFTING CHARLES

See under Charles Tyler

DRIFTING SLIM

See under Elmon Mickle

DRIFTING SMITH

See under Elmon Mickle

DRINK SMALL & HIS GUITAR

Vcl/gtr. with org(-1); pno(-2); el-bs; dms.

New York City, 1958

SDS-70669	I Love You Alberta -1	Sharp 101
SDS-70670		
SDS-70671	Cold, Cold Rain -2	Sharp 101

JOHN DUDLEY

Vcl/gtr.

Parchman Farm, Miss.,1959

	Cool Water Blues	Atlantic LP 1352
	Po' Boy Blues	Prestige International 25010

DUKE BAYOU & HIS MYSTIC 6

Jack Dupree, vcl (-1)/pno; Brownie McGhee, gtr; Bobby Harris, vcl(-2)/bs; wbd; dms.

New York City, 1949

R 1391	Rub A Little Boogie -1	Apollo 440
R 1392		
R 1393		
R 1394	Doomed -2	Apollo 440

SCOTT DUNBAR

Born on Deer Park Plantation, Wilkinson County, Mississippi in 1906.

		Old River Lake, Miss. June 24, 1954
	Memphis Mail	Folkways FP 654
		Pond, Miss. June 25, 1954
	Forty Four	Folkways FP 654
Add Celeste Dunbar, vcl; Rosie Dunbar, dancing		Folkways FP 654
Same, but Rosie Dunbar, vcl.		
	Goin' Back to Vicksburg	Folkways FA 2659

ANDREW DUNHAM

Vcl/gtr.

		Detroit, late 1949
B 7044	Sweet Lucy	Sensation 23
B 7045	Hattie Mae	–

FRED DUNN & HIS BARRELHOUSE RHYTHM

Vcl/pno. with bs; dms.

		New York City, 1946
SRC-570-RRB	Railroad Blues	Signature 32010, Guest Star 1901
SRC 571	Fred's Boogie Woogie	Signature 1026 –
SRC-572-RRA	Mountain Blues	Signature 32010 –
SRC-591	Blues Before Sunrise	Signature 1026 –
SRC-592-RRI	Baby Don't Feel Lowdown	Signature 1027 –
SRC-593-RR2	The Morning After	–

CHAMPION JACK DUPREE

Born in New Orleans on 4 July, 1910

Vcl/pno. with Sonny Terry, hca; Brownie McGhee, gtr.

		New York City, 1942
G 16266, FJ 2801	Slow Boogie	Folkways FJ 2801, FP 53
FJ 2804	Jitterbug	Folkways FP 59
FJ 2809	Mexican Reminiscences	Folkways FP 71

Vcl/pno. with gtr; bs; dms.

	Ain't That A Shame	Folkways FS 3825
	Talk To Me Baby	–
	Tell Me When	–
	Old Woman Blues	–
	Hard Feelings Blues	–
	Bus Station Blues	–
	Rattlesnake Boogie	–
	Black Wolf Blues	–
	Jail House	–
	Come Back Baby	– , Aravel 1004
	On My Way to Moe Asch	–

Vcl/pno.

		New York City, 1942/43
SO 17	Once I Had A Girl	Solo 10-014

Add Sonny Terry, hca.

SO 20	Black Woman Blues	Solo 10-014

Vcl/pno

		New York City, May 3, 1944
1229	Too Evil To Cry	Asch 550-2, Asch 2 1/2
	(rev. by Nora Lee King)	

CHAMPION JACK DUPREE TRIO
Vcl/pno. with Brownie McGhee, gtr; Count Edmonson, bs.

		New York City, 1945
HS 3929	Let's Have A Ball	Continental 6065
HS 3930	Going Down Slow	Continental 6066, LP 16002
HS 3931	Hard Feeling	Continental 6065, –
HS 3932	How Long, How Long Blues	Continental 6064, –
HS 3933	Mean Old Frisco	Continental 6066, Lenox, 511, –
HS 3934		
HS 3935	I Think You Need A Shot	Continental 6064
	When You Ain't Got A Dime	Lenox 511

Note:Lenox 511 issued as by Blind Boy Johnson & His Rhythms.

same:

HS 4021	Bad Whiskey And Wild Women	Lenox 505, Continental LP 16002
HS 4022		
HS 4023		
HS 4024	Bus Station Blues	Lenox 505, Continental LP 16002

Note: Reverse of LP 16002 is by Sonny Boy & Lonnie. Later issued on Maple Leaf LP 220 with all items retitled.

Vcl/pno.

		New York City, c. 1946
	Rum Cola Blues	Joe Davis 5100
	She Makes Good Jelly	–
	Johnson Street Boogie Woogie	Joe Davis 5101
	I'm Going Down With You	–
	F. D. R. Blues	Joe Davis 5102
	God Bless Our New President	–
5103A	County Jail Special	Joe Davis 5103
5103B	Fisherman's Blues Take 1	–
	Fisherman's Blues Take 2	Joe Davis 5103
DA 3-5	Lover's Lane	Joe Davis 5104
DA 3-6	Black Wolf	–
	Walkin' By Myself	Joe Davis 5105
	Outside Man	–
DA 3-1	Forget It Mama	Joe Davis 5106
DA 3-2	You've Been Drunk	–
	Santa Claus Blues	Joe Davis 5107
	Cin Mill Sal	– , 5103
DA 504	Love Strike Blues	Joe Davis 5108
DA 505	Wet Deck Mama	–
DA 506	Big Legged Mama	Celebrity 2012
DA 507	I'm A Doctor For Women	–

Note: Reissue of JD 5103 on Jazz Parade gives recording date as December, 1944.

WILLIE JORDAN & HIS SWINGING FIVE
Vcl/pno. With Jesse Powell, ten; Brownie McGhee, gtr; Count Edmonson, bs; Melvin Merritt, dms.

		New York City, 1946
207A	Cecelia, Cecelia	Alert 207
207B	Going Down To The Bottom	–

JACK DUPREE & HIS QUARTET
Same, but omit Brownie McGhee, gtr;

4217A	Fifth Avenue Blues	Alert 421
421B	Highway 51	–

CHAMPION JACK DUPREE & HIS COUNTRY BLUES BAND
Vcl/pno. With Mickey Spider, tpt; Jesse Powell, ten; Brownie McGhee, gtr; Cedric Wallace, bs; Gene Moore, dms.

		New York City, 1949
R 1325-2	Come Back Baby	Apollo 407
R 1326		
R 1327		
R 1328	Chittlin's And Rice	Apollo 407

JACK DUPREE & HIS BAND
Vcl/pno(-1) with Jesse Powell, ten; Lonnie Scott, pno; Brownie McGhee, gtr; Cedric Wallace, bs; Melvin Merritt, dms.

R 1362	One Sweet Letter -1	Apollo 413
R 1363		
R 1364	Lonesome Bedroom Blues	Apollo 421
R 1365	Old Woman Blues	
R 1366	Mean Mistreatin' Mama (no sax)	Apollo 413

BROTHER BLUES & THE BACK ROOM BOYS
Vcl/pno. with Brownie McGhee, gtr; bs. New York City, 1949

G 738	Featherweight Mama	Abbey 3015
G 739	Day Break	—

CHAMPION JACK DUPREE WITH BIG CHIEF ELLIS & HIS BLUES STARS
Vcl. with Al King, ten; Wilbert Ellis, pno; Brownie McGhee, gtr; Thomas Barney, bs; Ernest Hayward, dms. New York City, 1950

R 1446	Deacon's Party	Apollo 426
R 1447	My Baby's Comin' Back Home	Apollo 428
R 1448	Just Plain Tired	—
R 1449	I'm Gonna Find You Someday	Apollo 426

MEAT HEAD JOHNSON
Vcl/pno. with Brownie McGhee, Sticks McGhee, gtrs; Melvin Merritt, dms.

MHJ5	Old, Old Woman	Gotham 514
MHJ6	Mean, Black Woman	—
JD1	Goin' Back To Louisiana	Apex 1110
JD2	Barrelhouse Mama	—

LIGHTNIN' JR. & THE EMPIRES
Vcl/pno. with ten; gtr; bs; dms; vcl. grp. New York City, 1952

DA 774	Ragged And Hungry	Harlem 2334
DA 775	Somebody Changed The Lock On My Door	—

CHAMPION JACK DUPREE
Vcl/pno. with Sonny Terry, hca (-1): Sticks McGhee, gtr; Bob Harris, bs; Willie Jones, dms.
New York City, early 1953

R 3010	Stumblin' Block Blues	Red Robin 109
R 3011	Highway Blues -1	Red Robin 112, Everlast 5032
R 3012	Shake Baby Shake	—
R 3013	Number Nine Blues -1	Red Robin 109

Same:

R3076	Drunk Again	Red Robin 130
R 3077	Shim Sham Shimmy	—

CHAMPION JACK DUPREE

Vcl/pno. with Sidney Grant, ten; Mickey Baker, gtr; Cedric Wallace, bs; John Taylor dms.
New York City, April 7, 1953

K 8391-1	Ain't Noe Meat On De Bone	King 4651
K 8392-1	The Blues Got Me Rockin'	King 4633, LP 735
K 8393-1	Tongue Tied Blues	—
K 8394-1	Please Tell Me Baby	King 4651, LP 859

Vcl/pno. with Alexander Lightfoot, hca; Charles W. Connor, sax: Edwin Moire, gtr; Nathaniel Perillat, bs; Milton Batiste, dms. Cincinnati, December, 1, 1953

K 9344-1	Walkin' Upside Your Head	King 4695, LP 735
K 9345-1	Rub A Little Boogie	King 4706
K 9346-1	Hard Feeling	King 4706, LP 735

Vcl/pno. with Sidney Grant, ten; Jerome Darr, gtr; Cedric Wallace, bs; Cornelius Thomas, dms.
New York City, February, 15, 1955

K 8524-1	Harelip Blues	King 4797, LP 735, Audio Lab AL 1512
K 8525-1	Two Below Zero (no ten) Federal 12408	King 4779, LP 735, Bethlehem LP 6071
K 8526-1	Let The Doorbell Ring	King 4797
K 8527-1	Blues For Everybody (Everybody Blues)	King 4779, LP 735, Audio Lab AL 1512

CHAMPION JACK DUPREE & MR. BEAR
Vcl./pno. with Mr. Bear (Teddy McRae), vcl; Joe Williams, bs; George DeHart, dms.

		Cincinnati, May 29, 1955
K 9652-1	Walking The Blues	King 4812, Audio Lab AL 1512
K 9653-1	Daybreak Blues	—

Note: issued as by "Mr. Bear".

CHAMPION JACK DUPREE
Vcl/pno. with Mickey Baker, gtr; Ivan C. Rolle, bs; Calvin Shields, dms.

		New York City, June 27, 1955
K 8563-1	That's My Pa	King 4827, LP 735
K 8564-1	She Cooks Me Cabbage	— —

Same, but add Willis Jackson, ten; Robert C. Johnson, gtr(-1):

		New York City, June 29, 1955
K 8567-1	Failing Health Blues -1	King 4876, LP 735
K 8568-1	Stumbling Block -1	King 4827, —
K 8569		
K 8570-1	Mail Order Woman	King 4958, LP 735

Vcl/pno. with Lloyd Trotman, bs; Cliff Leeman, dms.   New York City, September 28,1955

K 8597-1	Silent Partner	King 4859, Lp 735, Audio Lab 1512
K 8598-1	House Rent Party	King 4885
K 8599-1	Big Leg Emma's	King 4958, LP 735

Note: 8598 issued as by Babs Gonzales.

JACK DUPREE
Vcl/pno. with George Smith, hca; Barney Richmond, bs; Alfred Dreares, dms.

		Cincinnnati, November 9, 1955
K 9705	Overhead Blues	King 4906, Audio Lab AL 1512
K 9706	Me And My Mule	King 4876, LP 735
K 9707	So Sorry, So Sorry	King 4906
K 9708	Sharp Harp	King LP 735

JACK DUPREE AND MR BEAR
Vcl/pno. with Mr. Bear (Teddy McRae), vcl; Larry Dale, gtr; Al Lucas, bs; Gene Moore, dms.

		New York City, September 17, 1956
G5-JB-7293	The Ups	Unissued
G5-JB-7294	Lonely Road Blues	Groove 4G-0171

McRae out:

G5-JB-7295	Story Of My Life	unissued
G5-JB-7296	When I Got Married	Groove 4G-0171

CHAMPION JACK DUPREE AND HIS COMBO
Vcl/pno. with Larry Dale, gtr; Al Lucas, bs; Gene Moore, dms.

		New York City, January 22, 1957
H4-PW-1226	Dirty Woman	Vik X-0260
H4-PW-1227	Old Time Rock & Roll	Vik X-0279
H4-PW-1228	Down The Lane	unissued
H4-PW-1229	Rocky Mountain	Vik X-0279
H4-PW-1230	Just Like A Woman	Vik X-0260

Vcl/pno. with Larry Dale, Sticks McGhee, gtrs; Al Lucas, bs; Willie Jones dms.

		New York City, August 20, 1957
H4-PW-6155	Shake Baby Shake	unissued
H4-PW-6156	The Wrong Woman	unissued
H4-PW-6157	You're Always Cryin'The Blues	unissued
H4-Pw-6158	Woman Trouble Again	unissued

McGhee out, Add Pete Brown, alt: New York City, October 15, 1957

H4-PW-7500	My Baby's Like A Clock	unissued
H4-PW-7501	Hello Darlin'	unissued
H4-PW-7502	Lollipop Baby	Vik X-0304
H4-PW-7503	Shake Baby Shake	—

Vcl/pno. with Pete Brown, alt(-1); Larry Dale (as Ennis Lowery), gtr; Wendell Marshall, bs;
Willie Jones, dms.   New York City, February 4, 1958

A 2952	Strollin'	Atlantic 2032, LP 8019
	Frankie And Johnny -1	–
A 5333	My Mother-in-Law	Atlantic 2095
A 5334	Evil Woman -1	– , LP 8019
	T. B. Blues -1	Atlantic LP 8019
	Can't Kick The Habit	–
	Nasty Woman -1	–
	Junker's Blues -1	–
	Bad Blood -1	Atlantic LP 8019
	Goin' Down Slow	–
	Stack-O-Lee -1	–

Vcl/pno. with Alexis Korner, gtr (-1); Jack Fallon, bs. London, 1959

	Seafood Blues	Atlantic LP 8045
	Death of Big Bill Broonzy -1	–
	Don't Leave Me Mary -1	–
	Rampart Street Special	–
	How Long Blues	–
	Bad Life -1	–
	Mother-In-Law Blues -1	–
	Slow Drag	–
	Dennis Rag	–
	Bad Luck Bound To Change -1	–

Vcl/pno. Copenhagen, December 29, 1959

	Gravier Street Rag	unissued
	Old Woman Blues	unissued
	Roll Me Over And Roll Me Slow	Storyville SLP 107, Atlantic LP 8056
	Daybreak Stomp	– – –
	That's All Right	– .. –
	Reminiscin' With Champion Jack Dupree	– – –
	I Had A Dream	– – –
	House Rent Party	– – –
	Snaps Drinking Woman	– – –
	One Sweet Letter From You	– – –
	Johnson Street Boogie Woogie	– – –
	Misery Blues	– – –
	Misery Blues	unissued
	New Vicksburg Blues	unissued
	New Vicksburg Blues	Storyville SLP 107, Atlantic LP 8056

Vcl/pno. Copenhagen, December, 13, 1960

	Midnight Hour Blues	Storyville SEP 381
	Blues Before Sunrise	–
	Blues Before Sunrise	Storyville SLP 187
	In The Evening	Storyville SEP 381
	Shirley May	Sotryville A 45051, SLP 193
	Shirley May	Storyville SLP 183
	Shirley May	unissued
	My Baby's Gone	Storyville SLP A
	I'm A Gamblin' Man	Storyville SLP 161
	Lonesome Bedroom Blues	
	Whiskey Head Woman	Storyville A 45051, SLP 193
	41 Highway	unissued
	Old Woman Blues	unissued
	My Baby's Coming Home	Storyville SLP A
	Shake, Baby, Shake	unissued
	Number 9	unissued
	How Long Blues	Storyville SEP 381

Vcl/pno. with H. Lange, gtr. except on (-1) Copenhagen, October, 3, 1961

	Schoolday Blues	Storyville SLP 145
	Everything I Do Is Wrong	Storyville SLP 151
	Alberta	Storyville SLP A

	I Feel Like A Millionaire	unissued
	I Feel Like A Millionaire -1	unissued
	I Feel Like A millionaire -1	unissued
	I Feel Like A Millionaire -1	unissued
	When A Young Girl Is Eighteen	unissued
	When A Young Girl Is Eighteen -1	Storyville SLP 145
	Carolina Sunrise	unissued
	Carolina Sunrise -1	Storyville SLP 145
	Champion Jack's Guitar Blues	unissued
	Automobile Blues	unissued
	I Ain't Goin' To Be Your Lowdown Dog -1	unissued
	I Ain't Goin' To Be Your Lowdown Dog -1	Storyville SLP 145
	You Can Make It If You Try -1	–
	Gravier Street Special -1	unissued
	Gravier Street Special -1-	unissued
	Drinkin' Wine Spodee–O–Dee -1	unissued
	Drinkin' Wine Spodee–O–Dee -1	unissued
	Drinkin' Wine Spodee–O–Dee -1	unissued
Same:		Copenhagen, October 4, 1961
	Fisherman's Blues	Storyville SLP 151
	You've Been Drunk -1	–
	Broken Hearted Blues	Storyville SLP 145
	I Love To Be With You	–
	Big Fat Mama	unissued
	Rocky Mountain Blues	unissued
	Deep Sea Diver	unissued
	Rock Me Mama	unissued
	Rock Me Mama	unissued
	Mean Mistreater	Storyville SLP 151
	Trouble Trouble	Storyville SLP 145
	Oh Baby Blues -1	unissued
	Cryin' Woman Blues	Storyville SLP 145
	My Heart Beats For You	unissued
	My Heart Beats For You	unissued
	My Heart Beats For You	Storyville SLP 145
	Free And Equal	–
	President Kennedy And Krutchev Blues	unissued
	Three O'Clock In The Morning	Storyville SLP 193
	Kind Hearted Woman	unissued
	Holiday Blues	Storyville SLP 193
	Poor House Blues	unissued
Vcl/pno.		Copenhagen, June 5, 1962
	I Hate To Be Alone	unissued
	Calcutta	unissued
	In The Dark	unissued
	Tomorrow Night	unissued
	Tomorrow Night	unissued
	I Just Want To	unissued
	Storybook	unissued
	T. V. Mama	unissued
	Suicide Blues	unissued
	Gravier Street Special	unissued
	Truckin' On Down	unissued
	Drive 'em Down Special	Storyville A 45088, A, SLP 155
	My Mother Is Gone	unissued
	Lover's Lane	unissued
	Wedding Day Blues	unissued
	Poor Boy Blues	unissued
Vcl/pno. with Mogena Seidelin, bs.		Copenhagen, June 14, 1962
	Storyville Special	unissued
	Cabbage Greens No. 3	unissued
	Cabbage Greens No. 3	unissued
	Daybreak Blues (acc. dms)	Storyville SLP 183
	I Hate To Be Alone	Storyville SLP 161

76

Calcutta Blues	Storyville SLP A	
T. V. Mama	Storyville SLP 168	
See See Rider	unissued	
One Wine	unissued	
One Wine	unissued	
Storybook	Storyville SLP 191	
When I've Been Drinking	Storyville SLP 161	
Diggin' My Potatoes	Storyville SLP 151	
Christine, Christine Blues	unissued	
Door To Door Blues	Storyville SLP 161	
Sleeping In The Street	Storyville SLP 161	
Sportin' Life Blues	Storyville SLP 151	
Mercy On Me	Storyville SLP 161	

Same: Copenhagen, June 15, 1962

Don't Ever Believe	Storyville SLP 168
Tomorrow Night	unissued
Tomorrow Night	Storyville SLP 151
In The Dark	unissued
In The Dark	Storyville SLP 151
Tomorrow Night	unissued
Christine, Christine Blues	Storyville SLP 188
Cabbage Greens No. 3	Storyville SLP 151
See See Rider	unissued
See See Rider	Storyville SLP 151
The Cold Ground Is My Bed	Storyville SLP 161
Keep Your Big Mouth Shut	unissued
Keep Your Big Mouth Shut	Storyville SLP 155
A Good Man Is Hard To Find	Storyville SLP 161
Careless Love	Storyville SLP 151
One By One Blues	Storyville SLP A
Everyday I Have The Blues	Storyville SLP 193
Please Send Me Someone To Love	unissued
Please Send Me Someone To Love	unissued
Please Send Me Someone To Love	Storyville SLP 187
Tee-Na-Nee-Na	Storyville SLP A
Please Don't Dog Your Woman	–
Bring Me Flowers When I'm Living	Storyville SLP 151
Oh Lawdy	Storyville SLP 193
Don't Worry	unissued

Same: Copenhagen, June 18, 1962

Drivin' Me Mad	unissued
That's All Right, Baby	Storyville SLP A
Young Girl Blues	Storyville SLP 193
You're So Fine	unissued
Please Send Me Someone To Love	unissued
Sportin' Life Blues	Storyville A 45088
Sportin' Life Blues	unissued
I'll Bet My Money	unissued
Sweet Mama	unissued
My Mother Is Gone	Storyville SLP A
I Just Want To Be Free	Storyville SLP 168
Back Door Special	Storyville SLP 155
People Talk	Storyville SLP 193
Rock Me Baby (Goin' Down The River)	unissued
I'm Going To Look The World Over	unissued
Dirty Mistreater	unissued
Dirty Mistreater	unissued
Work House Blues	Storyville SLP 187
Federal Man Blues	Storyville SLP 193
Fine And Mellow	–
Ain't That A Hard Pill To Swallow	unissued
Things I Used To Do	unissued
I'm Growing Older Everyday	Storyville SLP 161
Goin' To Denmark	unissued

	Self Pity	unissued
	I'm Crazy About You	Storyville SLP A
	It's Too Late	–
	I Feel So Good	unissued
	You Got Me Way Down Here	Storyville SLP 187
	Hand In Hand	unissued
	I Want To Settle Down	unissued
	Have You Ever Been Alone	unissued
	You Got To Do As I Tell You	unissued

Vcl/pno. with Ole Christiansen, bs; Alex Tiel, dms. Copenhagen, 1963

	I Feel Like A Millionaire	Storyville SLP 194
	Chicken Shack	–
	Gin Mill Sal	–
	Drinkin' Wine Spodee-O-Dee	–
	Talkin' Out Of My Head	unissued
	Talkin' Out Of My Head	Storyville SLP 194
	Anybody Here Want To Buy Cabbage	unissued
	Anybody Here Want To Buy Cabbage	Storyville SLP 194
	I Got A Little Girl	–
	Come Back Baby	–
	Please Send Me Someone To Love	–
	She Said No	–
	24 Hours	–
	Piano Solo	unissued
	When I'm Drinkin'	unissued
	It's Too Late	unissued
	Keep On Goin'	unissued
	In Prison Too Long	unissued
	Miss Ada Blues	unissued
	Doctor Dupree Blues	unissued

Vcl/pno. with Bob Carter, bs; Joe Harris, dms. Koblenz, January 3, 1963

	Wine, Whiskey And Gin Head Woman	Impulse LP 1037

Vcl/pno. with Keith Smith's Climax Jazz Band: London, June 26, 1964

DR. 33475	I'm A Prisoner	Decca LK 4681
DR. 33476	Track Number Nine	Decca DFE 8586
DR. 33477	London Special	–
DR. 33478	Fine And Mellow	, LK 4681

Vcl/pno. with John Mayall, hca; Eric Clapton, Tony McPhee, gtrs; Malcolm Pool, bs–gtr;
Keef Hartley, dms. London, 1966

DR. 36835	24 Hours	Ace Of Clubs ACL 1220
DR. 36836		
DR. 36837	Shim-Sham-Shimmy	Decca LK 4747
DR. 37031	Third Degree	–
DR. 39339	Calcutta Blues	Ace of Clubs ACL 1220

Omit Mayall and Clapton:

DR. 36838	He Knows The Rules	Decca LK 4747

Vcl/pno. with Tony McPhee, gtr; Bill Short, wbd (–1).

DR. 36839	Ain't That A Shame -1	Decca LK 4747
DR. 36840	Gimme A Pigfoot And A Bottle Of Beer -1	–
DR. 36841	She's All In My Life	–
DR. 36842	Won't Be A Fool No More	–
DR. 36843		
DR. 36844		
DR. 36845	(Goin' Down To) Big Leg Emma's	Decca LK 4747
DR. 36846	Take It Slow And Easy	–

Vcl/pno. On (–1) Dupree, vcl. only with Tony McPhee, gtr.

DR. 37032	T. V. Mama	Decca LK 4747
DR. 37033	Ooh La-La	–
DR. 37034	Poor Poor Me	–
DR. 37035	Down In The Valley -1	–
DR. 37036	Too Early In The Morning	–

78

Vcl/pno.

	Jack's Blues	unissued
	Shake Baby Shake	unissued
	Stuttering Blues	unissued
	Doctor Dupree	unissued
	Yella Pocahontas	unissued
	Too Late To Cry	unissued

L. DURST

Real name Lavada Durst.
Vcl/pno. with   Austin, c. 1949
    Hattie Green   Uptown?
L. DURST -1
DR. HEPCAT -2
Vcl/pno. with saxes; gtr; bs; dms.   Houston, 1949
ACA 1300   Hattie Green -1   Peacock 1509
ACA 1301   I Cried -2
    Note: Durst is Austin DJ "Dr. Hep Cat" on KVET Radio.

E

JIMMY EAGER

See under Tampa Red.

FORD EAGLIN

See under Snooks Eaglin.

SNOOKS EAGLIN

Real name Ford Eaglin. Born New Orleans in 1936.

BLIND SNOOKS EAGLIN
Vcl/gtr.   New Orleans, February, 1958
    Mean Old Frisco   Folkways FA 2461

SNOOKS EAGLIN
Vcl/gtr.   New Orleans, March, 1958

	Careless Love	Folkways FA 2476
	Come Back Baby	–
	High Society	–
	Let Me Go Home Whiskey	–
	Trouble In Mind	–
	St. James Infirmary	–
	I Got My Questionaire	–
	Driftin' Blues	–
	Rock Island Line	–
	Everyday I Have The Blues	–
	Sophisticated Blues	–
	See See Rider	–
	One Scotch, One Bourbon, One Beer	–
	A Thousand Miles Away From Home	–

| | I'm Lookin' For A Woman | – |
| | Look Down That Lonesome Road | – |

Vcl (–1)/gtr. with Lucius Bridges, vcl (–2)/gtr/wbd; Percy Randolph, vcl (-3)/hca (–4)/wbd.

		New Orleans,
	Possum Up A Simmon Tree -2	Folk-Lyric FL-107
	That's All Right -1, 4	– , Bluesville BVLP 1046
	Veal Chop And Pork Chop -3	Folk-Lyric FL-107
	I Ain't Gonna Study War No More -1	–
	Model T and The Train -4	–
	Jack O'Diamonds -3	–
	Death Valley Blues -1	–
	This Train -1, 2	–
	Bottle Up And Go -2	– , Bluesville BVLP 1046
	Mardi Gras Mambo -1, 2	Folk-Lyric FL-107
	Rock Me, Mama -1	–
	John Henry -2	–
	Lonesome Train -1	–
	I Had A Little Woman -1	–
	Don't Leave Me Mama -2	–
	Down By The Riverside	–

Same:

	Malaquena	Bluesville BVLP 1046
	Who Can Your Good Man Be	–
	I Must See Jesus	–
	Give Me The Good Old Box Car	–
	Mama Don't You Tear My Clothes	–
	She's A Black Rat	–
	Who's Been Fooling You	–
	Don't You Lie To Me	–
	Blue Shadows Blues (When Shadows Fall)	–
	Walkin' Blues	–
	Mean Old World	–
	Every Day	–
	(Well) I Had My Fun	–
	Fly Right (Back) Baby	–
	Mailman Passed & Didn't Leave No News	Storyville SLP 140
	Brown Skin Woman (Mama)	–
	One More Drink	–
	I Got A Woman	–
	Mama, Talk To Your Daughter	–
	Country Boy	Storyville 45056, SLP 146
	Alberta	–
	I Don't Know	Storyville SLP 146
	When They Ring Them Golden Bells	–
	Went Out Walkin'	–
	Remember Me	–

FORD EAGLIN

Vcl/gtr. with saxes; pno; bs; dms.

		New Orleans, 1960/61
IM 2618	Yours Truly	Imperial 5671
IM 2619	Nobody Knows	–
IM 2620	That Certain Door	Imperial 5692
IM 2621	By The River	–
IM 2882	If I Could	Imperial 5736
IM 2883	Guess Who	–
IM 3036	I've Been Walking	Imperial 5857
IM 3037	My Head Is Spinning	Imperial 5765
IM 3038	Would You	Imperial 5857
IM 3039	Travelin' Mood	Imperial 5765
IM 3207	Going To The River	Imperial 5802
IM 3208	I'm Slippin' In	–
IM 3209	Nothing Sweet As You	Imperial 5823

IM 3210	Don't Slam That Door	–
IM 4245	People Are Talking	Imperial 5866
IM 4246	Long Gone	Imperial 5890
IM 4247	Willy Lee	–
IM 4248	Reality	Imperial 5866
IM 5607	Little Eva	Imperial 5946
IM 5608	Cover Girl	–
IM 2884	See See Rider	Imperial unissued
IM 2885	Talk To Your Daughter	–
IM 5609	Is It True	–
IM 5610	Down Yonder	–

AMOS EASTON

Born in Georgia on May 7, 1905.

BUMBLE BEE SLIM
Vcl. with pno; gtr; bs; dms.   Los Angeles, 1951
A   Lonesome Old Feeling   Fidelity 3004
B   Ida Red   –

AMOS EASTON & HIS ORCH.
Add saxes.
A   Strange Angel   Speciality 410
B   Lonesome Trail Blues   –

KING BUMBLE BEE SLIM & HIS PACIFIC COAST SENDERS
Vcl/gtr. with ten (–1); Kid "Sharkey" Hall, gtr; pno; bs; dms.Los Angeles,
MGR 100-4   Two Guitar's Battle   Marigold (no number)
MGR 101-4   Twin Beds -1   –

BUMBLE BEE SLIM
Vcl/gtr. with Les McCann, pno; Leroy Vinnegar, bs; Ron Jefferson, dms.
                                             Los Angeles, 1962
            Direct South   Pacific Jazz 910
            Driftin' Blues
            Midnight Special   –
Vcl. with Teddy Edwards, ten; Richard Holmes, org; Joe Pass, gtr.
            Puppy Love   Pacific Jazz 910
            In The Evening
Add Lou Blackburn, tbn (–1); Leroy Vinnegar, bs; Ron Jefferson, dms.
            Wake Up In The Morning   Pacific Jazz 910
            New B & O Blues   –
            Meet Me In The Bottom   –
            Wee Baby Blues   –
            I'm The One   –

CLARENCE EDWARDS

Vcl/gtr. with Butch Cage, vln; Cornelius Edwards, gtr.   Baton Rouge, La., 1960
            You Don't Love Me Baby   Folk-Lyric FL-111
            Smokes Like Lightnin'   –
            Stack O'Dollars   –
            Mean Old Frisco   Storyville SLP 129
            Miss Sadie Mae   –
            Stagalee   –
            I Can't Quit You Baby   –
            This Is My Life   –

FRANK EDWARDS

Vcl/hca. with 2 gtrs.   Atlanta, 1950
1264   Love My Baby   unissued
1265   Gotta Get Together   Savoy MG 16000
            Note: Guitarists probably Willie McTell and Curley Weaver.

HONEYBOY EDWARDS

Real name David Edwards. Born in Shaw, Mississippi on April 28, 1915.

Vcl/gtr/hca (–1).   Clarksdale, Miss.,July 20, 1942

6610A1	Interview	unissued
6610A2	Spread My Raincoat Down	–
6610B1	Interview	–
6610B2	You Got To Roll	–
6610B3	You Got To Roll	–
6610B4	Stagolee	–
6610B5	Just A Spoonful	–
6611A1	I Love My Jelly Roll	–
6611A2	Interview	–
6611A3	Hellatakin' Blues	–
6611A4	Interview	–
6611 B	Interview	–
6612A1	Worried Life Blues	Library Of Congress L59
6612A2	Watercourse Blues	unissued
6612B1	The Army Blues -1	–
6612B2	Tear It Down	–
6612B3	Ragtime Selection	–

Vcl/gtr/hca (–1).   Delta Tourist Camp, Miss. July
                                                     22, 1942

6614A/B	Toasts, Folk Tales, Interview	unissued
6615A1	Interview	–
6615A2	Interview	–
6615A3	Do You Want A Little Bit Of This	–
6615B3	Wind Howlin' Blues -1	–
6615B4	Roamin' And Ramblin' Blues	–

Vcl/gtr. with Thunder Smith, pno (–1).   Houston, 1951

ARC 102A	Build A Cave	Artist Record Co. 102
ACA 1665	Early In The Morning	unissued
ACA 1666	Who May Your Regular Be -1	Artist Record Co. 102
ACA 1667	Who Could Be Loving You Tonight	unissued

Vcl/gtr. with John Lee Henley, hca.   Chicago, March 17, 1964

1	My Baby's Gone	unissued
2	Angel Child	–
3	Highway 61	Milestone LP 3002
4	Love Me Over Slow	unissued

Vcl/gtr.   Chicago, July 29, 1967

1	Just Like Jesse James	unissued
2	Sweet Home Chicago	–
3	Blues Like Showers Of Rain	–
4	Long Tall Woman Blues	–
5	Love Me Over Slow	–
6	Crawling King Snake	–
7	Skin And Bone Blues	–
8	Bull Cow Blues	–

Note: Releases as David Edwards on Library Of Congress, Mr. Honey on Artist
Record Co., and Honeyboy Edwards on Milestone.

J. D. EDWARDS

Vcl/gtr. with pno; gtr; dms.   New Orleans? May, 1953

IM 581	Cryin'	Imperial 5245
IM 582	Playboy Blues	unissued
IM 583	Hobo	Imperial 5245
IM 584	Cold In The Evening	unissued

Note: IM 583 is credited to S. Hopkins.

WILBERT ELLIS

BIG BOY ELLIS & HIS RHYTHM
Vcl/pno. with gtr.   New York City, 1945

82

| A 4166 | Dices Dices | Lenox 521, Continental LP 16003 |
| A 4167 | I Love You Baby | – – |

BIG CHIEF TRIO -1
BIG CHIEF & HIS TRIO -2
Vcl/pno. with Brownie McGhee, gtr; bs.   New York City, 1949
2004	Big Chief's Blues -1	SIW 523
2005	She's Gone -1	–
C 2027	Poor Man's Blues -2	SIW 530
C 2028	Mr. Radio Announcer -2	–

PERLINE ELLISON

Vcl. with Sam Price, pno; Abe Bolar,bs; Hal West, dms.   New York City, March 9, 1944
| 71848 | Now That Ain't Right | Decca 7910, 48064 |
| 71849 | Razor Totin' Mama | – – |

LEROY ERVIN

Vcl/pno.   Houston, 1947
| 415A, 828A | Rock Island Blues | Swing 415, Gold Star 628 |
| 415B, 628B | Blue, Black, Evil | – – |

ODIE ERVIN

No details: Oakland, 1954
| | She's A Bad, Bad Woman | Big Town 111 |
| | Note Pinned On My Bed | – |

SLEEPY JOHN ESTES

Born
Vcl/gtr. with Ed Wilkenson, bs (−1).   Saukville, Wisc.,March 23, 1962
	Someday Baby	Delmark 603
	Death Valley Blues -1	–
	Down South Blues -1	–
	Milk Cow Blues	–

Vcl/gtr. with Hammie Nixon, hca; Knocky Parker, pno (−1); Ed Wilkinson, bs.
                                             Saukville, Wisc. June 3, 1962
	Rats In My Kitchen -1	Delmark 603
	Stop That Thing -1	–
	Diving Duck Blues -1	–
	Married Woman Blues	–
	Who's Been Telling You -1	–
	Drop Down Mama	–
	You Got To Go	–
	I'd Been Well Warned	–

Vcl/gtr. with Hammie Nixon, hca; Yank Rachell, mdln/gtr; Mike Bloomfield, gtr (−1).
                                             Chicago, 1963?
	Broke And Hungry	Delmark 608
	Black Mattie	–
	3.00 Morning Blues -1	–
	Beale Street Sugar -1	–
	Olie Blues	–
	Freedom Loan	–
	The Girl I Love	–
	Electric Chair	– –
	Sleepy John's Twist	–

Vcl/gtr.
| | So Glad I'm Livin' | Delmark 608 |

Vcl/gtr. with Hammi Nixon, hca/jug; Yank Rachell, mdln.   Newport, R.I.,July 25, 1964
	Sleepy John's Twist	Vanguard 9180
	Mailman Blues	–
	Drop Down Mama	–

Clean Up At Home	–
Corinna	Vanguard 9184

Vcl/gtr. with Hammie Nixon, hca; Yank Rachell, mdln/gtr; Ed Wilkenson or Ransom
Knowling, bs.

	Chicago,
The Girl I Love	Delmark 613
City Hall Blues	–
Government Money	–
Working Man Blues	–
Mailman Blues	–
Mary Come On Home	–
Pat Mann	–
Vassie Williams	–
Young Lawyer	Delmark 613
Al Rawls	–
Lawyer Clark	–
Martha Hardin	–

Vcl/gtr. with Hammie Nixon, hca/jug.

	London, October 9, 1964
Needmore Blues	Storyville 172
Who's Been Telling You	–
Airplane Blues	–
Vernita	–
Denmark Blues	–
I'M A Tearing Little Daddy	–
You Stayed Away Too Long	–
Drop Down Mama	–
The Woman I Love	–
You Oughtn't Do That	–
Easin' Back To Tennessee	–
City Hall Blues	Storyville 188

Same:	Hamburg, October 9, 1964
I'm A Tearing Little Daddy	Fontana TL 5225

Note: Estes sides on Ebony are "doctored" pre-war items.

ANDREW EVERETT

Vcl/gtr.

	Houston, 1959
K. C. Ain't Nothing But A Rag	"77" LA 12/2
Hello Central, Gimme 209	–

F

THE FAT MAN

with Sunnyland Slim Trio:
Alfred Wallace, vcl/dms. with Sunnyland Slim, pno.

	Chicago, 1950
MRS-32781 You've Got To Stop This Mess	J.O.B. 103, Nashboro 516
MRS-32782 Glad I Don't Worry No More	– –

FENTION & THE CASTLE ROCKERS
See under Fention Robinson

TEE BEE FISHER
Vcl. with saxes; pno; gtr; bs; dms.

		Pasadena, Texas, 1964
JS 17 LH 1071	Sweet Little Angel	Jet Stream 709
JS 18, LH 1072	Five Long Years	—

FLASH TERRY
Vcl. with ten; pno (-1); gtrs; dms.

		Los Angeles, 1961
LV-6009	Her Name is Lou -1	Lavender 5
LV-6010	Cool It	—

CANRAY FONTENOT
See under Alphonse Ardoin.

FOREST CITY JOE (The Late)
Real name Joe Pugh. Born ?; Died Hughes, Arkansas in 1959.
Vcl/hca. with gtr.

		Chicago, 1949
U 7164	Memory Of Sonny Boy	Aristocrat 3101, Blues Classics 15
U 7165		
U 7166		
U 7167	A Woman On Every Street	Aristocrat 3101
Vcl/hca.		Hughes, Arkansas,1959
	Levee Camp Reminiscence	Atlantic LP 1348
	Train Time	—

Add Sonny Boy Rogers, gtr; Thomas Martin, dms.

	Drink On Little Girl	Atlantic LP 1348
	She Lived Her Life Too Fast	Atlantic LP 1352
	She Don't Love Me That Way	—
	Stop Breaking Down	—
	Forest City Jump	—
Vcl/pno.		
	Red Cross Store	Atlantic LP 1352

Note: See also Chicago Sunny Boy.

R. C. FOREST
Vcl/gtr. with Gozy Kilpatrick, hca.

		Houston, March, 1959
	Cryin' Won't Make Me Stay	"77" LA 12/2
	Tin Can Alley	"77" LA 12/3

JESSIE FORTUNE
Vcl. with hca. Lafayette Leake, pno; Buddy Guy, gtr; Jack Meyers, bs-gtr; Willie Smith, dms. Willie Dixon, 2nd vcl(-1).

		Chicago, April 26, 1963.
779	Good Things	USA 747
780	God's Gift To Man -1	—
781	Too Many Cooks	USA 738
782	Heavy Heart Beat	—

Note: Real name Jessie Anderson?

LEROY FOSTER
Born c. 1920 in Mobile, Alabama. Died Chicago in 1961.

LEROY FOSTER & MUDDY WATERS
Vcl/gtr. with Muddy Water, gtr; Big Crawford, bs.

Chicago, 1949

| U 7154 R | Locked Out Boogie | Aristocrat 1234 |
| U 7155 R | Shady Grove Blues | – |

BABY FACE LEROY OR VOCALIST BABY FACE

Vcl/gtr. with Little Walter, hca; Muddy Waters, gtr.

Chicago, 1950

| 100 A | My Head Can't Rest Anymore | Job 100, Chess 1447 |
| 100 B | Take A Little Walk With Me | – – |

BABY FACE LEROY TRIO

Vcl/dms. with Little Walter, vcl(-1)/gtr(-2)/hca; Muddy Waters, gtr.

Chicago, 1950

H 511, H 1004	I Just Keep Loving Her -1	Parkway 502, Herald 403
H 512, H 1007	Boll Weevil	Parkway 104, Herald 404
H 513, H 1006	Rollin' And Tumblin' Pt. 1	Parkway 501, –
H 514	Rollin' And Tumblin' Pt. 2	–
H 515, SBL 4460	Red Headed Woman	Parkway 104, Savoy 1122
H 516		
H 517, SBL 4459	Moonshine Blues (or Baby) -1,2	Parkway 502, Savoy 1122
H , H 1005	Take A Walk With Me -1,2?	Parkway ?, Herald 403

Note: Parkway 502 and Herald 403/404 issued as by Little Walter. Savoy 1122 as by Baby Face. H 512/3/4 on Blues Classics BC-8. There is a possibility that on H 1005 is "Muskadine Blues" by Little Walter on Regal 3296.

BABY FACE & SUNNYLAND TRIO

Vcl. with Sunnyland and Slim, pno; Robert Lockwood Jr., gtr; dms.

Chicago, 1952

| MRS 35224 | Pet Rabbit | JOB 1002 |
| MRS 35225 | Louella | – |

LITTLE WILLIE FOSTER

Vcl/hca. with Little Brother Montgomery, pno; gtr; dms.

Chicago, 1953

| P53-222 | Falling Rain Blues | Parrot 813 |
| P53-223 | Four Day Jump | |

Different session:
Vcl/hca. with Lazy Bill Lucas, pno; Floyd Jones, gtr; Ray Scott, dms.

| P53-222 | Falling Rain Blues | Blue Lake,113 |
| P53-223 | Four Day Jump | |

same:

Chicago 1957

| C 1010 | Crying The Blues | Cobra 5011 |
| C 1011 | Little Girl | – |

THE FOX

See under Eugene Fox

EUGENE FOX
THE SLY FOX

Vcl/gtr. with pno; bs; dms.

Los Angeles,1954

LS 17	Hoodoo Say	Spark 108
LS 18	I'm Tired of Beggin'	–
LS 19	My Four Women	Spark 112

add tpt; 2nd pno:

| LS 20 | Alley Music | Spark 112 |

THE FOX -1
EUGENE FOX -2
Vcl/gtr. with various vocals & sound effects: Los Angeles,1954
MM 2133   The Dream Part 1 -1   RPM 420
MM 2134   The Dream Part 2 -1   –
U 7607   Sinner's Dream -2   Checker 792

Vcl/gtr. with ten; pno; bs; dm:
U 7606   Stay At Home   -2   Checker 792

MABEL FRANKLIN

Born New Orleans on Augst 24, 1919
Vcl. with D. C. Bender, gtr; C. W. Thornton, dms.   Houston,1965
1002-1   Let's Do The Wiggle   Ritzy 1002
1002-2   Dream I Had Last Night   –

    Note: Also recorded as Sister Mabel Franklin.

PETE FRANKLIN

Born Indianapolis on January 16, 1927
No details: 1947
    Casey Brown Blues   Victor 22-0012
    Down Behind The Rise   –
Vcl/gtr/pno(-1)   Indianapolis, July 12, 1961
    I Got To Find My Baby   Bluesville BVLP 1068
    Lonesome Bedroom Blues -1   –
    Prison Bound   –
    Black Gal -1   –
    Grievin' Me   –
    Rocky Mountains   –
    Six White Horses -1   –
    Sail On   –
    My Old Lonesome Blues -1   –
    Guitar Pete's Blues   –

SONNY BOY FRANKLIN ORCHESTRA

Pee Wee Bell, vcl. with tpts; saxes; pno; Sonny Boy Franklin, gtr; bs; dms.
                                                            Houston, 1949
A   Jumping The Blues   Eddie's 1204
B   Merry Go Round   –

LAWRENCE FRAZER

Vcl. with Roosevelt Sykes, pno.   Chicago,
    Mean Man   unissued

    Note: Recorded by Jump Jackson.

CALVIN FRAZIER

Vcl/gtr. with T. J. Fowler's Band; John Lawton, tpt; Lee Gross, alt/bari; Walter Cox, ten;
T. J. Fowler, pno; Hand Ivory, bs; Clarence Stamps, dms.   Detroit, c. 1952
SCF-4215   Got Nobody To Tell My Troubles To   Savoy 858
SCF-4216   Little Baby Child   –

Vcl/gtr. with Washboard Willie, wbd/dms.   Detroit, 1956
49 A   Rock House   JVB 49
49 B   We'll Meet Again   ,–

    Note: Recorded Live at Palmer House. "Rock House" is almost identical with
    "Washboard Shuffle" by Washboard Willie (JVB 59)

Vcl/gtr. with ten(-1); pno; gtr; bs; dms.   Detroit, 1958/9
86 A   Have Blues Must Travel -1   JVB 86, Checker 908
86 B   Lilly Mae   –   –

    Note: Checker issue titled "Have Blues Will Travel"/"Track Down".

DAVID FREEMAN
Vcl/gtr.

Untraced records, reputedly for the Memphis Stomper Time label.

JOE FRITZ (Or Joe (Papoose) Fritz)
Vcl/ten. with pno; gtr; bs; dms. Houston, 1950

ACA 1497, MM 1339	Wrong Doing Woman	Modern 20-750
ACA 1498, MM 1338	If I Be Lucky	–
ACA 1499	Better Wake Up Girl	Peacock 1606
ACA 1500	Real Fine Girl	–

Vcl/ten. with Willie Johnson, pno; Donald Cooks, bs; Ben Turner, dms.

		Houston, 1951
2096	Please Get Off My Mind	SIW 559
2105	I Love My Darling	–
2211	I'm So Sorry	SIW 584
2212	I Do Love You	–
2228	Bad Woman Blues	SIW 574
2229	I've Tried Not To Love You	SIW 591
2238	Please Me Darling	SIW 602
2239	They Were Right	–
2247	Cool Cool Baby Blues	SIW 574
2276	Lady Bear Boogie	SIW 594

Vcl/ten. with Houston, 1951

ACA 1873	My Heart Belongs To You	unissued
ACA 1874	Don't You Dance	–
ACA 1875	My Baby Has Everything	–
ACA 1876	Tell Me Darling	–
ACA 1877	Double Crossin' Boogie	–
ACA 1878	Make Her See Things My Way	Peacock 1581
ACA 1920, 1997	Cerelle	Peacock 1640
ACA 1921	If I Didn't Love You So	–
ACA 1922	(by Paul Monday)	
ACA 1923	(by Paul Monday)	
ACA 1924	Summer's Coming On	Peacock 1574
ACA 1925	In Misery	–
ACA 1926	I'm Not Suspicious, But	Peacock 1581
ACA 1927	Stable Pony	unissued
ACA 1928	If You Were Mine	

Vcl/ten. with Johnny Otis Orch. Houston, 1954

ACA 2707	Lonesome Train	unissued
ACA 2708	Honey, Honey,	Peacock 1627
ACA 2709	Woman I Love	–
ACA 2710	Whiskey Blues	unissued

Vcl/ten. with tpt; pno; gtrs; el-bs; dms. Pasadena, Texas 1966

JF 1	Good Doctor, Sweet Soul	Jet Stream 732
JF 2	Aww She's A Stepper	–

FRANK FROST

Vcl/hca/gtr. with Jack Johnson, lead gtr; Sam Carr, dms. Memphis, 1963

P-421	Crawlback	Phillips Int. 3578
P-422	Jelly Roll King	–
	Everything's Alright	Phillips Int. LP 1975
	Lucky To Be Living	–
	Baby You're So Fine	–
	Gonna Make You Mine	–
	Now Twist	–
	Big Boss Man	–
	Jack's Jump	–

	So Tired Of Living By Myself	–
	Pocket Full of Shells	–
	Now What You Gonna Do	–
	Just Come on Home	–

Vcl/gtr/hca(-1) with ? Williams, hca; gtr; dms.   Memphis, 1966

1540	My Back Scratcher	Jewel 764
1541	Harp And Soul -1	
TM 1761	Things You Do	Jewel 771
TM 1762	Harpin' On It	–

Note: Lula, Mississippi artist.

JESSE FULLER

Born Jonesboro, Georgia on March 12, 1896
Vcl/gtr/hca/Kazoo/fotdella/cymbals   Oakland, Aprill 22, 1955

	Leavin' Memphis, Frisco Bound	Cavalier 5006, 6009, Arhoolie R 2009
	Got A Date, Half Past Eight	– – –
	Hump On My Back	– – –
	Flavour In Your Cream	– – –
	Motherless Children	– – –
	Amazing Grace	– – –
	Hark From The Tomb	– – –
	As long As I Feel The Spirit	– – –
	Finger Twister	Cavalier, 6009, Arhoolie R 2009
	Cincinnati Blues	– – –
	Just a Closer Walk	– – –
	Just Like A Ship On The Deep Blue Sea	– – –

Same: San Francisco, January 19, 1958

	I'm Going To Meet My Lovin' Mother	Good Time Jazz 12031
	Tiger Rag	–
	Memphis Boogie	–
	Bye And Bye	–
	Fingerbuster	–
	Stagolee (Stackolee)	–
	Hesitation Blues	–

Same: San Francisco, January, 25, 1958

	Take This Hammer	Good Time Jazz 12031
	Linin' Track (Linin' Up This Track)	–
	Raise A Ruckus	–

Same: San Fransisco, April 12, 1958

| | 99 Years (And One Dark Day) | Good Time Jazz 12031 |

Same: San Fransisco, 1960

	Leavin' Memphis, Frisco Bound	Good Time Jazz 12039
	Take It Slow And Easy	–
	The Monkey And The Engineer	–
	New Corrine	–
	Guitar Blues	–
	Runnin' Wild	–
	Hey, Hey	–
	In That Great Land	–
	The Way You Treat Me	–
	Down Home Waltz	–
	Beat It On Down The Line	–
	Buck And Wing	–

Same:

	San Fransisco Baby Blues	Good Time Jazz 12051
	Jesse's New Midnight Special	–
	Mornin' Blues	–
	Little Black Train	Good Time Jazz 12051
	(Sleeping In The) Midnight Cold	–
	Whoa Mule	–
	John Henry	–

89

```
            I Got A Mind To Ramble                          —
            Crazy 'Bout A Woman                             —
            Where Could I Go But To The Lord                —
            Stealin' Back To My Old Time Used To Be         —
            Brown Skin Girl                                 —
from Good Time Jazz sessions:
            Moving On Down The Line                 Topic 12T 134
            Stealing                                        —
            Animal Fair                                     —
            Railroad Worksong                               —
            Railroad Blues                                  —
            Hanging Round The Skin Game                     —
Same:                                               San Fransisco, November, 1962
            Crazy About A Woman                     Folk-Lyric FL-126
            See See Rider                                   —
            Ninety Nine Years                               —
            Stranger's Blues                                —
            I Want A Girl                                   —
            Old Cincinnati Blues                            —
            Long As I Can Feel The Spirit                   —
            Black And Blue                                  —
            Brownskin Woman                                 —
            I Got My Eyes On You                            —
            Preacher Lowdown                                —
            Bill Bailey                                     —
            San Francisco Bay Blues                         —
Same:                                               1963
            San Fransisco Bay Blues                 Bluesville BVLP 14006
            Everybody Works At Home But My Old Man          —
            Beale Street Blues                              —
            'et Me Hold You In My Arms Tonight              —
            Where Could I Go But To The Lord                —
            You're No Good                                  —
            I Want A Girl Just Like The Girl That Married
                        Dear Old Dad                        —
            Old Man Mose                                    —
            Crazy Waltz                                     —
            Brother Lowdown                                 —
            The Dozens                                      —
            I've Been So Doggone Lonesome                   —
            Animal Fair                                     —
Same:                                               1964
            Red River Blues                         Prestige 7368
            How Long, How Long Blues                        —
            You Can't Keep A Good Man Down                  —
            Key To The Highway                              —
            Picking The Strings                             —
            Midnight Special                                —
            Stranger Blues                                  —
            Fables Aren't Nothing But Doggone Lies          —
            Brownskin Gal, I Got My Eyes On You             —
            Cincinnati Blues                                —
            Hump On Your Back                               —
            Trouble If I Don't Use My Head                  —
Same:                                               London, October 26, 1965
            Bye and Bye                             Fontana TL 5313
            Stagolee                                        —
            Crazy 'Bout A Woman                             —
            Hesitation Blues                                —
            99 Years And One Dark Day                       —
            How Long Blues                                  —
            San Francisco Bay Blues                         —
            Fingerbuster                                    —
            Going Back To My Old Time Used To Be            —
```

JOHNNY FULLER   (see also in Appendix)

Vcl/gtr. with org; vibes; bs; dms.   Oakland, 1954/55

SF 2349	Fool's Paradise	Rhythm 1767, 1782, Aladdin 3278
	First Stage Of The Blues	– , Irma 110
SF 2348	Johnny Ace's Last Letter	Rhythm 1782, Aladdin 3278
	Johnny Ace's Last Letter (Alt. take)	Palace LP M-724
A	Lovin' Lovin' Man	Rhythm 1777
B	Remember	–

Note: Band on above session is probably Candyman McGuirt's Band.

Vcl/gtr. with Walter Robertson, hca; George Hurst, pno; R. Dixon, bs; T. Ramerson, dms.

| R 1773A | Train, Train Blues | Rhythm 1773, Hollywood 1043 |
| R 1773B | (Black Cat) Bad Luck Overtook Me | –   – |

Similar but no hca. Add saxes (-1):

HO 618	Mean Old World -1	Rhythm 1779, Hollywood 1057
HO 619	How Long -1	–
HO 620	Sunny Road	Hollywood 1084
HO 621	I Can't Succeed	–
HO 679	Too Late To Change	Hollywood 1077, Palace LP M-724
HO 680	Roughest Place In Town	Hollywood 1063
HO 681	My Mama Told My	Hollywood 1077, Palace LPM-724
HO 682	Comin' Round The Corner	Hollywood 1063

Vcl/gtr. with pno; bs; dms; unk. 2nd vcl (-1):

| FL-210 | Buddy -1 | Flair 1054 |
| FL-211 | Hard Times | – |

Omit pno;

| A | I Walk All Night | Money 206 |
| AA | These Young Girls | – |

Vcl/gtr. With Walter Robinson, hca; pno; bs; dms.

| | It's Your Life | Flair unissued |

Note: Gospel and later recordings not included

PLAYBOY FULLER

See under Rocky Fuller

ROCKY FULLER

Vcl/gtr.   Detroit 1952

| C 1020 | Soon One Morning | Checker 753 |
| C 1021 | Come On Baby, Now | – |

PLAYBOY FULLER
Vcl/gtr. with hca; pno.

| OP 246 | Gonna Play My Guitar | Fuller OP 171 |
| OP 247 | Sugar Cane Highway | – |

LOWELL FULSON (Or Lowell Fulsom)

Born Tulsa, Oklahoma in 1921.

> Note' All Fulson's early sides were recorded by Bob Geddins in Oakland California.
> As his first sides appeared in 1946 on both Swing Time and Geddins' labels, it is
> presumed that Geddins leased all Lowell's first sides to Jack Lauderdale. Though
> the titles as first are exactly the same and were recorded at the same sessions they
> are, as far as is known, alternate takes or variations of the original on Swing Time.
> Several items have been checked and are different; but not all, so this theory can-
> not be taken as definite. To simplify this discography Swing Time releases are included
> with the others. In 1949 Fulson finished with Geddins and became a permanent
> Swing Time artist until the label folded.

LOWELL FULSON on Big Town

LOWELL FULSON & TRIO on Swing Time
Vcl/gtr. with Eldridge McCarthy, pno. + bs; dms. on (-1)   Oakland, 1946

BT 1068, 4096	Crying Blues (Street Walking Woman)	Big Town 1068, Gilt Edge 5041
110 A	Crying Blues -1	Swing Time 110
BT 1069	You're Going To Miss Me When I'm Gone	Big Town 1068
110 B	You're Going To Miss Me When I'm Gone -1	Swing Time 110

Add Big Dad. bs + dms. on (-1):

BT 1070A, 4095	Miss Katie Lee Blues (Katie Lee Blues)	Big Town 1070A, 1071B, Gilt Edge 5041
	Miss Katie Blues -1	Swing Time 111, Down Beat 111
BT 1071A, 5079	Rambling Blues (Crying Won't Make Me Stay)	Big Town 1071A, 1071A, Gilt Edge 5050
	Ramling Blues -1	Swing Time 111, Down Beat 111
BT 1071B, 5080	Fulson's Blues (Bad Luck And Trouble)	Big Town 1071B, 1072A, Gilt Edge 5050
	Fulson's Blues	Swing Time 112
BT 1072B	San Fransisco Blues	Big Town 1072B, 1072B
	San Fransisco Blues -1	Swing Time 112

Note: Gilt Edge 5043 credited to Lowell Fulson is actually by K. C. Douglas, q.v.

Vcl/gtr. with Rufus J. Russell, pno; Arthur Robinson, bs; Asal C. Carson, dms.

MT 1074A	Trouble Blues	Big Town 1074
114 A	Trouble Blues	Swing Time 114
MT 1075	I'm Going To See My Baby	Big Town 1074
114 B	Want To See My Baby	Swing Time 114
BT 1076	Black Widow Spider Blues	Big Town 1077
	Black Widow Spider Blues	Swing Time 115
Bt 1077	Don't Be So Evil	Big Town 1077
	Don't Be So Evil	Swing Time 115
ST 103, JH 102	Scotty's Blues	Scotty's Radio 101
ST 104, JH 101	The Train Is Leaving	–

LOWELL FULSON & THE FUL-TONES on Trilon

LOWELL FULSON & TRIO on Swing Time
Vcl/gtr. with Eldridge McCarthy, pno; Bob Johnson, bs; Dickie Washington dms.
Oakland, 1947

T-1154-3	Jelly Jelly	Trilon 185
T-1155-2	Mean Woman Blues	–
	Mean Woman Blues	Swing Time 113
T-1156-2	9. 30 Shuffle	Trilon 186
T-1157-2	Thinkin' Blues	–
	Thinkin Blues	Swing Time 117
	Down Beat Shuffle	–
	Fulson Boogie	Swing Time 113

LOWELL FULSON & HIS ORCHESTRA on Trilon

LOWELL FULSON & TRIO on Swing Time
Probably same as last:

T-1191-4	Trynin' To Find My Baby (add ten)	Trilon 192
116 B	Trying To Find My Baby	Swing Time 116, Down Beat 116
T-1192	Let's Throw A Boogie-Woogie (add ten)	Trilon 192
T-1193-2	Highway 99	Trilon 193
116 A	Highway 99	Swing Time 116, Down Beat 116
T-1194-2	Whiskey Boogie	Trilon 193

LOWELL FULSON & HIS TRIO
Probably as last:

| 118A | Midnight Showers Of Rain | Swing Time 118 |
| 118 B | So Long, So Long. | – |

119 A	Wee Hours In The Morning	Swing Time 119, Down Beat 119
119 B	My Gal At Eight	–
120 A	Bad Luck Blues	Swing Time 120, Down Beat 120
120B	I'm Going Away	–

Vcl/gtr. with Ellis "King" Solomon, pno; Asal "Count" Carson, dms.

| 121A | The Blues Got Me Down | Swing Time 121, Down Beat 121 |
| 121B | Black Cat Blues | –   – |

Vcl/gtr. with same:

122A	Just A Poor Boy	Swing Time 122
122B	My Baby	–
123A	Blues And Women	Swing Time 123
123B	Sweet Jenny Lee	

LOWELL FULSON
Vcl/gtr. with Ellis "King" Solomon, pno; Asal "Count" Carson, dms.

133A	Television Blues	Swing Time 133
133B	Don't You Hear Me Calling You	–
134A	Demon Woman	Swing Time 134, Swing 134
134B	Tears At Sunrise	– –

TULSA RED & HIS TRIO
Vcl/gtr. with same:

| 135A | Blues And Misery | Swing Time 135 |
| 135B | Jam That Boogie | – |

LOWELL FULSON & HIS TRIO
Vcl/gtr. with same:

| 230A | Come Back Baby | Swing Time 230 |
| 230B | Country Boy | – |

LOWELL FULSON
Vcl/gtr. with Martin Fulson, gtr.   Oakland, 1948/49

| DT-1 | Three O'Clock Blues | Down Town 2002, Arhoolie R 2003 |
| DT-2 | I'm Wild About You | –   – |

LOWELL FULSON & TRIO
Vcl/gtr. with Ellis "King" Solomon, pno; Asal "Count" Carson, dms.

| 167A | Three O'Clock In The Morning | Swing Time 167, 290 |
| 167B | I'm Wild About You Baby | –   – |

LOWELL FULSON
Vcl/gtr. with Martin Fulson, gtr.

| 2021A, MM 1152 | I'm Prison Bound | Down Town 2021, RPM 305, Colonial 122 |
| 2021B, MM 1153 | My Baby Left Me | –   –   –   – |

Note: RPM issue as By Lowell Fulsom. 2021A retitled "Doin' Time Blues" with guitar intro shorted on RPM. 2021B retitled " Some Old Lonesome Day" on RPM, and "Goodbye, Goodbye" on Colonial.

CAV 100, SF 1746	Night And Day	Aladdin 3104
CAV 101, SF 1661	Double Trouble Blues	Aladdin 3088
CAV 125, SF 1745	Stormin' And Rainin'	Cavatone 250, Aladdin 3104
CAV 126, SF 1662	Good Woman Blues	Aladdin 3088, Arhoolie F 1006

Note: rev. of Cavatone 250 by Ulysses James, q.v.

LOWELL FULSON WITH GUITAR
Vcl/gtr. with Martin Fulson, gtr.

201A	Western Union Blues	Swing Time 201, Arhoolie R 2003
201B	Lazy Woman Blues	– –
202A	River Blues Part 1	Swing Time 202, –
202B	River Blues Part 2	– –

LOWELL FULSON & HIS ORCHESTRA
Vcl. with Vernon Smith, tpt; Don Hill, alt; Maxwell Davis, ten; Jay McShann, pno; Tiny Webb, gtr; Ralph Hamilton, bs; Jessie Sales, dms.

203A	Jimmy's Blues	Swing Time 203
203B	Ain't Nobody's Business	–

LOWELL FULSON WITH GUITAR
Vcl/gtr. with Martin Fulson, gtr.

219A	I Walked All Night	Swing Time 219, Arhoolie R 2003
219B	Midnight And Day	– –
220A	The Blues Is Killing Me	Swing Time 220, –
220B	Did You Ever Feel Unlucky	– –

VARIOUS CREDITS - USUALLY "WITH ORCHESTRA"
Vcl/gtr. with Earl Brown alt; Lloyd Glenn, pno; Billy Hadnott, bs; Bob Harvey, dms.

Los Angeles 1950

196A	Rocking After Midnight	Swing Time 196, Elko 154
196A+	Everyday I Have The Blues	– , Hollywood 1029, 1103, Nashville NLP 2030, Elko 254
197A	Cold Heated Woman	Swing Time 197
197B	Mama Bring Your Clothes Back Home	–
226A	Blue Shadows	Swing Time 226, Cash 1051
226A	Low Society Blues	– , Nashville NLP 2030
227A	Baby Won't You Jump With Me	Swing Time 227
227A+	Back Home Blues	–

Note: Elko 254 as by L. C. Robinson

Omit Earl Brown, alt:

	Rainey Day	Swing Time 231
	Miss Lillie Brown	–
237A+	Sinner's Prayer	Swing Time 237
	(rev. by Lloyd Glenn)	
272A	Blues With A Feelin'	Nashville NLP 2030
325A	Let Me Ride Your Automobile	Swing Time 325

Add Earl Brown, alt;

242A+	(Original) Lonesome Christmas Part 1	Swing Time 242, Hollywood 1022
242A	(Original) Lonesome Christmas Part 2	– –
243A+	I'm A Night Owl Part 1	Swing Time 243
243A	I'm A Night Owl Part 2	–
272A	Why Can't You Cry For Me	Swing Time 272

As last:

Los Angeles, 1951/52

289A+	Let's Live Right	Swing Time 289
295A	Guitar Shuffle	Swing Time 295, Hollywood 1029 1103, Nashville NLP 2030
295A+	Mean Old Lonesome Song	Swing Time 295
301A+	The Highway Is My Home	Swing Time 301
	(rev. by Lloyd Glenn)	
	Black Widow Spider -1	Swing Time 308
	Midnight Showers of Rain -1	–

-1. May be reissues from Swing Time 115, 118.

As last, but add Dell Graham, vcl(-1):

315A+	Raggedy Daddy Blues -1	Swing Time 315
315A	Goodbye -1	–
320A	Ride Until The Sun Goes Down	Swing Time 320
325A+	Upstairs	Swing Time 325
330A	I Love My Baby	Swing Time 330
338A	I've Been Mistreated	Swing Time 338, Parrot 787

Vcl/gtr. with 2 tens; pno; bs; dms.

Los Angeles, 1953

320A+	Good Party Shuffle (Christmas Party Shuffle)	Swing Time 320
330A+	Th' Blues Come Rollin' In	Swing Time 330
335A	Cash Box Boogie (Lowell Jumps One)	Swing Time 335, Arhoolie R 2003
	Juke Box Shuffle	Swing Time 338, Parrot 787

Add org. Earl Brown, vcl (-1):

289A	Best Wishes -1	Swing Time 289
335A+	My Daily Prayer	Swing Time 335
	There Is A Time For Everything	Arhoolie R 2003

LOWELL FULSON & HIS ORCHESTRA
Vcl/gtr. with 2 saxes; pno; bs; dms.   New Orleans, October, 19, 1953

NO 2232	Don't Leave Me Baby (ensemble vcl)	Aladdin 3217
NO 2233	Blues Never Fail	Aladdin 3233
NO 2234	Chuck With The Boys	Aladdin 3217
NO 2235	You've Got To Reap	Aladdin 3233

LOWELL FULSON
Vcl/gtr. with saxes; pno; bs; dms.   Los Angeles, 1954

7711	Reconsider Baby	Checker 804
7712	I Believe I'll Give It Up	—

Same, Eddie Chamblee, ten;   Los Angeles, 1955

7762	Lonely Hours	Checker 820
7763	Check Yourself	Checker 812
7764	Loving You	—
7765	Do Me Right	Checker 820
7882	Trouble, Trouble	Checker 829, Argo LP 4042
7883	I Still Love You Baby	—

Same: LosAngeles, 1956

8018	It's All Your Fault Baby	Checker 841
8019	Tollin' Bells	—
8020		
8021	It Took A Long Time	Checker 937
8334	Blues Rhumba	Checker 854
8335		
8336	Baby Please Don't Go	Checker 854

Same: Los Angeles, 1957

8502	Don't Drive Me Baby	Checker 865
8503	You're Gonna Miss Me	—

Same: Los Angeles, 1958

8612	I Want To Make Love To You	Checker 882
8613	Rock This Morning	—
8614	That's All Right	Checker 937

Same: Los Angeles, 1959

10056	Comin' Home	Checker 952
10057	Have You Changed Your Mind	—

Vcl/gtr. with Earl Brown, alt; Louis Williams, ten; Jim Wynn, bari; Lloyd Glenn, pno; Billy
Hadnott, bs; Robert "Snake" Sims, dms.   Los Angeles, June 2, 1960

10242	I'm Glad You Reconsidered	Checker 959
10243		
10244	Blue Shadows	Checker 959
10245-1	I Want To Know Part 1	Checker 972
10245-2	I Want To Know Part 2	

Similar: Los Angeles, 1961

U 11064	So May Tears	Checker 992
U 11065	Hung Down Head	—

Similar: Los Angeles, 1962

U 11839	Shed No Tears	Checker 1027
U 11840	Can She	
U 11841	Trouble With The Blues	Checker 1046
U 11842	Love Grows Cold	—

LOWELL FULSOM
Vcl/gtr. with Leon Blue & His Band: Unk. hca; Dave White, pno; Leon Blue, bs-gtr;
Clifton Young, dms.   Los Angeles, 1964
A   Stop And Think   Movin' 128
Omit hca. Add Tricky Jones, tpt; Brother Heanley, ten; James Curry, tbn;
B   Baby   Movin' 128

LOWELL FULSOM
Vcl/gtr. with

	Everytime It Rains	Kent 395, KLP5016
	My heart Belongs To You	–
401-1	Too Many Drivers	Kent 401, Kent 5027, 5016
401-2	Key To My Heart	–
410-1	Strange Feeling	Kent 410
410-2	What's Gonna Be	–

Vcl/gtr. with tpt: saxes; pno; bs; dms.   Los Angeles, 1965/66

	Night Spot Part 1	Modern 1009
	Night Spot Part 2	–
	No More Part 1	Kent 422
	No More Part 2	–
	Black Nights	Kent 431, KLP 5020, 5016
	Little Girl (Angel)	– , KLP 5016
440-1	Shattered Dreams	Kent 440, KLP 5016
440-2	Sittin' Here Thinkin'	–
443-1	Blues Around Midnight	Kent 443, –
443-2	Talkin' Woman	– , –
448-1	Change Your Ways	Kent 448, –
448-2	My Aching Back	– , –
452-1	Ask At Any Door In Town	Kent 452, –
452-2	Trouble I'm In	– , –
456-1	Tramp (no brass)	Kent 456, KLP 5020
456-2	Pico (no brass)	–
	Make A Little Love	Kent 463
	I'm Sinking	– , KLP 5020
	No Hard Feelings	Kent KLP 5020
	Lonely Day	–
	Hustlers Game	–
	Get Your Game Up Tight	–
	Back Door Key	–
	Goin' Home	–
	Year Of '29	– , A-Bet LP 401
	Two Way Wishing	Kent KLP 5016
	Just One More Time	Ride 139
	You Gonna Miss Me	–
	Tomorrow	

BOB GADDY

BOB GADDY & HIS ALLEY CATS
Vcl/pno. with Sonny Terry, hca; Brownie McGhee, gtr; dms. New York City, c. 1952
M 45   I (Believe You Got A Sidekick)   Jackson 2303
M 46
M 47   Bicycle Boogie   Jackson 2303

Unk. ten. replace Terry. Add Bob Harris, bs; George Wood, dms.
      New York City, 1952
J 4053   No Help Wanted (add vcl. chorus)   Jax 308
J 4054   Little Girl's Boogie   –

BOB GADDY & HIS KEYS
Similar to last:
D-760   Blues Has Walked In My Room   Harlem 2330
D-761   Slow Down Baby   –

Vcl/pno. with ten; Brownie McGhee, gtr; bs; dms.   New York City, 1956
OT 855   Operator   Old Town 1031
OT 856   I Love My Baby   –

Vcl. with Jimmy Wright, ten; Jack Dupree, pno; Larry Dale, gtr; Al Hall, bs; Gene Moore, dms.
      New York City, 1957
OT 871   Paper Lady   Old Town 1039, 1064
OT 872   Out Of My Name   –

Dupree out. Gaddy, vcl/pno:
OT 893   Woe Woe Is Me   Old Town 1050
OT 894   Rip And Run   –

Same: New York City, 1958
OT 909   You Are The One   Old Town 1057, 1074
OT 910   Take My Advice   –   –
OT 923   What Would I Do   Old Town 1064

Vcl/pno. with   New York City, 1959/60.
OT 934   Till The Day I Die   Old Town 1070
OT 935   I'll Go My Way   –
OT 948   Early One Morning   Old Town 1077
OT 949   What Wrong Did I Do   –
      Don't Tell Her   Old Town 1085
      Could I   –

DENNIS GAINUS

Vcl/gtr.   Houston, May 1, 1959
      You Gonna Look Like A Monkey   "77" LA 12/2

GANDY DANCERS

Group vcl.   Frisco Line, Ala., 1954
      Let's Move It   Folkways FA 2659

CECIL GANT

Born Nashville, Tennessee in 1915. Died New York City in 1951.

PVT. CECIL GANT "THE G.I. SING-STATION"
Vcl/pno. with bs (−1); dms (−2) for LP versions only.   Los Angeles, 1944/46
CG-1 (?)   Cecil Knows Better Now   Gilt Edge 508
CG-1   I Wonder -2   Gilt Edge 501, Bronze 117, 4
      Star 1159, 24, Sound 601,
      Decca 30320
CG-2   Cecil (or Cecil's) Boogie -2   Gilt Edge 501, Bronze 120, 4
      Star 1159, 24, Sound 601,
      Decca 30320
CG-3   Wake Up Cecil, Wake Up -1, 2   Gilt Edge 502, 4 Star 1205,
      Sound 601
CG-4   You're Going To Cry   Gilt Edge 508
CG-5

CG-6		
CG-7		
CG-8		
CG-9		
CG-10	Boogie Blues	Gilt Edge 502, 4 Star 1205
CG-11	Put Another Chair At The Table -2	Gilt Edge 503, Sound 601
CG-12	Cecil Boogie No. 2 (New Cecil Boogie) -1	Gilt Edge 503, 4 Star 25
CG-13	The Grass Is Getting Greener Ever Day	Gilt Edge 505
CG-14	Killer Diller Boogie (Syncopated Boogie)	Gilt Edge 505
CG-14A	Killer Diller Boogie	4 Star 1221, 24
CG-14A	Jam Jam Blues	Gilt Edge 516
CG-14B	Jam Jam Blues (Lightning Blues)	Gilt Edge 517
CG-15		
CG-16		
CG-17		
CG-18	Cecil's Mop Mop -1	Gilt Edge 504
CG-19	Are You Ready	Gilt Edge 506
CG-20	I'm Tired	–
CG-21		
CG-22		
CG-23	I'll Remember You	Gilt Edge 504, 4 Star 1339
CG-24	If I Had A Wish	Gilt Edge 518
CG-25	Fit As A Fiddle (add ten; bs; dms.)	Gilt Edge 509
CG-26	I Believe I Will	–
CG-26 (?)	In A Little Spanish Town	Gilt Edge 511
CG-27, A 1713		
	Rhumba Boogie Woogie	Gilt Edge 512
CG-28	Way Down	Gilt Edge 513
CG-29	Blues In Los Angeles	Gilt Edge 510
CG-30		
CG-31	Make Believable Girl	Gilt Edge 515
CG-32	Stuff You Gotta Watch (add ten; bs; dms. on LP	
		Gilt Edge 515, Sound 601, 4 Star 25
CG-33	Hey Boogie	Gilt Edge 511
CG-34	It's A Great Life	Gilt Edge 518
CG-35	What's On Your Worried Mind	Gilt Edge 514
CG-36		
CG-37	Nothing Bothers Me	Gilt Edge 513
CG-38	I Got A Gal	Gilt Edge 514
CG-39	I Feel It	Gilt Edge 516
CG-40	When I Wanted You	Gilt Edge 510
CG-41, A 1710		
	Little Baby, You're Running Wild	Gilt Edge 512
CG-42	Solitude	Gilt Edge 517, Sound 601
CG-43		
CG-44		
Add alt; gtr; bs; dms.		
CG-45	Midnight On Central Avenue	Gilt Edge 519, Sound 601
CG-46	Am I To Blame	Gilt Edge 525, 4 Star 1243, 24
CG-47	Stella	Gilt Edge 525
CG-48	Hey Little Baby	Gilt Edge 534
CG-49	How Can I Sleep (no alt.)	Gilt Edge 519, Sound 601
CG-50	In The Evening When The Sun Goes Down	Gilt Edge 534
Same:		
V 181	Rainy Weather For Me	Gilt Edge 534, 4 Star 1221
V 182		
V 183		
V 184		
V 185		
V 186	Hit That Jive Jack	Gilt Edge 534, 4 Star 1221, 24, Sound 601
V 192	Special Delivery (no alt.)	4 Star 1176, 25
V 193		

V 194		
V 195		
V 196	Jump Jack Jump	4 Star 1176, 25, Sound 601

From Gilt Edge sessions:
Vcl/pno.

	My Last Goodbye	Bronze 117
	It's All Over Now (or Darling)	Bronze 119, Bop Features 106
	Soft And Mellow	— , 4 Star 1243, 24
	Goodbye Baby	Bronze 120
	My Baby Changed	4 Star 1526
	Can't Get You Off My Mind	
2074	Time Will Tell (add vibes)	4 Star 1584, Sound 601
2075		
2076		
2077		
2078		
2079	Vobology	4 Star 1377
3046	Where I Belong	4 Star 1584
3047	Long Distance Call (add vibes)	4 Star 1377, Sound 601
4062	Rocking The Boogie	4 Star 1561
4063	I Will Go On Lovin' You	—
	I'm Losing You	4 Star 1606
	Peace And Love	—
	Coming Round The Mountain (rev. by	4 Star 1452
	Ivory Joe Hunter)	
	I'm Travellin' Alone	4 Star 1284, 25, Bop Features 106
	God Bless My Daddy	4 Star 1284
	Fare Thee My Baby	4 Star 1339

Vcl/pno.   1947

K 5459	Hogan's Alley	King 4231
K 5460	Why	

Vcl/pno. with bs; dms.   Nashville? 1947/49

A	Nashville Jumps	Bullet 250
B	Loose As A Goose	—
A	Train Time Blues	Bullet 255, Dot 1121, Record Shop Special 1
B	Sloppy Joes	issues as above
	Boogie Woogie Baby	Bullet 256
	If It's True	—
	I'm All Alone Now	Bullet 257
	Anna Mae	—
A	Ninth Street Jive	Bullet 258
B	It's The Girl	—
	Boozie Boogie	Bullet 264
	Every Minute Of The Hour	—
	Go To Sleep Little Baby	Bullet 265
	My My My	—
	I Wonder	Bullet 272
	I Believe I'll Go Back Home	—
	Another Day, Another Dollar	Bullet 280
	Three Little Girls	—
A	I'm A Good Man, But A Poor Man	Bullet 289
	(vcl. duet with Dorothy?)	
B	Cecil's Jam Session	Bullet 289
A	I Ain't Gonna Cry No More	Bullet 299
B	Screwy Boogie	—
	I Hate To Say Goodbye	Bullet 300
	My Little Baby	—
	Rose Room	Bullet 313
	I'm Singing The Blues Today	—
	What's The Matter	Bullet 320
	You Can't Do Me Right	—

Note: Dot purchased and reissued Bullet masters. From above sessions:

A	Crying To Myself	Dot 1016
B	Nobody Loves You	–
A	Waiting For My Train	Dot 1030
B	Cindy Lou	–
11	I'm Still In Love With You	Dot 1053
111	Alma	–
A	Goodbye Baby	Dot 1069
B	Raining Blues	–

CECIL GANT & HIS TRIO
Vcl/pno. with Tiny Webb, gtr; Ralph Hamilton, bs; Jessie Sailes, dms.

Los Angeles, 1949

	Deal Yourself Another Hand	Down Beat 209
	All Because Of You	–
	You're Going To Cry	Swing Time 302
	Baby I'm Losing You	–

CECIL GANT
Vcl/pno. with

New Orleans? February 21, 1950

IM 156	When You Left Me Baby	Imperial 5066
IM 157	Blues By Cecil	Imperial 5112
IM 158	Come Home	–
IM 159	You'll Be Sorry	Imperial 5066

GUNTER LEE CARR
Vcl/pno. with gtr; bs; dms.

New York City, July, 1950

76570	Goodnight Irene	Decca 48167
76571	My House Fell Down	–
76572	We're Gonna Rock	Decca 48170
76573	Yesterday	–

CECIL GANT
Vcl/pno. with dms.

New York, August 7, 1950

W.76710	Someday You'll Be Sorry Pt. 1	Decca 48171
W.76711	Someday You'll Be Sorry Pt. 2	–
W.76712	Owl Stew	Decca 48231
W.76713	Playin' Myself The Blues	–

Vcl/pno. with org.

New York, September, 1950

W.81539	God Bless My Daddy	Decca 48249
W.81540	The Grass Is Gettin' Greener	–

No details:

New York, October 13, 1950

W.80031	Train Time Blues No. 2	Decca 48190
W.80032	It Ain't Gonna Be Like That	–
W.80033	It's Christmas Time Again	Decca 48185
W.80034	Hellow Santa Claus	–

Vcl/pno. with gtr; bs; dms.

New York, January 19, 1951

W.80423	Shot Gun Boogie	Decca 48200
W.80424	Rock Little Baby	–
W.80425	My Little Baby	Decca 48212
W.80426	Don't You Worry	–

From unk. session:

	I Wonder	National 9003
	(rev. Hank D'Amico)	

WILLIE GARLAND

Vcl/hca. with pno; gtr; bs–gtr; dms.

Los Angeles, 1966

461-1	Black Widow Spider	Kent 461
461-2	Soul Blues	–

CLARENCE GARLOW (see also in APPENDIX)

Born Welsh, Louisiana in 1911.

CLARENCE GARLOW & HIS GUITAR
Vcl/gtr. with Hilmer Shakesliner, ten; Mildred Smith, pno; Johnny Marshal, dms.

Houston, 1949

ACA 1223	Bound To Lose My Mind	unissued
ACA 1224	In A Boogie Mood	Macy's 5002
ACA 1235	Jumpin' For Joy	unissued
ACA 1236	She's So Fine	Macy's 5001
ACA 1237	Blues As You Like It	–

Johnnie Mae Brown, pno. replaces Mildred Smith:

ACA 1268	Bon Ton Roula	Macy's 5002, Arhoolie 1009
ACA 1269	Too Many Women, Too Much Beer	unissued
ACA 1270	I Have Lost My Trust In You	unissued
ACA 1271	She Tore Up My Picture	unissued
ACA 1272	My Life Story	unissued

CLARENCE GARLOW & HIS ORCH.
Vcl/gtr. with Curtiss Babino, ten; Shelby Lackey, ten; Emma Del Lee, vcl/pno; Bill Parker, dms.
Crowley, La., 1951

| B-1000A | New Bon Ton Roula | Feature 1000 |
| B-1000B | Let Me Be Your Santa | – |

CLARENCE "BON TON" GARLOW, HIS GUITAR & ORCH.
Same – Curtiss Babino, vcl (–1):　Lake Charles, La., 1951

A	Louisiana Blues	Lyric 100
B	Watch Your Business -1	–
A	Wrong Doing Woman -1	Lyric 101
B	Trouble With My Woman	–

CLARENCE GARLOW
Vcl/gtr. with unk. ten; Emma Del Lee, vcl (–1)/pno; bs; dms.
New Orleans, 1952

NO 2094	New Bon Ton Roula	Aladdin 3179
NO 2095	You Got Me Crying -1	Aladdin 3225
NO 2096	Dreaming	Aladdin 3179
RR 2181	I'm Hurt	Aladdin 3225

Vcl/gtr. with Curtiss Babino, Shelby Lackie, tens; Anna Mae Rogers, vcl/pno; Bill Parker, dms.
Crowley, La., 1954

| A | If I Keep On Worrying | Feature 3005 |
| B | I Called You Up Daddy | – |

CLARENCE "BON TON" GARLOW
Vcl/gtr. with Maxwell Davis, ten; Willard McDaniel, pno; Red Callender, bs; Peppy Prince, dms.
Culver City, Calif., 1954

| FL 145 | Crawfishin' | Flair 1021 |
| FL 146 | Route 90 | – |

CLARENCE GARLOW & HIS ACCORDIAN
Vcl/accdn. with Darnell Jackson, pno; Chester Randle, gtr; Garen Joseph, bs; Matthew Colbert, dms.
Lake Charles, La., 1954

| A | Za Belle | Folk Star 1130 |
| B | Made Me Cry | – |

CLARENCE GARLOW, HIS GUITAR & ORCH.
Vcl/gtr. with Lionel Prevo, ten; Darnell Jackson, pno; Garen Joseph, bs; Matthew Colbert, dms.

| A | No, No Baby | Folk Star 1199 |
| B | I Feel Like Calling You | – |

'Ice Water', bs. replaces Joseph:　Lake Charles, La., 1956

A	Purty Little Doolie (sic)	Goldband 1043
B	Sundown	–
	Sunday Morning (no ten.)	unissued

Vcl/gtr. with Lionel Prevo, ten; Katie Webster, pno; 'Ice Water', bs; Little Brother Griffin, dms.
Lake Charles, La., 1957

| A | Bon Ton Roula | Goldband 1065 |
| B | Sound The Bell | – |

Vcl/gtr. with T. Baby Green Orch:　Beaumont, Texas, 1962

| | Sound The Bell | Bon-Ran? |
| | Train Fare Home | – |

Note: This artist is a resident and D.J. in Beaumont, Texas.

BILLY GARNER

Vcl/gtr. with   Memphis, 1961
| | That's What I Want To Do | Mojo 2171 |
| | Little Schoolgirl | – |

ROBERT GARRETT

Vcl/gtr. with pno; gtr; dms.   Nashville? 1962
| A | Quit My Drinkin' | Excello 2216 |
| B | Do Remember | – |

LEROY GARY

Vcl.   Lambert, Miss., 1959
| | Mama Lucy | Prestige LP 25010 |

BOB GEDDINS (or Robert Geddins)

BOB GEDDINS

Turner Willis, vcl. with pno; gtr; bs;   Oakland, 1945?
| 1064 | Irma Jean (rev. by Turner Willis) | Trilon 1058, Big Town 1058 |

BOB GEDDINS & HIS CAVALIERS

Vcl. ensemble. with Sherman Louis, pno; Lafayette Thomas, gtr; B. Bostic, bs.

                                                Oakland, 1949
| CT5A | Thinkin' And Thinkin' (rev. by Sherman's Trio) | Cavatone 5, Modern 20-685 |

BOB GEDDINS' CAVALIERS

Jimmy Wilson, vcl. with V. Eldmich, ten; Sherman Louis, pno; Lafayette Thomas, gtr; B. Bostic, bs.
| A | I'm A Stranger | Cavatone 103 |
| B | St. Louis Blues | – |

J. C. GENT

No details: Belleville, Ill., 1960
| | Bad Gal Blues | Marlo 1501 |
| | Wonder Why | – |

LLOYD GEORGE

Vcl/hca. with pno; gtrs; dms.   1962
| IM 3391 | Lucy Lee | Imperial 5837 |
| IM 3392 | Sing Real Loud | – |

Similar: 1963
IM 5325	Hold Me Close	unissued
IM 5326	Come On Train	Post 1006
IM 5327	Frog Hunt	–
IM 5328	Forever More	unissued

DADDYO GIBSON

No details: 1956
| 8140 | Behind The Sun | Checker 848 |
| 8141 | Night Train | – |

Note: May not be of interest.

GRANDPAPPY GIBSON

Real name Clifford Gibson.

Vcl/gtr. with gtr (–1); dms.   St. Louis, 1960
| 13940-1 | It's Best To Know Who You're Talking To | Bobbin 124 |
| 13940-2 | I Don't Want No Woman –1 | – |

add pno; bs.
| 127-1 | The Monkey Likes To Boogie | Bobbin 127 |
| 127-2 | No Success Blues | – |

EARL GILLIAM

Vcl/pno. with B. J. Brooks, ten; gtr; bs; dms.   Houston, 1962
I 343   Just You And I (rev. by B. J. Brooks) Ivory 1-343

Vcl/pno. with Lucian Davis Orch: saxes; gtr; bs; dms. Houston, 1966
ACA 7791 Don't Make Me Late Baby Sarg 128
ACA 7792
ACA 7793 Nobody's Blues Sarg 128
ACA 9117 Wrong Doing Woman Sarg 133
ACA 9118
ACA 9119 Petite Baby Sarg 133

JAZZ GILLUM

Born Indianola, Mississippi on September 11, 1904.
Vcl/hca. with Roosevelt Sykes, pno; Big Bill Broonzy, gtr; Ransom Knowling, bs.

            Chicago, September 26, 1945
D5-AB-312 Go Back To The County Bluebird 34-0730
D5-AB-313 Five Feet Four   –
D5-AB-314 Afraid To Trust Them Bluebird 34-0741
D5-AB-315 Whiskey Headed Buddies –

Vcl/hca. with Big Maceo, pno; Leonard Caston, gtr; Alfred Elkins, bs.
            Chicago, February 18, 1946
D6-AB-1816 Reckless Rider Blues Victor 20-1974
D6-AB-1817 Fast Woman Bluebird 34-0747
D6-AB-1818 All In All Blues Victor 20-2232
D6-AB-1819 Keep On Sailing Bluebird 34-0747
D6-AB-1820 Look On Yonder Wall Victor 20-1974
D6-AB-1821 Long Razor Blues Victor 20-2120

Vcl/hca. with James Clark, pno; Willie Lacey, gtr; Ransom Knowling, bs; Judge Lawrence
Riley, dms.   Chicago, September 18, 1946
D6-VB-1949 I'm Gonna Train My Baby Victor 20-2405
D6-VB-1950 Roll Dem Bones Victor 20-2580
D6-VB-1951 Can't Trust Myself Victor 20-2232
D6-VB-1952 I'm Not The Lad Victor 20-2120

Eddie Boyd, pno. replaces Clark: Chicago, April 24, 1947
D7-VB-704 The Blues What Am Victor 20-2580
D7-VB-705 Gonna Take My Rap Victor 20-2783
D7-VB-706 You Got To Run Me Down Victor 20-2405
D7-VB-707 Chauffeur Blues Victor 20-2783

Vcl/hca. with Robert Call, pno; Willie Lacey, gtr; Ransom Knowling, bs; Judge Lawrence
Riley, dms.   Chicago, October 2, 1947
D7-VB-1056 Hand Reader Blues Victor 20-2964
D7-VB-1057 Country Woman Blues Victor 20-0005
D7-VB-1058 You Should Give Some Away Victor 20-2964
D7-VB-1059 Take A Little Walk With Me Victor 20-3250

Same: Chicago, November 10, 1947
D7-VB-1145 What A Gal Victor 20-3118
D7-VB-1146 Signifying Woman Victor 20-3250, 50-0004
D7-VB-1147 The Devil Blues Victor 20-3118
D7-VB-1148 Jazz Gillum's Blues Victor 20-0005

Vcl/hca. with Robert Call, pno; LeMont Franklin, gtr; Ransom Knowling, bs; Judge Lawrence
Riley, dms.   Chicago, January 25, 1949
D9-VB-343 Take One More Chance With Me Victor 22-0033, 50-0017
D9-VB-344 Gonna Be Some Shooting Victor 22-0051, 50-0035
D9-VB-345 Look What You Are Today Victor 22-0033, 50-0017
D9-VB-346 A Lie Is Dangerous Victor 22-0051, 50-0035

Omit Franklin: Chicago, March 21, 1950
EO-VB-3411 I'm Still Going Down Slow unissued
EO-VB-3412 Don't Think I'm Buster Brown unissued
EO-VB-3413 Floating Power unissued
EO-VB-3414 Broadcasting Mama unissued

Vcl/hca. with Memphis Slim, pno/org (−1); Arbee Stidham, gtr (−2).

		New York City, 1961
	The Race Of The Jim Lee And The Katy Adam	Folkways FS 3826
	A Small Town They Call Bessemer -1	−
	Walkin' The Blues Away -1	−
	My Last Letter	−
	Key To The Highway	−
	Harmonica Boogie	−
	Gillum Blues -2	−

Note: See also Memphis Slim and Arbee Stidham.

BOYD GILMORE

Vcl/gtr. with Ike Turner, pno; poss. Joe Harris, dms.

		Clarksdale? 1952
MM 1780	Ramblin' On My Mind	Modern 860, Blues Classics 15
MM 1781	Just An Army Boy	−
MM 1837	All In My Dreams	Modern 872
MM 1838	:Take A Little Walk With Me	−

Note: MM 1838 has the introduction and solo from Elmore James' "Please Find My Baby" dubbed on.

Same:

		Clarksdale, April 13, 1952
	If That's Your Girl	Modern unissued
	If That's Your Girl (alt. take)	−
	I Love My Little Woman	−

GOLDRUSH

Vcl/pno.   Oakland, c. 1948

JG-7-1149   All My Money Is Gone (rev. by Black Diamond)Jaxyson 6A

GOOD JELLY BESS

Vcl/hca. with 2 gtrs; dms.   Nashville, 1962

NRS107A, VE 805

    A Little Piece At A Time   Hermitage 775

NRS107B, VE 806

    Come And Get It   −

Note: Male vocalist.

GOOD ROCKIN' SAMMY T.

No details: 1960

    Good Rockin' Mama   Junior 500

    Sweet Mama   −

JOHN LEE GRANDERSON

Born Ellendale, Tennessee?

Vcl/gtr.   Chicago, 1964

    A Man For The Nation   Testament S-01

    Good Morning Little Schoolgirl   Storyville SLP 181

Vcl/gtr. with Prezs Thomas, hca; Jimmy Walker, pno; William Mack, gtr.

                                 Chicago, 1965

    I Don't Feel Good   Testament T-2203

Vcl/gtr. with Bill Foster, gtr.

    My Home Ain't Here   Milestone LP 3002

JUNIOR GRAVELY

No details: 1959

    You Lied To Me Honey   Velatone 796

    Take My Hands

LEE GRAVES

No details: 1949

Cloudy Weather Blues	Mercury 8214
Papa Said Yes, Mama Said No, No, No	—
I'm From Texas	Mercury 8222
Sixty Years And A Day	—

ARVELLA GRAY

Born South Texas in 1910.
Vcl/gtr.   Chicago, July 11, 1960

	Corrine, Corinna	Heritage HLP 1004
	Have Mercy Mr. Percy	—
	Have Mercy Mr. Percy No. 2	—
	Railroad Songs And John Henry	—

Vcl/gtr.   Chicago, c. 1965

A	Freedom Riders	Gray 100
B	Freedom Bus	—

add Jimmy Brewer, gtr.

G 1313	You Are My Dear	Gray 13
G 1314	Deborah	—
G 1315	John Henry	Gray 14
G 1316	The Walking Blues	—

BOY GREEN

Vcl/gtr. with poss. 2nd gtr.   New York City, 1944

1103-S	A And B Blues	Regis 120
1104-S	Play My Juke Box	—

CLARENCE GREEN

Vcl/pno. with John Fontenett, ten; Horace Richmond, bs; Rigs Bolden, dms.

                                           Houston, 1948

A	Green's Bounce	Eddie's 1207
B	Galveston	—

Vcl/pno. with saxes; gtr; bs; dms.   Houston, 1951

ACA 1767	Heartaches	Peacock unissued
ACA 1768	I Just Found Out	—
ACA 1775	Hard Headed Woman	Peacock 1557
ACA 1776	Until The End	—
ACA 1915	Boogie Woogie Soldier	Peacock unissued
ACA 1916	Rock And Ride	unissued
ACA 1917	Oh What A Feelin'	unissued
ACA 1918	These Blues	unissued
ACA 1919	Hard To Satisfy	unissued

GALVESTON GREEN

Vcl/pno. with Rathe Lee, ten; Henry Bailey, bs; Lawrence Harms, dms.

                                           ? 1952

CG 1	My Time Is Your Time	Essex 701
CG 2	Bye-Baby-Bye	—
	Later records not included.	

GALVESTON GREEN

See under Clarence Green.

L. C. GREEN

Vcl/gtr. with Sam Kelley, hca.   Detroit, Summer, 1952

M 6009	When The Sun Is Shining	Dot 1103
M 6010	Little School Girl	Dot 1128
M 6011	Remember Way Back	— , Blues Classics BC-12
M 6012	Little Machine	Dot 1147

M 6013	Come Back Sugar Mama	–
M 6014		
M 6015		
M 6016	Hold Me In Your Arms -1	Dot 1103
	-1 No hca. Add 2nd gtr.	

Same:
| A | Going Down To The River Blues | Von 42 |
| B | Ramblin' Around Blues | – |

LARRY (MR. G) GREEN

Vcl/gtr. with tpts; saxes; pno; bs; dms.   Los Angeles, 1966
| A | Movin' The Blues | Movin' 133 |
| B | Bad Business | – |

R. GREEN & TURNER

See under Slim Green.

SLIM GREEN

Born Christian, Oklahoma?

R. GREEN & TURNER
Vcl/gtr. with ? Turner, hca.   Los Angeles, 1948
A	Alla Blues	J & M Fullbright 123
B	Central Ave. Blues	–
	Note: "Turner" was Green's girlfriend.	

SLIM GREEN
Vcl/gtr. with Louis Jackson, pno; Junior Hampton, dms.   Los Angeles, 1948
| A | Baby I Love You | Murray 501 |
| B | Tricky Woman Blues | – |

Vcl/gtr. with pno; bs.   Los Angeles, 1957
| 17233 | My Woman Done Quit Me (rev. by Al Simmons) | Dig 142 |

Vcl/gtr. with pno; gtr; dms.   Los Angeles,
| A | Shake 'Em Up | Canton 1789 |
| B | Jerico Alley | – |

GUITAR SLIM GREEN
Shelton Phillips, vcl (–1); pno (–2); Slim Green, gtr; 2nd gtr.
| G-1604 | Rock The Nation -2 | Geenote 907 |
| G-1603 | Movin' Out Baby -1 | – |

C. C. GRIFFIN

No details: Los Angeles, 1961
| | Storm Clouds | Joyce 1001 |
| | I Want To Be With You | – |

Vcl. with small band.   1963/64
| A | I Do Believe | Allegro R & B 2001 |
| B | Sitting Here Waiting | – |

LITTLE JIMMY GRIFFIN

Vcl. with saxes; pno; gtr; bs; dms.   Kansas City, c. 1962
| R 221 | I'm Search'n | R 508 |
| R 222 | If Things Don't Change | |

SHIRLEY GRIFFITHS

Born Brandon, Mississippi on 26 April, 1907.

J. T. ADAMS & SHIRLEY GRIFFITHS
Shirley Griffiths, vcl (–1)/gtr. with J. T. Adams, vcl (–2)/gtr.

           Indianapolis, 1961

106

	Walkin' Blues -1	Bluesville BVLP 1077
	Match Box Blues -2	—
	Indiana Avenue Blues	—
	In The Evening	—
	'A' Jump	—
	O Mama How I Love You -1	—
	Kansas City -2	—
	Bright Street Jump	—
	Done Changed The Lock On My Door -1	—
	Blind Lemon's Blues -2	—
	Naptown Boogie	—

SHIRLEY GRIFFITHS
Vcl/gtr.   Indianapolis, 1961

	Meet Me In The Bottom	Bluesville BVLP 1087
	River Line Blues	—
	Shirley's Jump	—
	Take Me Back To Mama	—
	Saturday Blues	—
	Left Alone Blues	—
	Big Road Blues	—
	Bye Bye Blues	—
	Hard Pill To Swallow	—
	Maggie Campbell Blues	—
	My Baby's Gone	—

GROOVY FIVE

See under Willie Johnson.

GROOVY TRIO

See under Willie Johnson.

GUITAR DAVE

Featuring hca. & gtrs.   1961

| | Zoro Pt. 1 | Central 291 |
| | Zoro Pt. 2 | — |

GUITAR NUBBITT

Real name Alvin Hankerson. Born in Fort Lauderdale, Florida in 1923.
Vcl/gtr.   Boston, 1962/64

M 5004	New Orleans	Bluestown 705, LP 7001
M 5005		
M 5006	Evil Hearted Woman	Bluestown 701
M 5007		
M 5008	I've Got The Blues	Bluestown 705
M 5009-1	Hard Road	Bluestown 702, LP 7001
M 5010	Laura	Bluestown 701
M 5011-1	Georgia Chain Gang	Bluestown 702, LP 7001

Add 2nd gtr. – prob. Alabama Watson:

| M 5075 | Big Leg Woman | Bluestown 707 |
| M 5076 | Crying Blues | — |

From above sessions:

	Traveller's Aid	Bluestown LP 7001
	Mean Ole Train	—
	Meltonia	—
	Sinner's Prayer	—
	I've Got A Feeling	—
	Evil Woman Blues	—

GUITAR SHORTY

Real name David William Kearney.
Vcl/gtr. with John Tinsley, ten; Lafayette Leake, pno; Willie Dixon, bs; Odie Payne or
Billie Stepney, dms.   Chicago, 1957
C-1022   You Don't Treat Me Right   Cobra 5017
C-1023   Irma Lee   –
Vcl/gtr. with brass; pno; bs; dms,   Los Angeles, 1959
P-301-A   Hard Life   Pull 301
P-301-B   Ways Of A Man   –
P-302-A   How Long Can It Last   Pull 302
P-302-B   Love Loves   –

GUITAR SLIM

See under Alec Seward.

GUITAR SLIM

See under Eddie Jones.

BOBBY GUITAR

See under Bobby (Guitar) Bennett.

ARTHUR GUNTER

Vcl/gtr. with Skippy Brooks, pno; bs; dms.   Nashville, 1955
A   Baby Let's Play House   Excello 2047, LP 8001
B   Blues After Hours   –
A   She's Mine All Mine   Excello 2053
B   You Are Doing Me Wrong   –
Omit pno. add Al Gunter, gtr.
A   Honey Babe   Excello 2058
B   No Happy Home   –
Same: Nashville, 1956/57
A   Trouble With My Baby   Excello 2073
B   Baby You Better Listen   –
Vcl/gtr. with tpt; Louis Brooks, ten; Skippy Brooks, pno; Al Gunter, gtr; dms; bs;
10266   Hear My Plea Baby (no pno.)   Excello 2084
10267   Love Has Got Me   –
Tpt; ten. out: Nashville, 1958
17955   Baby Can't You See   Excello 2125
17956   You're Always On My Mind   –
Vcl/gtr. with Louis Brooks, ten (–1); Skippy Brooks, pno; bs; dms.
                                                          Nashville, 1959
A   Ludella -1   Excello 2137
B   We're Gonna Shake -1   –
A   Don't Leave Me Now (add 2nd gtr.)   Excello 2147
B   Crazy Me (add 2nd gtr.)   –
A   No Naggin', No Draggin'   Excello 2164
B   I Want Her Back   –
Same: Nashville, 1960/61
A   Little Blue Jeans Woman   Excello 2191
B   Mind Your Own Business Babe   –
A   My Heart's Always Lonesome   Excello 2201
B   Love's Got Me (I'm Falling)   –
A   Who Will Ever Move Me From You   Excello 2204
B   Workin' For My Baby   –
            Note: Gunter now lives in Detroit.

BUDDY GUY

Born Lettsworth, Louisiana on July 30, 1936.

B. GUY & HIS BAND
Vcl/gtr. with Bob Neely, ten; McKinley Easton, bari; Otis Rush, gtr; Willie Dixon, bs; Odie Payne, dms.   Chicago, 1958

C 1042	Sit And Cry	Artistic 1501
C 1043	Try To Quit You Baby	–
C 1060	You Sure Can't Do	Artistic 1503
C 1061	This Is The End	–

BUDDY GUY
Vcl/gtr. with Jarrett "Gerry" Gibson, Donald Hankins, tens; Otis Spann, pno; Jack Meyers, bs–gtr; Fred Below, dms.   Chicago, 1960

U 10043	Slop Around	Chess 1759
U 10044	Broken Hearted Blues	–
U 10045	I Got My Eyes On You	Chess 1735
U 10046	First Time I Met The Blues	–

Same or similar to above. Add Junior Wells, hca (–1).   Chicago, 1961

10622	Let Me Love You Baby -1	Chess 1784
10623		
10624		
10625	Ten Years Ago -1	Chess 1784, Argo LP 4027
U 11358	Stone Crazy	Chess 1812
U 11359	Skippin' (Scrapin')	– , 1899

Vcl/gtr. with Sonny Turner, Murray Watson, tpts; Jarrett Gibson, Abe Locke, tens; Lafayette Leake, pno/org; Lefty Bates, gtr; Jack Meyers, bs–gtr; Phil Thomas, dms.
Chicago, September, 1962

11802	Hard But It's Fair	Chess 1878
11803		
11804	When My Left Eye Jumps	Chess 1838
	Baby Baby Baby	unissued

Similar:

U 11902	The Treasure Untold	Chess 1838

Vcl/gtr. with Bob Neely, ten; Jarrett Gibson, bari; Lafayette Leake, pno; Lacy Gibson, vcl (–1)/gtr; Jack Meyers, bs–gtr; Al Duncan, dms.   Chicago, February 7, 1963

12184	American Bandstand	unissued
12185	No Lie	Chess 1878
12186	100 Dollar Bill	unissued
12187	My Love Is Real -1	unissued

Vcl/gtr. with Donald Hankins, Jarrett Gibson, saxs; Otis Spann, pno; Jack Meyers, bs–gtr; Fred Below, dms.   Copa Cabana, Chicago, July 26, 1963

	Worried Blues	Argo LP 4031
	Don't Know Which Way To Go	–

   Note: Other tracks on above LP by other artists, all backed by the Buddy Guy band.

Vcl/gtr. with Sonny Boy Williamson, hca (–1); Jarrett Gibson, bari (–2); Lafayette Leake, pno; Jack Meyers, bs–gtr; Clifton James, dms.   Chicago, Summer, 1964

13209	I Dig Your Wig -1	Chess 1899
13271	My Time After Awhile	–

Vcl/gtr. with saxs; pno; gtr; bs–gtr; dms.   Chicago, 1965

	Leave My Girl Alone	Chess 1936
	Crazy Music	–
	Every Girl I See	Chess
	Too Many Ways	–

BUDDY BOY

Vcl/gtr. with Eddie Boyd, pno; Jimmy Lee Robinson, bs–gtr; Fred Below, dms.
Hamburg, October 7, 1965

	First Time I Met The Blues	Fontana TL 5286

No details:

		Chicago, 1966
15052	My Mother	Chess 1974
15053		
15054	Mother-In-Law Blues	Chess 1974

Vcl/gtr. with saxes; pno; el-bs; dms.   Chicago, 1963

12624	untitled	Chess unissued
12625	Stick Around	unissued
12621	untitled	unissued
12627	Moanin'	unissued

H

VERA HALL

Vcl.   Livingstone, Ala., 1959

Boll Weevil Holler	• Atlantic LP 1346
Trouble So Hard	–
Wild Ox Moan	Atlantic LP 1348

WALTER HAMILTON

Vcl/gtr. with Wallace Stevens, pno; and others.   Detroit, 1959

F 171	Sherry Blues	Fortune 849
F 172	Peaches And Cream	–

STICK HORSE HAMMOND

Vcl/gtr.   Chicago, 1950

JB100A	Gambling Man	J.O.B. 100
JB100B	Alberta	–
JB SHH 105A, RR906A		
	Highway 51	J.O.B. 105, Royalty 906
JB SHH 105B, RR906B		
	Too Late Baby	– –

Vcl/gtr.

SHH 1	Little Girl	Gotham 504
SHH 2	Truck 'Em On Down	–

JUNIOR HAMPTON

Dms. with Louis Jackson, pno; Slim Green, gtr.   Los Angeles, 1948

A	J. H. Stomp (rev. by Louis Jackson, q.v.)	Murray 500

TYE TONGUE HANLEY

Vcl. with ten (−1); pno; gtr; dms.   Detroit, 1957

88A	I'll Try To Understand	JVB 88
88B	You Got My Nose Wide Open -1	–

HARLEM STARS

Big Mama Thornton, vcl. with ten; pno; bs.   Houston, c. 1951

A	All Right Baby	E & W 100
B	Bad Luck Got My Man	–

HARMONICA BLUES KING

No details: Chicago, 1956

I Need You Pretty Baby	Ebony 1003
Blues King Mongo	–

HARMONICA FATS

Vcl/hca. with saxes; pno; gtr; bs; dms.   1962
SD600, 45837
        Tore Up   Darcey 5000, Skylark 600
SD601, 45837X
        I Get So Tired   —
        Mama Talk To Your Daughter   Darcey

HARMONICA FRANK

Real name Frank Floyd.
Vcl/gtr/hca (−1).   Memphis, 1951
U 80   Swamp Root   Chess 1475
U 81   Goin' Away Walkin' -1   —   , Blues Classics 15
U 82   Step It Up And Go -1   —
        Note: U 80 issued with U 81 or U 82 on reverse.

Same: Memphis, 1951
1504A   Howlin' Tomcat -1   Chess 1494, Blues Classics BC-7
1504B   She Done Moved (add traps)   —

Same: Memphis, 1954
U 124   The Great Medical Menagerist   Sun 205
U 125   Rockin' Chair Daddy -1   —

FRANK FLOYD
Vcl (−1)/gtr. with gtr; dms. Larry Kennon, vcl (−2).   Memphis,
F 303   Monkey Love -2   F & L 100
F 304   Rock A Little Baby -1   —

HARMONICA HARRY

See under Elmon Mickle.

HARMONICA JOE

Vcl/hca. with org; gtr; bs; dms.   New York City, 1964
583   That's No Big Deal   Skymac 1008
584   Look Here Mama   —

HARMONICA KING

See under George Smith.

HARMONICA SLIM

Vcl/hca. with saxes; pno; gtr; bs; dms.   Los Angeles, February 20, 1956
MR 2652 Mary Helen   Aladdin 3317
MR 2653 Lonely Hours   —
Same: Los Angeles, c. 1956
P 103A   Thought I Didn't Love You   Spry 103
P 103B   Going Back Home   —
Same: Los Angeles, 1957
A   My Girl Won't Quit Me   Vita 138
B   You Better Belive It   —
A   Drop Anchor   Vita 146
B   Do What You Want To Do   —
    Note: Real name may be Travis Blaylock. Also recorded with The Daybreakers.

HARP BLOWING SAM (Fowler)

See under Joe Williams Recordings (unissued).

HARPER – BRINSON BAND

Talking with Buddy Harper, hca; Lady Will Carr, pno; ? Brinson, bs; Rabon Tarrant, dms.

		Los Angeles, 1957
5031	Harper's Express	Specialty 593
5032		
5033	Harper's Return	Specialty 593

BEN HARPER & THE CINCO'S

Vcl/hca. with ten; pno; gtr; dms.

		Los Angeles, 1960
T 106	Drive Way Blues	Talent 106
T 106X	Here Comes My Gal	–

SONNY HARPER

Vcl/hca. with ten; pno; bs; dms.

		Los Angeles, c. 1962
A	Lonely Stranger	Ball 1011
AA	Going Back Home (Good Ole Memphis, Tenn.)	– , JRM 001

> Note: Harper is probable pseudonym for Ira Amos. Credits to J. Gray. JRM 001 issued as by Sander King (i.e. Saunders King!)

BOB HARRIS

Vcl/bs. with ten; Jack Dupree, pno; Brownie McGhee, gtr; Gene Moore, dms. Little Boy Blue, vcl (–1).

		New York City, 1951
D 765	Baby Say You Love Me	Derby 770
D 766	Up And Down The Hill	Derby 773
D 767	Drinkin' Little Woman -1	Derby 770
D 768	Doggin' Blues	Derby 773

> Note: Little Boy Blue is actually Danny Taylor (see Volume 2).

LITTLE BOBBY HARRIS

Vcl. with saxes; pno; gtr; bs; dms.

		New York City, c. 1952
M-40	Love, Love, Love	Jackson 2301
M-41	Friendly Advice	–

BOB HARRIS

Vcl/bs. with pno; gtr.

		New York City, 1952
1310	Heavyweight Mama	Par 1304
1311	Total Stranger	–

> Note: See also Duke Bayou, q.v.

HOMER HARRIS

No details:

		Chicago, September 27, 1946
CCO 4649	I'm Gonna Cut Your Head	Columbia unissued
CCO 4650	Atomic Bomb Blues	–
CCO 4651	Tomorrow Will Be Too Late	–

PEPPERMINT HARRIS

See under Peppermint Nelson.

WILLARD HARRIS

No details:

		1955
	Straighten Up Baby	Ekko 20001
	Talking Off The Wall	–

WILLIE LEE HARRIS

Born Artesia, Mississippi in ?. See under Big Joe Williams.

CASEY HART

Vcl/org. with Sonny Terry, hca: Lord Westbrook, gtr: Joe Benjamin, bs: Bobby Donaldson, dms.

New York City, 1961

| SOA 14A | Call Today | Choice 14 |
| SOA 14B | Blues For My Baby | – |

CLEO HARVES

WITH LIGHTNING GUITAR

Vcl/gtr. with bs.

Lake Charles, 1949

| A | Skinny Woman Blues | O. T. 105 |
| B | Crazy With The Blues | – |

ROY HAWKINS

Vcl/gtr. with saxes; pno; bs; dms.

Oakland, 1948

2018A	Christmas Blues	Down Town 2018
2018B	Roy's Boogie	–
2020A, MM 1178		
	It's Too Late To Change	Down Town 2020, Modern 20-705
2020B, MM 1179		
	West Express	–
2024A	Forty Jim	Down Town 2024
2024B	I Don't Know Why	–
2025A, MM 1151		
	Quarter To One	Down Town 2025, Modern 20-695
2025B, MM 1150		
	Strange Land	– –
2026A	Easy Going Magic Pt. 1	Down Town 2026
2026B	Easy Going Magic Pt. 2	–

No details:

Los Angeles, 1949

MM 1230-4	Sleepless Nights	Modern 20-720
MM 1231		
MM 1232		
MM 1233-3	Mistreatin' Baby	Modern 20-720
MM 1286-2	Where You Been	Modern 20-752
MM 1287-2	On My Way	–
MM 1288	Why Do Things Happen To Me	Modern 20-734
MM 1289	Royal Hawk	–

Los Angeles, 1950

MM 1364-1	Just A Poor Boy	Modern 20-777
MM 1365-1	My Temper Is Risin'	Modern 20-765
MM 1366-2	You Had A Good Man	Modern 20-777
MM 1367-1	Wine Drinkin' Woman	Modern 20-765

Vcl. with ten; pno; gtr; bs; dms.

Los Angeles, 1950

MM 1418-1	You're The Sweetest Thing	Modern 20-812
MM 1419-1	I'm Never Satisfied	–
MM 1420-6	Blues All Around Me	Modern 20-794
MM 1421-4	Mean Little Girl	–

Los Angeles, 1951

MM 1548	The Thrill Is Gone	Modern 826
MM 1549-5	Trouble Makin' Woman	–
MM 1550		
MM 1551-2	I Walk Alone	Modern 842

Los Angeles, 1951

MM 1678	I Don't Know Just What To Do	Modern 853
MM 1679-4	Gloom And Misery All Around	Modern 842
MM 1680		
MM 1681	You're A Free Little Girl	Modern 853

Vcl/gtr. with alt; ten; pno; bs; dms.		Los Angeles, 1952
MM 1771	Highway 59	Modern 859
MM 1772	Would You	–
MM 1823	Doin' All Right	Modern 869
MM 1824	The Thrill Hunt	–
		Los Angeles, 1954
MM 2225	Is It Too Late	RPM 440
MM 2226	If I Had Listened	–

Note: Last six sides possibly from earlier sessions.

From unknown sessions:

	Trouble In Mind	Kent 376
	What A Fool I Was	–
	Bad Luck Is Falling	Modern 898
	The Condition I'm In	–

Note: See also The Royal Hawk.

BILL HAYES

See under Henry Hayes.

HENRY HAYES

HENRY HAYES FOUR KINGS
Willis Threats, vcl. with Henry Hayes, alt; Lloyd Glenn, pno; Gene Phillips, gtr; Herman Washington, dms.

		Los Angeles, Sept. 10, 1946
A 5	All Alone Blues	Aladdin 157
B 6	Hayes Boogie	–
A 7	Angel Child Blues	Aladdin 158
B 8	Kickin' My Love Around	–

HENRY HAYES
Unk. vcl. with Henry Hayes, alt; pno; gtr; bs; dms.

		Houston, 1948
A	Bowlegged Angeline	Gold Star 633, Swing 414
B	Baby Girl Blues	– –

BILL HAYES
Perry Cain, vcl (– 1); Henry Hayes, alt; Ed Wiley, ten; Buster Pickens, pno; Donald Cooks, bs; Ben Turner, dms.

		Houston, 1950
2039	I Want To Cry -1	SIW 551
2051	I'm Sorry I Was Reckless -1	SIW 560
2057	Highway 75	SIW 551
2060	South Texas Blues	SIW 560
	If It's True What They Tell Me	Jade 211
	Just	–

Aladdin sides also issued as Willis Threats or The Four Kings. Later sides not included. See also Elmore Nixon, Goree Carter, Carl Campbell.

EDWARD HAZLETON

Vcl/hca.

	Los Angeles, March 1, 1960
Mocking The Train, Mocking The Dogs	Portents LP 2
Motherless Children Have A Hard Time	–
Poor Boy Travelling From Town To Town	–

SID HEMPHILL

Vcl/quills.

	Senatobia, Miss., 1959
Old Devil's Dream	Prestige Int. 25010

Add Lucius Smith, dms:

Come On Boys, Let's Go To The Ball	Atlantic LP 1346

JESSE "G.I. JAZZ" HENDRICKS
Lead vcl. with Albert Spencer, Louis "Bacon and Porkchops" Houston, Venesty Weles, David Walker, D. J. Miller, Matt Williams, James Hampton, Lee Curtis Tyler, C. B. "Smiffy" Kimble, James A. Champion, vcls.

	Ramsey Farm, Unit 1, Texas, 1951
Rattler	Elektra EKL-296

ROBERT HENRY

Vcl/hca. with pno; bs; dms.   Detroit, 1953

B 9253	Miss Anna B.	King 4624
B 9254-1	Old Battle Ax	King 4646
B 9255-1	Early In The Morning	
B 9256	Something's Wrong With My Lovin' Machine	King 4624

HERBY JOE

Vcl. with saxes; pno; gtr; bs; dms.   Chicago, 1956

U 3059	Smokestack Lightning	Abco 101
U 3060	Dreamed Last Night	–

ARCHIE LEE HILL

Vcl.   Livingstone, Ala., Jan/Feb. 1950

EF 130	She Done Got Ugly	Ethnic Folk Library 01483

HARVEY HILL JR.

Music By THE HARVEY HILL STRING BAND
Vcl/gtr. with hca; gtr; bs; dms.   Detroit? early '50's

A	Boogie Woogie Woman	SRC 104
B	She Fool Me	–

    Note: Ypsilanti, Michigan artist.

HENRY HILL

Vcl. with Lorenzo Holderness, ten; Devonia Williams, pno; Carl 'Pete' Lewis, gtr; Mario Delagarde, bs; Leard Bell, dms.   New York City, March, 1951

F 136	Wandering Blues	Federal 12030
F 137	My Baby's Back Home	Federal 12083
F 138	Sunday Morning Blues	Federal 12030
F 139	If You Love Me	Federal 12044

Same:

F 144	What's The Matter Mama	Federal 12044
F 145	Hold Me Baby	Federal 12037
F 146	Since You've Been Gone	–
F 147	Give Me Something Called Love	Federal 12083

ROSALIE HILL

Vcl/gtr.   Senatobia, Miss., 1959

	Bullyin' Well	Atlantic LP 1352

WILLIE HILL

Vcl/hca/gtr.   Gainesboro, Georgia, 1954

	2 untitled blues	Elko unissued

OTIS HINTON

Vcl/gtr. with pno; dms.   New York City, late 1953

507	Walkin' Down Hill	Timely 1003
508	Emmaline	–

CARL HODGES

Vcl/gtr.   Philadelphia, 1961

	Blues All Around My Bed	Storyville SLP 181
	Standing At The Greyhound Bus Station	Milestone LP 3002

    Note: Virginia artist.

CHA CHA HOGAN

Vcl. with pno; gtr; bs; dms.   Dallas, 1950

301	My Baby Loves Me	Talent 810
302	My Walking Baby	—

SILAS HOGAN

Vcl/gtr. with Whispering Smith, hca; Al Foreman, gtr; Bobby McBride or Rufus
Thibodeaux, bs–gtr; Austin Broussard, dms.   Crowley, La., 1962/63

A	You're Too Late Baby	Excello 2221
B	Trouble At Home Blues	—
A	Airport Blues	Excello 2231
B	I'm Gonna Quit You Pretty Baby	—

Same: Crowley, La., 1964

A	I'm Going In The Valley	Excello 2241
B	Lonesome La La	—
A	Dark Clouds Rollin'	Excello 2251
B	I'm In Love With You Baby	—
A	Everybody Needs Somebody	Excello 2255
B	Just Give Me A Chance	—

Same: Crowley, La., 1965/66

A	Baby Please Come Back To Me	Excello 2266
B	Out And Down Blues	—
A	Every Saturday Night	Excello 2270
B	So Long Blues	—
A	Early One Morning	Excello 2271
B	If I Ever Needed You Baby	—

Note: Baton Rouge artist.

ANDREW HOGG

Real name Andrew Hogg. Born Cushing, Texas on January 27, 1914. Died in Texas c. 1960.

SMOKEY HOGG ON (–1) OR ANDREW HOGG ON (–2)
Vcl/gtr.   Los Angeles, 1947

EXC 1345-2	Restless Bed Blues -1	Exclusive 95X -1
EXC 1346-2	My Last Blues -1	—
EXC 1347-1	He Knows How Much We Can Bear -2	Exclusive 89 -2
EXC 1348-1	I Don't Want Nobody's Bloodstains On My Hands -2	

SMOKEY HOGG

Vcl/gtr. with pno.   Dallas? 1948

BU 285A	Hard Times	Bullet 285
BU 285B	Goin' Back Home	—

Vcl/gtr. with bs.   Dallas, 1948

BB 1	To Many Drivers (Little Car Blues)	Modern 20-532, 833

Vcl/gtr. with pno.

BB 2	Country Gal	Modern 20-532, 833

Vcl/gtr. with pno; gtr; bs.

BB 3	Skinny Leg'd Woman	Modern 20-556
BB 4	Unemployment Blues	

Note: Above masters are from Blue Bonnet Records in Dallas.

Vcl/gtr. with pno; dms.   Los Angeles, 1948

MM 675-2	Anytime Is The Right Time	Modern 20-563
MM 676-1	My Christmas Baby	Modern 20-630
MM 677		
MM 678-1	New Year's Eve Blues	Modern 20-630
MM 679-1	High Priced Meat	Modern 20-815

Add bs.

MM 696-3	Jivin' Little Woman (I Don't Want You)	Modern 20-596, Kent 5024
MM 697		
MM 698-4	Golden Diamond Blues	Modern 20-606

MM 699-4	Where Did My Boogie Go (I Wonder)	Modern 20-563, Kent 5024
Add tbn.		Los Angeles, 1948
MM 723-4	What More Can A Woman Do	Modern 20-735
MM 724-1	My Baby's Worrying Me	Modern 20-615, Crown 5226
MM 725-1	Oh, Woman! Oh, Woman!	Modern 20-606
MM 726		
MM 727-1	Worrying Over You	Modern 20-596
MM	You Just Gotta Go	Crown CLP 5226

> Note: The above is an alternate take of MM 727. MM 724 is the untitled track on Crown CLP 5226.

Vcl/gtr. with Hadda Brooks, pno; Bill Davis, bs; Al Wichard, dms.

		Los Angeles, 1949
MM 753-2	Everybody Got A Racket	Modern 20-735
MM 754-2	By My So And So	Modern 20-615
	Worrying Mind (alt. take)	Crown CLP 5226
MM 755-1	Little School Girl	Modern 20-704, LP 2004
	Good Morning Little School Girl (alt. take)	Crown CLP 5226, Kent 5024
MM 756-1	Long Tall Mama	Modern 20-574
MM 757		
MM 758-1	I Feel Good	Modern 20-574
	Worryin' Mind (alt. take)	Kent LP 5024

Omit pno.

MM 977-2	Suitcase Blues (Lowdown Blues)	Modern 20-704, Kent LP 5024

Add 2nd gtr. (-1).

MM 1077	I'm Gonna Find Your Trick	Modern 20-667
MM 1078	Who's Heah -1	–
MM 1310-3	The Way You Treat Me (I Got Your Picture)	Modern 20-758, Crown 5226
MM 1311-1	You Gonna Look Like A Monkey (When You Get Old)	
		Modern 20-758, Crown 5226
MM 1312		
MM 1313		
MM 1314		
MM 1315	Smokey's Back In Town (She's My Baby)	Modern 20-802, Kent LP 5024

Omit bs.

	Runaway	Crown CLP 5226

> Note: MM 1311 has MM 1313-1 on the label.

Vcl/gtr. with pno; bs.

		1949
A	Nobody Treats Me Right	Specialty 321
B	I Want A Roller	–
A	Evil Mind Blues	Specialty 334
B	I'm Through With You	–
A	You Better Watch That Jive	Specialty 369
B	What's On Your Mind	–

Add dms.

A	I Want My Baby For Christmas	Specialty 342
B	Going Back To Texas (no pno)	–
A	Low Down Woman Blues	Specialty 356
B	Gonna Leave Town	-

> Note: Hogg may not play guitar on 356.

Vcl/gtr. with pno (−1); bs.

		Houston, 1949
ACA 1411	Change Your Ways	Macy's 5008
ACA 1412	Baby, Baby -1	
ACA 1413	Misery Blues	Independent 300
ACA 1414	Blues Oh Blues Pt. 1	unissued
ACA 1415	Blues Oh Blues Pt. 2	unissued
ACA 1416	(by Milton Willis)	
ACA 1417	Worried Blues -1	Independent 300
ACA 1418	You Gotta Go	Macy's 5003
ACA 1419	Leaving You Baby -1	–

Vcl/gtr. with Hadda Brooks, pno; Bill Davis, bs; Al Wichard, dms.

		Los Angeles, 1950
	You Can't Keep Your Business Straight	Crown CLP 5226
MM 1390-4	Possum Hunt	Modern 20-783
MM 1391		
MM 1392		
MM 1393-1	Let's Get Together And Drink Some Gin	Modern 20-783
MM 1394-1	Late Prowlin' Girl	Modern 20-802
MM 1395-1	Sleepless Blues	Modern 20-815
MM 1396-1	Classification Blues	Modern 20-770
MM 1397		
MM 1398-1	You Brought It On Yourself	Modern 20-770
MM 1399		
	Coming Back Home To You Again	Crown CLP 5226
	Goin' Back To Chicago	–

Omit bs.

	Look In Your Eyes Pretty Mama	Crown CLP 5226

Same: (From previous sessions)

	I Want My Baby	Kent LP 5024
	No Matter What You Do	–
	Come On Home	–
	When The Sun Goes Down	–
	I Bleed Through My Soul	–
	You Can't Tell Them Where I'm Going	–

Same:

IM 229	Up Today – Down Tomorrow	Imperial 5106
IM 230	Great Big Mama	Imperial 5111
IM 231	Worryin' Blues	Imperial 5106
IM 232	Need My Help	Colony C-103
IM 233	(not allocated)	
IM 234	In This World Alone	Colony C-103
IM 235	Key To My Door	Imperial 5111

Note: The following Modern sides though issued in 1951/52 are probably from earlier sessions. All cut in Los Angeles.

Vcl/gtr. with ten; pno; bs; dms.

MM 1692	You've Been Gone Too Long	Modern 844
MM 1693	Patrol Wagon Blues	–
	It' Raining Here	Crown CLP 5226

Vcl/pno. with unk. gtr; Bill Davis, bs; Al Wichard, dms.

MM 1892	Baby Don't You Tear My Clothes	Modern 884
MM 1893	Highway 51	–
MM 1908	Too Late Old Man (no gtr.)	Modern 896
MM 1917	River Hip Mama (no gtr.)	–
MM 2051	Can't Do Nothin'	Modern 924
MM 2052	I Just Can't Help It	–

SMOKY OR SMOKEY HOGG

Vcl/gtr. with Ed Wiley, ten; Willie Johnson, pno; Donald Cooks, bs; Ben Turner, dms.

		Houston, 1950
ME 3869	Miss Georgia	Mercury 8235
ME 3870	She's Always On My Mind	Mercury 8228
ME 3871	Dirty Mistreater	Mercury 8235
ME 3872	I'm Looking For Baby	Mercury 8228
2085	Why Should I Love You (2396)	SIW 555, 632
2087	You Won't Stay Home	–
	You Won't Stay Home (alt. take)	
	(Wanna Stay Home)	Time LP 6
	Saved All My Money	–
	I'm In Love With You	–
	Why Should I Worry	–

Vcl/gtr. with Joe Fritz, ten (–1); Willie Johnson, pno; Donald Cooks, bs. Ben Turner, dms.

		Houston, 1951
2206	I Love You Baby Pt. 1	SIW 565

2207	I Love You Baby Pt. 2	− , Time LP 70006
2227	I'm Leaving	SIW 632, Time LP 6
2237	Go Home With Me -1 (no pno.)	SIW 575
	Shake A Leg (alt. take) -1 (no pno.)	Time LP 70006

Vcl. with Joe Fritz, vcl (−1); Willie Johnson, pno; Goree Carter, gtr; Donald Cooks, bs;
Ben Turner, dms.

2225	I Have Often Wondered (no pno.)	Jade 212
2226	What In The World Am I Gonna Do (no pno.)	Jade 210
	What In The World Am I Gonna Do (no pno.− alt. take)	Time LP 6
2236	Back To The Country -1	SIW 575
	Let's Go Back To The Country -1 (alt. take)	Time LP 6
2260	She's The Girl I Need (no gtr.)	SIW 615

Add Joe Fritz, ten; omit pno.

2273	Comin' Out Blues (That's My Baby)	Jade 210, Time LP 6
2274	Lovin' Money Blues	SIW 615
2295	I Love Her Every Day	Jade 212
	Hello Baby	Time LP 6

Add pno.

	What You Gonna Do	Time LP 6
	I Often Wonder	−
	I'm So Lonely	Time LP 6

Vcl/gtr. with ten; bs; pno; dms.　　　　　Los Angeles, 1952

| A | Crawdad | Fidelity 3006 |
| B | Born On The 13th | − |

Vcl/gtr.　　　　　San Diego, 1952

| A,TXR 34 | Penitentiary Blues Pt. 1 | Ray's Record 33, Top Hat 1020, RIH 170, Blues Classics 16 |
| B,TXR 35 | Penitentiary Blues Pt. 2 | issues as above |

　　　Note: Aurally the Top Hat etc. reissues are dubbed from the Ray's version.

Vcl/gtr. with gtr; dms.

| A | I've Been Happy | Ray's Record 35 |
| B | I Used To Be Rich | − |

Vcl/gtr.　　　　　Los Angeles, 1952

TXR 42	Baby Shake Your Leg	Top Hat 1023
TXR 43	Fortune Teller Blues	−
JD-130A	You'll Need My Help Someday	RIH 130
JD-130AA	Somebody New	−
JD-131A	Ain't You Sorry Baby	RIH 131
JD-131AA	Ruby	−

Vcl/gtr. with ten(-1); pno; bs; dms.

JP 4A	Oohw Baby	Combo 4
JP 4B	Bottle Up And Go	−
JP 9A	Hello Little Girl -1	Combo 9
JP 9B	My Woman	−

Vcl. with ten; pno; gtr; bs; dms.　　　　　Los Angeles, January 1953

F 292-1	Keep A-Walking	Federal 12109, Bethlehem LP 6071
F 293	Your Little Wagon	Federal 12117
F 294	Penny Pinchin' Mama	
F 295-1	Do It No More	Federal 12109

Omit ten:

F 300-1	Gone, Gone, Gone	Federal 12127
F 301		
F 302		
F 303-1	I Ain't Got Over It Yet	Federal 12127

Same:　　　　　Los Angeles, late 1953

IM 673	When I've Been Drinking	Imperial 5269
IM 674	I Gotta Ride	unissued
IM 675	Tear Me Down	Imperial 5269

IM 676	Train Whistle	Imperial 5290
IM 677	My Baby's Gone	–
IM 678	Peace Of Mind	unissued
IM 679	Oo-Oo-Wee	unissued

ANDREW HOGG ON CROWN OR SMOKEY HOGG ON METEOR

Vcl/gtr. with pno; gtr; bs; dms.   Los Angeles, 1954

| (JB) 390 | I Declare | Crown 122, Meteor 5021 |
| (JB) 391 | Dark Clouds | – |

SMOKEY HOGG

Vcl/gtr. with ten; pno; bs; dms.   Los Angeles, late 1954

| ST 1004 | Ain't Gonna Play Second No Mo' | Show Time 1101 |
| ST 1005 | No More Whiskey | – |

Vcl. with hca; pno; gtr; bs; dms. .   Los Angeles, 1958

| 18625 | Sure'Nuff | Ebb 127 |
| 18626 | Good Mornin' Baby | – |

JOHN HOGG

Born West Connie, Texas in 1912
Vcl/gtr.   Houston, early 1951

| 3875 | Got A Mean Woman | Mercury 8230 |
| 3876 | Why Did You Leave Me | – |

Vcl/gtr.   Los Angeles, 1951

OCT-200-2	West Texas Blues	Octive 706A, Blues Classics 16
OCT-200-3	Black Snake Blues	Octive 705B, –
OCT-200-2	Worryin' Blues	Octive 706B
	(rev. by Norman Alexander)	
	Denver Blues	unissued

SMOKEY HOGG

See under Andrew Hogg

BILLY HOKE

WITH JAMES WAYNE & THE NIGHTHAWKS

Vcl. with pno; gtr; bs; dms.   Newark, N. J. 1965

101	I Wonder	D. W. 101/2
102	I Don't Want No Other Woman	–
1227	In My Own Special Way	D. W. 103
1228	Crying and Wonderin'	–

ACE HOLDER

Vcl/hca. with Gus Jenkins, pno; gtr; bs; dms.   Los Angeles, 1961

| A | Lonesome Highway | Pioneer 1004 |
| B | Homeless Boy | – |

Vcl/hca. with saxes; pno; gtr; bs; dms.   Los Angeles, 1962

	Leave My Woman Alone	Vanessa 100
	Wabba Suzy–Q	
	When You Hang Around	Vanessa 102
	Happy Anniversary	–

Same: Los Angeles, 1964

| D301 | Encourage Me Baby | Lulu 1124 |
| D300 | I'm In Love With You | – |

Vcl/hca. with 2 gtrs; bs-gtr; dms.   Los Angeles, 1966

| M-142-A | Sorry I Had To Leave | Movin' 142 |
| M-142-B | The Eatingest Woman | – |

Note: Band on Movin' is led by Curtis Tillman (el-bs).

WILLIE HOLIDAY

Vcl. with Eric Von Schlitz & His Big Six: saxes; pno; gtr; bs; dms.

		Houston, 1949
ACA 1476	Wake Up Little Girl	unissued
ACA 1477	I Saw The Blues	unissued
ACA 1478	My Woman Put Me Down	Peacock 1531
ACA 1479	I've Played This Town	–

Vcl. with
		Houston, 1950
ACA 1631	Midnight And Morning	Peacock unissued
ACA 1632	Willie's Blues	unissued
ACA 1633	I Don't Have To	unissued

LONNIE HOLMES & HIS DELTA BOYS

No details:

	unissued titles	Trumpet

SONNY BOY HOLMES

Vcl/gtr. with hca; pno; gtr; dms.

		Los Angeles, 1952
0-95	Walking And Crying Blues	Recorded in Hollywood 223
0-96	I've Got The $64 Question Blues (no hca)	–

Vcl/gtr.
225A	I Got Them Blues	Recorded in Hollywood 225
225AA	T-N-T Woman	–

WRIGHT HOLMES

Born Hightower, Texas on July 4, 1905
Vcl/gtr.

		Houston, 1947
	Alley Special	Gold Star unissued
	My Own Lonesome Blues	–

Vcl/gtr.
		Houston, 1947
Hu 205B	Alley Special	Miltone 5221, Gotham 511, Blues Classics BC-7
Hu 206	Good Road Blues	Miltone 5221, Gotham 508
WH 2	Drove From Home Blues	Gotham 508
	The Midnight Rambler	unissued

Note: Rev. Gotham 511 by Sonny Boy Johnson, q.v.

HOMER THE GREAT

See under Pee Wee Crayton

HOMESICK JAMES

See under James Williamson

HONEYBOY

See under Frank Patt

HOOKER JOE JR.

On Post. Pre-war sides by Walter Davis and Jesse James reissued.

EARL HOOKER

No details:

		1952
15083-1	Sweet Angel	Rockin' 519
15084-1	On The Hook	–

Gtr. with pno; bs; dms.
		1953
K 9218	Race Track	King 4600. LP 727
K 9219		

K 9220	Blue Guitar Blues	King 4600, LP 727
	Shake 'Em Up (Poor Joe)	King LP 727
	Happy Blues (Stomp Boogie)	–

Note: King LP 727 by John Lee Hooker, with the above tracks included using titles in brackets.

Gtr. with pno; bs; dms. Chicago, 1959
| 106B | Dynamite | Bea & Baby 106, Checker 947 |
| | (rev. by Bobby Saxton) | |

Same: Chicago, 1960
| 25-146 | Blues in D Natural | Chief 7016, 7039 |
| | (rev. by Junior Wells) | |

EARL HOOKER & HIS ROADMASTERS
Vcl/gtr; with Lafayette Leake, pno; bs; dms. Chicago. 1960
| 613 A | Do The Chicken | C. J. 613 |
| 613 B | Yea, Yea | – |

Vcl/gtr. with pno; gtr; bs; dms. Chicago, 1961
| 25-195 | Apache War Dance | Age 29101 |
| | (rev. by A. C. Reed). | |

No details: Chicago, 1962
| U-11786 | Tanya | Checker 1025 |
| U-11787 | Put Your Shoes On Willie | – |

As last: Chicago, 1962
	Blue Guitar	Age 29106
	Swear To Tell The Truth	–
26-121	How Long Can This Go One	Age 29111
26-125	These Cotton Pickin' Blues	–

Vcl/gtr. with Moose John, pno; gtr; bs; dms. The Earlettes, Vcl.

Chicago, 1963
26-132	Win The Dance	Age 29114
26-133		
26-134	That Man	Age 29114

Vcl/gtr. with tpt; ten; org; el-bs; dms. Chicago, 1966
| A | Wild Moments | C. J. 643 |
| B | Chicken | – |

JOHN LEE HOOKER

Born Clarksdale, Mississippi on 22 August, 1917

JOHN LEE HOOKER
Vcl/gtr. Detroit, November, 1948
B 7003	Sally Mae	Modern 20-627, 5, Crown CLP 5157, United 725, Kent KLP 5025
	Sally Mae (alt. take)	Crown CLP 5353, United 731
B 7004	Highway Blues	unissued
B 7005	Wednesday Evening Blues	unissued
B 7006	Boogie Chillen	Modern 20-627, 893, 5, Kent 332, Crown CLP 5157, 5238, United 718, 725, Kent KLP 5025, 5027

Note: Moder 893 is titled "New Boogie Chillen" with matrix MM 1926, edited into a different verse sequence. Reverse, titled "I Tried" though credited to Hooker is in fact by Sylvester Cotton.

TEXAS SLIM
Vcl/gtr. Detroit, prob. December 1948
| 5590 | Stomp Boogie | King 4283, 4504, LP 859, Bethlehem BCP 6071 |

122

| 5591 | | |
| 5592 | Black Man Blues | King 4283 |

Note: King 4504 as by John Lee Cooker. 5590 on LP 859 mislabeled as "Flub" by Memphis Slim.

DELTA JOHN -1

BIRMINGHAM SAM AND HIS MAGIC GUITAR -2

Vcl/Gtr. — Detroit, Dec. 1948early 1949

D 1102	Helpless Blues	Regent 1001 -1
D 1103		
D 1104	Goin' Mad Blues	Regent 1001 -1
D 1105		
D 1106	Low Down Midnite Boogie	Savoy 5558 -2
D 1107	Landing Blues	—

JOHN LEE HOOKER

Vcl/gtr. — Detroit, early 1949

B 7007	Drifting From Door To Door	Modern 20-714, Crown CLP 5232, Custom 1048, United 727, Kent KLP 5025
B 7008B	Hobo Blues	Modern 20-663, Crown CLP 5157, United 725
B 7009		
B 7010		
B 7011	Howlin' Wolf (I'm a Howling Wolf)	Modern 20-730, Crown CLP 5353, United 731
B 7012	Crawling Kingsnake	Modern 20-714, Crown CLP 5157 United, 725, Kent KLP 5025

JOHNNY WILLIAMS

Vcl/gtr. — Detroit, c. 1949

| | Miss Rosie Mae | Staff 704, Prize 704 |
| | Highway Blues | — — |

JOHN LEE HOOKER

Vcl/gtr. — Detroit, 1949

B 7033	Whistlin' And Moaning Blues	Modern 20-688, Crown CLP 5157, United 725, Kent KLP 5025
B 7034		
B 7035		
B 7036B	Hoogie Boogie	Modern 20-663, Crown CLP 5157, United 725

Note: Some Copies of Modern 20-663 may be titled "Rhythm No. 2", and may be an alternate take of B 7036.

Vcl/gtr. with Eddie Burns, hca.

| B 7039, R 1354 | Miss Eloise | Sensation 34, Regal 3295 |
| B 7040 | Burnin' Hell | Sensation 21 |

TEXAS SLIM

Vcl/gtr. — Detroit, 1949

5769	Nightmare Blues	King 4323, LP 727, Audio Lab AL 1520
5770-3	Late Last Night	King 4366, Federal 12377, King LP 727, 859, Bethlehem BCP 6071, Audio Lab AL 1520
5771	Wandering Blues	King 4334, LP 727
5772	Don't Go Baby	King 4334, — Audio Lab AL 1520
5773	Devil's Jump	King 4315, LP 727, Audio Lab AL 1520
5774	I'm Gonna Kill That Woman	King 4323, LP 727

| 5775-2 | Moaning Blues | King 4377, 4504, LP 727, 725, Audio Lab AL 1520 |
| 5776 | The Numbers | King 4315, LP 727 |

Note: King 4504 as by John Lee Cooker. Drums dubbed on 5770-3 on Federal 12377 and LP's.

JOHN LEE HOOKER
Vcl/gtr.   Detroit, late 1949

| B 7053B | Weeping Willow Boogie (Weepin' Willow on LP) | Modern 20-688, Crown CLP 5157, United 725, Kent KLP ⁵025 |
| B 7054 | Miss Sadie Mae | Sen- sation 21 |

TEXAS SLIM
                                                          Detroit, 1949/50

| 5790 | Heart Trouble Blues | King 4329, LP 727 |
| 5791 | Slim's Stomp | – |

JOHN LEE HOOKER
Vcl/gtr. with James Watkins, pno(-1)   Detroit, 1950

B 8010	No Friend Around	Modern 20-746
B 8011	Wednesday Evening	– , Crown CLP 5232, 5353, Custom 1048, United 727, 731
B 8012	Canal Street Blues	Sensation 26
B 8013	Playin' The Races	Modern 20-730
B 8014	Huckle Up Baby	Sensation 26
B 8015		
B 8016		
B 8017	Let Your Daddy Ride -1	Sensation 30
B 8017	Let Your Daddy Ride -1 (alt. take)	Modern 20-790, Crown CLP 5232, Custom 1048, United 727, Kent KLP 5025
B 8018	Goin' On Highway 51	Sensation 30

Note: B 8011 retitled "She Left Me On My Bended Knee" on CLP 5232, Custom 1048, United 727, and "She Left Me" on CLP 5353, United 731.

JOHNNY WILLIAMS
Vcl/gtr.   Detroit, 1950

| JW 710 A | Wandering Blues | Staff 710, Gotham 506 |
| JW 710 B | House Rent Boogie | –   – |

JOHN LEE HOOKER
Vcl/gtr.

B 8035	My Baby's Got Something	Sensation 33
B 8036	Decoration Day Blues	–
B 8037, R 1355	Boogie Chillen 2	Sensation 34, Regal 3295
B 8038		
B 8039		
B 8040	Roll 'n' Roll	Modern 20-767
B 8041		
B 8042	One More Time	Modern 20-790, Crown CLP 5353, United 731, Kent KLP 5025

Note: B 8042 retitled "Let's Talk It Over" on LP. It is not the same as MM 2099 on Modern 935 and corresponding LP's.

Vcl/gtr.   Detroit, late 1950

B 8047	Give Me Your Phone Number	Modern 20-767
B 8040, 1400	Notoriety Woman	Regal 3304
B 8049, 1401	Never Satisfied	–

124

JOHNNY WILLIAMS
Vcl/gtr. with Boogie Woogie Red, pno; Curtis Foster, dms.
718A 266A   Prison Bound   Staff 718, Swing Time 266
718B, 266A+Bumble Bee Blues   −   −

    Note: Other issues on Staff and Swing Time by Johnny Williams are by
    Baby Boy Warren, q.v.

TEXAS SLIM
Vcl/gtr.   Detroit, 1950/1
5890-2   Thinking Blues   King 4377, LP 727, Audio Lab
                                                  Al 1520
5891-1   Don't You Remember Me   King 4366, Federal 12377,
                                                  King LP 727, 875

    Note: Drums dubbed on 5891-1 on Federal 12377 and King LP 727.

JOHN LEE BOOKER
Vcl/gtr.   Detroit, 1951
U 60   Mad Man Blues   Gone 60, Chess 1462, LP 1454
U 61   Boogie Now (Hey Boogie on LP)   Gone 61,   −   −

JOHN LEE HOOKER
Vcl/gtr.   Detroit, prob. early 1951
B 9001 John L's House Rent Boogie   Modern 814, Crown CLP 5157
        (House Rent Boogie on LP)   United 725
B 9002 Queen Bee   Modern 814, Crown CLP 5157,
                                                  United 725, Kent KLP 5025
        Don't You Remeber Me   Crown CLP 5232, Custom 1048,
                                                  United 727.

THE BOOGIE MAN -1

JOHN LEE BOOKER
Vcl/gtr.   Detroit, c. 1951
JB 1403 Morning Blues   Acorn 308 -1
U 1948   Miss Lorraine   Chance 1108
U 1949   Talkin' Boogie   −
U 1986   Graveyard Blues   Chance 1110
U 1987   I Love To Boogie   −

    Note: Above recorded at one session.

JOHN LEE HOOKER
Vcl/gtr. with Eddie Kirkland, gtr.(-1)   Detroit, mid 1951
MM 1560 Women In My Life -1   Modern 829
MM 1561 Tease Me Baby (Tease Your Daddy)   United 731

THE BOOGIE MAN -1

JOHN L BOOKER
Vcl/gtr. with James Watkins, pno; Curtis Foster, dms.   Detroit, 1951
JB 1404 Do The Boogie   Acorn 308 -1
U 2060   609 Boogie   Chance 1122, Constellation CS 6
U 2061   Road Trouble   −   −

    Note: Audience applause dubbed on beginning and end of U 2060

JOHN LEE HOOKER

JOHN LEE HOOKER on Chess 1482

JOHN L' HOOKER on Modern 852
Vcl/gtr. with Eddie Kirkland, gtr.(-1)   Detroit, 1951
U 7326   Louise -1   Chess 1482, Modern 852,
                                                  Chess LP 1438
U 7327   High Priced Woman -1   Chess 1505, LP 1438
U 7328   Union Station Blues   −   −
U 7329

U 7330	Ground Hog Blues	Chess 1482, Modern 852, Chess LP 1438
U 7331	Leave My Wife Alone	Chess 1467, LP 1438, Argo LP 4042
U 7332		
U 7333	Ramblin' By Myself	Chess 1467, LP 1438
9553	Down At The Landing	Chess LP 1438
	Dreaming Blues	Chess LP 1454

Note: Modern 852 remastered with matrixes BS 7551/7550 respectively.

JOHN LEE HOOKER
Vcl/gtr. with Eddie Kirkland, gtr.   Detroit, late 1951

| MM 1635 | How Can You Do It | Modern 835, Crown CLP 5353, United 731 |
| MM 1636 | I'm In The Mood | Modern 835, 24, Kent 332, Crown CLp 5157, 5238, United 725 |

JOHN L. HOOKER
As above   Detroit, early 1952

| MM 1637 | Anybody Seen My Baby | Modern 847, Crown CLP 5157, United 725 |
| MM 1638 | Turn Over A New Leaf | Modern 847, Crown CLP 5232, Custom 1048, United 727 |

JOHN LEE HOOKER
Vcl/gtr. with Buddy Johnson, org; vibes (-1): Jimmy Turner, dms.

| MM 1797 | Cold Chills All Over Me (Cold Chills on LP) | Modern 862, Crown CLP 5157 United 725 |
| MM 1798 | Rock Me Mama (Good Rockin' Mama on LP) | Modern 862, Crown CLP 5232, Custom 1048, United 727 |

JOHN LEE HOOKER AND 'LITTLE' EDDIE KIRKLAND
Vcl/gtr. with Eddie Kirkland, vcl(-1)/gtr. Org. dubbed on (-1).

| MM 1857 | It Hurts Me So -1 | Modern 876, Crown CLP 5353, United 731 |
| MM 1858 | I Got My Eyes On You | issues as above |

JOHN LEE HOOKER
Vcl/gtr. with Eddie Kirkland, vcl (-1)/gtr.

| MM 3013 | Key To The Highway -1 | Modern 886, Crown CLP 5353, United 731 |
| MM 3014 Re | Bluebird Blues | Modern 886 |

JOHN LEE HOOKER
Vcl/gtr. Speeded-up gtr. dubbed on (-1)   Detroit, late 1952

U 7432	Walkin' The Boogie -1	Chess 1513, LP 1438, Argo LP 4026
U 7433	Sugar Mama	– – Argo LP 4027
9548	Love Blues	Chess LP 1438
9546	The Journey	Chess LP 1454
9547	Bluebird	

Same, prob. Eddie Kirkland, bs-gtr.(-1).

9544	I Don't Want Your Money	Chess LP 1454
9545	Hey, Baby	–
9552	Worried Life Blues	–
9549	Apologize	–
9550	Lonely Boy Boogie	–
9551	Please Don't Go	–
	Just Me And My Telephone -1	–

Vcl/gtr. with Eddie Kirkland, lead gtr.

| MM 1929 | Rock House Boogie | Modern 897, Crown CLP 5295, United 729 |
| MM 1952 | It's Stormin' And Rainin' | Modern 901 |

JOHNNY LEE
Vcl/gtr. with Eddie Kirkland, lead gtr.   Detroit, 1952/3

| GV-2-113 | I Came To See You Baby | DeLuxe 6009 |

GV-2-114   I'm A Boogie Man   –

JOHNNY WILLIAMS
Vcl/gtr.   Philadelphia, 1952/3

BL-1	Questionnaire Blues	Gotham 509
BL-2	Real Gone Gal	–
BL-3	Little Boy Blue	Gotham 513
BL-4	My Daddy Was A Jockey	–

JOHN LEE
Vcl/gtr

BL-6-1	Mean Old Train	Gotham 515
BL-7-1	Catfish	–

JOHN LEE HOOKER
Vcl/gtr. with Johnny Hooks, ten; Boogie Woogie Red, pno; Jimmy Turner, dms.
                                                  Detroit, 1953

MM 1928 Re	It's Been A Long Time Baby	Modern 897
MM 1951	Ride Till I Die	Modern 901
MM 2098	I Tried Hard	Modern 935

Vcl/gtr. with Jimmy Miller, tpt; Johnny Hooks, ten; Joe Woods, pno; Tom Whitehead, dms.

50-48	Boogie Rambler	JVB 30
50-49	No More Doggin'	–

JOHN LEE HOOKER
Vcl/gtr. with Eddie Kirkland, gtr; Boogie Woogie Red, pno; Tom Whitehead dms.
                                                  Detroit, June 26, 1953

MM 1970	Love Money Can't Buy	Modern 908
MM 1971Re	Please Take Me Back	–

Vcl/gtr. with Eddie Kirkland, gtr.		Detroit, 1953
MM 2016	Too Much Boogie	Modern 916
MM 2017	Need Somebody	–
MM 2088	I Wonder Little Darling	Modern 931
MM 2089	Jump Me (One More Time)	–

JOHN LEE BOOKER on Deluxe & Rockin

JOHN LEE HOOKER on Chart & Atco
Vcl/gtr. with Eddie Kirkland, vcl(-1)/gtr.(-1)/bs-gtr(-2)   Cincinnati, 1953

GR 15118-1	My Baby Don't Love Me	DeLuxe 6046, Atco LP 151
GR/C 15119 -1	Blue Monday (I Ain't Got Nobody)*	DeLuxe 6004, Chart 614
C 15120-1 15121	Misbelieving Baby	Chart 614
C 15122-1	Wobbling Baby -2	Chart 609
GR 15123-1	Pouring Down Rain -2	DeLuxe 6032, Rockin' 525, Atco LP 151
C 15124-1	Goin' South	Chart 609
GR 15125-1	Real Real Gone	DeLuxe 6046, Atco LP 151
GR 15126-1	Lovin' Guitar Man -1	DeLuxe 6004, –
GR 15127-1	Stuttering Blues	DeLuxe 6032, Rockin' 525, Atco LP 151
	Love My Baby	Atco LP 151
	I Ain't Got Nobody	–
	Misbelieving Baby	–

      Note: GR 15123 retitled "Wobbling Baby" on Atco LP 151. This and C 15122
      are alternate takes, the latter at a slower tempo. GR/C 15119/15120 are totally
      different to same titles on LP.

JOHN LEE HOOKER
Vcl/gtr. with Eddie Kirkland, gtr.   Detroit, 1953

MM 2049	Down Child	Modern 923, Crown CLP 5269, United 729
MM 2050	Gotta Boogie (Gonna Boogie on LP)	issues as above

| MM 2128 | Bad Boy | Modern 942, Crown CLP 5269 |
| | | United 729 |

Kirkland, vcl(-2):   Detroit, 1954

MM 2099	Let's Talk It Over -1	Modern 935, Crown CLP 5295,
		United 729
MM 2127	Cool Little Car	Modern 942
MM 2277	Lookin' For A Woman	Modern 978, Crown CLP 5295,
		United 729

Note: Voices double-tracked on MM 2099/2277 on single releases only.

Same:

| MM 2148 | Half A Stranger | Modern 948, Crown CLP 5295, |
| | | United 729 |

Vcl/gtr. with Johnny Hooks, Otis Finch, tens; Bob Thurman, pno; Eddie Kirkland, gtr;
Tom Whitehead, dms.

| MM 2149 | Shake, Holler And Run | Modern 948, Crown CLP 5295, |
| | | United 729 |

Vcl/gtr. with prob. Bob Thurman, pno. Hca dubbed on*.   Detroit, 1954

U 7597	It's My Own Fault -1	Chess 1562, LP 1438, Fortune
		LP 3002*
	Blues For Big Town	Fortune LP 3002
	Juke Bug	–

Add gtr; dms.

| U 7598 | Women And Money | Chess 1562, LP 1438 |

Note: Hooker states that Fortune sold the tracks on Chess 1562 to Chess and
subsequently dubbed hca on U 7597 and 'Juke Bug'.

Vcl/gtr. with Eddie Kirkland, gtr.

MM 2187	You Receive Me	Modern 958
	Baby You Ain't No Good	Crown CLP 5295, United 729
	Baby I'm Gonna Miss You	– –
		Kent KLP 5025

Vcl/gtr. with Otis Finch, ten; Bob Thurman, pno; Eddie Kirkland, gtr; Tom Whitehead, dms.

MM 2186	Taxi Driver	Modern 958
MM 2278	I'm Ready	Moder 978
	I Need Love So Bad	Crown CLP 5353, United 731,
		Kent KLP 5025

Vcl/gtr. with Eddie Kirkland, lead gtr; bs; dms.   New Jersey, c.1954

| | When My Wife Quit Me | Savoy MG 16000 |

Note: 4 or 6 titles were recorded at this session.

Vcl/gtr. with Otis Finch, ten; Bob Thurman, pno; Tom Whitehead, dms.

MM 2216	Hug And Squeeze (You)	Modern 966, Crown CLP 5232,
		Custom1048, United 727
	I Love You Baby (alt. of above)	Crown CLP.5232, Custom 1048,
		United 727
MM 2217	The Syndicator (The Syndicate)	Modern 966, Crown CLP 5232,
		Custom 1048, United 727, Kent
		KLP 5025

JOHN LEE HOOKER

Vcl/gtr.(-1). with Otis Finch, ten(-2); Boogie Woogie Red, pno; Tom Whitehead, dms.

Detroit, Sept/Oct. 1954

| SP 528 | Everybody's Blues -1 | Specialty 528 |
| XSP 528 | I'm Mad -2 | – |

Vcl/gtr. with Jimmy Reed, hca: Eddie Taylor, bs-gtr; George Washington, bs;
Tom Whitehead, dms.   Chicago, October, 19, 1955

55-336	Unfriendly Woman	Vee Jay 265
55-337	Wheel And Deal	Top Rank (F) RES-136
55-338	Mambo Chillen	Vee Jay 164
55-339	Time is Marching	– , LP 1007, 8502

Omit Reed:		Chicago, March 27, 1956
56-443	I'm So Worried Baby	Vee Jay 233
56-444	Baby Lee	Vee Jay 205, LP 1007
56-445	Dimples	− − ,1049, 1074
56-446	Every Night	Vee Jay 188, −
56-447	The Road Is So Rough	Vee Jay 233, −
56-448	Trouble Blues	Vee Jay 188

Vcl/gtr. with Otis Finch, ten; Eddie Taylor, bs-gtr; George Washington, bs;
Tom Whitehead, dms.   Chicago, June 7, 1956

56-479	Don't Get Tired	unissued
56-480	Stop Talking	unissued
56-481	Time And A Half	unissued
56-482	Lonely Blues	unissued

Vcl/gtr. with Johnny Hooks, ten (-1); Boogie Woogie Red, pno; Tom Whitehead, dms.
                                       Detroit, 1956/57

F 159	(Miss Said Mae) Curl My Baby's Hair	Fortune 846, LP 3002
F 160	609 Boogie	−

Vcl/gtr. with Eddie Taylor, bs-gtr; Quinn Wilson, bs; Tom Whitehead, dms.
                                       Chicago, March 1, 1957

57-633	Everybody Rockin'	Top Rank(F) RES-136
57-634	I'm So Excited	Vee Jay 245, LP 1007
57-635	I'See You When You're Weak	−
57-636	Mean Old Shake	Top Rank (F) RES-136
	('Crawlin' Black Spider' on RES 136)	

Vcl/gtr. with Frankie Bradford, pno; Eddie Taylor, bs-gtr; Everett McCrary, bs;
Richard Johnson, dms.   Chicago, July 23, 1957

57-717	Little Wheel	Vee Jay 255, LP 1007, 1049, 1074
57-718	Little Fine Woman	Unissued
57-719	Rosie Mae	Vee Jay 255
57-720	You Can Lead Me Baby	Vee Jay 265

Vcl/gtr. with Joe Hunter, pno; Everett McCrary, bs-gtr; Richard Johnson
                                       Chicago, June 10, 1958

58-927	I Love You Honey	Vee Jay 293, LP 1007
58-928	You've Taken My Woman	−
58-929	Mama You Got A Daughter	unissued

Vcl/gtr. with Eddie Taylor, bs-gtr(-1); Earl Phillips, dms(-2). Chicago, January 22, 1959

59-1067	Maudie -1,2	Vee Jay308, LP 1007, 8502
59-1068	Tennessee Blues -1,2	Vee Jay 319
59-1069	I'm In The Mood -1	Vee Jay 308, LP 1007, 1049
59-1070	Boogie Chillun	Vee Jay 319, − −
59-1071	Hobo Blues	Vee Jay 331, − −
59-1072	Crawlin' King Snake	− − −

Vcl/gtr. saxes; bs; dms. dubbed on issued marked*.   Culver City prob. early 1959

B-6101	Ballad To Abraham Lincoln	Lauren 361, Galaxy 201
B-6102	Mojo Hand	− −
	(retitled "Risin' Sun (Louisiana Voo-Doo)" on LP)	
B-6102-4	Lost My Job (I Lost My Job)	Lauren 362, Galaxy 716*, 201*
B-6102-6	Deep Down In My Heart	− , Galaxy 201
	Shake It Up And Go	Galaxy 716*, 201*
	Might As Well Say We're Through	Galaxy 201
	Left My Wife And Baby	−
	Travelin' Day And Night	−
	Fire At Natchez	−
	Sweetest Girl I Know	−
	Mad With You Baby	−
	My Mother-In-Law Moved In	−

Note: New matrixes for Galaxy 716 are F 2212/2211 respectively.

Vcl/gtr.   Detroit, April, 1959

	Black Snake	Riverside RLP 12-838, Battle 6114
	How Long Blues	− −

	Wobblin Baby	–	–
	She's Long, She's Tall, She Weeps Like A Willow Tree	–	–
	Pea Vine Special	–	–
	Tupelo Blues	–	–
	I'm Prison Bound	–	–
	I Rowed A Little Boat	–	–
	Water Boy	–	–
	Church Bell Tone	–	–
	Bundle Up And Go	–	–
	Good Mornin' Lil' School Girl	–	–
	Behind The Plow	–	–

Vcl/gtr. with Jimmy Miller, tpt; Johnny Hooks, ten; Bob Thurman, pno; Tom Whitehead, dms.

Detroit Nov/Dec. 1959

F 191	Cry Baby	Fortune 853
F 192	Love You Baby	–
H 50	Big Fine Woman	Hi-Q 5018, Elmor 303, Fortune LP 3002
H 51	Blues For Christmas	Hi-Q 5018, Elmor 303

Note: New Matrixes on Elmor 303 are 61-M-7 and 61-M-8 respectively.

Vcl/gtr.

New York City, February 9, 1960

	Come On And See About Me	Riverside RLP 12-321, Battle 6113
	Democrat Man	–
	That's My Story	–

Add Sam Jones, bs; Louis Hayes, dms.

RF 89	I Need Some Money	Riverside 45-438, RLP 12-321, Battle 45901, LP 6113
RF 90	No More Doggin'	issues as above
	I'm Wanderin'	Riverside RLP 12-321, Battle 6113
	I Want To Talk About You	–
	Gonna Use My Rod	–
	Wednesday Evening Blues	–
	One Of These Days	–
	I Believe I'll Go Back Home	–

Vcl/gtr.

1960?

	Burning Hell	Riverside RLP 008
	Graveyard Blues	–
	Baby Please Don't Go	–
	Jackson, Tennessee	–
	You Live Your Life And I'll Live Mine	–
	Smokestack Lightnin'	–
	How Can You Do It	–
	I Don't Want No Woman If Her Hair Ain't No Longer Than Mine	–
	I Rolled And Turned And Cried The Whole Night Long	–
	Blues For My Baby	–
	Key To The Highway	–
	Natchez Fire	–

Vcl/gtr. with Lefty Bates, gtr; Sylvester Hickman, bs; Jimmy Turner, dms. Vcl/gtr. only on -1.

Chicago, March 1, 1960

60-1373	I Wanna Walk	Vee Jay LP 1023
60-1374	Canal Street Blues	–
60-1375	I'll Know Tonight	–
60-1376	I Can't Believe -1	–
60-1377	Going To California	–
60-1378	Whiskey And Women	– , 1049, 8502
60-1379	Run On	Vee Jay LP 1023
60-1380	Solid Sender	Vee Jay 349, LP 1025
60-1381	Sunny Land	Vee Jay LP 1023
60-1382	Dusty Road	Vee Jay 366, LP 1023
60-1383	I'm A Stranger	Vee Jay LP 1023
60-1384	No Shoes	Vee Jay 349, LP 1023

Vcl/gtr. with Bill Lee, ns.   Newport, R.I. June 25, 1960
60-1622   The Hobo   Vee Jay LP 1033, Vanguard VRS 9083
60-1623   Maudie   Vanguard VRS 9083
60-1624   Tupelo   Vee Jay 366, LP 1033, 1049,
                                                               Vanguard VRs 9083

    Note: 60-1622 retitled "hobo Blues (or Dusty Road)" on Vanguard.
    60-1624 retitled "Tupelo (or Backwater Blues)".

SIR JOHN LEE HOOKER
Vcl/gtr. with Roy Hooker, lead gtr; Boogie Woogie Red, pno; Tom Whitehead, dms.

                                                         Chicago, June/July, 1960
F 205   Crazy About That Walk   Fortune 855
F 206   We're All God's Chillun   –

JOHN LEE HOOKER
Vcl/gtr. with Jimmy Reed, gtr/hca(-1); Lefty Bates, gtr; Quinn Wilson, bs; Earl Phillips, dms.

                                                        Chicago, January 4, 1961
61-1715   Want Ad Blues   Vee Jay 397, LP 1033, 8502,
                                                               Oldies 33 8005
61-1716
61-1717   I'm Going Upstairs   Vee Jay 379, LP 1033
61-1718
61-1719
61-1720   I'm Mad Again   Vee Jay 379, LP 1033
            Hard Hearted Woman -1   Vee Jay LP 1033

Vcl/gtr. same session:
61-1775   Take Me As I Am   Vee Jay 397, LP 1033
            Five Long Years   Vee Jay LP 1033
            I Like To See You Walk   –
            Wednesday Evening Blues   –   , 8502
            My First Wife Left Me   –   –
            You're Looking Good Tonight   –

No details'   1959/61
            Come And Ride With Me   Prestige unissued
            Dirty Ground Hog   –
            I Like to See You Walk   –
            My Heart's In Misery   –
            Moanin' Blues   –
            She Loves My Best Friend   –
            Sally Mae   –
            Take Me As I Am   –
            When My First Wife Left Me   Prestige unissued
            Wednesday Evening Blues   –
            You're Gonna Miss Me When I'm Gone   –
            You're Looking Good Again Tonight   –

    Note The above session was reported by Neil Slaven from "what appeared to be a
    list of Prestige tunes". Most of the other items in this list did tie up with actual
    Presige LP issues. It seems most likely that the above were recorded during this
    period.

Vcl/gtr. with bs-gtr.   Florida July 7, 1961
            Talk About Your Baby   Atco LP 151
            Don't Turn Me From Your Door   –
            You Lost A Good Man   –
            Drifting Blues   –
            Teachin' The Blues   Guest Star LP 1902
            Stand By Me Blues   –
            Baby Please Don't Go   –
            Two White Horses   –
            Talkin' 'Bout My Baby   –

Vcl/gtr. with saxes: pno: gtr; hs; dms.   Chicago, 1961
61-2204   Boom Boom   Vee Jay 438, LP 1043, 1049,
                                                               1074, 8502, Oldies 33 8005, 33
                                                               8007, Imperial al 1003
61-2205
61-2206
61-2207   She's Mine   Vee Jay 453, LP 1043
61-2208
61-2209   A New Leaf   Vee Jay 453, LP 1043
61-2210
61-2211   Drug Store Woman   Vee Jay 438, LP 1043, 1049,
                                                               Imperial Al 1003
             Process   Vee Jay LP 1043
             Lost A Good Girl   —
             Blues Before Sunrise   —   , 8502
             Let's Make It   —
             Thelma   —
             Keep Your Hands To Yourself   —
             What Do You Say   —

        Note:"Process" is listed on both sleeve and label of LP 8502 but is not actually
        on the record.

Vcl/gtr. with saxes; pno; bs-gtr; dms.   Chicago, 1962
62-2654   Send Me Your Pillow   Vee Jay 575, LP 1058
             Old Time Shimmy   Vee Jay LP 1058
             You Know I Love You   —
             Onions   —

Vcl/gtr. with tpt; saxes; org; pno(-1); gtr; bs-gtr; dms. The Vandellas, vcl. grp. Omit vcl. grp
(-2). Omit Saxes (-3); tpt(-4). Org; bs-gtr; dms. and hand clapping only (-5).
                                                               Chicago, 1962
62-2799   I Love Her -1,3   Vee Jay 493, LP 1058
62-2800
62-801   Take A Look At Yourself -4   Vee Jay 493, LP 1058
             Frisco(San Fransisco)   Vee Jay LP 1058
             She Shot Me Down   —
             Big Soul   —
             Good Rocking Mama -2   —
             No One Told Me   -5   —

Vcl/gtr. with T-Bone Walker, pno; Willie Dixon, bs; Jump Jackson, dms.
                                                               Hamburg, October 18, 1962
             Let's Make It   Polydor 46.23.7597
             Shake It Baby   —   —
             The Right Time   —
             I Need Your Love So Bad   unissued

Vcl/gtr. with saxes; pno; gtr; bs-gtr; dms; The Vandellas, vcl grp. Omit vcl. grp (-1);
saxes (-2).   Chicago, 1963
63-3310   I'm Leaving -1,2   Vee Jay 538, LP 1066, Oldies 324
63-3311   Birmingham Blues -1   —   —   —
63-3312   Don't Look Back   Vee Jay 575, —   —
             Love Is A Burning Thing   Vee Jay LP 1066
             I Want To Shout   —
             I Want To Hug You   —
             Poor Me   —

Vcl/gtr. with dms.   Chicago, 1963
             I Want To Ramble   Vee Jay LP 1066
             Half A Stranger   —
             My Grinding Mill   —
             Bottle Up And Go   —
             One Way Ticket   —

Vcl/gtr.   Newport, R.I. 1964
             I Can't Quit You Now Blues   Vee Jay LP 1078
             Stop Baby Don't Hold Me That Way   —
             Tuplo   —

132

	Bus Station Blues	–	, Vanguard
		VRS 9145	
	Freight Train Be My Friend	–	
	Boom Boom Boom	–	
	Talk That Talk Baby	–	, 8502
	Sometimes You Make Me Feel So Bad	–	, Vanguard
		VRS 9145	
	You've Got To Walk Yourself	–	
	Let's Make It	–	
	The Mighty Fire	–	, 8502

Note: "Sometimes" is listed on sleeve and label of LP 1078 as "Sometimes You Make Me" and "Feel So Bad".

Vcl/gtr. with gtr; bs–gtr; dms. Chicago, 1964

64-4427	Big Legs, Tight Skirt	Vee Jay 670
64-4428	Flowers On The Hour	Vee Jay 708
64-4429	It Serves Me Right	–
64-4430		
64-4431		
64-4432		
64-4433		
64-4434	Your Baby Ain't Sweet Like Mine	Vee Jay 670

Vcl/gtr. with The Groundhogs: pno; Tony McPhee, gtr; bs–gtr; dms. Org (–1). Omit McPhee (–2). London, May/June 1965

1F	Mai Lee	Planet PLF 114, Verve-Folkways
		LP 3003
2F 114	Don't Be Messing With My Bread	issues as above
	Bad Luck And Trouble -1	Verve-Folkways LP 3003
	Waterfront -1, 2	–
	No One Pleases Me But You -1	–
	It's Raining Here	–
	It's A Crazy Mixed Up World	–
	Seven Days And Seven Nights	–
	I'm Losin' You	–
	Little Girl Go Back To School	–
	Little Dreamer	–

Vcl/gtr. with Buddy Guy, bs–gtr; Fred Below, dms. Hamburg, October 7, 1965

| | King Of The World | Fontana 885.422 |
| | Della May | – |

Vcl/gtr. with Dicky Wells, tbn (–1); Barry Galbraith, gtr; Milt Hinton, dms. Omit Galbraith (–2). New York, November 23, 1965

	Shake It Baby	Impulse LP 9103
	Country Boy	–
	Bottle Up And Go	–
	You're Wrong	–
	Sugar Mama -2	–
	Decoration Day -2	–
	Money (That's What I Want) -1	–
	It Serve You Right To Suffer	–

Vcl/gtr. with pno; Eddie Burns, lead gtr; bs–gtr; dms. Hooker, vcl/gtr (–1). Chicago, mid 1966

	Let's Go Out Tonight	Chess 1965, LP 1508
	In The Mood (omit pno; gtr.)	– –
	Peace Lovin' Man	Chess LP 1508
	I Put My Trust In You	–
	Stella Mae	–
	You Know, I Know	–
	I'll Never Trust Your Love Again	–
	One Bourbon, One Scotch, One Beer	Chess LP 1508
	The Waterfront -1	–

Vcl/gtr. with collective personnel: Otis Spann, pno; Muddy Waters, Sammy Lawhorn, Luther Johnson, gtrs; Mac Arnold, bs–gtr; Francis Clay, dms. New York, August 1966

| | I'm Bad Like Jesse James | Bluesway BL 6002 |
| | She's Long, She's Tall | – |

133

When My First Wife Left Me	–
Hearaches And Misery	–
One Bourbon, One Scotch, One Beer	–
I Don't Want No Trouble	–
I'll Never Get Out Of These Blues Alive	–
Seven Days	–

Note: The above album was recorded live in Greenwich Village. Although mentioned on the sleeve, George Smith does not appear.

EDDIE HOPE & THE MANISH BOYS

Vcl (−1)/hca. with unk. vcl (−2); 2 gtrs; dms.   Miami? 1956

| C-174 | A Fool No More -1 | Marlin 804 |
| C-175 | Lost Child -2 | – |

CLYDE HOPKINS

Vcl. with brass; pno; gtr; bs/gtr; dms.   Memphis, 1966

| 101A | Fatten Pin | Black Gold 305 |
| 101B | Santa Fe | – |

JOEL HOPKINS

Vcl/gtr.   Dickinson, Texas, June 12, 1959

Good Times Here, Better Down The Road	"77" LA 12/2
Pretty Mama Let Me Be	unissued
Thunder In Germany	Heritage HLP 1001
I Ain't Gonna Roll For The Big Hat Man No More	–
Accused Me Of Forgin' Can't Even Write My Name	–
Sittin' Here Wonderin' What My Baby Done	unissued
Buck Dance Tune	unissued

Vcl/gtr.   Dickinson, October 31, 1959

'Lectric Chair Blues	unissued
Ain't Got No Momma Now (Black Snake Moan)	unissued
Match Box Blues	unissued
Stick Dance	unissued
Good Morning Blues	unissued
'Lectric Chair Blues	unissued
Match Box Blues	Heritage HLP 1001
Ain't Got No Momma Now	unissued
Monologue on Blind Lemon	unissued
Autobiographical Monologue	unissued

See also Lightnin' Hopkins.

LIGHTNIN' HOPKINS (see also in APPENDIX)

Real name Sam Hopkins. Born Centerville, Texas on 15 March, 1912.

"LIGHTNIN' " HOPKINS AND THUNDER SMITH

Thunder Smith, vcl/pno. with Lightnin' Hopkins, gtr; unk. dms.

Los Angeles, November 9, 1946

| 52-3 | Can't You Do Like You Used To Do | Aladdin 165 |
| 53-1 | West Coast Blues | – |

54/55 by Thunder Smith

Hopkins, vcl:

| 56-1 | Katie Mae Blues | Aladdin 167, Score LP 4022 Imperial LP 9180, 9259 |

57-2, IM 3613

	(I) Feel So Bad	Aladdin 168, Imperial 5834, LP 9180, 9259
58-1	That Mean Old Twister	Aladdin 167
59-1	Rocky Mountain Blues (I Can't Stay Here In Your Town)	Aladdin 168, Imperial LP 9211

LIGHTNIN' HOPKINS
Vcl/gtr. with Thunder Smith, pno (−1); unk. dms (−2).   Los Angeles, August 15, 1947
219   Short Haired Woman   Aladdin 3005, Score LP 4022,
    Imperial LP 9180
220   Big Mama Jump (Little Mama Blues) -2   Aladdin 3005, Score LP 4022
221   Down Now Baby (Down Baby)   Aladdin 209, Imperial LP 9186
222   (Let Me) Play With Your Poodle -1, 2   —
223   Fast Mail Rambler   Aladdin 204,   —
224   Thinkin' And Worryin'   —   —

Vcl/gtr. with Joel Hopkins, gtr.   Quinn Studio, Houston, 1947
3131A   Short Haired Woman   Gold Star 3131, Modern 20-529,
    Short Haired Woman (alt. take)   Dart LP-8000, Verve LP 8453
3131B   Big Mama Jump   Gold Star 3131, Modern 20-529,
    Arhoolie LP 2006

Vcl/gtr.   Quinn Studio, Houston, 1947/48
613A   Ida Mae   Gold Star 613, Modern 20-543,
    Arhoolie LP 2007
613B   Shining Moon   Gold Star 613, Modern 20-543
616A   Mercy   Gold Star 616, Modern 20-552
616B   What Can It Be   —   —   ,
    Arhoolie LP 2007
624A   Lonesome Home (Ain't It Lonesome)   Gold Star 624, Modern 20-568,
    Crown LP 5224, 5369, Custom
    LP 2014, United LP 713
624B   Appetite Blues   Gold Star 624, Modern 20-568
634A   Walking Blues   Gold Star 634, Modern 20-594,
    Arhoolie LP 2007
634B   Lightning Blues   Gold Star 634, Modern 20-594
637A   No Mail Blues   Gold Star 637, Modern 20-621
637B   Ain't It A Shame   —   —
640A   Tim Moore's Farm   Gold Star 640, Modern 20-673,
    Dart LP 8000, Verve LP 8453
640B   You Don't Know   Gold Star 640, Modern 20-673
641A   Treat Me Kind   Gold Star 641
641B   Somebody's Got To Go
646A   Baby Please Don't Go   Gold Star 646
646B   Death Bells   —   , Arhoolie LP
    2006

Same: Quinn Studio, Houston, 1949
652A   Mad With You   Gold Star 652, Arhoolie LP
    2007
652B   Airplane Blues   —   —
656A, 1056, 1258
    Unsuccessful Blues -1   Gold Star 656, Lightning 104,
    Dart 123, LP 8000, Verve LP
    8453
656B   Rollin' Woman Blues -1   Gold Star 656
    −1 small combo heard in background.

Vcl/gtr/org (−1). with unk. hawaiian gtr (−2); L. C. Williams, tap dancing (−3).
662A   Jailhouse Blues -2   Gold Star 662, S.I.W. 644,
    Dart LP 8000, Verve LP 8453
    Traveller's Blues -2   Dart LP 8000, Verve LP 8453
662B   T Model Blues   Gold Star 662, S.I.W. 644
664A, DA739K
    Lightnin's Boogie (or Blues) -3   Gold Star 664, Dart LP 8000,
    (or Bad Man's Blues)   Verve LP 8453, Time LP
    N90P 1385, Harlem 2324
664B   Unkind Blues   Gold Star 664, Arhoolie LP
    2007
665A, DA766M
    Fast Life (Woman)   Gold Star 665, Harlem 2331,
    Dart LP 8000, Verve LP 8453,
    Time LP N90P 1385

135

665B	European Blues	Gold Star 665, Time LP N90P 1384
666A	Automobile (Blues)	Gold Star 666, Jax 318, Arhoolie LP 2007
666B	Zologo (Organ Blues) -1	Gold Star 666, Jax 318, Arhoolie 1009
	Organ Boogie -1	Arhoolie LP 2007
669A, DA776M		
	Old Woman Blues (Good Old Woman)	Gold Star 669, Harlem 2336
669B, DA777M		
	Untrue Blues	— —
		Time LP N90P 1384
671A	Henny Penny Blues	Gold Star 671
671B	Jazz Blues	—
673A, DA567		
	Jackstropper Blues (The Jackstropper)	Gold Star 673, Harlem 2331, Dart LP 8000, Verve LP 8453
673B. 1057, 1259, DA740K		
	Grievance Blues (Grieving Blues) (or Nobody Cares For Me)	Gold Star 673, Lightning 104, Dart 123, Arhoolie LP 2006, Harlem 2324

From various Quinn sessions:
Vcl/gtr.

	Penitentiary Blues	Dart LP 8000, Verve LP 8453
	Racetrack Blues	— —
	Somebody's Got To Go -1	Arhoolie LP 2007
	Bluebird Blues	—
	Seems Funny Baby	—
	Coolin' Board Blues	—
	Goin' Back And Talk To Mama	—
	I Just Don't Care (Candy Kitchen)	Imperial LP 9211
	Tell It Like It Is (Whiskey Blues)	— , Arhoolie LP 2007
	Sugar Mama (Sugar On My Mind)	Aladdin 3015, Imperial LP 9211
	Miss Loretta (Sugar Mama No. 2) (Loretta Blues)	Imperial LP 9211, Arhoolie LP 2007

−1 Completely different to same title on Gold Star 641.

(MODERN RECORDS PURCHASED 32 MASTERS FROM QUINN IN 1951)

MM 1652	Beggin' You To Stay (Someday)	RPM 337, Crown LP 5224, 5369, Custom LP 2014, United LP 713
MM 1653	Don't Keep My Baby Long -1	RPM 351, Crown LP 5224, 5369, Custom LP 2014, United LP 713, Kent 5027
MM 1654		
MM 1655	Bad Luck And Trouble	RPM 337
	−1 edited on LP.	
MM 1664	Last Affair	RPM 351, Crown LP 5224, 5369, Custom LP 2014, United LP 713, Jewel 5000
MM 1665	Jake Head (Boogie)	RPM 346, Crown LP 5224, 5369 Custom LP 2014, United LP 713
MM 1666		
MM 1667	Lonesome Dog (Blues)	RPM 346, Crown LP 5224, 5369, Custom LP 2014, United LP 713, Jewel 5000
MM 1846	Needed Time	RPM 359
MM 1847	One Kind Favor	
MM 1902	Another Fool In Town	RPM 378
MM 1903	Candy Kitchen (Hopkins, pno.)	—
MM 1972	Mistreater Blues (Mistreated)	RPM 388, Score LP 4022, Imperial LP 9180
MM 1973	Black Cat	RPM 388

MM 2032	Santa Fe (Blues)	RPM 398, Crown LP 5224, 5369, Custom LP 2014, United LP 713
MM 2033	Someday Baby	RPM 398
	Tell Me (Pretty Mama)	Crown LP 5224, 5369, Custom LP 2014, United LP 713
	Give Me Back That Wig	issues as above
Vcl/gtr.		Houston, February 25, 1948
, IM 3761	Picture On The Wall	Aladdin 3015, Imperial 5852, LP 9186
3028A	Nightmare Blues	Aladdin 3028
3028B	Woman Woman (Change Your Way)	− , Imperial LP 9211
3035A	Morning Blues	Aladdin 3035, Imperial LP 9186
3035B	Have To Let You Go	−
3052A	Baby Child (Mama's Baby Child)	Aladdin 3052, Imperial LP 9211
3052B	Changing Weather Blues (Unpredictable Woman)	Aladdin 3052, Imperial LP 9211
Same:		Houston, 1948/49
4002A	Whiskey Headed Woman (Drinkin' Woman)	Score 4002, Imperial LP 9211
4002B, IM3686		
	Lightnin's Boogie (Sis Boogie)	− , Imperial 5852, LP 9186
	Rollin' Blues (Rollin' And Rollin')	Aladdin 3063, Score LP 4022, Imperial LP 9180
, IM 3619	Shotgun (Blues)	Aladdin 3063, Score LP 4022, Imperial 5834, LP 9180, 9259
509A	Moonrise Blues	Aladdin 3077
HTN 3	Honey, Honey Blues (Honey Babe)	− , Score LP 4022, Imperial LP 9180
HTN L8-B	Abilene	Aladdin 3096, Imperial LP 9180
HTN 501-1	Miss Me Blues (You're Gonna Miss Me)	Aladdin 3096, Imperial LP 9211
453Q	You Are Not Going To Worry My Life Anymore (Worried Life Blues)	Aladdin 3117, Imperial LP 9186, 9211
509X	Daddy Will Be Home One Day	− −
668 HTN 4	So Long	Aladdin 3262, Score LP 4022, Imperial LP 9180
670 HTN 2	My California	Aladdin 3262, Score LP 4022, Imperial LP 9180, 9259
	See See Rider	Score LP 4022, Imperial LP 9180
	Come Back Baby	Imperial LP 9186
	Baby You're Not Going To Make A Fool Out Of Me	−
	Someday Baby	Imperial LP 9211
Vcl/gtr/tap dancing (−1), with Donald Cooks, bs.		ACA Studio, Houston, 1950/51
J 478	You Caused (My Heart To Weep)	SIW 642, Jax 642, Time LP N90P 1385
J 479	Tap Dance Boogie -1	− − −
J 480		
J 481		
J 482 HO	I Wonder (Why)	SIW 660, Jax 660, Time LP 70006
J 483	Papa Bones Boogie (Buck Dance Boogie) -1	SIW 652, Time LP 70006
J 484	(by L. C. Williams)	
J 485	No Good Woman (Home In The Woods)	Jax 315, Time LP N90P 1385
J 486	Gone Again (Lightnin's Gone Again)	SIW 661, Jax 661, Time LP N90P 1385
J 487		
J 488	Dirty House	SIW 647, Time LP 70004, Mainstream LP 56040
J 489	Bald Headed Woman	SIW 647
J 490		
J 491	Everything Happens To Me	SIW 652, Time LP 70004, Mainstream LP 56040
J 492	Freight Train Blues	SIW 658, Time LP 70004

J 493, 4072	I've Been A Bad Man (Mad Blues) -1	SIW 660, Jax 315, 660
J 494, 294	New Worried Life Blues	SIW 649, Jax 649
J 495	One Kind Of Favor	— — , Time LP N90P 1385
J 496	(by Peppermint Harris)	
J 497		
J 498		
J 499		
J 500	Broken Hearted Blues	SIW 658, Time LP N90P 1385
	Worried Blues	Time LP N90P 1385
	Don't Think I'm Crazy	Time LP 70004, Mainstream LP 56040

Same:		New York City, 1950
4038	Down To The River (no bs.)	SIW 661, Jax 661
4069	Contrary Mary (Crazy Mary)	Jax 321, Harlem 2321
4070		
4071	I'm Begging You	Jax 321, Harlem 2321
4243	You Do Too (I'll Never Forget The Day)	Mercury 8252, Time LP N90P 1385
4244	Everybody's Down On Me	— , Time LP 70004, Mainstream LP 56040

Same:		New York City, c. Nov. 1950
2326	Coffee Blues	SIW/Jax 635, Time LP 70004, Mainstream LP 56040
2327	Praying Ground Blues	SIW 599, Time LP 70004, Mainstream 56040
2328	Gotta Move (Boogie) -1	— —
2329		
2330		
2331		
2332, K90W 2922		
	Give Me Central 209 (Hello Central)	SIW 621, Time LP 70004, Shad 5011, Mainstream LP 56040
2333	Long Way From Texas	SIW 611, Time LP 70004, Mainstream 56040
2334, K90W 2923		
	Tell Me Boogie (Mad As I Can Be) -1	SIW 611, Time LP 70004, Shad 5011, Mainstream LP 56040
2335	New Short Haired Woman	SIW/Jax 635, Time LP 70004, Mainstream LP 56040

| Same: | | New York City, c. Dec. 1950 |
| 2387 | New York Boogie -1 | SIW 621 |

Same:		ACA Studios, Houston, 1952
9104	Sad News From Korea	Mercury 8274
9105	Let Me Fly Your Kite -1	—
YB 9223	Gone With The Wind -1	Mercury 8293
YB 9224	She's Almost Dead	—
9406	Ain't It A Shame (no bs.)	Mercury 70081
9407	Crazy About My Baby (no bs.)	—
YB 9688	My Mama Told Me -1	Mercury 70191
YB 9689	What's The Matter Now	—

Add Connie Kroll, dms:		New York City, July 29, 1953
84970	Highway Blues	Decca 48312
84971	I'm Wild About You Baby	Decca 48321
84972	Bad Things On My Mind	Decca 48321, LP 4434
84973	The War Is Over	Decca 48842, 28841
84974	Policy Game	— —
84975	Merry Christmas	Decca 48306
84976	Happy New Year	—
84977	Cemetry Blues -1	Decca 48312

-1 Crying dubbed on.

Vcl/gtr. with Donald Cooks, bs; Gene ?, dms.   ACA Studios, Houston, 1954
H 1074   I Love You Baby   Herald 476
H 1075   Shine On Moon   Herald 490, Mercury LP 25011
H 1076, 1341
            Lightnin's Boogie (Boogie Woogie Dance)   Herald 425, 504, LP 1012,
                                                                Mount Vernon LP 104, Folk Art
                                                                LP 5003, Mercury LP 25003
H 1077   Lonesome In Your Home   Herald 471, LP 1012, Mount
                                                                Vernon LP 104, Folk Art LP
                                                                5003, Mercury LP 25002
H 1078   Remember Me   Herald 497
H 1079   Sittin' Down Thinkin'   Herald 490, LP 1012, Mount
                                                                Vernon LP 104, Folk Art LP
                                                                5003
H 1080, 1452
            Lightnin's Special (Flash Lightnin')   Herald 428, 547, LP 1012,
                                                                Mount Vernon LP 104, Folk Art
                                                                LP 5003
H 1081   Please Don't Go Baby   Herald 497
H 1082, 1342
            Don't Think 'Cause You're Pretty (Blues Is A
            Mighty Bad Feeling) -1   Herald 425, 504, LP 1012,
                                                                Mount Vernon LP 104, Folk Art
                                                                LP 5003
H 1083, 1451
            Life I Used To Live (Gonna Change My Ways)   Herald 428, 547, LP 1012,
                                                                Mount Vernon LP 104, Folk Art
                                                                LP 5003

            −1 re-edited on Herald 504.
Same:
H 1098, 1423
            Grandma's Boogie (Lightnin's Stomp)   Herald 476, 531
H 1099   My Baby's Gone   Herald 456, LP 1012 Mount
                                                                Vernon LP 104, Folk Art LP
                                                                5003
H 1100, 1424
            Early Mornin' Boogie (Hear Me Talkin')   Herald 443, 531
H 1101, 1449
            Sick Feeling Blues (I'm Achin')   Herald 436, 542, LP 1012,
                                                                Mount Vernon LP 104, Folk Art
                                                                LP 5003
H 1102, 1450
            Moving Out Boogie (Let's Move)   Herald 436, 542
H 1103   Hopkins Sky Hop   Herald 471
H 1104   Evil Hearted Woman   Herald 449, LP 1012, Mount
                                                                Vernon LP 104, Folk Art LP
                                                                5003
H 1105   Don't Need No Job   Herald 456
H 1106   Blues For My Cookie   Herald 465, LP 1012, Mount
                                                                Vernon LP 104, Folk Art LP
                                                                5003
H 1107   Had A Girl Named Sal   Herald 465
H 1108   They Wonder Who I Am   Herald 449
H 1109-1   Nothin' But The Blues   Herald 443, LP 1012, Mount
                                                                Vernon LP 104, Folk Art LP
                                                                5003
H 1110   That's All Right Baby -1   Herald 483
H 1111   Finally Met My Baby -1   −
            −1 add Ruth Ames, vcl.
1396, ACA 3313
            My Little Kewpie Doll (Wonder What Is Wrong
            With Me)   Herald 520, LP 1012, Ace 516,
                                                                Mount Vernon LP 104, Folk Art
                                                                LP 5003, Teem LP 5005

1397, ACA 3314
| | Lightnin' Don't Feel Well (Bad Boogie) | Herald 520, Ace 516 |
Same:
C-193	Walkin' The Streets	Chart 636
C-194	Mussy Haired Woman	–
	Walkin' The Streets	Guest Star LP 1902
	Mussy Haired Woman	

Vcl/pno.
ACA Studios, Houston, 1954
"77" LA 12/1
| | Goin' To Galveston | |
| | Met The Blues On The Corner | |

Vcl/gtr.
ACA Studios, Houston, 1953
8002-1	Late In The Evening	TNT 8002, Blues Classics 16
8003-2	Lightnin's Jump	
8003-1	Leavin' Blues	TNT 8003
8004-2	Moanin' Blues	–

Same:
Houston, January 16, 1959
	Penitentiary Blues	Folkways FS 3822, RBF 202, Verve Folkways 9000, 5003
	Bad Luck And Trouble	issues as above
	Come Go Home With Me	–
	Trouble Stay 'Way From My Door	Folkways FS 3822, Verve-Folkways 9000, 5003
	See That My Grave Is Kept Clean	Folkways FS 3822, Verve-Folkways 9000, 5003
	One Kind Favor	RBF 202
	Goin' Back To Florida	Folkways FS 3822, RBF 202, Verve Folkways 9000, 5003
	Reminiscences Of Blind Lemon	Folkways FS 3822, Verve-Folkways 9000, 5003
	Fan It	issues as above + Aravel LP 1004
	Tell Me Baby	Folkways FS 3822, Verve-Folkways 9000, 5003
	She's Mine	issues as above

Vcl/gtr. with Luke Miles, vcl (–1).
Houston, February 16, 1959
1	Till The Gin Gets Here	Tradition LP 1035
2	So Long Baby	Tradition LP 1040
3	Bunion Stew	Tradition LP 1035
4	You Got To Work To Get Your Pay	–
5	Go Down Ol' Hannah	
6	Santa Fe Blues	Tradition LP 1040
7	Hear My Black Dog Bark	Tradition LP 1035
8	Black And Evil -1	unissued
9	Walkin' With Frankie -1	unissued

Same:
Houston, February 26, 1959
10	Long Time	Tradition LP 1035
11	Rainy Day Blues	–
12	Worryin' My Mind	–
13	Baby -1	–
14	Long Gone With A Turkey In The Corn	–
15	See See Rider	
16	How Many Days Must I Wait	"77" LA 12/1
17	Prison Blues Come Down On Me -1	Tradition LP 1035
18	That Mean Old Twister (Backwater Blues)	–
19	Gonna Pulla Party	–
20	Bluebird, Bluebird	–

Vcl/gtr.
Houston, May 12, 1959
21	Beggin' Up And Down The Streets	"77" LA 12/1
22	Black Snake	–
23	Get Off My Toe	Tradition LP 1040
24	Mama And Papa Hopkins	–
25	Short Haired Woman	–

140

26	If You Ever Been Mistreated	"77" LA 12/1
27	Children's Boogie	—
28	When The Saints Go Marching In	Tradition LP 1040
Same:		Houston, July 13, 1959
29	Dig Me In The Morning	"77" LA 12/1
30	Back To Arkansas	—
31	In The Evening When The Sun Goes Down	Tradition LP 1040
32	Corinne Corinne	Candid 8026
33	The Foot Race Is One	Tradition LP 1040
34	Have You Ever Seen A One-Eyed Woman Cry	"77" LA 12/1
Same:		Houston, July 16, 1959
35	Hard Headed Children	"77" LA 12/1
36	Tom Moore's Farm	"77" LA 12/3
37	Blues Jumped The Rabbit	unissued
38	Bottle Up And Go	Tradition LP 1040
39	Blues For Queen Elizabeth	"77" LA 12/1
40	That Gamblin' Life	Tradition LP 1040
41	Hello England	"77" LA 12/1
42	75 Highway	Tradition LP 1040
43	The Dirty Dozens	Raglan LP 51
Same:		Houston, July 20, 1959
44	Trouble In Mind	Tradition LP 1040
45	When The Saints Go Marching In	"77" LA 12/1
46	Blues Come Late In The Evening	unissued
Same:		Houston, November 19, 1959
47	Long Way From Texas	Heritage LP 1001
48	Red River Valley	unissued
49	Ella Speed	unissued
50	Motherless Child	unissued
51	Look Out Settegast, Here Me And My Partner Come	Heritage LP 1001
52	Jack O'Diamonds	unissued
53	Make Me Some Changes Soon	unissued
54	Farmer's Wife Come Creeping In Her Sleep	unissued
55	No Hair At All	unissued
56	Getting Out Of Th e Bushes Tap Dance	Heritage LP 1001
57	Sad Hours Of Night	unissued
58	Whiskey, Whiskey	Heritage LP 1001
59	Boogie Improvisation	unissued
60	Suicide Blues	Heritage LP 1001
Same:		Houston, December 8, 1959
61	Oh My Baby Take Me Back (Candy Man)	unissued
62	Minnie Lee	unissued
63	Mister Charlie Your Rolling Mill Is Burning Down	unissued
64	Natural Blues	unissued
65	Houston Boogie	unissued

Vcl/pno. with Melvin "Jack" Jackson, vcl/pno. (duet) Houston, January 25, 1960
The Slop "77" LA 12/3

Vcl/gtr. with Sonny Terry, vcl/hca; Brownie McGhee, vcl/gtr; Big Joe Williams, vcl/gtr;
Jimmy Bond, bs. Los Angeles, July 6, 1960
First Meeting -1 World Pacific 1296, 1817,
  Kimberley 2017

How Long Has It Been Since You Been Home
-2 issues as above
Ain't Nothing Like Whiskey —
Penitentiary Blues —
Chain Gang Blues Society LP 1029
If You Steal My Chickens You Can't Make 'Em
Lay World Pacific 1296, 1817,
  Kimberley 2017

Wimmen From Coast To Coast issues as above

Four Friends Blues	unissued
Friends And Pals	unissued
New Car Blues (Brand New Car) -3	Society LP 1015, 1020
You Gonna Need Somebody To Go Your Bond (I've Been Buked)	Society LP 1020
Blues From The Bottom	unissued
Three Aces On The Bottom Of The Deal (Blues For Gamblers)	Vee Jay LP 1138, Horizon LP 1617, Society LP 1009, 1020
I'm Gonna Mourn On That Shore	issues as above
Razor Sharp Blues -1	Society LP 1029

−1 Hopkins and McGhee only.
−2 Hopkins only.
−3 Williams and Terry only.
−4 Williams only.

Vcl/gtr.		Ash Grove, Los Angeles, July 6/7, 1960
	Introduction (Lightnin' Talks)	Vee Jay LP 1138, Horizon LP 1617, Society LP 1009
	Big Car Blues	issues as above
	Coffee House Blues	−
	Stool Pigeon Blues	−
	Ball Of Twine	−
Vcl/gtr. with Luke Miles, vcl/hca; L. C. Williams, vcl/dms.		Houston, c. October, 1960
	When Mother's Dead And Gone	unissued
Vcl/gtr. with Leonard Gaskin, bs; Belton Evans, dms.		New Jersey, October, 1960
	Automobile Blues	Bluesville BVLP 1019, Prestige 343
	You Better Watch Yourself	−
	Mean Old 'Frisco	−
	Shinin' Moon	−
	Come Back Baby	−
	Thinkin' About An Old Friend	−
	The Walkin' Blues	− , LP 1084, 821
	Back To New Orleans	− − , 817
	Katie Mae	Bluesville 825, BVLP 1019
	Down There Baby	Bluesville BVLP 1019
Add Sonny Terry, hca (−1)/vcl (−2):		
	Rocky Mountain Blues	Bluesville BVLP 1029, 1081, SP 101
	Got To Move Your Baby -1	Bluesville 813, LP 1029, 1081, 1084, SP 101
	So Sorry To Leave You -1	− − − SP 101
	Last Night Blues -1	Bluesville 821, − − 1084, SP 101
	Lightnin's Stroke -1	Bluesville BVLP 1029, 1081, SP 101
	Hard To Love A Woman -1	Bluesville 817, LP 1029, 1081, 1084, SP 101
	Conversation Blues -1, 2	Bluesville BVLP 1029, 1081, SP 101
	Take A Trip With Me	− −
Vcl/gtr/pno (−1), with bs; dms.		New York City, November, 1960
FM 171	Mojo Hand	Fire 1034, LP 104, Sphere-Sound 7001, Mercury MG 20826
FM 172	Glory Bee	Fire 1034, LP 104, Sphere-Sound 7001
	Coffee For Mama	Fire LP 104, SphereSound 7001
	Awful Dream	− −
	Black Mare (Trot)	− −

Have You Ever Loved A Woman -1	Fire LP 104, SphereSound 7001	
Sometimes She Will	–	–
Shine On Moon	–	–
Santa Claus (Blues)	–	–
How Long Has The Train Been Gone	–	,
	701	

Vcl/gtr. or Vcl/pno (–1), or Vcl/pno/gtr (–2).   New York City, November 15, 1960

The Trouble Blues	Candid LP 8010
Lightnin's Piano Boogie -1	–
Wonder Why	–
Mister Charlie Ptl. & 2	– , 603
Take It Easy -2	–
Mighty Crazy	–
Your Own Fault Baby To Treat Me The Way You Do -1	–
I've Had My Fun If I Don't Get Well No More	–
Black Cat	Candid LP 8019

Vcl/gtr.   ACA Studio, Houston, July 7, 1961

Black Gal	Bluesville BVLP 1057
Baby Don' You Tear My Clothes	–
Good Morning Little Schoolgirl	–
Coffee Blues	–

Same: ACA Studio, Houston, July 26, 1961

Buddy Brown's Blues	Bluesville BVLP 1045
Wine Spodee-O-Dee	–
Sail On Little Girl, Sail On	– , 814
Death Bells	Bluesville BVLP 1045, 814
DC 7	–
Going To Dallas To See My Pony Run	–
Jailhouse Blues	–
Blues In The Bottle	–
Beans Beans Beans	–
Catfish Blues	–
My Grandpa Is Old Too	–

Vcl/gtr/pno (–1), with Barbara Dane, 2nd vcl (–2); Gino Landry, bs; Victor Leonard, mds.
Berkeley, November 26, 1961

Bald Headed Woman	Arhoolie F 1011
Burnin' In L. A.	–
Speedin' Boogie	–
Once Was A Gambler	–
Do The Boogie -1	–
Goin' Out	–
Wine Drinkin' Woman	Arhoolie F 1012
Hurricane Carla	unissued
Candy Kitchen	unissued
Jesus Won't You Come By Here -2	Arhoolie F 1022

Vcl/gtr.   Berkeley, December 2, 1961

California Showers	Arhoolie F 1011

Vcl/gtr. with Spider Kilpatrick, dms.   ACA Studio, Houston, Jan. 23, 1962

Meet You At The Chicken Shack	Arhoolie F 1011
Ice Storm Blues	
Candy Wagon	Arhoolie F 1018
Down Home Blues	unissued

No details:

Organ Boogie	Arhoolie F 1009

Vcl/gtr. with Billy Bizor, hca (–1)/vcl (–2); Spider Kilpatrick, dms.
ACA Studio, Houston, Feb. 17, 1962

How Many More Years I Got To Let You Dog Me Around	Bluesville BVLP 1057

Black Cadillac	Bluesville BVLP 1057	
Walking This Road By Myself -1	–	
The Devil Jumped The Black Man -1	–	
My Baby Don't Stand No Cheating (My Babe)	Bluesville BVLP 1061, 825	
You Is One Black Rat	–	
The Fox Chase -1, 2	–	
Mojo Hand	–	, 1084,
	Prestige 343	
Mama Blues -1, 2	–	
My Black Name	Bluesville BVLP 1070	
Ida Mae	–	

Vcl/gtr. with Buster Pickens, pno; Donald Cooks, bs; Spider Kilpatrick, dms.

	ACA Studio, Houston, Feb. 20, 1962	
Prison Farm Blues	Bluesville BVLP 1070	
Worried Life Blues	Bluesville BVLP 1057	
Happy Blues For John Glenn (Pts. 1 & 2)	–	, 820
Sinner's Prayer	Bluesville BVLP 1061, 1084, 822	
Angel Child	–	
I Got A Leak In This Old Building	–	
Pneumonia Blues	–	
Have You Ever Been Mistreated	–	

Vcl/gtr.			
1530	Mary Lou	Houston, c. 1962	
		Dart 152, Vee Jay LP 1044	
1531	Want To Come Home	–	
	Please Don't Quit Me	Vee Jay LP 1044	
	Devil Is Watching You	–	
	Heavy Snow	–	
	Coon Is Hard To Catch	–	
	Rolling And Rolling	–	
	Walking Around In Circles	–	

Vcl/gtr. with Elmore Nixon, pno; Ivory Lee Semien, dms.   Houston, 1961

132B	War Is Starting Again	Ivory 91272, Vee Jay LP 1044	
132A	Got Me A Louisiana Woman	–	–

Vcl/gtr.			
		Houston, c. 1962	
	T Model Blues	Bluesville BVLP 1070	
	Jackstropper Blues	–	
	You Cook All Right	–	
	You Never Miss The Water	–	
	Let's Do The Susie Q	–	
	Smokes Like Lightnin'	–	

Vcl/gtr. with Leonard Gaskin, bs; Herbie Lovelle, dms.   New Jersey, c. 1963

Business You're Doin'	Bluesville BVLP 1073, 1084, 823	
Wake Up Old Lady	–	–
Stranger Blues	–	
Don't Embarass Me Baby	–	
Little Sister's Boogie	–	
Goin' Away	–	, 824
You Better Stop Here	–	–
I'm Wit' It	–	
Let's Go Sit On The Lawn	Prestige LP 1086, 326	
I Woke Up This Morning (no bs; dms.)	–	
I Got Tired	–	
I Like To Boogie	–	, 326
I Asked The Bossman	–	
I'm Taking The Devil Of A Chance	Prestige 1086	
Just A Wrist Watch On My Arm	–	
I Was Standing On 75 Highway (no bs; dms.)	–	
Get It Straight	–	

Vcl/gtr.		"The Second Fret", Phila-
		delphia, c. 1963
	Blues Is A Feeling	Prestige 14021
	Me And Ray Charles	–
	In The Evening	–
	Ain't It Crazy	–
	Last Night I Lost The Best Friend I Ever Had	–
	Everything	–
	I Work Down On The Chain Gang	–
	Meet Me In The Bottom	–
Vcl/gtr.		The Bird Lounge, Houston,
		1964
	I Heard My Children Crying	Guest Star 1459
	Leave Jike Mary Alone	–
	You Treat Po' Lightning Wrong	–
	I'm Gonna Meet My Babe Somewhere	–
	There's Good Rockin' Tonight	–
	Don't Treat That Man 'Way You Treat Me	–

Vcl (–1)/gtr. with John Henry Hopkins, vcl(–2)/gtr; Joel Hopkins, vcl (–3)/gtr.

		Waxahachie, February 16, 1964
	I Want To Go Fishing -1, 2	unissued
	Little Letter -2	unissued
	Hey Baby Hey -1, 2	unissued
	Saddle Up My Grey Mare -2	unissued
	Hot Blooded Woman Blues -1, 2	Arhoolie F 1022
	Tell Me, Tell Me -2	unissued
	Two Little Chickens -2	unissued
	Mary -1	unissued
	Little Girl -1	unissued
	I Got A Brother In Waxahachie -1	unissued
	See About My Brother John Henry -1	Arhoolie F 1022
	Black Hannah -1, 2	–
	Come On Down To My House -1	unissued
	Hey Mr. Buzzard -3	unissued
	I Walked From Dallas -3	Arhoolie F 1022
	Grosebeck Blues -1, 3	unissued
	Mama Don't Treat Your Daughter Mean	unissued
	Good Times Here Better Down The Road	unissued

Vcl/gtr. with Barbara Dane, vcl/gtr.		Berkeley, June 18, 1964
	Shake That Thing	unissued
	Sometimes She Loves Me	Arhoolie F 1022
	You Got Another Man	–
	I'm Going Back Baby	–
	Mother Earth	–

Vcl/gtr.		Hamburg, October 9, 1964
	Ain't It A Pity	Fontana TL 5225, TL 681.522
	Baby Please Don't Go	– –

Vcl/gtr.		New York City, late 1964
	I Don't Want To Do Nothing With You	Prestige 7370
	You Is One Black Rat	–
	Got Nowhere To Lay My Head	–
	Just Boogyin'	–
	Take Me Back	–
	I Was Down On Dowling Street	–

Talking to Sam Charters:
	I Growed Up With The Blues	Prestige 7370
	My Family	–
	I Learn About The Blues	–
	I First Came Into Houston	–
	I Meet Texas Alexander	–
	There Were Hard Times	–
	I Make My First Record And Get My Name	–
	My Thoughts On The Blues	–

Vcl/gtr.

How Have You Been	Pickwick LP 33 PC 3013
Take It If You Want It	–
The Crazy Song	–
Lightnin's Love	–
I Wish I Was A Baby	–
Christmas Time Is Coming	–
This Time We're Gonna Try	–
Come On Baby Let's Work Awhile	–
The Jet	–
I Don't Need You Woman	–

Vcl/gtr. with Joel Hopkins, gtr;   Houston, March 17, 1965
Going Back To Baden Baden   Arhoolie F 1022

Vcl/gtr. with Harold "Frenchie" Joseph, dms.   Houston, March 18, 1965

Monkey Taker	Arhoolie 513
Come On Baby	
Mama's Fight	Arhoolie 508
My Woman	–
Gabriel	unissued
Penitentiary Blues	unissued

Vcl/gtr. with Jimmy Bond, bs; Earl Palmer, dms. (Don Crawford, hca. dubbed on –1).
Los Angeles, October 4/5, 1965

Mojo Hand -1	Verve-Folkways 9022, Verve 5014	
Little Wail (Lightnin's Blues)	–	–
Cotton	–	–
Take Me Back	–	–
Nothin' But The Blues -1	–	–
Hurricane Betsy	–	–
Guitar Lightnin' (One More Time)	–	–
Woke Up This Morning (Crying The Blues) -1	–	–
Shake Yourself (Make It Move) -1	–	–
Goin' To Louisiana	Saga ERO 8001	
Down Home Blues	–	
Back To Arkansas	–	
Blues In The Rain	–	

Vcl/gtr. with Elmore Nixon, pno; dms.   Houston, 1965

Wig Wearing Woman	Jewel LP 5000
Morning Blues	–
Gambler's Blues	–

Vcl/gtr. with pno; dms.

Found My Baby Crying	Jewel LP 5000
Back Door Fr iend	–
Move On Out Pt. 1	–
Move On Out Pt. 2	–
Fishing Clothes (no pno.)	–

Vcl/gtr. with Leonard Gaskin, bs; Herbie Lovelle, dms.   New York City, 1965

I'm Going To Build A Heaven Of My Own	Prestige 7377, 405
Pts. 1 & 2	
My Babe	–
Too Many Drivers	–
I'm A Crawling Blacksnake	–
Rocky Mountain Blues	–
I Mean Goodbye	–
The Howling Wolf	–
Black Ghost Blues	–
Darling Do You Remember Me	–
Lonesome Graveyard	–

Vcl/gtr. with John Ewing, tbn; Jimmy Bond, bs; Earl Palmer, dms.
Los Angeles, c. Oct., 1965

Shaggy Dad	Verve-Folkways 3013
I'll Be Gone	–
Shining Moon	–

146

Talk Of The Town	Verve-Folkways 3013
Don't Wake Me	–
What'd I Say	–
Good Times	–
Goin' Back Home	–
Shake It Baby	–

Vcl/gtr. with Francey Clay, dms.   Berkeley, April 15, 1966

Last Night	Arhoolie F 1030
Going To Louisiana	–
Black Cadillac	–
Short Haired Woman	–
Lightnin's Boogie	–

(rev. of LP by Clifton Chenier and Mance Lipscomb.)

J. D. HORTON

Vcl/hca. with gtr; bs; dms.   Nashville, 1952

BU 437	Cadillac Blues	Bullet 350
BU 438	Why Don't You Let Me Be	–

SHAKEY HORTON

See under Walter Horton.

WALTER HORTON

Born Horn Lake, Mississippi in 1918.

MUMBLES
Vcl/hca. with pno (−1); Jimmy DeBerry, gtr; Joe Hill Louis, gtr/traps (where heard).
Memphis, early 1951

MM 1506-1	Little Boy Blue	Modern 20-809
MM 1507		
MM 1508-2	Now Tell Me Baby -1	Modern 20-809
MM 1619	Black Gal	RPM 338
MM 1620		
MM 1621	Jumpin' Blues	RPM 338

WALTER HORTON
As last: Memphis, 1952

1041	Walter's Boogie	Chess 1529
1042	West Winds Are Blowing	–

No details: Memphis, 1953

	unissued titles	Sun

BIG WALTER & HIS COMBO
Vcl/hca. with Red Holloway, John Cameron, tens; Lafayette Leake, pno; Lee Cooper, gtr;
Willie Dixon, bs; Fred Below, dms.   Chicago, late 1954

1496	Hard Hearted Woman	States 145, Blues Classics BC-8
1497	Back Home To Mama	–

Vcl/hca. with Harold Ashby, ten; Lafayette Leake, pno; Otis Ru sh, gtr; Willie Dixon, bs;
Al Duncan, dms.   Chicago, 1956

U 3238	Have A Good Time	Cobra 5002
U 3239	Need My Baby	–

Vcl/hca. with Henry Grey, pno; gtr; bs−gtr; Clifton James, dms.
Chicago, 1964

	Have A Good Time	unissued
	Can't Help Myself	Decca LK 4748

Vcl/hca. with Bobby Buster, org; Buddy Guy, gtr; Jack Meyers, bs−gtr; Willie Smith, dms.
Willie Dixon, vcl (−1).   Chicago, late 1964

12915	Good Moanin' Blues -1	Argo 5476, LP 4037
12917	Groove Walk	–
	Friday Night Stomp	Argo LP 4037
	Gonna Bring It On Home -1	–
	La Cucuracha	–
	Wee Baby Blues	–

	It's Alright	Argo LP 4037
	Wrinkles	–
	Hard Hearted Woman	–

Vcl/hca. with Jimmy Walker, pno; Johnny Young, gtr. Chicago, 1965
        Everybody's Fishing   Testament T-2205
        Hard Hearted Woman   –

HOT ROD HAPPY

See under Country Jim.

SON HOUSE

Born Lyon, Mississippi on March 21, 1902. Real name Eddie House.
Vcl/gtr. with Al Wilson, gtr (–1)/hca (–2).   New York City, 1965
        Death Letter   Columbia 2417
        Pearline   –
        Louise McGhee   –
        John The Revelator (no gtr.)   –
        Empire State Express -1   –
        Preachin' Blues   –
        Grinnin' In Your Face (no gtr.)   –
        Sundown   –
        Levee Camp Moan -2   –

Vcl/gtr.   New York City, November, 1966
        Levee Camp Moan   Verve FTS-3010

LAWYER HOUSTON

Vcl/gtr.   Dallas? 1950
A 451   Dallas Be Bop Blues   Atlantic 916
A 452   Western Rider Blues   Atlantic 971, Melodeon LP
                                                       7234
A 453   Hug Me Baby   –
A 454
A 455
A 456   Lawyer Houston Blues   Atlantic 916
        Note: Atlantic 971 issued as by Soldier Boy Houston.

SOLDIER BOY HOUSTON

See under Lawyer Houston.

JOHNNY HOWARD

Vcl/gtr. with pno.   Detroit, 1953
C2-144-1   Vacation Blues   Deluxe 6044
C2-149-1   Hastings Street Jump   –

PEG LEG HOWELL

Real name Joshua Barnes Howell. Born Edmonton, Ga. on 5 March, 1888.
Vcl/gtr.   Atlanta, April 11, 1963
        Blood Red River   Testament 204
        John Henry   –
        Uncle Sam Blues   –
        Jack Rabbit Blues   –
        Worried Blues   –
        Jelly Roll Blues   –
        Jo Jo Blues   –
        Skin Game Blues   –
        Coal Man Blues   –
        Let Me Play With Your Yo Yo   –

HOWLIN' WOLF

Real name Chester Burnett. Born Aberdeen, Mississippi on June 10, 1910.
Vcl/hca. with James Cotton, hca (–1); Ike Turner, pno; Willie Johnson, gtr; Willie Steel, dms.

		West Memphis, 1948 (?)
1028	Saddle My Pony	Chess 1515
1029	Worried All The Time	–

Cotton out: Memphis, 1951
| U 83 | Moanin' At Midnight (no pno.) | Chess 1479, LP 1434 |
| U 84 | How Many More Tears | –   – |

Vcl/hca. with unk. pno; 2 gtrs; Joe Martin, dms.
| | Keep What You Got | Crown CLP 5240, Custom 2055, United 717 |

Vcl/hca. with Ike Turner, pno; Willie Johnson, gtr; Willie Steel, dms.
MM 1674	Riding In The Moonlight	RPM 333, Crown CLP 5240, Custom 2055, United 717, 718, Kent 5027, Modern 12
MM 1685	Passing By Blues	RPM 340
MM 1748	My Baby Stole Off	RPM 347
MM 1749	I Want Your Picture	–
	Dog Me Around	Crown CLP 5240, Custom 2055, United 717, 718
	Worried About My Baby	Crown CLP 5240, Custom 2055, United 717
	Brownskin Woman	Crown CLP 5240, Custom 2055, United 717, Modern 12

Vcl/hca. with unk. pno; Willie Johnson, gtr; bs; Willie Steel, dms.
		Memphis? 1951
MM 1684	Crying At Daybreak (no pno.)	RPM 340, Crown CLP 5240, Custom 2055, United 717
	House Rockin' Boogie (no hca.)	Crown CLP 5240, Custom 2055, United 717

Vcl/hca. with Willie Johnson, Pat Hare, gtrs; Willie Steel, dms.
| MM 1677 | Morning At Midnight | RPM 333, Crown CLP 5240, Custom 2055, United 717, 718 |

Unk. hca; gtr; dms.
| | Backslide Boogie | Crown CLP 5240, Custom 2055, United 717 |
| | Twistin' And Turnin' | as above |

Note: Though credited to Wolf, the artist on these two tracks is either Joe Hill Louis or Shakey Horton. Crown 5240 also on Kent 5026.

Hare out. Add Ike Turner, pno: Memphis, 1952
| F 1005 | Howlin' Wolf Boogie | Chess 1497 |
| 1038 | My Last Affair | Chess 1528 |

Same but add Charles, tbs; Jayne, unk. ten:
| 1037 | Oh! Red | Chess 1528 |

Vcl/hca. with unk. pno; gtr; dms.   Memphis? 1952
F 1004	The Wolf Is At Your Door	Chess 1497
	Work For Your Money	Chess LP 1512
	I've Got A Woman	–

Vcl/hca. with Hosea Lee Kennard, pno; Jody Williams, Hubert Sumlin, gtrs; Fred Below, dms.
		Chicago, 1953
U 7246	Getting Old And Grey	Chess 1510
U 7427	Mr. Highway Man	–
U 7565	All Night Boogie	Chess 1557, LP 1434
U 7566	I Love My Baby	– , LP 1512
	Just My Kind	Chess LP 1512

Vcl/hca. with Otis Spann, pno; Lee Cooper, 1st gtr; Hubert Sumlin, 2nd gtr; Willie Dixon, bs; Earl Phillips, dms.   Chicago, 1954
U 7618	No Place To Go	Chess 1566, LP 1512
U 7619		
U 7620		

U 7621	Rockin' Daddy	Chess 1566, LP 1512
	Neighbours	Chess LP 1512
	I'm The Wolf	–

Same except Jody Williams, gtr. replaces Cooper:

| 7657 | Baby How Long | Chess 1575, LP 1434 |
| 7658 | Evil Is Going On ("Evil" on LP) | –   – , LP 4027 |

Same: Chicago, 1955

| 7740 | I'll Be Around | Chess 1584, LP 1512 |
| 7741 | Forty Four | – , LP 1434 |

Same but Henry Gray, pno. replaces Spann:

7795	Who Will Be Next	Chess 1593, LP 1512
7796	I Have A Little Girl	– –
7797	(by Muddy Waters)	
7798	Come To Me Baby	Chess 1607
7799	Don't Mess With My Baby	–

Vcl/hca. with Hosea Lee Kennard, pno; Hubert Sumlin, gtr; Earl Phillips, dms.
                                                                            Chicago, 1956

| 7985 | Smoke Stack Lightning | Chess 1618, LP 1434 Argo LP 4026 |
| 7986 | You Can't Be Beat | – , LP 1512 |

Vcl/hca. with Hosea Lee Kennard, pno; Willie Johnson, 1st gtr; Otis "Smokey" Smothers, 2nd gtr; Earl Phillips, dms.
                                                                            Chicago, May 1956

8175	I Asked For Water	Chess 1632, LP 1434, Argo LP. 4034
8176	So Glad	–
8177		
8178	The Natchez Burning	Chess 1744, LP 1502

Similar or same, but add Adolph "Billy" Dockins, ten (–1):
                                                                            Chicago, December 1956

8352	Going Back Home	Chess 1648
8353		
8354	My Life -1	Chess 1648
8355		

Similar or same: Chicago, 1957

8528	Who's Been Talking	Chess 1750, LP 1469
8529	Tell Me	– –
8530	Somebody In My Home	Chess 1668, LP 1434
8531	Nature	

Vcl/hca. with Hosea Lee Kennard, pno; Jody Williams, Hubert Sumlin, gtrs; Earl Phillips, dms.
                                                                            Chicago, 1957

8615		
8616	Poor Boy	Chess 1679, LP 1502
8617		
8618	Sitting On Top Of The World	Chess 1679, LP 1502

Same: Chicago, 1958

| 8774 | I Didn't Know | Chess 1695 |
| 8775 | Moanin' For My Baby | – , LP 1434 |

Vcl/hca. with Abe Locke, ten; Hosea Lee Kennard, pno; Hubert Sumlin, gtr; Alfred Elkins, Willie Dixon, bs; S. P. Leary, dms.

| 8789 | | |
| 8790 | I Better Go Now | Ch ess 1726 |

Vcl/hca. with Hosea Lee Kennard, pno; L. D. McGhee, gtr; Willie Dixon, bs; S. P. Leary, dms.

9150	I'm Leaving You	Chess 1712, LP 1434
9151		
9152	Change My Way	Chess 1712

Vcl/hca. with Hosea Lee Kennard, pno; Hubert Sumlin, gtr; S. P. Leary, dms.
                                                                            Chicago, 1959

| 9272 | Howlin' Blues | Chess 1726 |
| 7618 | You Gonna Wreck My Life | Chess 1744, LP 1434 |

Note: 2nd title above is a remake of "No Place To Go", using the old master number. There is no proof that it is from the session above but it is very likely.

150

Same, but add Abe Locke, ten:
9583	I've Been Abused	Chess 1753
9584	Howlin' For My Darling (no hca.)	Chess 1762, LP 1469
9585		
9586	Mr. Airplane Man	Chess 1753

Vcl. with Otis Spann, pno; Hubert Sumlin, gtr; Willie Dixon, bs; Fred Below, dms.
Chicago, 1960
10262		
10263	Wang Dang Doodle	Chess 1777, LP 1469
10264	Back Door Man	— —
10265	Spoonful	Chess 1762, — , Argo LP 4026

Vcl. with Johnny Jones, pno; Jimmy Rogers, 1st gtr; Hubert Sumlin, 2nd gtr; Willie Dixon, bs; Sammy Lewis, dms.
Chicago, 1961
10913	Little Baby	Chess 1793, LP 1469
10914		
10915		
10916		
10917	Down In The Bottom	Chess 1793, LP 1469

Vcl/gtr (−1), with Johnny Jones, pno; Hubert Sumlin, gtr; Willie Dixon, bs; Sammy Lay, dms.
10937	Shake For Me	Chess 1804, LP 1469
10938	The Red Rooster -1	—

Vcl/gtr. with Henry Gray, pno; Hubert Sumlin, gtr; Jimmy Rogers, bs−gtr; Willie Dixon, vcl (−1)/bs; Sammy Lay, dms.
Chicago, December, 1961
11377	You'll Be Mine	Chess 1813, LP 1469
11378	Just Like I Treat You	Chess 1823
11379	I Ain't Superstitious	—
11380	Goin' Down Slow -1	Chess 1813, LP 1469

Vcl/gtr. with J. T. Brown, ten; Johnny Jones, pno; Hubert Sumlin, gtr; Willie Dixon, bs; Junior Blackman, dms.
Chicago, September 1962
11914	Mama's Baby	Chess 1844
11915	Do The Do	

Vcl/hca. with Jarrett Gibson, Donald Hankins, saxes; Otis Spann, pno; Buddy Guy, gtr; Jack Meyers, bs−gtr; Fred Below, dms.
Copa Cabana, Chicago, July 26, 1963
	Sugar Mama	Argo LP 4031
	May I Have A Talk With You	—

Vcl. with J. T. Brown, ten; Donald Hankins, bari; Lafayette Leake, pno; Hubert Sumlin, gtr; Buddy Guy, bs−gtr; Sammy Lay, dms.
Chicago, August 14, 1963
12616	Tail Dragger	Chess 1890, LP 1502
12617	Hidden Charms	—
12618	300 Pounds Of Joy	Chess 1870, LP 1502
12619	She Brought Joy To My Soul	unissued
12620	Built For Comfort	Chess 1870, LP 1502

Vcl. with Arnold Rogers, ten; Donald Hankins, bari; Johnny Jones, pno; Hubert Sumlin, gtr; Andrew Palmer, bs−gtr; Willie Dixon, bs; Sammy Lay, dms. Chicago, 1964
	Shake It	unissued

Vcl. with Arnold Rogers, ten; Donald Hankins, bari; Lafayette Leake, pno; Hubert Su mlin, Buddy Guy, gtrs; Jack Meyers, bs−gtr; Clifton James, dms.   Chicago, 1964
	Shake It	unissued

Vcl/hca. with Arnold Rogers, ten; Donald Hankins, bari; Johnny Jones, pno; Hubert Sumlin, gtr; Andrew Palmer, bs−gtr; Willie Dixon, bs; Sammy Lay, dms.
Chicago, August, 1964
	Love Me Darlin'	Chess 1911
	My Country Sugar Mama	— , LP 1502

Vcl/gtr. with Hubert Sumlin, gtr; Willie Dixon, bs; Clifton James, dms.
Hamburg, October 9, 1964
	Dust My Broom	Fontana TL 5225

Vcl. with
Chicago, 1965
	Killing Floor	Chess 1923, LP 1502
	Louise	— —

13383	Tell Me What I've Done	Chess 1928, LP 1502
13385	Ooh Baby	— —
		Chicago, 1966
13882	I Walked From Dallas	Chess 1945
13883	Don't Laugh At Me	

LUTHER HUFF

Born Hinds County, Mississippi on December 5, 1910.
Vcl/mdln. with Percy Huff, gtr.

		Jackson, Winter, 1950
DRC-1-23-2	(She's Got A) Dirty Disposition	Trumpet 132
DRC-1-24-2	1951 Blues	—
DRC-1-25		
DRC-1-26		
DRC-1-27	Bull Dog Blues	Trumpet 141, Blues Classics 15
DRC-1-28	Rosalie Blues	Trumpet 141

WILLIE B. HUFF

WITH J. FULLER ORCH.
Vcl. with Johnny Fuller, gtr; dms.

		Oakland, 1953
1770A	Beggar Man Blues	Rhythm 1770
1770B	I've Been Thinkin' And Thinkin'	—

Add ten; pno:

6264	I Love You Baby	Big Town 105
6265	Operator 209	—

PEE WEE HUGHES & THE DELTA DUO

Vcl/hca. with gtr; dms.

		New Orleans, 1949
1012	(I'm A) Country Boy	DeLuxe 3228, Savoy LP 16000
1013	Santa Fe Blues	—

D. A. HUNT

Vcl/gtr.

		Memphis, 1953
U 69, S 12130		
	Lonesome Ol' Jail	Sun 183
U 70, S 12131		
	Greyhound Blues	—

SLIM HUNT

Vcl. with alt; pno; gtr; dms.

		Nashville, 1955
A	Welcome Home Baby	Excello 2055
B	Lonesome For My Baby	—
	Note: alto is very indistinct.	

LONG JOHN HUNTER

See under Lost John Hunter.

LOST JOHN HUNTER

LOST JOHN HUNTER & THE BLIND BATS
Vcl/pno. with gtr; dms.

		Los Angeles, 1950
3726	Cool Down Mama	4 Star 1492
3727	School Boy	—
3772	Y-M & V Blues	4 Star 1511, Blues Classics BC-14
3773	Boogie For Me Baby	—

LONG JOHN
Vcl/pno. with alt; ten; gtr; bs; dms.

		Houston, 1953
ACA 2720	Crazy Girl	Duke 122
ACA 2721	She Used To Be My Woman	—

152

LONG JOHN HUNTER
As last   1960

A	El Paso Rock	Yucca 132
B	Midnight Stroll	–
A	Ole Rattler	Yucca 138
B	Grandma	–

LEE HUNTER
Vcl/pno.   Houston, 1948

651A	Lee's Boogie	Gold Star 651
651B	Back To Santa Fe	– , Arhoolie R 2006

Note: This is the brother of **Ivory Joe Hu nter**

MISSISSIPPI JOHN HURT

Born Teoc, Mississippi in March, 1894. Died November, 3, 1966

Vcl/gtr.   Washington, D.C. March 24, 26, 29 &
                                                           April 2nd, 1963

Avalon Blues	Piedmont 13157
Richland Woman	–
Spike Drive Blues	–
Salty Dog	–
Cow Hooking Blues	–
Spanish Fandange	–
Casey Jones	–
Louis Collins	–
Cand Man Blues	–
My Creole Belle	–
Liza Jane	–
God's Unchanging Hand	–
Joe Turner Blues	–

Vcl/gtr.   Newport, R.I. July 25, 1964

Candy Man	Vanguard VRS 9145
Trouble, I've Had It All My Days	–
Frankie	–

Vcl/gtr.   Falls Church, Va. March 14, 15, 21, 1964

Lazy Blues	Piedmont 13161
Farther Along	–
Sliding Delta	–
Nobody Cares For Me	–
Cow Hooking Blues No. 2	–
Talkin' Casey	–
Weeping And Wailing	–
Worried Blues	–
Oh Mary, Don't You Weep	–
I Been Cryin' Since You Been Gone	–

Vcl/gtr.

Pay Day	Vanguard CRS 9220
I'm Satisfied	–
Candy Man	–
Make Me A Pallet On The Floor	–
Talking Casey	–
Corrina, Corrina	–
Coffee Blues	–
Louis Collins	–
Hot Time In The Old Town Tonight	–
If You Don't Want Me Baby	–
Spike Driver's Blues	–
Beulah Land	–

Vcl/gtr.   Newport, R.I. Ju ly 25, 1964

Spike Driver's Blues	Vanguard VRS 9145
See See Rider	–

| | Stagolee | Vanguard VRS 9145 |
| | Coffee Blues | –   , 9183 |

J. B. HUTTO

Born Augusta, Georgie on April 26, 1929. Full name Joseph Benjamin Hutto

J. B. & HIS HAWKS
Vcl./gtr. with George Maywether, hca; Joe Custom, bs-gtr; Porkchop, wbd/dms.

		Chicago, 1954
C 5118	Pet Cream Man	Chance 1160
C 5119	Lovin' You	–
C 5120	Now She's Gone	Chance 1155
C 5121	Combination Boogie	–

J. B. HUTTO
As last, but add Johnny Jones, pno.

U 5152	Price Of Love	unissued
U 5153	Things Are So Slow	Chance 1165, Blues Classics BC-8
U 5154	Dim Lights	– –
U 5155	Thank You For Your Kindness	unissued
U 5156	Mouth Harp Mambo	unissued

J. B. HUTTO
Vcl/gtr. with Herman Hassell, bs-gtr; Frank Kirkland, dms.

		Chicago, late 1965
	Going Ahead	Vanguard VRS 9216
	Please Help	–
	Too Much Alchohol	–
	Married Woman Blues	–
	That's The Truth	–

I

IVORY LEE

See under King Ivory Lee

J. B. & HIS BAYOU BOYS

See under J. B. Lenoir

J. B. & HIS HAWKS

See under J. B. Hutto

BILL JACKSON

Born Granite, Maryland, in 1911.
Vcl/gtr.   Philadelphia, 1962

Old Rounder Blues	Testament T-201
Long Steel Rail	—
Last Go Round	—
Careless Love	—
Titanic Blues	—
Freight Train Runs So Slow	—
Blues In The Morning	—
You Ain't No Woman	—
Freight Train Blues	— , Milestone LP3002
Moaning Guitar Blues	—
Goin' Back South	—
Blood Red River	—
Don't Put Your Hands on Me	—
Trouble In Mind	Storyville SLP 181

Vcl/gtr.   late 1963

The 22nd Day Of November	Testament S-01

BROTHER JACKSON

See under Louis Jackson

HANDY JACKSON

Vcl. with ten; pno; gtr; dms.   Memphis, 1953

U 55	Got My Application Baby	Sun 177
U 56	Trouble (Will Bring You Down)	—

JOHN JACKSON

Born Rapahannock County, Virginia in 1924
Vcl/gtr/bjo(-1)   Fairfax. Va., April 19, 1965

Nobody's Business But My Own	Arhoolie F 1025
Going Down To Georgia On A Horn	—
Black Snake Moan	—
Flat Foot And Buck Dance	—
If Hattie Wanna Lu, Let Her Lu Like A Man -1	—
T. B. Blues	—
I'm A Bad, Bad Man	—
Rattlesnakin' Daddy	—
Poor Boy	—
Boat's Up The River	—
Steamboat Whistle Blues	—
John's Rag -1	—
Cindy	—
John Henry	—

JOHN HENRY JACKSON

Vcl/gtr. with A. C. Craig, gtr.   Angola, 1959

My Baby Got To Go	Storyville SLP 125
Tell Me Pretty Baby	—

JOHNNY JACKSON

Lead vcl. with James W. Hobbs, Houston Page, William Evans, vcls.

		Ramsey Farm, Unit 1, Texas 1951
	Raise 'Em Up Higher	Elektra EKL-296
	Hammer Ring	–

LEE JACKSON

Born St. Louis, Mo. on September 26, 1907
Vcl/gtr. with John Tinsley, Harold Ashby, tens; Little Willie Foster, hca; Sunnyland Slim, pno; Willie Dixon, bs; Joe Harris, dms.

		Chicago, 1957
C-1002	Fishin' In My Pond	Cobra 5007
C-1003	I'll Just Keep Walking	–

Vcl/gtr. with J. T. Brown, Boyd Atkins, tens; Johnny Jones, pno; Eugene Pierce, gtr; Bob Anderson, bs-gtr; Jump Jackson, dms.

		Chicago, 1960
115A	Juanita	Keyhole 115
115B	Please Baby	–

LIL' SON JACKSON

Born Tyler, Texas on August, 17, 1916. Real name Melvin Jackson.

LITTLE SON JACKSON
Vcl/gtr.

		Houston, 1948
638A	Roberta Blues	Gold Star 638, Time LP 4, Folkways RBF 202
632B	Freedom Train Blues	Gold Star 638
642A	Ground Hog Blues	Gold Star 642
642B	Bad Whiskey,-Bad Women	–
Same:		Houston, 1949
653A	Gone With The Wind (She's Gone)	Gold Star 653, Time LP 4
653B	No Money, No Love	–
MM 1672	Talkin' Boogie	Modern 840
MM 1673	Milford Blues	
663A	Cairo Blues	Gold Star 663
663B	Evil Blues	–
668A	Gambling Blues	Gold Star 668, Dot 1051, S.I.W. 643
668B	Homeless Blues	– –

Note: 668B as "Homeless" on Dot or "Homesick Blues" on S.I.W. Gold Star 668 also on Arhoolie R 2006

LIL' SON JACKSON
Vcl/gtr.

		Los Angeles, 1950
IM 206	Ticket Agent Blues	Imperial 5100
IM 207	True Love Blues	–
IM 208	Evening Blues	Imperial 5108
IM 209	Spending Money Blues	Imperial 5237
IM 210	Tough Luck Blues	Imperial 5108
Same:		Los Angeles, December 16, 1950
IM 241	Peace Breaking People	Imperial 5113
Im 242	Rockin' And Rollin'	– , LP 9142, LP 9210
IM 243	Two Timin' Women	Imperial 5119, –
IM 244	Rocky Road	– –
IM 245	Disgusted	unissued
IM 246	Travelin' Alone	Imperial 5125, 5192, LP 9142
IM 247	New Year's Resolution	Imperial LP 9142
IM 248	Young Woman Blues	Imperial 5125, 5192, LP 9142

LIL' SON JACKSON & HIS ROCKIN' & ROLLERS
Vcl/gtr. with ten; Boston Smith, pno; Booker T. Everhart, bs; Be Bop McKinley dms.

		Dallas, 1951
IM 281	Mr Blues	Imperial 5131, LP 9142
IM 282	Time Changes Things	– –

LIL' SON JACKSON
Vcl/gtr. with Booker T. Everhart, bs.

IM 283	Wondering Blues	Imperial 5137, LP 9142
IM 284	Restless Blues	— —
IM 285	All Alone	Imperial 5237

Vcl/gtr. with Henry Jenkins, alt; Al Calloway, pno; Booker T. Everhart, bs; Be Bop Mckinley, dms.

| IM 319 | Everybody's Blues (bs only) | Imperial 5156, LP 9142 |
| IM 320 | Travelin' Woman | — |

LIL' SON JACKSON & HIS ROCKIN & ROLLERS
Same:

| Im 321 | Red Light | Imperial 5144 |
| IM 322 | Achin' Heart | — ; LP 9142 |

Omit bs:

| IM 369 | Upstairs Boogie | Imperial 5165 |
| IM 370 | All My Love | — |

Omit sax. Add 2nd gtr.

| IM 371 | **Big Gun** Blues | Imperial 5175 |
| IM 372 | My Little Girl | — |

LIL' SON JACKSON
Vcl/gtr. with Junior Herman Williams, Henry Jenkins, saxes (-1); Boston Smith, pno; Booker T. Everhart, bs; Johnny Shields, dms.   Fort Worth, June 2, 1952

IM 445	Get High Everybody -1	Imperial 5300
IM 446	Let Me Down Easy	—
IM 447	My Younger Days	Imperial 5319
IM 448	I Wish To Go Home	—

Vcl/gtr. with Al Calloway, pno; Booker T. Everhart, bs; Be Bop McKinely dms.
Forth Worth, October 1952

IM 489	Black And Brown	Imperial 5218
IM 490	Journey Back Home	Imperial 5204
IM 491	Sad Letter Blues	Imperial 5218
IM 492	Rockin' And Rollin' No. 2	Imperial 5204

Add J. B. Anderson, ten; Boston Smith, pno. replaces Calloway:
1953

IM 527	Lonely Blues	Imperial 5229, Post 2014
IM 528	Freight Train Blues (No Money)	—
IM 529	How Long	Imperial 5312
IM 530	Good Ole Wagon (no ten)	—
IM 531	Blues By The Hour (no ten)	Imperial 5286
IM 532	Pulpwood Boogie	unissued
IM 533	Losin' My Woman	unissued
IM 534	Trouble Don't Last Always	Imperial 5286

Note: Im 528 has been edited on Post 2014

Vcl/gtr.   Dallas, June 1953

IM 605	Movin' To The Country	Imperial 5248
IM 606	Thrill Me Baby	Imperial 5267
IM 607	Confession	Imperial 5248
IM 608	Doctor, Doctor.	Imperial 5267

Add unk. beating sticks (-1);   Dallas September, 1953

IM 636	Piggly Wiggly -1	Imperial 5276
IM 637	Dirty Work -1	Imperial 5259
IM 638	Little Girl	—
IM 639	Big Rat -1	Imperial 5276

Sticks out: Dallas, late 1954

IM 829 re	Sugar Mama	Imperial 5339-x
IM 830-re	Messin' Up	—
IM 831	Prison Bound	Imperial 5963
IM 832	Rolling Mill	

Vcl/gtr.   Dallas, July 10, 1960

	Blues Came To Texas (Walked To Dallas)	Arhoolie F 1004
	Cairo Blues	–
	Ticket Agent Blues	–
	Louise Blues	–
	Sugar Mama	–
	The Girl I Love	–
	Santa Fe Blues	–
	Turn Your Lamp Down Low	–
	Ground Hog Blues	–
	Gambling Blues	–
	Charley Cherry 1	–
	Charley Cherry 11	–
	West Dallas Blues	–
	Rollin' Mill Went Down	–
	Red River Blues	–
	Roberta Blues	–
	Johnnie Mae	Arhoolie F 1006

LOUIS JACKSON

BROTHER JACKSON
Pno. with Slim Green, gtr: Junior Hampton, dms.   Los Angeles, 1948

B	L. J. Boogie	Murray 500
	(rev. by Junior Hampton q.v.)	

LOUIS & FROSTY
Vcl/pno. with William Pyles, vcl/gtr.   Los Angeles,

C 1208, 8028	Lonesome And Confused	C-Note 109
C 1209, 8030	Train Time	–

LOUIS JACKSON

	Tweedle Woofin' Boogie	C-Note 110
	Fran's Mood	

MONROE "MOE" JACKSON

Vcl/gtr. with Mason Brown, pno(-1).   1949

2204	Move It On Over -1	Mercury 8127
2205	Go'Way From My Door	– , Blues Classics BC-5

DONNIE JACOBS

Vcl/gtr. with Jerry Devillier, hca; gtr; dms.   Ville Patte, La. 1966

J30X	If You Want Good Lovin'	Jin 201
J31X	Street Walkin' Woman	

Note: Ville Platte artist.

BETTY JAMES

Vcl. with 2 gtrs. bs; dms;   New York City, 1961

CJ 8174, 11193	I'm A Little Mixed Up	Cee Jay 583, Chess 1801, Argo LP 40
CJ 8175, 11194	Help Me To Find My Love	– –
Same:		1962
U 11684	Henry Lee	Chess 1837
U 11689	I'm Not Mixed Up Anymore	
Same:		1966
14943	I Like The Way You Walk	Chess 1970
14944	Salt In Your Coffee	–

ELMER JAMES

See under Big Boy Crudup.

ELMORE JAMES (or Elmo James)

Born Canton, Mississippi on January 18, 1918.
Died Chicago, Illinois on May 23, 1963
Vcl/gtr. with Sonny Boy Williamson, hca; Odie Johnson, bs. Jackson, Miss. 1952

DRC 52, A-60	(ACA 2026) Dust My Broom	Trumpet 146, Ace 508, Jewel 764
	(I Believe) My Time Ain't Long	Blues Classics BC-5, Teem LP5005
DRC 53, A-61	(ACA 2028) Catfish Blues	Trumpet 146, Ace 508, Jewel 783
	(I Wish I Was A Catfish)	

Note: DRC 53 is not by James, but by an unidentified vocalist/guitarist. Reverse of both Jewel issues are by Big Boy Crudup.

Vcl/gtr. with J. T. Brown, ten; Johnny Jones, pno; Odie Payne, dms.

Chicago early 1953

MR 5000	Baby What's Wrong	Meteor 5003
MR 5001	I Believe	Meteor 5000
MR 5002	Sinful Woman	Meteor 5003
MR 5003	I Held My Baby Last Night	Meteor 5000

Note: Other sides on Meteor credited to James are actually by J. T. Brown.

ELMORE JAMES & HIS BROOMDUSTERS
Vcl/gtr. with J. T. Brown, ten; Johnny Jones, pno; bs; Odie Payne, dms.

Chicago, 1954/56

FL-123	Early In The Morning	Flair 1011
FL-124	Hawaiian Boogie	–
FL-131	Can't Stop Lovin'	Flair 1014
FL-132	Make A Little Love	–
U-4321	Country Boogie	Checker 777
	My Best Friend	unissued
	I See My Baby	unissued
U-4324	She Just Won't Do Right	Checker 777
	Whose Muddy Shoes	unissued

Add Boyd Atkins, alt/ten;

FL-148	Strange Kinda Feeling	Flair 1022
FL-217	Standing At The Crossroads	Flair 1057, Kent 433
MM 2285	Wild About You	–
MM 2286	Long Tall Woman	–

Add unk. tpt; bar;

FL-162	Make My Dreams Come True	Flair 1031
FL-182	Sho'Nuff I Do	Flair 1039
FL-183	1839 Blues	–
FL-200	Dark And Dreary	Flair 1048, Crown CLP 5168
FL-201	Rock My Baby Right	–
FL-225	Late Hours at Midnight	Flair 1062
FL-226	The Way You Treat Me (Mean And Evil)	– , Crown CLP 5168
FL-240	Happy Home	Flair 1069, Crown CLP 5168, Kent 331, 394, Modern 15, United LP 718
FL-241	No Love In My Heart	Flair 1069, Crown CLP 5168

Rhythm only:

FL-147	Please Find My Baby	Flair 1022, Blues Classics 15
FL-161	Hand In Hand	Flair 1031
FL-216	Sunnyland	Flair 1057, Crown CLP 5168, Kent 433, 465

Vcl/gtr. with Johnny Jones, pno; Homesick James, gtr; Odie Payne, dms. Vcl.gtp (-1).

FL-250	Dust My Blues	Flair 1074, Crown CLP 5168, Kent 331, 394, Modern 15, United LP 718
FL 251	I Was A Fool	Flair 1074, Crown CLP 5168

FL-260	Blues Before Sunrise	Flair 1079 Crown CLP 5168
FL-261	Goodbye Baby -1	− −
		Kent 465.

Note: Crown CLP 5168 reissued on Custom LP 1054 and United LP 716.

ELOMORE JAMES & HIS BROOMDUSTERS
Vcl/gtr. with J. T. Brown, ten; Johnny Jones, pno; gtr; dms.

Chicago, 1957

C 2402, 57-699	The Twelve Year Old Boy	Chief 7001, Vee Jay 249
C 2403, 57-700	Coming Home	− −
C 2404, 57-741	It Hurts Me Too	Chief 7004, Vee Jay 259
C 2405		
C 2406, 57-740	Elmore's Contribution to Jazz	Chief 7004, Vee Jay 159

Vcl/gtr. with J. T. Brown, ten; Johnny Jones, pno; Eddie Taylor, gtr; dms.

| 12406, 25-117 | Cry For Me Baby | Chief 7006, Vee Jay 269, USA 815, S&M 101, M-Pac 7231 |
| 12407, 25-118 | Take Me Where You Go | issues as above |

ELMORE JAMES
Vcl/gtr. with J. T. Brown, ten; Johnny Jones, pno. Homesick James, gtr;

Chicago, 1959

U 10109. 35261	I Can't Hold Out	Chess 1756
U 10110, 35261X	The Sun Is Shining	−
	The Sun Is Shining (alt. take)	Argo LP 4034
	Stormy Monday Blues/Madison Blues	unissued

ELMORE JAMES & HIS BROOMDUSTERS
Vcl/gtr. with J. T. Brown & others, saxes; Johnny Jones, pno; Homesick James, gtr; dms.

Chicago, 1959

FM 123	Make My Dreams Come True -1	Fire 1011, Sphere Sound 7002, 7008, Mercury LP 20826
FM 124	Bobby's Rock	Fire 1011, Shpere Sound 7002
FM 133, 6431	The Sky Is Crying	Fire 1016, Flashback 15, Sphere Sound 7002
FM 134	Held My Baby Last Night	Fire 1016, Sphere Sound 7002

Note -1 Aurally this is the same take as on Flair 1031.

ELMORE JAMES
Vcl/gtr. with J. T. Brown, ten; Johnny Jones, pno; gtr; dms. Chicago, 1960

| 25-139 | Calling The Blues -1 | Chief 7020 |
| 25-154 | Knocking At Your Door | − |

Note: -1 This is not by James at all, but by Junior Wells with Earl Hooker.

ELMO JAMES
Vcl/gtr. with saxes,pno; Homesick James or Spruce Johnson, gtr; bs; dms.

New York City, 1961

FM-151	Rollin' And Tumblin'	Fire 1023, Sphere Sound 7002
FM-152	I'm Worried	− −
FM-165	Done Somebody Wrong	Fire 1031, −
FM-166	Fine Little Mama	− −
	Pickin' The Blues	Enjoy 2015

ELMORE JAMES
Vcl/gtr. with Sammy Myers, hca (-1); pno; Homesick James, gtr; dms.

Jackson, Miss. 1961

| FM-193 | Look On Yonder Wall -1 | Fire 504, Enjoy 2022, Sphere Sound 708, 7008 |

| FM-194, 6516 | Shake Your Moneymaker | Fire 504, Enjoy 2022, Sphere Sound 708, 7008 |

Vcl/gtr. with Danny Moore, tpt; saxes; Johnny Acey, pno; Riff Ruffin, gtr; Paul Williams, bs; ? Williams, dms.   New York City, 1962

FM 301	Stranger Blues	Fire 1503
FM 302	Anna Lee	–
ZTSP 98-718, 6326	(My) Bleeding Heart	Enjoy 2015, Sphere Sound 702, 700
6432	Standing At The Crossroads	Enjoy 2020, Sphere Sound 7002
	Dust My Broom	Flashback 15, Sphere Sound 702, 7002

From unknown Fire sessions:

	It Hurts Me Too	Enjoy 2015
ZTSP 105797	Mean Mistreater Mama	Enjoy 2020
EN 34578	Everyday I Have The Blues	Enjoy 2027
EN 34579	Dust My Broom	–

Add saxes; bs:

6327	One Way Out	Sphere Sound 702, 7002
	I Can't Stop Loving You	Sphere Sound 7002
6517	I Need You	Sphere Sound 708, 7008
	Got To Move	Sphere Sound 7008
	Something Inside Of Me	–
	Strange Angels	–
	Early One Morning	Sphere Sound 7008
	She Done Moved	–
	Baby Please Set A Date	–

Note: The following is the correct session data for one Flair date. See also previous details   Chicago, April 1, 1956

Make My Dreams Come True (7 takes)	Flair 1031 (take 7)
Strange Kinda Feeling (6 takes)	Flair 1042 (take 6)
Dark And Dreary (5 takes)	Flair 1048 (take 4)
So Mean To Me (4 takes)	unissued
Wild About You (22 takes)	Mod. 983 (take 4)
Untitled Instrumental (4 takes)	unissued
Long Tall Woman (2 takes)	Mod. 983 (take 2)

Session commenced 6.30 p.m. at United Studio. Supervision by Joe Bihari.

JESSE JAMES

SUNNY JAMES

Vcl/gtr. with Thunder Smith, pno; Luther Stoneham, gtr.   Houston, 1948

| DT 20010A | Please Mam Forgive Me | Down Town 2010 |
| DT 20010B | Excuse Me Baby | – |

JESSE JAMES

Vcl/gtr. with Willie Johnson pno; Donald Cooks, bs;   Houston, 1951

| 2223 | Forgive Me Blues | SIW 569 |
| 2224 | Corrina's Boogie | – |

Note: No connection with any other Jesse James on record.

SKIP JAMES

Born Benotonia, Mississippi on June, 9, 1902
Vcl/gtr.   Falls Church, Va. 1964

Hard Time Killing Floor Blues	Melodeon 7321
Sickbed Blues	–
Washington D.C. Hospital Centre Blues	–
Devil Got My Woman	–
Illinois Blues	–
I Don't Want No Woman To Stay Out All Night Long	–
Cherry Ball Blues	–
All Night Long	–

161

Vcl/pno(-1)/gtr(-2)		Boston, November 1964
L-756A	Four O'Clock Blues -1	Herwin 92402
L-757A	Drunken Spree -2	Herwin 92403
L-758A	Illinois Blues -2	–
L-764A	How Long Blues -1	Herwin 92402
Vcl/pno/gtr. with Russ Savakus, bs (-1)		New York City, 1965
	Hard Time Killing Floor Blues	Vanguard VRS 9219
	Crow Jane	–
	Washington D. C. Hospital Centre Blues	–
	Special Rider Blues	–
	Drunken Spree	–
	Cherry Ball	–
	How Long -1	–
	All Night Long	–
	My Gal	–
	Cypress Grove	–
	I'm So Glad	–
	Look Down The Road	–
Vcl/gtr.		New York City, November 24/ 27, 1966
	Devil Got My Woman	Verve Folkways FTS-3010

SUNNY JAMES

See under Jesse James

ULYSSES JAMES

Vcl/gtr. with ten; pno; bs; dms.		Oakland, 1948
133	Poor Boy	Cava-Tone 250
	(rev. by Lowell Fulson)	

JAMIN' JIM

See under Carolina Slim

JELLY BELLY

See under Alec Seward

BO BO JENKINS

Real name J. P. Jenkins. Born in Arkansas in 1917.
Vcl/gtr. with Robert Richard, hca; Albert Witherspoon, gtr; Harry Fleming, dms.

		Detroit, 1954
U 7614	Democrat Blues	Chess 1565, Blues Classics BC-6
U 7615	Bad Luck And Trouble	

Vcl/gtr. with Willie Johnson, Eddie Taylor, gtrs; unk. dms.

		Chicago, 1955
BX 307A	Nothing But Love	Boxer 202, Duchess 101
BX 307B	Tell Me Who	– –

Vcl/gtr. with Robert Richard, hca; unk. pno; gtr; Ted Walker, dms.

		Detroit, 1956
F 127	Baby Don't You Want To Go	Fortune 838, Blues Classics BC-12
F 128	Ten Below Zero	–

Note: 45 rpm version of above features alternate takes of both sides.

Vcl/gtr. with Walter Cox, pno; unk. gtr; dms.

		Detroit, c. 1964
CP 4535	You Will Never Understand	Big Star 001
CP 4536	Tell Me Where You Stayed Last Night	–

ESSIE JENKINS

Vcl/pno.		Berkeley, March 17, 1962
	Influenza Blues	Arhoolie F 1018

162

GUS JENKINS

LITTLE TEMPLE & HIS "88"
Vcl/pno. with hca; Dave ? gtr; bs; dms   Los Angeles, 1954

SP 475	I Ate The Wrong Part	Specialty 475
XSP 475	Cold Love (no gtr)	–

THE YOUNG WOLF
Vcl(-1)/pno. with saxes(-2); poss. Frank Patt, vcl(-3)/gtr; bs; dms.

2897	Worries And Troubles -3	Combo 88
2898	I Tried -1, 2	Combo 88

     Note: Matrices reported also as 2894, 2896 on above.

GUS JINKINS
Pno. with saxes; prob. Frank Patt, Vcl(-1)/gtr. bs; dms.   Los Angeles 1956

A	You Told Me -1	Flash 115
B	Tricky	–

GUS JINKINS
Vcl/pno. (-1) with saxes; gtr; bs; dms. bongo; castinets (-2)

A	I Remember Last Xmas	Flash 116
A	So What	–
B	Spark Plug	–

same.   Los Angeles 1957/58

A	Pay Day Shuffle Part 1	Flash 123
B	Pay Day Shuffle Part 2	–

Add bongo, omit saxes; gtr(-1)

A	Stand By Me	Flash 126
B	Copper Tan -1	–
E 2024	Hit The Road	Flash 128
E 2025	Road Runner	–

Mamie Perry, vcl (-1); tpt; alt; ten; bari; Gus Jenkins, pno; gtr; bs; dms.

E 2556	I'm Hurted -1	Flash 130
E 2557	My Baby Waited Too Long -1	–
E 2558	Slow Down	Flash 131
E 2559	Drift On	–

Vcl/pno. with tpt; saxes; gtr; bs; dms.   Los Angeles, 1959/60

A	Spanky	Pioneer 101
B	Gonna Take Time	–
A	Cuttin' Out	Pioneer 103
B	Signin' On	–

Same   Los Angeles, 1961/62

	You Made Me	Pioneer 1006
	Vine Street Shuffle	–

BLUES SLIM
Same

A	Let's Talk It Over	Pioneer 1007
B	Tell The Truth Baby	–

GUS JINKINS
Same

	Jealous Of You Baby	Pioneer 1009
	Off The Road	–
	Too Tough	Pioneer 10011
	Right Messy	–
	Celebrate Part 1	Pioneer 10013
	Celebrate Part 2	–

Add Tuba (-1)'   Los Angeles, 1963

A	The New Tricky	Catalina 711
B	Tuba Twist -1	–

Vcl/pno. with tpt; saxes; gtr; bs-gtr; dms.   Los Angeles, 1964/65
60018   Chittlins   Tower 107, General Artists 1003
60019   You'll Be The One   — —
60055   Frosty   Tower 122
60056   You Used Me   —
G-1001   Right Shakey   General Artists 1001/2, Sar 149
G-1002AA   Don't Get Sassy   General Artists 1001/2, Sar 149

Note: Complete discography included as good blues sides mixed throughout.

ROBERT JENKINS

Gtr. with hca(-1); gtr; dms.   Chicago, 1950
P 105   Steelin' Boogie Pt. 1   Parkway 103
P 106   Steelin' Boogie Pt. 2 -1   —

WILBERT JENKINS

Born New Orleans ?
Vcl/gtr. with Press Thomas, hca; Tommy Allen, gtr.   Chicago, 1964
Married Woman Blues   Testament T-2203
Crawling King Snake   —

JESSE & BUZZY

See under Jesse Perkins

JIMMY & WALTER

See under Jimmy DeBerry

GUS JINKINS

See under Gus Jenkins

BILL JOHNSON & HIS STIRCATS

See under Willie Johnson

BLIND BOY JOHNSON

See Under Jack Dupree.

CONRAD JOHNSON

Born Victoria, Texas on November 15, 1915.

CONRAD JOHNSON
Alt. with Jimmy Vincent, tpt; Sam Williams, ten; Ed Harris, bari; unk. pno; gtr; bs; dms;
ensemble vcl.   Houston, 1947
A   Howling On Dowling   Gold Star 622
B   Fisherman Blues   —

CONNIE'S COMBO
Similar: Houston, 1948
ACA 1062   Ugly Mae   Freedom 1508
ACA 1063   Shout It Out   —

See also L. C. Williams.

HARRY "SLICK" JOHNSON

Vcl. with   Houston, 1951
ACA 1829   Goodbye, Blues, Goodbye   unissued
ACA 1830   No One Can Take Your Place   Peacock 1560
ACA 1831   She's My Weakness   unissued
ACA 1832   My Baby's Coming Home   Peacock 1560
ACA 1833   Medium Baby Blues   unissued
ACA 1834   Tired of Travelin'   unissued

164

ACA 1948	45 Blues	unissued
ACA 1949	Your Time Is Out	unissued
ACA 1950	Heartbreaker	unissued
ACA 1951	You'll Need A Friend	unissued
ACA 1974	Trouble Is Hard	unissued
ACA 1975	The Old Roof Rocker	unissued
ACA 1976	Tired of Being Alone	unissued

HENRY JOHNSON

See under Big Bill Broonzy.

JOE JOHNSON

Vcl/gtr. with pno; gtr; bs; dms.　　　　　　　　　　Crowley, La., late 1966
| A | Santa Bring My Baby Back | A-Bet 9417 |
| B | Dirty Woman Blues | – |

JOSEPH "CHINAMAN" JOHNSON

Vcl. with W. D. Alexander, Mack Maze, Arthur Sherrod, L. Z. Lee, Jesse Lee Warren, vcls.

Ellis Farm, Texas, 1951

Move Along 'Gator　　　　　　　　　　　　Elektra EKL-296
Just Like A Tree Planted By The Water　　　Elektra EKL-296

Vcl. with R. G. Williams Group, vcls.　　　　Ramsey Farm, Texas, March 17, 1951

Shake It Mr. Gator　　　　　　　　　　　　"77" LA 12/3

LARRY JOHNSON

Vcl/gtr.　　　　　　　　　　　　　　　　　New York City, 1966
| BS-1 | Catfish Blues | Blue Soul 100 |
| BS-2 | So Sweet | – |

Vcl/gtr. with Hank Adkins, gtr.　　　　　　New York City, 1966
	Four Women Blues	Prestige 7472
	The Captain Don't 'Low Me Here	–
	Tell You Women 'Bout Me	–
	Watch Dog Blues	–
	Death Call	–
	Two Gun Green	–
	When I'm Drinking	–
	Whiskey Store Blues	–
	If You Don't Want Me Baby	–
	My Gal Ain't Fat	–
	Country Road Blues	–
	Take These Blues Off My Mind	–

LEROY JOHNSON

LEROY "COUNTRY" JOHNSON
Vcl/gtr. with Louis "Nunu" Pitts, bs.　　　Houston, 1949
| 1064 (ACA) | No One To Love Me | Freedom 1509 |
| 1065 (ACA) | Loghouse On The Hill | – |

LEROY JOHNSON
Vcl/gtr. with tpt; 2 saxes; pno; bs; dms.　New York City, June 29, 1951
CO-46460	Unlucky Blues	Okeh 6813
CO-46461		
CO-46462	Home Town Woman	Okeh 6813

LONNIE JOHNSON (see also in APPENDIX)

Born New Orleans, La. on February 8, 1889.
Vcl/gtr. with Blind John Davis, pno; Ransom Knowling, bs.　Chicago, December 14, 1944
| D4-AB-328 | Some Day Baby | Bluebird 34-0732 |
| D4-AB-329 | My Love Is Down | Bluebird 34-0742, Victor 20-1890, 22-0116 |

| D4-AB-330 | The Victim Of Love | Bluebird 34-0742 |
| D4-AB-331 | Watch Shorty | Bluebird 34-0732, Victor 20-3165 |

Vcl/gtr. with Blind John Davis, pno; Omit Davis (−1). No vcl (−2).

New York City, July 15, 1946

D 484	My Last Love	Disc 5061
D 485	Keep What You Got	Disc 5062
D 486	Solid Blues	Disc 5063, 710, Arco 1227
D 487	I'm In Love With You	Disc 5060, Arco 1227
D 488	Drifting Along Blues	Disc 5064, 710, Holiday 5001, Asch LP 2 1/2
D 489	How Could You Be So Mean	Disc 5061
D 490	Why I Love You	Disc 5062
D 491	Tell Me Why	Disc 5060
D 492	Rocks In My Bed -1	Disc 5063, 710
D 493	Blues For Everybody -2	Disc 5065, −
D 494	In Love Again -1	Disc 5064, − , Holiday 5001
D 495	Blues In My Soul -2	Disc 5065, −

Vcl/gtr. with poss. Blind John Davis, pno; bs.

		Chicago, June 2, 1947
	How Could You	Aladdin 197, Score 4005
	Love Is The Answer	− −
	Blues For Lonnie	Aladdin 3029
	Don't Blame Her	−
	You Know I Do	Aladdin 3047
	Your Last Time Out	−

Vcl/gtr. with John Hughes, pno; Roy Coulter, bs.

Cincinnati, Dec. 10/11/14, 1947

5310-1	I Am So Glad	King 4212
5311-1	What A Woman	King 4201
5312-	Happy New Year Darling	King 4251, 4492
5313-1	Tomorrow Night	King 4201, 4758, LP 520, Bethlehem LP 6071
5323	Friendless Blues	Federal 12376
5334	My Baby's Gone	unissued
5335	I Want My Baby	King 4225
5336	What A Real Woman	Federal 12376
5337	Love That Gal	unissued
5338	It's Been So Long	King LP 520
5339	Be Sweet To Me	Parlophone 8663
5340	(by The Ravens)	
5341	Don't Be No Fool	unissued

Vcl/gtr. with Allen Smith, pno; Monte Morrison, bs.

		same date
5350	Falling Rain Blues	King 4450
5351		
5352		
5353-2	Drunk Again	King 4388, LP 520, 859
5374	Jelly Roll Baker	King 4388, LP 520
5445-1	Working Man's Blues	King 4212, LP 520
5446	Chicago Blues	unissued
5447	Lazy Woman	unissued
5448	In Love Again	King 4225

Vcl/gtr. with Herman Smith, pno; Monte Morrison, bs.

		Cincinnati, August 13, 1948
5547	Pleasing You	King 4245, 4758, LP 520
5548	Good Night Darling	King 4450
5549	Feel So Lonesome	King 4245
5550	It's Too Late To Cry	unissued
5551	You're Mine You	King 4278
5552	I Know It's Love	King 4261
5553	Baby Ain't I Loving You	unissued
5554	Tell Me Little Woman	King 4263
5555	Call Me Darling	King LP 520
5556	Tomorrow	−
5557	Lonesome Road	−

5558	So Tired	King LP 520
5559	Backwater Blues	King 4251, LP 520
5560	Careless Love	King LP 520
5575	Bewildered	King 4261

Same: Cincinnati, November 19, 1948

5580	So Tired	King 4263
5581	My My Baby	King 4278

Vcl/gtr. with Frank Payne, pno; Earl Monroe Wood, gtr; Edwyn Conley, bs.

Cincinnati, April 8, 1949

5720	I Found A Dream	King 4297
5721	Don't Play Bad With My Love	King 4317
5722		

Vcl/gtr. with Frank Payne, pno; Jerry Lane, gtr; Edwyn Conley, bs.

Cincinnati, April 9, 1949

5723	You Take Romance	King 4297
5724	She's So Sweet	King 4317

Vcl/gtr. with Simeon Hatch, pno; Franklyn Skeete, bs; Leon Abramson, dms.

Cincinnati, November 29, 1949

5803	Troubles Ain't Nothing But The Blues	King 4346
5804	Confused	King 4336
5805	I'm So Afraid	King 4346
5806	Blues Stay Away From Me	King 4336

Vcl/gtr. with Simeon Hatch, pno; Paul Parks, bs; Nelson Burton, dms.

Cincinnati, September 14, 1950

5955	I'm So Crazy For Love	King 4411
5956	Nobody's Lovin' Me	King 4432
5957-2	Little Rockin' Chair	King 4423
5958	Nothin' Clickin' Chicken	King 4411

Same: Cincinnati, September 20, 1950

5959	Nothing But Trouble	King 4432
5960		
5961-2	When I'm Gone (Will It Still Be Me)	King 4423
5962	What Have I Got Pretty Baby	unissued

Vcl/gtr. with Ray Felder, ten; Eddie Smith, Tommy Smith, Willie Wilkins, pno; bs; dms.
in unk. order. Cincinnati, February 26, 1951

9024	Why Should I Cry	King 4459
9025-1	It Was All In Vain	King 4473
9026-1	You Only Want Me When You're Lonely	—
9027	Tell Me I'm Yours	King 4459

Vcl/gtr. with Red Prysock, ten; Jimmy Robinson, pno; Clarence Mack, bs; Calvin Shields, dms.
Cincinnati, October 26, 1951

9092	Darlin'	King 4503
9093	My Mother's Eyes	King 4510
9094	Me And My Crazy Self	—
9095	Seven Long Days	King 4503

Vcl/gtr. with Charlie Hooks, tpt; Holley Dismukes, alt; Louie Stephens, ten; Teddy Buckner, bari;
Todd Rhodes, pno; Joe Williams, bs; Bill Benjamin, dms. Cincinnati, June 3, 1952

9144	I'm Guilty	King 4553
9145-1	Just Another Day	King 4572
9146-1	You Can't Buy Love	—
9147	Can't Sleep Any More	King 4553

No details:

	Tomorrow Night	Parade 110
	(rev. by George Dawson's Chocolateers)	
	Lonesome Day Blues	Paradise 123
	Tell Me Baby	—

Vcl/gtr. with ten; pno; bs; dms. 1956

RR-18	Don't Make Me Cry Baby	Rama 9
RR-19	My Woman Is Gone	
	This Love Of Mine	Rama 20
	I Love A Dream	—

RR-29

167

RR-29	Will You Remember	Rama 14
RR-30	Stick With It Baby (no pno.)	–

Vcl/gtr. with Hal Singer, ten; Claude Hopkins, pno; Wendell Marshall, bs; Bobby Donaldson, dms.   Englewood Cliffs, March 8, 1960

126	Don't Ever Love	Bluesville BVLP 1007, 806
127	Big Leg Woman	–
128	No Love For Sale	–
129	She Devil	–
130	One Sided Love Affair	–
131	Blues Around My Door	–
132	You Will Need Me	–
133	There Must Be A Way	–
134	I Don't Hurt Any More	–
135	There's No Love	–
136	She's Drunk Again	–
137	You Don't Move Me	, 806

Vcl/gtr. with Elmer Snowden, gtr; Wendell Marshall, bs.   Englewood Cliffs, May 16, 1960

138	Haunted House	Bluesville BVLP 1011
139	Memories Of You	– , 812
140	I'll Get Along Somehow	– , –
141	I Found A Dream	–
142	St. Louis Blues	–
143	Backwater Blues	–
144	Jelly Roll Baker	– , 1055
145	Savoy Blues	–
146	Blues For Chris	–
147	Elmer's Blues	–

Vcl/gtr/pno (–1).

	New Orleans Blues	Bluesville BVLP 1024
	My Little Kitten Susie	–
	Evil Woman -1	–
	What A Difference A Day Makes	–
	Moaning Blues	–
	Summertime	–
	Lines In My Face	–
	Losing Game	–
	New Year's Blues	–
	Slow And Easy	–
	Four Walls And Me	–
	You Won't Let Me Go	–

Vcl (–1)/gtr. with Victoria Spivey, vcl (–2)/pno (–3); Cliff Jackson, pno.
Englewood Cliffs, July 13, 1961

270	Long Time Blues -2	Bluesville BVLP 1044
271	Idle Hours -2	–
272	Leave Me Or Love Me -1	–
273	Darling I Miss You So	–
274	Please Baby -1	–
275	End It All -1	–
276	Good Luck Darling -1	–
277	You Are My Life -1	–
278	Oh Yes, Baby -1	–
279	No More Cryin' -1	–
280	You Have No Love In Your Heart -1	–
281	I Got The Blues So Bad -2, 3	–

Vcl/gtr.

	Another Night To Cry	Bluesville BVLP 1062
	I Got News For You Baby	–
	Blues After Hours	–
	You Didn't Mean What You Said	–
	Fine Booze And Heavy Dues	–
	I've Got To Get Rid Of You	–
	Bow-Legged Baby	–
	Make Love To Me Baby	–

	Lots Of Loving	Bluesville BVLP 1062
	A Story About Barbara	–
	Goodbye Kitten	–
Vcl/gtr.		
	Johnson Swings	Xtra 1037
	Some Day Baby	–
	Lonesome Road	–
	When You're Feeling Low Down	–
	I Ain't Gonna Be Your Fool	–
	Get Yourself Together	–
	Roamin' Rambler	–
	The Last Call	–
	My Love Is Down	–
	Nuts About That Gal	–
	Fly Right Baby	–
	Swingin' The Blues	–
Vcl/gtr.		New York City, c. 1963
	Stick By Me Baby	Spivey LP 1004
	Stop Talking	–
	Four Shots Of Gin	–
	Mr. Johnson's Guitar Talks	–
Vcl/gtr.		Bremen, October 13, 1963
	It's Too Late To Cry	Fontana TL 5204
Vcl/gtr. with Otis Spann, pno.		Copenhagen, October 16, 1963
	Tomorrow Night	Storyville SLP 162
	Clementine Blues	–
	See See Rider	–
	Raining On The Cold Cold Ground	–
	Too Late To Cry	–
	Call Me Darling (no pno.)	–
	Why Did You Go	–
	Swingin' With Lonnie	–
	Please Help Me	
	My Baby Is Gone	Storyville SLP 166
	You Don't Know What Love Is	–
	Don't Cry Baby	Storyville SEP 415, SLP 188

Vcl/gtr. with Little Brother Montgomery, pno; Sonny Greer, dms.

		New York City, April/June, 1965
	My Baby Isn't Here	Spivey LP 1006

MEAT HEAD JOHNSON

See under Jack Dupree.

RAY JOHNSON

No details: c. 1952

	House Of Blues	Mercury 70203
	I'll Never Let You Go	–
	Boogin' The Blues	Mercury 70231
	Smilin' Blues	–

Note: Is this Red Johnson?

RED JOHNSON

No details: c. 1952

YB 9349	West Coast Blues	Mercury 70141
YB 9402	Mama Does The Boogie	– , 70194
	On My Way To California	Mercury 70194

ROCKHEART JOHNSON

Vcl. with unk. hca; Jeanne Jamerson, pno; George Callendar, bs; E. J. Harper, dms.

		Los Angeles? July 22, 1952
E2-VB-5395	Black Spider	Victor 20-5136
E2-VB-5396	Evilest Woman In Town	Victor 20-4967
E2-VB-5397	Midnight Rambler	Victor 20-5136
E2-VB-5398	Rockheart's Blues	Victor 20-4967

SAM (SUITCASE) JOHNSON

Vcl/gtr.

		Houston, 1951
2362	Sam's Coming Home	SIW 608
2363	Sam's Boogie	–

SHERMAN JOHNSON

Vcl/pno. with

		Nashville, 1951
A	Back Alley Boogie	Nashboro 507
B	Nashville After Midnigh.	–

Vcl/pno. with

		Jackson, 1952
ACA 2135	Saving My Love	unissued
no mx	Married Man Blues	unissued
no mx	Annie Ruth	unissued
no mx	Country Girl	unissued
no mx	Sooner Or Later	unissued

SHERMAN JOHNSON & HIS CLOUDS OF JOY

Vcl/pno. with ten; gtr; bs; dms.

		Jackson, 1953
DRC-134	Pretty Baby Blues	Trumpet 189
DRC-135	Sugar Mama	–
DRC-136	Hot Fish	Trumpet 190
DRC-137, ACA 2353		
	Lost In Korea	–

Note: Resident of Meridian, Mississippi.

SONNY BOY JOHNSON

Vcl/hca. with 2 gtrs.

		Los Angeles, 1947
TV 301A	Quinsella	Miltone 301, Gotham 511

SONNY BOY JOHNSON & HIS BLUE BLAZERS
Vcl/hca. with Beverley Scott, Ernest McClay, gtrs; Dig Moore, pno;

		Los Angeles, 1948
A	Come And Go With Me	Murray 505
B	Come And Go With Me	–
A	Swimming Pool Blues	Murray 507, Blues Classics BC-14
B	I'm Drinking My Last Drink	Murray 507

Note: Gotham 511 issued as by Wright Holmes. Miltone 301 not yet traced. Murray 505 issued with same label on each side. Title is correct for Side B only.

TOM JOHNSON

See under Mississippi String Band.

TYLER JOHNSON

See under Moochie Reeves.

WILLIE JOHNSON

THE GROOVY TRIO ON GROOVY OR BILL JOHNSON ON IMPERIAL
Vcl/pno. with bs; dms.   Houston, 1949
ACA 1392, IM 338

	Too Late Baby	Groovy 101, Imperial 5148
ACA 1393, IM 337		
	Squeeze My Baby	– –

170

THE GROOVY FIVE
Vcl/pno. with ten; gtr; bs; dms.   Houston, 1950

ACA 1515	Sinkin' Blues	Groovy unissued
ACA 1516	End Of Be Bop	–
ACA 1619	Lost Baby	Groovy 103
ACA 1620	Wrong Love Blues	–
ACA 1621	Jeff's Boogie	unissued
ACA 1622	Strange, Strange Woman	unissued
ACA 1623	Lonesome Blues	unissued
ACA 1624	Please Me Baby	unissued

WILLIE JOHNSON
Pno. with Henry Hayes, alt; Ed Wiley, ten; Donald Cooks, bs; Ben Turner, dms.

2059	Sampson Street Boogie	SIW 570

BILL JOHNSON
Vcl/pno. with ten; gtr; bs; dms.   Houston, 1951

ACA 1699	Bill's Boogie	Groovy unissued
ACA 1700	Worried Blues	–
ACA 1838	Sad And Blue	Lucky 7 unissued
ACA 1901	Rocket 88	Lucky 7 unissued
ACA 1902	Changing Blues	–
ACA 1903, IM 340	I'm So Happy	Imperial 5163
IM 339	Tears Come Falling Down	–

WILLIE JOHNSON
Hubert Robinson, vcl (–1); Slim Reese, vcl (–2); Henry Hayes, alt; Ed Wiley, ten; Goree
Carter, gtr; Donald Cooks, bs; Ben Turner, dms.

2209	Boogie In Blues	Jade 201
2213	Got The Boogie Woogie Blues -1	SIW 570
2219	Weeping Little Woman	Jade 201
2269	That Boy's Boogie	Jade 209
2270	Shout It Out -2	–

Vcl/pno. with Thelma, vcl (–1); saxes; gtr; bs; dms.   Houston, 1952

SWJ 4288	Here Comes My Baby -1	Savoy 881
SWJ 4289	Sometimes I Wonder Why	Savoy 894
SWJ 4290	Love Me Till Dawn	–
SWJ 4291	Don't Tell Mama -1	Savoy 881

      Note: Band on Savoy session is probably Henry Hayes 4 Kings.

Similar: Houston, 1954

	That Night	Specialty 493
	Say Baby	–

BIRMINGHAM JONES

Vcl/hca. with 2 tens; pno; 2 gtrs; bs–gtr; dms.   Chicago, 1965

	I'm Glad	Vivid unissued
	Drinking Again	–
	Birmingham Bounce	–
	Chills And Fever	–

CURTIS JONES

Born Naples, Texas on August 18, 1906.
Vcl/pno. with Lorenzo King, ten; L. C. McKinley, gtr; Alfred Elkins, bs; Judge Riley, dms.

                                      Chicago, 1953

U 2570	Wrong Blues	Parrot 782
U 2571	Cool Playing Blues	–

Vcl/pno. with Robert Banks, org; Johnny "Moose John" Walker, gtr (–1); Leonard Gaskin,
bs; Belton Evans, dms.   New York, November 9, 1960

	Lonesome Bedroom Blues	Bluesville BVLP 1022
	A Whole Lot Of Talk For You -1	–
	Suicide Blues -1	–
	Please Say Yes (no org.)	–
	Weekend Blues -1	–

	Good Woman Blues -1	Bluesville BVLP 1022
	Trouble Blues	–
	Love Season	–
	Low Down Worried Blues	–
	Good Time Special	–
	Fool Blues -1	–

Vcl/pno.   Chicago, January 12, 1962

	Lonesome Bedroom Blues	Delmark DL-605
	Highway 51	–
	Stackolee	–
	She's Got Good Business	unissued
	Tin Pan Alley	Delmark DL-605
	Curtis Jones Boogie Woogie	–

Same: Chicago, January 28, 1962

	Evil Curse Blues	Delmark DL-605
	Black Magic Blues	–
	Tour Blues	–
	Gut Bucket Blues	–
	Love Fake Blues	–
	Gut Bucket Blues	unissued
	Runnin' The Blues	Delmark DL-605

Vcl/pno. with Bob Carter, bs; Joe Harris, dms.   Koblenz, January 3, 1963
| | Lots Of Talk For You | Impulse LP 1037 |

Vcl/pno. with Alexis Korner, gtr (−1); Jack Fallon, bs; Eddie Taylor, dms.
                                                                   London, November 27/8, 1963

DR. 32316	Shake It Baby -1	Decca LK 4587, 4681
DR. 32317	Lonesome Bedroom Blues -1	–
DR. 32318	Dust My Broom -1	–
DR. 32319	Good Woman Blues -1	–
DR. 32320	Young Generation Boogie (omit bs.)	–
DR. 32321	Alley Bound Blues	–
DR. 32322	Don't Leave Me Baby	unissued
DR. 32323	Syl-Vous Play Blues	Decca LK 4587

Vcl/pno/gtr (−1).
DR. 32324	Roll Me Over	Ace Of Clubs ACL 1220
DR. 32325	Curtis Jones Boogie	Decca LK 4587
DR. 32326	Please Send Me Someone To Love	–
DR. 32327	Jinney	unissued
DR. 32328	The Honeydripper	Decca LK 4587
DR. 32329	Red River Blues -1	–
DR. 32330	Skid Row -1	–
DR. 32331	You Got Good Business	Ace Of Clubs ACL 1220

DOC JONES

See under Willie "Doc" Jones.

EDDIE JONES

Born Greenwood, Mississippi on 10 December, 1926. Died New York City on February 7, 1959.

EDDIE JONES & HIS PLAYBOYS – on 5134

GUITAR SLIM – on 5278, 5310
Vcl/gtr. with pno; bs; dms.   New Orleans, 1951
IM 299	Bad Luck Is On Me (Woman Troubles)	Imperial 5134, 5278
IM 300	New Arrival	– , 5310
IM 301	Standin' At The Station	Imperial 5310
IM 302	Cryin' In The Mornin'	Imperial 5278

EDDIE (GUITAR SLIM) JONES
Vcl/gtr (−1), with alt; ten; pno; bs; dms; vcl. grp (−1).   Nashville, 1952
| Nash-3 | Feelin' Sad | Jim Bullet 603 |
| Nash-4 | Certainly All -1 | – |

GUITAR SLIM & HIS BAND

Vcl/gtr. with tpt; prob. Lee Allen, ten; Alvin Tyler, ten/bars; Ray Charles, pno; Frank Fields, bs; Earl Palmer, dms.　　　　　　　　　　　　　　New Orleans, 1954/56

XSP-482	The Things That I Used To Do	Specialty 482
SP-482	Well I Done Got Over It	–
XSP-490	The Story Of My Life	Specialty 490
SP-490	A Letter To My Girlfriend	--
XSP-527	Later For You Baby	Specialty 527
SP-527	Trouble Don't Last	–
XSP-536	Sufferin' Mind	Specialty 536
SP-536	Twenty Five Lies	–
XSP-542	Our Only Child	Specialty 542
SP-542	Stand By Me	–
XSP-551	I Got Sumphin' For You	Specialty 551
SP-551	You're Gonna Miss Me	–

Vcl/gtr. with similar:

XSP-557	Quicksand	Specialty 557
SP-557	Think It Over	–
XSP-569	Sum'thin' To Remember You By	Specialty 569
SP-569	You Give Me Nothin' But The Blues	–

Vcl/gtr. with brass; pno; bs; dms.　　　　　　　　　　　New York City, 1956

S 1935	Down Through The Years	Atco 6072
S 1936	Oh Yeah!	–

same:　　　　　　　　　　　　　　　　　　　　　　New York City, 1957

57-C-230-12	If I Should Lose You	Atco 6097
57-C-231-11	It Hurts To Love Somebody	–

GUITAR SLIM WITH LLOYD LAMBERT & HIS ORCH.

Vcl. with unk. personnel except Les Spann, gtr.　　　　　New York City, 1957

57-C-307	I Won't Mind At All	Atco 6108
57-C-308	Hello, How You Bin, Goodbye	–

No details:　　　　　　　　　　　　　　　　　　　　New York City, 1958

58-C-346-11	When There's No Way Out	Atco 6120
58-C-347-11	If I Had My Life To Live Over	–

EDDIE "ONE STRING" JONES

Vcl/one-string gtr.　　　　　　　　　　　Los Angeles, February 14, 1960

	"One String Three-Quarter Banjo Picker".	Portents 2
	Rolling And Tumbling Blues	–
	Come Back Baby	–
	I'll Be Your Chauffeur	–
	It's Raining Here	–
	The Dozens	–

FLOYD JONES

Born Marinia, Arkansas on July 21, 1917.
Vcl/gtr. with Snooky Pryor, hca; Moody Jones, bs.　　　Chicago, 1947

M 1312	Stockyard Blues	Marvel ? Old Swingmaster 22
M 1313	Keep What You Got	– –

Note: M 1312 also on Blues Classics BC-8.

Vcl/gtr. with Billy Howell, tpt (–1); Sunnyland Slim, pno; Moody Jones, gtr; Elgar Edmonds, dms.　　　　　　　　　　　　　　　　　　　　　　　　Chicago, 1952

MRS 1001A	Big World -1	JOB 1001
MRS 1001B	Dark Road	– , Blues Classics BC-8

Vcl/gtr. with Little Walter, hca; Jimmy Rogers, gtr; Willie ?, dms.

　　　　　　　　　　　　　　　　　　　　　　　　　Chicago, 1952

F 1006	Dark Road	Chess 1498
F 1007	Big World	–

Vcl/gtr. with Little Walter, hca; dms.　　　　　　　　　Chicago, 1953

U 7480	You Can't Live Long	Chess 1527
U 7481	Early Morning	–

FLOYD JONES & HIS TRIO
Vcl/gtr. with Sunnyland Slim, pno; Moody Jones, gtr; Elgar Edmonds, dms.
Chicago, 1953

U 2365	Skinny Mama	JOB 1013
U 2366		
U 2367	On The Road Again	JOB 1013

Vcl/gtr. with Snooky Pryor, hca; Sunnyland Slim, pno; Eddie Taylor, gtr; Alfred Wallace, dms.
Chicago, February 3, 1955

55-128	Schooldays On My Mind	Vee Jay 111
55-129	Ain't Times Hard	–
55-130	Floyd's Blues	Vee Jay 126
55-131	Any Old Lonesome Day	–

JIMMY JONES & HIS TRIO

Vcl/pno. with gtr; bs; dms.
New York City, 1949

| HOL-109 | Trouble Blues | Holiday 702 |
| HOL-110 | Red Beans And Rice | – |

LITTLE JOHNNY JONES

Born prob. Jackson, Mississippi c. 1924. Died Chicago, November 1964.

LITTLE JOHNNY
Vcl/pno. with Muddy Waters, gtr; Leroy Foster, gtr/bs–dms. Chicago, 1950

| U 7214 | Big Town Playboy | Aristocrat 405 |
| U 7215 | Shelby County Blues | – |

LITTLE JOHNNY JONES WITH THE CHICAGO HOUND DOGS
Vcl/pno. with J. T. Brown, ten; bs; Odie Payne, dms. Chicago, 1953

| FL-121 | Sweet Little Woman (Dirty By The Dozen) | Flair 1010 |
| FL-122 | I May Be Wrong | – |

LITTLE JOHNNY JONES
Vcl/pno. with ten; gtr; dms. Chicago? 1954

A 1336	Hoy, Hoy	Atlantic 1045
A 1337		
A 1338	Doin' The Best I Can	Atlantic 1045

SUNNY JONES

Vcl/gtr.
Baltimore, ?

| 201 | Don't Want Pretty Women | Orchid 1211 |
| 202 | Leaving Home Blues | |

WILLIE JONES

Vcl/gtr. with Joe B. Pugh, hca; Roland Hayes, dms.
Hughes, Ark., 1959
| | You Got Dimples In Your Jaw | Prestige Int. 25005 |

WILLIE "DOC" JONES

No details:
Houston, 1950

ACA 1544	Railroadin' Papa	unissued
ACA 1545	Wolf Song	Peacock 1540
ACA 1546	Doc Gets The Blues	unissued
ACA 1547	Sure Cure For The Blues	unissued
ACA 1548	Do You Want To Roll	Peacock 1540
ACA 1549	Cold Blooded Woman	unissued

Houston, 1951

ACA 1789	Fine As Wine	unissued
ACA 1790	Louise	unissued
ACA 1791	My Baby's Comin' Home	unissued

DOC JONES
No details:
1954

| SDJ 4598 | My Promise | Savoy 1173 |
| SDJ 4599 | I'm Gonna Love And Be Loved | – |

174

WILLIE JORDAN
See under Jack Dupree.

DOC BILL JOSEPH
Vcl. with Lafayette Leake, pno; gtr; bs; dms.   Chicago, 1963
7828   Sittin' Thinkin'   Flyght 911
            (rev. by Chris Haley)
790   How It Hurt Me   Flyght 917
791   I Don't Like It   −

JUNIOR BLUES
No details.   1950
            Whiskey Head Woman   RPM 320
            Young And Good Lookin'   −

K

BOB KELLY & THE BOB KATS
Vcl. with 2 gtrs; dms.   Detroit, 1962
9049   Malinda   Bango 501
9050   She's My Baby   −

ROBERT KELTON & HIS TRIO
Irving Young, vcl. with Rufus J. Russel, pno; Robert Kelton, gtr; Edward W. Wallace, Jnr., bs.
                                                                San Francisco, Feb. 21, 1950
SF 1601   Muddy Shoes   Aladdin 3054
SF 1603   Try Me One More Time   −
SF 1604   No No Baby   Aladdin 3187
SF 1602   Don't Care What You Say   −
            Note: Kelton was Jimmy McCracklin's first guitarist.

KENNY & MOE – THE BLUES BOYS
Vcl. with hca; pno; gtr; bs−gtr; dms.   1956
7049-1   Can't Help Myself   DeLuxe 6101
7050-1   You're Gonna Miss Me When I'm Gone   −

Omit hca;   1957
7107   I'm All Alone   DeLuxe 6122
7108-1   Big Joe   DeLuxe 6134
7109   I Want To Love You   DeLuxe 6122
7110-1   I Sing This Song   DeLuxe 6134
7164   Double Talk Baby   DeLuxe 6154
7165   So Long I'm Gone   −
7166-1   There's Something About You   DeLuxe 6139
7167-1   Yes I will   −

ROBERT KETCHUM

Born Richmond, Texas in 1930
Vcl/pno. with ten; gtr; bs; dms.   Houston, 1953
ACA 2535   Ooh Gee, Ooooh Gee   unissued
ACA 2536   Near To Me   unissued
ACA 2537   Stockade   Peacock 1623
ACA 2538   She's Gone From Me   –

GOZY KILPATRICK

Vcl/hca. with R. C. Forest, gtr.   Houston, March 1959
            Goin' To The River   "77" LA 12/3

KING CHARLES

Left Hand Charlie, vcl. with King Charles, tpt(-1); ten; pno; gtr; bs; dms. .
                                                     Lake Charles, La 1954
1131-1   Bop Cat Stomp -1   Folk Star 1131
1131-2   But You Thrill Me (no ten)   –

KING DAVID

Real name David Crockett.
Vcl/hca.   Chicago, July, 1960
            Fanny Mae   Heritage HLP 1004
            Sugar Mama   –
            Good Mornin', Little Schoolgirl   –
            38 Pistol   –
            44 Blues   –

KING IVORY LEE

Real name Lee Semiens. Born Washington, La. on September, 13, 1931
Vcl. with Henry Hayes ten; Elmore Nixon, pno; O. C. Jackson, gtr; Oscar "Yogi" Adams,
bs; Ben Turner, dms.   Houston, 1954
ACA 2927   Mary Where You Been So Long   Alameda   ?
ACA 2928   Feel I Want To Cry   –
Same: Houston, 1957
ACA 3189   Let Me Get You Told   Alameda   ?
ACA 3190   Mean And Mistreated   –
Vcl/dms. with Henry Hayes, ten; Elmore Nixon, pno; Hop Wilson, gtr; Clarence Green, bs.
                                                     Houston, 1958
ACA 3657   Rockin' In The Cocanut Top   Trey 1003
ACA 3658   Fuss Too Much   –
no mx   I'm So Lonely   unissued
no mx   Ace In The Hole   unissued

IVORY LEE
Vcl/dms. with B. J. Brooks, ten; pno; Little Arch, gtr; bs.   Houston, 1962
LH 1236   Broke And Hungry   Ivory 1-1236
LH 1237   Alley Oop   Ivory 1-1237

KING TUT

Vcl. with Ed Wiley, ten; Henry Hayes, alt; Willie Johnson, pno; Donald Cooks, bs;
Ben Turner dms.   Houston, 1950
            Inquisitive Man   SIW 542
            Lonely Blues   –
2032   Why Did You Leave Me Baby   SIW 550
2053   You've Been Fiddling Around   –

            Note: see also Ed Wiley

AL KING

Vcl. with saxes; pno; gtr; bs; dms.   Los Angeles? 1965

SH-7714	Reconsider Baby	Shirley 117
SH-7715	On My Way	

Note: Guitarist on the Sahara issue is JOHNNY HEARTSMAN.

New York City, 1966

SA 23661	Think Twice Before You Speak	Sahara 111
SA 23662	The Winner	–
SA 49661	My Money Ain't Long Enough	Sahara 113
SA 49662	Blue Shadows	–
SA 910661	Everybody Ain't Your Friend	Sahara 114
SA 910662	This Thing Called Love	–

Note: Credits to Al K. Smith. Guitarist on Shirley is Johnny Heartsman.

ALBERT KING (see also in Appendix)

Born Indianola, Mississippi on April, 25, 1924

Vcl/gtr. with Johnny Jones, pno; gtr; bs; dms.   Chicago, December, 1953

U 53177	Bad Luck Blues	Parrot 798
U 53178	Be On Your Merry Way	

Vcl/gtr. with saxes; Sam Wallace, pno; bs; dms.   St. Louis, 1959

13566-1	Ooh-ee Baby	Bobbin 114, King LP 852
13566-2	Why Are You So Mean To Me	–
13566-1	Need You By My Side	Bobbin 119
13566-2	The Time Has Come	
129-1	I Walked All Night Long	Bobbin 129, King LP 852
129-2	I've Made Nights By Myself	–
143-1	Old Blue Ribbon	Bobbin 143
143-2	I've Made Nights By Myself	

James Vaughan, pno. replaces Wallace.   St. Louis, 1960

14064-A	Let's Have A Natural Ball	Bobbin 126, King LP 852
14064-B	Blues At Sunrise	–

Johnny Johnson, pno; replaces Vaughan.   St. Louis, 1961/2

no mx	I Get Evil	Bobbin 135, King LP 852
no mx.	What Can I Do To Change Your Mind	–
1634-1	I'll Do Anything You Say	Bobbin 141
1634-2	Got To Be Some Changes Made	Bobbin 141
K-10989	Don't Throw Your Love On Me So Strong	King 5575, LP 852
K-10990	This Morning	–
K-10997	Travelin' To California	King 5588, LP 852
K-10998	Dyna Flow	–

Same Add vcl/grp(-1)   St. Louis, 1963

K-11544	Had You Told It Like It Was	King 5751, LP 852
K-11545	This Funny Feeling -1	–
	The Big Blues	King LP 852

Vcl/gtr. with saxes; Don James, org; bs; dms.   East St. Louis, 1965

RK4M 6443	C.O.D.	Coun-tree 1006
RK4M 6444	Lonesome (no saxes)	Coun-tree 1007
RK4M 6445	You Threw Your Love On Me Too Strong	Coun-tree 1006
RK4M 6446	Worsome Baby	Coun-tree 1006

Vcl/gtr. with saxes; Booker T., pno; el-bs; Al Jackson, dms.   Memphis, 1966

STX 10119	Laundromat Blues	Stax 190
STX 10120	Overall Junction	–
STX 10594	Oh Pretty Woman	Stax 197
STX 10595	Funk-shun	–
STX 11128	Crosscut Saw	Stax 201
STX 11129	Down Don't Bother Me	–

B. B. KING (See also in Appendix)

Real name Riley B. King. Born September, 16, 1925 in Itta Bena, Mississippi.

Notes: Due to the many and varied reissues of King's recordings it has been impossible to check everything for alternate takes and retitling.

Vcl/with ten; tbn; Phineas Newborn pno; Tuff Green bs; dms. Memphis, late 1949

A	Miss Martha King	Bullet 309
B	When Your Baby Packs Up And Goes	–
A	Got The Blues	Bullet 315
B	Take A Swing With Me	–

Vcl/gtr. with Willie Mitchell, tpt; Ben Branch, ten; Hank Crawford, alt; Phineas Newborn, pno (-1); Ike Turner, pno (-2); Calvin Newborn, gtr; Tuff Green, bs; Earl Forest or Ted Curry, dms.

Memphis 1950/51

MM 1404	Mistreated Woman -1	RPM 304
MM 1405	B. B. Boogie -1	–
MM 1438-2	The Other Night Blues -1	RPM 311
MM 1439-1	Walkin' And Cryin' -1	–
MM 1469	My Baby's Gone -2	RPM 318
MM 1470	Don't You Want A Man Like Me -2	–
MM 1489	B. B. Blues -2	RPM 323
MM 1490		
MM 1491	Fine Looking Woman -2	RPM 348
MM 1563	She's Dynamite -2	RPM 323
MM 1604	She's A Mean Woman -2	RPM 330
MM 1605	Hard Working Woman -2	–

Same: Phineas Newborn out.   Memphis, 1952

MM 1682	3 O'ClockBlues	RPM 339, Crown 5020, 5238, 5405, Kent 5012, 5027, 339, Modern 9, Galaxy 202.
MM 1683	That Ain't The Way To Do It	RPM 339, Kent 339, Crown 5020
MM 1752	She Don't Love Me No More	RPM 348
MM 1805	Shake It Up And Go	RPM 355
MM 1806	My Own Fault Darling	–
MM 1843	Someday, Somewhere	RPM 360
MM 1844	Gotta Find My Baby	–
MM 1865	You Didn't Want Me	RPM 363
MM 1866	You Know I Love You	– , Crown 5020, Kent 5012, Modern 19

Same   Los Angeles? 1953

MM 1924	Story From My Heart And Soul	RPM 374
MM 1925	Boogie Woogie Woman	– , Crown 5063

Vcl/gtr. with Johnny Ace, pno. and others   Covington, Tenn., 1953

ACA 2398	Remember Me	Peacock unissued
ACA 2399	What A Difference	–
ACA 2400	I Don't Believe It	–
ACA 2401	I Can't Put You Down	–
ACA 2594	I Did Everything I Could	Peacock unissued
ACA 2595	I've learned My Lesson	–
ACA 2596	Come On Baby Take A Swing With Me	–

Vcl/gtr. with Floyd Jones, tpt. George Coleman, alt/ten; Bill Harvey, ten; Connie McBooker, pno; James Walker, bs; Ten Curry, dms; Charles Crosby, conga.

Houston, 1953

MM 1940	Woke Up This Morning	RPM 380. Kent 340, 5012, Crown 5020, Modern 3, Galaxy 202 United 718, Custom 1056
MM 1941	Don't Have To Cry	RPM 380

Similar:

MM 1960	Please Love Me	RPM 386, Kent 336, Crown 5020 Modern 1
MM 1961	Highway Bound	RPM 386
MM 2014	Neighbourhood Affair	RPM 391
MM 2015	Please Hurry Home	–
MM 2024	Why Did You Love Me	RPM 395
MM 2025	Blind Love	– , Kent 337, Crown 5020
MM 2053	Praying To The Lord	RPM 403
MM 2054	Please Help Me	–

178

B. B. "BLUES BOY" KING

Similar		Houston? 1954/55
MM 2069	I Love You Baby	RPM 408
MM 2070	The Woman I Love	− , Kent 325
MM 2090	Everything I Do Is Wrong	RPM 411
MM 2091	Don't You Want A Man Like Me	− , Crown 5063
MM 2100	When My Heart Beats Like A Hammer	RPM 412, Kent 383, 5012, Crown 5063, Modern 11
MM 2101	Bye Bye Baby	RPM 412
MM 2121	You Upset Me Baby	RPM 416, Crown 5020, 5238, 5405, Kent 337, 5012, Modern 11, Galaxy 202
MM 2122	Whole Lot Of Love	RPM 416, Kent 388, 5013
MM 2139	Sneaking Around	RPM 421, Kent 5012, Crown 5143, Galaxy 202.
MM 2140	Everyday I Have The Blues	RPM 421, Crown 5020, Kent 5012, Galaxy 202
MM 2162	Lonely And Blue	RPM 425
MM 2163	Jump With Me Baby	− , Crown 5249
MM 2188	Shut Your Mouth	RPM 430, Crown 5230
MM 2189	I'm In Love	− −

Note: RPM 430 has matrix numbers 2062/63 shown on label and scratched out in wax. MM 2188 possibly on Crown 5230.

MM 2206	Talkin' The Blues	RPM 435
MM 2207	Boogie Rock	−
MM 2212	What Can I Do (Just Sing The Blues)	RPM 437, Crown 5063, 5143
MM 2213	Ten Long Years (I Had A Woman)	RPM 437, Kent 338, 339, 5012, Crown 5020, 5063, 5143, Modern 19.

Vcl/gtr. with tpt; saxes; pno; bs; dms.		Los Angeles? 1956
MM 2261-4	Crying Won't Help You	RPM 451, Kent 336, Crown 5020 Modern I
MM 2264	Cracking Up Over You	RPM 450
MM 2265	Ruby Lee	− , Crown 5063
MM 2268-1	Sixteen Tons	RPM 451
MM 2270-1	Can't We Talk It Over	−
MM 2281	Did You Ever Love A Woman	RPM 457, Crown 5020, Kent 346, 5012, Galaxy 202
MM 2282	Let's Do The Boogie	RPM 457
MM 3006	Dark Is The Night Part 1	RPM 459
MM 3007	Dark Is The Night Part 2	−

Vcl/gtr. with Kenny Sands, tpt; Lawrence Burdine, alt; Johnny Board, ten; Floyd Newman, bari; Millard Lee, pno; Jymie Merritt, bs; Ted Curry, dms. Los Angeles, 1956

MM 3057-2	Sweet Little Angel	RPM 468, Kent 346, 5012, Crown 5020, Galaxy 202,
MM 3058-1	Bad Luck	RPM 468, Crown 5020, Galaxy 202
MM 3084	On My Word Of Honour	RPM 479
MM 3085	Bim, Bam	−

Similar:		Los Angeles, 1957
MM 3123	Early In The Morning	RPM 486, Crown 5063
MM 3124	You Don't Know	−
MM 3139-1	How Do I Love You	RPM 490
MM 3140-3	You Can't Fool My Heart	−
MM 3151	I Want To Get Married	RPM 492, Crown 5063
MM 3152	Troubles, Troubles (Troubles)	−, −
MM 3163	(I'm Gonna) Quit My Baby	RPM 494, Ket 5013, Crown 5143
MM 3164	Be Careful With A Fool	RPM 494, Crown 5143
	I Wonder	RPM 498
	I Need You So Bad	−
MM 3179	The Key To My Kingdom	RPM 501
MM 3180	My Heart Belongs To You	−

Vcl/gtr. with Kenny Sands or Henry Boozier, tpt; Lawrence Burdine, alt; Johnny Board, ten; Herman Green, Fred Ford or Barney Hubbard, bari; Millard Lee, pno; Marshall York, el-bs; Ted Curry, dms.   Los Angeles, 1958/59

Why Do Everything Happen To Me	Kent 301, 429, 5012, Crown 5063
You Know I Go For You	Kent 301, Crown 5063
Don't Look Now But You Got The Blues	Kent 307
Days of Old	– , Crown 5143
I Am	Kent 317
Worry, Worry	–
The Fool	Kent 319, Crown 5115
Come By Here	–
A Lonely Lover's Plea	Kent 321
Time To Say Goodbye	Kent 327, Crown 5115
Please Accept My Love	Kent 315
You've Been An Angel	–
Sugar Mama	Kent 329
Mean Old Frisco	–
Past Day	Crown 5063

Vcl. with Joe Newman, Snooky Yound, John Anderson, Pete Candoli, tpts; Henry Coker, Dick Nash, Tommy Peterson, tbns; Marshall Royal, Jewel Grant, alts; Frank Foster, Frank Wess, Ten?s Charlie Fowlkes, bari; Milt Raskin, pno; Herman Mitchell, gtr; Eddie Jones, bs; Sonny Payne, dms; Maxwell Davis, arr/cond.   Los Angeles, January, 1959

Everyday I Have The Blues	Kent 327, 338, 5012, Crown 5111

Vcl/gtr. with Kenny Sands, Henry Boozier, tpts; Pluma Davis, tbn; Lawrence Burdine, alt; Johnny Board, ten; Barney Hubert, bari; Millard Lee, pno; Marshall Yor, el-bs; Sonny Freeman, dms   Los Angeles, 1959

Sweet Thing	Crown 5115
I've Got Papers On You Baby	–
Tomorrow Is Another Day	–
I Love You So	–
We Can't Make It	–
Treat Me Right (add 2nd gtr)	–
The Woman I Love (no saxes)	–

Vcl/with org. pno. bs; dms; tambourine; Charioteers, vcl/grp.

Precious Lord	Crown 5119, Kent 392
Army Of The Lord	–
Save A Seat For Me	–
Ole Time Religion	–
Sweet Chariot	–
Servant's Prayer	–
Jesus Gave Me Water	–
I Never Heard A Man	–
I'm Willing To Run All The Way	–
I'm Working On The Building	–

Vcl/gtr. with Kenny Sands, Henry Boozier, tpts; Pluma Davis, tbn; Lawrence Burdine alt; Johnny Board, ten; Barney Hubertm bari; Millard Lee, pno; Marshall York, el-bs; Sonny Freeman, dms.   Los Angeles, 1960

Sweet Sixteen Part 1	Kent 330, 5012, 5027, Crown 5143, Galaxy 202, Modern 5, A-Bet 401
Sweet Sixteen Part 2	Kent 330, 5012, Crown 5143
I Was Blind	Crown 5143
Whole Lot Of Lovin'	–
Someday Baby	–
I Had A Woman	–
(I've)Got A Right To Love My Baby	Kent 333, Crown 5167
My Fault	– , Galaxy 202
Dry Bones	–
Good Man Gone Bad	Kent 346, Crown 5167
Partin' Time	– –
What Way To Go	Crown 5167
Long Nights	–

180

Feel Like A Million	Crown 5167
I'll Survive	–
If I Lost You	–
You're On Top	–
I'm King	–

Vcl/gtr. with LLoyd Glenn, pno; Ralph Hamilton, bs; Jessie Sailes, dms.

	Los Angeles, 1960
You Done Lost Your Good Thing Now	Kent 350, Crown 5188
Walking Dr. Bill	– – , Kent 5013
Hold That Train	Kent 358, – –
Understand	– –
Someday Baby	Kent 360, –
Mr. Pawn Broker	Crown 5188, Kent 5013
Driving Wheel	–
My Own Fault Baby	–
Cat Fish Blues	–
Please Set A Date	–

Vcl/gtr. with Kenny Sands & Another, tpts; Johnny Board & others, saxes; Millard Lee, pno; unk. el-bs; Sonny Freeman, dms.

Things Are Not The Same	Kent 351
Fishin' After Me	–
Bad Luck Soul	Kent 353, Crown 5230
Get Out Of Here	– –
Bad Case Of Love	Kent 362, 5012, Crown 5230, Modern 3
You're Breaking My Heart	Kent 362, Crown 5230, Galaxy 202

Same:	Los Angeles, 1961
Blues For Me	Crown 5230
Just Like A Woman	– , Kent 441

Note: The two remaining tracks on Crown 5230 are by a different artist.

Vcl/gtr. with Kenny Sands, tpt; Johnny Board, ten; Duke Jethro, org; Leo Lauchie? el-bs; Sonny Freeman, dms.

Lonely	Kent 365
My Sometimes Baby	–
Hully Gully (Twist)	Kent 372, Crown 5286
Gonna Miss You Around Here	–
Mashed Potatoe Twist	Kent 373
Three O'Clock Stomp	–
Mashing The Popeye	Kent 381
Tell Me Baby	–
Going Down Slow	Kent 383, Galaxy 202
Three O'Clock Blues	Kent 386
Your Letter	– , Crown 5309
Christmas Celebration	Kent 387, 412
Easy Listening (Blues)	– – , Crown 5286
Down Now	Kent 388
Trouble In Mind	Kent 389
Long Nights	–

Add 2nd tpt. & 2 saxes

The Road I Travel	Kent 390
My Reward (no gtr, brass)	– , Crown 5230
The Letter	Kent 391, Crown 5359
You Better Know	–

Vcl/gtr. with Jimmy McCracklin, pno; bs; dms.

Rock Me Baby	Kent 393, 5012, United 718 Custom 1044, 1056
I Can't Lose	Kent 393

181

Vcl/gtr. with prob. Kenny Sands, tpt; Johnny Board, Bobby Forte, tens; Duke Jethro,
pno/org; Leo Lauchie, el-bs; Sonny Freeman, dms.

You're Gonna Miss Me	Kent 396, 5013, Crown 5309
Let Me Love You	— —
I Can't Explain	Kent 5013, Crown 5309
Troubles Don't Last	
Beautician Blues	Kent 403, 5021
I Can Hear My Name	— —
The Worst Thing In My Life	Kent 415, 5021
Got 'Em Bad (omit tpt)	— —, Crown 5309
Please Love Me	Kent 421, 5012, Custom 1041
Baby Look At You	—, Crown 5230
Blue Shadows	Kent 426, 5021
And Like That	
Just A Dream	Kent 429, 5012,
Eyesight To The Blind	Kent 441, 5021
Broken Promise	Kent 435
Have Mercy Baby	
Five Long Years	Kent 445, 5021
Love Honour And Obey	—
Ain't Nobody's Business	Kent 447, 5021
I Wonder	—
The Jungle	Kent 462, 5021
Long Gone Baby	— —
Blues Stay Away	Kent 458
It's A Mean World	—, 5021

No details

Blues For Me	Crown 5286
Night Long	—
Confessin'	—
Don't Touch	—
Slow Walk	—
Walkin'	—
Shoutin' The Blues	—
Rambler	
The Wrong Road	Crown 5309
I Need You Baby	—
So Many Days	—
Down Hearted	—
Strange Things	—
Going Home	Crown 5359
You Never Know	—
Please Remember Me	—
Come Back Baby	—
You Won't Listen	—
Sundown	—
You Shouldn't Have Left	Crown 5359
House Rocker	—
Shake Yours	—

Vcl/gtr. (-1). with Maxwell Davis Orch. unk. tpts; William Green, Jewel Grant, alts; unk. tens;
Floyd Turnham, bari; Lloyd Glenn, pno; Ralph Hamilton, bs; Jessie Sales, dms.

Los Angeles, March 1, 1962

10797	My Baby's Coming Home -1	ABC 10334
10798	Blues At Midnight -1	—, LP 456
10799	I'm Gonna Sit In Till You Give In	ABC 10316
10800	You Ask Me	—
10801		
10802	Slowly Losing My Mind	ABC 10486
	Sneakin' Around	ABC 10361, LP 456
	Chains Of Love	— —
	Little Mama	unissued

Vcl/gtr. with Belford Henricks Orch.		1962
11100	Tomorrow Night	ABC 10367
11101	Guess Who	ABC 10390
11102	By Myself	– 'LP 456
11103	Mother's Love	ABC 10367, –
Vcl/gtr. with Teacho Wiltshire Orch.		New York City, 1963
11446	Young Dreams	ABC 10455, LP 456
11447	How Do I Lose You	ABC 10486
11448	On My Word Of Honour	ABC 10455
Vcl/gtr. with		1963
11796	How Blue Can You Get	ABC 10527
11797		
11798	Please Accept My Love	ABC 10527
Vcl/gtr. with		1964/65
	Help The Poor	ABC 10552
	I Woudn't Have It Any Other Way	–
	The Hurt	ABC 10576
	Whole Lotta Lovin'	–
	Never Trust A Woman	ABC 10599
	Worryin' Blues	
	Please Send Me Someone To Love	ABC 10616
	Stop Leading Me On	–
	Night Owl	ABC 10675
	Tired Of Your Jive	–
	I Need You	ABC 10710
	Never Could Be You	–
	All Over Again	ABC 10724
	The Things You Put Me Through	–

Vcl/gtr. with Johnny Board, Bobby Forte, tens; Kenny Sands, tpt; Duke Jethro, org; Leo Lauchie, el-bs; Sonny Freeman, dms. Chicago, November 21, 1964

	Everyday I Have The Blues	ABC 509, 10634
	Sweet Little Angel	–
	It's My Own Fault	–, 10634
	How Blue Can You Get	–
	Please Love Me	–
	You Upset Me Baby	–
	Worry, Worry	–
	Woke Up This Morning	
	You Done Lost Your Good Thing Now	–
	Help The Poor	–
Vcl/gtr. with		1966
	I'd Rather Drink Muddy Water	ABC 528, 10754
	Goin' To Chicago Blues	– –
	See See Rider	–
	Do You Call That A Buddy	–
	Wee Baby Blues	–
	In The Dark	–
	Confessin' The Blues	–
	I'm Gonna Move To The Outskirts Of Town	–
	How Long, How Long Blues	–
	Cherry Red	–
	Please Send Me Someone To Love	–
Vcl/gtr. with		
	You're Still A Square	ABC 10766
	Tormented	

Vcl/gtr. with Duke Jethro, org; Leo Lauchie, el-bs; Sonny Freeman, dms.

13432A	Don't Answer The Door Pt. 1	ABC 10856
13432B	Don't Anwer The Door Pt. 2	–

Vcl/gtr. with Kenny Sands, tpt; Bobby Forte, ten; Duke Jethro, org; Louis Satterfield, el-bs; Sonny Freeman, dms. Chicago, November 5, 1966

	Waitin' For You	Bluesway 6001, ABC 10889
	Gambler's Blues	–
	Tired Of Your Love	–
	Night Life	– , ABC 10889
	Buzz Me	–

Don't Answer The Door	Bluesway 6001
Blind Love	−
I Know What You're Putting Down	−
Baby Get Lost	−
Gonna Keep On Loving You	−

B. B. KING REISSUES

The Following Crown LPs have been reissued several times. To Simplify matters we list all known reissues here:

```
Crown 5020 = United 726
Crown 5063 = United 732
Crown 5115 = United 711, Custom 1049
Crown 5119 = United 723, Custom 1059
Crown 5143 = United 728
Crown 5157 = United 730
Crown 5188 = United 724
Crown 5230 = United 708, Custom 1046
Crown 5286 = United 705
Crown 5309 = United 703, Custom 1040
Crown 5359 = United 714, Custom 1052
```

B.B.KING JR. & THE BLUES MESSENGERS

Vcl/gtr. with saxes; pno; bs; dms.   New York City 1964

101A	I'm So Glad It's All Over	L. Brown 101
101B	Ain't That Loving You Baby	−

EDDIE KING

Vcl/gtr. with   Chicago, 1960

Shakin' Inside	J.O.B. 1122
Love You Baby	−

Note: Is this Eddie King Milton? See also Little Mack

FREDDY KING

Born Gilmer, Texas on September 30, 1934
Vcl/gtr. with Margaret Whitfield, vcl(-1); Earl E. Payton, hca; Milton Rector, bs-gtr;
Robert Elam, bs; Thomas J. McNulty, dms. Chicago, 1956/57

LB 157	Country Boy -1	El-Bee 157
LB 158	That's What You Think	−

Vcl/gtr. with Gene Redd, Clifford Scott, reeds; Sonny Thompson, pno; Bill Willis, bs-gtr;
Phillip Paul dms.   Cincinnati, August, 25, 1960

K 4882	See See Baby	Federal 12428
K 4883	You've Got To Love Her With A Feeling	Federal 12384, King LP 762
K 4884	Have You Ever Loved A Woman	−
K 4885	Hide Away	Federal 12401, King LP 856
K 4886	I Love The Woman	− , King LP 762

Add Fred Jordan, gtr;		
F 1368-2	Lonesome Whistle Blues	Federal 12415, King LP 762
F 1369	If You Believe	Federal 12443, −
F 1370		
F 1371		
F 1372-2	It's Too Bad	Federal 12415, King LP 762
F 1373	I'm Tore Down	Federal 12432, − , 792
	You Know That You Love Me	King LP 762
	You Mean, Mean Woman	−
	Let Me Be	−

Gtr. with Fred Jordan, gtr; Bill Willis, bs-gtr; Phillip Paul dms.

                Cincinnati, April 5, 1961

F 1390-1	Onion Rings	Federal 12529
F 1391	Sen-Sa-Shun	Federal 12432, King LP 773, 856, 964
F 1392		

F 1393		
F 1394	Side Tracked	Federal 12456, King LP 773, 856
F 1395	The Stumble	Federal 12450, – –
F 1396	San-Ho-Zay	Federal 12428, – –
F 1397		
F 1398	Just Pickin'	Federal 12470, King LP 773, 856. 964
F 1399	Heads Up	Federal 12443, – –
	Wash Out	King Lp 773, 856
	Swooshy	– –
	Out Front	– –
	Butter Scotch	– –

Vcl/gtr. with Gene Redd, Clifford Scott, reeds; Sonny Thompson, pno; Fred Jordan gtr; Bill Willis, bs-gtr; Phillip Paul, dms.   late 1961

F 771	Takin' Care Of Business	Federal 12450, King LP 762
F 772		
F 773		
F 774	In the Open	Federal 12475, King LP 773, 856
	Christmas Tears	Federal 12439
	I Hear Jingle Bells	–
	Say Hay Pretty Baby	Federal 12477

Same, Gene Redd also tpt: Cincinnati, early 1962

F 1423	High Rise (Closed Door)	Federal 12521, King LP 819
F 1424-2	Texas Oil	Federal 12462
F 1425	She Put The Whammy On Me	Federal 12521
F 1426	I'm On My Way To Atlanta	Federal 12475
F 1427		
F 1428	Driving Sideways	Federal 12518
F 1429-1	Sittin' On The Boat Dock	Federal 12456
F 1430	Come One	Federal 12470

Add Lula Reed, vcl(-1):   Cincinnati, March 1962

F 1431-1	Do The President Twist -1	Federal 12457, King LP 777
F 1432-2	(Let Your Love) Watch Over Me -1	Federal 12471, –
F 1433 -1	You Can't Hide -1	– –
F1434-1	It's Easy Child -1	Federal 12477, – , 964
F 1435-1	Your Love Keeps A-Working on Me -1	Federal 12457
F 1436-2	What About Love	Federal 12462

Same: omit saxes (-1);

F 804		
F 805	The Bossa Nova Watusi Twist	Federal 12482, King LP 821
F 806		
F 807	Someday After A While	Federal 12518, King LP 821
F 808		
F 809-1	You're Barkin' Up The Wrong Tree	Federal 12499, King LP 821
F 810		
F 811-1	(The Welfare) Turns Its Back On You	Federal 12499, King LP 821
F 812		
F 813	Look Ma I'm Crying	Federal 12482, King LP 821
F 814-1	I'd Love To Make Love To You	Federal 12491, –
F 815-2	One Hundred Years	– –
	I Hurts To Be In Love	King LP 821
	You Walked In	–
	Bossa Nova Blues	–
	Walk Down The Aisle (Honey Chile)	–
	Is My Baby Mad With Me -1	–

Vcl/gtr. with ten; pno; Bobby King, gtr; Benny Turner, bs-gtr; dms.
    Cincinnati, 1963

F 851-1	Now I've Got A Woman	Federal 12529, King LP 964
F 852	Surf Monkey	Federal 12509, King LP 928
F 853	If You Have It	Federal 12535
F 854		
F 855		

F 856	Monkey Donkey	Federal 12509
F 857	Meet Me At The Station	Federal 12515, King LP 964
F 858	Full Time Love	Federal 12537
F 859	King-A-Ling	Federal 12515, King LP 928

Gtr. with pno; Bobby King, gtr; Benny Turner, bs-gtr; dms.

	Freeway 75	King LP 928
	Low Tide	–
	The Sad Nite Owl	–
	Funny Bone (no pno)	–
	Nickel Plated	–
	Freddy's Midnite Dream	–
	Fish Fare	–
	Cloud Sailing	–
	Remington Ride	–

Vcl/gtr. with Lonnie Mack's Band; Saxes; org; Lonnie Mack, gtr; bs-gtr; dms.

F 884	I Love You More Every Day	Federal 12535
F 885		
F 886	Some Other day, Some Other Time	Federal 12532
F 887	She's The One	Federal 12537
F 888		
F 889	Man Hole (no saxes)	Federal 12532, King LP 928, 864

Vcl/gtr. with Lonnie Mack's Band: saxes; org; Lonnie Mack, gtr; bs-gtr; Frank Charles, dms.

	Double-Eyed Whammy	Federal
	Use What You Got	
	You Got Me Licked	
	Girl From Kookamonga	

JULIUS KING

Vcl/gtr/kazoo   Nashville, 1952
E2-KB-2227	If You See My Lover	Tennessee 123
E2-KB-2228	I Want A Slice Of Your Pudding	–

RICHARD KING & HIS ORCHESTRA

Vcl. with alt; pno; bs; dms.   Lake Charles, La 1951
KH 800A	Banks Of The River	Khoury's 800
KH 800B	Ride, Daddy, Ride	–

EDDIE KIRK

See under Eddie Kirkland

WEE WILLIE KIRK

No details'   1952
	Come On Home And Quit Your Lookin'	Bullet 340
	Your Love Was So Nice And Warm	–

EDDIE KIRKLAND

Born New Orleans, Louisiana on August, 26, 1928

LITTLE EDDIE KIRKLAND
Vcl/gtr. withJohn Lee Hooker, gtr.   Detroit, 1952
MM 1872	It's Time	RPM 367
MM 1873	That's All Right	–

EDDIE KIRKLAND
Vcl/gtr. with dms   Detroit, 1953
K 9305	Please Don't Think I'm Nosey	King 4680
K 9306	No Shoes	King 4659, LP 875, Blues Classics BC-12
K 9307	Mistreated Woman	King 4680
K 9308	Time For My Lovin' To Be Done	King 4659

Note: Alternate take of 9306 on LP 875

EDDIE KIRKLAND & HIS HOUSE ROCKERS

Vcl/gtr. with Johnny Hooks, ten; Joe Dooms. pno; Jimmy Parner, dms.

Detroit, 1959

F-169	I Need You Baby	Fortune 848
F-170	I Must Have Done Somebody Wrong	–

EDDIE KIRKLAND

Vcl/hca/gtr. with King Curtis' Band: King Curtis, Oliver Nelson, ten; Herman Foster, pno;
Billy Butler, gtr; Jimmy Lewis, bs-gtr; Ray Lucas dms.　　New York City, Dec. 8 1961

3301	I Tried	Tru-Sound 15010
3302	Man Of Stone	–
3303	Oh Baby Please	unissued
3304	Train Done Gone	Tru-Sound 409, 15010
3305	I'm Goin' To Keep Lovin' You	Tru-Sound 15010
3306	Something's Gone Wrong In My Life	Tru-Sound 409, 15010
3307	Baby You Know It's True	Tru-Sound 15010

George Stubbs, pno. replaces Foster:　　New York City, March 9, 1962

3423	Saturday Night Stomp	Tru-Sound 15010
3424	I'm Gonna Forget You	–
3425	Down On My Knees	–
3426	Don't Take My Heart	–
3427	Daddy Please Don't Cry	–
3428	Have Mercy On Me	–

EDDIE KIRK

Vcl/hca(-1). with tpt?; ten; bari; pno; gtr; bs; dms. fem. Choir (-2)

Los Angeles?, 1964

BS-16137	Let Me Walk With You -2	King 5895
BS-16138		
BS 16139	Monkey Tonight -1	King 5895
BS-16140		

Eddie Kirk
Vcl/hca/gtr. with el-bs; dms.

		1965
	The Hawg Part 1	Volt 106
	The Hawg Part 2	–
	The Bones	Volt 111
	I Found A New Love	–

L

ERNEST LANE

Vcl/pno. with tpt; ten; gtr; bs; dms.　　Clarksdale, Miss. 1951

MM 1788	What's Wrong Baby	Blues & Rhythm 7000
MM 1789	Little Girl, Little Girl -1	–

　　Note -1 omit brass. Lane is a member of Ike Turner's Band. He now lives in
　　Los Angeles.

WILLIE LANE (LITTLE BROTHER)

Vcl/gtr.   Dallas, 1949
167   Prowlin' Ground Hog   Talent 805
168   Too Many Women Blues   –
169
170
171   Howling Wolfe Blues (sic)   Talent 806
172   Black Cat Rag   –

      Note: Fort Worth, Texas artist.

BILLIE LANGFORD - "EMPEROR OF THE BLUES"

Vcl. with tpt; pno; bs.   New York City, 1946
JM 12   Mean And Evil Woman   Harlem 1002
JM 13
JM 14   Let Me Grease Your Griddle   Harlem 1102

BILLY LANGFORD COMBO

Vcl. with ten; pno; bs; dms.   New York City, 1945
HS 4018   Blues In Nashville   Lenox 504
HS 4019   Be Bop On The Boogie   –

      Note: Aurally not the same artist as Billie Langford

CHARLES LAVERNE

Vcl/gtr. with   1957
    Hudson River Blues   Mark 117
    La Verne's Boogie

LAZY BILL & HIS BLUE RHYTHMS

Real name Bill Lucas. Born Caldwell, Arkansas on May 29, 1918
Vcl/pno. with Homesick James, gtr. dms.   Chicago, 1954
C 5074   She Got Me Walkin'   Chance 1148
C 5075   I Had A Dream
C 5076   My Baby's Gone   unissued
C 5077   I Can't Sleep, I Can't Eat   unissued

      Note: See Also The Blues Rockers.

LAZY LESTER

Real name Leslie Johnson. Born Baton Rouge, La. in 1936.
Vcl/hca. with Guitar Gable, gtr; Fats Perrodin, bs–gtr; Bruce Broussard, dms.
                                        Crowley, La., 1958
A   I'm Gonna Leave You Baby   Excello 2095
B   Lester's Stomp   –   , LP 8006
Vcl/hca. with Al Foreman, Bobby McBride, gtrs; Warren Storm, dms.
A   Go Ahead   Excello 2107
B   They Call Me Lazy   –

                                        Crowley, La., 1959
A   I Told My Little Woman   Excello 2129
B   Tell Me Pretty Baby   –
A   I'm A Lover Not A Fighter   Excello 2143, LP 8006
B   Sugar Coated Love   –   –

                                        Crowley, La., 1960
A   I Hear You Knockin'   Excello 2155, LP 8006
B   Through The Goodness Of My Heart (no hca.)   –
A   I Love You, I Need You   Excello 2166
B   Late, Late In The Evening   –

                                        Crowley, La., 1961
A   Bye Bye Baby (Gonna Call It Gone)   Excello 2182, LP 8006
B   A Real Combination For Love   –

Add Katie Webster, pno:		
A	You Got Me Where You Want Me	Excello 2197
B	Patrol Blues	–
Add Lionel Torrence, ten:		Crowley, La., 1962
A	I'm So Glad (My Baby's Back Home)	Excello 2206, LP 8006
B	Whoa Now	–

Vcl/hca. with Al Foreman, gtr; Bobby McBride or Rufus Thibodeaux, bs–gtr; Austin Broussard, dms.

A	If You Think I've Lost You (You're As Wrong As You Can Be)	Excello 2219, LP 8006
B	I'm So Tired	–
Add unk. wbd (–1):		Crowley, La., 1963
A	Lonesome Highway Blues - 1	Excello 2230, LP 8006
B	I Made Up My Mind	–
A	You Gonna Ruin Me Baby	Excello 2235
B	Strange Things Happen	–
Same:		Crowley, La., 1964
A	A Word About Woman	Excello 2243
B	Could Happen To You	Excello 2243, LP 8006
		Crowley, La., 1966
A	Take Me In Your Arms	Excello 2274
B	You Better Listen (To What I Said)	–
Vcl/hca. with Katie Webster, org; 2 gtrs; dms.		
A	Because She's Gone	Excello 2277
B	Ponderosa Stomp	–

LAZY SLIM JIM

See under Carolina Slim.

LEADBELLY

Real name Huddie Leadbetter. Born Mooringsport, La. c. 1888. Died New York City December 6, 1949.

> Note: As this artist has mainly recorded in the true folk vein, only sessions thought to be of interest to blues collectors are listed.

Vcl/gtr. with Sonny Terry, hca.		New York City, Summer 1943
SC 258	On A Monday	Asch 343-3, Stinson 17
SC 259	John Henry	– – , Design 903, 247
SC 260	How Long Blues	Asch 343-1, – , –
SC 261, A 467	Irene (Goodnight Irene)	Asch 343-2, Atlantic 917, Stinson 17
	Irene (alt. take)	Melodisc 1151
SC 262	Ain't You Glad	Asch 343-2, Stinson 17, Design 903, 247
SC 263, A 468	Good Morning Blues	Asch 343-1, Atlantic 917, Stinson 17
Vcl/gtr. with Paul Howard, zither.		Hollywood, October 4, 1944
CAP 397-4	Ella Speed	Capitol H 369, EAP2-369, T 1821
CAP 398-3	Rock Island Line	Capitol 10021, H 239, T 1821
CAP 399-1	Tell Me Baby	Capitol H 369, EAP1-369, T 1821
CAP 400-1	Take This Hammer	Capitol H 369, EAP1-369, T 1821
same:		Hollywood, October 5, 1944
CAP 413-3	Irene	Capitol 40130, H 369, EAP1-369, T 1821
CAP 414-2	Western Plain	Capitol H 369, EAP2-369, T 1821

| CAP 415-2 | On a C hristmas Day | Capitol H 369, EAP1-369, T 1821 |
| CAP 416-3 | Back Water Blues | Capitol 40130, H 369, EAP1-369, T 1821 |

Vcl/gtr/pno (−1)   Hollywood, October 27, 1944

CAP 457-2	Eagle Rock Rag (Eagle Rocks)	Cap 10021, H 239, T 1821
CAP 458-3	Hot Piano Rag -1	Capitol T 1821
CAP 459-2	Sweet Mary Blues	Capitol 40038, H 369, EAP2-369, T 1821
CAP 460-3	Grasshoppers In My Pillow	Capitol 40038, T 1821

THE LEAPFROGS

See under Louis Campbell.

DAVIE LEE

Vcl.   Marian, Miss., Jan/Feb., 1950

Meet Me In The Bottoms   Folkways FE 4474, P 474

EMMA DELL LEE & TRIO

Vcl/pno. with Curtiss Babino, ten; unk. bs; Bill Parker, dms.   Lake Charles, La., 1951

| A | How Much I Love You | Khoury's 900 |
| B | No Good Daddy | − |

See also Clarence Garlow.

JIMMIE LEE

See under Jimmy Lee Robinson.

JOHN LEE

Real name John Lee Henley. Born Canton, Mississippi on February 13, 1919.
Vcl/hca. with Robert Lockwood, Jr., Johnny Holloway, gtrs; (Moody?) Jones, bs;
"Zona", dms.   Chicago, 1952

| U 4911 | Rhythm Rockin' Boogie | JOB 114 |
| U 4912 | Knockin' On Lula Mae's Door | − |

Note: U 4912 has voices heard faintly in background.

Vcl/hca. with Honeyboy Edwards, gtr.   Chicago, March 17, 1963

Blue And Lonesome   Testament unissued
Ida Lou   −
Ida Lou   −

Hca. solos.   Chicago, November 30, 1965

Slidin' Devil   Testament unissued
Slidin' Devil   −
Devil's Dream   −
Fox Chase   −

JOHN LEE

Vcl/gtr.   Montgomery, Ala., July, 1951

F-170	Baby Blues	Federal 12089
F-171		
F-172	Down At The Depot	Federal 12054
F-173	Alabama Boogie	−
F-174	Blind's Blues	Federal 12089, Blues Classics BC-5

JOHN LEE (Gotham Records)

See under John Lee Hooker.

JOHNNY LEE

See under John Lee Hooker.

LONESOME LEE

See under Jimmy Lee Robinson.

ROOSEVELT LEE

Vcl. with Skippy Brooks, pno; gtr; bs; dms.　　　　　　　　Nashville, 1954
| A | Lazy Pete | Excello 2022 |
| B | I'm So Sad | — |

TOMMY LEE

Real name Tommy Lee Thompson.
Vcl/gtr. with pno (–1); gtr; dms.　　　　　　　　Jackson, Miss., 1953
| ACA 2511 | Packing Up My Blues -1 | Delta 403 |
| ACA 2512 | Highway 80 Blues | — |

  Note: This artist also recorded for Ace, but no titles were issued.

J. B. LENOIR (see also in Appendix)

Born Monticello, Mississippi on March 5, 1929. Died Champaign, Illinois on April 29, 1967.
Vcl/gtr. with Sunnyland Slim, pno; Alfred Wallace, dms.　　　Chicago, 1952
| J 42342 | People Are Meddlin' In Our Affairs | JOB 112 |
| J 42343 | Let's Roll | — |

J. B. LENORE & HIS BAYOU BOYS
As last, but add Leroy Foster, gtr.　　　　　　　　Chicago, 1951
JB-31641	Deep In Debt Blues	Chess 1463
JB-31642	Carrie Lee-Oo	—
JB-31643	My Baby Told Me	Chess 1449
JB-31644	Korea Blues	—

J. B. & HIS BAYOU BOYS
As last, but omit Foster.　　　　　　　　Chicago, 1952
1009	The Mountain	JOB 1008
1010	I'll Die Trying	JOB 1016
1011	How Much More	JOB 1008

J. B. LENORE & HIS COMBO
Vcl/gtr. with J. T. Brown, ten; Sunnyland Slim, pno; Alfred Wallace, dms.
　　　　　　　　　　　　　　　　　Chicago, 1953
U-2319	The Mojo	JOB 1012, Constellation CS-6
U-2320	Slow Down Woman	Constellation CS-6
U-2321	I Want My Baby	JOB 1016, Constellation CS-6
U-2322	How Can I Live	JOB 1012, —

Similar:　　　　　　　　　　　　　　Chicago, 1954
| 2707 | Play A Little While | JOB 1102 |
| 2708 | Louise | — |

J. B. LENOIR
Vcl/gtr. with Lorenzo Smith, ten; Joe Montgomery, pno; Al Galvin, dms.
　　　　　　　　　　　　　　　　　Chicago, 1954
P-53202	I'm In Korea	Parrot 802
P-53203	Eisenhower Blues	—
P-53214	Man Watch Your Woman	Parrot 809
P-53215	Mama Talk To Your Daughter	—
P-53203	Tax Paying Blues	Parrot 802*

  * "Eisenhower Blues" was banned shortly after release. "Tax Paying Blues" was
  remade with slightly different lyrics. Same personnel and matrixes were used.

Vcl/gtr. with Alex Atkins, alt; Ernest Cotton, ten; Joe Montgomery, pno; Al Galvin, dms.
　　　　　　　　　　　　　　　　　Chicago, Spring, 1955
P-55224	Mama Your Daughter Is Going To Miss Me	Parrot 814
P-55225	What Have I Done	—
P-55275	Fine Girls	Parrot 821
P-55276	I Lost My Baby	—

J. B. LENORE
Vcl/gtr. with Alex Atkins, alt; Ernest Cotton, ten; Joe Montgomery, pno; Willy Dixon, bs;
Al Galvin, dms.   Chicago, 1956
7902   Let Me Die With The One I Love   Checker 844
7903   If I Give My Love To You   —

Same: Chicago, December, 1956
8360   Don't Touch My Head   Checker 856
8361
8362   I've Been Down So Long   Checker 856
8363   What About Your Daughter   Checker 874

Vcl/gtr. with alt; ten; pno; bs; dms;   Chicago, 1957
8490   Five Years   Checker 874
              Note: Matrix on label of Checker 874 is 8463.

As above, but add Leonard Caston, org; vcl. grp (−1).   Chicago, 1958
8728   Daddy Talk To Your Son   Checker 901
8729   She Don't Know -1   —

J. B. LENORE
Vcl/gtr. with Junior Wells, hca; Ernest Cotton, ten; Joe Montgomery, pno; Jesse Fowler, dms.
                                                                      Chicago, ? August 11, 1958
K90W-2914   Back Door   Shad 5012
K90W-2915   Lou Ella   —

J. B. LENOIR
Vcl/gtr. with Alex Atkins, alt; Ernest Cotton, ten; Joe Montgomery, pno; Jesse Fowler, dms.
                                                                      Chicago, May 10, 1960
60-1428   Oh Baby   Vee Jay 352
60-1429   It's The Thing   unissued
60-1430   What Can I Do   unissued
60-1431   Do What I Say   Vee Jay 352, LP 1020

Vcl/gtr.   Chicago, July 17, 1960
              Move To Kansas City   Decca LK 4664
              I Been Down So Long   —
(BH-103)   Mojo Boogie   Blue Horizon 1004
(BH-104)   I Don't Care What Nobody Say   —

J. B. LENOIR & HIS AFRICAN HUNCH RHYTHM
Vcl/gtr. with Jarrett Gibson, ten; Lafayette Leake, pno; Milton Rector, bs−gtr; Willie Smith,
dms. "Peeples", bongo (−1).   Chicago, July 23, 1963
789,18928   I Sing Um The Way I Feel -1   USA 744
790,18929   I Feel So Good   —

Vcl/gtr. with Fred Below, dms (−1).   Chicago, May 5, 1965
              Alabama Blues   CBS 62593
              The Mojo Boogie -1   —
              God's Word   —
              The Whale Has Swallowed Me   —
              Move This Rope   —
              I Feel So Good -1   —
              Alabama March   —
              Talk To Your Daughter -1   —
              Mississippi Road   —
              Good Advice   —
              Vietnam   —
              I Want To Go -1   —

Vcl/gtr. with Shakey Horton, hca.   Hamburg, October 7, 1965
              Slow Down   Fontana 885.422 TY

BUDDY LEWIS

See under Ernest Lewis.

ED LEWIS

Vcl.   Lambert State Pen., Miss., 1959

          Lucky Holler   Atlantic LP 1346

Vcl. with Johnny Lee Moore, James Carter, Henry Mason, vcls.

          Tom Devil   Prestige Int. 25005

          Stewball   –

          I Be So Glad When The Sun   Goes Down   Atlantic LP 1346

ERNEST LEWIS

BUDDY LEWIS

Vcl/gtr. with pno; bs; dms.   Los Angeles, 1952/53

ST 312A   You've Got Good Business   Swing Time 312

ST 312A +   Lonesome Bedroom   –

WEST TEXAS SLIM

Vcl/gtr.

1007A   Lou Della   Flame 1007

1007A +   Little Mae Belle   –

ERNEST LEWIS

Vcl/gtr. with hca.

E 4191   No More Lovin'   Parrot 791

E 4192

E 4193   West Coast Blues   Parrot 791

COUNTRY SLIM

Vcl/gtr. with pno.

H 514   What Wrong Have I Done   Hollywood 1005

MISS COUNTRY SLIM

Vcl. with pno; Ernest Lewis, gtr.

H 515   My Girlish Days   Hollywood 1005

FURRY LEWIS

Vcl/gtr.   Memphis, February 18, 1959

          I'm Going To Brownsville   Folkways FS 3823

                                               Memphis, February 24, 1959

          John Henry   RBF RF 202

          Casey Jones   –

                                               Memphis, October 3, 1959

          You Can Leave Baby   RBF RF 202

          Warm Up   –

          Longing Blues   Folkways FS 3823

          John Henry   –

          I Will Turn Your Money Green   –

          Pearlee Blues   –

          Judge Boushay Blues   –

          Casey Jones   –

          East St. Louis Blues   –

          Early Recording Career   –

          The Medicine Shows

Vcl/gtr.

          John Henry   Bluesville BVLP 1036

          When My Baby Left Me   –

          Shake 'Em On Down   –

          Big Chief Blues   –

          Old Blue   –

          I'm Going Back To Brownsville   –

          Back On My Feet Again   –

          White Lightnin'   –

          Roberta   –

          St. Louis Blues   –

          Baby You Don't Want Me   Bluesville BVLP 1037

          Done Changed My Mind   –

          Goin' To Kansas City   –

	Judge Boushay Blues	Bluesville BVLP 1037
	Casey Jones	–
	This Time Tomorrow	–
	I Will Turn Your Money Green	–
	Frankie And Johnny	–
	Longing Blues	–
	Long Tall Gal Blues	–

JOHNNY LEWIS

See under Joe Hill Louis.

PETE (GUITAR) LEWIS

Real name Carl Lewis.
Vcl/gtr/hca (−1). with Gerald Wilson, Don Johnson, tpts; George Washington, John
Pettigrew, tbns; Ben Webster, Curtis Lowe, Lorenzo Holderness, tens; Floyd Johnson, alt/bari;
Devonia Williams, pno; Mario Delagarde, bs; Leard Bell, dms. Los Angeles, January 4, 1952

F 220	Louisiana Hop	Federal 12066
F 221	Raggedy Blues	Federal 12076
F 222	Crying With The Rising Sun	Federal 12066
F 223	Harmonica Boogie -1	Federal 12076, King LP 859

similar: Los Angeles, 1952

F 284	The Blast -1	Federal 12112
F 285	Ooh Midnight	Federal 12103, King LP 528
F 286	Scratchin' Boogie	–
F 287	Chocolate Pork Chop Man	Federal 12112

Vcl/gtr. with Don Johnson, tpt; George Washington, tbn; James Von Streeter, ten; Fred Ford,
bari; Devonia Williams, pno; Albert Winston, bs; Leard Bell, dms.
Los Angeles, August, 1952

| R 090-1 | Goin' Crazy | Peacock 1624 |
| R 091-1 | Back Door Troubles | – |

SAMMY LEWIS (the late)

Vcl (−1)/hca. with Willie Johnson Combo: Albert Joiner, pno (−2); Willie Johnson, vcl (−2)/
gtr; Joe Willie Wilkins, gtr; Joe Nathan, dms. Memphis, 1954

| U-146 | I Feel So Worried -1 | Sun 218 |
| U-147 | So Long Baby Goodbye -2 | – |

LICK, SLICK & SLIDE

No details: 1954

| WW 592 | I Got Drunk | Savoy 1150 |
| WW 593 | I Love My Baby | – |

PAPA LIGHTFOOT

Real name Alexander Lightfoot.
Vcl/hca. with Houston, 1949

| ACA 1318 | Papa George Blues | Peacock ? |
| ACA 1319 | Lightfoot Boogie | – |

Hca. with pno; gtr (−1); bs; dms. New Orleans, November 19, 1952
RR 2056, NO 2509

	After-While (Blue Lights)	Aladdin 3171, 3304
NO 2507	Jumpin' With Jarvis -1	Aladdin 3304
NO 2508	Fast Jump	unissued
NO 2509	P. L. Blues	Aladdin 3171

Note: Matrix nos. appear to be wrong on labels. Aurally all same session.

Vcl/hca. with gtr; dms. New Orleans, 1954

IM 714	Wine, Women, Whiskey	Imperial 5289
IM 715	When The Saints Go Marching In	unissued
IM 716	Mean Old Train	Imperial 5289
IM 717	Jump The Boogie	unissued

194

Vcl/hca. with pno; Paul "Guitar Red" Johnson, gtr; bs; dms. Atlanta, 1954
SPL 7201   Mean Old Train   Savoy 1161, MG 16000
SPL 7202   Wildfire   –

LIGHTNIN' GUITAR'S BAND

See under Sonny Boy and Lonnie.

LIGHTNIN' JR.

See under Jack Dupree.

LIGHTNIN' LEON

Vcl/gtr. with hca; pno; bs–gtr; dms.   Memphis, 1960
R 105   Dark Muddy Bottom   Rita 1005
R 106   Repossession Blues   –
            Note: Reputed to have also recorded for Bluestown.

LIGHTNIN' SLIM (see also in Appendix)

Real name Otis Hicks. Born St. Louis, Missouri in 1915.
Vcl/gtr. with Wild Bill Phillips, hca; Diggy Do, dms.   Crowley, La., 1954
ACA 2814   Bad Luck   Feature 3006
ACA 2815   The Blues Are Back Again   unissued
F 3006 Re   Rock Me Mama   Feature 3006
Vcl/gtr. with Henry Clement, hca; Sammy Drake, dms.   Crowley, La., 1954
F 507   I Can't Live Happy   Feature 3008
F 508   New Orleans Bound   –
Vcl/gtr. with Schoolboy Cleve, hca; unk. dms.
F 527   Bugger Bugger Boy   Feature 3012
F 528   Ethel Mae   –
Vcl/gtr. with hca; dms.   Jackson, Miss. 1954
3034   Bad Feeling Blues   ACE 505, Teem LP 5005
3035   Lightnin' Slim Boogie   –
Vcl/gtr. with Slim Harpe, hca; 'Jockey', dms.   Crowley, La. Late 1955
A   Lightnin' Blues   Excello 2066
B   I Can't Be Successful
Same: Crowley La, 1956
A   Sugar Plum   Excello 2075
B   Just Made Twenty One   –
A   Goin' Home   Excello 2080
B   Wonderin' And Goin'
Vcl/gtr. with Lazy Lester, hca; Warren Storm, dms; woodblocks or wbd.
                                                   Crowley, La 1957/58
11857   Bad Luck And Trouble   Excello 2096
11858
11859   Have Your Way   Excello 2096
A   Mean Old Lonesome Train   Excello 2106, LP 8004
B   I'm Grown (add female vcl)   –
A   I'm A Rollin' Stone   Excello 2116
B   Love Me Mama   , LP 8004
Same: Crowley, La 1959
18974   Hoo Doo Blues   Excello 2131, LP 8000
18975   It's Might Crazy   –
23620   My Starter Won't Work   Excello 2142, LP 8000
23621   Long Leanie Mama   –   –
26977   I'm Leavin' You Baby   Excello 2150, LP 8000
26978   Feelin' Awful Blue   –   –
A   Sweet Little Woman   Excello 2160, LP 8000
B   Lightnin's Troubles
Same: Crowley La, 1960
32184   Rooster Blues   Excello 2169, LP 8000
32185   G. I. Slim   –   –

195

A	Tom Cat Blues	Excello 2173, LP 8000
B	Bed Bug Blues	– –
A	Too Close Blues	Excello 2179
B	My Little Angel Child	–

Vcl/gtr. with Lazy Lester, hca; Al Foreman, Bobby McBride, gtrs; Warren Storm, dms.

Crowley, La 1961

A	Cool Down Baby	Excello 2186
B	Bothing But The Devil	–
A	I Just Don't Know	Excello 2195, LP 8004
B	Somebody Knockin'	–
A	I'm Tired Waiting Baby	Excello 2203
B	Hello Mary Lee	–

Vcl/gtr. with Katie Webster, pno (-1); Bobby McBride, bs-gtr; Warren Storm, dms.

Crowley, La. 1962

A	Mind Your Own Buesiness -1	Excello 2215
B	You're Old Enought To Understand	–

Webster out. Add Lazy Lester, hca;

A	I'm Warning You Baby	Excello 2224
B	Wintertime Blues	– , LP 8004

Vcl/gtr. with Lazy Lester, hca; Al Foreman, gtr; Bobby McBride or Rufus Thibodeaux, bs-gtr; Austin Broussard, dms.

Crowley, 1963

A	I'm Evil	Excello 2228
B	If You Ever Need Me	– , LP 8004
A	You Know You're So Fine	Excello 2234
B	Loving Around The Clock	–

Same:

Crowley, La. 1964

A	Blues At Night	Excello 2240
B	Don't Mistreat Me Baby	–
A	The Strangest Feeling	Excello 2245
B	You Give Me The Blues	– , LP 8004
A	Greyhound Blues (no bs-gtr)	Excello 2252
B	She's My Crazy Little Baby	– , LP 8004

Add Katie Webster, org:

A	Baby Please Come Back	Excello 2258, LP 8004
B	You Move Me Baby	– –

Same

Crowley, La. 1965

A	Have Mercy On Me Baby	Excello 2262, LP 8004
B	I've Been A Fool For You Darling	–

Webster out:

A	Can't Live This Life No More	Excello 2267
B	Bad Luck Blues	–

Add Katie Webster, pno;

A	Don't Start Me Talking	Excello 2269, LP 8004
B	Darling, You're The One	–

Same, omit pno(-1):

Crowley, La 1966

A	Love Is Just A Gambie -1	Excello 2272, LP 8004
B	I Would Hate To See You Leave	
A	Just A Lonely Stranger	Excello 2276
B	Goin' Away Blues -1	–

Note: Real matrix numbers on Excello issues are only stamped on 78 rpm issues.

LILY MAE & THE HOUSE ROCKERS

Full name Lily Mae Kirkman
Vcl. with Alex Atkins, alt; Ernest Cotton, ten; Memphis Slim, pno; Ernest Crawford, bs.

Chicago, 1948

24407	Lovin' Man Blues	Miracle, M 129
24408	Lonesome	–

196

MANCE LIPSCOMB

Born Navasota, Texas on April, 8 1895

ANONYMOUS
Vcl/gtr.   Houston, June 30, 1960
    Tom Moore's Farm   "77" LA 12/3 Blues Classics 16

MANCE LIPSCOMB
Vcl/gtr.   Navasota, August, 11 1960
    Freddy   Arhoolie F 1001
    Sugar Babe   —
    Going Down Slow   —
    Baby Please Don't Go   —
    Rock Me All Night Long   —
    Ain't Gonna Rain No More   —
    Jack O'Diamonds Is A Hard Card To Play   —
    Shake, Shake Mama   —
    Ella Speed   —
    One Thin Dime   —
    Going To Louisiana   —
    Mama Don't Allow   —
    Ain't It Hard   —
    'Bout A Spoonful   —
    Backwater Blues   Arhoolie F 1006

                                     Navasota, August 13, 1960
    Evil Heart Blues   Decca LK 4664
    Blues In The Bottle

Vcl/gtr.   Houston, July 7, 1961
391-2   Captain, Captain   Reprise 2012

                                     Houston, July 8, 1961
396-2   Careless Love   Reprise 2012
397-2   Alabama Bound   —
398
399-1   Trouble In Mind   Reprise 2012
400-8   Ballad Of The Boll Weevil   —
401-2   Which-A-Way Do Red River Run   —
402-2   Johnnie Take A One On Me   —
403
404-2   Motherless Children   Reprise 2012
405-1   When Death Come Creeping In Your Room —

                                     Houston, July 9, 1961
409-6   Rock Gravel Makes A Solid Road   Reprise 2012
422-2   Buck Dance
423
424
425
426-1   Night Time Is The Right Time   Reprise 2012

Note: Numbers 387 to 439 were assigned to the selections recorded July 7-10, 1961. There are from 1 to 4 complete takes on each selection. There is enough material for two more albums.

Vcl/gtr.
    Joe Turner Killed A Man   Arhoolie F 1023
    Bumble Bee   —
    Silver City   —
    If I Miss The Train   —
    Alabama Jubilee   —
    God Moves On The Water (The Titanic)   —
    Come Back Baby   —
    Charlie James   —
    Boogie In A   —
    Key To The Highway   —
    Cocaine Done Killed My Baby   —
    Spanish Flang Dang   —

	You Got To Reap What You Sow	Arhoolie F 1023
Vcl/gtr.		Cabale Club, Berkely,
	Take Me Back Babe	Arhoolie F 1026
	Shine On Harvest Moon	–
	Rag In G	–
	Heel And Toe Polka	–
	Big Boss Man	–
	You Gonna Quit Me	–
	Blues In G	–
	Mama Don't Dog Me	–
	Polly Wolly Doodle All Day	–
	Tell Me Where You Stay Last Night	–
	Knockin' Down windows	–
	Nobody's Fault But Mine	–
	Motherless Children	–
Vcl/gtr.		Berkeley, April 15, 1966
	Stop Time	Arhoolie F 1030
	I Ain't Got Nobody	–
	Take Your Arms From Around My Neck	–
	Sugar Babe	–
	When The Saints Go Marchin In	–

TIPPO LITE & HIS ALL STARS

Vcl. with saxes; pno; gtr; bs; dms.		Memphis, early '50s
	Dark Skin Woman Blues	Back Alley 202
	Jumping This Morning	–

LITTLE AL (The late)

Real name Al Gunter

Vcl/gtr. with Arthur Gunter, gtr; dms.		Nashville, 1957
A	Little Lean Woman	Excello 2098
B	No Jive	–

Vcl/gtr. with pno; dms.		Nashville 1958
18110	Every Day Brings About A Change	Excello 2128
18111	Easy Ridin' Buggy	–

LITTLE BOY BLUES

See under Bob Harris

LITTLE BOY FULLER

Real name Rich Trice

Vcl/gtr.		New York City, 1947
S-3392	Shake Your Stuff	Savoy 5535
S-3393		
S-3394	Lazy Bug Blues	Savoy 5535

LITTLE DAVID

Vcl/gtr. with ten(-1); pno		Los Angeles, 1952
A	Macayo	International 104, RPM 371
B	Crying Blues -1	– , –

LITTLE DAVID

Real name David Wylie

Vcl/gtr.		1950
1262	Shackles Round My Body	Regal 3271
1263	You're Gonna Weep And Moan	– , Savoy MG 16000

LITTLE HUDSON'S RED DEVIL TRIO

Real name Hudson Showers
Vcl/gtr. with Lee Eggleston (Akerson?), pno; Jesse ? , dms.   Chicago, 1953
U 2359   Rough Treatment   JOB 1015
U 2360   I'm Looking For A Woman   –

LITTLE JOE

See under Joe Hill Louis

LITTLE JOE BLUE

Real name Joe Vallery. Born Vicksburg, Mississippi on September 23, 1934
Vcl. with 2 saxes; pno; Larry Green, gtr; Curtis Tillman, bs-gtr; Chuck Thomas, dms.

		Los Angeles, 1966
M 132A	Dirty Work Going On	Movin' 132, Checker 1141
M 132B	Pretty Woman	–
14928	My Tomorrow	Checker 1150
14929		
14930	Once A Fool	Checker 1150
	Little Baby	Movin' 135
	Just Look At You Woman	–

Note: Produced by Fats Washington.

LITTLE JOHNNY

See under Little Johnny Jones

LITTLE JUNIOR'S BLUE FLAMES

See under Little Junior Parker.

LITTLE LARRY

Vcl. with pno; gtr; ns-gtr; dms.   Des Moines, 1965

ZTSC 90116-2KA	Loretta	Success 103
ZTSC 90117-1KA	Ride With Me	–

Note: Both sides credited to Hudson.

LITTLE MAC (or MACK)

Real name Mack Simmons, Born Arkansas in 1933.

LITTLE MACK (1)

MACK SIMMON & HIS BOYS (2)
Vcl/hca with ? Cook, hca (-1); pno (-2); Eddie King, gtr; Bob Anderson, bs-gtr;
Robert Whitehead, dms.   Chicago, 1959

606 A	Come Back	C. J. 606 (1)
606 B	My Walking Blues	–
101A, 231M	Jumping At The Cadillac -1	C. J. 607B (2)
201B, 231M	I Need You -2	– A

LITTLE MAC

ST' LOUIS MAC (B&B 113)
As above, with Emery Williams, pno;   Chicago, January 15, 1960

109 A	Time Is Getting Tougher	Bea & Baby 109
109 B	Don't Come Back	–
113 A	You Mistreated Me	Bea & Baby 113, Jaybird 4001
113 B	Broken Heart	– –

LITTLE MACK

Same or similar to above:

118 A	Let's Hootenanny Blues (Out of Jail)	Bea & Baby 118
118 B	I'm Your Fool	–

Add saxes, onit pno;   Chicago, 1961

11237, 404-84X	I'm Happy Now	Checker 991
11238, 404-84	Don't Leave Me Now	–
	I Need Love	unissued
	Played For Keeps	unissued

MAC SIMS

Prob. Mack Simmons Vcl/hca; with 2 tens; pno; gtr; bs; dms.

Chicago, 1961

S 2064	Drivin' Wheel	Pacer 1201
S 2065	Broken Hearted	–

LITTLE MILTON

Milton Campbell Not included in this volume.

LITTLE MILTON

Real name Milton Anderson
Vcl(-1)/hca; with pno; gtr; dms; Eddie White, vcl (-2)

Jackson, 1953

ACA 2406	Little Milton's Boogie -1	Delta 403
ACA 2407	Boggie Woogie Baby (sic) -2	–

Eddie White, vcl. with Milton Anderson, hca; gtr; dms.

no mx	Mistreated Baby Blues	Delta dub
no mx	Baby Don't You Know	–

> Note: Dub has 416 pencilled on, but this number was used for a Tabby Thomas release. Probably not issued.

LITTLE MOJO

See under Mojo Buford.

LITTLE PAPA JOE

See under Jody Williams.

LITTLE RED WALTER (S)

Vcl/hca. with saxes; pno; gtr; bs; dms.   New York City, 1965

711A	Aw Shucks Baby	Le Sage 711
711B	I'm Mad	–
TC731A	Pickin' Cotton	Le Sage 73 1
TC731B	Ain't Nothing But Gossip	–

LITTLE SAM

See under Big Bill Broonzy

LITTLE SON

See under Big Bill Broonzy

LITTLE SONNY

Real name Aaron Willis. Born Greensboro, Alabama on October 6, 1932.
Vcl. with Chuck Smith, pno; James ? , gtr; Jim Due Crawford, dms.

Detroit, April 1958

21839, FR 3060	I Gotta Find My Baby	Duke 186

| 21840, FR 3061 | Hear My Woman Calling | Duke 186 |

Vcl/hca. with Eddie Burns, gtr; Jim Due Crawford, dms.   Detroit, April 1958.

| 5001A | Love Shock | JVB 5001, Excello 2209 |
| 5001B | I'll Love You Baby | — |

Hca. with brass; gtr; bs-gtr; dms.   Detroit, 1966

| ZTSC 126449 | The Creeper | Revilot 209 |
| ZTSC 126450 | Latin Soul | — |

LITTLE T-BONE

Vcl/gtr. with pno.   Houston, 1947

| Hu 209 | Love-s A Gamble | Miltone 5223 |
| Hu 210 | Christmas Blues | — |

LITTLE TEMPLE & HIS "88"

See under Gus Jenkins

LITTLE WALTER (see also in Appendix)

Real name Marion Walter Jacobs. Born Alexandria, Louisiana on May 1, 1930

> Note: For other vocal sides see Sunnyland Slim and Leroy Foster, where they
> are listed to avoid confusion.

Vcl(-1)/hca. with Othum Brown, vcl(-2)/gtr.   Chicago, 1947

| 711A, U 2108 | Ora Nelle Blues (That's Alright) -2 | Ora Nelle 711, Chance 1116 |
| 711B U 2109 | I Just Keep Loving Her -1 | — — |

LITTLE WALTER TRIO
Vcl/gtr. with Muddy Waters, gtr; Leroy Foster, dms.

Chicago, 1950

| R 1356 | Muskadine Blues | Regal 3296, Blues Classics BC-S |
| R 1357 | Bad Acting Woman | — |

> Note: The above are Parkway masters.

LITTLE WALTER & HIS NIGHT CATS
Vcl/hca. with Louis Miles, David Miles, gtrs; Fred Below, dms.

Chicago 1952

| U 7437 | Juke | Checker 758, LP 1428, 2973 |
| U 7438 | Can't Hold Out Much Longer | — — |

LITTLE WALTER & HIS NIGHT CAPS
Same:

Chicago, 1952

| 1052 | Mean Old World | Checker 764, LP 1428 |
| 1053 | Sad Hours | — — , 2973 |

LITTLE WALTER & HIS JUKES
Same:

Chicago, 1953

U 4343	Don't Have To Hunt No More	Checker 767
U 4344	Crazy Legs	Cgecker 986
U 4345	Tonight With A Fool	Checker 767
U 4346	untitled	unissued
U 4347	Oh Brother Jack	unissued
U 4348	Off The Wall	Checker 770, LP 1428
U 4349	Tell Me Mama	— —

> Note: There is an alternate take of U 4348 on an English Pye LP

Same:

Chicago 1954

U 4394	Quarter To Twelve	Checker 780
U 4398	Blues With A Feeling	— , LP 1428
U 4399	Last Boogie	unissued

U 4400	Too Late	Checker 825
U 4401	Fast Boogie	unissued
U 4402	Lights Out	Checker 786
U 4403	Fast Large One	unissued
U 4404	You're So Fine	Checker 786, LP 1428
U 4416	Last Night	Checker 805, LP 1428
		Argo LP 4042
U 4417	Mellow Down Easy	Checker 805

Note: The version of U 4416 on Argo LP 4042 is an alternate take minus harmonica.

LITTLE WALTER
Vcl/hca. with Louis Miles, Robert Lockwood, Jr., gtrs; Willie Dixon, bs; Fred Below, dms.

		Chicago 1954
7604	Rocker	Checker 793
7608	Oh Baby	–

Add Otis Spann, pno;
| 7653 | I Got To Find My Baby | Checker 1013 |

Vcl/hca. with Robert Lockwood, Jr., David Miles, gtrs; Fred Below, dms.
| U 7673 | You'd Better Watch Yourself | Checker 799, LP 1428 |
| U 7674 | Blue Light | – – |

Vcl./hca. with Leonard Caston, Robert Lockwood, Jr., gtrs; Willie Dixon, bs; Fred Below, dms.
| | | Chicago, 1955 |
| 7776 | Thunder Bird | Checker 811 |

Omit Caston, Lockwood plays both gtr; and bs-gtr;
| 7777 | My Babe | Checker 811, LP 1428 |
| | | Argo LP 4025 |

Vcl Chorus dubbed on:
| 7777R | My Babe | Checker 955 |

Vcl/hca. with Bo Diddley, gtr(-1); Robert Lockwood Jr., gtrs; Willie Dixon, bs; Fred Below, dms;
| U 7827 | Roller Coaster -1 | Checker 817 |
| U 7828 | I Got To Go | – |

Vcl/hca. with Robert Lockwood Jr., David Miles, gtrs; Willie Dixon, bs; Fred Below, dms;
| U 7874 | Crazy For My Baby | Checker 986 |
| U 7888 | I Hate To See You Go | Checker 825 |

Same
		Chicagom 1956
U 7966	One More Chance With You	Checker 838
U 7967	Who	Checker 833
U 7968	Boom, Boom Out Goes The lights	Checker 867, Argo LP 4042
U 7969	It Ain't Right	Checker 833
8068	Flying Saucer	Checker 838

Vcl/hca. with Robert Lockwood Jr., Luther Tucker, gtrs; Willie Dixon, bs; Fred Below dms.
8191	It's Too Late Brother	Checker 852
8192	Teenage Beat	Checker 845
8193	Take Me Back	Checker 852
8194	Just A Feeling	Checker 845

Same:
		Chicago 1957
8433	Nobody But You	Checker 859
8434		
8435	Shake Dancer	Checker 1071
8436	Everybody Needs Somebody	Checker 859
8525	Temperature	Checker 867
8526	Ah'w Baby	Checker 945
8527	I've Had My Fun	–

Fred Robertson, gtr; replaces Lockwood.
		Chicago, 1958
8644	The Toddle	Checker 890
8645	Confessin' The Blues	–

Vcl/hca. with Otis Spann, pno; Muddy Waters, Luther Tucker, gtrs; Willie Dixon, bs; George Hunter, dms.
| 8981 | Key To The Highway | Checker 904, Argo LP 4027 |
| 8982 | Rock Bottom | – |

Fred Robertson, gtr. replaces Waters:

9244	Everything's Gonna Be Alright	Checker 930
9620	Mean Old Frisco	Checker 1117
9621	Back Track	Checker 930
9655	Blue And Lonesome	Checker 1117

Same: Chicago, 1960/61

| 9810 | Me And Piney Brown | Checker 939 |
| 9811 | Break It Up | – |

Spann out:

10208	Blue Midnight	Checker 955
10593	I Don't Play	Checker 968
10594	As Long As I Have You	–
10595		
10596	Just You Fool	Checker 1013

Vcl/hca. with Jarrett Gibson, Ten/bari; Lafayette Leake, pno; Billy Emerson, org;
Buddy Guy, gtr; Jack Meyers, bs-gtr; Al Duncan, dms.

Chicago, February 5, 1963

12168	Up The Line	Checker 1043
12169	I'm A business Man	Checker 1081
12170	Dead Presidents	–
12171	Southern Feeling	Checker 1043

LITTLE WALTER J

See under Little Walter.

LITTLE WALTER JR.

See under George Smith.

LITTLE WILLIE LITTLEFIELD

Vcl/pno. with Don Wilkerson, ten(-1); dms.   Houston 1948/49

ACA 1031	Little Willie's Boogie	Eddie's 1202
ACA 1032	My Best Wishes	
ACA 1033	Medley Boogie	unissued
ACA 1034	Chicago Bound	Eddie's 1205
ACA 1046	Littlefield Boogie	Freedom 1502
no mx	What's The Use	Eddie's 1205
no mx	Swanee River (pno solo)	Eddie's 1212
no mx	Boogie Woogie Playgirl -1	–

> Note: Leroy Ervin, gtr; on one session. Rev. Freedom 1502 by Goree Carter
> who is possibly guitarist on the Littlefield side. Freedom issue advertised in
> Billboard March 26, 1949.

Vcl/pno. with tpt; saxes; gtr; bs; dms. (On Modern sessions backing is prob, Maxwell Davis'
or Wardell Gray's band.   Los Angeles, 1949

MM 1115	Midnight Whistle	Modern 20-686
MM 1116	It's Midnight	–
MM 1117	Drinkin' Hadacol	Modern 20-709
MM 1143	Come On Baby	Modern 20-716, 20-785
MM 1144	Farewell	Modern 20-709
MM 1220-3	The Moon Is Risin'	Modern 20-726
MM 1221-1	Merry Xmas	Modern 20-716, 20-785
MM 1226-3	Tell Me Baby	Modern 20-747
MM 1227-2	Your Love Wasn't So	Modern 20-729
MM 1255-2	Frightened	Modern 20-726
MM 1256-2	Why Leave Me All Alone	Modern 20-747
MM 1281-3	Once Was Lucky	Modern 20-801
MM 1282-4	Trouble All Around Me	Modern 20-775
MM 1283-2	Rockin' Chair Mama	Modern 20-729
MM 1284-3	Hit The Road	Modern 20-775
MM 1375-3	Cheerful Baby	Modern 20-754
MM 1376-2	Happy Pay Day	–

Vcl/pno. with Lora Wiggins, vcl(-1); others unk.		Los Angeles, 1950
MM 1434-1	I've Been Lost -1	Modern 20-801
MM 1435-3	Ain't A Better Story Told -1	Modern 20-781
MM 1436	Life Of Trouble	Modern 854
MM 1437-1	You Never Miss A Good Woman Till She's Gone	Modern 20-781

Vcl/pno. with ten; gtr; bs; dms.		Los Angeles, 1951
MM 1647	Lump In My Throat	Modern 837
MM 1648	Mean Mean Woman	–
MM 1649	Too Late For Me	Modern 854

Vcl/pno. with Maxwell Davis, ten; Jewel Grant, alt/bari; Herman Mitchell, gtr; Ralph Hamilton bs; Jesse Sailes, dms.　Los Angeles, August, 18, 1952

F-276	Sticking On You Baby	Federal 12101
F-277	Blood Is RedderThan Wine	–
F-278-1	K. C. Loving	Federal 12110, 12351
F-279-1	Pleading At Midnight	–

Vcl./pno. with Rufus Gore, ten; Charlie Grayson, gtr; Edwyn Conley, bs; Bill Douglas, dms.　Cincinnati, June 9, 1953

F-1107	The Midnight Hour Was Shining	Federal 12137, 12351, King LP 859
F-1108-1	Miss K. C.'s Fine	Federal 12148
F-1109-1	Rock A Bye Baby	–
F-1110	My Best Wishes And Regards	Federal 12137
F-1111-1	Jim Wilson's Boogie	Federal 12221
F-1112-1	Sitting On The Curbstone	–

Vcl/pno. with Wardell Gray, ten; Jesse Irvin, gtr; Mario Delagarde, bs; Bill Douglas, dms.　Los Angeles, October 30, 1953

F-379	Please Don't Go-o-o-o-oh	Federal 12163
F-380	Falling Tears	Federal 12174
F-381	Goofy Dust Blues	–
F-382	Don't Take My Heart Little Girl	Federal 12163

Vcl/pno. with gtr; bs-gtr. dms; chorus 9-10		1956
1018	Ruby-Ruby -1	Bulls-Eye 1005, Rhythm 108.
1019	Easy Go	– –

ROBERT LOCKWOOD JR.

Born Marvell, Arkansas on March 27, 1915

Vcl/gtr. with Sunnyland Slim, pno; bs; dms.		Chicago, November, 1951
4538	I'm Gonna Dig Myself A Hole	Mercury 8260
4539	Dust My Broom (duet)	–

ROBERT JR. LOCKWOOD

Vcl/gtr. with		Chicago, 1954
3003	Aw, Aw Baby	J.O.B. 1107
3004	Sweet Woman From Maine	–

Vcl/gtr. with Sunnyland Slim, pno.		Chicago, July 13, 1960
	Take A Little Walk With Me	Decca LK 4664
	Boogie	unissued

Note: Cleveland, Ohio based artist. See also under Otis Spann q.v.

CRIPPLE CLARENCE LOFTON (The Late)

Vcl (-1)/pno.		Chicago, December 1943
127	Policy Blues -1	Session 10-014
128	I Don't Know -1	–
129	The Fives	Session 10-005
130	Deep End Boogie	–
140	In The Mornin'	Session 10-006
141	Early Blues	–
142	I Don't Know -1	Session 12-005
143	Streamline Train	J 1224

BERT LOGAN (The Late)

Vcl/gtr. with Big Joe Williams, gtr; Russ Logan, wbd.   Crawford, Miss., 1965
	Don't You Want To Be A Member	Testament T-2209
	Four O'Clock In The Morning	Storyville SLP 180

RUSS LOGAN

Vcl/wbd. with Big Joe Williams, gtr;   Crawford, Miss., 1965
	Annie Mae	Testament T-2209

CLARENCE LONDON

Vcl/gtr.   Dallas, 1953
A	Goin' Back To Mama	Fidelity 3009
B	One Rainy Morning	—

LONESOME LEE

See under Jimmy Lee Robinson

LONESOME SUNDOWN

Real name Cornelius Green. Born Donaldsonville, La. in 1931.
Vcl/gtr. with ? Miller, pno. "Jockey", dms.   Crowleym La. late 1956
A	Leave My Woman Alone	Excello 2092
B	Lost Without Love	

Vcl/gtr. with Lazy Lester, hca (-1); ? Miller, pno. "Jockey", dms. vcl. grp (-2)
     Crowley, la. 1957
A	My Home Is A Prison	Excello 2102
B	Lonesome Whistler (no pno)	
A	Don't Say A Word -1	Excello 2117
B	I've Got The Blues -2	—

Vcl/gtr. with Lazy Lester, hca; Katie Webster, pno; Bobby McBride bs-gtr; Warren Storm, dms/wbd.   Crowley, La. 1958
18976	Lonely, Lonely Me	Excello 2132
18977	I'm A Mojo Man	
A	I Stood By (no hca)	Excello 2145
B	Don't Go	—

Same: Crowley, La, 1959
A	No Use To Worry	Excello 2154
B	You Know I Love You	
A	If You See My Baby (no hca)	Excello 2163
B	Gonna Stick To My Baby	—

Same: Crowley, La. 1960
A	Love Me Now	Excello 2174
B	Learn To Treat Me Better	—

Same, but add Lionel Torrence, ten;   Crowley, La, 1961
A	Lonesome Lonely Blues	Excello 2202
B	I'm Glad She's Mine	—

     Crowley, La, 1962
A	My Home Ain't Here	Excello 2213
B	I Woke Up Crying (Oh What A Dream)	—

     Crowley, La, 1963
A	When I Had I Didn't Need	Excello 2236
B	I'm A Samplin' Man	—

Vcl/gtr. with Lionel Torrence, ten; Katie Webster, pno; Bobby McBride, or Rufus Thibodeaux, bs-gtr; Austin Broussard, dms.   Crowley, La. 1964
A	Guardian Angel	Excello 2242
B	I Wanta Know Why	—
A	I Had A Dream Last Night	Excello 2249
B	I Got A Broken Heart	—

Add Lionel Prevo, ten;		Crowley, La, 1965
A	You're Playing Hookey	Excello 2254
Omit saxes. Add hca;		
B	Please Be On That "5.19"	Excello 2254
Add Saxes (-1);		
A	Hoodoo Woman Blues	Excello 2259
B	I'm Gonna Cut Out On You -1	–
A	It's Easy When You Know How	Excello 2264
B	Gonna Miss You When You're Gone	–

LONG JOHN

See under Lost John Hunter

LONG TALL LESTER

Real name Lester Foster.
Vcl with hca; pno; bs-gtr; dms

		Houston, 1958
FR 3084-1	All Because Of You	Duke 197
FR 3085-1	Working Man (no pno)	–

Note: Aurally the hca is played by Lazy Lester. This artist lives in Ripley, Arkansas.

JEWELL LONG

Born Sealy, Texas on June 30, 1908
Vcl/pno/gtr.(-1)

		Sealy, August. 13 1960
	Frankie And Albert	VJM VEP 4
	My Pony Run Blues -1	–
	Sealy Rag -1	–
	Muddy Shoes Blues	–
	untitled piano blues	unissued
	Ella Speed -1	unissued

LOUIS & FROSTY

See under Louis Jackson

JOE HILL LOUIS (See also in APPENDIX)

Born ?   Died Memphis c. 1958
Vcl/hca/gtr./dms. with bs

		New York City, November 21, 1949
CO 41942	Don't Trust Your Best Friend	Columbia 30221
Co 41943	Railroad Blues	Columbia 30182
CO 41944	A Jumpin' And A Shufflin'	
CO 41945	Joe's Jump	Columbia 30221
Vcl/hca/gtr/hi-hat or traps		Memphis, 1950
MM 1459	I Feel Like A Million	Modern 20-795, Blues Classics 15
MM 1460	Heartache Baby	–
Same:		Memphis 1951
MM-1492	Boogie In The Park	Modern 20-813
MM-1493	Cold Chills	
MM-1540	Walkin'Talkin' Blues	Modern 20-822
MM-1541	Street Walkin' Woman	–
Add Ford Nelson, pno(-1).		
MM-1564	Eyesight To The Blind -1	Modern 20-828
MM-1565	Goin' Down Slow	–
MM-1629	Gotta Go Baby	Modern 839
MM-1630	Big Legged Woman	–
Same:		Memphis 1952
MM-1750	Peace Of Mind	Modern 856
MM-1751	Chocolate Blonde	–

JOHNNY LEWIS
Vcl/gtr. with ten; pno; d,s

GR 15065	She's Taking All My Money	Rockin' 517

GR-15066   Jealous Man   Rockin' 517

JOE HILL LOUIS
Vcl/gtr./traps. with Walter Horton, hca(-1)
C-1035A   Dorothy May -1   Checker 763
C-1036A   When I'm Gone   –

Vcl/hca/gtr. with Billy "Red" Love, pno; Willie Nix, dm.   Memphis 1953
U 57   We All Gotta Go Sometime   Sun 178
U 58   She May Be Yours   –
           Tiger Man (no hca)   unissued

Vcl/gtr. with ten; pno; bs; dms.   1954
H-410-C   Bad Woman Blues   Big Town 401
H-411-C   Hydromatic Woman   –

Vcl/gtr. with bs; dms.   West Memphis, c. 1954
           I'm Leaving Tomorrow   Ace unissued
           Get Up Off It   –
           Sweetest Woman I Ever Seen   –

Add pno. 2nd gtr.
           4th And Beale   Ace unissued
           Ruthy Mae   –
           J. H. Boogie   –

LITTLEJOE
Vcl/gtr. with ten; pno; bs; dms.   Memphis, 1957
1000A   Glamour Girl   House Of Sound C&S 500
1000B   Keep Your Arms Around Me -1   –
           -1 no ten

JOE HILL LOUIS
Vcl/hca/gtr/dms.   Memphis, February 24, 1953
           Woodchopper's Ball   Modern unissued
           Boogie   –
           I Love My Baby   –
           Western Union Man   –
           She Got Me Walkin'   –
           She Broke Up My Life   –
           Keep Away From My Baby   –
           Good Morning Little Angel   –
           Boogie No. 2.   –

LESLIE LOUIS

Vcl. with ten; pno; Joe Hill Louis, hca/gtr. dms.   Memphis, 1952
GR 15053-1 Ridin' Home   Rockin' 509
GR 15054-1 Don't Do It Again   –

TOMMY LOUIS & THE RHYTHM ROCKERS

Vcl. with hca; gtr; bs; dms.   early '60's
           The Hurt Is On   Muriel 1001
           I Love You so   –

LOUISIANA RED

Real name Red Minter Born Bessemer, Alabama
Vcl/hca (where hear)/gtr. with saxes; pno; bs; dms.   New York City, 1960
1246-1   I Done Woke Up   Atlas 1246
1246-2   I Had A Feeling

Vcl/hca/gtr. with bs-gtr; dms.   New York City, 1962
           Red's Dream   Roulette 4469, LP 25200,
                                                              Foru, Circle LP 9100
           Ride On, Red, Ride On   issues as above.
           Keep Your Hands Off My Woman   Roulette LP 25200, Forum LP 910
           I'm Louisiana Red   –   –

207

	Sweet Alesse	Roulette LP 25200, Forum LP 9100
	Working Man Blues	– –
	I'm A Roaming Stranger	– –
	I Wonder Who	– –
	The Seventh Son	– –
	Sad News	– –
	Don't Cry	– –
	Two Fifty Three	– –

Same:		New York City, 1964
GP 1014	I'm Too Poor To Die	Glover 3002
GP 1015	Sugar Hips	–

Note: Glover 3002 may be from Roulette sessions

HOT SHOT LOVE

Vcl/hca. with gtr; dms.		Memphis, 1954
F-12	Wolf Call Boogie	Sun 196
F-13	Harmonica Jam	–

JASPER LOVE

Born Lambert, Mississippi in 1915.
Vcl/pno. with Columbus Jones, vcl(-1)

		Clarksdale, July 23, 1960
	Santa Fe Blues	Decca LK 4664
	Love's Honeydripper	Arhoolie FS 101
	Desert Blues	Arhoolie F 1005
	The Slop -1	

WILLIE LOVE

Born Lambert, Mississippi in 1911. Died 1957

WILLIE LOVE'S THREE ACES
Vcl/pno. with ten; Little Bill, gtr; bs; dms.

		Jackson, Miss. Summer 1951
DRC 1-37	Take It Easy Baby	Trumpet 137
DRC 1-38	Little Car Blues	–

Omit ten(-1):

DRC 48	Everybody's Finshing -1	Trumpet 147
DRC 49		
DRC 50	My Own Boogie	Trumpet 147

WILLIE LOVE & HIS THREE ACES
Vcl/pno. with Joe Willie Wilkins, gtr; bs; dms.

		Jackson, Miss. 1952
DRC 100, ACA 2129	Feed My Body To The Fishes	Trumpet 172
DRC 101, ACA 2130	Fallin Rain	–
DRC 102, ACA 2131	Vanity Dresser Boogie	Trumpet 173
DRC 103, ACA 2134	Seventy Four Blues	– , Blues Classics 15
DRC 104, ACA 2133	21 Minutes to 9	Trumpet 174
DRC 105, ACA 2132	Shady Lane Blues	–
DRC 106, ACA 2147	Nelson Street Blues	Trumpet 175
DRC 107, ACA 2148	V-8 Ford	–

Vcl/pno. with ten; bs; dms.

		Jackson, Miss. late 1953
DRC 174B ACA 2558	Shout Brother Shout	Trumpet 209
DRC 175 ACA 2559	New Worried Blues	unissued

208

DRC 176, ACA 2556 DRC 177	Wonderful Baby	unissued
DRC 178, ACA 2557	Willie Mae	unissued
DRC 175B, ACA 2916	Way Back (add gtr)	Trumpet 209

Note; Tenor on above is aurally Duke Huddleston.

LONNIE LYONS (The Late)

LONNIE LYONS COMBO
Vcl/pno. with Nelson Mills, tpt; Conrad Johnson, atl; Sa, Williams, ten; Goree Carter, gtr;
Louis "Nunu" Pitts, bs; Allison Tucker, dms.   Houston, 1949

4*1029(ACA)		
	Lonely Heart Blues	Freedom 1504
4*1030(ACA)		
	Barrelhouse Night Cap	–
F 1059(ACA)		
	Far Away Blues	Freedom 1507
F 1060(ACA)		
	Fly Chick Bounce	–
ACA 1082	Neat And Sweet Part 1	Freedom 1512
ACA 1083	Neat And Sweet Part 2	–

LONNIE LYONS, HIS PIANO AND ORCH:
Same: Houston, 1949

SMK-1162 (ACA)		
	Helpless	Freedom 1519
SMK-1163 (ACA)		
	Down In The Groovy	–

Omit Brass (–1):

SMK-1227	Betrayed -1	Freedom 1523
SMK-1228	Sneaky Joe	
ACA 1216	She's My Best Bet	Freedom unissued
ACA 1217	It's Just A Dream	–
ACA 1218	Tall, Tan And Terrific	–

LONNIE LYONS
Vcl/pno. with Ed Wiley, ten; Henry Hayes, alt; Donald Cooks, bs; Ben Turner, dms.
                                                                          Houston, 1951

	I Need Romance	SIW 566
	I'm Waiting Baby	–

SMILING SMOKEY LYNN

Vcl (–1). with Don Johnson Band: Tpts; ten; bar; pno; bs; dms.

		Los Angeles, 1949
A	State Street Boogie -1	Specialty 323
B	Jackson's Blues	–

Vcl. with Wallace Sandford's Orch.; saxes; pno; gtr; bs; dms. Houston, 1951

ACA 1770	Unfaithful Woman	Peacock 1555
ACA 1771	Goin' Back Home	–

Prob. same:

ACA 1779	Time For Me To Go	Peacock unissued
ACA 1780	We'll Rock It	–

Vcl. with Bill Harvey's Band: saxes; pno; gtr; bs; dms.   Houston, 1952

ACA 2000	Love Is A Funny Thing	unissued
ACA 2001	Leave My Girl Alone	Peacock 1579
ACA 2002	Born To Rock	unissued
ACA 2003	Straighten Up Pretty Baby	Peacock 1579

M

WILLIE MABON (see also in APPENDIX)

Born Memphis, Tennessee on October 24, 1925.

BIG WILLIE
Vcl/pno. with hca (−1); gtr.   1949
R-1389   Bogey Man -1   Apollo 450
R-1390   It Keeps Raining   −

WILLIE MABON & HIS COMBO
Vcl/pno. with Ernest Cotton, ten; bs; dms.   Chicago, 1953
U 4314   Worry Blues   Parrot 1050, Chess 1531
U 4315   I Don't Know   −   −
                                                                   Chess LP 1439, Argo LP 4042
U 4328   I'm Mad   Chess 1538, LP 1439
U 4331   Night Latch   −

Vcl/pno. with tpt; alt; bar; gtr; bs; dms.
U 7528   You're A Fool   Chess 1548
U 7529   Monday Woman   −
U 7571   I Got To Go   Chess 1554
U 7572   Cruisin'   −

Same: Chicago, 1954
U 7611   Would You Again   Chess 1564
U 7612   Late Again   −

Similar:
U 7678   Come On Baby   Chess 1592
U 7722   Poison Ivy   Chess 1580, LP 1439
U 7723   Say Man   −

Similar: Chicago, 1955
U 7782   Whow, I Feel So Good   Chess 1592
U 7871   The Seventh Son   Chess 1608
U 7872   Lucinda   −

Similar: Chicago, 1956
U 8119   Knock On Wood   Chess 1627
U 8120   Got To Let You Go   −

Vcl/pno. with Ellis Hunter, gtr; Lannie Lee Evan, Norman J. Davis, bs. & dms (in unk. order)
                                                                   Chicago, August 16, 1957
U 575   Light Up Your Lamp   Federal 12306, Delta 3004
U 576   Rosetta, Rosetta   −   −
U 577   It's Gonna Hurt You   unissued
U 578   Got To Find My Baby   unissued

Vcl/pno. with ten (−1); Robert Lockwood, Jr., gtr; Otis Tucker, bs−gtr; Jimmy Bolden, dms.
                                                                   Chicago, 1960
U 537   I Don't Know -1   Mad 1300
U 538   I Gotta Go Now   Mad 1298
U 539   I Got To Have Her -1   Mad 1300
U 540   Michell   Mad 1298

Vcl/pno. with Billy Emerson, org; Eugene Pierson, gtr; Jimmy Lee Robinson, bs−gtr;
Clifton James, dms.   Chicago, 1962
S-2125   Got To Have Some   Formal 1016
S-2126   Why Did It Happen To Me   −

Omit Emerson. Add 2nd gtr (−1):

FR-1051B	Mean Mistreater	Formal 1018
FR-1051A	Fannie Mae -1	−

Vcl/pno. with saxes (−1); Billy Emerson, org; Lacy Gibson, gtr; Jack Meyers, bs−gtr; Al Duncan, dms.   Chicago, February 7, 1963

USA 2557	That's No Big Thing	USA 735
USA 783	Too Hot To Handle -1	USA 741
	Click-Ed Clack	unissued
USA 2556	Just Got Some	USA 735

        Note: titles listed as in Willie Dixon files.

Same: Chicago, 1963

USA 786	I'm The Fixer	USA 741

Omit org:

USA 800	Ruby's Monkey -1	USA 750
USA 801		
USA 802	I'm Hungry	USA 750

Vcl/pno. with saxes; gtr; bs; dms.   Chicago, 1964

USA 813	New Orleans Blues	USA 759
USA 814	Some More	−

Vcl/pno. with hca; gtr; bs; dms.

820	Somebody Gotta Pay	USA 767
821	Harmonica Special	−

Vcl/pno. with tpt; saxes; tbn; gtr; bs; dms.   Chicago, 1965

862	Lonesome Blue Water	USA 787
863	Some Time I Wonder	−

CONNIE McBOOKER

CONNIE McBOOKER
L. C. Williams, vcl. with Connie McBooker, pno; Eddie Green, dms.

    Houston, 1949

A	Short Baby Boogie	Eddie's 1928
B	Rich Woman Blues	−

CONNIE MAC BOOKER ORCH.
Vcl/pno. with saxes; gtr; bs; dms. ensemble vcl (−1).   Houston, 1949

SMK 1194	Loretta	Freedom 1520
SMK 1195	Come Back Baby -1	−

CONNIE MACK BOOKER
Same: Houston, 1951

MM 2042	Love Me Pretty Baby	RPM 401
MM 2043	All Alone	−

JAMES "JACK OF ALL TRADES" McCAIN

Vcl/hca. with pno; bs.   Chicago, 1945

B	Good Mr. Roosevelt	Chicago 103
	(rev. by Big Joe Williams, q.v.)	

JERRY McCAIN

JERRY (BOOGIE) McCAIN
Vcl/hca. with poss. Duke Huddleston, ten; gtr; bs; tamb; dms.

    Jackson, early 1954

DRC , ACA 2765		
	Oh Wee Baby	unissued
DRC , ACA 2767		
	Feel Just Like I'm In Love	unissued
DRC 189, ACA 2766		
	East Of The Sun	Trumpet 217
DRC 190, ACA 2768		
	Wine-O-Wine	−

No details:		Jackson, late 1954
DRC 217, ACA 3021		
	Stay Out Of Automobiles	Trumpet 231
DRC 218, ACA 3024		
	Love To Make Out	–
ACA 3025		
	Crazy About That Mess	unissued
ACA 3026		
	Fall Guy	unissued

JERRY McCAIN & HIS UPSTARTS

Vcl/hca. with pno; gtrs; dms. Nashville, 1956/59

A	That's What They Want (no pno.)	Excello 2068
B	Courtin' In A Cadillac	– , 2268
A	If It Wasn't For My Baby	Excello 2079
B	You Don't Love Me No More	–
A	Run, Uncle John, Run	Excello 2081
B	Things Ain't Right	–
A	Trying To Please	Excello 2103
B	My Next Door Neighbor	–
A	Listen Young Girls	Excello 2111
B	Bad Credit	–
18509	Groom Without A Bride	Excello 2127
18510	The Jig's Up	–

Note: rev. Excello 2268 by The Blues Rockers, q.v.

JERRY McCAIN

Vcl/hca. with Robert McCoy, pno; "Bo Diddley", gtr; Ivory Williams, bs; Leon Davis, dms.

Birmingham, Ala., 1961

S 888	She's Tough	Rex 1014
S 889	Steady	–

Vcl/hca. with ten; pno; gtr; bs–gtr; dms. Nashville, 1962

ZTSP 56742	Red Top	Okeh 7150
ZTSP 56743	Twist '62	–

Same: Nashville, 1962

ZTSP 57687	Jet Stream	Okeh 7158
ZTSP 57714	Popcorn	–

Same: Nashville, December 26, 1962

ZTSP 59462	Turn The Lights On Popeye	Okeh 7170
ZTSP 59463	Hop Stroll	–

Vcl/hca. with Tpts; pno; gtr; bs; dms; Chorous. Nashville, 1965

10095	Here's Where You Get It	Ric S-153-65
10096	Pokey	–

Vcl/hca. with ten; pno; gtr; bs; dms; vcl. grp. Birmingham, Ala., 1965

S-1321	Love Me Right	Continental 777
S-1322	Ting-Tang-Tagalu	–

Vcl/hca. with ten; pno; gtr; bs; dms. Nashville, 1965

MW 596	728 Texas	Jewel 753
MW 597	Homogenized Love	–

Same: Nashville, 1966

TM 1524	Sugar Baby	Jewel 761
TM 1525	Honky Tonk	–

Note: McCain also recorded for Reed Records in Alabama.

ERNEST McCLAY & HIS TRIO

Vcl/gtr. with Louis Jackson, pno; Beverley Scott, gtr. Los Angeles, 1948

A	Big Timing Woman	Murray 506
B	Night Working Woman	–

ROBERT McCOY

Vcl/pno. Birmingham, Ala., 25 December, 1958

	Louise Blues	Vulkan 2501

	Jingle Bells	unissued
	Bye Bye Baby	–
	Right String But The Wrong Yo Yo	–
	Don't The Moon Look Lonesome	–
	Ain't Misbehavin'	–

Vcl/pno.   Birmingham, Ala., Summer, 1962
| | Bob's Boogie (Bye Bye Baby) | Vulkan 2503 |

Vcl/pno.   Birmingham, Ala., Fall, 1962
	Bye Bye Baby	rejected
	Dyin' Slow Blues	rejected
	Louise Blues No. 2	Vulkan 2501
	Bob's Stomp Down	rejected
	Washington Heights	Vulkan 2501
	Let's Get Together	–
	Pratt City Special	–
	Call The Wagon	–

Vcl/pno.   Birmingham, Ala., Winter, 1962
	Church Bell Blues	Vulkan 2501
	Bye Bye Baby	–
	Dyin' Slow Blues	–
	Bessemer Rag	–

Vcl/pno.   Birmingham, Ala., Summer, 1963
| | 44 Blues | Vulkan 2503 |
| | There'll Be Some Changes Made | Vulkan 2504 |

Vcl/pno.   Birmingham, Ala., October 11,
                                              1963
	Prison Bound Blues	Vulkan 2502
	Original Cow Cow Blues	–
	How Long Blues	–
	Florida Bound Blues	–
	Pinetop's Boogie Woogie	–
	McCoy Boogie	–
	Dirty Dozens	–
	DuPree Blues	–
	Honky Tonk Train	–
	44 Blues	–
	Yancey Special	–
	Mr. Freddy Blues	–

Vcl/pno. with Weyman Marshall, ten (–1); Pat Cather, vcl (–2)/pno (–3); Birmingham Sam,
comb (–4); Dave Miles, hca (–5).   Birmingham, Ala., March 14,
                                              1964
	Shake Your Moneymaker -1, 2	unissued
	Gone Mother Blues	–
	Mr. Redcap Porter, -1, 4	–
	Red's Blues	–
	All In All Baby	–
	All Night Long	–
	What'd I Say (Weyman Marshall, vcl) -2	
	Key To The Highway -5	rejected
	Key To The Highway -5	rejected
	Bye Bye Baby -3	rejected
	Straight Alky	unissued
	Trouble, Trouble, Trouble	–

ROBERT McCOY & HIS FIVE SINS
Vcl/pno; Frank Adams, ten/clnt (–1); King Jesse Ellston, org (–2); Frank Walton, tpt;
Pat Cather, pno (–3); David McConico, gtr; Ivory Williams, bs; James Summerfield, dms;
Marcus Ingram, vcl (–4); 2 girl sgrs, vcls (–5).   Birmingham, Ala., July 15, 1964
0001-1	Louise -2	rejected
0001-2	Louise -2	Soul-O 112
0002-1	Bye Bye Baby -2, 4, 5	–
0002-2	Bye Bye Baby -2, 4, 5	unissued
0003-1	There'll Be Some Changes Made	rejected
0003-2	There'll Be Some Changes Made	rejected

0003-3	There'll Be Some Changes Made	unissued
0004-1	Cherry -2	unissued
0004-2	Cherry -2	rejected
0004-3	Cherry -2	unissued
0005-1	Goodbye -2, 4, 5	rejected
0005-2	Goodbye -2, 4, 5	Soul-O 114
0006-1	Goodbye Pt. 2 -2, 4, 5, 3	–
0006-2	Goodbye Pt. 2 -2, 3, 4, 5	unissued
0006-3	Goodbye Pt. 2 -2, 3, 4, 5	unissued

RUBE McCOY

Born Booneville, Mississippi in 1922.
Vcl. with Big Joe Williams, gtr.   East St. Louis, 1965

	Black Mary	Testament T-2209
	Rising Sun Shine On	–
	Rising Sun Blues	Storyville SLP 180

JIMMY McCRACKLIN (see also in Appendix)

Born St. Louis, Mo.   Los Angeles, 1945

APP 100A	Miss Mattie Left Me	Globe 102
APP 100B	Mean Mistreated Lover	–
APP 301	Highway 101	Globe 104
APP 302	Baby Don't You Want To Go	
1-MC	Achin' Heart	Globe 109
4-MC	Street Loafin' Woman	– , Preview 107

Vcl. with David Blunston, pno.   Los Angeles, 1945
| 182A | You Deceived Me | Excelsior 182 |
| 182B | Blunston's Boogie | – |

Vcl. acc. includes John "Shifty" Henry, bs; Alray "Jo-Jo" Kidd, dms.
| SA 298-7 | Special For You | Courtney 123 |
| SA 297-5 | You Had Your Chance | – |

Vcl/pno. with Robert Kelton, gtr; bs.   Oakland, 1947
CAV 128, SF 1664
| | Railroad Blues | Cavatone 130, Aladdin 3089 |
CAV 129
CAV 130, SF 1663
| | Bad Luck And Trouble | ?   , Aladdin 3089 |
| CAV 131 | Jimmy's Blues | Cavatone 251 |

JIMMY McCRACKLIN & HIS BLUES BLASTERS
Vcl/pno. with Robert Kelton, gtr; Little Red, dms.   Oakland, 1948
Q11, MM 1180
| | Bad Condition Blues | Down Town 2023, Modern 20-806 |

Q12, MM 1181
	Blues Blasters Shuffle	– –
SR 104A	Low Down Mood	Down Town 2027
SR 104B	She's My Baby	–

Vcl/pno. with Little Red, dms.   Oakland, 1949
| T-120066 | Rock And Rye | Trilon 197 |
| T-120177 | Miss Minnie Lee Blues | – |

No details:
T-1287-3	Playin' On Me	Trilon 231
T-1288-5	Big Foot Mama	–
T 1304	When I'm Gone	Trilon 245, Old Swingmaster 25
T 1305	South Side Mood	Trilon 244, Old Swingmaster 24
T 1306	Listen Woman	Trilon 245, Old Swingmaster 25
T 1307	I Can Understand Love	Trilon 244, Old Swingmaster 24

No details: Oakland, 1949/50
MM 1185-3	Love When It Rains	RPM 317
MM 1186-2	Your Heart Ain't Right	–
MM 1235-2	Just Won't Let Her Go	Modern 20-762

214

MM 1236-2	Rockin' All Day	Modern 20-762
MM 1237-2	I Think My Time Is Here	Modern 20-728
MM 1238-2	Deceiving Blues	–
MM 1239-1	Beer Drinking Woman	Modern 20-722
MM 1240-2	Up And Down Blues	–
MM 1290-5	Gotta Cut Out	Modern 20-741
MM 1291		
MM 1292-1	Bad Health Blues	Modern 20-741

JIMMY McCRACKLIN & HIS ORCHESTRA
Vcl/pno. with Joe Conwright, alt; Charles Sutter, ten; Lafayette Thomas, gtr; Joe Toussaint, bs; San Frisco Jeff, dms.   Los Angeles, 1951

260A	You Don't Love Me	Swing Time 260
260A +	Looking For A Woman	–
264A	True Love Blues	Swing Time 264
264A +	I'm Gonna Have Fun	–
	Rockin' Man	Swing Time 270, JMC 209
	I'm Tired	– –
285A	That's Life	Swing Time 285
285A +	What's Your Phone Number	–
286A	I Found That Woman	Swing Time 286, Hollywood 1025
286A +	Blues For The People	– , Hollywood 1025,
		Nashville NLP 2030
291A	Movin' On Down The Line	Swing Time 291
291A +	House Rockin' Blues	–

Johnny Parker, alt. & unk. ten. replaces Conwright & Sutter: Houston, 1952

ACA 2201	Chancing My Love	unissued
ACA 2202	My Days Are Limited	Peacock 1605
ACA 2203	She's Gone	–
ACA 2204	Better Have Your Fun	unissued

Same: Houston, 1953

ACA 2341	Share And Share Alike	Peacock 1615
ACA 2362	The Cheater	Peacock 1639
ACA 2410	She Felt Too Good	Peacock 1615
ACA 2411	I've Been Deceived	unissued

No details: Oakland, 1953

ACA 2597	I Want You To Love Me	unissued
ACA 2598	You Better Think Awhile	unissued
ACA 2599	You Don't Score No More	unissued
ACA 2600	Jockey Blues	unissued
ACA 2601	Do You Remember	unissued
ACA 2602	Waste Of Time	unissued
ACA 2603	Just A Feeling	unissued
ACA 2604	Blow Jay, Blow	unissued
ACA 2707	Pleasin' Papa	unissued

No details: Oakland, 1954

ACA 2809	The End	unissued
ACA 2880	My Story	Peacock 1639
ACA 2881	I Want No Woman	unissued
ACA 2882	Blues And Troubles	unissued
ACA 2883	Hello Baby	unissued
ACA 2920	Every Time	unissued
ACA 2921	Night And Day	unissued
ACA 2922	You're So Fine	unissued

JIMMY McCRACKLIN
Vcl/pno. with saxes; Lafayette Thomas, gtr; bs; dms.   Oakland, 1954

MM 2063	Blues Blasters Boogie	Modern 926
MM 2064	The Panic's On	
MM 2096	Darlin' Share Your Love	Modern 934
MM 2097	Give My Heart A Break	–
	Oh Baby	Crown CLP 5244
	You Don't Seem To Understand	–
	Reelin' And Rockin' Twist	–

| MM 2160 | Please Forgive Me Baby | Modern 951, Crown CLP 5244 |
| MM 2161 | Couldn't Be A Dream | −   − |

Vcl/hca/pno. with Lafayette Thomas, gtr; bs; dms.   Oakland, 1955

MM 2218	Gonna Tell Your Mother	Modern 967, Kent 369, Crown CLP 5244
MM 2219	That Ain't Right	− − −
	I Can't Tell	Crown CLP 5244
	My Mother Says	− , Kent 5027

Vcl/hca. with Lafayette Thomas, gtr; bs; dms.

| HO 656 | Fare You Well | Hollywood 1054 |
| HO 657 | It's All Right | −   , LP 503, Nashville NLP 2030 |

> Note: Crown CLP 5244 also issued on Custom LP 2057 and United LP 719. See Vol. Later recordings not included.

WILLARD McDANIEL

Pno. with bs; dms.   Los Angeles, 1951

A	Blues On The Delta	Specialty 415
B	3 A.M. Boogie	− , 105
A	Ciribiribin Boogie	Specialty 424, −
B	Blues For Mimi	−

> Note: Later records by this artist not included.

FRED McDOWELL

Born near Memphis, Tennessee on January 12, 1904.

Vcl/gtr.   Como, Miss., 1959

Keep Your Lamps Trimmed And Burning	Atlantic LP 1346, Prestige Int. 25010
Been Drinkin' Muddy Water Out Of A Hollow Log	Atlantic LP 1348
Freight Train Blues	−
Drop Down Mama	Atlantic LP 1352
When You Get Home, Write Me A Few Little Lines	−
You Done Tol' Everybody	Prestige Int. 25005
61 Highway Blues	Prestige Int. 25010
Soon One Mornin'	−

Add Fannie Davis, comb; Miles Pratcher, gtr (−1):

| Fred McDowell Blues | Prestige Int. 25010 |
| Shake 'Em On Down -1 | Atlantic LP 1348 |

Vcl/gtr. with Annie Mae McDowell, vcl (−1).   Como, Miss., February 13, 1964

Write Me A Few Lines	Arhoolie F 1021
I Heard Somebody Call	−
61 Highway	−
Mama Don't Allow Me	−
Kokomo Blues	−
Fred's Worried Blues	−
You Gonna Be Sorry	−
Shake 'Em On Down	−
My Trouble Blues	−
Black Minnie	−
That's Alright	−
When I Lay My Burden Down -1	−

Vcl/gtr.   Newport, R.I., July 24, 1964

I'm Going Down South	Vanguard VRS 9180
61 Highway Blues	−
If The River Was Whiskey	−
Fred's Rambling Blues	Vanguard VRS 9182
Shake 'Em On Down	−
Louise	Vanguard VRS 9186

Vcl/gtr. with Annie Mae McDowell, vcl (−1).   Como, Miss., November 24, 1963

	Waiting For My Baby	Testament T-2208
	I'm In Jail Again	–
	The Girl I'm Loving	–
	Going Down South, Carrying My Whip	–
	Diving Duck Blues	–
	The Sun Rose This Morning	–

Add Annie Mae McDowell, vcl.   Como, Miss., February 24, 1964

	Get Right Church	Testament T-2208
	Amazing Grace	–
	Jesus Gonna Make Up My Dyin' Bed	–
	Where Could I Go	–
	The Lord Will Make A Way -1	–
	Keep Your Lamp Trimmed And Burning -1	–
	When The Saints -1	–
	Kokomo (vcl. Fred only)	Testament T-2209
	Louise (vcl. Fred only)	–

Vcl/gtr.   Hamburg, October 7, 1965

	Highway 61	Fontana 681.529 TL

Vcl/gtr. with Eli Green, vcl (−1).   Como, Miss., 1966

	I Ain't Gonna Be Bad No More	Arhoolie F 1027
	Where Were You	–
	I Looked At The Sun	–
	Do My Baby Ever Think Of Me	–
	Brooks Run Into The Ocean -1	–
	Bull Dog Blues -1	–
	I Walked All The Way From East St. Louis	–
	Red Cross Store Blues	–
	Gravel Road Blues	–
	Frisco Lines	–
	You Got To Move	–
	I Wish I Was In Heaven Sitting Down	–

BROWNIE McGHEE

Real name Walter Brown McGhee. Born Knoxville, Tennessee in November, 1915.

BROWNIE McGHEE & SONNY TERRY
Vcl/gtr. with Terry, hca.   New York, December 12, 1944

S 5760	That's The Stuff (Watch Out)	Savoy 5533, 826
S 5761	Knockabout Blues (Carolina Blues)	– –
S 5762	Easy Ridin' Buggy	Savoy 5534
S 5763	Woman Lover Blues	–

BROWNIE McGHEE
Vcl/gtr. with (collective personnel): Sonny Terry, hca; Melvin Merritt, pno; Pops Foster or Count Edmondson, bs; Sticks Evans, dms.   New York City, 1946

402	Going Down Slow	Alert 405
403-Z	Brownie's Guitar Boogie	Alert 403, 405
404	Rock Me Mama	Alert 402
405	Night Time Is The Right Time	Alert 404
406 (403-Y)	Worried Life Blues	Alert 403
407	Lovin' With A Feeling	Alert 404
408	No Worries On My Brain	Alert 402
500	Key To The Highway	Alert 400
501	Mean Ole Frisco	Alert 401
502		
503	Rum Cola Blues	Alert 400
508	Sportin' Life Blues	Alert 401, RBF 202
	Bad Blood	Alert 406
	I Don't Care	–
	Strange Woman	Alert 407
	Big Legged Woman	–
408A	Grehound Bus	Alert 408
408B	Confusin' Blues	–

409 Y	B. M. Blues	Alert 409
409 Z	Evil But Kindhearted	–
	Shake It Up And Go	Alert 410
	Brownie Blues	–
411 Y	Got Stem Winder	Alert 411
411 Z	My Mary Blues	
412 Y	Best Jelly Roll In Town	Alert 412
412 Z	Seaboard And Southern	–
413 A	Dissatisfied Woman	Alert 413
420 A	Hello Blues	Alert 420
420 B	How Can I Love You	–

Add Jesse Powell, ten:

| 413 B | Baseball Boogie | Alert 413 |

Vcl/gtr.　　　　　　　　　　　　　　　　　New York City, Summer, 1947

D 786	Lonesome Blues	Disc 6057
D 787	Me And My Dog	
D 788	Secret Mojo Blues	Disc 6058
D 789	Pawnshop Blues	– , Asch LP 2 1/2
D 790	The Way I Feel	Disc 6059
D 791	Go On Blues	–

Note: Matrices reversed on labels of Disc 6059.

Add Melvin Merritt, pno:

| D 879 | Telegram Blues | Disc 6088 |
| D 880 | Good Boy | |

Vcl/gtr. with Jack Dupree, pno; Baby Dodds, dms.　　New York City, May 26, 1947

S 3428	Auto Mechanic Blues	Savoy 5541
S 3429	I'm Talking About It	
S 3430	Dollar Bill	Savoy 5538
S 3431	Country Boy Boogie	Savoy 5538

Vcl/gtr. with Melvin Merritt, pno; Arthur Herbert, dms.　　New York, August, 1947

S 3436	First And Fifteenth Stuff	Savoy 5548
S 3437	Three Women Blues	Savoy 5565
S 3438	Running Away From Love	Savoy 5559
S 3439	Good Thing Gone	Savoy 5561

Similar: Add bs (−1).　　　　　　　　　　　　New York, October, 1947

S 3475-2	Mabelle -1	Savoy 5548
S 3458		
S 3459	Poor Boy Blues	Savoy 5565

Vcl/gtr. with Lonnie Scott, pno; bs; dms.　　　　New York, December, 1947

S 3507	Good Roller Blues	Savoy 714
S 3508	Wrong Man Blues	Savoy 5559
S 3509	I Know My Baby	Savoy 714
S 3510-2	Married Women Blues	Savoy 5551

Vcl/gtr. with Hal Singer, ten (−1); Sonny Terry, hca (−2); Tiny Parker, pno; Bob Harris, bs; dms.　　　　　　　　　　　　　　　　　　　　New York City, 1948

S 23000	Bad Nerves	Savoy 872
S 23001	Sweet Baby Blues -2	Savoy 899
S 23002	Don't Mistreat Me	unissued
S 23003	Four O'Clock In The Morning -2	Savoy 899
S 23014	Brownie's New Worried Life Blues	Savoy 747
S 23015	I Was Fooled -1	Savoy 5557
S 23016	Confused -1	–

Vcl/gtr. with Milt Larkins, tbn; Hal Singer, ten; Harry Van Walls, pno; bs; dms. The X-Rays, vcl. grp.

27142	You Got To Love Me Baby	Savoy 760
27143		
27144		
27145	Feed Me Baby	Savoy 760

Vcl/gtr. with Hal Singer, ten; Lonnie Scott, pno; bs; dms.

| S 35112-2 | Robbie-Doby Boogie | Savoy 5550 |
| S 35113-1 | My Fault | Savoy 5551 |

S 35114
S 35115-1   Hard Bed Blues   Savoy 5550

Vcl/gtr. with Freddie Groom, pno; bs; dms.
S 35166   Dreaming And Crying   Savoy 704
S 35166   Wholesale And Retail   –

Vcl/gtr. with ten; pno; bs; dms.   New York, April, 1948
36120   New Baseball Boogie   Savoy 5561

Vcl/gtr. with Harry Van Walls, pno; Bill Caples, gtr; bs; dms.
36142   True Blues   Savoy 778
36143-A-1   My Consolation   –
36144   C. C. Baby   unissued

Vcl/gtr. with poss. Wilbert Ellis,pno; Gene Ramey, bs.   New York City, 1948
C 414   My Bulldog Blues   SIW 517
C 415
C 416   Gin Headed Woman   SIW 517

BLIND BOY WILLIAMS & HIS BLUES BAND (OR GUITAR)
Vcl/gtr. with Sticks McGhee, gtr.   New York City, 1948
J 4008   Just Drifting   SIW 538, Jade 708
J 4011   Yesterday   –   –

BROWNIE McGHEE
Vcl/gtr. with Al King, ten; Harry Van Walls, pno; Thomas Barney, bs; Ernest Hayward, dms.
                                           New York, January, 1951
50785   I'm Gonna Cross The Water   London 980
50786   Buggy Boogie   –

Vcl/gtr. with ten; pno; bs; dms. vcl. grp (–1).   New York City, 1951
D 783   I'm Gonna Move Cross The River   Derby 776
D 784   Sleepless Nights -1   –

Vcl/gtr. with ten; pno; Cedric Wallace, bs; dms.
D 767   Woman I Love   Derby 783
D 768   All Night Party   –

BIG TOM COLLINS
Vcl (–1)/gtr. with Jack Dupree, vcl (–2)/pno; Cedric Wallace, bs; Earl A. Johnson, dms.
                                           New York, July 11, 1951
K 8057-1   Heart Breaking Woman -2   King 4568
K 8058-1   Watchin' My Stuff -2   –
K 8059-1   Heartache Blues -1   King 4483
K 8060-1   Real Good Feeling -1   –   , LP 875

BROWNIE McGHEE
Vcl/gtr.   New York, January 3, 1952
PR 285   Heart In Sorrow   Par 1301
PR 286   Operator Long Distance   –

BROWNIE McGHEE AND HIS JOOK BLOCK BUSTERS
Vcl/gtr. with Sonny Terry, vcl (–1)/hca; Bob Gaddy, pno; Bob Harris, bs; George Wood,
dms. Vcl. by band (–2).   New York City, 1952
J 497   A Letter To Lightnin' Hopkins   SIW 302, Mainstream LP 56049
            (Lightnin's Blues)
J 498   Smiling And Crying Blues   –   –
            (Crying The Blues)
JA 4009   Meet You In The Morning -2   Jax 307, Mainstream LP 56049
JA 4010   I Feel So Good (Feel So Good)   Jax 304,   –
JA 4011   Key To The Highway   –
JA 4012
JA 4013
JA 4014   Brownie's Blues   Jax 307
JA 4015
            Forgive Me   Mainstream LP 56049
            The Woman Is Killing Me -1   –

Vcl (–1)/gtr. with Sonny Terry, vcl (–2)/hca.
JA 4016   Stranger's Blues -1, 2   Jax 310, Mainstream LP 56049
            (Stranger Blues)

219

JA 4017		
JA 4018	Man Ain't Nothin' But A Fool -2	Mainstream LP 56049
JA 4019		
JA 4020	New Bad Blood (Bad Blood) -1	Jax 322, Mainstream LP 56049
	Mean Old Frisco -1	Mainstream LP 56049
	Mean Old Frisco (alt. take) -1	Time LP T 7006
	Sittin' On Top Of The World -1, 2	Mainstream LP 56049
	Goin' Down Slow -2	– , Time LP T 7006

Vcl/gtr. with Sonny Terry, hca; Bob Gaddy, pno; Bob Harris, bs; George Wood, dms.

JA 4031	Dissatisfied Woman	Jax 310
JA 4032	Pawnshop Blues	Jax 322

Add ten:

JA 4055	I'm 10,000 Years Old	Jax 312
JA 4056	Cherry Red	–

Similar, add 2 saxes (–1):

DA 731	Christina	Harlem 2323
DA 732	Worrying Over You	–
DA 762K	Bluebird -1 (ensemble vcl.)	Harlem 2329
DA 763K	My Confession (I Want To Thank You) -1	–

BROWNIE McGHEE & HIS JOOK BLOCK BUSTERS
Vcl/grt. with 2 tens; pno; bs; dms.   1953

E3 QB 5314, M 8186		
	Cheatin' And Lying	Dot 1184
E3 QB 5315, M 8169		
	Need Someone To Love Me	–

Vcl/gtr. with pno; bs.

BME 102	High Price Blues	Encore 102
BME 103	Black, Brown And White Blues	–

Vcl/gtr. with Sonny Terry, hca; Jack Dupree, pno; Bob Harris, bs; Daddy Merritt, dms.
New York City, 1953

R 3016	Don't Dog Your Woman	Red Robin 111
R 3017	Daisy	–

Vcl/gtr. with Sonny Terry, hca; bs; dms.   New York City, 1954

SBM 5100	Bottom Blues	Savoy 844, MG 14019, Sharp 2003
SBM 5101	Tell Me Baby	Savoy 872, – –
	Sittin' Pretty	Savoy MG 14019, –
SBM 5103	Gone, Baby, Gone	Savoy 844, MG 14019, –

Vcl/gtr. with Sticks McGhee, gtr; dms.

SBM 5517	Diamond Ring	Savoy 835, MG 14019, Sharp 2003
SBM 5518		
SBM 5519	So Much Trouble	Savoy 835, MG 14019, Sharp 2003
	Dissatisfied Blues	Savoy MG 14019, –
	The Way I Feel	– –

Vcl/gtr. with Sonny Terry, hca; Ernest Hayes, pno; Mickey Baker, lead gtr; Leonard Gaskin, bs; Gene Brooks, dms.   New York City, October, 1955

SBM 6754	When It's Love Time	Savoy 1185, MG 14019, Sharp 2003
SBM 6755	I'd Love To Love You	Savoy 1177, – –
	Love's A Disease	Savoy 1185, MG 14019, –
SBM 6757	My Fault No. 2 (My Fault)	Savoy 1185, MG 14019, –
SBM 6758	Anna Mae	Savoy 1177

Vcl/gtr. with Sticks McGhee, gtr; pno; dms.

	Living With The Blues	Savoy MG 16000

Vcl/gtr. with Sonny Terry, vcl/hca; Coyal McMahan, vcl/maraccas.
New York City,

	The Midnight Special	Folkways FP 28, FA 2028
	Pick A Bale Of Cotton	– – ,
		Verve 9010

I Shall Not Be Moved	Folkways FP 28, FA 2028,	
Raise A Ruckus Tonight (Raise The Roof)	–	–

Omit McMahan, vcl:

Mamma Blues No. 2	Folkways FP 28, FA 2028,	
	Verve 9010	

Sonny Terry, vcl/hca. with Brownie McGhee, gtr; Coyal McMahan, maraccas.

A Man Is Nothing But A Fool	Folkways FP 28, FA 2028	
Rising Sun (no maraccas)	–	– ,
	Verve 9010	

Coyal McMahan, vcl. with Brownie McGhee, gtr; Sonny Terry, hca.

In His Care	Folkways FP 28, FA 2028,	
	Verve 9010	
Preachin'	–	–

Vcl/gtr.

New York City, 1955

Careless Love	Folkways FA 2030
Good Morning Blues	–
Sporting Life	–
Me And Sonny	–
Pawnshop Blues	–
Move To Kansas City	–
Betty And Dupree	–
Worried Mind	–

Vcl/gtr. with Sonny Terry, vcl/hca; Gene Moore, vcl/dms.

New York City, November, 1957

Better Day	Folkways FA 2327
Confusion	–
Dark Road	–
John Henry	–
Let Me Make A Little Money	–
Old Jabo	–
If You Lose Your Way	–
Guitar Highway	–
Heart In Sorrow	–
Preachin' The Blues	–
Can't Help Myself	–
I Love You Baby	–
Best Of Friends	–

Vcl/gtr. and Sonny Terry, vcl (−2)/hca. with Chris Barber's Jazz Band: Pat Halcox, tpt; Chris Barber, tbn; Monty Sunshine, clt; Eddie Smith, bjo; Dick Smith, bs; Graham Burbidge, dms.

London, May 2, 1958

Betty And Dupree -1	Nixa NJT 515	
No Worries On My Mind -1		
This Little Light Of Mine -2	–	
Glory -2	–	, NJE 1073

Vcl (−1)/gtr. and Sonny Terry, vcl (−2)/hca. with Monty Sunshine, clt (−3); Eddie Smith, bjo (−4); Pat Halcox, tpt (−5); Chris Barber, bs (−6).

Custard Pie -2, 3, 6	Nixa NJT 515, NJE 1073	
Key To The Highway -1, 4	–	–
If I Could Only Hear My Mother Pray -1, 5, 6	–	–

Vcl (−1)/gtr. with Sonny Terry, vcl (−2)/hca; Dave Lee, pno. (a) Omit Lee, McGhee, plays pno (b) Omit McGhee (c) Omit Lee (d) McGhee, vcl. only with Lee and Terry.

London, May 7, 1958

Auto Mechanic Blues -1	Nixa NJE 1060
Wholesale And Retail -1	–
Black Horse Blues -2	–
Brownie's Blues -1 (a)	Nixa NJL 18
Sonny's Blues -2 (b)	–
Southern Train -1 (c)	–
Treated Wrong -1, 2 (c)	–

Same:

London, May 8, 1958

Woman's Lover Blues -1	Nixa NJE 1060	
Change The Lock -2 (c)	Nixa NJL 18	
You'd Better Mind -1, 2 (a)	–	, NJE 1074

Cornbread, Peas And Black Molasses -1, 2	Nixa NJL 18, NJE 1074	
I Love You Baby -2	–	–
That's How I Feel -1 (d)	–	–
Climbing On Top Of The Hill -1, 2 (c)	–	–
Ju st A Dream	–	
Gone But Not Forgotten -1 (d)	–	

Vcl/gtr. with Ernest Hayes, pno; Roy Gaines, Carl Lynch, gtrs; Al Lucas,bs; Bobby
Donaldson, dms.　　　　　　　　　　　　　　　　　　New York City, September 22,
　　　　　　　　　　　　　　　　　　　　　　　　　　1958

Living With The Blues	Savoy 1564
Be My Friend	–
I Love You Cindy	unissued
Death Of Big Bill	unissued

Vcl/gtr.　　　　　　　　　　　　　　　　　　　　　Oaksdale, September, 1958

Take This Hammer	Metrojazz 2-E 1009
I'm Gonna Tell How Good You Treat Me	–
See See Rider -1	–

　　　-1 Add Milt Hinton, bs; Don Lamond, dms.

Vcl/gtr.　　　　　　　　　　　　　　　　　　　　　New York, December 26, 1958

Poor Boy	Folkways FG 3557
Memories Of My Trip	–
Walking Blues	–
Hard Feeling	–
A Hard Road To Travel	–
You Don't Know My Mind	–
Brownie's Blues	–
A Face In The Crowd	– , Aravel LP 1004
Blues Singer's Prayer	–
I Ain't Gonna Scold You	–
A Cheater Can't Win	–
Big Wide World	– , Aravel LP 1004
How Long	–
Gone But Not Forgotten	–

Vcl/gtr.　　　　　　　　　　　　　　　　　　　　　New York City, 1959

Cholly Blues	Folkways FA 2421
Pinetop's Blues	–
Hangman's Blues	–
Jelly Roll Baker	–
Loving Mama Blues	–
Backwater Blues	–
Four Day Creep	–
Black Snake Moan	–
Long Gone	–
Freight Train Blues	–
Last Mile Blues	Folkways FA 2422
Poor Man's Blues	–
St. James Infirmary	–
Grievin' Hearted Blues	–
Pallet On The Floor	–
Please Don't Dog Your Woman	–
Good Morning Blues	–
Brownie's Deep Sea River	–
No Gooder's Blues	–
Hard Times Blues	–

BROWNIE McGHEE & SONNY TERRY
Vcl/gtr. with Sonny Terry, hca; Bob Gaddy, pno; bs; dms.　　1959

944	She Loves So Easy	Old Town 1075
945	I Need A Woman	–

222

Vcl/gtr. with Sonny Terry, vcl/hca.   Newport, July 11/12, 1959

      Pick A Bale Of Cotton   Vanguard VRS 9063, VSD 2054

      My Baby Done Changed The Lock On The Door   −   −

      Midnight Special   Folkways FA 2432

      Living With The Blues   −

Same: New York City, 1959

      Pick A Bale Of Cotton   Choice 1, LP 100, Sound of
                                   America 2001

      John Henry   −   −

      Take This Hammer   Choice LP 100,   −

      Rock Island Line   −   −

      I Will Send   −   −

      I'm Gonna Tell God   −   −

      Skip To My Lou   −   −

      Wee Little Sally Walker   −   −

      Cindy, Cindy   −   −

      Old McDonald   −   −

      King William   −   −

      Around The Crab Apple Tree   −   −

      Go In And Out The Window   −   −

      My Mommy Told Me   −   −

Vcl (−1)/gtr. with Sonny Terry, vcl (−2)/hca; with Dave Lee, pno (−3).

                               London, October 7, 1959

      Rockin' And Whoopin' -2, 3   Columbia DB 4433, SEG 8226,
                               33SX 1223

      Talking Harmonica Blues -2   −   −

      I Was Born With The Blues -1, 3   Columbia 33SX 1223

      Jet Plane Blues -2   −

      I'll Put A Spell On You (McGhee only)   −

      Hound Dog Holler -2   −

      Fighting A Losing Battle -1, 2, 3   −

      I Need A Lover (McGhee only)   −

      Crazy Man Blues -2, 3   −

      Doctor Brownie's Famous Cure -1, 3   −

      Sonny's Easy Rider -1, 2, 3   −

      Walk On -1, 3   , SEG 8226

Vcl (−1)/gtr. with Sonny Terry, vcl (−2)/hca.   Los Angeles, December 29, 1959

      Key To The Highway -1   World Pacific WP 1294

      Lose Your Money -1, 2   −

      Louise -2   −

      Sporting Life -1   −

      New Harmonica Breakdown   −

      Prison Bound -1   −

      Livin' With The Blues -1   −

      Blowin' The Fuses   −

      Baby, Please Don't Go -1, 2   −

      Twelve Gates To The City -2   −

      Pawnshop Blues -1   −

      Brownie's Guitar Blues   −

Same: New York City, 1960

      Pawnshop   Bluesville LP 1002, 809,
                                   Prestige 14013

      Let Me Be Your Dog   −   , 802,

                                   −

      You Don't Know   −

      Betty And Dupree's Blues   −

      Back To New Orleans   −

      Stranger Here   −   , 802,

      Fox Hunt   −

      I'm Prison Bound   −

Louise Louise	Bluesville LP 1002, Prestige 14013
Baby, How Long	–
Freight Train	– , 818, –

Same:

Too Nicey Mama -1, 2	Bluesville BVLP 1005, 809
Sonny's Squall -1	–
Red River Blues -1, 2	–
Black Gal -1	–
Blues Before Sunrise -1	–
Sweet Lovin' Kind -1, 2	–
Midnight Special -1, 2	–
Take This Hammer -1, 2	–
Meet Me Down At The Bottom -1	–
Tryin' To Win -1, 2	–

Same:

Blues All Round My Head	Bluesville BVLP 1020
East Coast Blues	–
Muddy Water	
Beggin' And Cryin'	Bluesville BVLP 1020, 818
My Plan	–
Trying To Destroy Me	–
Everything I Had Is Gone	–
Jealous Man	
Understand Me	–
Blues Of Happiness	–

Vcl/gtr. with Sonny Terry, vcl/hca.

Walk On	Vee Jay LP 1138, Horizon WP 1617
Blues For The Lowlands	– –
Down By The Riverside	– –
Blowin' The Fuses	– –
Just Rode In Your Town	Society 1015
Sun's Gonna Shine	–
Po' Boy	–
Drinkin' In The Blues	–

Vcl/gtr. with Sonny Terry, vcl/hca; Roy Haynes, dms (–1).   New York City, 1961

I Got A Woman	Bluesville BVLP 1033
Hold Me In Your Arms	–
The C. C. And O. Blues	–
That's Why I'm Walkin -1	–
Wrong Track -1	–
Blue Feeling -1	–
House Lady -1	–
I Know Better -1	–
The Devil's Gonna Get You	–
Don't You Lie To Me	–

Vcl/gtr. with Memphis Slim, pno; Willie Dixon, bs; Jump Jackson, dms.
Hamburg, October 18, 1962

Crying At The Station	Polydor 4M 46397

Vcl/gtr.

Jump Little Children	Bluesville BVLP 1042
Lonesome Day	–
One Thing For Sure	–
The Killing Floor	–
Little Black Engine	–
I Don't Know The Reason	–
Trouble In Mind	–
Everyday I Have The Blues	–
Door To Success	–

Vcl/gtr. with Sonny Terry, vcl/hca.   Newport, 1963

	Long Gone	Vanguard VRS 9145
	Key To The Highway	–
	Walk On	–

Note: See also Sonny Terry, Lightnin' Hopkins. Also recorded as Brothers McGhee and Terry and with Andy Griffiths. See also Harry Van Walls.

STICKS McGHEE

Real name Granville McGhee. Born Knoxville, Tennessee in 1917. Died New York, August, 1961.

STICKS McGHEE & HIS BUDDIES

Vcl/gtr. with Brownie McGhee, gtr; unk. bs.   New York City, 1947

N 74860	Drinkin' Wine Spo-Dee-O-Dee	Decca 48104
N 74861	Baby, Baby Blues	–
16A	Blues Mixture	Harlem 1018
16B	Drinkin' Wine Spo-Dee-O-Dee	–

Note: N 74860 may be a reissue of Harlem 16B.

STICKS McGHEE

Vcl/gtr. with Wilbert "Big Chief" Ellis, pno; Brownie McGhee, gtr; Gene Ramey, bs; unk. dms.

New York, February, 1949

A189	Drinkin' Wine Spo-Dee-O-Dee	Atlantic 873
A190		
A191	Lonesome Road Blues	Atlantic 881
A192	Blues Mixture	Atlantic 873
A193	I'll Always Remember	Atlantic 881
A194	Blue And Brokenhearted	Atlantic 926

Add unk. tpt; alt: New York, October, 1949

A316	My Baby's Coming Back	Atlantic 909
A317	Drank Up All That Wine	Atlantic 898
A318	Venus Blues	Atlantic 909
A319	Southern Menu	Atlantic 898

Vcl/gtr. with Sonny Terry, hca; Harry "Van" Walls, pno; unk. bs; dms.

New York, March, 1950

A416	Let's Do It	Atlantic 912
A417	She's Gone	–
A418	House Warmin' Boogie	Atlantic 926
A419	Blue Barrelhouse	Atlantic 937

Vcl/gtr. with ten; pno; bs; dms.

A537	One Monkey Don't Stop No Show	Atlantic 937
A538	Tennessee Waltz Boogie	Atlantic 926

STICKS McGHEE & HIS ORCH.

Vcl/gtr. with Al King, ten; Van Walls, pno; Brownie McGhee, gtr; prob. Thomas Barney, bs; Ernest Hayward, dms.   New York, January, 1951

50723	You Gotta Have Something On The Ball	London 978
50724	Oh What A Face	–

STICKS McGHEE & HIS BUDDIES

Vcl/gtr. with ten; bari; Van Walls, pno; bs; dms.   New York, November, 1951

A747	Wee Wee Hours Part 1	Atlantic 955
A748	Wee Wee Hours Part 2	–
A749	New Found Love	Atlantic 991
A750	Meet You In The Morning	–

STICKS McGHEE & HIS BUDDIES

Vcl/gtr. with bs.   New York City, 1952

709A	My Little Rose	Essex 709
709B	No More Reveille	–

STICKS McGHEE

Vcl/gtr. with Ed Wanderveer, tpt; Charles Rawlins, Maxwell Lucas, tens; Douglas Blackman, pno; Clifford Bryan, bs; George Ward, dms.   New York, January 14, 1953

K 8346	Little Things We Used To Do	King 4610, Bethlehem LP 6071
K 8347	Blues In My Heart	King 4628

| K 8348 | Whiskey Women And Loaded Dice | King 4628, Audio-Lab AL 1520 |
| K 8349 | Head Happy With Wine | King 4610,   – |

Vcl/gtr. with James Buchanan, ten; Sir Charles Thompson, pno; Mickey Baker, gtr; Carl Pruitt, bs; Specs Powell, dms.   New York, September 2, 1953

K 8438	I'm Doin' All The Time	King 4700
K 8439	Dealin' From The Bottom	King 4672, Audio-Lab AL 1520
K 8440	The Wiggle Waggle Woo	King 4700
K 8441	Jungle Juice	King 4672, Audio-Lab AL 1520

Vcl/gtr. with Jimmy Wright, ten; Herbert "Duke" Parham, pno; Prince Babb, bs; Gene Brooks, dms.   New York, February 23, 1955

K 8543	Double Crossin' Liquor	King 4783
K 8544	Six To Eight	
K 8545	Get Your Mind Out Of Th e Gutter	King 4800, Audio-Lab AL 1520
K 8546	Sad, Bad, Glad	–

Note: Rev. Audio-Lab AL 1520 by John Lee Hooker, q.v.

STICKS McGHEE & THE RAMBLERS

No details: New York City, 1955

SMM7905	Things Have Changed	Savoy 1148
SMM7906		
SMM7907	Help Me Baby	Savoy 1148

STICKS McGHEE

Vcl/gtr. with Sonny Terry, hca; J. C. Burris, gtr; unk. dms.   New York City, 1960

| H 1468 | Money Fever | Herald 553 |
| H 1469 | Sleep In Job | – |

DAVID PETE McKINLEY

PETE McKINLEY

Vcl/gtr. with hca; dms.   1952

| A | Black Snake Blues | Fidelity 3008 |
| B | Crying For My Baby | – |

DAVID PETE McKINLEY

Vcl/gtr.

| APM 1 | Shreveport Blues | Gotham 505 |
| APM 2 | Ardelle | – |

Note: Texas or Louisiana Artist probably.

L. C. McKINLEY

Born Winona, Mississippi.

L. C. McKINLEY AND HIS ORCHESTRA

Vcl/gtr. with Ernest Cotton, ten; Eddie Boyd, pno; bs; dms.   Chicago, 1953

| 1412 | Companion Blues | States 135 |
| 1413 | Weeping Willow Blues | – |

L. C. McKINLEY

Vcl/gtr. with Red Holloway, Johnny Board, tens; Bob Call, pno; James Lee, bs; Vernell Fournier, dms.   Chicago, January 25, 1955

55-236	Good Lover Blues	unissued
55-237	Strange Girl	Vee Jay 133
55-238	Blue Evening	unissued
55-239	She's Five Feet Three	Vee Jay 133

Vcl/gtr. with Ernest Cotton, ten; John A. Gordon, alt/bari; Bob Call, pno; Lafayette ?, gtr; Odie Payne, dms.   Chicago, August 18, 1955

55-300	My Eyes Jumped Out	unissued
55-301	I'm So Satisfied	Vee Jay 159
55-302	Down With It	unissued
55-303	Lonely	Vee Jay 159

Vcl/gtr. with alt; ten; bari; pno; bs; dms.   Chicago, 1959

| A | Nit Wit | Bea & Baby 102 |
| B | Sharpest Man In Town | – |

226

PETE McKINLEY

See under David Pete McKinley.

CAB McMILLAN & HIS FADEAWAYS

Vcl. with tpt; ten; pno; gtr; bs; dms.　　　　　　　Houston, 1950
　　　　　I'm Young and Able　　　　　　　　　　Macy's 5011
　　　　　Three Women Blues　　　　　　　　　　　—

DENNIS McMILLON

Vcl/gtr.　　　　　　　　　　　　　　　　　　　　Linden, N.J., 1950
R 1055　　I Woke Up One Morning　　　　　　　　Regal 3257,
AM 1056　Poor Little Angel　　　　　　　　　　　Regal 3232, Savoy MG 16000
R 1057　　Paper Wooden Daddy　　　　　　　　　Regal 3257, Melodeon LP 7324
AM 1058　Goin' Back Home　　　　　　　　　　　Regal 3232, Blues Classics 14
　　　　　Note: North Carolina artist.

BLIND WILLIE McTELL

BARRELHOUSE SAMMY (THE COUNTRY BOY)

Vcl/gtr.　　　　　　　　　　　　　　　　　　　　Atlanta, 1949
A 320　　Broke Down Engine Blues　　　　　　　Atlantic 891, Blues Classics BC-7
A 321
A 322
A 323　　Kill It Kid　　　　　　　　　　　　　　Atlantic 891, Blues Classics BC-7

PIG 'N' WHISTLE BAND – 1
BLIND WILLIE –2
BLIND WILLY McTELL –3
PIG 'N' WHISTLE RED –4
Vcl/gtr. with Curley Weaver, gtr*.　　　　　　　　Atlanta, 1950
1266　　Don't Forget　　　　　　　　　　　　unissued
1267　　A To Z Blues -4　　　　　　　　　　　Savoy MG 16000
1268　　Good Little Thing　　　　　　　　　　unissued
1269　　You Can't Get Stuff No More　　　　　unissued
1270　　Love Changing Blues* -1　　　　　　　Regal 3277
1271　　Savannah Mama　　　　　　　　　　　unissued
1272　　Talking To You Mama -1　　　　　　　Regal 3277
1273　　East St. Louis　　　　　　　　　　　　unissued
1279　　Honey It Must Be Love　　　　　　　　unissued
1280　　Sending Up My Timber　　　　　　　　unissued
1281　　Lord Have Mercy If You Please　　　　unissued
1282　　Climbing High Mountains　　　　　　　unissued
1283　　River Jordan -2　　　　　　　　　　　Regal 3260
1284　　How About You -2　　　　　　　　　　—
1285　　It's My Desire -3　　　　　　　　　　Regal 3272
1286　　Hide Me In Thy Bosom -3　　　　　　　—
Vcl/gtr.　　　　　　　　　　　　　　　　　　　　Atlanta, 1956
　　　　Baby It Must Be Love　　　　　　　　　Bluesville BVLP 1040
　　　　Dyin' Crapshooter's Blues　　　　　　　—
　　　　Pal Of Mine　　　　　　　　　　　　　—
　　　　Don't Forget It　　　　　　　　　　　—
　　　　Kill It Kid　　　　　　　　　　　　　　—
　　　　That Will Never Happen No More　　　　—
　　　　My Blue Heaven　　　　　　　　　　　unissued
　　　　Beedle Um Bum　　　　　　　　　　　Bluesville BVLP 1040, 1055
　　　　A Married Man's A Fool　　　　　　　　—
　　　　A to Z Blues　　　　　　　　　　　　—
　　　　Goodbye Blues　　　　　　　　　　　　—
　　　　Basin Street Blues　　　　　　　　　　unissued
　　　　Salty Dog　　　　　　　　　　　　　　Bluesville BVLP 1040
　　　　Wabash Cannonball　　　　　　　　　　—
　　　　St. James Infirmary　　　　　　　　　　unissued
　　　　If I Had Wings　　　　　　　　　　　　unissued

| | Instrumental Blues | unissued |
| | Easy Life | Bluesville BVLP 1040 |

PAUL McZIEL ZYDECO BAND

Vcl./accdn. with Wallace Gergner, wbd. Lafayette, La. July 23, 1961
	Allons A Lafayette	Arhoolie F 1009
	Tap Dance	–
	I'm Sad And I'm Blue	Arhoolie F 1012

SHORTSTUFF MACON

Real name John Wesley Macon. Born Crawford, Mississippi in 1933

MR. SHORTSTUFF
Vcl/gtr. with Big Joe Williams, vcl (-1)/gtr. New York, May 23, 1964
213	Old Gray Mule	Spivey LP 1005
214	I Want A Little Bit	–
215	I Want To Love	–
216	Moanin'	–
217	Cotton Pickin'	–
218	Great Big Legs	–
219	Don't Want	–
220	No Special Woman	–
	Didn't Know Right From Wrong -1	–
	What Make A Man Sleep So Sound -1	–
	If You Can't Fly A Plane -1	–
	Toledo To Buffalo -1	–

SHORTSTUFF MACON
Same:
	My Jack Don't Drink Water	Xtra 1009, Folkways 1004
	Corrina	–
	Hell Bound Blues	–
	Messing With That Thing	–
	Rock Road, Bad Feeling	–

Note: Interjections on various tracks above by Williams.

MAGIC SAM

Real name Sam Maghett. Born Granada, Mississippi on February 14, 1937

MAGIC SAM
Vcl/gtr. with Little Brother Montgomery, pno; Mack Thompson, bs-gtr; Billie Stepney, dms.
Chicago , 1957
1014	All Your Love	Cobra 5013
1015	Love Me With A Feeling	–
1030	Everything Gonna Be Alright	Cobra 5021
1031	Look Watcha Done	–

Vcl/gtr. with Harold Burrage, pno; Mack Thompson, bs-gtr; Willie Dixon, bs; Odie Payne, dms.
Chicago, 1958
1038	All Night Long	Cobra 5025
1039	All My Whole Life	–
C 1054	Easy Baby	Cobra 5029
C 1055	Twenty One Days In Jail	–

Vcl/gtr. with Boyd Atkins, ten; Johnny Jones, pno; Odell Campbell, bs; S. P. Leary, dms.
Four Duchesses, vcl. grp. Ammons Sisters, vcl. grp (-1) Chicago, 1960/61
25-131	Mr. Charlie -1	Chief 7013
25-132	You Don't Have To Work -1	Chief 7033
25-133		
25-134	My Love Is Your Love -1	Chief 7013
25-141	Square Dance Rock Part 1	Chief 7017
25-141	Square Dance Rock Part 2	–
25-176	Every Night About This Time	Chief 7026
25-177		
25-178	Do The Camel Walk	Chief 7026
25-179	Blue Light Boogie	Chief 7033

Vcl/gtr. with org; bs; dms.   Chicago, 1964

	High Heel Sneakers	CBS 144
	All Your Love	

Vcl/gtr. with saxes; pno; bs-gtr; dms.   Chicago, 1966

21500A	Out Of Bad Luck	Crash 425, The Blues
21500B	She Belongs To Me	— —

SIDNEY MAIDEN

Born Mansfield, Louisiana
Vcl/hca. with The Blues Blowers: San Francisco, April 15, 1952

IM 432	Honey Bee Blues	Imperial 5189
IM 431	Thinking The Blues	

Vcl/hca. with pno; Slim Green, gtr; dms.   Los Angeles, 1957

15890	Hand Me Down Baby	Dig 138
	(rev. by Al Simmons)	

Vcl/hca. with Haskell Sadler, gtr; Bee Brown, dms.   Los Angeles, 1957

A	Hurry, Hurry Baby	Flash 101
B	Everything Is Wrong	—

Vcl/hca. with K. C. Douglas, gtr.   Berkeley, April 16, 1961

	Buy Me An Airplane	Bluesville BVLP 1035
	Sweet Little Woman	—
	My Black Name	—
	Sidney's Fox Chase	—
	San Quentin Blues	—
	Tell Me Somebody	—
	Blues An' Trouble	—
	Hand-Me-Down Baby	—
	Sidney's Worried Life Blues	—
	Me And My Chauffeur	—
	Coal Black Mare	—
	I'm Going Back Home	—
	Sweet Little Woman	unissued
	Sugar Mama	unissued
	Bottle Up And Go	unissued
	Bottle Up And Go	unissued
	Sidney's Shuffle	unissued
	Me And My Chauffeur	unissued

Note: The 78 rpm and 45 rpm issues of Dig 138 are alternate takes.

Note: Add to Imperial session

IM 429	Working Woman	Imperial unissued
IM 429A	Up The River Blues	—
IM 430	Broke And Busted	—
IM 430A	Harpin' The Boogie	—
no mx	Wake Up Wicked Woman	—
no mx	I'm Putting My Woman Down	—

TOMMIE 'BLIND TOM' MALONE

w. Bill Reese Band - "Shake" calling by Little Arch:
Vcl/pno. with gtr; bs; dms.   Chicago, c. 1960

1055A	Cow Cow Shake	Ebony 1055
1055B	Worried Life	—

SYLVIA MARS

Vcl. with Mitch Greenhill, gtr; (-1) Gordie Edwards, hca (-2). Abbeville, S.C.?

	Walk Right In -1	Folk-Lyric FL 124
	Trouble, Trouble, Trouble	—
	Lowdown Death	—
	Back Water Blues -2	—
	He's Got Me Goin' -2	—
	Things About Comin' My Way -1	—

Note: Other titles on this album are Spirituals.

MATTHEW 'HOGMAN' MAXEY
Born Haynesville, Louisiana on January 18, 1917.
Vcl /gtr.

	Angola, 1959
Stagolee	Folk-Lyric LFS A-3
Black Night Falling	—
Duckin' And Dodging	Storyville SLP 125
Rock Me Mama	—
Hard Headed Woman	—

MAXWELL STREET JIMMY
See under Maxwell Street Jimmy Davis.

MACK MAZE
Vcl.

	Ellis Farm, Texas 1951
If You See My Mother	Elektra EKL-296

MEMPHIS EDDIE
See under Memphis Eddie Pee.

MEMPHIS JIMMY
See under James Clark.

MEMPHIS MINNIE (see also in APPENDIX)
Born Algiers, Louisiana on June 24, 1900
Vcl/gtr. with Ernest Lawlar, gtr; dms.

		Chicago, December 19, 1944
C 4302	Fashion Plate Daddy	unissued
C 4303	When You Love Me	Okeh 06733, Columbia 37455, 30022
C 4304	Please Set A Date	Columbia 36895, 30003
C 4305	Mean Mistreater Blues	Columbia 37295, 30015
C 4306	Love Come And Go	Okeh 06733, Columbia 37455, 30022
C 4307	True Love	Columbia 36895, 30003
C 4308	When My Train Comes Home	unissued

Vcl/gtr. with Ernest Lawlar, gtr; bs.

		Chicago, February, 26, 1946
CC 04504	I'm So Glad	Columbia 37295, 30015
CC 04505	Hold Me Blues	unissued
CC 04506	Killer Diller	unissued
CC 04507	Moaning Blues	unissued
CC 04508	Got To Leave You	unissued
CC 04509	The Man I Love	unissued

Add dms.

		Chicagom September, 20, 1946
CC 04625	Got To Leave You	unissued
CC 04626	Killer Diller Blues	Columbia 37977, 30102
CC 04627	Moaning Blues	unissued
CC 04628	Hold Me Blues	Columbia 37977, 30102
CC 04629	Fish Man Blues	Columbia 37597, 30054
CC 04630	Wester Union	Columbia 30134
CC 04631	My Man Is Gone	unissued
CC 04632	Lean Meat Won't Fry	Columbia 37579, 30054

Vcl/gtr. with Blind John Davis, pno; Ernest Lawlar, gtr; bs; dms.

		Chicago, December 27, 1947
CC 04968	Three Times Seven Blues	Columbia 38099, 30111
CC 04969	Daybreak Blues	Columbia 30120
CC 04970	Million Dollar Blues	—
CC 04971	Shout The Boogie	Columbia 38099, 30111

MEMPHIS MINNIE AND LITTLE SON JOE
Vcl/gtr. with Ernest Lawlar, gtr.

		Chicago, February 1949
CC 05043	Tears On My Pillow	Columbia 30176

CC 05044	Sweet Man	Columbia 30176
CC 05045	Tonight I Smile On You	Columbia 30146
CC 05046	Jump Little Rabbit	–

MEMPHIS MINNIE
Vcl/gtr. with Sunnyland Slim, pno; bs; dms.　　　　　Chicago, 1950

1216	Why Did I Make You Cry	Regal 3259
1217	Kidman Blues	– , Savoy MG 16000

MEMPHIS MINNIE WITH LITTLE JOE AND HIS BAND
Vcl. with pno(-1): Joe Hill Louis, hca/gtr; dms.　　　　Memphis 1952

1024	Broken Heart -1	Checker 771
1027	Me And My Chauffeur	–

Note: Wax give matrix numbers as 1124/27

MEMPHIS MINNIE AND HER COMBO
Vcl/gtr. with pno; gtr; dms.　　　　　　　　　　Chicago? 1954

2606	Kissing In The Dark	JOB 1101
2607	World Of Trouble	

MEMPHIS SLIM

Real name Peter Chatman. Born September 3, 1916 in Memphis, Tennessee. Vcl/pno. with
Alex Atkins, alt; Ernest Cotton, ten; Ernest Crawford, bs.　Chicago, 1946

1167H	Mistake In Life	Hy-Tone 10, Melody Lane 10
1168H	Grinder Man Blues	– –
	Slim's Boogie	Hy-Tone 17
	Little Mary	

MEMPHIS SLIM & HIS SOLID BAND

19A HYI	Cheatin' Around	Hy-Tone 19
19B HY18	A Letter Home	–

Note: Actual title of label Melody Lane Is Melody Lane Record Shop

MEMPHIS SLIM & HIS HOUSE ROCKERS
Willie Dixon, bs. replaces Crawford:　　　　　　　Chicago, 1947

UB 2650	Kilroy's Been Here	Miracle M102
UB 2651	Rockin' The House	Miracle M103
UB 2652	Lend Me Your Love	– , Federal 12033
UB 2653, F 1046-1	Darling, I Miss You	Miracle M102, – King LP 885

Charlie Jenkins bs. replaces Dixon:

UB 21179	Pacemaker Boogie	Miracle M110, Federal 12015, King LP 885
UB 21180	Motherless Child	issues as above
UB 21181	Harlem Bound	Miracle M111, King LP 885
UB 21182	Life Is Like That	– , Federal 12007

Ernest Crawford, bs, replaces Jenkins:　　　　　　Chicago, 1948

UB 21744	Nobody Loves Me	Miracle M145, Federal 12007
UB 21745	Believe I'll Settle Down	Master 1010, Old Swingmaster 1010
UB 21746		
UB 21747	Throw This Poor Dog A Bone	Miracle M 153
UB 21748	Help Me Some	Miracle M 136

Same:

UB 21938	Country Girl	Master 1010, Old Swingmaster 1010
UB 21939		
UB 21940	Blue And Lonesome	Miracle M 136
UB 21941	Angel Child	Miracle M 145

Same'

UB 22322	Midnight Jump	Miracle M125, Federal 12021
UB 22323		
UB 22324		
UB 22325	Messin' Around	Miracle M125, Federal 12021

Same:		Chicago, 1949
UB9-1280	You And I	Miracle M153

Timothy Overton, ten. replaces Cotton:

UB 10001	Frisco Baby	Miracle M132
UB 10002		
UB 10003	Timsy's Whimsey	Miracle M132

Prob. same, except Ernest Cotton, ten. replaces Overton'

MS1	Restless Nights	Master 1020
MS2	If You Live That Life	–
MS3		
MS4	Love At Sight	Master 1030
MS5		
MS6		
MS7	Jumping Bean	Master 1030

MEMPHIS SLIM
Vcl/pno. with Alex Atkins, alt. Timothy Overton, ten; Betty Overton, bs.

		Cincinnati, January 1949
K 5662	Cheatin' Around	King 4284
K 5663	A Letter Home	King 4312, LP 885, Bethlehem 6071
K 5664	Now I Got The Blues	King 4284, –
K 5665	Grinder Man Blues	King 4327, –
K 5666	Don't Ration My Love	– –
K 5667	Slim's Boogie	King 4312, –
K 5668	Little Mary	King 4324,
K 5669	Mistake In Life	– ,LP 859, 885
	Poor Joe	King LP 885

Note: "Flub" on LP 859 credited to Slim is actually "Stomp Boogie" by John Lee Hooker, q.v. Other two tracks on King LP 885 are by Earl Hooker, q.v.

Vcl/pno. with Alex Atkins, alt; Timothy Overton, ten; Alfred Elkins, bs; Leon Hooper, dms.

		Houston, 1949
ACA 1320	My Baby Don't Love Me No More	unissued
ACA 1321	Texas Boogie	unissued
ACA 1322	The Girl I Love	Peacock 1517
ACA 1323	Mean Little Woman	–
ACA 1328	Confessions Of A Playboy	unissued
ACA 1329	Blues And Temptation	unissued
ACA 1330	Tired Of Your Running Around	unissued
ACA 1331	Funny Feeling Blues	unissued

MEMPHIS SLIM & THE HOUSE ROCKERS
Same

		Chicago, 1950
PR 80	Slim's Blues	Premium 860, Chess LP 1455
PR 81	Havin' Fun	– –

Same, but add The Vagabonds, vcl. grp(-1). Memphis Slim vcl. Floyd Hunt, Pno(-2)

UN50-212	Flock Rocker	Premium 850
UN50-213	I Guess I'm a Fool -1	– , Chess LP 1446, 1455, Argo LP 4042
UB50-217	Really Got The Blues -2	Premium 867, Chess LP 1455
UB50-221	Mother Earth	– , Chess LP 1446, 1455

Vcl/pno. with Alex Atkins, alt; Timothy Overton, ten; Ike Perkins, gtr; Alfred Elkins, bs; Oscar Larkin, dms.

		Chicago, 1951
UB51-130	Trouble, Trouble	Premium 873
UB51-131	'Fore Day	–
UB51-132	My Baby Left Me	Premium 878
UB51-133	Feelin' Low	–

Vcl/pno; with Neil Green, Purcell Brockenborough, tens; Ransom Knowling, bs; Oscar Larkin, dms. Terry Timmons, vcl (-1)

		Chicago, 1951
YB 4194	Train Is Comin'	Mercury 70063
YB 4195	The Question -1	Mercury 8281

Nelson Berry, ten; John Frazier, bs; replaces Brockenborough And Knowling, bs;

YB 4238	Drivin' Me Mad	Mercury 70063
YB 4239	Never Let Me Love	Mercury 8281
YB 4240	Train Time	Mercury 8251
YB 4241	Blue Evening -1	–

Henry Taylor, bs replaces Frazier:

YB 4542	No Mail Blues	Mercury 8266
YB 4543	Gonna Need My Help Someday	–

Purcell Brockenborough, ten. replaces Berry: Houston 1952

ACA 2072	My Two Way Girl	unissued
ACA 2073	Binghampton Bounce	unissued
ACA 2074	My Lucky Day	unissued
ACA 2075	Don't You Know	unissued
ACA 2076	Sittin' And Thinkin'	Peacock 1602
ACA 2077	The Blacks	unissued
ACA 2078	Lonely Boy	unissued
ACA 2079	Dorie Boogie	unissued
ACA 2080	New Orleans	unissued
ACA 2081	Living Like A King	Peacock 1602
ACA 2082	Blue Memory	unissued
ACA 2083	Weak And Helpless	unissued

MEMPHIS SLIM & HIS HOUSE ROCKERS

Vcl/pno. with Neil Green, Charles Ferguson, tens; Henry Taylor, bs; Otho Allen, dms.
Terry Timmons, vcl(-1) Cleveland, 1952

FL 210	Tia Juana	Premium 903, Chess 903, LP 1455
FL 213	I'm Crying -1	– –
U 7395	Walking Alone	Chess 1491
U 7396	Rockin' Chair	–

Details unknown;

	Marack	Chess LP 1455
	Rockin' The Pad	–
	Reverend Bounce	–
	Blues For My Baby	–

Vcl/pno. with Neil Green, Purcell Brockenborough, tens; Matt Murphy, gtr; Henry Taylor, bs; Otho Allen, dms. Chicago, 1952

1168	Back Alley	United U138
1174	Living The Life I Love	–

Ernest Cotton, ten; Curtis Mosley, bs. replace Brockeborough and Taylor;
 Chicago, 1953

1335	The Comeback	United U156
1336	Five O'Clock Blues	–
1337	Call Before You Go Home	United U166
1338	This Is My Lucky Day	–

Vcl/pno. with Neil Green, Jimmy Conley, tens; Matt Murphy, gtr; Henry Taylor, bs; Otho Allen, dms. Chicago, 1954

1430	Wish Me Well	United U176
1431		
1432		
1433	Four Years Of Torment	United U182
1434	Sassy Mae	United U176

Same:

1482	Memphis Slim U.S.A.	United U186
1483	She's Alright	United U189
1484	Two Of A Kind	–
1485		
1486	Blues All Around My Head	United U186

No details:

	Got To Find My Baby	United 201
	Blue And Lonesome	–

Vcl/pno. with ten; gtr; bs; dms. Los Angeles? 1954

A	My Country Gal	Money 212
AA	Treat Me Like I Treat You	–

MEMPHIS SLIM & HIS ORCHESTRA

Vcl/pno. with John Calvin, alt; Matt Murphy, gtr; Sam Chatman, bs; Billie Stepney, dms.

Chicago, January 8, 1958

58-816	What's The Matter	Vee Jay 294
58-817	She Keeps Me Crying	Top Rank RES-116
58-818	Chicago Is The Place For Me	unissued
58-819	This Time I'm Through	Vee Jay 294
58-820	Stroll On Little Girl	Vee Jay 271
58-821	Guitar Cha Cha	−

Vcl/pno. with prob. Muddy Waters, gtr; Al Hall, bs; Shep Sheppard, dms.

Carnegie Hall, April 3, 1959

Boogie Woogie Memphis	United Artists UAS 3050
The Saddest Blues	−
How Long	−

No details, prob. for same session:

All This Piano Boogie	United Artists UAS 3137
How Long	−
Stackholes	−
John Henry	−
Bye Bye Baby	−
Love My Baby	−
When The Sun Goes Down	−
Someday Baby	−
Slim's Slow Blues	−
Gee, Ain't It Hard To Find Somebody	−

Vcl/pno.

New York City, July, 19, 1959

Walkin' The Boogie	Folkways FG 3524
Cow Cow Blues	−
Jefferson County Blues	−
Four O'Clock Blues	−
Mister Freddie	−
Trouble In Mind	−
44 Blues	−
88 Boogie	−
Sail On Blues	−
Down Home Blues	−
Down That Big Road	−
Roll And Tumble	−
Crowing Rooster	−
Woman Boogie Blues	−

MEMPHIS SLIM & HIS ORCHESTRA

Vcl/pno. with Alex Atkins, alt; John Calvin, Ernest Cotton, tens; Matt Murphy, gtr; Sam Chatman, bs; Billie Stepney, dms.

Chicago, August 18, 1959

59-1231	Messin' Around	Vee Jay VJLP 1012, 1020
59-1232	The Come Back	Vee Jay 343, VJLP 1012
59-1233	Wish Me Well	Vee Jay VJLP 1012
59-1234	Slim's Blues	Vee Jay 343, VJLP 1012
59-1235	Gotta Find My Baby	Vee Jay VJLP 1012
59-1236	My Gal Keeps Me Crying	Vee Jay 330, VJLP 1012
59-1237	Sassy Mae	Vee Jay VJLP 1012
59-1238	Rockin' The House (Beer Drinkin' Woman)	−
59-1239	Lend Me Your Love	−
59-1240	Misery	−
59-1241	Blue And Lonesome	−
59-1242	Steppin' Out	Vee Jay 330, VJLP 1012
59-1243	Mother Earth	Vee Jay VJLP 1012

MEMPHIS SLIM & WILLIE DIXON

Vcl/pno. with Willie Dixon, vcl/bs.

New York City, 1959

Joogie Boogie	Folkways FA 2385
Stewball	−
John Henry	−
Kansas City 1	−

Kansas City 2	Folkways FA 2385
Kansas City 3	–
Have You Ever Been To Nashville Pen	–
Roll And Tumble	–
Beer Drinking Woman	–
Chicago House Rent Party	–
44 Blues	–
Unlucky	–

MEMPHIS SLIM
Vcl/pno.   New York City, 1959/60

The Bells	Folkways FG 3535
The Lord Have Mercy On Me	–
My Baby Don't Love Me No More	–
I Left That Town	–
Boogie After Midnight	–
The Train Is Gone	–
Pinetop's Boogie	–
Whiskey Drinking Blues	–
San Juan Blues	–
In The Evening	–
How Long Blues	– ,Aravel 1004
Sail On Little Girl	–
John Henry	–

MEMPHIS SLIM & WILLIE DIXON
Vcl(-1)/pno. with Willie Dixon, vcl(-2)/bs.   New York City, January 1960

Choo Choo -1	Verve MGV 3007
4 O'Clock Boogie	–
Rub My Root -2	–
C Rocker	–
Home To Mama -2	–
Shaky -2	–
After Hours	–
One More Time -2	–
John Henry -1,2	–
Now Howdy -1, 2	–

MEMPHIS SLIM, WILLIE DIXON & PETE SEEGER
Vcl/pno. with Willie Dixon, vcl/bs; Pete Seeger, vcl.   New York City, April, 1960

I'm On My Way	Folkways FA 2450
Hileland Laddie	–
Tina Singu	–
Sweet Potatoes	–
Worried Man Blues	Folkways FA 2450
Oh, Mary Don't You Weep	–
Pretty Polly	–
Jacob's Ladder	–
Times Are Getting Hard	–
Bayeza	–
The Quizmasters	–
New York City	–
Midnight Special	–
Somebody Tell That Woman	Folkways FA 2386
My Baby Don't Stand No Cheating	–
Stewball	–
Slop Boogie	–
Misery Falls Like Rain	–
Wish Me Well	–
T For Texas	–
I Just Want To Make Love To You	–
Try To Find My Baby	–
One More Time	–
Nobody Loves Me	–
We Are Going To Rock	–

Note: FA 2450 issued as by "Pete Seeger at the Village Gate with Memphis Slim and Willie Dixon". It is not known if Slim and Dixon are heard on all tracks.

MEMPHIS SLIM
Vcl/pno. with Alexis Korner, gtr; Stan Grieg, dms. Omit gtr(-1); dms(-2).

London, July 14, 1960

Memphis Slim U.S.A.	Collector JGN 1004
Caught The Old Coon At Last	−
Whiskey And Gin	−
Two Of A Kind	−
I Love You More And More	−
Chicago Stomp	−
Don't Think You're Smart -1	−
Memphis, Tennessee -1, 2	−
Misery	−
Bertha May -1, 2	−
Me Myself And I	−
Rock Me Baby -1, 2	Collector JGN 1005
Ain't Nobody's Business If I Do	−
Sun Gonna Shine In My Back Door	−
In The Evenin' -2	−
Frisco Baby -1	−
I Believe I'll Settle Down -2	−
Darlin' I Miss You So -2	−
Roll And Tumble -2	−
Blue This Evening-1, 2	−
Pinetop's Blues	Collector JDN 102
How Long	−
Sad And Lonesome	Collector JEN-5
Kansas City	−
Slow And Easy -1	−

Vcl/pno.

Copenhagen, August 25, 1960

Reminiscin' With Memphis Slim	Storyville SLP 118
Memphis Boogie	−
St. Louis Boogie	−
Santa Fee Boogie	−
Chicago, New Home Of The. Blues	−
Chicago Rent Party Blues	−
Arkansas Road House Blues	−
Midnight Jump	−
Goodbye Blues	−
Good Rockin' Blues	Storyville SEP 385
Blues Confession	−
Boogie Woogie	−
Worried All The Time	− , SLP 187

Add Erik Molbach, bs; Jorn Elniff, dms;

Copenhagen, August 26, 1960

I'm So All Alone	Storyville SLP 138
Four Walls (This Is A Good Time To Write A Song)	−
El Capitan	Storyville A45055, SLP 138
The Question	unissued
Misery	unissued
Born With The Blues	unissued
True Love	Storyville SLP 138
You're Gonna Worry Too	unissued
Whizzle Wham	unissued
Two Of A Kind	unissued
Big City Girl	Storyville A45055, SLP 138
Fattening Frogs For Snakes	Storyville SLP 138
Whizzle Wham	unissued

Vcl/pno. with Arbee Stidham, gtr; Armand "Jump" Jackson, dms.

Chicago, October 1960

Alberta	Folkways FG 3536
Boogie Woogie Piano Styles	−

Scandinavian Boogie	Folkways FG 3536
Down South	—
The Big Race	—
Chicago Rent Party	—
Between Midnight And Dawn	—
46th Street	—

Vcl/pno. with 2 gtrs. one poss. Matt Murphy: c. 1960

Mean Old Frisco	Xtra 1008, Disc 1105

Vcl/pno. with Matt Murphy, gtr.

If A Rabbit Had A Gun	Xtra 1008, Disc 1105
You'll Never Make It	—

Vcl. with Matt Murphy, gtr.

What Makes You Do Me Like You Do	Xtra 1008, Disc 1105
I Ain't Bad	—
I Love You Baby	—

Vcl/pno. with dms.

Alberta	Xtra 1008

Pno. with bs.

A Short One	Xtra 1008, Disc 1105
Number Nine	—
4 O'Clock In The Morning	—

from Folkways sessions:

You Should See My Brother	Disc 1105
You Name It	—
Relaxin'	—
Have Mercy	—
Mum's The Word	—
Dedication To Pete Johnson	—
Down For The Count	—

Vcl/pno. New York City, 1960

Beer Drinking Woman	Bluesville BVLP 1018
Just Blues	—
Blue And Disgusted	—
When Your Dough Roller Is Gone	—
Hey Slim	—
Darling I Miss You So	Bluesvill BVLP 1031
You're Gonna Need My Help One Day	—
Fast And Free	—
My Baby Left Me	—

Add Buster 'Harpie' Brown, hca;

The I. C. Blues	Bluesville BVLP 1018
Motherless Child	—
Lonesome Traveler	Bluesville BVLP 1031
Angel Child	—

Brown Out, Add Lafayett Thomas, gtr; Wendell Marshall, bs;

Teasing The Blues	Bluesville BVLP 1018
Baby Doll	—
Blue Brew	—
Rack 'Em Back Jack	—
Brenda	—
No Strain	Bluesville BVLP 1031
Don't Thing You're So Smart	—
Raining The Blues	—
Lucille	—
Nice Stuff	—

Vcl/pno.

Blues Is Troubles	Bluesville BVLP 1053	
Grinder Man Blues	—	
Three-In-One Boogie	—	
Letter Home	—	
Churnin' Man Blues	—	, 1055

237

Two Of A Kind	Bluesville BVLP 1053,
The Blacks	—
If You See Kay	— , 1055
Frankie And Johnny Boogie	—
Mother Earth	—

Vcl/pno./org(-1)

Steady Rollin' Blues	Bluesville BVLP 1055, 1075
Sweet Root Man	—
Mean Mistreatin' Mama	Bluesville BVLP 1075
Soon One Morning -1	—
Cella's Boogie -1	—
Big Legged Woman	—
Rock Me Mama	—
Goin' Down Slow -1	—
Mr. Freddie Boogie -1	—
Three Women Blues	—

Vcl/pno. with Jazz Gillum, vcl(-1)/hca; Arbee Stidham, vcl(-2)/gtr.

	New York City,.January 16, 1961
I Feel So Good	Candid CM 8023
Rockin' Chair Blues -2	—
Baby Gone -1	—
Cow Cow Blues	—
Miss Ida B	—
44 Blues	—
Trouble In Mind	—
Worried Life Blues	—
I Don't Want My Rooster Crowin' -1	—
Lonesome In My Bedroom	—
Diggin' My Potatoes -2	—
In The Evening	—

Same:

Born With The Blues	Candid CM 8024
Just Let Me Be	—
Red Haired Boogie	—
Blue And Disgusted	—
New Key To The Highway	—
I'd Take Her To Chicago	—
Harlem Bound	—
El Capitan	—
I Just Landed In Your Town	—
John Henry	—
I Believe I'll Settle Down	—
Bad Luck And Trouble	—
Late Afternoon Blues	—
Memphis Slim, U.S.A.	—

MEMPHIS SLIM AND HIS BAND
Vcl/pno. with John Calvin, alt; Johnny Board, ten; Matt Murphy, gtr; Sam Chatman, bs;
Billie Stepney, dms.

	Chicago, 1961
Lonesome	Strand 25041, LP 1046
Four Walls	— —
Cold Blooded Woman	Strand LP 1046
One Man's Mad	—
Let The Good Times Roll Creole	—
What Is The Mare-Rack	—
Pigalle Love	—
It's Been Too Long	—
Big Bertha	—
I'm Lost Without You	—
I'll Keep On Singing The Blues	—
True Love	—

MEMPHIS SLIM
Vcl/pno.

		London, April 17, 1961
	I Feel So Good	Fontana 688.701
	Plowhand Blues	–
	Keep Your Hand On Your Heart	unissued
	Rocking Chair	unissued
	Prison Bound	unissued
	Highway 51	Fontana 688.701
	Lonesome Bedroom	unissued
	Sitting On Top Of The World	Fontana 688.701
	Sunnyland Train	–
	Goin' To The River	–
	Love To You	–
	Sweet Root Man	unissued
	I Can Hear My Name A-Ringing	unissued
	Black Cat Blues	unissued
	Going Down Slow -1	Fontana 688.701
	Big Bill's Blues	unissued
	Rock Me Baby	Fontana 688.701

Note: Add Josh White, introduction and humming.

Vcl/pno.

		Bayonne, May, 1961
	Every Day	Agorilla AG 33-02
	When I've Been Drinking	–
	Pinetop's Boogie Woogie	–
	Sail On Blues	–
	Memphis Slim U.S.A.	–
	In The Evening	–
	Instrumental Boogie	–
	You Don't Know My Mind	–
	St. Louis Blues	–
	Wish Me Well	–
	Piney Brown Blues	–
	Pigalle Love	• –

Vcl/pno/cel.

		Copenhagen, June 5, 1961
	Three Woman Blues	Storyville SLP 138
	3 And 1 Boogie	
	Frankie And Johnny	unissued
	Medium And Rare	Storyville SLP 155
	A Letter Home	Storyville SLP 168
	Funky (Slow And Easy)	unissued
	Boogie Woogie For Piano And Celeste	Storyville SLP 155
	Bertha May	Storyville SLP 188
	Bertha May	Storyville SLP 138
	Celeste Boogie	Storyville SLP 183
	Celeste Boogie	Storyville SLP 138
	Mean Mistreatin' Mama	Storyville SLP 155
	Gone Mother Blues	Storyville SLP 187

Pno/cel (–1).

		Paris, July 7, 1961
	Panic Street	Odeon XOC 181
	The Hustler	–
	Carried Away	–
	Bluesnick	–
	Back Home	–
	Olympia Boogie	–
	Sonophonic Boogie -1	–
	Blue Slim	–
	Musing -1	–
	West Side Trot	–
	Hotfan's Delight	–

Vcl/pno. with T-Bone Walker, gtr; Willie Dixon, vcl (–1)/bs; Armand "Jump" Jackson, dms.

		Hamburg, October 11, 1962
	We're Gonna Rock	Polydor 46.397
	Stewball -1	–
	Bye Bye Baby	–

239

Vcl (−1)/pno. with Willie Dixon, vcl (−2)/bs; Phillippe Combelle, dms.

		Paris, November 15/16, 1962
	Rock And Rolling The House -1, 2	Polydor 46.131
	Baby Please Come Home	−
	How Make You Do Me Like You Do -1	−
	The Way She Loves A Man -2	−
	New Way To Love -2	−
	African Hunch With A Boogie Beat -2	−
	Shame Pretty Girls -2	−
	Baby-Baby-Baby -2	−
	Do De Do -2	−
	Cold Blooded -2	−
	Just You And I -1, 2	−
	Pigalle Love -1	−
	All By Myself -1, 2	−

Vcl/pno. with Matt Murphy, gtr; Willie Dixon, bs; Billie Stepney, dms.

		Bremen, October 18, 1963
	Wish Me Well	Fontana TL 5204

Vcl/pno. with Sonny Boy Williamson, vcl (−1)/hca; Matt Murphy, gtr (−2).

		Copenhagen, November 1, 1963
	Early One Morning	Storyville SEP 415
	Rebecca Blues -1	Storyville SLP 168
	Copenhagen Woman -2	Storyville SLP 188

Vcl/pno.		New York City, April/June, 1965
	T. B. Blues	Spivey LP 1006

MEMPHIS WILLIE B.

See under Memphis Willie Borum.

MERCY BABY

Real name Jimmy Mullins.
Vcl/dms. with B. J. Brooks, Jack White, saxes; Willie Taylor, pno; Frankie Lee Sims, gtr;
Ralph Morgan, bs.

		Dallas, 1957
3388	Marked Deck	Ace 528
3389	Rock And Roll Baby	−
3402	Silly Dilly Woman	Ace 535
3403	Mercy's Blues	−

Similar:

3435	Pleadin'	Ric 955
3436	Don't Lie To Me	−

Vcl/dms. with saxes; pno; gtr; bs. Dallas, 1958

501 −	You Ran Away	Mercy Baby 501
501 +	Love's Voodoo	−
502 −	The Rock And Stomp	Mercy Baby 502
502 +	So Lonesome	−

MERCY DEE

Full name Mercy Dee Walton. Born Waco, Texas on August 13, 1915. Died Stockton, California on December 2, 1962.

Vcl/pno.		Los Angeles, 1949
11-001-A, A 859		
	Baba-Du-Lay Fever (G.I. Fever)	Spire 101, 11-001
11-001-B, A 860		
	Lonesome Cabin Blues *	− −
11-002-A	Evil And Hanky	Spire 102, 11-002
11-002-B	Travellin' Alone Blues	− −
*	Also on Blues Classics 16.	

Vcl/pno. with gtr; bs.		Los Angeles, 1950
IM 225	Honely Baby	Imperial 5104
IM 226	Empty Life	− , Colony 111

IM 227	Please Understand	Bayou 003
IM 228	Birdbrain Baby	Imperial 5110, Colony 111
Same:		
IM 249	Big Foot Country	Imperial 5110
IM 250, FK 19		
	Danger Zone (Crepe On Your Door)	Imperial 5127, Bayou 013
IM 251	Roamin' Blues	Imperial 5118
IM 252	Straight And Narrow	Colony 102
IM 253	Bought Love	Imperial 5118
IM 254	Old Fashioned Ways	Colony 107
IM 255, FK 20		
	Happy Bachelor (Blues)	Colony 102, Bayou 013
IM 256	Pay Off (Anything In The World) *	Imperial 5127, Colony 107, Bayou 003 *

Vcl/pno. with dms; "Thelma", vcl (−1); "Lady Fox", vcl (−2).

Los Angeles, 1953/4

XSP 458	One Room Country Shack	Specialty 458
SP 458	My Woman Knows The Score	−
XSP 466	Rent Man Blues -1	Specialty 466
SP 466	Fall Guy	−
XSP 481	Get To Gettin' -2	Specialty 481
SP 481	Dark Muddy Bottom	−

Vcl/pno. with L. C. Robinson, gtr; dms.

Los Angeles, 1954

A	Trailing My Baby	Rhythm 1774
B	The Main Event	

Note: Although the label indicates the above personnel, "The Main Event" is an instrumental featuring ten; pno; gtr; bs; dms. with a "live" audience.

Vcl/pno. with ten (−1); gtr; 2nd gtr (−2); bs; dms. Ensemble vcl. (−3).

Los Angeles, 1955

FL-244	Romp And Stomp Blues -1	Flair 1073
FL-245	Oh Oh Please	−
FL-256	Come Back Maybellene -2	Flair 1077
FL-257	True Love -3	−
FL-258	Have You Ever	Flair 1078
FL-259	Stubborn Woman	−

Vcl/pno. with Sidney Maiden, hca; J. C. Douglas, gtr; Otis Cherry, dms.

Stockton, February 5, 1961

	Jack Engine	Arhoolie F 1007
	Brown Gal	Arhoolie F 1017
	Lady Luck	unissued
	Call The Asylum	Arhoolie F 1007
	Mercy's House Party	−
	Walked Down So Many Turnrows	
	My Little Angel	unissued
	Eighth Wonder Of The World	unissued
	I Been A Fool	Arhoolie F 1006
	Red Light	Arhoolie F 1007

Omit Maiden:

Stockton, February 12, 1961

	Mercy's Troubles	Arhoolie F 1007
	The Drunkard	unissued
	Troublesome Mind	Arhoolie F 1007
	You Don't Know My Mind	unissued
	Mercy's Boogie	unissued

Same:

Stockton, March 12, 1961

	Pity And Shame	unissued
	Way Out In The Country	unissued
	After The Fight	unissued
	After The Fight	unissued
	Fairweather Mama	unissued
	Birdbrain Baby	Arhoolie F 3001
	K.C. And Mercy's Wail	unissued
	Shady Lane	unissued
	Your Friend And Woman	unissued

Vcl/pno. with Sydney Maiden, hca; Otis Cherry, dms; Marcellus Thomas, vcl (−1).

		Berkeley, April 16, 1961
	Call The Asylum	unissued
	Lady Luck	Arhoolie 501, F 1007
	Betty Jean	−
	Mad Blues -1	unissued
	Pity And A Shame	Bluesville BVLP 1039
	Shady Lane	−
	After The Fight	−
	Your Friend And Woman	−
	One Room Country Shack	−
	The Drunkard	−
	Five Card Hand	−
	Have You Ever Been Out In The Country	−
	My Little Angel	−
	Sidney And Mercy's Shuffle	unissued
	Sugar Daddy	Arhoolie F 1012

DADDY MERRITT QUINTET

Tiny Parker, vcl. with Melvin Merritt, pno; Brownie McGhee, gtr; bs; dms.

		New York City, 1950
	Knockout Blues	Monogram 203
	My Daddy Loves It	−

LOUIE MEYERS & THE ACES

Louis Miles, hca. with David Miles, Syl Johnson, gtrs; Willie Dixon, bs; Fred Below, dms.

		Chicago, 1956
3126	Just Wailing	Abco 104
3127	Bluesy (no 2nd gtr.)	−

ELMON MICKLE (see also in APPENDIX)

Born Keo, Arkansas on February 24, 1919.

DRIFTIN' SLIM or SMITH
Vcl/hca. with Baby Face Turner, Junior Brooks, gtrs; Bill Russell, dms.

		North Little Rock, 1951
MM 1733	My Little Machine	Modern 849
MM 1734	Down South Blues	−

Brooks out. Add Sunny Blair, hca; Ike Turner, pno:

		North Little Rock, May 6, 1952
MM 1874	Good Morning Baby	RPM 370, Blues Classics 15
MM 1875	My Sweet Woman	−

ELMON MICKLE
Vcl/hca. with Philip Walker, gtr; Bobby Tinsley, dms.

		Los Angeles, November, 1959
003A	Flatfoot Sam	Elko 003
003B	I Got To Get Some Money	−
004A	Lonesome Highway	E.M. 132
004B	Jackson Blues	−

Vcl/hca/gtr. with Ernie Pruitt, vcl; dms (−1).

		Los Angeles,
B	Short 'n' Fat	E.M. 132, EM & EP 133
A	Whatever You're Doing, Keep On Doing It To Me -1	EM & EP 133

      Note: E.M. 132A issued with either reverse.

ELMON MICKLE & HIS RHYTHM ACES
Vcl/hca. with org (−1); gtr; bs−gtr; dms.

		Los Angeles,
J 610	Independent Walk -1	J Gems 1908, Soulin' 100
J 611	Short And Fat	−

      Note: J 610 on Soulin' as "Nothin' But The Blues" by Harmonica Harry.

MODEL T. SLIM
Vcl/hca. with Jack Wall, gtr; bs; dms. Los Angeles, 1966
X-1883   Shake Your Boogie   Wonder 15001/2
X-1884, 68003X
              Good Morning Little Schoolgirl   −   , Magnum 739
68003   Jackson, Tennessee   Magnum 739
Vcl/hca/gtr. with Bill Baucomb, vcl (−1). Los Angeles, December 3, 1966
              Sugar Mama   unissued
              Hunting Somebody   unissued
              Jackson Blues   unissued
              Hoodoo Man Blues   unissued
              13 Highway -1   unissued
              You Oughta See My Baby   unissued
              Mama Don't Allow   unissued
              You Said You Love Me   unissued
              She Don't Want Me No More unissued
              Train Fare Home   unissued
              Watchin' My Stuff   unissued
              Standin' Around Cryin'   unissued
              I Done Tore Your Playhouse Down unissued

AMOS MILBURN (see also in APPENDIX)

Born Houston, Texas c. 1924.
Vcl/pno. with bs; dms. Add ten (−1). Los Angeles, 1945/46
A   After Midnight   Aladdin 159, AL 503
B   Amos' Blues -1   −
A   My Baby's Boogie   Aladdin 160
B   Darling How Long   −
A   Down The Road Apiece   Aladdin 161, AL 704, 707
B   Don't Beg Me   −
        Amos' Boogie   Aladdin 173, AL 704
        Operation Boogie   Aladdin 174, AL 703
        Cinch Blues   −
Vcl/pno. with Maxwell Davis, ten; gtr; bs; dms. Los Angeles, 1947
157   My Love Is Limited   Aladdin 201
158   Blues At Sundown (no ten.)   −
159   Money Hustlin' Woman   Aladdin 191
        Sad And Blues   Aladdin 202
        That's My Chick   −
166   Real Gone   Aladdin 191
254   Chicken Shack Boogie   Aladdin 3014, AL 704, Score
                                         LP 4012, Imperial LP 9176, 017
273   It Took A Long, Long Time   Aladdin 3014
        Roomin' House Boogie   Aladdin 3032, AL 704
Omit Davis: Los Angeles, October 27, 1947
403   Train Time Blues   Aladdin 206
404   What Can I Do   Aladdin 3197
405   Bye Bye Boogie (add ten.)   Aladdin 206, AL 704, 707
        Fool Playing Blues   Aladdin 211
        I Still Love You   −
Add Davis, ten: Los Angeles, 1947
RR 664 My Luck Is Bound To Change   Aladdin 3150
3026B   Pot Luck Boogie   Aladdin 3026, AL 704
No details: Los Angeles, 1948
3018A   Bewildered   Aladdin 3018, Imperial 017
3018B   A And M Blues   −
        Jitterbug Parade   Aladdin 3023
        Hold Me Baby   −
3026A   In The Middle Of The Night   Aladdin 3026
        Empty Arm Blues   Aladdin 3032
        Note: Later recordings not included.

LUKE 'LONG GONE' MILES

Born Lachute, Louisiana on May 8, 1925.
Vcl. with Sonny Terry, hca; Brownie McGhee, gtr.

		Los Angeles, 1961
YW 23840	Long Gone	Smash 1755
YW 23845	War Time Blues	–

Vcl. with Willie Chambers, gtr; Leroy Vinnegar, bs.

		Los Angeles, February 5, 1964
	I Feel Alright	World Pacific 1820
	Things That I Used To Do	–
	No Money, No Honey	– , 408
	Miss Hazel Mae	–
	Long Gone	– , 408
	Barefoot Rock	–
	Bad Luck	–
	Mercury Jump	–
	Long Distance Call	–
	So Sorry For To Leave	–

& THE BOYS FROM 25TH STREET

Vcl. with Bruce Bromberg, J. C. Warner, gtrs; D. L. Walker, bs–gtr; K. Sawyer, dms.

		Los Angeles, May 17, 1965
A	Lena Mae	Two Kings 100
B	38 Pistol	–
A	Losing My Mind	Two Kings 101
B	Early One Morning	–

BIG JOHN HENRY MILLER

Born Starkville, Mississippi?
Vcl/gtr. with Jimmy Lee Miller, gtr.

		Mississippi? 1965
	Down Here By Myself	Storyville SLP 180

LEROY MILLER

Lead vcl. with hoeing group, vcls.

		Parchman Farm, Miss., 1959
	Berta, Berta	Prestige Int. 25010

TAL MILLER

Vcl/pno. with gtr; bs; Wilson Semien, dms.

		Lake Charles, La., 1957
H08W-2027	Life's Journey	Goldband 1059
H08W-2028	Mean Old Kokamoo	–

Note: Later sides not included. Opelousas, La. based artist.

MISSISSIPPI SHIEKS

Walter Vincson, vcl/gtr; Jesse Coleman, pno; Sammy Hill, gtr; Pops Foster, bs; Earl Watkins, dms.

		Chicago, September 8, 1961
396	A Wonderful Thing	Riverside RLP 403
397	Things About Comin' My Way	Riverside RLP 389, 403
398	I Knew You Were Kiddin'	Riverside RLP 403

MISSISSIPPI STRING BAND

Tom Johnson, vcl (–1)/gtr (–2)/mand (–3); John Copeland, mand (–4)/gtr (–5).

		Vicksburg, Miss., June 6, 1954
	Blues -2, 4	Folkways FP 654
	Hootchie Kootchie -3, 5	–
	It's Tight Like That -1, 2, 4	–
	See See Mama -1, 2, 4	–

MISS PEACHES

Real name Elsie Griner, Jr.
Vcl. with pno.

		Atlanta? 1954
E4 3593	Calling Moody Field Part 1	Groove 0009
E4 3594	Calling Moody Field Part 2	–

244

LONNIE MITCHEL

Vcl/accdn. with pno; Ivory Semien, dms.　　　　　　Houston, 1961
| L136 | Watusi Beat | Ivory 136 |
| L137 | Louisiana Slo-Drag | Ivory 137 |

WALTER MITCHELL

Vcl/hca. with Robert Richard, hca; Boogie Woogie Red, pno; bs.
　　　　　　　　　　　　　　　　　　　　　　　Detroit, 1948
| DE-1 | Stop Messing Around | JVB 75827 |
| DE-2 | Pet Milk Blues | – |

Note: See also Robert Richard.

MOBILE STRUGGLERS

James Fields, vcl (−1); Lee Warren, vcl (−2). with 2 vlns; mand; tub or sbs (−1); gtr (−2).
　　　　　　　　　　　　　　　　　　　　　Mobile Ala.? July, 1949
| 984 | Memphis Blues -1 | American Music 104 |
| 985 | Fattenin' Frogs -2 | – |

Note: Probable recording date July 26/7. 980/1 recorded July 12. 982/3 recorded July 19.

MODEL T. SLIM

See under Elmon Mickle.

MOJO

See under Mojo Buford.

LITTLE BROTHER MONTGOMERY

Real name Eurreal Montgomery. Born Kentwood, Louisiana on May 17, 1907.

LITTLE BROTHER MONTGOMERY QUINTET
Vcl/pno. with Lee Collins, tpt; Oliver Alcorn, ten/clt; Ernest Crawford, bs; Jerome Smith, dms.
　　　　　　　　　　　　　　　　　　　　　Chicago, 1947
1-DS	El Ritmo	Century 4009
2-DS	Swingin' With Lee	Century 4010
3-DS	Long Time	Century 4009
4-DS	That Woman I Love	Century 4010
No details:		Chicago, 1950
	unissued titles	Savoy

LITTLE BROTHER MONTGOMERY
Vcl/pno.
　　　　　　　　　　　　　　　　　　　　　Chicago, c. 1954
	Mule Face Blues	Windin' Ball WS104
	Cow Cow Blues	–
	Vicksburg Blues	–
	Crescent City Blues	–

LITTLE BROTHER MONTGOMERY & HIS VICKSBURGERS
Vcl/pno. with dms.　　　　　　　　　　　　　　Chicago, 1956
	Cow Cow Blues	Ebony 1000, 1002
	Vicksburg Blues	–
	Fever	Ebony 1002

LITTLE BROTHER MONTGOMERY & HIS BOGALUSA BOYS
Vcl/pno. with bs; dms; George Blunt, shouting (−1).
| A | Pinetop's Boogie -1 | Ebony 1005 |
| B | Arkansas Blues | – |

LITTLE BROTHER MONTGOMERY
Vcl/pno.
　　　　　　　　　　　　　　　　　　　　　Chicago, 1960
	Pleading Blues	Folkways FG 3527
	Vicksburg 44	–
	Early One Morning	–
	Now About That Prisoner	–

	Crescent City Blues	Folkways FG 3527
	Pallet On The Floor	–
	West 46th Street Boogie	–
	Louisiana Rag	–
	I Ain't No Bulldog	–
	Mean Old Mama	–
	London Shout	–
	Storyville Blues	–
	L & N Boogie	–
	It's All Over Now	–

Vcl/pno.   Chicago, July 14, 1960

	Dud Low Joe	Decca LK 4664
	Trembling Blues	"77" LA 12/21
	No Special Rider Here	–
	Crescent City Blues	unissued
	Original Vicksburg Blues	Decca LK 4664
	Balling The Jack	unissued
	I'm Sure Of Everything But You	unissued
	My Electrical Invention	"77" LA 12/21
	House Rent Boogie	unissued
	Coonjine Baby	unissued
	Bob Martin Blues	"77" LA 12/21
	That's Why I Keep Drinking	–

Vcl/pno. with Lafayette Thomas, gtr; Julian Eull, bs.   New York City, July 1960

	Tasty Blues	Bluesville BVLP 1012
	Santa Fe	–
	How Long Brother	–
	Pleading Blues	–
	No Special Rider	–
	Brother's Boogie	–
	Sneaky Pete Blues	–
	Something Keeps Worrying Me	–
	Cry, Cry Baby	–
	Satellite Blues	–
	Deep Fried	–
	Vicksburg Blues	–

Vcl/pno. with Ken Colyer, tpt (-1); Jack Fallon, bs(-2)   London, August 18/20, 1960

	Farish Street Jive Take 1	Columbia 33SX 1289
	Farish Street Jive Take 3	–
	New Vicksburg Blues	–
	Chinese Man Blues	–
	Canadian Sunset	–
	Cow Cow Blues	– , DB 4594
	Just The Blues -1	–
	I Ain't Gonna Give Nobody -1	–
	Buddy Bolden's Blues -1	–
	Pinetop's Boogie Woogie -2	– , DB 4594

Add Alexis Korner, gtr; Bob Guthrie, dms:

	I Keep Drinkin'	Columbia 33SX 1289
	Old Man Blues	–

LITTLE BROTHER MONTGOMERY AND FRIENDS

Vcl/pno. with Ted Butterman, cnt; Bob Gordon, clt; Bob Shriver (as "Rufus Brown"), ten (-1)
Mike McKendrick, bjo; Elaine McFarland, vcl. pno. solo (-2). Chicago, September 6, 1961

343	Saturday Night Function -1	Riverside RLP 390
344	Satellite Blues -1	–
344-1	New Satellite Blues -1	Riverside RLP 403
345	Twelfth Street Rag -1	rejected.
346	Cooter Crawl	Riverside RLP 390
347	Up The Country Blues	unissued
348	Michigan Water Blues	unissued
349	Prescription For The Blues	unissued
350	Home Again Blues -2	unissued

351	Riverside Boogie -2	unissued
352	Trouble In Mind	unissued
353	Somethin' Keep On Worryin' Me	Riverside RLP 389
354	Sweet Daddy, Your Mama's Done Gone Mad	unissued
355	Oh Daddy	unissued
356	44 Vicksburg -2	unissued

LITTLE BROTHER MONTGOMERY
Vcl/pno. with Lil "Hardin" Armstrong, Hardinaires & The Folk Jazz Hootenannies:
Chicago, 1960

| 1030A | Gonna Raise Rukus Tonight | Ebony 1030 |

LITTLE BROTHER MONTGOMERY & HIS JAZZ BLUES BAND
| 1030B | In The Evening | Ebony 1030 |

LITTLE BROTHER MONTGOMERY
Vcl/pno. with Lonnie Johnson, gtr; Sonny Greer, dms.   New York, Apr/June 1965
| | New Black Snake Blues | Spivey LP 1006 |
| | West Texas Blues | |

Vcl/pno.   Chicago, 1966
| A | All My Love | F. M. 1000 |
| B | She's My One And All Desire | – |

Note: Gospel sides made for Folkways not included

ALEXANDER MOORE (see also in APPENDIX)

Born Dallas, Texas on November 22, 1899
Vcl/pno. with poss. Smokey Hogg, gtr; dms.   Dallas ? 1951
| MM 1614-1 | If I Lose You Woman | RPM 326 |
| MM 1615 | Neglected Woman | – |

WHISTLING ALEX MOORE
Vcl/pno.   Dallas, July 30, 1960
	Wake Up Old Lady	Arhoolie F 1006
	That's Disgustin'	unissued
	Chock House Boogie	unissued
	Rubber Tyred Hack	Arhoolie F 1008
	Miss No Good Weed	–
	You Say I'm A Bad Feller	–
	Goin' Back To Froggy Bottom	–
	Frisky Gal	–
	Pretty Woman With A Sack Dress On	–
	Raggin' At Minnie's Tea Room	unissued
	Black Eyed Peas And Hog Jowls	Arhoolie F 1008
	Whistling Alex Moore's Blues	–
	From North Dallas To The East Side	–
	West Texas Woman	–
	July Boogie	–
	Boogie In The Barrel	–
	Liverpool	unissued
	Crazy Mixed Up Boogie	Decca LK 4664

JOHNNY LEE MOORE

Vcl. with Convict Group, vcls (-1)   Lambert, Miss. 1959
	Levee Camp Holler	Atlantic LP 1348
	Eighteen Hammers -1	–
	Early In The Morning	Prestige LP 25009

MOZELLE MOORE

Vcl(-1) hca.   Perry County, Ala? April 1954?
	When The Saints Go Marching In	Folkways FA 2659
	I'm Going To Pack Up My Things, And Back	
	Down The Road I'm Goin' -1	–

247

Jug with Phillip Ramsey, Sr., gtr; Phillip Ramsey, Jr. wbd; Dancing and handclapping by Horace Sprott and others.

Good Times   Folkways FA 2659

MOOSE JOHN

Real name John Walker
Vcl/pno. with gtrs: dms.   Los Angeles, 1955

7919	Wrong Doin' Woman	Ultra 102
7920	Talkin' About Me	−

Note: Also known as Big Moose, Later records not included

LEO MORRIS

WITH MARCEL & HIS BAND
Vcl/gtr. with accdn; gtr; dms.   Houston 1961

ACA 4686	Wanta Know How You Feel	Ivory 4-1-465
ACA 4687	I Don't Need You	−

MR. BO & HIS BLUES BOYS

Vcl. with tpt; ten; pno; gtr; bs-gtr; dms.   Detroit, 1966

A	I Ain't Gonna Suffer	Big D 851
B	If Trouble Was Money	−

MR. HONEY

See under Honeyboy Edwards, q.v.

MR. PERCY

No details.   1954

E4KB 3119	Full Of Misery	Dot 1205
E4KB 3120	Somebody Help Me Out	−

MR. SHORTSTUFF

See under Shortstuff Macon.

MUDDY WATERS (see Also in Appendix)

Real name KcKinley Morganfield. Born Rolling Fork, Mississippi on April 4, 1915

MCKINLEY MORGANFIELD
Vcl/gtr.   Stovall, Miss. summer 1941

4769-A-1,	Country Blues	Library of Congress AAFS 18,
A4377		L4, Testament T-2210
4769-A-2,	I Be's Troubled	issues as above
A4378		

SON SIMMS FOUR
Vcl(-1)/gtr. with Percy Thomas, vcl(-2)/gtr; Son Simms, vln; Louis Ford, vcl(-3)/mdln.
                                             Stoval, July 24, 1942

6628-A-6	Rambling Kid Blues -1	Testament T-2210
6628-A-7	Rosalie -1	−
6628-A-8	Joe Turner Blues -3	−
6628-B-1	Pearlie May Blues -2	−

Vcl/gtr. with Son Simms, gtr(-1); Charles Berry, gtr;(-2)

6628-B-2	Take A Walk With Me -1	Testament T-2210
6628-B-3	Burr Clover Blues -1	−
6629-A-1,2	I Be Bound To Write To You -2	−
6629-A-3	You Gonna Miss Me When I'm Dead And Gone	−

Vcl/gtr.   Clarksdale, August 1942

6666-A-3	You Got To Take Sick And Die Some Of These Days	Testament T-2210
6666-B-1	Why Don't You Live Right So God Can Use You	

| 6666-B-2 | Country Blues | Testament T-2210 |

Note: Son Simms is belived to be Henry Sims.

Vcl/gtr.   Chicago, September 27, 1947

CCO 4652	Jitterbug Blues	Columbia unissued
CCO 4653	Hard Days Blues	–
CCO 4654	Buryin' Ground Blues	–

Vcl/gtr. with Sunnyland Slim, pno; Big Crawford, bs.   Chicago, 1947

| U 7058 | Gypsy Woman | Aristocrat 1302, Chess LP 1501 |
| U 7059 | Little Anna Mae | – |

Slim Out: Chicago , 1948

| U 7112 | I Can't Be Satisfied (Looking For My Baby) | Aristocrat 1305, Chess 1514, LP 1427 |
| U 7113 | I Fee Like Going Home | Aristocrat 1305 |

Same:

U 7131-R	Train Fare Home	Aristocrat 1306, Chess LP 1511
U 7132		
U 7133		
U 7134-R	Sittin' Here And Drinkin' (Whiskey Blues)	Aristocrat 1306, Chess LP 1511
	Down South Blues	Chess LP 1511
	Kind Hearted Woman	–

Vcl/gtr. with Leroy Foster, gtr; Big Crawofrd, bs.   Chicago, 1949

U 7148	You're Gonna Miss Me	Aristocrat 1307
U 7149	Mean Red Spider	–
U 7150		
U 7151-R	Streamline Woman	Aristocrat 1310
U 7152		
U 7153-R	Muddy Jumps One	Aristocrat 1310

Foster Out

| U 7199 | Little Geneva | Aristocrat 1311, Chess LP 1501 |
| U 7200 | Canary Bird | –   – |

Vcl/gtr. with Johnny Jones, pno; Leroy Foster, dms.   Chicago, 1950

| U 7215 | Screamin' And Cryin' | Aristocrat 406, Chess LP 1501 |
| U 7216 | Where's My Woman Been | – |

Vcl/gtr. with Big Crawford, bs;

U 7235	Rollin' And Tumblin' Part 1	Aristocrat 412, Chess LP 1501
U 7236	Rollin' And Tumblin' Part 2	–
U 7237	Rollin' Stone	Chess 1426, LP 1427, Argo LP 4034
U 7238	Walkin' Blues	Chess 1426, LP 1501

Add Little Walter, hca;

U 7261	You're Gonna Need My Help I Said	Chess 1434, LP 1511
U 7262	Sad Letter Blues	– –
U 7263	Early Morning Blues	Chess 1490, –
U 7264	Appealing Blues (Hello Little Girl)	Chess 1468, –

Same, add wbd (-1);

| U 7275 | Louisiana Blues -1 | Chess 1441, LP 1427 |
| U 7276 | Evan's Shuffle | |

Walter Horton, hca replaces Walter: Chicago, 1951

| U 7304 | Long Distance Call | Chess 1452, LP 1427 |
| U 7305 | Too Young To Know | –   , LP 1511 |

Horton Out, Add Jimmy Rogers, gtr;

| U 7306 | Honey Bee | Chess 1468, LP 1427, 1511 |

Vcl/gtr. with Little Walter, hca; Elgar Edmonds, dms. Add Jimmy Rogers, gtr(-1).

U 7357	Country Boy	Chess 1509
U 7358	She Moves Me	Chess 1490, LP 1427
U 7359	My Fault	Chess 1480
U 7360	Still A Fool -1 (no hca)	– , 1921, LP 1427

Vcl/gtr. with Little Walter, hca; Jimmy Rogers, gtr; Elgar Edmonds, dms.

U 7439	Please Have Mercy	Chess 1514

Add Otis Spann, pno

U 7476	Who's Gonna Be Your Sweet Man	Chess 1542
U 7477	Standing Around Crying	Chess 1526, LP 1427
U 7478	Gone To Main Street	–

	Spann out:	Chicago, 1953
U 4334	She's All Right	Chess 1537
	She's All Right (alt. take)	Chess LP 1511
U 4335	Sad, Sad Day	Chess 1537
	My Life Is Ruined	Chess LP 1511

Add Big Crawford, bs;

U 7501	Turn The Lamp Down Low	Chess 1542
U 7502	Loving Man	Chess 1585

Walter Horton, hca; replaces Walter:

U 7551	Blow Wind Blow	Chess 1550
U 7552	Mad Love (I Just Want You To Love Me)	– , LP 1427
U 7589	I'm Your Hoochie Coochie Man	Chess 1560, LP 1427
U 7590	She's So Pretty	–

Little Walter, hca; replaces Horton'

U 7630	Just Make Love To Me	Chess 1571, LP 1427
U 7631	Oh Yeah	–

Vcl. with Walter Horton or Little Walter, hca; Jimmy Rogers, gtr; Luther Tucker, bs; Fred Below, dms.

		Chicago, 1954
U 7697	I'm Ready	Chess 1579, LP 1427
U 7698		
U 7699	I Don't Know Why	Chess 1579

Note: On last session Horton And Walter blew alternate solos.

Add Otis Spann, pno. (-1)

U 7746	I'm A Natural Born Lover -1	Chess 1585
U 7747	Ooh Wee	Chess 1724

Vcl. with Little Walter, hca; Otis Spann, pno. Jimmy Rogers, gtr; Willie Dixon, bs; Francey Clay, dms.

		Chicago, 1955
U 7784	Young Fashioned Ways	Chess 1602
U 7785	I Want To Be Loved	Chess 1596
U 7786	My Eyes (Keep Me In Trouble)	–

Walter Horton, hca. replaces Horton.

U 7937	I Got To Find My Baby	Chess 1644
U 7938	Sugar Sweet	Chess 1612
U 7939	Trouble No More	–
U 7940	Clouds In My Heart	Chess 1724

Vcl. with Walter Horton, hca(-1); Little Walter, hca (-2); James Cotton, 2nd. hca(-3); Jimmy Rogers, gtr; Willie Dixon, bs; Francey Clay, dms.

		Chicago, 1956
8012	40 Days And £0 Nights -1	Chess 1620, LP 1501
8013	All Abourd -2, 3	

Same, but Walter Horton, hca. Add Otis Spann, pno:

8147	Just To Be With You	Chess 1644, LP 1501
8148	Don't Go No Farther	Chess 1630
8149	Diamonds At Your Feet	–

James Cotton, hca; replaces Horton:

		Chicagom 1957
8388	I Live The Life I Love	Chess 1680
8389	Rock Me	Chess 1652
8390		
8391		
8392	Look What You've Done	Chess 1758
8393	Got My Mojo Working	Chess 1652

Vcl. with Marcus Johnson, ten; James Cotton, hca; Otis Spann, pno. Pat Hare, gtr; Fracney
Clay, dms;

8510	Good News	Chess 1667
8511	Evil	Chess 1680
8512	Come Home Baby	Chess 1667

Omit ten. Add Willie Dixon, bs;   Chicago, 1958

8732	I Won't Go	Chess 1692
8733	She's Got It	–
8979	She's 19 Years Old	Chess 1704, Argo LP 4042
8980	Close To You (add ten)	

Andrew Stephens, bs. replaces Dixon: Chicago 1958/59

| 9140 | Walking Thru The Park | Chess 1718, LP 1501 |
| 9194 | Mean Mistreater | Chess 1718 |

Same, but Willie Smith or Francey Clay, dms.

9504	Take The Bitter With The Sweet	Chess 1733
9505	She's Into Something	–
9511	I Feel So Good	Chess 1748, Lp 1444
9512		
9513	Love Affair	Chess 1758
8514	Recipe For Love	–

Smith Out:

9640	Tell Me Baby	Chess 1739, LP 1444
9641	When I Get To Thinking	Chess 1748, –
	Southbound Train	Chess LP 1444
	Just A Dream	–
	Double Trouble	–
	I Done Got Wise	–
	Mopper's Blues	–
	Lonesome Road Blues	–
	Hey Hey	–

Note: Willie Smith stated that 12 sides were cut at 9504/14 session, of which he
played on six and Clay on six.

Vcl/gtr. with James Cotton, hca; Memphis Slim, pno; Al Hall bs; Shep Sheppard, dms.

Carnegie Hall, New York, April 3, 19:

	Hoochie Coochie Man	United Artists UAL 3050
	Goin' Down	–
	Rock Me	United Artists UAL 3137
	Sunrise Blues	–

Note: Last two titles credits to Memphis Slim.

Vcl. with Little Walter, hca; Otis Spann, pno; Jimmy Rogers, gtr; Willie Dixon bs; Francey Clay, dms

Chicago, April 23, 1960

| 10032 | I'm Your Doctor | Chess 1752 |
| 10033 | Read Way Back | -- |

Vcl. with James Cotton, hca; Otis Spann, pno; Pat Hare, gtr; Andrew Stephens, bs;
Willie Smith, dms.   Chicagom 1960

10293	Tiger In Your Tank	Chess 1765
10294		
10295	Meanest Woman	Chess 1765
10296/99		
10300	Woman Wanted	Chess 1774

Vcl/gtr. with James Cotton, hca. Otis Spann, vcl(-1)/pno. Pat Hare, gtr; Andrew Stephens, bs;
Francey Clay, dms.   Newport, July 3, 1960

	I Got My Brand On You	Chess 1449
	I'm Your Hoochie Coochie Man	–
	Baby Please Don't Go	–
	Soon Forgotten	–
	Tiger In Your Tank	–
	I Feel So Good	Chess LP 1449
10544	Got My Mojo Working Part 1	– , 1774, Argo LP 4027
	Got My Mojo Working Part 2	–
	Goodbye Newport Blues -1	–

251

Vcl. with J. T. Brown, Boyd Atkins, tens; Otis Spann, pno; Matt Murphy, gtr; Milton Rector, bs-gtr; Al Duncan, dms. Chicago, 1961

| 11013 | Lonesome Room Blues | Chess 1796 |
| 11014 | Messin' With The Man | – |

Vcl. with J. T. Brown, Ernest Cotton, tens; John Walker, org(-1)/pno.(-2); Earl Hooker, gtr; Willie Dixon, bs; Casey Jones, dms. Chicago, 1962

U 11446	Going Home	Chess 1819
U 11447		
U 11448	Muddy Waters Twist -1	Chess 1827
U 11449	Tough Times	Chess 1819

Same: Chicago, June 1962

| U-11711 | You Shook Me -1, 2 | Chess 1827 |

Same: Chicago, 1962

| U-11836 | You Need Love | Chess 1839 |
| U-11837 | Little Brown Bird | – |

Vcl. with James Cotton, hca; Otis Spann, pno. Luther Tucker, gtr; Willie Dixon, bs; Willie Smith, dms. Chicago, 1963

U-12442	Five Long Years	Chess 1862
U-12443		
U-12444	Twenty Four Hours	Chess 1862

Vcl. with Jarret Gibson, ten; Donald Hankins, bari; Otis Spann, pno; Buddy Guy, gtr; Jack Meyers, bs-gtr; Fred Below, dms. Cop Cobana, Chicago, July 26, 1963

	Sitting And Thinking	Argo LP 4031
	Clouds In My Heart	–
	Got My Mojo Working	–
	19 Years Old	–

Add Buddy Guy, Willie Dixon, vcls:

| | Wee Wee Baby | Argo LP 4031 |

Vcl/gtr. with Otis Spann, pno; Willie Dixon bs; Billie Stepney, dms.
 Bremen October 13, 1963

| | Five Long Years | Fontana TL 5204 |

Vcl/gtr. with Buddy Guy, gtr(-1). Chicago, 1964

	Feel Like Going Home	Chess LP 1483
	Cold Weather Blues –1	–
	Big Leg Woman -1	–
	My Captain -1	–

Vcl/gtr. with Buddy Guy, gtr; Willie Dixon, bs; Clifton James, dms.

	Country Boy	Chess LP 1483
	My Home Is In The Delta	–
	Long Distance	–
	Good Morning Little School Girl	–
	You Gonna Need My Help	–

Vcl/gtr. with James Cotton, hca; Otis Spann, pno; gtr; bs; dms.
 Chicago, 1964

| 13150 | The Same Thing | Chess 1895, LP 1501 |
| 13151 | You Can't Lose What You Never Had | – – |

Vcl/gtr. with J. T. Brown, ten(-6)/vlt(-2); Otis Spann, pno; gtr; bs; dms.
 Chicago, 1965

13475	Put Me In Your Lay Away	Chess 1921
13932	My Dog Can't Bark	Chess 1937
13935	I Got A Rich Man's Woman	–

Vcl. with tpt; tbn; alt; ten ;bari; Otis Spann, pno; org; Jimmy Cotton, hca; gtr; bs-gtr; dms.
 Chicago, June 1966

14866	Corina, Corina	Chess 1973, LP 1507
	Piney Brown Blues	Chess LP 1507
	Black Night	–
	Trouble In Mind	–
	Going Back To Memphis	–
	Betty And Dupree	–
	Sweet Little Angel	–
	Take My Advice	–

	Trouble	Chess LP 1507
	Hard Loser	–
15035	Hootchi Kootchie Man	Chess 1973

Note: 15035 is actually 7589 with brass dubbed on.

MUDDY WATERS BLUES BAND

Otis Spann, vcl.(-1)/pno/org; George Smith, vcl(-2)/hca; Sammy Lawhorn, Main Stream (Muddy Waters), gtrs; Luther Johnson, vcl (- 3)/bs-gtr; Francey Clay, dms; Victoria Spivey, vcl(-4)

New York City, Nov. 25, 1966

Chicago Slide	Spivey LP 1008
Creepin' Snake -3	–
Look Out Victoria -2	–
You Done Lost Your Good Thing Now -1	–
Take Webster's Word For It -4	–
Theme	–
Ain't Nobody's Business What I Do -1	–
Born In Georgia -3	–
Trouble Hurts -4	–
Watermelon Man	–
Old Ugly Man Like Me -2	–
Gave It All To Me -4	–

MUDDY WATERS JR.

See under Mojo Buford.

MUMBLES

See under Walter Horton.

"MURDERERS' HOME" (or NEGRO PRISON SONGS)

Various solo or group vocals, largeley unaccompanied.

Parchman Farm, Miss. 1947

Road Song	Tradition 1020
No More My Lawd	–
Katy Left Memphis	–
Old Alabama	–
Black Woman	–
Jumpin' Judy	–
Whoa Back	–
Prettiest Train	–
Old Dollar Mamie	–
It Makes A Long Time Man Feel Bad	–
Rosie	–
Leave Camp Holler	–
Early In The Morning	–
Tangle Eyes Blues	–
Stackerlee	–
Prison Blues (acc. hca)	–
Sometimes I Wonder (acc. 2 gtrs)	–
Bye Bye Baby (acc. 2 gtrs.)	–

MATT MURPHY

Born Sunflower, Mississippi on December, 27, 1929
Vcl/gtr.

Copenhagen, 1963

| Gravel Road | Storyville SLP 166 |

Vcl/gtr. with Memphis Slim, pno; Willie Dixon, bs; Billy Stepney, dms.

Bremen, October, 13, 1963

| Matt's Guitar Boogie | Fontana 681,510,ZL |

SAMMY MYERS

SAMMY MYERS WITH KING MOSE ROYAL ROCKERS
Vcl/hca. with pno; gtr; dms.

Jackson, 1957

| 3404 | My Love Is Here To Stay | Ace 536 |
| 3405 | Sleeping In The Ground | – |

SAMMY MYERS
Vcl/hca. with pno; 2 gtrs; dms.   New Orleans? 1960
| FM 159 | Sad, Sad Lonesome Day | Fury 1035 |
| FM 160 | You Don't Have To Go | |

SAMMIE (LITTLE JOHN) MYERS
Vcl(-1); brass; organ; pno; gtr; el-bs; dms.   1966
| LH 2597 | Little John -1 | Soft 1003 |
| LH 2598 | Boss Bag | – |

BIG BOY MYLES

BIG BOY MYLES & THE SHA-WEES
Vcl. with ten; Professor Longhair, pno; gtr; bs; dms.   New Orleans, 1955
SP 564	That Girl I Married	Specialty 564
XSP 564	Who's Been Fooling You	
5017	Hickory Dickory Dock	Specialty 590
5018	Just To Hold My Hand	–

Note: Real Name Edgar Miles. Later recordsnot of any interest. Also recorded with The Sha-Weez.

N

LEMON NASH

Vcl/ukl. with Henry Thomas, gtr;   Baton Rouge, La. C. 1958
New Orleans Blues   Storyville SLP 129

NEGRO PRISON SONGS

See under "Murderer's Home" q.v.

PEPPERMINT NELSON

Real name Harrison Nelson
Vcl/gtr. with Elmore Nixon, pno;   Houston, 1947
| A | Pepermint Boogie | Gold Star 626 |
| B | Houston Blues | – |

PEPPERMINT HARRIS

Vcl/gtr. with Henry Hayes, alt; Ed Wiley, ten; Willie Johnson, pno; Donald Cooks, bs; Ben Turner, dms.   Houston 1950
2034	Raining In My Heart	SIW 543
2035	My Blues Moved, Rolled Away	
2056	This Is Goodbye Baby	SIW 554
2063	Texerkana Blues	SIW 568
2064	The Blues Pick On Me	SIW 597
2065	Reckless Lover	SIW 578
2067	Mabel, Mabel	SIW 554, Time LP 5
2083	Gimme, Gimme, Gimme	SIW 576

Add tpt.		Houston, 1951
2208	Fat Girl Boogie	SIW 568
2239	Hey Sweet Thing	SIW 576
2246	Oo Wee Baby (Love With A Thrill)	SIW 578
2279	Let's Ride	SIW 597, Time LP 5
2368	I Always End Up Blue	SIW 612
2370	I Screamed And I Cried	–
2388	She's My Baby	SIW 623, Time LP 5
2389	I Wake Up Screaming	–
2411	Please Let Me Come Home	SIW 638
2412	I'm Going Crazy Baby	–
3006	I'm Telling You People	SIW 587
3007	How Long Must I Suffer	–
J 496	Got A Big Fine Baby	SIW 650, Time LP 5
J 501	I Will Always Think Of You	–
MM 2108	Bye, Bye, Fare Thee Well	Modern 936
MM 2109	Black Cat Bone	–

From above sessions:

	These Are My Blues	Time LP 4
	Evil Woman Blues	–
	I Have Often Wondered	Time LP 5
	Too Late To Worry	–
	Oh, I Got The Blues	–
	Please Tell Me Baby	–
	Gonna End My Worries	–
	Want To See You Baby	–
	I'm Writing You Baby	–

Vcl. with Maxwell Davis & others, saxes, pno; gtr; bs; dms.		Los Angeles, June 16, 1951
RR 1697	It's You, Yes, It's You	Aladdin 3097
RR 1698	I Got Loaded (no saxes)	–

Same:		Los Angeles, August 29, 1951
RR 1741	Wasted Love	Aladdin 3177
RR 1742	I Sure Do Miss My Baby	Aladdin 3154
RR 1743	(not allocated)	
RR 1744	I Never Get Enought Of You	Aladding 3206

Same:		Los Angeles, October 5, 1951
RR 1762	Have Another Drink And Talk To Me	Aladdin 3107
RR 1763	Middle Of Winter	–
RR 1764	P. H. Blues	Aladdin 3108
RR 1765	Let The Back Door Hit You	–

Same:		Los Angeles, April 8/9 1952
RR 1910	I Cry For My Baby	Aladdin 3141
RR 1911	Hey Little Schoolgirl	Aladdin 3154
RR 1912	There's A Dead Cat On The Line	Aladdin 3147
RR 1914	Right Back On	Aladdin 3130
RR 1915	Maggie's Boogie	–
RR 1912	Every Dog Has His Day	unissued

Same:		Los Angeles, May 29, 1953
RR 1937	Goodbye Blues	Aladdin 3177
RR 1938	Don't Leve Me All Alone	Aladdin 3183
RR 1936	Wet Rag	

		Los Angeles, August 25, 1953
RR 2211	Three Sheets In The Wind	Aladdin 3206

Vcl. with saxes; pno; gtr; bs; dms		Los Angeles, 1954
A	Cadillac Funeral	Money 214, Cash 1003
AA	Treat Me Like I Treat You	–

Same:		Los Angeles, 1955
F4PB 3544	Need Your Lovin'	"X" 0142
F4PB 3545	Just You And Me	

Vcl. with Ten; pno; gtr; bs; dms.		Lake Charles, c. 1960
DD 1	Messing Around With The Blues	Dart 103
DD2	You Got Me Wonderin'	–

255

Same:		Houston, 1960
ACA 3992	Angel Child	Duke 319
ACA 3993	Ain't No Business	–
Vcl. with ten(-1); pno; gtrs; dms.		Tyler, Texas 1965
TM 1071	Marking Time -1	Jewel 742
TM 1072	Bad, Bad Woman	–
Same:		Memphis, 1966
	Ma Ma -1	Jewel 747
	Aything You Can Do -1	–
TM 1520	Raining In My Heart -1	Jewel 762
TM 1521	My Time After Awhile -1	–

NEW ORLEANS SLIM

See under Ira Amos

MANNY NICHOLS

Vcl/gtr.		Houston, 1949
no mx	Walkin' Blues	FBC dub
no mx	untitled blues	–
ACA 1436	Walking Talking Blues	FBC 125
ACA 1437	Tall Skinny Mama Blues	–
ACA 1438,		
IM 353	Get Going (Throw A Little Boogie)	Imperial 5162, Arhoolie F 1018
ACA 1439,		
IM 356	Worried Life Blues	Imperial 5173
ACA 1440,		
IM 355	Forgive Me Blues	–
ACA 1441,		
IM 354	No One To Love Me	Imperial 5162

Note: Nicholls is a resident of Victoria, Texas.

THE NIGHTHAWKS (Essex)

See under Bob Camp

THE NIGHTHAWKS (Aristocrat)

See under Robert Nighthawk.

ROBERT NIGHTHAWK

Real name Robert McCullum. Born Helena, Arkansas on November 30, 1909
Died Helena, Ark. in late 1967.

Vcl/gtr. with pno; Willie Dixon, bs.		Chicago, 1948
U 7130	My Sweet Lovin' Woman	Chess 1484
Same:		Chicago, 1949
U 7195	Black Angel Blues -1	Aristocrat 2301
U 7196	Annie Lee Blues -1	–
U 7197	Return Mail Blues	Chess 1484
Same:		Chicago, 1950
U 7227	Six Three 0 -1	Aristocrat 413
U 7228		
U 7229	Jackson Town Gal -1	Aristocrat 413

Note: -1 Issued as by The Nighthawks.

Vcl/gtr. with Bob Call, pno; Ransom Knowling, bs; dms.		Chicago, 1951
1005	Feel So Bad	United 105
1006	Kansas City Blues	United 102, Blues Classics BC-8
1007	Cryin' Won't Help You	–
1008	Take It Easy Baby	United 105

256

ROBERT NIGHTHAWK & HIS NIGHTHAWKS BAND

Same: Chicago, 1953
1151   The Moon Is Rising   States 131
1152   Maggie Campbell   –

Vcl/gtr. with Walter Horton, hca; Henry Gray, pno; Willie Dixon, bs; Clifton James, dms.
                                                               Chicago, 1964
           Lula Mae   Decca LK 4748
           Merry Christmas   –

Vcl/gtr. with Johnny Young, gtr; John Wrencher, hca.   Chicago, 1964
           Blues Before Sunrise   Testament T-2203

WILLIE NIX

Born Memphis, Tennessee in 1923.
Vcl/dms. with Albert Joiner, pno; Willie Johnson, gtr.   Memphis, 1951
MM 1608   Lonesome Bedroom Blues   RPM 327
MM 1609   Try Me One More Time   –

Add hca.   Memphis, 1952
C 1026   Truckin' Little Woman   Checker 756
C 1027   Just One Mistake   –

WILLIE NIX – THE MEMPHIS BLUES BOY
Vcl/dms. with Walter Horton, hca; Billy "Red" Love, pno; Joe Hill Louis, gtr.
                                                               Memphis, 1953
U 59   Seems Like A Million Years   Sun 179
U 60   Baker Shop Boogie   –

WILLIE NIX & HIS COMBO
Vcl. with Snooky Pryor, hca; Sunnyland Slim, pno; Eddie Taylor, gtr; Alfred Wallace, dms.
                                                               Chicago, late 1953
C 5062   Nervous Wreck   Chance 1163
C 5063   No More Love   –
C 5064   Just Can't Stay   Sabre 104
C 5065   All By Myself   –

ELMORE NIXON

Born Crowley, Louisiana on November 17, 1933.
No details.   Houston, 1949
ACA 1398   Take Me Back Again   Lucky 7 ?
           Note: This odd side is probably connected with those by Milton Willis, q.v.

WITH HENRY HAYES 4 KINGS
Vcl/pno. with Henry Hayes, alt; ten; gtr; bs; dms.   Houston, 1950
ACA 1550   Alabama Blues   Peacock 1537
ACA 1551   My Wish For You (add tpt.)   –

& HIS HADACOL BOYS
Vcl/pno. with Henry Hayes, alt; Ed Wiley, ten; Donald Cooks, bs; Ben Turner, dms.
2040   Foolish Love   SIW 546
2041   It's A Sad, Sad World   –

WITH HENRY HAYES & HIS RHYTHM KINGS
As last, but add Goree Carter, gtr.   Houston, 1951
2249   I Went To See A Gypsy   SIW 601
2250   Shout And Rock   –
2254   Searching Blues   SIW 580
2255   I'm Moving Out
YB 9390   Playboy Blues   Mercury 70061
YB 9391
YB 9392-8 Million Dollar Blues   Mercury 70061

Vcl/pno. with Henry Hayes, alt; ten; gtr; bs; dms.
ACA 1879   California, I Love   unissued
ACA 1880   You See Me Smiling   Peacock 1572
ACA 1881   It's Hard To Love A Woman   unissued
ACA 1882   A Hep Cat's Advice   Peacock 1572

As last:		Houston, 1952
ACA 2320	Over Here Pretty Baby	Savoy 878
ACA 2321	If You'll Be My Love	Savoy 1105
ACA 2322	Forgive Me Baby	Savoy 878
SHH 4292	Elmore's Blues (Prob. ACA 2323)	Savoy 889
SHH 4293	Last Nite (Prob. ACA 2324)	Savoy 1105
SHH 4294	Sad And Blue (Prob. ACA 2319)	Savoy 889

Vcl/pno. with saxes; gtr; bs; dms.		Houston, September, 1955
IM 920	Don't Do It	Post 2008
IM 921	The Women	
IM 918	A Broken Heart	Imperial 5388
IM 919	You Left Me	–

ALLAN NURSE'S BLUES BAND

Vcl/pno. with		1944/45
UN 26	Black Snake Blues	Ebony 1030
UN 27	There's Only One Man	–
	I Love To Read The Funnies	Southern 114
	Jelly Shakin' Blues	Southern 123
	Bye Bye Mary	–

O

LILLIAN OFFITT

Born Nashville, Tennessee on November 4, 1933.

Vcl. with ten; pno; gtr; bs; dms.		Nashville, 1957/58
A	Miss You So	Excello 2104
B	If You Only Knew	–
A	Just Lonesome That's All	Excello 2124
B	Darling I'll Forgive You	–
A	Darlin' Please Don't Change	Excello 2139
B	Can't Go On	–

Vcl. with ten; pno; Earl Hooker, gtr; bs; dms.		Chicago, 1959/60
25-123	The Man Won't Work	Chief 7012
25-124	Will My Man Be Home Tonight	–
25-137	Oh Mama	Chief 7015
25-138	My Man Is A Lover	–
25-188	Troubles	Chief 7029
25-191	Shine On	–

OLE SONNY BOY

Vcl/hca. with pno; gtr; dms.		Nashville, 1956
A	Blues And Misery	Excello 2086
B	You Better Change	–

Note: Credits on both sides to C. Grossley.

ONE STRING SAM

Vcl/1-string gtr.		Detroit, c. 1956
A	My Baby Ooo	J.V.B. 40
B	I Need A Hundred Dollars	– , Blues Classics BC-12

LARRY O'WILLIAMS

Vcl/gtr. with org; bs–gtr; dms.   Houston, 1966
519-1 That's My Girl   Arhoolie 519
519-2 Hear Me Calling Baby   —

P

MEMPHIS EDDIE P.

See under Memphis Eddie Pee.

LIL PALMORE & HER CALDONIA BOYS (or CAL PALMER)

Vcl. with   1948
C 104 I Believe I'll Go Back Home Ebony 1004, SIW 540, 10000
C 107 Lil's Caldonia Boogie   — — —

CAL "CALDONIA" PALMER

Vcl. with John Sellers, vcl (–1). & Little Brother's Jazz Blues Band: tpt; Eurreal Montgomery, pno; bs; dms.
A Busy Bootin' And You Can't Come In -1 Ebony 1040
B Michigan Water Blues   —

PAPA GEORGE

Vcl/hca/wbd. with   Natchez, Miss., 1950
                Sultan 1425

LITTLE JUNIOR PARKER

Born West Memphis, Arkansas on March 3, 1927.

LITTLE JNR. PARKER & HIS BLUE FLAMES

Vcl. with ten; Matt Murphy, gtr; Ike Turner, pno; unk. bs; L. C. Dranes, dms.
                Memphis, 1952
MM 1809 You're My Angel   Modern 864
MM 1810 Bad Women, Bad Whiskey —

LITTLE JUNIOR'S BLUE FLAMES

Vcl. with Raymond Hill, ten; Bill Johnson, pno; Floyd Murphy, Pat Hare, gtrs; poss. John Bowers, dms.   Memphis, late 1953
U 77 Feelin' Good (no ten; pno.) Sun 187
U 78 Fussin' And Fightin'   —
U 88 Love My Baby (no ten; pno.) Sun 192
U 89 Mystery Train   —

LITTLE JNR. PARKER WITH BILL JOHNSON'S BLUE FLAMES

Vcl. with Bill Johnson, pno; Pat Hare, gtr. and others. Houston, 1954
ACA 2723 Please Baby Blues   Duke 127
ACA 2724 Dirty Friend Blues   Duke 120
ACA 2725 Can't Understand   —
ACA 2726 Sittin' Drinkin' And Thinkin' Duke 127

LITTLE JNR. PARKER & THE BLUE FLAMES
Vcl. with Jimmy Stewart, tpt; Joe Fritz, alt; Jimmy Johnson, ten; Ray Fields, bari; Dale McJown, pno; Pat Hare, gtr; Hamp Simmons, bs; Sonny Freeman, dms.

		Houston, 1954
ACA 2903	Can You Teach Me Baby	unissued
ACA 2904	Bachelor's Blues	unissued
ACA 2905	Backtrackin'	Duke 137
ACA 2906	I Wanna Ramble (rhythm only)	–

LITTLE JNR. PARKER & HIS ORCH.
As above:

		Houston, 1955
ACA 3101	Driving Me Mad	Duke 147
ACA 3102	There Better Not Be No Feet (In Them Shoes)	Duke 147
ACA 3103	I'm Tender	unissued
ACA 3104	Pretty Baby	unissued

LITTLE JNR. PARKER WITH BILL HARVEY'S BAND
Vcl/hca. with Joe Scott, tpt; Pluma Davis, tbn; Bill Harvey, ten; Connie McBooker, pno; Pat Hare, gtr; Hamp Simmons, bs; Sonny Freeman, dms.

		Houston, May 7, 1956
FS 3002-1	Mother-In-Law Blues (no brass)	Duke 157
FS 3003-1	That's My Baby	

As above:

		Houston, December 12, 1956
FS 3016	Dolly Bee	Duke 164
FS 3017	Next Time You See Me	–

LITTLE JNR. PARKER & HIS COMBO
Vcl/hca. with Connie McBooker, pno; Pat Hare, gtr; Otis Jackson, bs; Sonny Freeman, dms.

		Houston, 1957/58
FR 3024-3	Pretty Baby	Duke 168
FR 3025-2	That's Alright	–

LITTLE JNR. PARKER & THE AL SMITH ORCH.
Vcl/hca. with similar to last, including Al Smith, bs.

OV 3042	Peaches	Duke 177
OV 3043	Pretty Little Doll	–

LITTLE JNR. PARKER & HIS BAND
Vcl/hca. with tpt; saxes (–1); pno; gtr; bs; dms.

FR 3056-4	Wondering -1	Duke 184
FR 3057-4	Sitting And Thinking	–

As before:

FR 3062-X	Barefoot Rock	Duke 193
FR 3077	What Did I Do	–

Vcl/hca. with pno; gtr; bs; dms.

FR 3092	Sometimes	Duke 301
FR 3093	Sweet Home Chicago	–

Note: Later records not included.

MONISTER PARKER
Vcl/gtr. with bs.

		Houston, late 1951
ACA 1987	Black Snake Blues	Nucraft 100
ACA 1988	You Gonna Need Me	–

TINY PARKER
See under Daddy Merritt.

WILLIS PARKER
Vcl. with Henry Hayes, alt; Ed Wiley, ten; Willie Johnson, pno; Donald Cooks, bs; Ben Turner, dms.

		Houston, 1951
2271	733 Blues	SIW 589
2272	5 Will Get 10	–

FRANK PATT

HONEYBOY

Vcl/gtr. with hca; Gus Jenkins, pno; bs; dms.   Los Angeles, 1954

XSP 476	Bloodstains On The Wall	Specialty 476
SP 476	My Time Ain't Long	–

FRANK PATT ORCHESTRA

Vcl/gtr. with ten; Gus Jenkins, pno; bs; dms.   Los Angeles, 1957

A	You Going To Pay For It Baby	Flash 117
AA	Gonna Hold On	–

Note: See also Gus Jenkins.

EARL PAYTON & HIS BLUES CATS

Vcl/hca. with Freddy King, gtr; Robert Elam, bs-gtr; Thomas J. McNulty, dms.

Chicago, 1954

unissued titles	Parrot

MEMPHIS EDDIE PEE

Vcl/gtr. with alt; Prince Albert, pno; bs; dms.   Los Angeles, 1945

APP 201	Mistreated All The Time	Globe 103
APP 202	Goin' Back To Smokey Mountain	–

Same, William Bates, sax;

APP 8A	Big Leg Mama	Globe 108
APP 8B	My House Fell Down	–

MEMPHIS EDDIE P & HIS TRIO

Vcl/gtr. with pno; bs.   Los Angeles, 1948

TV 222A	Trouble Blues	Foto 222
TV 222B	Hep Chick	–

MEMPHIS EDDIE

Vcl/gtr. with ten; pno; bs. dms.   Los Angeles, 1950

MM 1377-2	Velma Lee	RPM 301
MM 1378-1	Lonesome Change	
	I Believe	RPM 308
	Mercy Blues	–
	Good Time Woman	RPM 310
	Highway 61	
MM 1432-3	Real Fine Girl	RPM 315
MM 1433-2	Baby Lou	–

PEETIE WHEATSTRAW'S BUDDY

No details: Chicago, 1947

U 1231	Dog Eatin' Men	Hy Tone 38
U 1232	Miss Irene	–

Note: Possibly Harmon Ray, q.v.

MORRIS PEJOE (See also in APPENDIX)

Vcl/gtr. with Henry Grey, pno; Jody Williams, bs-gtr; Frank Kirkland, dms.

Chicago, 1954

U 7490	Tired Of Crying Over You	Checker 766
Y 7491	Gonna Buy Me A Telephone	–

Vcl/gtr. with ten; pno; gtr; dms.

4892	Can't Get Along	Checker 781
4896	I'll Plumb Get It	–

Same: Chicago, May 9, 1955

55-266	You Gonna Need Me	Vee Jay 148
55-267	Hurt My Feelings	–

Vcl/gtr. with saxes; pno; bs; dms   Chicago, c. 1956

U 3195	Screaming And Crying	Abco 106
U 3196	Maybe Blues	

Same: Chicago, c. 1960
410A   She Walked Right In   Atomic H A-1-410
410B   You Gone Away   – B-2-411

JERRY PERKINS & HIS BLUES BLASTERS

Vcl. with pno; gtr;   Los Angeles, early '50s
203 A   Katherine Blues   W & W 204
203 B   Knocking The Boogie   –

JESSE PERKINS

JESSE & BUZZY
Vcl/hca. with Buzzy, gtr; dms.   1959/60
SJP 70395   Without Your Love   Savoy 1556
SJP 70396   Going Back To Orleans   –

JESSE PERKINS & THE BAD BOYS
Vcl/hca. with pno; Buzzy, gtr; bs; dms.
SJB 70680   Madly In Love   Savoy 1584
SJB 70679   One More Kiss   –

VIRGIL PERKINS

Vcl/wbd. with JackSims, gtr;   Houston, November, 6, 1955
          Goin' Around The Mountain   Folkways FA 2610
          John Henry   –
          Interview   –
          Trouble In Mind -1   RBF 202

          Note: -1 Perkins also plays kazoo.

Vcl/wbd.
          Solo   RBF 202

BLIND JAMES PHILLIPS

Born Birmingham, Alabama on April 20, 1914
Vcl/gtr.   Birmingham, August 24, 1962
          Night Is Falling   Arhoolie F 1012
          No Lovin'   Arhoolie F 1018

PIANO RED

Real name Willie Perryman.
Vcl/pno. with W. J. Jones, bs; William R. Green, dms   Atlanta, July 25, 1950
EO-VB-5220 Jumpin' The Boogie   Victor 22/50-0118
EO-VB-5221 Rockin' With Red   Victor 22/50-0099,
                                                   Groove 5000, EGA-7
EO-VB-5222 Let's Have A Good Time   Victor 22/50-4265
EO-VB-5223 Red's Boogie   Victor 22/50-0099,
                                                   Groove 5000

W. Harper, dms. replaces Green: Atlanta, October 18, 1950
EO-VB-5949 The Wrong Yoyo   Victor 22/50-0106
EO-VB-5950 My Gal Jo -1   –
EO-VB-5951 Baby, What's Wrong -1   Victor 22/50-0130
EO-VB-5952 Well, Well, Baby -1   unissued

          Note: -1 Add L. Johnson, alt.
Vcl/pno. with Wesley Jackson, gtr; W. J. Jones, bs; J Williams, dms.
                                                   Atlanta, February 22, 1951
E1-VB-1319 Just Right Bounce   Victor 22/50-0118,
                                                   Grove EGA-3
E1-VB-1320 Diggin' The Boogie   Victor 22/50-4265
E1-VB-1321 Layin' The Boogie   Victor 22/50-0130,
                                                   Groove EGA-3
E1-VB-1322 Bouncin' With Red   Victor 20/47-4524

262

Vcl/pno. with Wesley, Jackson, gtr; George Miller, bs; F. M. Hawkins, dms.

		Atlanta, October 17, 1951
E1-VB-3777	It Makes No Difference Now	Victor 20/47-4380
E1-VB-3778	Hey Good Lookin'	Victor 20/47-4380
E1-VB-3779	Count The Days I'm Gone	Victor 20/47-4524
E1-VB-3780	My Boogie	unissued

Vcl/pno. with B. Mays, tpt; F. Taylor, D. Henderson Jr., saxes; Wesley Jackson, gtr; C. Holloway Jr., bs; L Lawson, dms.

		Atlanta, May 10, 1952
E2-VB-6227	The Sales Tax Boogie	Victor 20/47-4766
E2-VB-6228	Voo Doopee Doo	Victor 20/47-4957
E2-VB-6229	Daybreak	–
E2-VB-6230	She Walks Right In	Victor 20/47-4766

Vcl/pno. with Budd Johnson, alt/ten; Rene Hall, gtr; Doles Dickens, bs; Charlie Smith, dms.

		New York, November 6, 1952
E2-VB-7734	I'm Gonna Tell Everybody	Victor 20/47-5224
E2-VB-7735	I'm Gonna Rock Some More	Victor 20/47-5101
E2-VB-7736	She's Dynamite	Victor 20/47-5224
E2-VB-7737	Everybody's Boogie	Victor 20/47-5101, Groove EGA-3

Add Al Sears, ten;

		New York, March 26, 1953
E3-VB-1009	Your Mouth's Got A Hole	Victor 20/47-5337
E3-VB-1010	Right And Ready	Victor 20/47-5544
E3-VB-1011	Taxi, Taxi 6963	–
E3-VB-1012	Decatur Street Boogie	Victor 20/47-5337

Vcl/pnol withClyde William Lynn, saxes; Wesley Jackson, gtr; George Miller, bs; James Jackson, dms.

		Atlanta, November 10, 1953
E3-VB-2616	Sober	unissued
E3-VB-2617	She Knocks Me Out	unissued
E3-VB-2618	Going Away Baby	unissued
E3-VB-2619	Chitlin' Hop	unissued

vcl/pno. with Buddy Lucas, ten; Rene Hall, gtr; Edward Small, bs; Marty Wilson, dms.

		New York, March 17, 1954
E4-VB-3848	Decatur Street Blues	Groove G-0023
E4-VB-3849	Big Rock Joe From Kokomo	

Vcl/pno. with Clyde Lynn, saxes; Wesley Jackson, gtr; George Miller, bs; James Jackson, dms.

		Nashville, February 14, 1955
F5-JB-0244	Pay It No Mind	Groove G-0101, LG 1002
F5-JB-0245	Jump Man Jump	– – ,EGA-3
F5-JB-0246	Do She Love Me	Groove EGA-6
F5-JB-0247	She Knocks Me Out	Groove G-0136

Same:

		Nashville, July, 25, 1955
F5-JB-5356	Peachtree Parade	Victor 20/47-6933
F5-JB-5357	Red's Blues	Groove G-0126
F5-JB-5358	Six O'Clock Boogie	Groove G-0118, EGA-7, LG 1002
F5-JB-5359	Jumpin' With Daddy	Groove G-0136, EGA-8, –
F5-JB-5360	Gordy's Rock	Groove G-0126
F5-JB-5361	Real Good Thing	Groove EGA-6, LG 1002
F5-JB-5362	Goodbye, Goodbye, Goodbye,	Groove G-0118, EGA-8, LG 1002
F5-JB-5363	Please Tell Me Baby	Groove EGA-7, LG 1002

Probably the same:

		Magnolia Ballroom, Atlanta, March 5 1956
G5-JB-2621	I'm Nobody's Fool	Groove G-0145
G5-JB-2622	Wrong Yo-Yo	Groove EGA-6, LG 1002
G5-JB-2623	Umph-Umph-Umph	Groove EGA-7
G5-JB02624	That's My Desire	Groove G-0145
G5-JB-2625	Got You On My Mind	Groove EGA-7, LG 1002
G5-JB-2626	Fattin' Frogs For Snakes	Groove EGA-8, LG 1002
G5-JB-2627	Rockin' With Red	Groove LG 1002
G5-JB-2628	Red's Boogie	unissued
G5-JB-2629	Don't Get Around Much Anymore	Groove EGA-6, LG 1002
G5-JB-2630	It's Time To Boogie	unissued
G5-JB-2631	Hey Good Lookin'	unissued
G5-JB-2632	Teen Age Bounce	unissued

263

Vcl/pno. with Charlie O'Kane, alt/bari; Elliott Lawrence, pno; Mary Osborne, gtr; Russ
Saunders, bs; Osie Johnson, dms.   New York, September 13, 1956
G5-JB-7262 You Were Mine For Awhile   Groove G-0169
G5-JB-7263 Sweetest Little Something   unissued
G5-JB-7264 Since I Fell For You   unissued
G5-JB-7265 Woo-Ee   Groove G-0169

Vcl/pno. with Kenny Burrell, Skeeter Best, Leroy Kirkland, gtrs; Milst Hilton, bs; Gus
Johnson, dms. vcl. choir.   New York, February 5, 1957
H2-WB-1431 Rock Baby   Victor 20/47-6859
H2-WB-1432 Teach Me To Forget   unissued
H2-WB-1433 Wild Fire   Victor 20/47-6856
H2-WB-1434 Please Don't Talk About Me   Victor 20/47-6953

Vcl/pno. with Budd Johnson, ten; Ben Smith, bari; Carl Lynch, Eddie Thomas, gtrs; Doles
Dickens, bs; Gus Johnson, dms.   New York, August 30, 1957
H2-JB-6277 South   Victor 20/47-7065
H2-JB-6278
H2-JB-6279 Co Cha   Victor 20/47-7065
H2-JB-7280 Dixie Roll   unissued
H2-JB-7281 Boston Scored   unissued

Vcl/pno. with Clyde Lynn, Horace Prayer, saxes; Wesley Jackson, George Adams, gtrs; George
Miller, Bs; Bobby Tuggle, Marion Booker, dms.   Nashville, March 2, 1958
J2-WB-0446 One Glimpse Of Heaven   Victor 20/47-7217
J2-WB-0447 Blue Blues   unissued
J2-WB-0448 Work With It   unissued
J2-WB-0449 Eighter From Decatur   unissued
J2-WB-0450 Please Come Back Home   unissued
J2-WB-0451 Comin On   Victor 20/47-7217

Vcl/pno. with gtr; bs-gtr; dms. vcl.grp   1958
NR-112   This Old World   Jax 1000
NR-113   I Feel Good   –

No details
U 9124   Get Up Mare   Checker 911
U 9129   So Worried   –

Note: Later records by this artist as Doctor Feelgood not included.

FATS PICHON

See under Walter Pichon

WALTER PICHON (The Late)

WALTER "FATZ" PICHON
Vcl(-1)/pno.   New Orleans 1945?
A 3361   Fat And Greasy -1   Raynac 1101
A 3362   Deep South Boogie   –

FATS PICHON
Pno. with bs; dms.   New Orleans, 1947
354   Outskirts Of Town   DeLuxe 3072
355
356
357   Cherry   DeLuxe 3072
358   Deep South Boogie   DeLuxe 3069
359   Pinetop's Boogie   –

Note: Later recordings not included

BUSTER PICKENS

Born In Texas in 1915. Died Houston, Texas in October, 1964.
Vcl/pno.   Houston, August 9, 1960
            Barrelhouse Man   unissued
            Back Door Blues   unissued
            Back Door Blues   Heritage HLP 1008

	She Caught The L & N	Heritage HLP 1008
	Ain't Nobody's Bizness If I Do	–
	Colorado Springs	–
	Hattie Green	–
	Santa Fe Blues	–
	Remember Me	–
	Ma Grinder	unissued
	Shorty George	unissued
	D. B. A. Blues	Heritage HLP 1008
	Stagolee	unissued
	Mountain Jack	Heritage HLP 1008
	Santa Fe Train	–
	Rock Island Blues	–
	Four Ten Blues	unissued
	No Name Rag	unissued
Same:		Houston, August, 17, 1960
	Raise Your Window	unissued
	The Cows	unissued
	Back Water Blues	unissued
	Blues In The Bottom	unissued
	Shorty George	unissued
	Hattie Green	unissued
	Stavin' Chain	unissued
	How Long, How Long	unissued
	You Better Stop Your Women	Heritage HLP 1008
	Ma Grinder	–
	The Cows	unissued
Same:		Houston, May 4, 1961
	Jim Nappy	Heritage HLP 1008
	Women In chicago	–

SLIM PICKENS

See under Eddie Burns

DAN PICKETT

Vcl/gtr. with 2nd gtr (-1)		Philadelphia, 1948
DP1	Laughing Rag	Gotham 201
DP2	That's Grieving Me	–
DP3	Baby How Long	Gotham 542, Blues Classics BC-6
DP4	You Got To Do Better	–
DP5	Ride To A Funeral In A V-s	Gotham 510
DP6	Early One Morning	–
DP7	Something's Gone Wrong	Gotham 512
DP8	Chicago Blues	–
DP9	Lemon Man	Gotham 516
DP10	Number Writer -1	–

Note: Second guitarist may be Tampa Red. Alabama Artist.

PIG & WHISTLE BAND

See under Blind Willie McTell.

PIG 'n' WHISTLE RED

See under Blind Willie McTell

PINETOP SLIM (See also in APPENDIX)

Vcl/gtr.		Atlanta 1949
MM 1035	Applejack Boogie	Colonial 106, Blues Classics BC-6
MM 1036	I'm Gonna Carry On	–

POLKA DOT SLIM

Vcl/hca. with 2 gtrs; dms.   Detroit, 1963
165-1199   Ain't Broke, Ain't Hungry   Instant 3269
165-1200   A Thing You Gotta Face   –

     Note : Both sides credited to Sax Kari (see Volume 2)

POOR BOB

Real name Bob Woodfork. Born Lake Village, Arkansas on March 13, 1925.
Vcl/gtr. with Henry Gray, pno; Buddy Guy, Mighty Joe You, gtrs; Clifton James, dms.

                                    Chicago, 1965
        I Won't Be Happy   Decca LK 4748
        The Sun Is Rising   –

POOR BOY

See under St. Louis Jimmy.

POPPA (or POPPY) HOP

See under Hop Wilson

CLARENCE POSEY

Pno. with Henry Smith, gtr.   Detroit, 1952
802B   Rockin' Chair Boogie   Fortune 802
        (rev. by Henry Smith)

TINY POWELL

Real name Vance Powell. Born Warren, Arkansas in late 'twenties.
Vcl. with tpt; saxes; Johnny Heartsman, gtr; el-bs; dms.   Oakland, 1964
101A   My Time After Awhile   Wax 101, 14
101B   Take Me With You -1   – –
        -1 Add vcl. grp.

Same: Oakland, 1965
        I Done Made It Over   Ocampo 101
Vcl. with Eddie Foster's Band   Los Angeles, 1965
        I Done Made It Over   Ocampo 101
        ?   –

     Note: Ocampo 101 issued both takes simultaneously.

MILES PRATCHER

Vcl(-1)/gtr. with Bob Pratcher, vln;   N. Mississippi, 1959
        All Night Long -1   Atlantic LP 1348
        Buttermilk   Prestige Int. 25005
        I'm Gonna Live Anyhow 'Till I Die -1   Prestige Int. 25010

PRETTY BOY

Vcl. with Johnny Fuller's Band   Oakland, 1954
        I'm Bad   Rhythm 1768
        Find My Baby   –

PREZ KENNETH

Vcl. with saxes; hca; bs-gtr; dms.   Chicago, 1965/66
        I Am The Man Downstairs   Biscayne 005
        I'm Looking For My Baby   –
3987 01A   Devil Dealing Part 1   Biscayne 009
3987 01B   Devil Dealing Part 2   –

You Left Me To Cry   Biscayne 015
            ?   —

        Note: Real name is Kenneth Kidd.

PRINCE ROBINSON

Vcl/pno. with gtr; bs; dms.   Chicago,
            Thunderbird   unissued
            My Baby's Got Another Man   unissued
            What You Got On Your Mind   unissued
            Mary Lou   unissued

        Note: Recorded by Jump Jackson.

AL PRINCE & HIS ORCH'

No details.   Los. Angeles, 1952
            Don't Love A Married Woman   Swing Time 318
            Wine   —

        Note: See Also Little Willie Cotton.

WES PRINCE & HIS RHYTHM PRINCES (The Late)

V. Mears, pno; Harold Grant; vcl/gtr; Wesley Prince, bs; F, Parker, dms.

                                                      Los. Angeles, 1946
            Doghouse Blues   Excelsior 167
            I Ain't Gonna Move   —
            Pop Fly Blues   Excelsior 170
            Sizzling Papa Blues   /   —

"PRISON WORKSONGS"

Big Louisiana (Rodney Mason), Reverend Rogers, Roosevelt Charles, vcls.
                                                      Angola, La. 1959
            Berta   Folk Lyric FL-
Guitar Welch, Hogman Maxey, Andy Mosley, vcls.
            Take This Hammer
            Alberta Let Your Bang Hang Low
Big Louisiana, Reverend Rogers, Jose Smith, vcls.
            Stewball
Odea Matthews, vcl.
            Five Long Years For One Man
            Somethin' Within Me
James Russell & Gang, vcl.
            I Had Five Long Years
Johnny Butler & Gang, vcls.
            Early In The Mornin'
Big Louisiana, Rossevelt Charles, Arthur Davis, vcls.
            All Teamed Up In Angola's Mule Lot
Willy Rafus & Gang, vcls.
            I Got A Hurtin' In My Right Side
Big Louisiana, Arthur Davis, Willy Rafus, vcls.
            Let Your Hammer Ring
Andy Mosley, Johnny Butler, Willy Rafus, vcls.
            Cleanin' This Highway
Guitar Welch, Hogman Maxey, Robert Pete Williams, vcls.
            John Henry
Murray Macon, vcl.
            Jesus Cares

PROFESSOR LONGHAIR

See under Roy Byrd.

267

SNOOKY PRYOR

Real name James Pryor
SNOOKY & MOODY
Vcl/hca. with Moody Jones, gtr.   Chicago, 1948
PL 101   Boogie   Planet 101, Old Swingmaster 18
PL 102   Telephone Blues   Planet 102,   –

Note: PL 102 also issued as "Calling Up My Baby Blues".

SNOOKY PRYOR
Vcl/hca. with Leroy Foster, gtr; bs;   Chicago, 1950
JB 101A   Boogy Fool   JOB 101
JB 101B   Raisin' Sand   –

Vcl/hca. with Sunnyland Slim, pno; Eddie Taylor, gtr; Moody Jones, bs;
                                                                      Chicago, 1052
JB 48881   I'm Getting Tired (no pno)   JOB 115
JB 48882   Going Back On The Road   –

Same: Chicago, 1953
P53-206   Crosstown Blues   Parrot 807
P53-207   I Want You For Myself   –
JOB 3006   Cryin' Shame   JOB 1014
JOB 3011   Eighty Nine Ten

Vcl/hca. with Lee Cooper, gtr; Earl Phillips, dms.   Chicago, July 17, 1956
56-500   Someone To Love Me   Vee Jay 215
56-501
56-502   Judgement Day   Vee Jay 215

Note: Johnny Young claims to play guitar on above session.

Vcl/hca. with Big Bill ?, hca; gtr; dms.   Chicago, 1963
2001   Uncle Sam Don't Take My Man   JOB 1126
2002   Boogie Twist   –

See also Floyd Jones and Johnny Young

JOE PULLUM with trio.

Born Texas?; Died Los Angeles, c. 1965
Vcl. with pno; gtr; dms.   Los Angeles, 1948
267A+   My Woman Pt. 1   Swing Time 267
267A   My Woman Pt. 2   –

DOUG QUATTLEBAUM

Born Florence, South Carolina in 1927
Vcl/gtr.   Philadelphia, 1953
DQ1   Don't Be Funny Baby   Gotham 519
DQ2   Lizzie Lou   –
Same: Philadelphia, July 6, 1961
            Walking Blues   unissued
            Good Woman Blues   Storyville SLP 181
            Baby Please Don't Go   unissued
            Let's Talk It Over   unissued
            What You Want Me To Do   unissued
            If You Ever Been Mistreated   unissued
            Lizzie Lou   unissued
            Drifting Blues   unissued
            Tell Me What'd I Say   unissued
            Make Me Feel Good, Kiddie-o   unissued
            Adam And Eve   unissued
            Nobody's Fault But Mine   unissued
Same: Philadelphia, November 27, 1961
            Sweet Little Woman   Bluesville BVLP 1065
            Whiskey Headed Woman   –
            Trouble In Mind   –
            You Is One Black Rat   –

268

On My Way To School	Bluesville BVLP 1065
You Ain't No Good	–
Come Back Blues	–
Mama Don't Allow Me To Stay Out All Night	–
Big Leg Woman	–
Black Night Is Falling	–
Baby, Take A Chance With Me	–
So Sweet	–
Worried Life Blues	–

R

YANK RACHELL

Real name James Rachell. Born near Brownsville, Tennessee on March 16, 1908
Vcl/mdln. with Hammie Nixon, hca/jug; Sleepy John Estes, gtr; Big Joe Williams, gtr(-1):
Mike Bloomfield, gtr(-1)

	Chicago, 1964
Move Your Hand (Williams solo)	Delmark DL-606
Texas Tommy	–
Up And Down The Line -1	–
Shout Baby Shout	–
Bye Bye Baby	–
Stop Knockin' On My Door --1	–
Doorbell Blues -1	–
Lonesome Blues	–
I'm Gonna Get Up In the Morning	–
Get Your Morning Exercise	–

Note: See Aslo Sleepy John Estes.

PHILLIP RAMSEY

Vcl/gtr. with Horace Sprott, hca

| | Nr. Dobine Creek, Ala, Apr. 17, 1954 |
| I Feel Good Now Baby | Folkways FP 654 |

MRS. PHILLIP RAMSEY

Vcl/gtr.

| | Nr. Dobine Creek, Ala, Apr. 17 1954 |
| Me And My Short Box | Folkways FP 654 |

HENRY RATCLIFF

Vcl.

| | Parchman Farm Miss, 1959 |
| Louisiana | Prestige LP 25010 |

HERMAN "PETTIE WHEATSTRAW" RAY

Vcl. with ten; pno; gtr; bs; dms.

		New York City, May 20, 1949
74935	Working Man	Decca 48107
74936	Trouble Blues	Decca 48105
74937	President's Blues	Decca 48107
74938	I'm A Little Pice Of Leather	Decca 48105

OTIS READ

Vcl with ten(-1); hca (-2); gtrs; dms.
Los Angeles, 1961

NR–1118	Love Is A Serious Thing -2	Nanc 1118/9
NR-1119	Come On Baby -1	–

A. C. REED

Vcl. with pno; Earl Hooker, gtr; bs-gtr; dms.
Chicago, 1961/62

25-201	This Little Voice	Age 29101
	(rev. by Earl Hooker)	

No details
26-606	Come On Home	Age 29103
26-207	I Wanna Be Free	–

Vcl. with pno; Reggie Boyd, gtr; poss. Earl Hooker, gtr; dms; vcl. grp(-1).
26-123	Mean Cop -1	Age 29112
26-124	That Ain't Right	–

Vcl. with saxes; org; pno; gtr; bs; dms.
27-338	I Stay Mad	Age 29123
27-339	Lotta Lovin'	–

Note: Above probably Earl Hooker's band.

BOB REED & HIS BAND

No details: -vcl by "Ivory Lucky".
A-1021	I'm Leaving You	Melatone 1003, Dena ?
A-1022	I'm Going To Change My Way Of Living	–

JAMES REED & HIS BAND (The Late)

Vcl. with saxes; pno; gtr; bs; dms.
Oakland, 1954

	Roughest Place In Town	Rhythm 1775
	?	
A	Oh People	Money 201
AA	My Love Is Real	–
FL 176	This Is The End	Flair 1034
FL 177	My Mama Tole Me	–
FL 187	Dr. Brown	Flair 1042
FL 188	Better Hold Me	–
6409	Things Ain't What They Used To Be	Big Town 117, ET 1002
6639	You Better Hold Me	– –

Note: Above may not be the correct order of issue. Tenor solos on the above may be by
Que Martyn. The Only copy of Rhythm 1775 known is a one sided test.

JIMMY REED

Born Leland, Mississippi in 1926
Vcl/hca/gtr. with Eddie Taylor, bs-gtr; Morris Wilkerson, dms.

Chicago, December 29, 1953
53-104	High And Lonesome	Chance 1142, Vee Jay 100, LP 8501
53-105	Jimmy's Boogie	Vee Jay 105
53-106	Found My Baby	–
53-107	Roll And Rhumba	Chance 1142, Vee Jay 100, LP 1004, 1080, Oldies oL 8005

Vcl/hca/gtr. with Eddie Taylor, gtr; Morris Wilkerson, dms. Chicago, December 30, 1953
53-120	You Don.t Have To Go	Vee Jay 119, LP 1004, 1020, 1035, 1039
53-121	Boogie In The Dark	Vee Jay 119, LP 1004, 1035, 1039, 1073
53-122	Shot My Baby	unissued
53-123	Rockin' With Reed	Vee Jay 186, LP 1008

Vcl/hca/gtr. with Eddie Taylor, gtr; Ray Scott, dms. Chicagom January 18, 1955
55-229	You Upset My Mind	unissued

55-230	I'm Gonna Ruin You	unissued
55-231	Pretty Thing	unissued

Vcl/hca/gtr. with Eddie Taylor, gtr; Dave Ship, bs; Ray Scott, dms.
Chicago, March 24, 1955

55-248	I'm Gonna Ruin You	Vee Jay 132
55-249	Pretty Thing	–
55-250	instrumental	unissued
55-251	Come On Baby	unissued

Vcl/hca/gtr. with W. C. Dalton, gtr; Henry Gray, pno; Milton Rector, bs–gtr; Earl Phillips, dms.
Chicago, July 18, 1955

55-293	I Ain't Got You	Vee Jay LP 1022
55-294	She Don't Want Me No More	Vee Jay 153
55-295	Come On Baby	unissued
55-296	I Don't Go For That	Vee Jay 153

Vcl/hca/gtr. with Eddie Taylor, gtr; Vernell Fournier, dms.   Chicago, November 9, 1955

55-359	Lovin' You Baby	unissued
55-360	untitled	unissued

Same: Chicago, December 5, 1955

55-382	Baby, Don't Say That No More	Vee Jay 168, Oldies 114
55-383	Ain't That Lovin' You Baby	– , LP 1004, 1020, 1035, 1039, Oldies 114
55-384	Can't Stand To See You Cry	Vee Jay 186, LP 1004

Same: Chicago, June 11, 1956

56-483	When You Left Me	unissued
56-484	My First Plea	Vee Jay 203, LP 1004, 1080, Oldies OL 8005
56-485	You So Sweet	unissued
56-486	I Love You Baby	Vee Jay 203

Vcl/hca/gtr. with Eddie Taylor, gtr; Earl Phillips, dms.   Chicago, October 3, 1956

56-551	You Got Me Dizzy	Vee Jay 226, LP 1004, 1035, 1039
56-552	Honey Don't Let Me Go	–
56-553	instrumental	unissued
56-554	untitled	unissued

Same: Chicago, January 9, 1957

57-590	It's You Baby	unissued
57-591	Honey Where You Going	Vee Jay 237
57-592	Do The Thing	unissued
57-593	Little Rain	Vee Jay 237, LP 1004

Vcl/hca/gtr. with Eddie Taylor, gtr; Remo Biondi, gtr (–1); 'Levinsky', vln (–2); Earl
Phillips, dms.   Chicago, April 3, 1957

57-660	Signals Of Love	Vee Jay 253, Oldies OL 33
57-661	The Sun Is Shining	Vee Jay 248, LP 1035, 1039
57-662	Baby, What's On Your Mind	– , LP 1008
57-663	Honest I Do -1	Vee Jay 253, LP 1004, 1035, 1039, 1074, Oldies OL 33
57-664	instrumental	unissued
57-665	untitled	unissued
57-666	instrumental	unissued
57-667	Odds And Ends -2	Vee Jay 298, LP 1080

Same: Chicago, September 5, 1957

57-736	The Moon Is Rising	unissued
57-737	My Bitter Seed	Vee Jay LP 1008
57-738	Ends And Odds	Vee Jay 304, LP 1008
57-739	instrumental	unissued

Vcl/hca/gtr. with Eddie Taylor, gtr; Earl Phillips, dms.   Chicago, November 7, 1957

57-792	The Moon Is Rising	unissued
57-793	Down In Virginia	unissued
57-794	I'm Gonna Get My Baby	unissued

Vcl/hca/gtr. with Remo Biondi, gtr; Eddie Taylor, bs–gtr; Earl Phillips, dms.

		Chicago, December 12, 1957
57-809	The Moon Is Rising	unissued
57-810	You're Something Else	Vee Jay 270, LP 1004
57-811	A String To Your Heart (no hca.)	– , LP 1008
57-812	Down In Virginia	unissued

Same:

		Chicago, March 12, 1958
58-861	Go On To School	Vee Jay 275, LP 1004
58-862	You Got Me Crying	–
58-863	The Moon Is Rising	Vee Jay LP 1008
58-864	Down In Virginia	Vee Jay 287, LP 1008

Same:

		Chicago, May 28, 1958
58-920	I'm Gonna Get Me Baby	Vee Jay 298
58-921	I Wanna Be Loved	Vee Jay 326, LP 1008, Abner 1029
58-922	Caress Me Baby	Vee Jay 333, LP 1008, Oldies OL 19
58-923	I Know It's A Sin	Vee Jay 287, LP 1008

Same:

		Chicago, September 11, 1958
58-993	You In That Jack	unissued
58-994	Going To New York	Vee Jay 326, LP 1008, 1035, 1039
58-995	I Told You Baby	Vee Jay 304

Vcl/hca/gtr. with Lefty Bates, gtr; Eddie Taylor, bs–gtr; Earl Phillips, dms.

		Chicago, March 26, 1959
59-1101	Take Out Some Insurance (no hca.)	Vee Jay 314, LP 1008, 1035, 1039, 1073, Oldies 115
59-1102	You're Mine, Little Girl	unissued
59-1103	I'm Nervous	Vee Jay LP 1022
59-1104	You Know I Love You	Vee Jay 314, Oldies 115

Vcl/hca/gtr; with Lefty Bates, Eddie Taylor, gtrs; Marcus Johnson, bs–gtr; Earl Phillips, dms.

		Chicago, August 7, 1959
59-1211	Baby What You Want Me To Do	Vee Jay 333, LP 1021, 1022, 1035, 1039, 1074, 1073, 1080, Oldies OL 19, LP 1100
59-1212	Goin' By The River Pt. 1	Vee Jay LP 1022
59-1213	Goin' By The River Pt. 2	Vee Jay 357, LP 1022

Vcl/hca/gtr. with Philip Upchurch, gtr; Eddie Taylor, bs–gtr; Earl Phillips, dms.

		Chicago, August 25, 1959
59-1248	Where Can You Be	Vee Jay 347, LP 1022
59-1249	Hush Hush	Vee Jay 357, – , 1035, 1039
59-1250	I Was Wrong	Vee Jay LP 1021, 1022
59-1251	Blue Blue Water	Vee Jay LP 1035

Vcl/hca/gtr. with Lefty Bates, Eddie Taylor, gtrs; Earl Phillips, dms.

		Chicago, December 15, 1959
59-1318	Please Don't	unissued
59-1319	Found Love	Vee Jay 347, LP 1022, 1035, 1039
59-1320	You Gonna Need My Help	unissued

Vcl/hca/gtr. with Lefty Bates, Lee Baker, gtrs; **Curtis Mayfield**, bs–gtr; Earl Phillips, dms; Mama Reed, vcl (–1).

		Chicago, March 14, 1960
60-1403	Hold Me Close -1	Vee Jay LP 1035
60-1404 ?	You Don't Have To Go	unissued
60-1405 ?	Ain't That Lovin' You Baby	unissued

Vcl/hca/gtr. with Lefty Bates, gtr; poss. Curtis Mayfield, bs–gtr; Earl Phillips, dms.

		Chicago, 1960
	What's Wrong Baby	Vee Jay LP 1035
	Found Joy	–
	Kind Of Lonesome	–
	Blue Carnegie	– , 1073

Vcl/hca/gtr. with Lefty Bates, Lee Baker, gtrs; Willie Dixon, bs; Earl Phillips, dms;
Mama Reed, vcl (−1).   Chicago, March 29, 1960
60-1417   Come Love -1   Vee Jay LP 1022
60-1418   Big Boss Man -1   Vee Jay 380, LP 1022, 1035,
                                          1039, 1074, 1080, 1100,
                                          Oldies OL 75
60-1419   Meet Me   Vee Jay LP 1022

Vcl/hca/gtr. with Lefty Bates, Philip Upchurch, gtrs; Earl Phillips, dms.
                                          Chicago, June 29, 1960
60-1544   I Got The Blues   Vee Jay LP 1025
60-1545   Sugar Sugar   unissued
60-1546   Got Me Chasing You   Vee Jay LP 1025
60-1547   Down The Road   −
60-1548   Want To Be With You Baby   −
60-1549   Jimmy's Rock   −
60-1550   Laughin' At The Blues   Vee Jay 373, LP 1025
60-1551   You're My Baby   Vee Jay LP 1025
60-1552   That's It   unissued
60-1553   Ain't Gonna Cry No More   Vee Jay LP 1025
                You Know You're Looking Good   −

Vcl/hca/gtr. with Lefty Bates, gtr; unk. bs−gtr; Eddie Taylor, bs (−1); Earl Phillips, dms;
Mama Reed, vcl (−2); fem. chorus, (−3).   Chicago, December 13, 1960
60-1709   Close Together -1, 2, 3   Vee Jay 373, LP 1025, 1073
60-1710   Tell The World I Do   Vee Jay LP 1025
60-1711
60-1712   I'm A Love You (I'm In Love With You) -1, 3   Vee Jay 380, LP 1035, Oldies
                                          OL 75

Vcl/hca/gtr. with Lefty Bates, gtr; bs−gtr; Earl Phillips, dms; Mama Reed, vcl (−1).
                                          Chicago, 1961
61-2069   Tell Me You Love Me   Vee Jay 449, LP 1035
61-2070   Bright Lights, Big City -1   Vee Jay 398, LP 1035, 1073,
                                          Oldies OL 63
61-2071
61-2072   What's Wrong Baby -1   Vee Jay 425, LP 1035, 1080
61-2073   I'm Mr. Luck   Vee Jay 398, LP 1035, Oldies
                                          OL 63
61-2074   Aw Shucks Hush Your Mouth   Vee Jay 425, LP 1035, 1073

Vcl/hca/gtr. with Lefty Bates, gtr; Jimmy Reed Jnr., bs−gtr; Phil Upchurch, bs; Al Duncan,
dms.   Chicago, 1962
62-2465   Good Lover   Vee Jay 449, LP 1050
62-2466   Down In Mississippi   Vee Jay 616, LP 1080

Vcl/hca/gtr. with gtr; bs−gtr; dms. (prob. as last).   Chicago, 1962
62-2513   Too Much   Vee Jay 459, LP 1050, 1080

Vcl/hca/gtr. with gtr; bs−gtr; dms. Add tpts; ten; org. (−1).   Chicago, 1962
62-2561   I'll Change My Style   Vee Jay 459, LP 1050
                Let's Get Together   Vee Jay 473,   −
                Take It Slow   Vee Jay LP 1050
                In The Morning   −
                Back Home At Noon   −
                Kansas City Baby   −
                You Can't Hide   −
62-2568   Oh John   Vee Jay 473, LP 1050, 1080

Vcl/hca/gtr. with acc. prob. same as last.   Chicago, prob. 1963
                St. Louis Blues   Vee Jay 570, LP 1072, 1073,
                                          1080
                Trouble In Mind   Vee Jay LP 1072
                Wee Wee Baby   Vee Jay 584, LP 1072
                How Long, How Long Blues   Vee Jay LP 1072
                See See Rider   Vee Jay 584, LP 1072
                Roll 'Em Pete   Vee Jay LP 1072
                (I'm Gonna Move To) The Outskirts Of Town   Vee Jay 570, LP 1072, 1080
                The Comeback   Vee Jay LP 1072

	Cherry Red	Vee Jay LP 1072
	Worried Life Blues	–
	Five Long Years	–

Vcl/hca/gtr. with gtr; bs–gtr; dms.   Chicago, 1963

63-3067	Shame Shame Shame	Vee Jay 509, LP 1067, 1080
63-3068		
63-3069	There'll Be A Day	Vee Jay 509, LP 1067
	Mary, Mary	Vee Jay 552, LP 1067, 1080
	Ain't No Big Deal	Vee Jay LP 1067
	Baby's So Sweet	–
	Mixed Up	–
	Up Tight	–
	Cold And Lonesome	–
	I'm Gonna Help You	Vee Jay 552, LP 1067
	Upside The Wall	Vee Jay LP 1067
	I'm Trying To Please You	–

12-string gtr. with gtr; bs–gtr; dms.

| | New Chicago Blues | Vee Jay LP 1073 |
| | Blues For Twelve Strings | – |

Note: All other tracks on LP 1073 are dubs of the original recordings, with Reed's voice deleted and a 12-string gtr. overdubbed.

Vcl/hca/gtr. with gtr; bs–gtr; dms.   Chicago, 1964

64-3933	Help Yourself	Vee Jay 593, LP 1095
64-3934	Heading For A Fall	–
	Going Fishing	Vee Jay LP 1095
	Wear Something Green	–
	Fifteen Years	–
	Things Ain't What They Used To Be	–

Vcl/hca/gtr. with Johnny Jones, pno; Hubert Sumlin, gtr; Eddie Taylor, bs–gtr; unk. dms.
Chicago, July/August, 1964

64-4437	Left Handed Woman	Vee Jay 702, LP 1095
64-4438	I Wanna Be Loved	Vee Jay 642, LP 1095
64-4439		
64-4440	A New Leaf	Vee Jay 642, LP 1095
64-4441		
64-4442		
64-4443	I'm Going Upside Your Head	Vee Jay 622, LP 1095
64-4444	The Devil's Shoestring Pt. 2	– –

Vcl/hca/gtr. with gtr; bs–gtr; dms.

| | When You're Doing Alright | Vee Jay LP 1095 |
| | You've Got Me Waiting | – |

Note: All tracks on LP 1095 have a 'live' audience dubbed on.

Vcl/hca/gtr. with gtr; Jimmy Reed Jnr., bs–gtr; dms.   Chicago, 1965

65-8666	I'm The Man Down There	Vee Jay 702
65-8667	When Girls Do It	Vee Jay 709
65-8668	Don't Think I'm Through	–

Vcl/hca/gtr. with   Chicago, 1966

EX 1009	Knocking At Your Door	Exodus 2005
EX 1010	Dedication To Sonny	–
EX 1011	Cousin Peaches	Exodus 2008
EX 1012	Crazy About Oklahoma	–

Vcl/hca/gtr. with Lefty Bates, Jimmy Reed Jnr., gtrs; Jimmy Gresham, bs; Al Duncan, dms.
Chicago, November 4 & 8, 1966

13699	I Got Nowhere To Go	ABC-Paramount 10887, Bluesway BL 6004
13705	Two Ways To Skin A Cat	– –
	Big Boss Man	Bluesway BL 6004
	I Wanna Know	–
	Heartaches And Trouble	–
	Tell Me What You Want Me To Do	–
	Honey I'll Make Two	–
	You Don't Have To Go	–

	Don't Play Me Cheap	Bluesway BL 6004
	Two Sides To Every Story	–
	I'm Just Trying To Cop A Plea	–
	Two Heads Are Better Than One	–

DOC REESE

Vcl.

| | Ol' Hannah | Folkways FJ 2801, FP 53 |

Vcl. with unk. group, vcl (–1).
Newport, R.I. July 23/6, 1964

	Old Hannah	Vanguard VRS-9180
	Hey Rattler -1	–
	Oh My Lord -1	–

SLIM REESE

Vcl. with Henry Hayes, alt; Ed Wiley, ten; Willie Johnson, pno; Goree Carter, gtr;
Donald Cooks, bs; Ben Turner, dms.
Houston, 1951

| | Got The World In A Jug | SIW 581 |
| | I'm So Worried | – |

Note: See also under Willie Johnson.

MOOCHIE REEVES

Vcl/gtr/kazeo. with Ollie Crenshaw, vcl/gtr; Tyler Johnson, vcl/imit. bs.
Mobile, Ala., July 18, 1954

	Raise A Ruckus	Folkways FA 2610
	Rock Me Baby	–
	My Bonnie Lies Over The Ocean	–
	Trouble, It's Followed Me All My Days	–
	Key To The Highway	RBF 202

BIG JACK REYNOLDS & HIS BLUES MEN

Vcl/hca. with org; gtr; bs; dms.
Detroit, 1964

SK4M-7354, H-91
| | I Had A Little Dog | Hi-Q 5036 |
SK4M-7355, H-92
| | You Won't Treat Me Right | – |

TEDDY REYNOLDS

Vcl/pno. with Ed Wiley, ten; Henry Hayes, alt; Donald Cooks, bs; Ben Turner, dms.
Houston, 1950/51

2093	Walkin' The Floor Baby	SIW 571
2099	Why Baby Why	SIW 558
2101	Summer Is On Its Way	–
2220	Waitin' At The Station	SIW 613
2226	Right Will Always Win	SIW 571
2227	Strange Mysterious Woman	SIW 594
2257	Too Late To Change	SIW 594
	You Put A Voodoo Spell On Me	SIW 586
	My Heart's Full Of Misery	–
2369	Suicide Blues	SIW 613

Note: See also Ed Wiley.

EUGENE RHODES

Vcl/gtr.
Indiana State Pen., 29-31 March, 1962, 20-25 March, 1962 or 1-3 July, 1962

	If You See My Saviour	Folk Legacy FSA-12
	Blues Leaping From Texas	–
	Don't Talk Me To Death	–
	Talkin' About My Time	–

275

	Working On The Levee	Folk Legacy FSA-12
	Step It Up And Go	–
	Talk	–
	I Keep Wondering	–
	Jelly, Jelly	–
	Dough Rolling Papa	–
	Who Went Out The Back	–
	See That My Grave Is Kept Clean	–
	I'm Gonna Find Me A Woman	–
	If She's Your Woman	–
	Fast Life	–
	Whosoever Will, Let Him Come	–

RHYTHM WILLIE

Hca. with saxes; pno; bs; dms.   Chicago, 1950

UB50-1062, EO-OB-12973-1		
	Wailin' Willie	Premium 866
UB50-1063, EO-OB-12974-1		
	I Got Rhythm	–

RICHARD BROTHERS

See under Robert Richard.

ROBERT RICHARD

Vcl/hca. with Walter Mitchell, hca; Boogie Woogie Red, pno; Howard Richard, gtr; bs.
                                                                Detroit, 1948

K 5604	Wigwam Woman	King 4274
K 5608	Root Hog	– , LP 875
DE-4	Cadillac Woman	JVB 75828
	(rev. by Joseph Von Battle)	

RICHARD BROTHERS

Robert Richard, vcl/gtr. with Howard Richard, vcl/gtr.   Detroit, 1956

ST-1	Stolen Property	Strate-8 1500
ST-2	Drunk Driver's Coming	–

J. RIGGINS JR.

See under Floyd Dixon.

HUBERT ROBERSON

See under Hubert Robinson.

ROBERT JR.

See under Robert Lockwood Jr.

GIP ROBERTS

Vcl. with alt; pno; bs; dms.   Detroit, 1958

A	No One Monkey Goin' To Run My Show	J.V.B. 29
B	Sandman	–

WALTER ROBERTSON

Vcl/hca. with pno; Johnny Fuller, gtr; dms.   Oakland, 1954

FL 208	Sputterin' Blues (no hca.)	Flair 1053
FL 209	I've Done Everything I Can	–
	Note: Real name Walter Robinson. See also Robinson Brothers.	

ROBINSON BROTHERS

See under L. C. Robinson.

276

FENTION ROBINSON

Born Greenwood, Mississippi on September 23, 1935.

FENTION ROBINSON & HIS DUKES
Vcl/gtr. with pno; bs; dms. Add. saxes (−1).   Memphis, 1957
MR 5068   Tennessee Woman -1   Meteor 5041
MR 5069   Crying Out Loud   −

FENTION & THE CASTLE ROCKERS -1
DAVID DEAN'S COMBO -2
Vcl/gtr. with pno; Larry Davis, bs−gtr; dms; David Dean, ten; (−2).
                                                                Houston, 1958
FR 3071   The Feeze -1   Duke 190
FR 3072   The Double Freeze -2   −

FENTION ROBINSON & THE CASTLE ROCKERS
As above:
FR 3073-4 Mississippi Steamboat   Duke 191
FR 3074-4 Crazy Crazy Lovin'   −

FENTION ROBINSON
Vcl/gtr. with Booker T, pno. and unk. studio grp.   Houston, 1959
FR 7016   As The Years Go By   Duke 312
FR 7017   School Boy   −
FR 7050   Tennessee Woman   Duke 329
FR 7051   You've Got To Pass This Way Again   −

FENTON ROBINSON
Vcl/gtr. with saxes; pno; bs−gtr; dms.   Chicago, 1966
M-5899-03A-106
           Say You're Leavin'   USA 842
M-5899-03B-112
           From My Heart   −

HUBERT ROBINSON

HUBERT ROBERSON & ORCH.
Vcl. with saxes; pno; gtr; bs; dms.   Houston, 1949
no mx   H. R. Jumps   Eddie's 1211
no mx   Lonely Traveller   −

HUBERT ROBINSON
Vcl. with saxes; Elmore Nixon, pno; gtr; bs; dms.   Houston, 1950
ACA 1471   H. R. Boogie   unissued
ACA 1472   Central Station Blues   unissued
ACA 1473   Where Were You Pretty Baby   Macy's 5005
ACA 1474   Boogie The Joint   −
ACA 1475   Bad Luck And Trouble   Macy's 5010

Vcl. with tbn (−1); saxes; pno; gtr; bs; Elmore Nixon, dms.
ACA 1575   I Don't Love No Other Woman   unissued
ACA 1576   Answer To Wintertime Blues -1   Macy's 5007
ACA 1577   Old Woman Boogie   −
ACA 1578   I Love You Baby -1   Macy's 5015
ACA 1579   Room And Board Boogie   Macy's 5010
ACA 1580   High Class Woman -1   Macy's 5015

HUBERT ROBINSON & HIS YARDBIRDS
Vcl. with tpt; Henry Hayes, alt; Ed Wiley, ten; Willie Johnson, pno; Donald Cooks, bs;
Ben Turner, dms.   Houston, 1951
3003   Hard Lovin' Daddy   Jade 206
3004   Gas Happy Blues   −
           See also Curtis Amy, Willie Johnson and Milton Willis.

JAMES ROBINSON

Hca/gtr.
                                                                Camden, N.J., 1965
           Standing In My Back Door Crying   Storyville SLP 181

JAMES ROBINSON

Vcl/pno. St. Louis, 1957

      Bat's Blues Tone LP 1, Folk Lyric LP 117
      Four O'Clock   –   –
    Note: Known as Bat The Humming Bird.

JIMMY LEE ROBINSON

Born Chicago, Illinois on April 30, 1931.

LONESOME LEE
Vcl/gtr. with Luther Tucker, gtr; Bobby Perry, acc. gtr; unk. bs; Odie Payne, dms.
                                              Chicago, 1959
      Lonely Travellin' Bandera 2501
      Cry Over Me –

JIMMY LEE
Vcl/gtr. with Chuck Smith, ten (–1); Tall Paul Hankins, pno (–2); Clear Waters, bs;
Buddy Rogers, dms. Chicago, 1960
B-4552   All Of My Life -2 Bandera 2506
B-4553   Chicago Jump -1 –

JIMMY LEE ROBINSON
Vcl/gtr. with ten; gtr; bs; Odie Payne, dms; vcl. grp. Chicago, 1962
      Twist It Baby Bandera 2510
      Times Is Hard –

Vcl/gtr. with Fred Below, dms. Hamburg, October 7, 1965
      Rosa Lee Fontana 681.529 TL

L. C. ROBINSON

Born Sommerville, Texas ?

ROBINSON BROTHERS
Vcl/gtr. with Walter Robinson, hca; R. L. Daniels, pno. Los Angeles, 1945
319   I Got To Go Black & White 107
320   Hurry Hurry Baby Black & White 108
321   Come Back To Me Baby Black & White 107
322   L. C. Boogie Black & White 108

L. C. ROBINSON
The following is actually Swing Time 196 by Lowell Fulson.
101A   Rock With L. C. Elko 254
101B   Lonely Heart Blues –

Vcl/gtr. with Walter Robinson, hca; pno; bs; dms. Oakland, 1954
A   If I Lose You Baby Rhythm 1772
B   Why Don't You Write To Me –

ROCKIN' SYDNEY

Real name Sidney Semien. Born Lebeau, La., on April 9, 1938.
Vcl/gtr. with George Lewis, hca; Francis Semien, bs–gtr; Sherman Thomas, gtr; Roger
Semien, dms. Lake Charles, La., 1959
      She's My Morning Coffee Fame ?
      Calling You –
      Walked Out On You Fame ?
      Rock You –

ROCKIN' SYDNEY & HIS ALL STARS
Vcl/gtr. with saxes; pno; Francis Semien, bs–gtr; Roger Semien, dms.
                                              Ville Platte, La., 1959
J 7332   Don't Say Goodbye Jin 110
J 7333   My Little Girl –

Vcl/gtr. with George Lewis, hca; Sherman Thomas, gtr; Francis Semien, bs–gtr; Roger
Semien, dms. Ville Platte, La., 1963/64
J 7420   No Good Woman Jin 156, LP 4002, Sutton LP ?
J 7421   You Ain't Nothing But Fine –

J 7317	Send Me Some Lovin'	Jin 164
J 7318	Past Bedtime	–
J 7325	No Good Man	Jin 168
J 7326	If I Could, I Would	–

Vcl/gtr. with George Lewis, hca; Katie Webster, pno; Sherman Webster, bs-gtr; Roger Semion, dms.

| J 7329 | Let Me Cross Over | Jin 170 |
| J 7330 | You Don't Have To Go | – |

Vcl/gtr. with George Lewis, hca; Sherman Thomas, gtr; Francis Semien, bs-gtr; Roger Semion, dms.

J 7335	It Really Is A Hurtin' Thing	Jin 174
J 7336	Something's Wrong	–
J 7341	Wasted Days, Wasted Nights	Jin 177
J 7342	Ya Ya	–

COUNT ROCKIN' SIDNEY & HIS DUKES

Vcl/hca. with Katie Webster, pno; B Singleton, gtr; Rickey Kelly, bs-gtr; Charles Page, bs;
Little Brother Griffin, dms.   Lake Charles, June 1965

| SO:2653 | Actions Speak Louder Than Words | Goldband 1158 |
| SO:2654 | Lais Per La Patate | – |

Vcl/hca. with Danny Sonnier, gtr; Rickey Kelly, bs-gtr; Charles Page, dms.

| SO:2765 | Something Working Baby | Goldband 1159 |
| SO:2766 | My Poor Heart | – |

COUNT ROCKIN' SYDNEY

Vcl. with Katie Webster, org(-1)/pno. (-2) Rickey Kelly, gtr; Sherman Webster, bs;
Casa Blanca Club, New Iberia, 1966

| SO: 3004 | Dedie Dedie Da -1 | Goldband 1162 |
| SO:3005 | Life Without Love -2 | – |

Vcl/hca. with vcl. chorus & rhythm

| SO:3575 | Shed So Many Tears | Goldband 1170 |
| SO:3576 | Gonna Be Looking | – |

JIMMY ROGERS (see also In APPENDIX)

Real name   Born Atlanta, Georgia on June 3, 1924

JIMMY ROGERS & HIS TRIO

Vcl/gtr. with Little Walter, hca; Muddy Waters, gtr(-1); Big Crawford, bs.
Chicago, 1950

U7269	That's All Right	Chess 1435, LP 1446
U 7270	Ludella	–
U 7277	Going Away Baby -1	Chess 1442
U 7278	Today, Today Baby -1	–

JIMMY ROGERS & HIS ROCKING FOUR

Vcl/gtr. with ten; Eddie Ware, pno; bs; dms.   Chicago, 1951

U 7308	I Used To Have A Woman	Chess 1506
U 7309	The World Is In A Tangle	Chess 1453, LP 1446, Argo LP 4034
U 7310	She Loves Another Man	

Vcl/gtr. with Little Walter,hca(-1) Eddie Ware, pno(-2); Big Crawford, bs; dms.

U 7361	Money, Marbles And Chalk -2	Chess 1476
U 7362		
U 7363	Chance To Love -1	Chess 1476

Vcl/gtr. with ten; Eddie Ware, pno; bs; dms.   Chicago, 1952

| U 7424 | Back Door Friend | Chess 1506 |

Vcl/gtr. with Henry Gray, pno; poss. Muddy Waters, gtr(-1); bs; dms.

U 7445	The Last Time	Chess 1519
U 7446		
U7447	Out On The Road -1	Chess 1519

Omit pno.   Chicago, 1953

| U 7503 | Left Me With A Broken Heart | Chess 1543 |
| U 7504 | Act Like You Love Me | – |

Vcl/gtr. with Little Walter, hca; Henry Gray, pno; bs; dms.   Chicago, 1954

| 7591 | Blues All Day Long | Chess 1616 |
| 7592 | Chicago Bound | Chess 1574 |

Vcl/gtr. with Little Walter, hca; Otis Spann, pno; Willie Dixon bs; dms.
7632   Sloppy Drunk   Chess 1574

Omit Spann, pno;   Chicago, 1956
7970   You're The One   Chess 1616

JIMMY ROGERS

Vcl/gtr. with Walter Horton, hca; pno; Willie Dixon bs; dms.
8304   If It Ain't Me   Chess 1643
8305   Walking By Myself   – , LP 1446

Vcl/gtr. with Little Walter, hca; Otis Spann, pno. Wayne Bennett, gtr; Willie Dixon bs;
Fred Below, dms.   Chicago, 1957
8394   One Kiss   Chess 1659
8395   I Can't Believe   –

Similar, but Walter Horton, hca; Francey Clay, dms; vcl. grp (-1).
                                                 Chicago, 1958
8597   What Have I Done   Chess 1687
8598
8599   Trace Of You -1   Chess 1687

Vcl/gtr. with Otis Spann, pno; bs-gtr; Willie Dixon, bs; S. P. Leary, dms.
                                                 Chicago, 1959
9241   Rock This House   Chess 1721
9242   My Last Meal   –

DR. ROSS

Real name Isiah Ross. Born Tunica, Mississippi on October, 21, 1925

DR' ROSS & HIS JUMP & JIVE BOYS
Vcl/hca/gtr. with Wiley Galatin, gtr.   Memphis, 1952
F 1012   Country Clown   Chess 1504
F 1013   Dr. Ross Boogie   –

DOCTOR ROSS
Vcl/hca. with Wiley Galatin, gtr; Robert Moore, broom; Reuben Martin, wbd.
U 90   Come Back Baby   Sun 193 Memphis, 1954
U 91   Chicago Breakdown   –
               Shake 'Em On Down   unissued
               Deep Down In The Ground   unissued
               My Be Bop Gal   unissued
               Phillipine Jump   unissued
               That's Alright Mama   unissued

Vcl/hca/gtr. with Tom Troy, gtr; Bobby Parker, dms.   Memphis, 1954
U 136   The Boogie Disease   Sun 212
U 137   Juke Box Boogie + 7 unissued titles   –
               + 7 unissued titles

Vcl/hca(-1)/gtr/dms.   Flint, December 1958
D 1001,
KB 1190B   Industrial Boogie   D. I. R. A101
D 1002,
KB 1190A   Thirty-Two Twenty -1   – B102, Blues Classics 12

DR. ROSS & HIS ORBITS
Vcl/hca/gtr. with gtr; bs-gtr; dms.   Detroit, 1959
F 221   Cat Squirrel   Fortune 857
F222   The Sunnyland   –

Vcl/hca/gtr. with Little Joe's Band: gtr: bs-gtr: dms.   Detroit 1961
H 68   Cannonball   Hi-Q 5027
H 69   Numbers Blues   –

Vcl/Hca/gtr. with gtr; bs; gtr; dms.   Detroit, 1963
H 83   New York Breakdown   Hi-Q 5033
H 84   Call The Doctor -1   –

Note: -1 Vcl. not by Ross, Heard handclapping are William Carter, Ernest Jackson,
Charley Shannon and Solomon Brandage.

Vcl/hca/gtr/dm.	Flint, 1965	
Cat Squirrel	Testament T-2206	
Blues And Trouble	–	
Freight Train	–	
Illinois Blues	–	
Hobo Blues	–	, Milestone 3002
Mama Blues	–	
My Little Woman	–	
Dr. Ross Rock	–	
32-20	–	
Good Morning Little Schoolgirl	–	
China Blues	–	
Blues In The Night	–	
Going To The River	–	
Drifting Blues	–	
Fox Chase	–	

Vcl/hca/gtr.	London, October 20, 1965	
Flying Eagle Boogie	Blue Horizon LP 1, Xtra 1038	
Going Down Slow	–	
Something To Tell You (Want All My Friends To Know)	–	–
Tommy Dorsey Boogie	–	
Hobo Blues	–	
Mother Before This Time Another Year	–	
Bad Whiskey, Bad Women	–	–
Decoration Day	–	–
Too Close Together	–	
Rollin' And Tumblin'	–	–
Mean Old World	–	
Rock Me	–	
China Blues	unissued	
Industrial Boogie	unissued	
Cat Squirrel	unissued	
Blues In The Night	unissued	

Vcl/hca/kazoo/gtr/dm	Flint, January, 1966
Miss Elvira	Xtra 1038
Train Fare Home	
After Hours Blues	–
Sugar Gal	
Sweet Black Angel	–
Stop Cryin'	–
Miss Beatrice Blues	unissued
Don't Worry About The Mule	unissued
Good Rocking At Midnight	unissued
Sugar Mama Blues	unissued
Honey Bee Blues	unissued
Who Been Fooling You	unissued
Going Back To Germany	unissued
Who's Hat Is That	unissued
That's All Right Mama	unissued
Hobo Blues	unissued
Little Boy Blue	unissued
Harmonica Slide	unissued

Vcl/hca/gtr/dms	Hamburg, October 7, 1965
My Black Name Is Ringing	Fontana 681. 529TL

ROYAL HAWK

Vcl. with saxes; pno; gtr; bs; dms		1953
FL 127	Royal Hawk	Flair 1013
FL 128	I Wonder Why	–

Note Probably Roy Hawkins, q.v.

OTIS RUSH (see also in APPENDIX)

Born Philadelphia, Mississippi on April 29, 1934

OTIS RUSH & HIS BAND
Vcl/gtr. with Lucius Washington, Harold Ashby, tens; Lafayette Leake, pno; Willie Dixon, bs;
Al Duncan or Wayne Bennett, dms.   Chicago, 1956

U 3236, 11314	I Can't Quit You Baby	Cobra 5000, Chief 8000
U 3237, 11316	Sit Down Baby	– –

Same: Chicago, 3 months later 1956

U 3331, 13064	Violent Love	Cobra 5005
U 3332, 13066	My Love Will Never Die	–

OTIS RUSH
Vcl/gtr. with Shakey Horton, hca; Harold Ashby, ten; Lafayette Leake pno; Jody Williams,
gtr; Willie Dixon, bs; Odie Payne, dms.   Chicago, 1957

C 1008	Groaning The Blues	Cobra 5010
C 1009	If You Were Mine	–

Little Brother Montgomery, pno; Louis Miles, gtr; replace Leake & Williams;

C 1018	Love That Woman	Cobra 5015
C 1019	Jump Sister Bessie	–

Vcl/gtr. with Harold Ashby, ten; Lafayette Leake, pno; Reggie Boyd gtr; Willie Dixon, bs;
Odie Payne, dms.

C 1034	Three Times A Fool	Cobra 5023
C 1035	She's A Good 'un	–

Vcl/gtr. with Harold Ashby, ten; Little Brother Montgomery, pno; Louis Miles, gtr; Willie
Dixon, bs; Fred Below, dms.   1958

C 1046	It Takes Time	Cobra 5027
C 1047	Checking On My Baby	–

Vcl/gtr. with Ike Turner Band; Willie Dixon, bs; Odie Payne, dms.

C 1056	Double Trouble	Cobra 5030
C 1057	Keep On Loving Me Baby	–
C 1064	All Your Love	Cobra 5032
C 1065	My Baby Is A Good-Un	–

OTIS RUSH AND BAND
Vcl/gtr. with Bob Neely, ten; Lafayette Leake, pno; Matt Murphy, bs-gtr; Willie Dixon, bs; Odie
Payne, dms.   Chicago, January 1960

9966	So Many Roads, So Many Trains	Chess 1751, Argo LP 4027
9967	I'm Satisfied	–

Same:

U 10447	You Know My Love	Chess 1775
U 10448	I Can't Stop Baby	–

> Note: Rush Thinks that he has 4 unissued Chess sides - including a remade "All
> Your Love". Willie Dixon said he made 3 sessions of 4 numbers with Rush prior to
> 1962 - some with Matt Murphy, gtr;

OTIS RUSH AND BAND
Vcl/gtr. with King Kolax, Sonny Turner, Murray Watson, tpts; Milton Bland, tbn; Johnny Board,
Abe Locke, tens; Lafayette Leake, pno/org; Lefty Bates, gtr; Jack Meyers, bs-gtr; K. C. Jones, dms.
                                                          Chicago, September 6/7, 1962

UV 7110	Home Work	Duke 356
UV 7113	I Have To Laugh	–
	Don't Let It End This Way	unissued
	untitled	unissued

Vcl/gtr. with Robert Crowder, alt; Luther Tucker, gtr; Roger Jones, bs-gtr; Willie Lion, dms.
                                                          Chicago, late 1965

	Everything's Going To Turn Out Alright	Vanguard VRS 9217
	It's A Mean Old World	–

Rcok   Vanguard VRS 9217
It's My Own Fault   –
Vcl/gtr. with Little Brother Montgomery, pno; Jack Meyers, bs-gtr; Fred Below, dms.
                                                     Berling, October, 16, 1966
All Your Love   Fontana 885.43ITY
My Own Fault   –

HARRY RUTLEDGE

Dancing with Horace Sprott, hca   Nr. Cahaba River, Ala. April 10,
                                                     1954
Buck Dance   Folkways FP 654

S

HASKELL SADLER & HIS ORCHESTRA
Vcl/gtr. with saxes; Sidney Maiden, hca; pno; bs; Bee Brown, dms.
                                                     Los Angeles, 1957
A   Do Right Mind   Flash 103
B   Gone For Good   –

SAILOR BOY
Vcl/gtr. with saxes; bs; dms.   Los Angeles, 1956
10488   Country Home   Dig 116
             (rev. by Preston Love)
12769   What Have I Done Wrong   Dig 126
12770   What Have I Done Wrong   –

        Note: Dig 126 has same title on both labels.

CLARENCE SAMUELS
Vcl/gtr. with saxes; pno; bs; dms.   Los Angeles, 1948
             Household Troubles   Swing Time 131
             C. S. Jam   –
             Deep Sea Diver   Swing Time 149
             A. C. Boogie Blues   –
Vcl/gtr. with
             Boogie Woogie Blues   Aristocrat 1001
             Lollypop Mama   –
Vcl/gtr. with tpt; tbn; alt; ten; pno; bs; dms   Houston, 1949
ACA 1428   Lost My Head   Freedom 1533
ACA 1429   Lowtop Inn   –   , Bayou 010
ACA 1430   Stack 'Em Stack 'Em Pt. 1   unissued
ACA 1431   Stack 'Em, Stack 'Em Pt. 2   unissued

        Note: Rev. Boyou 010 by Goree Carter, q.v.
Same:
ACA 1527   I'm Gonna Leave You Baby   unissued
ACA 1528   (by Julius Stewart)

ACA 1529	Get Hep To Yourself	unissued
ACA 1733	She Walk, She Walk, She Walk, Part 1	Freedom 1541
ACA 1734	She Walk, She Walk, She Walk, Part 2	—
ACA 1759	Walk, Walk, Walk, Part 1	unissued
ACA 1760	Walk, Walk, Walk, Part 2	unissued
ACA 1820	Somebody Gotta Go	Freedom 1544
ACA 1821	Hey Joe	—

Vcl/gtr. with

		? 1950
970	Ginne	DeLuxe 3219
971	Stompin' At The Jubilee	—

Vcl/gtr. with

		New York City, June 1954
FUL 2291	Life Don't Mean A Thing	Lamp 8004
FUL 2292	Cryin'. 'Cause I'm Troubled	Lamp 8005
FUL 2293	Lightnin' Struck Me	—
FUL 2294	Crazy With The Heat	Lamp 8004

Vcl/gtr. with Saxes; pno; bs; dms.

		? 1956
B	Chicken Hearted Woman	Excello 2093
A	Got No place To Call My Own	—

Vcl/gtr. with

		?
	Without You	Apt 5028
	We're Going To The Hop	

Vcl/gtr. with

		Houston 1966
ACA 5431	Cryin' 'Cause I'm Troubled	Sharon?
ACA 1432	Charlie Loan Me 50¢	

BOBBY SANDS

See under John Bullard

ASHTON SAVOY

Born Opelousas, Louisiana in 1936

ASHTON SAVOY & HIS COMBO
Vcl/gtr. with Danny George, ten; Katie Webster, pno; Lightnin' Mitchell, dms.

		Lake Charles, 1957
713	Juke Joint	Hollywood 1081
714	Denga, Denga	—
	Rooster Strut	unissued

No ten; except (-1); add Lazy Lester, hca.

		Lake Charles, July 4, 1959
	Need Shorter Hours	Storyville SLP 177
	Want To Talk To You Baby	—
	Tell Me Baby -1	—

Note: See also Katie Webster. Now resident in Houston.

ALONZO SCALES

Vcl. with Sonny Terry, hca; pno; gtr; bs; dms.

		New York City, Dec. 30, 1955
WW 124	Hard Luck Child	Wing 90049
WW 125		
WW 126	We Just Can't Agree	Wing 90049

SCHOOLBOY CLEVE

Real name Cleve White
Vcl/hca. with Lightnin' Slim, gtr; unk. dms

		Crowley, La, 1954
F 529	She's Gone	Feature 3013
F 530	Strange Letter Blues	—

Note: Opelousas based artist.

BEVERLEY SCOTT & HIS TRIO

Vcl/gtr. with Louis Jackson, pno; Ernest McClay, gtr;

| | | Los Angeles, 1948 |
| A | Shaking The Boogie | Murray 503 |

B	Southern California Blues	Murray 503

LANNIE SCOTT TRIO

Real name Lonnie Scott
Pno. with   New York City, May 1946

59043	Lannie's Boogie Woogie	Savoy 614
59044	Barrelhouse Boogie	–

LEVI SEABURY (the late)

Vcl/hca. with pno; gtr; bs; dms.   Memphis, 1957

H 70B 2017	Boogie Beat	Blues Boy's Kingdom 101
H 70B 2018	Motherless Child	–

Note: This artist died soon after cutting these sides.

ALEC SEWARD & LOUIS HAYES

Alec Seward born Newport News, Virginia in 1901
Louis Hayes born Asheville, North Carolina in 1912

THE BLUES KING
Seward, vcl(-1)/gtr. with Hayes, vcl (-2)/gtr.   New York City, 1946/7

SO 5	Me And My Baby -1	Solo 10-003
SO 6	Good Boy -2	–

THE BLUES BOY: GUITAR SLIM & JELLY BELLY
Seward, vcl(-1)/gtr. with Hayes, vcl (-2)/gtr.

A	Up And Down Blues -1,2	Tru-Blue 100, Arhoolie R 2005
B	Crooked Wife Blues -2	– Arhoolie unissued
A	Snowin' And Rainin' Blues -1, 2	Tru-Blue 102, Arhoolie R 2005 '
B	Smilin' Blues -1	– Arhoolie unissued
A	Ungrateful Woman Blues -2	Tru-Blue 102, Arhoolie unissued
B	Keep Straight Blues -1, 2	– Arhoolie R 2005
	(prob. "No More Hard Times" on R 2005)	
A	Been Plowing Blues (Mike & Jerry)	Tru-Blue 103, Arhoolie R 2005
B	Don't Leave Me Blues -1	– Arhoolie unissued
A	(South) Carolina Blues -1, 2	Tru-Blue 104, Arhoolie R 2005
B	Baby Left Me -1	– Arhoolie unissued
MF 226-C1	In Love Blues -1, 2	Superdisc 1053
MF 227-C1	Worried Man Blues -1	

THE BACK PORCH BOYS
Same:

R 1258	Big Hip Mama -1	Apollo 392
R 1259	Be Kind Blues	Apollo 406
R 1260	Sweet Woman Blues	–
R 1261-KD	Water Trough Blues -2	Apollo 412
R 1262-KB	Sorry Women Blues -2	–
R 1263		
R 1264	King Kong Blues -1	Apollo 392

Note: Apollo 412 issued as by Jelly Belly & Slim Seward

GUITAR SLIM & JELLY BELLY

SLIM SEWARD & FAT BOY HAYES on MGM
Same:

107A	Big Trouble Blues	Arhoolie R 2005
107B	Humming Bird Blues	unissued
108A	Right and Wrong Woman	Arhoolie R 2005
108B	Southern Whistle Blues	
109A	Jail And Buddy Blues	–
109B	Mean Girl Blues	unissued
110A	Travelin' Boy's Blues	MGM 10306, Arhoolie R 2005
110B	Railroad Blues	MGM 10770,
11A	Yellow Brown Blues	Arhoolie F 1012

111B	Bad Acting Woman	Arhoolie R 2005
112A	Christmas Time Blues	MGM 10306, Arhoolie R 2005
112B	Cooking Big Woman	unissued
113A	Early Morning Blues	unissued
113B	My Isabel	unissued
114A	Hard Luck Blues	unissued
114B	Unhappy Home Blues	unissued
115A	Working Man Blues	MGM 10770, Arhoolie R 2005
115B	Oh Baby, Oh Baby	unissued
116A	I've Been Dreaming	unissued
116B	Dupree Blues (Betty And Dupree)	Arhoolie R 2005
117A	Why Oh Why	–
117B	Down South Blues	unissued
118A	Evil Woman Blues	unissued
118B	Honey Bee Blues	unissued

Seward, vcl/gtr. with Larry Johnson, hca (except on -1)   New York City, 1965

	Big Hip Mama	Bluesville BVLP 1076
	Evil Woman Blues	–
	Goin' Down Slow -1	–
	Sweet Woman	–
	Some People Say	–
	Creepin' Blues	–
	I Made A Mistake In Life	–
	Piney Woods -1	–
	Late One Saturday Evening	–
	Let A Good Thing Go	–

See also Sonny Terry. Records with Woody Guthrie not included.

WILL SHADE

Born Memphis. Tennesse on February 5, 1898. Died Memphis, November, 1966.

Hca. with Charlie Burse, gtr;   Memphis, December 5, 1956

	Harmonica And Guitar Blues	Folkways FA 2610

Vcl(-1)/hca. with Charlie Burse, vcl (-2)/gtr. Gus Cannon, jug.

	Tippin' around -2	Folkways FA 2610, RBF 202
	Take Your Fingers Off It -1	– –

Vcl/gtr. with Gus Cannon, vcl (-1)

	What You Gonna Do Baby -1	Folkways FA 2610
	I Can't Stand It	RBF 202

Vcl. with Charlie Burse. vcl

	Interview	Folkways FA 2610

Vcl/gtr.   Memphis, July 20, 1960

	Newport News Blues	Decca LK 4664

SHAKEY JAKE

Real name James Harris, Born Earle, Arkansas on April 12, 1921

Vcl. with Willie Dixon Band: Magic Sam, gtr; Syl Johnson, bs-gtr; Willie Dixon bs; dms.

Chicago, 1958

C 1048	Roll Your Moneymaker	Artistic 1502
C 1049	Call Me If You Need Me	–

Vcl/hca. with Jack McDuff, org; Bill Jennings, gtr.   New York City, 1959

	My Foolish Heart	Bluesville 807, BVLP 1008
	Jake's Blues	– –
	Worried Blues	Bluesville BVLP 1008
	Sunset Blues	–
	You Spoiled Your Baby (Omit org.)	–
	Teardrops	–
	Just Shakey	–
	Still Your Fool	–
	Keep A-Loving Me Baby	–
	Call Me When You Need Me	

| | Huffin' And Puffin' | Bluesville BVLP 1008 |
| | Good Times | – |

Vcl/hca. with Robert Banks, pno; Jimmy Lee Robinson, gtr; Leonard Gaskin bs; Junior
Blackman, dms.

		New York, November 1960
	Mouth Harp Blues	Bluesville BVLP 1027
	Love My Baby	–
	Jake's Cha Cha	–
	Gimme A Smile	–
	My Broken Heart	–
	Angry Love	–
	Things Is Alright	–
	Easy Baby	–
	Things Are Different Now	–
	It Won't Happen Again	–

Vcl/hca. with Memphis Slim, pno; T-Bone Walker, gtr; Willie Dixon bs; Jump Jackson, dms.

		Hamburg, October 18, 1962
	Hey Baby	Polydor 46.397
	Love My Baby	–

ROBERT SHAW

Vcl/pno.

		Austin, Texas, March 8, June 10, Aug. 9, 1963
	Whores is Funky	Almanac 10, Arhoolie F 1010
	The Cows	–
	Here I Come With My Dirty, Dirty Duckins On	– –
	The Clinton	– –
	Black Gal	– –
	Hattie Green	– –
	The Ma Grinder	– –
	People, People Blues	– –
	Put Me In The Alley	– –
	Piggly Wiggly Blues (Groceries On My Shelf)	– –
	Turn Loose My Tongue	Arhoolie F 1012

SHERMAN'S TRIO

Sherman Louis, pno; with Lafayette Thomas, gtr; B. Bostic, bs;

		Oakland, 1949
CT5B	Jumping For Julia	Cavatone 5, Modern 20-685
	(rev. by Bob Geddins)	

JOHNNY SHINES

Born Memphis, Tennessee on April 25, 1915
Vcl/gtr.

		Chicago, February 24, 1946
CCO 4496	Tennessee Woman Blues	Columbia unissued
CCO 4497	Delta Pine Blues	–
CCO 4498	Ride, Ride Mama	–
CCO 4499	Evil Hearted Woman Blues	–

SHOE SHINE JOHNNY

Vcl/gtr.

		Chicago, 1950
U 7279	Joliet Blues	Chess 1443
U 7280	So Glad I Found You	–

JOHNNY SHINES

Vcl/gtr. with Al Smith, bs.

		Chicago, 1952
JB 48885	Ramblin'	JOB 116, Blues Classics BC-6
JB 48886		
JB 48887	Cool Driver	JOB 116

Vcl/gtr. with Walter Horton, hca

		Chicago, early 1953
U 2337	Evening Sun	JOB 1010
U 2338	No Name Blues	unissued
U 2339	Brutal Hearted Woman	JOB 1010
U 2340	I'm Gonna Call The Angel	unissued

Vcl/gtr. with Walter Horton, hca; Charlie Musselwhite, hca (-1); Floyd Jones, bs; Frank
Kirkland, dms.   Chicago, 1965
        Dynaflow Blues   Vanguard VRS 9218
        Black Spider Blues   –
        Layin' Down My Shoes And Clothes   –
        If I Get Lucky   –
        Rockin' My Boogie -1   –
        Mr. Bo Weevil   –
        Hey, Hey

SHOE SHINE JOHNNY

See under Johnny Shines

J. D. SHORT

Born Port Gibson, Mississippi on December 26, 1902. Died St. Louis. Missouri, Oct/nov. 1962
Vcl/hca/gtr.   St. Louis, July 3, 1962
        So Much Wine   Folkways FS 1467
        Train, Bring My Baby Back (no gtr)   –
        You Been Cheating Me   –
        Charlie Patton (vcl. only)   –
        Fightin' For Dear Old Uncle Same   –

      Note: See also Big Joe Williams.

AL SIMMONS

WITH SLIM GREEN & THE CATS FROM FRESNO.
Vcl/gtr. with pno(-1); Slim Green, gtr; dms.   Los Angeles, 1956
15889   Old Folks Boogie -1   Dig 138
        (rev. by Sidney Maiden)
17234   You Ain't Too Old   Dig 142
        (rev. by Slim Green)

MACK SIMMONS

See under Little Mac

JIMMY SIMON

No details'
        Runnin' Blues   Phoenix 017/018
        Fine Baby Blues   –

FRANKIE LEE SIMS

Vcl/gtr. with bs.   Dallas, 1948
A   Home Again Blues   Blue Bonnet 147
B   Cross Country Blues   –
A   Don't Forget Me Baby   Blue Bonnet 148
B   Single Man Blues   –
Vcl/gtr. with bs; Hubert Washington, dms.   Dallas, 1953
SP 459   Lucy Mae Blues   Specialty 459, Blues Classics 16
XSP 459   Don't Take It Out On Me   –
SP 478   I'm Long Gone   Specialty 478, Blues Classics 16
XSP 478   Yeh Baby   –
SP 487   Rhumba My Boogie   Specialty 487
XSP 487   I'll Get Along Somehow   –

      Note: Above probably all cut at one session.

Vcl/gtr. with Willie Taylor, pno; Hubert Washington, dms.   Dallas, 1957
3381   Misery Blues   Ace 524
3382   What Will Lucy Do   –

Vcl/gtr. with Jack White, ten; Willie Taylor, pno; Ralph Morgan, bs; Jimmy Mullens, dms.

3386	Hey Little Girl	Ace 527
3387	Walking With Frankie	–, Teem LP 5005

Similar:

3414	My Talk Didn't Do Any Good	Ace 539
3415	I Warned You Baby	–
S138	She Likes To Boogie Real Low	Vin 1006
S 139	Well Goodbye Baby	–
	Come Back Baby	Ace unissued
	How Long	–

MAC SIMS

See under Little Mac

SIR ARTHUR

Vcl/hca. with org; gtr; bs; dms. vcl. grp (-1)

Los Angeles, 1965

1785	Stop Cheatin' On Me	Coleman 62865
1786	Do The Walk -1	–

Note: Probably Arthur Wright, q.v.

SKOODLE DUM DOO & SHEFFIELD

Real name Seth Richard
Vcl/gtr. with Sheffield hca/gtr. (-1)

New York City, late 1943

S 1079	Tampa Blues	Regis 107
S 1080	Gas Ration Blues	–
S 1084	Broome St. Blues	Manor 1056
S 1088	West Kinney St, Blues -1	–

SLEEPY JOE

See under Ralph Willis

SLIM HARPO

Real name James Moore. Born West Baton Rouge, La. on January 11, 1924
Vcl/hca. with Guitar Gable, gtr; Fats Perrodin, bs-gtr; "Jockey", dms.

Crowley, La. 1957

16007	I'm A King Bee	Excello 2113, LP 8001, 8003
16008	I've Got Love If You Want It	– , LP 8003

Vcl/hca. with Al Foreman, Bobby McBride, gtrs; Warren Storm, dms.

Crowley, La 1959

A	Wonderin' And Worryin'	Excello 2138
B	St range Love	–
A	You'll Be Sorry One Day	Excello 2162
B	One More Day	–

Same:

Crowley, La 1960

A	Buzz Me Babe	Excello 2171, LP 8003
B	Late Last Night	

Add Lionel Torrence, ten(-1);

A	Blues Hangover -1	Excello 2184, LP 8003
B	What A Dream	– –

Add Katie Webster, pno(-1):

Crowley La, 1961

A	Rainin' In My Heart	Excello 2194, LP 8003
	Rainin' In My Heart (alt. take)	Excello LP 8005
B	Don't Start Cryin' Now -1	Excello 2194, LP 8003
	My Home Is A Prison -2	Excello LP 8003
	Bobby Sox Baby -2	–
	Moody Blues	–
	Snoopin' Around	–
	Dream Girl	–

Vcl/hca. with Lionel Torrence, ten; Al Foreman, gtr; Bobby McBride or Rufus Thibodeaux,
bs-gtr; Austin Broussard, dms.   Crowley, La 1964
A   I Love The Life I'm Living   Excello 2239, LP 8005
B   Buzzin'   –
A   I Need Money   Excello 2246
B   Little Queen Bee   –   , LP 8005
A   We're Two Of A Kind   Excello 2253, LP 8005
B   Still Rainin' In My Heart   –
Same: Crowley, La 1965
A   Sittin' Here Wonderin'   Excello 2261
B   What's Going On Baby   –
A   Harpo's Blues   Excello 2265, LP 8005
B   Please Don't Turn Me Down   –
Vcl/hca. with Willie Parker, ten(-1); James Johnson, Rudolph Richard, gtrs; Katie Webster, pno;
Geese August, bs; Sammy Kaye, dms.   Crowley, La 1966
A   Baby Scratch My Back -1   Excello 2273, LP 8005, A-Bet LP 401
B   I'm Gonna Miss You (Like The Devil)   –   –
A   Shake Your Hips -1   Excello 2278, LP 8005
B   Midnight Blues   –   –
           Wonderin' Blues   Excello LP 8005
A   I'm Your Breadmaker Baby   Excello 2282
B   Loving You   –

Vcl/hca. with   New Orleans, 1962
IM 3040   Something Inside Me   Imperial unissued
IM 3041   Still Rainin' In My Heart   –
IM 3042   A Man Is Crying   –
IM 3043   Tonite I'm Lonely   –

THE SLY FOX

See under Eugene Fox.

AL SMITH

Real name Alonzo Smith
Vcl/hca/gtr. with pno; bs; dms.   Lake Charles, La 1959
A   If I Don't See You   Goldband 1092
B   I Love Her So   –

ARTHUR SMITH TRIO

No details   New York City, 1946
                                                       Superdisc 1032

          Note: This may be the same artist as Sonny Boy & Lonnie q.v.

COOL PAPA SMITH & HIS ORCH.

Vcl. with alt; ten; pno; gtr; bs; dms,   Austin, Texas c. 1949
A   You Better Change Your Ways Woman   Uptown 202
B   Christmas Blues   –

DRIFTING SMITH

See under Elmon Mickle

GEORGE SMITH

Born in Cairo, Illinois on April 7(?), 1924

LITTLE GEORGE SMITH
Vcl/hca with pno; Po' Bob Woodfork, gtr; bs; dms.   Kansas City, 1954/55
MM 2208   Blues In The Dark   RPM 434
MM 2209   Telephone Blues   –
MM 2242   Blues Stay Away   RPM 442
MM 2243   Oppin' Doopin' Doopin'   –

| MM 3042 | You Don't Love Me | RPM 478 |
| MM 3043 | Down In New Orleans | – |

Add brass;
| MM 3004 | Love Life | RPM 456 |
| MM 3005 | Cross Eyed Suzie Lee | – |

LITTLE WALTER JR.
Vcl/hca. with pno; bs; dms.   Los Angeles, 1955/56
| A | Miss O'Mally's Rally | Lapel 101 |
| B | Don't Know | |

HARMONICA KING
Vcl/hca. with ten; gtr; bs; dms.
| A | All Last Night | Lapel 103 |
| B | Hot Rolls | – |

GEORGE SMITH
Vcl/hca. with org; gtr; bs; dms
001	West Helena Blues	J & M
002	Go Ahead On Woman	–
008	Long As I Live	Carolyn 1420
009	Nobody Knows	–

Note: J & M Label gives no issue number.

GEORGE ALLEN
Vcl/hca. with pno; 2 gtrs; dms.   Oakland, 1957
| 1008 | Times Won't Be Hard Always | Sotoplay 0010,,0031/2 |
| 1009 | Tight Dress | |

Add org. vibes (-1);
| 10012 | Loose Screws -1 | Sotoplay 0012 |
| 10013 | The Time To Go On | |

Vcl/hca. with saxes; pno; gtr; bs-gtr; dms.
S-0021	Sometimes You Win When You Lose	Sotoplay 0021/2
S-0022	Come On Home	–
S-0023	You Can't Undo What's Been Done	Sotoplay 0023/4
S-0024	Rope That Twist	

GEORGE ALLEN
Vcl/hca. with ten; pno; gtr; bs; dms. vcl. grp.   Oakland, 1965
| S-0031 | I Must Be Crazy | Sotoplay 0031/2 |

Vcl/hca with pno; 2 gtrs; dms
| 55189A | Brown Mule | Sotoplay S-51 |
| 55189X | Good Things | – |

Note: "Loose Screws"/Tight Dress" also reissued, number unknown

HENRY SMITH

Vcl/gtr.   Detroit, 1952
| 802A | Dog Me Blues | Fortune 802 |
| | (rev. by Clarence Posey) | |

Vcl/gtr. with Eddie Burns, hca; Calvin Frazier, gtr; Washboard Willie, wbd.
                                                Detroit, 1954
E4KB-5072,		
M 8407	Good Rocking Mama	Dot 1220
E4KB-5073,		
M 8408	Lonesome Blues	–

ROBERT CURTIS SMITH

Born Mississippi in 1930
Vcl/gtr. with Wade Walton, vcl (-1)   Clarksdale, July 14, 1960
	I Hope One Day My Luck Will Change -1	Decca LK 4664
	Going Back To Texas	Arhoolie F 1005
	Lonely Widow	–

	Lost Love Blues	Arhoolie F 1005
	Stella Ruth	Arhoolie F 1006
Vcl/gtr.		Clarksdale, summer, 1962
	Catfish	Bluesville BVLP 1064
	Put Your Arms Around Me	–
	Rock Me Mama	–
	Council Spur Blues	–
	I Feel So Good	–
	I'm Going Away	–
	Ain't That Loving You Baby	–
	Get A Real Young Woman	–
	See My Chauffeur	–
	Sunflower River Blues	–
	Katy Mae	–
	Goody, Goody	–
	Can You Remember Me	–
	I Hate To Leave You With Tears In My Eyes	–
Add dms:		
A	We Love Each Other	Arhoolie 502
B	Please Don't Drive Me Away	– , F 1018

SHORTY SMITH

See under Sonny Boy & Lonnie

"RED" WILLIE SMITH

Vcl/gtr. with Huston Townsend, jug (-1).		York, Ala, Jan/feb. 1950
	Kansas City Blues	Folkways FE 4417, P 417
	Salty Dog -1	– –

THUNDER SMITH

Real name Wilson Smith. Born ? Died Houston, 1965

Vcl/pno. with Lightnin' Hopkins, gtr;		Los Angeles, November 9, 1946
54-1	L. A. Blues	Aladdin 166
55-1	Little Mama Boogie (Blues)	– , Imperial LP9180
Vcl/pno. with Luther Stoneham, gtr;		Houston, 1947
A	Cruel Hearted Woman	Gold Star 615
B	Big Stars Are Falling	– , Arhoolie 2006

THUNDER SMITH & ROCKIE

Vcl/pno. with Luther Stoneham, vcl(-1)/gtr.		Houston 1948
A	Thunder's Unfinished Boogie	Down Town 2011
B	The Train Is Leaving -1	–
A	New Worried Life Blues	Down Town 2012
B	Mable Blues -1	–
A	Low Down Dirty Ways	Down Town 2013
B	Water Coast Blues -1	–

THUNDER SMITH

Same:		Houston 1949
A	Santa Fe Blues (no gtr)	GoldStar 644, Arhoolie 2006
B	Temptation Blues	–

Note: See also under Lightnin' Hopkins q.v.

WHISPERING SMITH

Real name Moses Smith.

Vcl/hca. with Al Foreman, gtr; Bobby McBride or Rufus Thibodeaux, bs-gtr; Austin Broussard, dms.

		Crowley, La, 1963
A	Mean Woman Blues	Excello 2232
B	Hound Dog Twist	–
A	Don't Leave Me Baby	Excello 2237
B	Live Jive	–

292

Same:		Crowley, La 1964
A	I Tried So Hard	Excello 2250
B	Crying Blues	–
A	I Can't Take It Anymore	Excello 2260
B	Baby You're Mine	–

Note: Baton Rouge based artist.

WILLIE "LONG TIME" SMITH

Vcl. with Willie Lacey, gtr; Ransom Knowling, bs; Chuck Sanders, dms.

		Chicago, June 13, 1947
CCO 4800	No Special Rider Here	Columbia 37827, 30097
CCO 4801	My Buddy Doctor Clayton	Columbia 37990, 30104
CCO 4802	Due Respects To You	Columbia 37827, 30097
CCO 4803	I Love You Baby Boogie	Columbia 37990, 30104
Similar:		Chicago, December 27, 1947
CCo 4964	Dirty Deal Boogie	Columbia 30140
CCO 4965	Flying Cloud Boogie	–
CCO 4966	Devilment On My Mind	unissued
CCO 4967	Nameless Blues	unissued

SMOKY BABE

Real name Robert Brown. Born Itta Bena, Mississippi in 1927
Vcl/gtr. with Sally Dotson, vcl(-1); Henry Thomas, hca (-2); William Dotson, vcl (-3); Clyde Causey, hca (-4);

		Scotlandville, February, 1960
	Rabbit Blues -1	Folk-Lyric FL-108
	Too Many Women -2	–
	Two Wings -3	–
	Mississippi River -2	–
	I'm Broke And Hungry	–
	My Baby She Told Me -2	–
	Black Ghost -1	–
	Ain't Got No Rabbit Dog -4	–
	Bad Whisky	–
	Black Gal -4	–
	Goin' Back Home	–

Vcl/gtr.

		Baton Rouge, 1960
	Goin' Downtown Boogie	Folk-Lyric FL-111
	Boogy	Storyville SLP 129
	I Went Down 61 Highway	–
	Regular Blues	–
	Talkin' Baby	–

Vcl/gtr. with Clyde Causey, vcl/hca (-1); Henry Thomas, hca (-2);

		Baton Rouge, 1961
	Now Your Man Done Gone	Bluesville BVLP 1063
	Hottest Brand Goin'	–
	Something's Wrong With My Machine -2	–
	Insect Blues	–
	Long Way From Home	–
	I'm Going Back To Mississippi	–
	Melvanie Blues	–
	Locomotive Blues -1 (hca solo)	–
	Ocean Blues	–
	Boogy Woogy Rag	–
	Coon Hunt -1	–
	Cold Cold Snow	–

SMOKEY SMOTHERS

Real name Otis Smothers, Born Lexington, Mississippi on March 14, 1925. Vcl/gtr. with Freddy King, Fred Jordan, gtrs; Phillip Paul, dms.

		Cincinnati, August 25, 1960
K 4869	Smokey's Lovesick Blues	Federal 12405, King LP 779
K 4870	Crying Tears	Federal 12385, –

K 4871	Midnight And Day	Federal 12420, King LP 779
K 4872	Honey I Ain't Teasin'	–	–
K 4873	Blind And Dumb Man Blues	Federal 12441,	–
K 4874	What Am I Going To Do	Federal 12385,	–
K 4875	I've Been Drinking Muddy Water	Federal 12395,	–
K 4876	Monkey Man	–	–
K 4877	You're Gonna Be Sorry	Federal 12503,	–
K 4878	I Can't Judge Nobody	Federal 12441,	–
K 4879	Give It Back	Federal 12488,	–
K 4880	Come On Back Little Girl	Federal 12405,	–

Vcl/gtr. with hca; gtr; bs-gtr; dms.   1962

F 1451	Hello Little Schoolgirl	Federal 12466
F 1452	Way Up In The Mountains of Kentucky	Federal 12488
F 1453	The Case Is Closed	Federal 12503
F 1454	Twist With Me Annie	Federal 12466

SNOOKY & MOODY

See under Snooky Pryor or Floyd Jones

KING SOLOMON (or SOLOMAN)

Real Name Ellis Solomon

Vcl/pno. with Johnny Heartsman, gtr; bs;   Oakland, 1953

6246	Mean Train -1	Big Town 102
6247	Baby I'm Cutting Out	–
	–1 various sound effects added.	

Vcl/pno. with tpt; ten; gtr; bs; dms.   Los Angeles, 1960

| U 10927 | Non-Support Blues Pt. 1 | Ball 511, Checker 980 |
| U 10928 | Non–Support Blues Pt. 2 | – | – |

Tpt. out; ad 2nd gtr.   Los Angeles,

K-3201	Separation	Mader-D 301/2
K-3202	Little Dab Will Do It	–
MD-102	When A Man Loves A Woman	Mader-D 102
MD-103	I Don't Play That Way	–
1532A	I'm In Your Corner Baby	Tomsey 101
1532B	I'm In Love With You	–
303A	I Got To Move	Don-J 303
303B	Uncle John's Swinging Farm	–
X-217	Separation	Magnum 721, World's 122
X-218	I Want To Know	Magnum 720,	–
X-2032	Yodeling This Morning	Magnum 720
X-3009	Scratch My Back	Magnum 721

Vcl/pno. with tbn; ten; gtr; el-bs; dms.   Los Angeles, 1966

446-1	Please Mr. President	Kent 446
446-2	Mr. Bad Luck	–
451-1	S. K. Blues	Kent 451
451-2	New Figure	–
RR-001	Big Things	Resist 501
RR-002	You Ain't Nothing But A Teenager	–

Note: Guitarist on Big Town issue is JOHNNY HEARTSMAN.

SONNY & JAYCEE

See under Sonny Terry

SONNY BOY & LONNIE (Sonnie & Lonnie)

A. Smith vcl/gtr. with Lonnie Johnson, vcl/pno. Sam Bradley, vcl/gtr.; unk. dms.

New York City, 1945

	South West Pacific Blues	Continental 6050, LP 16002, LP 16003, Lenox 510
	Quincy Avenue Boogie	Continental 6050
	Wiggle Around Me Baby	Continental LP 16002, LP 16003, Lenox 510

W 3670	My Baby Blues	Continental 6053, LP 16002
W 3671	The Wide Boogie	Continental 6052, –
W 3672	I'll Water You Every Day	Continental 6054
W 3673	Bigheaded Woman	–
W 3674	Big Moose Blues	Continental 6053, LP 16002
W 3675	Talking Boogie	Continental 6052, –

SONNY BOY & SAM
Same:

UC 3757	I Wonder Who's Holding You	Continental 6055, LP 16003
UC 3758	Mama Blues	–

Notes: Lenox 510 issued as by Shorty Smith & His Rhythm. Continental LP 16002 reissued on Masterseal LP 220 with all tracks re-titled and credited to Lightnin' Guitar's Band. See also Arthur Smith Trio q.v. The Pianist has no connection with the Lonnie Johnson.

SONNY BOY & SAM

See under Sonny Boy And Lonnie.

SONNY BOY WILLIAMSON (See also in APPENDIX)

Real name Willie or Rice Miller. Born Glendora, Mississippi c. 1901
Died Helena, Arkansas on May, 25, 1965.
Vcl/hca. with pno; Cliff Bivens, bs; "Frock", dms.　　　　Jackson, early 1951

DRC-15-2	Eyesight To The Blind	Trumpet 129, Blues Classics 9
DRC-16-2	Crazy About You Baby	– –

Vcl/hca. with Dave Campbell, pno; Joe Willie Wilkins, gtr; Cliff Bivens, bs; "Frock", dms.

DRC-17, ACA2031	Stop Crying	Trumpet 140, Blues Classics 9
DRC-18, ACA2024	Do It If You Wanna	Trumpet 139, –
DRC-19 ACA2023	Cool, Cool Blues	– –
DRC-20 ACA 2032	Come On Back Home	Trumpet 140, –
DRC-21 ACA2030	I Cross My Heart	Trumpet 144, –
DRC-22 ACA 2029	West Memphis Blues	– , –

Note: ACA data from ACA Files

Vcl/hca. with Clarence Lonnie, pno; Joe Willie Wilkins, gtr; Cliff Bivens, bs; "Frock", dms.
　　　　　　　　　　　　　　　　　　　Jackson, late 1951

DRC-45 ACA 2027	Sonny Boy's Christmas Blues	Trumpet 145, Blues Classics 9
DRC-46 ACA 2025	Pontiac Blues	– –

Same: but Bivens replaced by vcl. bs.　　　　Jackson, January 31, 1952

DRC-88 ACA 2119	Might Long Time (no pno; gtr; dms.)	Trumpet 166, Blues Classics 9
DRC-89 ACA2117	Nine Below Zero (no gtr)	– –
DRC-90 ACA2118	She Brought Life Back To The Dead (no dms)	Trumpet 215, Blues Classics 9
DRC-91 ACA2122	Too Close Together (no pno)	Tpt 212, –
DRC-92 ACA2120	Stop Now Baby (no pno)	Trumpet 168, –
DRC-93, ACA2121	Mr. DownChild (no pno)	– , –

Note: Alternate take of DRC-90 on 45 rpm issue.

Vcl/hca, with Duke Huddleston, ten; Dave Campbell, pno; Joe Willie Wilkins, gtr; Oliver
Harris, bs; S. P., dms.   Jackson, late 1953

DRC-180		
ACA2560	Cat Hop	Trumpet 212
DRC-185,		
ACA2772	Gettin' Out Of Town (no pno)	Trumpet 215
DRC-186		
DRC-187		
ACA2771	Red Hot Kisses	Trumpet 216
DRC-188		
ACA 2769	Going In Your Direction	–
ACA 2770	Keep It To Yourself	unissued

Vcl/hca. with Clarence Lonnie, pno; B. B. King, gtr; Glen Ricketts, dms.
                                     Jackson 1954

DRC-211,		
ACA3036	Empty Bedroom	Trumpet 228
DRC-212		
ACA3037	From The Bottom	–

Vcl/hca withDave Campbell, pno; Joe Willie Wilkins, gtr; dms.

ACE 3201		
ACA 3246	Boppin' With Sonny (no pno)	Ace 511
ACE 3202		
ACA 3043	No Nights by Myself (no gtr)	–, Teem LP 5005

> Note: Sonny Boy claims to play drums on the above record. The above masters
> were leased by Ace from Trumpet. Twelve Trumpet sides remain unissued.

Vcl/hca. with Otis Spann, pno; Muddy Waters, Jimmy Rogers, gtrs; Fred Below, dms.
                                     Chicago, 1955

7890	Don't Start Me To Talkin'	Checker 824, LP 1437, Argo LP 4026
7891	All My Love In Vain	–

Vcl/hca. with Robert Lockwood, Jr., Luther Tucker, gtrs; Willie Dixon bs; Fred Below, dms.

7980	Let Me Explain	Checker 834, LP 1437
7981		
7982		
7983	Your Imagination	Checker 834, LP 1437
Same:		Chicago 1956
8205	Keep It To Yourself	Checker 847
8206		
8207	The Key To Your Door	Checker 847,LP 1437
Same:		Chicago 1957
8409	Fattening Frogs For Snakes	Checker 864, LP 1437, Argo LP 4034
8410	I Don't Know	– –

Add Otis Spann, pno;

8593	Cross My Heart	Checker 910, LP 1437
8594	Born Blind	Checker 883
8595	Ninety Nine	– , LP 1437
8596	Dissatisfied	Checker 910, –, Chess LP 1503

Vcl/hca. with Lafayette Leake, pno; Robert Lockwood, Jr; Gene ?, gtrs; Willie Dixon, bs;
Fred Below, dms.   Chicago, 1958

8753	Your Funeral And My Trial	Checker 894, LP 1437
8754		
8755	Wake Up Baby	Checker 894, LP 1437

Vcl/hca. with Otis Spann, pno; Robert Lockwood Jr., Luther Tucker, gtrs; Willie Dixon;
bs; Odie Payne, dms.   Chicago, 1959

9479	Let Your Conscience Be Your Guide	Checker 927
9480	Unseeing Eye	–

Fred Below, dms. replaces Payne:

9829	The Goat	Checker 943, Chess LP 1509
9830		
9831		
9832	It's Sad To Be Alone	Checker 943, Chess LP 1503

Vcl/hca. with Otis Spann, pno; Eddie King Milton, Luther Tucker, gtrs; Fred Below, dms.

		Chicago, 1960
10266	Temperature 110	Checker 956
10267		
10268	Lonesome Cabin	Checker 956

Vcl/hca. with Lafayette Leake, pno; Robert Lockwood, Jr., Luther Tucker, gtrs; Fred Below, dms.

10416	Trust Me Baby	Checker 963, Chess LP 1503
10417		
10418	Too Close Together	Checker 963

Vcl/hca. with Otis Spann, pno; Robert Lockwood, Jr., Gtr; Willie Dixon, vcl (-1)/bs; Odie Payne, dms.

		Chicago, 1961
10571	Stop Right Now	Checker 975, Chess LP 1509
10572	The Hunt -1	− −

Vcl/hca. with "Connon"?, pno; Robert Lockwood, Jr., Luther Tucker, gtrs; Willie Dixon, bs; Fred Below dms.

11226	One Way Out	Checker 1003
11227	Nine Below Zero	− , Chess LP 1509

Vcl/hca. with Lafayette Leake, org; Matt Murphy, gtr; Milton Rector, bs-gtr; Al Duncan, dms.

		Chicago, Jaunuary 11, 1963
12113	Got To Move	Chess LP 1503
12114	Bye Bye Bird	Checker 1036, Chess LP 1509
12115	Help Me	− −
12116	Bring It On Home	Checker 1134, Chess LP 1503, Argo, LP 4031
	Baby Let Me Please Come Home	unissued

Note: Crowd noises dubbed on 12116 on Argo LP 4031

Vcl/hca. with saxes; Lafayette Leake, pno; Buddy Guy, gtr; Jack Meyers, bs-gtr; Clifton James, dms.

		Chicago, September 6, 1963
12663	One Way Out	Chess LP 1503
12664	My Younger Days	Checker 1080, Chess LP 1509
12665	Trying To Get Back On My Feet	Checker 1065, −
1266	Decoration Day	− −

Note: Saxes Probably Jarret Gibson and Donald Hankins.

Omit saxes:

13211	I Want You Close To Me	Checker 1080, Chess LP 1509

From unknown sessions:

	Too Young To Die	Chess LP 1503
	Checkin' Up On My Baby	−
	Down Child	Checker 1134, Chess LP 1503
	Peach Tree	Chess LP 1503
	That's All I Want	−
	Too Old To think	−
	She's My Baby	Chess Lp 1509
	Somebody Help Me	−

Vcl/hca.

		Bremen, October 13, 1963
	Sonny Boy's Harmonica Boogie	Fontana681.510ZL

Add Otis Spann, pno; Matt Murphy, gtr; Willie Dixon bs; Billie Stepney, dms.

	I Don't Know	Fontana 681.510ZL

Vcl/hca. with Matt Murphy, gtr(-1)

		Copenhagen, November 1, 1963
	Don't Let Your Right Hand	Storyville SLP 158
	I Can't Understand	−
	Movin' Down The River	Storyville SLP 170
	The Lights Went Out	−
	The Sky Is Crying -1	Storyville SLP 158
	Coming Home To You Baby -1	−
	Gettin' Together -1	−
	Slowly Walk Close To Me -1	−
	Why Are You Crying -1	−
	Once Upon A Time -1	−
	Down And Out -1	Storyville SEP 415

Memphis Slim, pno. replaces Murphy:

	I Wonder Do I have A Friend	Storyville SLP 158
	Sonny Boy's Girlfriends	Storyville SLP 170
	Same Girl -1	–

Note: -1 Memphis Slim, vcl. also

Add Matt Murphy, gtr; Billie Stepney, dms. Omit Memphis Slim (-1)

	Little Girl	Storyville SLP 158
	I'm So Glad	–
	Chicago Bounce	–
	Movin' Out	–
	The Story Of Sonny Boy Williams -1	–
	On My Way Back Home -1	Storyville SLP 170

Vcl/hca. with gtr;   Copenhagen, November 1963

	Baby Let Me Come Back	Collector's Special 100
	November Boogie	–
	All Night Long	–
	Leavin' Blues	–

Vcl/hca. with Eric Clapton, Chris Dreja, gtrs; Paul Samwell-Smith, bs-gtr; Jim McCartney, dms; Vcl/hca. only (-1)   London, 1963

	Bye Bye Bird	Mercury MG 21071
	Mister Downchild	–
	Out On The Water Coast	–
	23 Hours Too Long	–
	Baby Don't Worry -1	–
	Pontiac Blues	Mercury Mg 21071
	Take It Easy Baby	–
	I Don't Care No More -1	–
	Do The Weston	–

Vcl/hca. with Memphis Slim, pno.   Paris, December 1, 1963

	The Skies Are Crying	Vogue 639-30
	Your Funeral And My Trial	–
	Explain Yourself To Me	–
	Nine Below Zero	–
	Fattening Frogs For Snakes	–
	My One Room Cabin	–
	Getting Out Of Town	–

Vcl/hca. with Hubert Sumlin, gtr;   Hamburg, October 9, 1964

	I'm Trying To Make London My Home	Fontana TL 5225

Add Sunnyland Slin, pno; Willie Dixon bs; Clifton James, dms.

	Dissatisfied	Fontana TL 5225

SONNY BOY WILLIAMSON

Vcl/hca. with pno; 2 gtrs; dms.   Shreveport, 1960

MS 146	Pretty Lil Thing	Ram 2501
MS 147	Mailman, Mailman	–

Note: This is neither of the two known Sonny Boy's, but a totally different artist.

OTIS SPANN

Born Jackson, Mississippi on 1931
Vcl/pno. with George Smith, hca(-1); poss. Robert Lockwood, Jr., gtr; Willie Dixon, bs;
Fred Below, dms.   Chicago, 1955

7738	It Must Have Been The Devil -1	Checker 807
7739	Five Spot	–

Note: Spann claims a fantastic peronnel for the above , but the artists listed are the only ones heard. Also according to Matrix listing, there could only have been these two sides cut at the session.

Vcl/pno. with Robert Lockwood Jr., vcl (-1)/gtr   New York City, 1960

	The Hard Way	Candid LP 8001
	Take A Little Walk With Me -1	

	Otis In The Dark	Candid LP 8001
	Little Boy Blue -1	—
	Country Boy	—
	Beat-Up Team	—
	My Daily Wish -1	—
	I Got Rambling On My Mind -1	—
	Worried Life Blues	—
	Great Northern Stomp	—

Vcl/pno. with J. T. Brown, ten; Sonny Boy Willimson, hca; Matt Murphy, gtr; Billie
Stepney, dms.   Chicago, September 21. 1963

	Skies Are Blue	Checker unissued
	My Baby Is Gone	—
	Love Is A Miracle	—
	No. No. No	—

Vcl/pno. with Sonny Boy Williamson, hca; Matt Murphy, gtr; Willie Dixon, bs; Billie
Stepney, dms.   Bremen, October 13, 1963

	Had My Fun	Fontana 681.510ZL

Vcl/pno. with Lonnie Johnson, gtr;(-1)   Copenhagen, October 16, 1963

	Good Morning Mr. Blues	Storyville SLP 157
	Love. Love, Love	—
	Riverside Blues	—
	Must Have Been The Devil	—
	Jelly Roll Baker	—
	Trouble In Mind -1	—
	Worried Life Blues	—
	T. B. Blues	—
	Spann's Boogie	—
	Don't You Know	—
	Goin' Down Slow	—
	The Skies Are Blues	Storyville SLP 168
	Keep Your Hand Out Of My Pocket	—
	Boots And Shoes	Storyville SLP 188

Vcl/pno. with Louis Miles, gtr; Willie Smith, dms,   Chicago, January 1964

	Lovin' Girl	One-Derful unissued
	The Name Of The Blues	—

Vcl/pno. with Muddy Waters (as "Brother"), gtr; Eric Clapton, gtr (-1) Ransom Knowling, bs;
Willie Smith, dms.   London May 4, 1964

DR.33230	Natural Days	Decca LK 4615
DR.33231	Meet Me In The Bottom	—
DR'33232	I Got A Feeling	—
DR.33234	Sarah Street	—
	Sarah Street (alt. take)	unissued
DR.32235	Jangleboogie	Decca LK 4615.
DR.33236	Nobody Knows	unissued
DR.33237	The Blues Don't Like Nobody	Decca LK 4615
DR.33238	T.99	—
DR.33239	My Home In The Desert	Ace Of Clubs ACL 1220
DR.33240	Mojo Rock'n' Roll	Decca LK 4681
DR.33241	Pretty Girls Everywhere -1	— ,Ace of Clubs ACL 1220
DR.33242	Country Boy	Ace Of Clubs ACL 1220
DR'33243	Spann's Boogie	Decca LK 4615
DR.33244	Stirs Me Up -1	Decca E 11972, LK 4681
DR.33245	I'd Rather Be The Devil	unissued
DR.'33246	I Came From Clarksdale	Decca LK 4615
DR.33247	Rock Me Mama	—
DR.33248	Get Out Of My Way	unissued
DR.33249	Lost Sheep In The Fold	Decca LK 4615
DR.33250	Keep Your Hand Out Of My Pocket	Decca F 11972
DR.33251	T.99	unissued
DR.39340	You're Gonna Need My Help	Ace OfClubs ACL 1220

Note: DR.33244, Jimmy Page, hca/gtr/bs-gtr dubbed on. DR.33250, Jimmy Page,
gtr dubbed on.

Vcl/pno. withJames Cotton, vcl(-1)/hca. James Madison, Muddy Waters, gtrs: Milton
Rector, bs-gtr; S. P. Leary, dms.   Chicago, c.February, 1965
          The Blues Never Die   Prestige PR 7391
          I Got A Feeling   –   , 348
          One More Mile To Go -1   –
          Feelin' Good -1   –
          After Awhile   –
          Dust My Broom -1   –
          Straighten Up Baby -1   –   , 348
          Come On   –
          Must Have Been The Devil   –
          Lightnin'   –
          I'm Ready -1   –

Vcl/pno.   Chicago, 1964
          Sad Day In Texas   Testament S-01

Vcl/pno. with Robert Whitehead, dms (-1)   Chicago, 1965
          Nobody Knows My Troubles   Testament T-2211
          Worried Life Blues   –
          You Can't Hide   –
          What's On Your Worried Mind   –
          Vicksburg Blues -1   –
          Spann's Boogie Woogie   –
          See See Rider   –
          One Room Country Shack   –
          Mr. Jelly Roll Baker   –

Vcl/pno./org(-1) with James Cotton, hca; Johnny Young, gtr; Jimmy Lee Morris, bs-gtr;
S. P. Leary, dms.   Chicago, November 22, 1965
          Get Your Hands Out Of My Pocket   Testament T-2211
          Sarah Street   –
          Jack Knife -1   –
          Who's Out There   –
          Lovin' You- 1   –

Vcl/pno. with S. P. Leary dms.   Chicago, 1966
          Marie   Vanguard VRS 9216
          Burning Fire   –
          S. P. Blues   –
          Sometimes I Wonder   –
          Spann's Stomp   –

     Note: Above may be from Testament sessions

Vcl/pno. with George Smith hca; Muddy Waters, Sammy Lawhord, Luther Johnson, gtrs;
Mac Arnold, bs-gtr; Francis Clay, dms.   New York City, August, 1966
          Popcorn Man   Bluesway BL-6003
          Brand New House   –
          Chicago Blues   –
          Steel Mill Blues   –
          Down On Sarah Street   –
          T'Ain't Nodbody's Biz-ness   –
          Nobody knows Chicago Like I Do   –
          My Home Is In The Delta   –
          Spann Blues   –

SPECKLED RED

Real name Rufus Perryman. Born Monroe, Louisiana in October 1892.
Vcl/pno.   St. Louis, September 2, 1956
1   Blues On My Brain   unissued
2   Wilkins Street Stomp   –
3   Cow Cow Blues   –
4   Blues On My Brain   –
5   Cow Cow Blues   Delmark DL 601 ?
6   Blues On My Brain   unissued
7   Fishtail Blues   –
8   Boogie Woogie   –

9	Shanty In Old Shanty Town	unissued
10	Right String But Wrong Yo Yo	Delmark DL 601
11	Baby Won't You Please Come Home	unissued
12	Dirty Dozens	Delmark DL 601
13	Talking Blues	unissued
14	Right String But Wrong Yo Yo	–
15	Jus Blues	
16	Highway 61 Blues	Delmark DL 601
17	Cuttin' For Kicks	unissued
18	After Dinner Blues	Delmark DL 601
19	Dad's Piece	Tone 1, Folk-Lyric FL 117
20	Wilkins Street Stomp	Delmark DL 601 ?
21	Oh Red	Tone 1, Folk-Lyric FL 117
22	Early In The Morning	– –
23	Blues On My Brain	Delmark DL 601 ?
24	If I Could Be With You	unissued
25	Oh Red	–
26	Red's Boogie Woogie	Delmark DL 601
27	It Feels So Good	unissued
Same:		St. Louis, November, 3 1956
28	Oh Red	unissued
29	Dirty Dozens	–
30	Fishtail Blues	–
31	Cow Cow Blues	–
32	Right String But The Wrong Yo Yo	–
33	Going Down Slow	–
34	Crying In My Sleep	–
35	Backwater Blues	–
36	Early In The Morning	–
37	Bugle Call Stomp	–
38 Wilkins	Wilkins Street Stomp	–
39	Milk Cow Blues	–
40	Just The Blues	–
41	Highway 61 Blues	–
42	After Dinner Blues	–
43	Ready For Anything Blues	–
44	Right String But The Wrong Yo Yo	–
45	Baby Won't You Please	–
46	Dirty Dozens	unissued
47	Talking Blues	–
48	Right String But The Wrong Yo Yo	–
49	Blues On My Brain (If You Ever Been Down)	–
50	Fishtail Blues	–
51	Boogie Woogie	–
52	Shanty In Old Shanty Town	–
53	Blues Warm Up	–
54	Wilkins Street Stomp	–
55	Cow Cow Blues	–
56	Speckled Red Blues	–
57	Cow Cow Blues	–
Same:		St. Louis, June 4, 1957
58	Dirty Dozens	unissued
59	Early In The Morning	–
60	Bugle Call Blues	–
61	Wilkins Street Stomp	–
62	Milk Cow Blues	–
63	Fishtail Blues	–
64	Cow Cow Blues	–
65	Right String But The Wrong Yo Yo	–
66	Going Down Slow	Delmark DL 601
67	Welfare Store Blues	unissued
68	Crying In My Sleep	Delmark DL 601
69	It Ain't No Good	unissued
70	Bugle Call Rag	–

71	Fishtail Blues	unissued
72	Wilkins Street Stomp	–
73	Dirty Dozens	–

Probably from the above sessions:
Vcl/pno.

| | Blues On My Brain | Euphonic 1204 |
| | All On Account Of You | – |

Vcl/pno.   London, 1960

	T'Ain't Nobody's Bizness If I Do	VJM VEP 26
	Oh Red	–
	Caldonia	–
	Early In The Morning	–

Vcl/pno.   Copenhagen, July 19, 1960

	Cow Cow Blues	Folkways FG 3555
	Tain't Nobody's Bizness	–
	How Long Blues	–
	Uncle Sam's Blues	–
	It Feels So Good	–
	If I Could Be With You	–
	If I Had A Million Dollars	–
	Why Don't You Practice	–
	You Ain't No Good	–
	Pinetop's Boogie Woogie	–
	I've Got A Feeling	–
	Baby Won't You Please Come Home	–
	Early In The Morning	Storyville SLP 117
	Dirty Dozens	–
	I've Had My Fun	–
	St. Louis Stomp	–
	Red's Own Blues	–
	I've Got The Right String	–
	Little Girl	–
	Oh Red	–
	Milk Cow Blues	–
	Dad's Piece	–
	Four O'Clock Blues	–
	Caldonia	–
	Talking	–

BIG BOY SPIRES

Real name Arthur Spires. Born Yazoo City, Mississippi in 1912.
Vcl/gtr. with Earl Dranes, Eddie Ell, gtrs; Willie Smith, dms.   Chicago, 1952

| C 1016 | One Of These Days | Checker 752 |
| C 1017 | Murmur Low | – |

BIG BOY SPIRES & HIS TRIO

Vcl/gtr. with John Lee Henley, hca; Johnny Williams, gtr; Johnny "Ted"?, dms.
Chicago, 1953

U 5000	About To Lose My Mind	Chance 1137
U 5001	Which One Do I Love	–
U 5002	Someday Little Darling	unissued
U 5003	My Baby Left Me	unissued
U 5004	Rhythm Rockers	unissued
U 5005	Tired Of Being Mistreated	unissued

Vcl/gtr. with Johnny Young, gtr.   Chicago, October 9, 1965

1	Twenty-One Below Zero	Storyville SLP 180
2	Evening Sun	unissued
3	What Did It	unissued
4	What About You	unissued
5	Stormy Night Blues	unissued
6	51 Highway Blues	unissued
7	Right Away	unissued

Water Coast Blues   unissued
              Note: Above recorded by Pete Welding.

HORACE SPROTT

Vcl/hca. with group vcl(-1)   Cahaba River. Ala. April 10, 1954
              Fox Chase   Folkways FP 654
              Take Rocks And Grave (To) Make A Solid
                           Road (Railroad Blues) -1   −
Vcl.
              Take This Hammer   Folkways FP 653
              Shine On, Rising Sun   −
Hca.
              Freight Train "The Southern"   Folkways FP 653
Vcl. with Marshall Ford, vcl. interjections.
              Smoke Like Lightening   Folkways FP 651
Hca. with Phillip Ramsey, gtr;   Dobine Creek, Ala, April 17, 1954
              Saturday Night Hoe-Down   Folkways FP 654
Vcl.   Huff Cabin, Ala, April 17, 1954
              Early One Morning, The Blues Come Falling
                           Down   Folkways FP 651
Vcl. with Bessie Ford, vcl(-1)   Marion, Ala. April 21, 1954
              Ain't This A Mean World   Folkways FP 651
              Oh, Glad, Oh, Free   −
Vcl. with Nellie Hastings, vcl.
              My Hoe Leadin' My Row   Folkways FP 651
Vcl.   Perry Co., Ala, c. April 1954.
              Luke And Mullen   Folkways FP 651
              Louisiana Blues   Folkways FP 652
              Say You Don't Know, Honey   −
              One Dollar Bill, Two Dollar Bill   −
              Baby, If I Don't Get Lucky Time   Folkways FP 653
              Black Snake Blues   −
              My Little Annie, So Sweet   Folkways FA 1659
Hca.
              The Frisco   Folkways FA 1659
Hca.   Sprott, Ala. c. April 1954
              The Hunt/Hunt Horn   Folkways FA 2659
Dancing with handclaps.   Cahaba River, Ala. May 8, 1954
              Buck Dance   Folkways FP 653
              See also Phillip Ramsey and Harry Rutledge.

ST. LOUIS JIMMY

Real name James Oden. Born Nashville, Tennessee on June 26, 1905
Vcl. with Roosevelt Sykes, pno; Ted Summit, gtr; Arman "Jump" Jackson, dms.
                                                   Chicago, December 14, 1944

D4-AB-
320-1   Strange Woman Blues   Bluebird 34-0727
D4-AB-
321-1   One More Break   −
D4-AB-
322-1   My Story Blues   unissued
D4-AB-
323-1   Bad Condition   Victor 20-2650

POOR BOY
Vcl. with Roosevelt Sykes, pno.   Chicago, 1945
QB 3352   New Going Down Slow   Black & White 106
              (rev. by Alton Redd)

ST. LOUIS JIMMY

Vcl. with J. T. Brown, alt; Roosevelt Sykes, pno; Willie Dixon, bs.

Chicago, October 18, 1945

D5-AB-0392	Mother's Day	unissued
D5-AB-0393	Trouble In The Land	unissued
D5-AB-0394	Dog House Blues	Victor 20-2650
D5-AB-0395	Make Up Your Mind	unissued

Vcl. with
Chicago, c.1946

UN 104, K 5053	Going Down Slow	unissued
UN 108, 5054	Together We Go	unissued

Vcl. with Roosevelt Sykes, pno; gtr; bs.
Chicago, 1947

UB 2765B	I Ain't Done Nothing Wrong	Bullet 270
UB 2768B	Going Down Slow	—
no mx	My Trouble	Bullet 278
no mx	Sittin' And Thinkin'	—
no mx	Now I'm Through	Bullet 291
no mx	Mr. Brown Boogie	—

> Note: UB 2765B has also been shown as UB 2766B. It has been suggested that the Bullet sides are actually by Walter Davis but this is not borne out by aural evidence.

Vcl. with Eddie Chamblee, ten; Roosevelt Sykes, pno; gtr; bs; dms.

Chicago, 1948

UB 9242	Biscuit Roller	Miracle 134
UB 9243	I'm Sorry Now	—

Vcl. with Muddy Waters & His Blues Combo; Oliver Alcorn, ten; Sunnyland Slim, pno; Muddy Waters, gtr; Ernest Crawford, bs.

UB 9290A	Florida Hurricane	Aristocrat 7001
UB 9293A	So Nice And Kind	—

Vcl. with Sunnyland Slim's Orch: Sunnyland Slim, pno;
Chicago, 1949

2572-1	Shame On You Baby	Mercury 8137
2573-1	I'll Never Be Satisfied	—

Vcl. with Sunnyland Slim, pno; Sam Casimir, gtr; Andrew?, bs;

Chicago, August 26, 1949

UB9-1032, R 1379	Mother's Day	JOB 101, Apollo 420
UB9-1033 R 1380	Jack L. Cooper Chicago Woman Blues	Apollo 420

Vcl. with Sunnyland Slim, pno; gtr; bs.
Chicago, 1951

	Tryin' To Change My Ways	Savoy MG 16000

Vcl. with pno; gtr; bs.
1953

H 1018	Hard Luck Boogie	Herald 407
H 1019	Good Book Blues	—

Vcl. with ten; Roosevelt Sykes, pno; gtr; bs; dms.
Chicago, 1953

HY40CF	Coming Up Fast	Opera OP-4
HY43DR	One Doggone Reason	—

Same:

ACA 2391	Drinkin' Woman	Duke 110
ACA 2392	Why Work	—

Vcl. with Red Saunders Band: brass; pno; gtr; bs;; Red Saunders, dms.

Chicago, 1955

B 823	Goin' Down Slow	Parrot 823
B 824	Murder In The First Degree	—

Vcl. with Robert Banks, pno; Jimmie Lee, gtr(-1); Leonard Gaskin, bs; Belton Evans, dms;
New York, November 19, 1960

	Poor Boy	Bluesville BVLP 1028
	Nothin' But The Blues	—

304

	Mother's Day	Bluesville BVLP 1028
	Some Sweet Day -1	—
	Dog House Blues -1	—
	My Heart Is Loaded With Trouble	—
	I'm Saint Louis Bound	—
	Goin' Down Slow	—
	Sweet As She Can Be	—
	Monkey Faced Woman	—

Vcl. with Roosevelt Sykes, pno
Chicago,

	Save Me A Drink	unissued
	The Girl I Love	unissued
	Poor Boy	unissued

Note: Recorded by Jump Jackson.

Vcl. with Roosevelt Sykes or Sunnyland Slim, pno; Homesick James, gtr/bs-gtr; (-1)
Chicago, May 17, 1963

	Complete This Order	Delmark rejected
	Monkey Faced Blues	—
	Resolution Blues	Delmark rejected
	Evil Ways	—
	Soon Forgotten -1	—
	Going Down Slow -1	—

Note: Bob Koester cannot recall which pianist played on which titles. Homesick James was playing a double-necked guitar.

Vcl. with Homesick James, Evans Spencer, gtrs; Washboard Sam, wbd; Willie Dixon, vcl. on Choruses (-1).
Chicago, March 25, 1964

178	Going Down Slow	unissued
179	Going Down Slow	Spivey LP 1003
180	Goody Goody Goody -1	unissued
181	Goody Goody Goody -1	Spivey LP 1003

ST. LOUIS MAC

See under Little Mac

JAMES STEWART (The Harmonica Cat)

Vcl(-1)/hca. with James Freeman, ten; Lewis Dervis, Vcl(-2)/gtr. Bill Parker dms.
Lake Charles, La. 1954

A	Sweet Woman -1	Folk Star 1192
B	Lover Blues -2	—

WILLIAM STEWART

Vcl/gtr.
Memphis c. 1953

no mx	I'm Going To Leave Here Walkin'	Sun test
no mx	Blues All Around My Bed	—

Note: Numbers shown on labels are TB 1030, 1040, 230

ARBEE STIDHAM (see also in APPENDIX)

Vcl. with Oett "Sax" Mallard, alt; Bill Casimir, ten; Bob Call, pno; Tampa Red, gtr; Ransom Knowling, bs; Judge Ruley, dms.
Chicago, September 18 1947

D7-VB-1032	In Love With You	Victor 20-2767
D7-VB 1033	I Found Out For Myself	Victor 20-2572, 20/47-4951, 50-0003
D7-VB-1034	I Don't Know How To Cry	Victor 20-2767
D7-VB-1035	My Heart Belongs To You	Victor 20-2572, 20/47-4951, 50-0003, Camden CAL 740

Vcl. with Lucky Millinder's Orchestra: Frank Galbreath, tpt; Tab Smith, Alt; Harold Clark, Hal Singer, tens; Sir Charles Thompson, pno; Mundell Lowe, gtr; H. Holmes, bs; G. Stanton, dms.
New York, December 21, 1948

D8-VB-4097	Your Heart Belongs To Me	Victor 22-0000
D8-VB-4098	Sitdham Jumps	—

| D8-VB-4099 | I Can't Explain My Love | unissued |
| D8-VB-4100 | unknown title | unissued |

Vcl. with Ellis "Stumpy" Whitlock, tpt; Oett "Sax" Mallard, alt; Eddie "Sugarman" Penigar, ten;
Bob Call, pno; Willi Lacey, gtr; Ransom Knowling, bs; Judge Riley, dms.

		Chicago, March 10, 1949
D9-VB-426	What The Blues Will Dow	Victor 22-0040, 50-0024
D9-VB-435	A Heart Full Of Misery	Victor 22-0018
D9-VB-436	Falling Blues	Victor 22-0040, 50-0024
D9-VB-437	You'll Be Sorry	Victor 22-0101, 50-0101
D9-VB-438	I've Got So Many Worries	Victor 22-0018

Calvin Ladner, tpt. replaces Whitlock:		Chicago, July 19, 1949
D9-VB-1135	So Tired Of Dreaming	Victor 22/50-0101
D0-VB-1136	Send My Regrets	Victor 22-0053, 50-0037
D9-VB-1137	Marcia	unissued
D9-VB-1138	Barbecue Lounge	Victor 22-0053, 50-0037

Vcl. with Ellis "Stumpy" Whitlock, tpt; Nat Jones, alt; Cyril "Cozy" Eggleston, ten; Bob Call,
pno; Willie Lacey, gtr; Ransom Knowling, bs; Judge Riley, dms.

		Chicago, March 21, 1950
EO-VB-3415	Feel Like I'm Losing You	Victor 20/50-0093
EO-VB-3416	Let My Dreams Come True	Victor 20/50-0083
EO-VB-3417	Squeeze Me Baby	Victor 20/50-0093
EO-VB-3418	Any Time Ring My Bell	Victor 20/50-0083

Vcl. with John Peck, tpt; Jesse "J. J." Jones, ten; Calvin Jones, pno; bs; dms.

		Chicago, 1951
2296	Nothing Seems Right	SIW 596
2299	Sixty Minutes To Wait	−

Same:		
2343	Feelin' Blue And Low	SIW 606, Time LP 2
2344	I've Got News For You Baby	−
2345	Bad Dreams Blues	SIW 617
2346	Why Did I Fall In Love With You	−

From above sessions:		
	I'm In The Mood	Time LP 2
	I Want To Rock	Time LP 4
	Feeling Blues And Low	−

Note: Last title is not same as 2343

Vcl. with Lefty Bates Band: ten; pno; Lefty Bates, gtr; bs; dms.

| 1634 | Look Me Straight In The Eye | States 164 |
| 1635 | I Stayed Away Too Long | − |

Vcl. with Andrew "Goon" Gardner, alt; Tommy "Madman" Jones, ten; Eddie Ware, pno;
Ransom Knowling, bs; Judge Riley, dms. Chicago, 1952

| C 1018 | Someone To Tell My Troubles To | Checker 751 |
| C 1019 | Mr. Commissioner | − |

Same:		
U 4367	Don't Set Your Cap For Me	Checker 778
U 4368	I Don't Play	−

Vcl. with		Chicago, 1956
3061	I'll Always Remember	Abco 100
3062	Meet Me Halfway	−

Vcl. with 2 hca. pno; gtr; dms.		
U 3207	When I Find My Baby	Abco 107
U 3208	Please Let It Be Me	−

Vcl/gtr. with King Curtis, tne; John Wright, pno; Leonard Gaskin, bs; Armand "Jump" Jackson, dms

		New York City 1960
	Last Goodbye Blues	Bluesville BVLP 1021
	You Can't Live In This World By Yourself	−
	Pawnshop	−
	I'm Tires Of Wandering	−
	I Want To Belong To You	−
	Wee Baby Blues	−

	You Keep Me Yearning	Bluesville BVLP 1021
	My Heart Will Always Belong To You	–
	People What Would You Do	–
	Teenage Kiss	–

Vcl/gtr. with Memphis Slim, pno/org; Armand "Jump" Jackson, dms.

New York City, 1960

	Good Morning Blues	Folkways FS 3824
	Falling Blues	–
	Blue And Low	–
	Misery Blues	–
	My Baby Left Me	–
	In The Evening	–
	Walking Blues	–
	I've Got To Forget You	–
	Standing In The Corner	–
	Careless Love	–
	Tell Me Mama	–

Vcl/gtr. with Jazz Gillum, hca; Memphis Slim, org.

New York City, 1961

	I Wonder Why	Folkways FS 3826, Aravel 1004
	You've Got To Reap Just What You Sow	–
	Let It Be Me	– , Aravel 1004
	I'll Always Remember You	–
	You've Got To Meet Me Half-Way)no hca)	–

Note: See also Memphis Slim

LUTHER STONEHAM

Born Walker County, Texas in 1913
Vcl/gtr.   Houston, 1951
9007   Sittin' And Wonderin'   Mercury 8275
9008   January 11, 1947 Blues   –

Note: See also Thunder Smith.

STORMY HERMAN & HIS MIDNIGHT RAMBLERS

Vcl/hca. with pno; gtr; bs; dms.   Los Angeles, 1955
A   The Jitterbug   Dooto 358
B   Bad Luck   –

BABE STOVALL

Born Tylertown, Mississippi on October 14, 1907
Vcl/gtr. with Gooson Phillips, bjo; Sylvester Handy, bs.   New Orleans, 1965
	I'm Gwine To New Orleans	Verve VPM 1
	Good Morning Blues	–
	Time Is Winding Up	–
	Salty Dog	–
	Corrine Corinne	–
	Careless Love	–
	Coal Black Mare	–
	Woman Blues	–
	If I Could Hear My Mother Pray	–

LEON STRICKLAND

Vcl/gtr. with Leslie Anders, gtr; Lucius Bridges, wbd.   Baton Rouge, 1960
| | I Won't Be Your Lowdown Dog No More | Folk-Lyric FL-111 |

SUGARCANE & HIS VIOLIN

Real name Don Harris
Vcl/vln. with saxes; pno; prob. Dewey Terry, gtr; bs; dms.   Los Angeles, c. 1961
35710   They Say You Never Can Miss   Eldo 103

| 35710x | Elim Stole My Baby (Boo Hoo) | Eldo 103 |
| | | |

Note: Also recorded as part of the Don & Dewey duo.

THE SUGARMAN

Vcl/gtr. with bs.   Houston? 1951
| 2364 | Which Woman Do I Love | SIW 609 |
| 2365 | She's Gone With The Wind | – |

DOUG SUGGS

Pno.   Chicago, 1956
| | Doug's Jump | Tone LP I, Folk Lyric LP117 |
| | Weet Patootie | – |

HUBERT SUMLIN

Born Greenwood, Mississippi on November 16, 1931
Gtr. with Sunnyland, Slim, pno; Willie Dixon, bs; Clifton James, dms.

Hamburg, October 9, 1964
| | No Title Boogie | Fontana TL 5225 |

Vcl(-1)/gtr.   East Berlin, November 1, 1964
	Love You, Woman -1	Amiga 8 50 043
	When I Feel Better	–
	I Love -1	–
	Hubert's Blues	–

Gtr. with Neil Slaven, gtr (-1)   Kenley, November 29, 1964
BH/VER-
| 100 | Across The Board -1 | Blue Horizon 1000 |
BH/VER-
| 101 | Sumlin Boogie | – |
| BH-102 | Hubert's Racket -1 | unissued |

SUNNYLAND SLIM (see also in APPENDIX)

Real name Albert Luandrew. Born Lambert, Mississippi on September 5, 1907

DOCTOR CLAYTON'S BUDDY
Vcl. with Blind John Davis, pno; Big Bill Broonzy, gtr; Ransom Knowling, bs; Judge Riley, dms.

Chicago, December 10, 1947
D7-VB-2362	Farewell Little Girl	Victor 20-3235
D7-VB-2363	Broke And Hungry	Victor 20-3085
D7-VB-2364	Illinois Central	Victor 20-2733
D7-VB-2365	Nappy Head Woman	Victor 20-2954

Same: Chicago, December 31, 1947
D7-VB-2390	Across The Hall Blues	Victor 20-3085
D7-VB-2391	Walking With The Blues	Victor 20-3255
D7-VB-2392	Sweet Lucy Blues	Victor 20-2733
D7-VB-2393	No Whiskey Blues	Victor 20-2954

SUNNYLAND SLIM & MUDDY WATER
Vcl/pno. with Muddy Waters, gtr; Big Crawford, bs.   Chicago, 1947
| U 7056 | Johnson Machine Gun | Aristocrat 1301 |
| U 7057 | Fly Right, Little Girl | – |

SUNNYLAND SLIM & MUDDY WATERS' COMBO
As above, but add Alex Atkins, atl: Chicago, 1948
| U 7110 | She Ain't Nowhere | Aristocrat 1304 |
| U 7111 | My Baby, My Baby | – |

SUNNYLAND SLIM & HIS SUNNYLAND BOYS
Floyd Jones, vcl/gtr. Sunnyland Slim, pno; Leroy Foster, dms.

Chicago, 1948
| A | Hard Times | Tempo Tone 1001 |
| B | School Days | – |

SUNNYLAND SLIM & MUDDY WATERS

As last, but add Little Walter, vcl/hca. Ensemble vcl(-1):

A	Blue Baby	Tempo Tone 1002
B	I Want My Baby -1	

SUNNYLAND SLIM & HIS SUNNY BOYS

Vcl/pno. with Lonnie Johnson, gtr; Andrew Hare, bs.   Chicago, 1949

UB 21608	Jivin' Boogie	Hytone 32
UB 21609	Brown Skin Woman	–
UB 21610	My Heavy Load	Hytone 33/34
UB 21611	Keep Your Hands Out Of My Money	–
UB 21612	Miss Bessie Mae	Hytone 33
UB 21612	The Devil Is A Busy Man	–

Note: Duplicate matrices and issue numbers noted for above session.

No details:

U 1226	5 Foot 4 Gal	Hytone 37
U 1227		
U 1231/2	by Pettie Wheatstraw's Buddy, q.v.	
U 1235	I've Done You Wrong	Hytone 37

Vcl/pno. with ten; Robert Lockwood Jr., gtr; bs.   Chicago, 1949

2574-1	Mud Kicking Woman	Mercury 8132
2575-1	Everytime I Got To Drinking	–

SUNNYLAND SLIM & HIS TRIO

Vcl/pno. with Sam Casimir, gtr; bs.   Chicago, c. March 1950

	Bad Times	Apollo 416
	I'm Just A Lonesome Man	–

Vcl/pno. with Robert Lockwood Jr., gtr; Moody Jones, bs.   Chicago, 1950

JB-32783	Down Home Child	JOB 102
JB-32784	Sunny Land Special	–

Vcl/pno. with Snooky Pryor, hca; Leroy Foster, gtr.   Chicago, 1950

EO-CB-4504 SS1A	Back To Korea Blues	Sunny 101
EO-CB-4505 SS1B	It's All Over Now	–

Vcl/pno. with ten; gtr; bs; dms.   1951

R 1513	Orphan Boy Blues	Regal 3327, Savoy MG 16000
R 1514A	When I Was Young	–

Vcl/pno. with Robert Lockwood, Jr., gtr; bs; dms.   Chicago, November 1951

4629	Ain't Nothing But A Child	Mercury 8277
4630	Brown Skinned Woman	–
4631	Hit The Road Again	Mercury 8264
4632	Gin Drinkin' Baby	–

SUNNYLAND TRIO

Vcl/pno. with Billy Howell, tpt(-1); Robert Lockwood Jr., gtr; bs.

Chicago, 1952

MRS 35226	Leaving Your Town	JOB 1003
MRS 35227	Mary Lee -1	–

DELTA JOE

Vcl/pno. with Leroy Foster, gtr;   Chicago, 1953

OP8A	Roll, Tumble And Slip	Opera OP-5
OP8B	Train Time	–
U 2121	4 O'Clock Blues	Chance 1115
U 2122	I Cried	–

Vcl/pno. with J. T. Brown, ten; J. B. Lenoir, gtr; bs; Alfred Wallace, dms.

Chicago, 1953

U 2323	When I Was Young	Constellation CS-6
U 2324	Bassology	–
U 2325	Worried About My Baby	–
U 2326	Living In The White House	–
U 2327	Please Don't	–

Vcl/pno. with Walter Horton, hca; Eddie Taylor, gtr.		Chicago, 1954
BL 54-109	Going Back To Memphis	Blue Lake 105, Blues Classics 15
BL 54-110	Devil Is A Busy Man	–
Add Big Crawford, bs/maraccas:		
BL 54-115	Shake It Baby	Blue Lake 107
BL 54-116	Bassology	–

Vcl/pno. with Snooky Pryor, hca; Floyd Jones or Eddie Taylor, gtr; Alfred Wallace, dms.

		Chicago, February 3, 1954
54-132	Troubles Of My Own	Vee Jay unissued
54-133	Worried About My Baby	–
54-134	I Done You Wrong	–
54-135	Be My Baby	–

SUNNYLAND SLIM & HIS BOYS
Vcl/pno. with Ernest Cotton, ten; Little Pete, gtr; Big Crawford, bs/maraccas; Alfred Wallace, dms.

1009A	Shake It Baby	JOB 1105
U-1016	Woman Trouble (Overnite)	– , 1011

Note: JOB 1011 issued as by John Brim who sings the reverse.

SUNNYLAND SLIM & HIS PLAYBOYS
Vcl/pno. with Ernest Cotton, ten; Robert Lockwood Jr. gtr(-1); Prince Candy, gtr(-2); bs; Alfred Wallace, dms.

JOB 2900	Four Day Bounce -2	JOB 1108
JOB 3001	That Woman -1	–

SUNNYLAND SLIM WITH LEFTY BATES COMBO
Vcl/pno. with Red Holloway, ten; Louis Miles, Lefty Bates, gtrs; bs; dms.

		Chicago, 1955
M 5003	Be Mine Alone	Club 51 C-106
M 5004	Sad And Lonesome	–

Vcl/pno. with Walter Horton, hca; Jimmy Rogers, gtr; Poor Bob Woodfork, bs-gtr; Willie Dixon bs; S. P. Leary, dms.

		Chicago, 1956
C-1000	It's You Baby	Cobra 5006
C-1001	Highway 51	–

Vcl/pno. with Corky Robertson, bs; Jump Jackson dms. Vcl with Little Brother Montgomery, pno (-1).

		Chicago, July 14, 1960
	One Room Country Shack	"77" La 12/21
	Brownskin Woman	–
	I Got The Blues About My Baby	–
	Devil Is A Busy Man	–
	La Salle Street Boogie	–
	Prison Bound - 1	–
	That's Why I Keep Drinkin' -1	"77" LA 12/21

Vcl./pno. with Gilbert Potter, Oett "Sax" Mallard, tens; Robert Lockwood, Jr., gtr; Lee Jackson, bs-gtr; Jump Jackson, dms.

		Chicago, 1961
A	Worried About My Baby	Miss 117
B	Drinking And Clowning	–

Vcl/pno. with King Curtis, ten; Robert Banks, org; Leonard Gaskin, bs; Belton Evans, dms.

		Newark, N. J. November 1960
	I'm Prison Bound (no ten)	Bluesville BVLP 1016, 816
	Slim's Shout	–
	The Devil Is A Busy Man	–
	Brownskin Woman	–
	Shake It	– , 816
	Decoration Day	–
	Baby How Long	– , 811
	Sunnyland Special	–
	Harlem Can't Be Heaven (no ten)	–
	It's You Baby	– , 811

Vcl/pno. with Homesick James Williamson, gtr/bs-gtr.

		Chicago, May 17, 1963
	Everytime I Get To Drinking	Delmark unissued
	Poor Boy	–
	Depression Blues	–
	I Done Wrong	–

Vcl/org. with Homesick James, Evans Spencer, gtrs; Washboard Sam, wbd.

Chicago, March 26, 1964

193	Won't Dp That No More	unissued
194	Won't Do That No More	Spivey LP 1003
195	Won't Do That No More	unissued;
196	Drinking	Spivey LP 1003
197	untitled organ instrumental	unissued

Vcl/pno. with Hubert Sumlin, gtr; Willie Dixon, bs; Clifton James, dms.

Hamburg, October 9, 1964

	Everytime I Get To Drinking	Fontana TL 5225

Vcl/pno.

Copenhagen, October 1964

Prison Bound Blues	Storyville SLP 169
Johnson Machine Gun	—
Miss Ida B	—
Sad And Lonesome Blues	—
That's Alright	—
Anna Lou Blues	—
I Done You Wrong	—
It's You Baby	—
Tin Pan Alley	—
Brown Skin Woman	—
You're The One	—
Goin' Down Slow	Storyville SLP 169
Woman Trouble Blues	Storyville SLP 168
Sittin' Here Thinkin'	—
One Room Country Shack	Storyville SLP 188

Vcl/pno. with Hubert Sumlin, gtr; Willie Dixon, bs; Clifton James, dms.

East Berlin, November 1, 1964

It's You, My Baby	Amiga 8 50 043
Everytime I Get To Drinking	—
We Gonna Jump	—
Too Late For Me To Pray	—

Omit Sumlin and James:

Leavy Camp Moan (sic)	Amiga 8 50 043

ROOSEVELT SYKES

Born Helena, Arkansas on January 31, 1901.

ROOSEVELT SYKES AND HIS PIANO
Vcl/pno. with Ted Summitt, gtr; Armand "Jump" Jackson, dms.

Chicago, December 15, 1944

D4-AB-344	Honeysuckle Rose	Bluebird 34-0729
D4-AB-345	Mellow Queen	Bluebird 34-0721
D4-AB-346	Jivin' The Jive	Bluebird 34-0729
D4-AB-347	I Wonder	Bluebird 34-0721

ROOSEVELT SYKES TRIO or
"THE HONEYDRIPPER" (Roosevelt Sykes)
Vcl/pno. with J. T. Brown, ten(-1); bs

Chicago, 1945

		Cincinnati 3500
QB 3349-1A	I Wonder -1	Black & White 100
QB 3350-1A	Tender Hearted Woman	Cincinnati 3500
		Black & White 100
QB 3351	This Tavern Boogie	

Vcl./pno. with J. T. Brown, alt; Willie Lacey, gtr; Armand "Jump" Jackson, dms.

Chicago, July 2, 1945

D5-AB-342	I'm In This Mess For You	unissued
D5-AB-343	Don't Push Me Around	Victor 20-2534
D5-AB-344	Little Sam	Bluebird 34-0745
D5-AB-345	Anytime Is The Right Time	

Vcl/pno. with J. T. Brown ten; Johnny Walker, clt; John Frazier, bs; Charles Saunders, dms.

Chicago, October 9, 1945

D5-AB-386	The Honeydripper	Bluebird 34-0737
D5-AB-387	Dare Bait	Victor 20-2051

| D5-AB-388 | High Price Blues | Bluebird 34-0737 |
| D5-AB-389 | Peeping Tom | Victor 20-2201 |

Vcl/pno. with Johnny Morton, tpt; Oett "Sax" Mallard, alt; Leon Washington, ten; Leonard Caston, gtr; Alfred Elkins, bs; Armand "Jump" Jackson, dms.

Chicago, February 18, 1946

D6-VB-1822	That's My Gal	Victor 20-1906
D6-VB-1823	Tonight	Victor 20-2051
D6-VB-1824	Living In A Different World	Victor 20-3315
D6-VB-1825	Sunny Road	Victor 20-1906

Vcl/pno. with Johnny Morton, tpt; Oett "Sax" 'allard, alt; Bill Casimir, ten; Sam Casimir, gtr; Ernest "Big" Crawford, bs; Armand "jump" Jackson dms.

Chicago, August 23, 1946

D6-VB-1935	Her Little Machine	unissued
D6-VB-1936	Flames Of Jive	Victor 20-2382
D6-VB-1937	Sneakin' And Dodgin'	Victor 20-3176
D6-VB-1938	Bop De Bip	Victor 20-2382

Vcl/pno. with Lucius Henderson, tpt; Martin Rough, Calmes Julian, saxes; Leonard Caston, gtr; Curtis Ferguson, bs; Heywood Cowan, dms.   Chicago, February 5, 1947

D7-VB-308	Bobby Sox Blues	Victor 20-2201
D7-VB-309	Kilroy's In Town	Victor 20-2534
D7-VB-310	BVD Blues	Victor 20-2658
D7-VB-311	I'm Her Honeydripper	–

Vcl/pno. with Johnny Morton, tpt; Oett "Sax" Mallard, alt; Bill Casimir, ten; Sam Casimir, gtr; Ernest "big" Crawford, bs; W. B. Nelson, dms.   Chicago, October 15, 1947

D7-VB-1070	Mama, Mama	Victor 20-3176
D7-VB-1071	I Got Eyes For You	unissued
D7-VB-1072	Doodle Rag	unissued
D7-VB-1073	Walkin' And Drinkin'	Victor 22-0011

Vcl/pno. with Johnny Morton, tpt; Oett "Sax" Mallard, alt; Walker Broadus, ten; Bill Casimir, ten; Emmanuel Sayles, gt; Ransom Knowling, bs; Judge Riley, dms. Omit tpt (-1)

Chicago, November 18, 1947

D7-VB-1169	Heavy Hearted Blues	unissued
D7-VB-1170	Boogie Honky Tonk	Victor 20-2902
D7-VB-1171	Roose Blues	–
D7-VB-1172	Time Wasted On You	Victor 20-3014
D7-VB-1173	What Is Your Aim Today -1	unissued
D7-VB-1174	Until The Cows Come Home -1	Victor 20-3315
D7-VB-1175	High As A Georgia Pine -1	Victor 20-3014
D7-VB-1176	I Know How You Feel -1	Victor 22-0041, 50-0025

Vcl/pno. with   Chicago, 1947

| | Candy Man Blues | Bullet 319 |
| | Why Should I Cry | – |

Vcl/pno. with gtr; bs; dms.   Chicago, December 30, 1948

D8-VB-3266	He's Just A Gravy Train	Victor 22-0011
D8-VB-3267	Southern Blues	Victor 22-0056
D8-VB-3268	Stop Her Poppa	Victor 22-0041, 50-0025

Vcl/pno. with Willie Lacey, gtr; J. C. Bell, bs; P. F. Thomas, dms.

Chicago, October 28, 1949

D9-VB-2003	How Am I To Know	unissued
D9-VB-2004	My Baby Is Gone	Victor 22-0056
D9-VB-2005	Mind Your Own Business	unissued
D9-VB-2006	All My Money Gone	unissued

Vcl/pno. with Armand "Jump" Jackson, dms.   Chicago, 1949

R 1224	Drivin' Wheel	Regal 3286
R 1225	Rock It	Regal 3269
R 1226	West Helena Blues	Regal 3286, Blues Classics 15
R 1227	Mailbox Blues	Regal 3306
R 1228	Wintertime Blues	
R 1229	Blues 'n' Boogie	Regal 3269

Add ten:

| R 1501 | Green Onion Top | Regal 3324 |
| R 1502 | Wonderin' Blues | – |

ROOSEVELT SYKES AND THE HONEYDRIPPERS

Vcl/pno. with Oett "Sax" Mallard, Robert "Sax" Crowder, saxes; gtr; Ernest "Big" Crawofrd, bs; Armand "Jump" Jackson, dms. Chicago, 1951/4

U 1001	Fine And Brown	United 101
U 1002	Lucky Blues	–
U 1003	Raining In My Heart	United 120
U 1004	Heavy Heart	–

Saxes out, Add vln(-1);

U 1126	Walkin' This Boogie	United 129
U 1129	Four O'Clock Blues -1	United 139
U 1131		
U 1132	Security Blues	United 129

Add ten (-1);

U 1290	Come Back Baby	United 152
U 1291		
U 1292		
U 1293	Tell Me True -1	United 152

Vcl/pno. with gtr; bs; dms. New Orleans, 1954

IM 833	You Can't Be Lucky All The Time	unissued
IM 834	Sweet Old Chicago	Imperial 5347
IM 835	Jail Bait	unissued
IM 836	Blood Stains	Imperial 5347

Same:

IM 914	Hush Oh Hush	Imperial 5367
IM 915	Cannon Ball	unissued
IM 916	I'm Tired	unissued
Im 917	Crazy Fox	Imperial 5367

Vcl/pno. with gtr; bs; dms; ten Memphis 1957

| 1006A | She's Jail Bait | House of Sound 505 |
| 1006B | Sputnick | – |

Vcl/pno. with Clarence Perry Jr., ten(-1); Frank Ingalls, Floyd Ball, gtrs; Armand "Jump" Jackson, dms. Vcl/pno. only (-2) New Yotk City, 1960

	Drivin' Wheel -1	Bluesville NVLP 1006
	Long Lonesome Night	–
	Set The Meat Outdoors -1	–
	Coming Home -1	–
	Stompin' The Boogie	–
	Number Nine -1	–
	Calcutta -1	–
	Selfish Woman -2	–
	Hangover (omit 1 gtr)	–
	Night Time Is The Right Time -1	–
	Runnin' The Boogie -1	–
	Hey Big Momma -1	–

Vcl/pno. with King Curtis, ten; Robert Banks, org (-1); Leonard Ga.kin, bs; Belton Evans. dms. Omit ten(-2) New York, Novembr 1960

	Miss Ida B	Bluesville BVLP 1014, 810
	Satellite Baby -1	–
	Mislead Mother -1	–
	Yes Lawd -1	–
	I Hate To Be Alone -1	–
	Jailbait -1	–
	Lonely Day -2	–
	Pocketful Of Money -1	–
	She Ain't For Nobody -1, 2	–

Vcl/pno. with Don Lawson, dms. London, January 21, 1961

	Monte Carlo Blues	Columbia 33SX 1343
	Pretty Woman	–
	Careless Love	–

313

Night Time Is The Right Time	—
Blues For Big Sid	—
Roll On	—
The Train Is Coming	—
Piano Solo	—
Pappa Low	—
On The Sunny Side Of The Street	—
Ice Cream Freezer	—

Vcl /pno. with Alexis Korner, gtr(-1); Phil Seamen, dms.　　London, January 21, 1961

Sweet Old Chicago -1	Columbia 33SX 1422
Mr. Sykes Blues	
Let It Rock	Columbia 33SX 1422, SEG 8226
Mistakes In Life	—
So Tired	—
Hot Nuts -1	—
Gulf Port Boogie	—
Unlucky Thirteen Blues	—
Three Handed Woman	—
Little And Low -1	—
Green Onion Top	—
How Long, How Long Blues -1	—

Vcl/pno.　　New York City, June 1961

Sweet Old Chicago	Folkways FS 3827
Don't Care Blues	—
47th Street Jive	—
Memphis Slim Rock	—
44 Blues	—
Security Rock	—
R. S. Stomp	—
Ran The Blues Out Of My Heart	—
All My Money's Gone	—
Woman In Helena, Arkansas	—
The Sweet Root Man	—
The Thing	—
Please Don't Talk About Me When I'm Gone	—

Vcl/pno.　　Chicago,

Love Disease	unissued
Jive Blues	unissued
Running The Boogie	unissued

Add 2 gtrs(-1); dms (-2)

Miss Mercy Lee Blues -1, 2	unissued
Miss Mercy Lee Blues	unissued
Miss Mercy Lee Blues -1	unissued

Vcl/pno. with ten; gtr; bs; dms.

I Got A Letter	unissued
The Devil's Eyes	unissued

Note: The above sides were recorded by Jump Jackson

Vcl/pno. with Oett 'Sax' Mallard, ten; Lee Jackson, gtr; Willie Dixon, bs; dms.　　Chicago, April/May, 1962

Slave For Your Love	Crown CLP 5287, Kent 384
Gone With The Wind	— ,Kent 434, 5027
Wild Side	— , Kent 384
Out On A Limb	— , Kent 434
Honey Child	—
Never Loved Like This Before	—
Last Chance	—
Casual Friend	—
Your Will Is Mine	—
Hupe Dupe Do	—

Vcl/pno. with Homesick James Williamson, gtr/bs-gtr(-1)　　Chicago, May 1963

Red-Eyed Jesse Bell	Delmark DL-607

	I Like What YouDo (When You Do What You Did Last Night)	–
	We Gotta Move -1	–
	North Gulfport Boogie	–
	Watch Your Step (If You Just Can't Be Good)-1	–
	Ho! Ho! Ho!	–
	Living the Right Life	–
	New Fire Detective Blues	–
	Run This Boogie -1	–
	Slidell Blues -1	–
	Mistake In Life	–
	She's Got Me Straddle A Log	–
	Dirty Motor Scooter	unissued.

Vcl/pno. with Pat Wilson, dms; Victoria Spivey, vcl(-1)   New York City, June 3, 1963

131	This Is A New World	Spivey LP 1004
132	This Is A New World	unissued
133	Mercy Dee Blues	unissued
134	Mercy Dee Blues	unissued
135	Let's Play Mommie And Daddy	Spivey LP 1004
136	Sleeping All Day Blues	unissued
137	Sleeping All Day Blues	unissued
138	Mother Fuyer	unissued
139	Mother Fuyer	unissued
140	Lake Charles Stomp	Spivey LP 1004
141	Stella	unissued
142	Bad Luck	unissued
143	New Poodle Dog	unissued
144	New Poodle Dog	unissued
145	On My Way To Gulfport	unissued
146	Thirteen Hours -1	Spivey LP 1004

Vcl/pno. with Buddy Guy, gtr; Jimmy Lee Robinson, bs-gtr; Fred Below, dms.
    Hamburg, October 7, 1964

	Come Back Home	Fontana TL 5286

Vcl/pno. with Jack Meyers, bs-gtr; Fred Below, dms.   Berlin, October 16, 1966

	Running The Boogie	Fontana 885.431TY

Vcl/pno.   Copenhagen, October 23, 1966

	Big Ben	Storyville SLP 189
	Boot That Thing	–
	Springfield Blues	–
	Henry Ford Blues	–
	I'm A Dangerous Man	–
	True Thing	–
	You Understand	–
	Whole Lot Of Children	–
	The Last Laugh	–
	Gold Mine	–
	44 Blues	–
	Sugar Cup	–
	Dog Finger Blues	Storyville SLP 183
	Under Eyed Woman	Storyville SLP 187
	The Way I Feel	Storyville SLP 188
	9 Hour Call	Storyville SLP 187

SONNY T.

See under Sonny Terry.

TABBY & HIS MELLOW, MELLOW MEN

See under Tabby Thomas.

TAMPA RED

Real name Hudson Whittaker.
Vcl/gtr/kazoo. with Blind John Davis, pno; Ransom Knowling, bs.

		Chicago, December 15, 1944
D4-AB-336	The Woman I Love	Bluebird 34-0724
D4-AB-337	Detroit Blues	Bluebird 34-0731
D4-AB-338	Sure Enough I Do	–
D4-AB-339	Lulu Mae	Bluebird 34-0724

Vcl/gtr/kazoo. with Big Maceo, vcl/pno; Tyrell Dixon dms. Chicagom July 5, 1945

D5-AB-346	Mercy Mama	Bluebird 34-0740, Victor 20-1887
D5-AB-347	I Can't Get Along With You	Bluebird 34-0748
D5-AB-348	Give Me Mine Now	unissued
D5-AB-349	Better Leave My Gal Alone	Bluebird 34-0740

Chick Sanders, dms. replaces Dixon: Chicago, October 19, 1945

D5-AB-1200	I'll Be Up Again Some Day	Victor 20-2147
D5-AB-1201	I Oughta Bite You	–
D5-AB-1202	Corrine Blues	Victor 20-2432
D5-AB-1203	Play Proof Mama	Victor 20-2249

Alfred Elkins, bs. replaces Sanders: Chicago, February 19, 1946

D6-VB-1826	Let's Try It Again	Victor 20-2597
D6-VB-1827	Maybe, Someday	Victor 20-1988
D6-VB-1828	Crying Won't Help You	–
D6-VB-1829	Please Be Careful	Victor 20-2249

Vcl/gtr/kazoo. with Oett "Sax" Mallard, alt/clt; Blind John Davis, pno; Ernest "Big" Crawford, bs; Armand "Jump" Jackson, dms. Chicago, September 16, 1946

D6-VB-1945	You May Be Down Someday	Victor 22-0009
D6-VB-1946	She's A Solid Killer Diller	Victor 20-2597
D6-VB-1947	Poor Stranger Blues	Victor 20-3309
D6-VB-1948	New Bad Luck Blues	Victor 20-2432

Vcl/gtr/kazoo. with Walter Williams, tpt; John Gardner, alt; Blind John Davis, pno; Ransom Knowling, bs; Judge Riley, dms. Chicago, September 23, 1947

D7-VB-1040	I Know My Baby Loves Me	Victor 20-3008
D7-VB-1041	Blue And All Alone	Victor 20-2849
D7-VB-1042	You Better Woo Your Baby	–
D7-VB-1043	Grieving Blues	Victor 20-3160

Vcl/gtr/kazoo. with Oett "Sax" Mallard, alt; Bill Casimir, ten; Bob Call, pno; Ransom Knowling, bs; Judge Riley, dms. Chicago, October 31, 1947

D7-VB-1114	Sugar Baby	Victor 20-3309
D7-VB-1115	Keep Jumping	Victor 22-0009
D7-VB-1116	I'll Dig You Sooner Or Later	Victor 20-3160
D7-VB-1117	Roaming And Rambling	Victor 20-3008

Vcl/gtr/kazoo. with Johnnie Jones, pno; Ransom Knowling, bs; Odie Payne, dms. Chicago, March 24, 1949

D9-VB-460	It's A Brand New Boogey	Victor 22-0043, 50-0027
D9-VB-461	Come On, If You're Coming	Victor 22-0035, 50-0019
D9-VB-462	Please Try To See It My Way	Victor 22-0071, 50-0056
D9-VB-463	When Things Go Wrong With You	Victor 22-0035, 50-0019

Add Sugarman Penigar, ten;

D9-VB-1147	Put Your Money Where Your Mouth Is	Victor 22-0043, 50-0027
D9-VB-1148	That's Her Own Business	Victor 22-0057, 50-0041
D9-VB-1149	It's Too Late Now	Victor 22-0071, 50-0056
D9-VB-1150	I'LL Find My Way	Victor 22-0057, 50-0041

Penigar out: Chicago, March 7, 1950

EO-VB-3394	1950 Blues	Victor 22/50-0084
EO-VB-3395	It's Good Like That	Victor 22-0094
EO-VB-3396	Love Her With A Feelin'	Victor 22/50-0084
EO-VB-3397	New Deal Blues	Victor 22-0094

Same: Chicago, November 7, 1950

EO-VB-4564	Midnight Boogie	Victor 22-0112
EO-VB-4565	Don't Blame Shorty For That	Victor 22-0107
EO-VB-4566	I Miss My Lovin' Blues	Victor 22-0112
EO-VB-4567	Sweet Little Angel	Victor 22-0107

Same:		Chicago, March 20, 1951
E1-VB-490	Since My Baby's Been Gone	Victor 22-0136
E1-VB-491	She's Dynamite	Victor 22-0123
E1-VB-492	Pretty Baby Blyes	Victor 22-0136
E1-VB-493	Early In The Morning	Victor 22-0123, Camden CAL 740

Same:		Chicago, July 28, 1951
E1-VB-2247	Boogie Woogie Woman	Victor 20-4275
E1-VB-2248	She's A Cool Operator	Victor 20-4399
E1-VB-2249	I Won't Let Her Do It	Victor 20-4275
E1-VB-2250	Green And Lucky Blues	Victor 20-4399

Add Bill Casimir, ten;		Chicago, April 21, 1952
E2-VB-5421	I'm Gonna Put You Down	Victor 20-4722
E2-VB-5422	Look A There, Look A There	Victor 20/47-4898
E2-VB-5423	True Love	–
E2-VB-5424	But I Forgive You	Victor 20-4722

Same:		Chicago, November 17, 1952
E2-VB-5465	Too Late Too Long	Victor 20/47-5134
E2-VB-5466	I'll Never Let You Go	Victor 20-5273
E2-VB-5467	All Mixed Up Over You	Victor 20/47-5134
E2-VB-5468	Got A Mind To Leave This Town	Victor 20-5273

JIMMY EAGER & HIS TRIO

Vcl/gtr. with pno; dms.		Chicago, 1953
U 2352	Please Mr. Doctor	Sabre 100
U 2353	I Should Have Loved Her More	–

TAMPA RED

Vcl/gtr. with Willie "Sonny Boy" Williams, hca; Johnnie Jones, pno; Willie Lacey,
gtr; Ransom Knowling, bs; Odie Payne, dms.

		Chicago, September 1, 1953
E3-VB-0268	We Don't Get Along No More	unissued
E3-VB-0269	So Crazy About You Baby	Victor 20-5523
E3-VB0270	So Much Trouble	–
E3-VB-0271	If She Don't Come Back	Victor 20-5594

Walter Horton, hca; replaces Williams		Chicago, December 4, 1953
E3-VB-2701	Big Stars Falling Blues	Victor 20-5594
E3-VB-2702	If I Don't Find Another True Love	unissued
E3-VB-2703	Rambler's Blues	RCA Victor RCX-7160
E3-VB-2704	Evalena	--

Vcl/gtr/kazoo (-1)		Chicago, ? 1960
	I'm A Stranger Here -1	Bluesville BVLP 1030
	Let Me Play With Your Poodle	– , 1055
	Goodbye Baby -1	–
	Things About Coming My Way -1	–
	Kansas City Blues	–
	You Better Do It Right -1	–
	Louise Blues	–
	It's Tight Like That -1	–
	You Got To Love Her With A Feeling	–
	Boogie Woogie Woman	–

Same:		
	How Long	Bluesville BVLP 1043
	Gin Headed Woman	–
	You Better Let My Gal Alone	–
	Don't Jive Me	–
	Dark And Stormy Night	–
	Don't You Lie To Me	–
	Georgia, Georgia	–
	Jelly Whippin' Blues	– , 1055
	Chicago Moan Blues	–
	Don't Dog Your Woman	–
	Drinkin' My Blues Away	–

TARHEEL SLIM

See under Allen Bunn

BABY TATE

Born Elberton, Georgia on January 28, 1916
Vcl/gtr.   Spartanburg, S. C. 1962
    Dupree Blues   Bluesville BVLP 1072
    See What You Have Done   —
    What Have I done To You   —
    Baby I'm Going   —
    Hey Mama, Hey Pretty Girl   —
    When Your Woman Don't Want You Around —
    My Baby Don't Treat Me Kind   —
    Trucking Them Blues Away   —
    Baby You Just Don't Know   —
    Lonesome Over There   —
    I Ain't Got No Loving Baby Now   —

BUDDY TATE

Vcl/gtr. (-1)/accdn(-2) with saxes; pno; gtr; bs; dms.   New Orleans, c. 1956
    Lifetime In Prison Pt. 1 -1   Ace unissued
    Lifetime In Prison Pt. 2 -2   —

COCOA (or KOKO) TAYLOR

Real name Cora Taylor (nee Walton). Born Memphis on September 28, 1935

KOKO TAYLOR
Vcl. with Jarrett "Gerry" Gibson, tan; Lafayette Leake, pno; J. B. Lenoir, gtr; Milton
Rector, bs-gtr; Willie Smith, dms.   Chicago, July 23, 1963
791, 4-
18924   Like Heaven To Me   USA 745
792, 4-
18925   Honky Tonky   —

COCOA TAYLOR
Vcl. with Homesick James, Evans Spencer, gtrs; Willie Dixon, tamb;
                                             Chicago, March 26, 1961
    What Kind Of Man Is This   Spivey LP 1003
    Which-A-Way To Go   —
    I'm Looking For A Man   Spivey LP 1009

KOKO TAYLOR
Vcl. with Shakey Horton, hca; Lafayette Leake, pno; Robert Nighthawk, Buddy Guy,
gtrs; Jack Meyers, bs-gtr; Clifton James, dms.   Chicago, July 1964
13306   I Got What It Takes   Checker 1092
13307   What Kind Of Man Is This

Vcl. with Willie Dixon vcl/bs; ten; gtrs; bs; dms.   Chicago, 1965/66
14389   Wang Dang Doodle   Checker 1135
14390   Blues Heaven   —
14391
14392   Tell Me The Truth   Checker 1148
14891   Good Advice   Checker 1148

EDDIE TAYLOR

Born Beneard, Mississippi on January 29, 1923
Vcl. with Snooky Pryor, hca; Sunnyland Slim, pno; Floyd Jones, gtr; Alfred Wallace, dms.
                                             Chicago, February 7, 1954
54-136   Steady Pistol   Vee Jay unissued
Vcl/gtr. with Jimmy Reed, hca/gtr; Ray Scott, dms.   Chicago, January 18, 1955
55-227   Bad Boy   Vee Jay 149
55-228   E. T. Blues   —

318

Vernell Fournier, dms. replaces Scott:		Chicago, December 5, 1955
55-385	Ride 'Em On Down	Vee Jay 185
55-386	Big Town Playboy	–

Vcl/gtr. with George Maywether, hca; Jimmy Lee Robinson, bs-gtr; Earl Phillips, dms.

		Chicago, July 9, 1956
560487	You'll Always Have A Home	Vee Jay 206
56-488	Don't Knock At My Door	–
56-489	Good Hearted	unissued
56-490	Bongo Beat	unissued

Omit Maywether:

		Chicago, November 5, 1957
57-765	I'm Gonna Love You	Vee Jay 267
57-766	Lookin' For Trouble	–
57-767	Find My Baby	unissued
57-768	Stroll Out Wench	unissued

Vcl/gtr. with Jimmy Reed, hca; Johnny Jones, pno; Hubert Sumlin, gtr; dms.

		Chicago, 1964
64-013	I'm Sitting Here	Vivid 104
64-014	Do You Want Me To Cry	–

HOUND DOG TAYLOR

Real name Theodore Roosevelt Taylor, Born Greenville, Mississippi on April 14, 1916.
Vcl/gtr. with Emery Williams Jr., pno; ? Emerson, bs; Levi Lewis, dms.

		Chicago, 1960
A	(Five) Take Five	Bea & Baby 112, Marjette 1102, Key 112
B	My Baby's Coming Home	– – –

Vcl/gtr. with Lafayette Leake, pno; Blind Jesse Williams, bs-gtr; dms.

		Chicago, 1962
A	Christine	Firma 626
B	Alley Music	–

MONTANA TAYLOR

Vcl/pno. with Almond Leonard, wbd(-1)

		Chicago, April 18, 1946
C 11	Low Down Boogie	Circle 1009. Riverside RLP 152
C 12	Toot Your Whistle	unissued
C 16	Sweet Sue -1	Circle 1010
C 17	In The Bottom	Circle 1008, Riverside RLP 152
C 18	Rotten Break Blues -1	Circle 1015, –
C 19	I Can't Sleep	Circle 1009, –

Same:

		Chicago, April 19, 1946
C 31	Montana Five	unissued
C 32	Memphis Four O'Clock	unissued
C 33	'Fo Day Blues	Circle 1010
C 34	Detroit Rocks	unissued
C 35	Indiana Avenue Stomp	Circle 1008, Riverside RLP 152
C 36	Montana's Blues	Circle 1015, –
C 37	Rag Alley Drag	unissued

JOHNNY TEMPLE

Vcl. with saxes; pno; bjo; bs; dms.

		1946
K 5146	Yum, Yum	King 4151, LP 859
K 5152	I Believe I'll Go Downtown	– , Bethlehem LP 6071

Vcl. with pno; gtr; bs; dms.

		Chicago c.1949
M 2000	Between Midnight And Day	Miracle 156
M 2001	Sit Right On It	–

THE TENNESSEE GABRIEL

Gospel items by Brownie McGhee. Not included in this volume.

NAT TERRY

Real name Nathaniel Terry
Vcl/gtr.   Dallas? 1951
IM 323   Take It Easy   Imperial 5150
IM 324   I Don't Know Why   –

SONNY TERRY

Real name Sanders Terrell. Born Georgia in 1911.
Vcl/hca. with Woody Guthrie, gtr;   New York City, 1944
            Glory   Asch 432-2
            Lonesome Train   Asch 550-3, LP 2 1/2
Vcl/hca. with Brownie McGhee, gtr;
S 5764   Run Away Women   Savoy 5549
S 5765   Shake Down   –
Same: New York City, 1945
SO7   Sweet Woman   Solo 10-004
SO8   Fox Chase (no gtr)   –
Add Baby Dodds, dms.   New York City, January 1947
1296   Whoopin' The Blues   Capitol 40003, T 793
1297   Leavin' Blues   Capitol 40043
1298   Riff And Harmonica Jump   Capitol 40061
1299   All Alone Blues   Capitol 40003
Vcl/hca. with Alan Gilbert, Lynn Murray's Singers and Orchestra, directed by Ray Charles:
                                                             New York City, March 30, 1947
CO37551   This Time Of The Year   Columbia 4392M
Vcl/hca. with Brownie McGhee, gtr; Baby Dodds, dms.   New York City, June 12, 1947
1725   Harmonica Rag   Capitol 15237
1726   Screamin' And Cryin' Blues   Capitol 40061
1727   Bear Garden Blues   Capitol 40097, TB01971-4
1728   Worried Man Blues   Capitol 40043
Vcl/hca. with Melvin Merritt, pno; Brownie McGhee, gtr;bs; dms.
                                                             New York, November 13, 1947
2508   Hot Headed Woman   Capitol 40122
2509   Custard Pie Blues   –
2510   Crow Jane Blues   Capitol 40097
2511   Early Morning Blues   Capitol 15237
Vcl/hca. with Wilbert Ellis, pno; Brownie McGhee, gtr; Melvin Merritt, dms.
                                                             New York City, early 1950
4339   Telephone Blues   Capitol 931
4340   Tell Me, Tell Me   unissued
4341   Dirty Mistreater   Capitol 931
Vcl/gtr. with Doc Bagby, org; Brownie McGhee, gtr; Melvin Merritt, dms.
                                                             New York City, 1951/2
ST1   Baby Let's Have Some Fun   Gotha, 517
ST2   Four O'Clock Blues   –
ST3   Harmonica Rhumba   Gotham 518
ST4   Lonesome Room   –
            No Love Blues   unissued?
            Wine Headed Woman   –
Vcl/hca. with Brownie McGhee, gtr; Coyal McMahan, bongoes.
GRC 1060   Hootin' Blues   Gramercy 1004
GRC 1061   Dangerous Woman   Gramercy 1005
Vcl/hca.   New York City, 1952
            Dirty Mistreater   Aravel LP 1004
            Alcholic Blues   Folkways FP 35, FA 2035
            Women's Blues (Corrina)   –   –
            Lost John   –   –
            Locomotive Blues   –   –
            Bad Luck Blues   –   –
            Harmonica Stomp   –   –

	Shortnin' Bread	Folkways FP 35, FA 2035
	Fine And False Voice	– –
	Beautiful City	
		Aravel LP 1004

Add Woody Guthrie, vcl/gtr.

	Silver Fox Chase	Stinson LP 55
	Don't You Hear Me Callin' You	–
	Worried And Lonesome Blues	–
	She's A Sweet Woman	–
	South Bound Express	–
	You Don't Want Me	–
	Tell Me Little Woman	–

Vcl/hca. with Brownie McGhee, Leadbelly, Cisco Houston, Pete Seeger or Woody Guthrie, gtrs.

	A Man Is Nothing But A Fool	Verve 9010
	Right On That Shore	–
	John Henry	–
	Louise	–
	Go Tell Aunt Rhody	–
	Good Morning Blues	–
	Twelve Gates To The City	–
	Easy Rider	–
	Careless Love	–
	Key To The Highway	–

Vcl/hca. with

	Cornbread And Molasses	Archive Of Folk Music 106
	Ham AndEggs	–
	Lost John	–
	Chain Gang Blues	–
	It Takes A Chain Gang Man	–
	Betty And Dupree	–
	Stackolee	–
	Rock Me Mama	–
	Chain Gang Special	–
	Long John	–
	Pick A Bale Of Cotton	Archive Of Folk Music 106
	Red River	–

Vcl/hca. with Brownie MgGhe, gtr.

| | Greyhound Bus station | Stinson LP 55 |

Vcl/hca. with wbd; washtub; bones; frying pans.

	The Woman Is Killing Me	Folkways FP 6, FA 2006
	Custard Pie Blues	– –
	Diggin' My Potatoes	– –
	Crazy Man Blues	– –
	Wine-Headed Woman	– –
	My Baby Done Changed The Lock On That Door	– –
	Sonny's Jump	– –

SONNY "HOOTIN'" TERRY
Vcl/hca. with Brownie McGhee, gtr;

| JA 4017 | I Don't Worry | Jax 305 |
| JA 4018 | Man Ain't Nothing But A Fool | – |

SONNY T & HIS BUCKSHOT FIVE
Vcl/hca. with Bob Gaddy, pno; Brownie McGhee, gtr; Bob Harris, bs; Gene Brooks, dms.

| DA 758 | Dangerous Woman | Harlem 2327 |
| DA 759 | I Love You Baby | – |

SONNY "HOOTIN' " TERRY & HIS NIGHT OWLS

M 42	That Woman Is Killing Me	Jackson 2302
M 43		
M 44	Harmonica Train	Jackson 2302

321

Vcl/hca. with Alex Seward, vcl (-1)/gtr.   New York City, 1953

Red River	Elektra 14, Washington 702
John Henry	– –
The Fox Chase	– –
Talking About The Blues	– –
Goodbye Leadbelly	– –
Moaning And Mourning Blues	– –
In The Evening	– –
Mama Told Me	– –
Louise Blues	Elektra 15, –
Chain The Lock On My Door	– –
Baby Baby Blues	– –
Custard Pie	– –
Kansas City	– –
Old Woman Blues	– –
Little Annie -1	–
Down In The Bottom Blues -1	–
Late One Saturday Evening (Night) -1	–
Hard Luck Blues -1	–

Note: All titles on Washington 702 also on Riverside 12-644.

Vcl/hca. with Jack Dupree, pno; Brownie McGhee, Sticks McGhee, gtrs; Willie Jones, dms.

R 3014	Harmonica Hop	Red Robin 110
R 3015	Doggin' My Heart Around	–

Vcl/hca. with Fletcher Smith, pno; Mickey Baker, gtr; Johnny Williams, bs; Marty Wilson, dms; Bobby Donaldson, bongos   New York, August 27, 1953

E3-VB-1902	Hootin' And Jumpin'	Victor 20/47-5492
E30VB-1903	Sonny Is Drowsing	Victor 20/47-5577
E3-VB-1904	I'm Gonna Rock My Wig	–
E3-VB-1905	Hooray, Hooray	Victor 20/47-5492

Vcl/hca. with Teddy Charles, vbs; Brownie McGhee, gtr; Lee Stanfield bs; Marty Wilson, dms.   New York February 1, 1954

E4-HB-3500	Lost Jawbone	Groove 0015
E4-HB-3501	Louise	–
E4-HB-3502	I Took You In Baby	unissued
E4-HB-3503	Juice Head Woman	unissued

Vcl/hca. with Brownie, McGhee, Sticks McGhee, gtrs; Milt Hinton, bs; Gene Brooks, dms.   New York, November 7, 1955

F5-JB-7740	Hootin' Blues No. 2	Groove 0135
F5-JB-7741	Throw This Old Dog A Bone	unissued
F5-JB-7742	Ride And Roll	Groove 0135
F5-JB-7743	Tell Me Why	unissued

Vcl/hca. with pno; gtr; bs; dms.   New York City, 1956

JOZ 192	Fast Freight Blues	Josie 828
JOZ 193	Dangerous Woman	–

Vcl/hca. with Bob Gaddy, pno; Brownie McGhee, gtr

OT 839	Uncle Bud	Old Town 1023
OT 840	Climbing On Top Of The Hill	–

Vcl/hca. with Brownie McGgee, Vcl/gtr.   San Francisco, March 15, 1957

I Got Fooled	Fantasy 3254
No Need Of Running	–
I Feel So Good	–
Thinkin' And Worryin'	–
I Love You Baby	–
California Blues	–
Walkin' And Lyin' Down	–
First And Last Love	–
Christine	–
I Have Had My Fun	–
Whoopin' And Squallin'	–
Water Boy Cry	–
Motherless Child	–
Sportin' Life	–

SONNY & JAYCEE
Vcl/hca. with J. C. Burris, gtr;   New York City, 1958
E-1369   Mister Froggie   Ember 1034
E-1370   Keep On Doggin' Me   –
Vcl/hca. with Sticks McGhee, gtr; J. C. Burris, bones
            Wail On   Folkways FA 2369
            Better Let It Go   –
            Poor Mand AndGood Man Blues   –
            Body Slap Blues   –
            Bone Solo   –
            Wine Blues   –
            My Baby's Leaving   –
            Easy Rider   –
            Whooping And Hollering Blues   –
            Jail House Blues   –
            I've Been A Long Long Ways   –
            Boys In My Room   –
            Keep On Dogging Me   –
            Pete's Jump   –
Add Belton Evans, dms.   New York City, 1959/60
            My Baby Done Gone   Bluesville BVLP 1025
            I Ain't Gonna Be Your Dog No More   –
            Worried Blues   –
            High Powered Woman   –
            Pepperheaded Woman   –
            Sonny's Story   –
            I'm Gonna Get On My Feet   –
            Four O'Clock Blues   –
            Telephone Blues   –
            Great Tall Engine   –
Vcl/hca. with Lightnin' Hopkins, gtr; Leonard Gaskin, bs; Belton Evans, dms.
                                                                  New York City, October, 1960
            One Monkey Don't Stop The Show   Bluesville BVLP 1059
            Changed The Lock On My Door   –
            Tater Pie   –
            She's So Sweet   –
            Diggin' My Potatoes   –
Vcl/hca. with Brownic McGhee, gtr;
            Sonny's Coming   Bluesville BVLP 1059
            Ida Mae   –
            Callin' Mama   –
            Bad Luck   –
            Blues From The Bottom   –
Vcl/hca. with Brownie McGhee, vcl/gtr.   San Fransisco,
            You Can't Hide   Fantasy 3296, 546
            I Shall Not Be Moved   –   –
            Just A Closer Walk   –
            Children Go Where I Send Thee   –
            What A Beautiful City   –
            Glory, Glory   –
            If I Could Hear My Mother pray   –
            I'm Going To Shout   –
            Packing Up   –
            Get Right Church   –
            Some Of These Days   –
            If You See My Saviour   –
            John Henry   Fantasy 3317
            I'm A Stranger   –
            Cornbread And Peas   –
            Louise   –
            I Done Done   –
            Meet You In The Morning   –
            Poor Boy From Home   –

323

	Hudy Leadbelly	Fantasy 3317
	Something's Wrong At Home	–
	Take This Hammer	–
	Baby's Gone	–
	Lose Your Money	–
		San Fransisco, December 1961
	Hooray, Hooray	Fantasy 3340, S8091
	This Woman Is Killing Me	– –
	Born To Live The Blues	– –
	Just About Crazy	– –
	I Got A Little Girl	– –
	Up, Sometimes Down	– –
	Keep On Walking Baby	– –
	I Knocked On Your Door	– –
	Baby I Got My Eye On You	– –
	I Feel All Right Now	– –
	Worry Worry Worry	– –
	Dupree	Choice 15
	Hootin'	–

TEXAS GUITAR SLIM

Pseudonym for Johnny Winters. White artist.

TEXAS RED

Vcl/gtr. with Sax Kari's Orch; alt; Ten; gtr; dms.   Detroit, 1956
| 5018 | Turn Around | Bullseye 1009 |
| 5019 | Coming Home | – |

TEXAS RED & JIMMY
Same: Detroit, 1957
| B | Black Snake Blues | Viceroy 3333, Checker 879 |
| | (Rev. by Katie Watkins q.v.) | – |

TEXAS RED & JIMMY

See under Texas Red

TEXAS SLIM

See under John Lee Hooker

R. B. THIBADEAUX

Vcl. with tpt; ten; pno; gtr; bs; dms.   Houston, 1949
ACA 1302	R. B. Boogie	Peacock 1513
ACA 1303	New Kind Of Loving	–
ACA 1380	Blues At Daybreak	unissued
ACA 1381	You Love So Good	unissued
ACA 1382	She's A Real Fine Woman	unissued
ACA 1383	Rain On My Window Pane	unissued

ALEXANDER "MUDCAT" THOMAS

Vcl/pno. with dms.   Atlanta, 1960
S 1075	12th Street Rag	NRC 062
S 1076	Step It Up And Go	–
Same:		Nashville,
	Mudcat Blues	Smash MP 27046
	My Blue Heaven	–
	Sugar Bee	–
	TennesseeWaltz	–
	Steel Guitar Rag	–
	When The Saints	–
	Tell Me What's On Your Mind	–
	Raunchy	–

324

	Worrisome Blues	Smash MP 27046
	The Story Of Boot Juice	—
	Back Door Man	—
	Weepin' Willow	—
	Step It Up And Go	—

ANDREW THOMAS

See under Andy Thomas

ANDY THOMAS

Vcl. with Thunder Smith, pno. Luther Stoneham, gtr
Houston 1948

A	Angel Chile	Gold Star 645
B	My Baby Quit Me Blues	—

Vcl. with Lightnin' Hopkins gtr;
Houston, 1949

A	In Love Blues	Gold Star 659
B	Walking And Crying	—

ANDREW THOMAS

Vcl. with Luther Stoneham, gtr;
Houston, 1949

no mx	I Love My Baby	Swing With The Stars 1038/39
no mx	Chicago Blues	—

BURT THOMAS & HIS BAND

Vcl. with Henry Hayes, alt. Ed Wiley; ten; Willie Johnson, pno; Donald Cooks, bs;
Ben Turner, dms;
Houston, 1951

2248	The Boston Hop	Jade 205
3001	Sad Conditions Blues	—

JESSE THOMAS

Born Loganport, Louisiana ?

JESSE THOMAS (THE BLUES TROUBADOR) & HIS GUITAR

Vcl/gtr.
Los Angeles, 1948

WP-232-A	Same Old Stuff	Miltone 232
WP-232-B	Double Due Love You	—
WP-233-A	Zetter Blues	Miltone 233
WP-233-B	Mountain Key Blues	—

JESSE THOMAS

Vcl/gtr.

JT-1A	Melody In C	Club
JT-1B	You Are My Dreams	—
1	I Wonder Why	Club
2	Another Friend Like Me	—

Note: Club labels show no issue numbers

Vcl/gtr. with ten; pno; bs; dms.
Houston 1949

1074	Guess I'll Walk Alone	Freedom 1513
1075	Let's Have Some Fun	—

Vcl/gtr.
Los Angeles, 1949

MM 1187	Gonna Write You A Letter	Modern 20-710
MM 1188	Meet Me Tonight Along The Avenue	unissued
MM 1189	Tomorrow I May Be Gone	unissued
MM 1190	Texas Blues	Modern 20-710

Vcl/gtr. with Lloyd Glenn, pno; Billy Hadnott, bs; Bob Harvey, dms.
Los Angeles, April 30, 1951

	Xmas Celebration	Swing Time 240
	I Can't Stay Here	—
	Now's The Time	Swing Time 241
	It's You I'm Thinking Of	—

Add ten:

Ho 697	Long Time	Hollywood 1072, LP 503

Ho 698	Cool Kind Lover	Hollywood 1072, LP 503

Vcl/gtr. with ten; pno; bs; dms.　　　　　　　Los Angeles, 1951

419A	When You Say I Love You	Specialty 419
419B	Jack Of Diamonds	—

Vcl/gtr. with hca; dms (-1)　　　　　　　Los Angeles, 1953

6342	Another Fool Like Me -1	Elke 107
6343	Gonna Move To California	—

KID THOMAS

Vcl/hca. with pno; gtr; dms.　　　　　　　Los Angeles, 1957

F 566	The Spell	Federal 12298
F 567	The Wolf Pack	—

Vcl/hca. (-1) with 2 gtrs; dms

32262	You Are An Angel	T. R. C. T-1012
32263	Rockin' This Joint To-Nite -1	—

L. J. THOMAS

Vcl. with ten; pno; gtr; bs;dms　　　　　　　Memphis, 1952

U 7393	Baby Take A Chance With Me	Chess 1493
U 7394	Sam's Drag	—

No details　　　　　　　Houston, 1953

ACA 2719	Night Or Day	Peacock unissued

LAFAYETTE THOMAS

Born Shreveport, Louisiana on June 13, 1932
Gtr. with ten; bari; bs; dms.　　　　　　　Oakland, c 1955

5000X	Cockroach Run	Jumping 5000

Vcl/gtr. with Sammy Price, pno; bs; Joe Belton, dms.　　New York City, July 1959

SLT 70603	Please Come Back To Me	Savoy 1574
SLT 70604	Lafayette's A-Comin'	—

> Note: Also recorded for Peacock, Star And Big Town. All either unissued or untraced.

MARCELLUS THOMAS & HIS RHYTHMS OF ROCKETTS

Vcl. with ten; pno; gtr; bs; dms.　　　　　　　Oakland,

A	Breather Blues	Ajax 104
B	Haller's 89 Whiskey Boogie	—

> See also Mercy Dee q.v.

MULE THOMAS

Vcl/gtr. with hca; bs　　　　　　　Shreveport, La. 1958

735	Take Some And Leave Some	Hollywood 1091, Palace LP 724
736	Blow My Baby Back Home	—　　　　　—

> + two unissued titles.

RUFUS THOMAS

Born Collierville, Tennessee on March 26, 1917.
Vcl. with Evelyn Young, ten; ? Bradshaw, pno; Robert Carter, gtr; Red Davis, dms

Memphis, 1950

332	I'll Be A Good Boy	Talent 807
333	I'm So Worried	—

Vcl. with Herman Green, ten; Houston Stokes, dms + others:

Memphis, 1952

U 62	Night Walkin' Blues	Chess 1466
U 63	Why Did You Dee Gee	—

326

Vcl. with brass; Billy "Red" Love, pno; gtr; bs; dms.
| U 7399 | No More Doggin' Around | Chess 1492 |
| U 7400 | Crazy 'Bout You Baby | — |

Vcl. with Richard Sanders, bari; Billy "Red" Love, pno; bs; dms.
| 1024 | Juanita | Chess 1517 |
| 1025 | Decorate The Counter | — |

Vcl. with Billy "Red" Love, pno; Joe Hill Louis, gtr; bs; Houston Stokes, dms.
Memphis, 1953
| U 63 | Bearcat | Sun 181 |
| U 64 | Walkin' In The Rain | — |

Same:
| U 79 | Tiger Man | Sun 188 |
| U 80 | Save That Money | — |

Note: later recordings by this artist are not included.
Unissued titles from Talent Sessions are:-
Who's That Chick
Double Trouble
Take Me Home, I'm Tired, He Lied
Paper Doll

TABBY THOMAS

TABBY & HIS MELLOW, MELLOW MEN
Vcl. with Buddy Stewart's Band; tpt; alt; ten; pno; gtr; bs; dms.

Jackson, Miss. 1953
| ACA 2669 | Thinking Blues | Delta 416 |
| ACA 2670 | Church Member's Ball | — |

TABBY THOMAS
Vcl. with Bob Johnson Orch.

Crowley La. 1954
| A | Tomorrow | Feature 3007 |
| B | Mmmm, I Don't Care | — |

Vcl. with ten: pno: gtr; bs; dms.

Crowley, la 1961
R 7020	Don't Say	Rocko 511
R 7021	Too Late Blues	—
Z 7472	My Baby's Got It	Zynn 1002
Z 7473	Tomorrow I'll Be Gone	—

Vcl. with Lazy Lester hca; Katie Webster, pno; gtr; bs; dms. Crowley, La. 1961
| A | Hoodoo Party | Excello 2212 |
| B | Roll On Ole Mule | — |

No details:
Crowley La, 1962
| | He's Got The Whole World In His Hands | Excello 2222 |
| | Popeye Train | — |

TAB THOMAS
No Details

Crowley, La 1965
| A | Play Girl | Excello 2281 |
| B | Keep On Trying | — |

WILLIE THOMAS

See under Butch Cage.

KID GUITAR THOMPSON

No details
1960
| | My Baby Done Me Wrong | Dore 881 |
| | | — |

ROCKY THOMPSON

See under Goree Carter.

WILLIE MAE " BIG MAMA " THORNTON

Born In Montgomery, Alabama on December 11, 1926

Note: Details listed as in ACA files in spite of conflictions with previous discographics.

Vcl. with Joe Scott, tpt; alt; ten; bari; pno; gtr; bs; dms		Houston, 1951
ACA 1861	Partnership Blues	Peacock 1567
ACA 1862	Mischievous Boogie	Peacock 1603
ACA 1863	Precious Daddy	unissued
ACA 1864	All Fed Up	Peacock 1567

Vcl. with tpt; Bill Harvey, ten; pno; gtr; bs; dms.		Houston 1952
ACA 2068	Cotton Picking Blues	Peacock 1621
ACA 2069	Everytime I Think Of You	Peacock 1603
ACA 2070	No Jody For Me	Peacock 1587
ACA 2071	Let Your Tears Fall Baby	–

Vcl. with Don Johnson, tpt; George Washington, tbn; James Von Streeter, ten; Fred Ford, bari; Devonia Williams, pno; Pete Lewis, gtr; Albert Winston, bs; Leard Bell, dms; Johnny Otis, vibes.

		Los Angeles, August 13, 1952
ACA 2256	They Call Me Big Mama	Peacock 1621
ACA 2257	Walking Blues	Peacock 1647
ACA 2258	Hound Dog (rhythm only)	Peacock 1612, Duke LP 73
ACA 2259	Just Can't Help Myself	unissued
ACA 2260	Nightmare	Peacock 1612
ACA 2261	Rockabye Baby	Peacock 1647
ACA 2262	Hard Times	unissued
ACA 2263	I've Searched The World Over	Peacock 1632

Same:		Los Angeles, 1953
RR 105-5	I Ain't No Fool Either	Peacock 1626
RR 106		
RR 107-9	The Big Change	Peacock 1626
RR 108-9	I Smell A Rat (rhythm only)	Peacock 1632

Vcl. with brass. Burt Kendricks, gtr; pno; bs; dms.		Houston, 1954
ACA 2832	Tarzan And The Dignified Monkey -1	Peacock 1654
ACA 2833	Where Are You Goin'	unissued
ACA 2834	Stop Hoppin' On Me	Peacock 1642
	-1 add Elroy Peace, vcl.	
ACA 2835	Story Of My Blues	Peacock 1642

Vcl. with Billy Harvey & others, saxes; pno; gtr; bs; dms.		Houston, 1955
ACA 3086	The Fish	Peacock 1650
ACA 3087	You Don't Move Me	unissued
ACA 3088	Laugh, Laugh, Laugh	Peacock 1650
ACA 3089	How Come	Peacock 1654

Same:		Houston 1957
FR 1034	Just Like A Dog	Peacock 1681
FR 1035	My Man Called Me	–

Vcl/hca. with pno; gtr; dms		Oakland, 1961
A	You Did Me Wrong	Bay Tone 107
B	Big Mama's Blues	–

Vcl. with saxes; pno; gtr; bs; dms.		Los Angeles, 1965
SO-0033	Summertime	Sotoplay 0033/£
SO-0034	Truth'll Come To The Light	–
S 0039	Tomcat	Sotoplay 0039
	(rev. not by Thornton)	

WITH JOHNNY TALBOT'S BAND

Vcl/hca (-1) with saxes; pno; gtr; bs-gtr; dms.		
424-1	Before Day -1	Kent 424
424-2	Me And My Chauffeur	–

Vcl. with Eddie Boyd, pno; Buddy Guy, gtr; Jimmy Lee Robinson, bs-gtr; Fred Below, dms.

		Hamburg, October 7, 1965
	Hound Dog	Fontana 681,529 TL

Vcl/hca(-1)/dms(-2). with Shakey Horton, hca (-3); Eddie Boyd pno/org (-4); Buddy Guy
gtr; Jimmy Lee Robinson, bs-gtr; Fred Below, dms.   London, October 20, 1965

	Swing It On Home	Arhoolie F 1028, 512
	Sweet Little Angel	–
	The Place	–
	Little Red Rooster -4	–
	Unlucky Girl -3	–
	Hound Dog -3	–
	Down Home Shake Down -1, 3, 4	–
	Your Love Is Where It Ought To Be -1, 2	–
	Session Blues -2, 3	–

Vcl. with Fred McDowell, gtr.

	My Heavy Load	Arhoolie F 1028, 512
	School Boy	–

Vcl/hca. with James Cotton, hca; Otis Spann, pno; Muddy Waters, gtr; unk. gtr; bs-gtr;
Francey Clay, dms   San Fransisco, April 25, 1966

	I'm Feeling Alright	Arhoolie F 1032
	Sometimes I Have A Heartache	–
	Black Rat	–
	Life Goes On	–
	Wrapped Tight	–
	Bumble Bee	–
	Gimme A Penny	–
	Looking The World Over	–
	I Feel The Way I Feel	–
	My Love	–

Note: See also Harlem Stars.

WILLIS THREATS

See under Henry Hayes.

BIG SON TILLIS & D. C. BENDER

Real names Ellas Tillis & D. C. Bendy
Tillis Vcl/hca/gtr. with Bendy, gtr;   Los Angeles, 1953

A	Rocks Is My Pillow	Elko 821
B	Zetela Blues	–

Lillian Tillis, vcl. with Tillis vcl(-1)/gtr. Bendy, gtr;

A	When I Get In This House Woman -1	Elko 822
B	Ten Long Years	–

Tillis, vcl(-1)/gtr. with Bendy Vcl(-2)/gtr.

A	Dayton Stomp -1	Elko 823
B	My Baby Wrote Me A Letter -2	–

Tillis Vcl/gtr. with Bendy, gtr.

	Tillis Stomp	Elko unissued
	Big Son's Blues	–
	Buaty Street (add wbd)	–
	I'm Going Upstairs	–
	I Got A Letter	–
	Cold Blues	–
	Texas Blues	–
	Tillis Boogie (add pno)	–
	Lonesome Road (vcl Lillian Tillis)	–

Note: Tillis also recorded before 1953 for Elko at Longview, Texas with Doc
Thomas' Band. These sides were not issued. See also D. C. Washington. Lillian
Tillis is from Dayton, Texas.

JAMES TISDOM

Born in Texas in 1912
Vcl/gtr. with gtr; bs(-1)   Los Angeles, late '40s

A	Model T Boogie	Universal-Fox 100

B	Last Affair Blues	Universal-Fox 100
A	Throw This Dog A Bone	Universal-Fox 101
B	Wine Head Swing	–
A	I Feel So Good -1	Universal-Fox 102
B	Overhaul Blues -1	–

JIMMY TOLIVER & HIS CALIFORNIA BLUES MEN

Pno. with ten; vibes; Edgar Rice, gtr; bs; dms.

		Los Angeles, c. 1963
A	Breaking Out	T & T 102
AA	Going Home	–

HENRY TOWNSEND

Born

Vcl/gtr. with Tommy Bankhead, gtr; Vcl/pno. only (-1)

	1961
Cairo's My Baby's Home	Bluesville BVLP
Tired Of Being Mistreated	–
Rocks Have Been My Pillow	–
The Train Is Coming	–
She Just Walked Away	–
I Asked Her If She Loved Me	–
I Got Tired	–
My Home Ain't Here	–
All My Money Gone -1	–
She Drove Me To Drinking	–
My Baby Have Come Back	–

TREE TOP SLIM (Willie Ealey)

See under Joe Williams Recordings (unissued).

JOE TUCKER

Dancing with Scott Dunbar, gtr;

	Nr. Pond, Miss. June 25, 1954
Buck Dance	Folkways Fp 654

TULSA RED

See under Lowell Fulson

BABY FACE TURNER

Vcl/gtr. with Sunny Blair, hca; Ike Turner, pno; Bill Russell, dms.

North Little Rock, May 6, 1952

MM 1876	Blue Serenade	Modern 882
MM 1877	Gonna Let You Go	– , Meteor 5006, Blues Classic
44 Blues		unissued

Note: Meteor 5006 issued as by Sunny Blair,
See also Sunny Blair, Elmon Mickle and Junior Brooks.

PETE TURNER & HIS BLUES BAND

No details.

		New York City, 1947
H.1943	Pete Turner Blues	Haven 3001
H.1944	Little Man Blues	–

WILLIE TURNER

Vcl.

	Nr. Livingstone, Ala. Jan/Feb. 1950
Captain Holler Hurry	Folkways FE 4474, P 474
John Henry	– –
Now Your Man Done Gone	Folkways FE 4417, P 417

T. V. SLIM

See under Oscar Wills.

CHARLES TYLER

DRIFTING CHARLES

Vcl/gtr. with Al Foreman, gtr; Rufus Thibodeaux, bs-gtr; Warren Storm, dms.

Crowley, La. May 1963

L-0157	Drifting Cloud	Lanor 515
L-0158	Evil Hearted Woman	–

Note: Other recordings not of interest. Opelousas artist.

V

HARRY VAN WALLS

"SPIDER SAM"

Brownie McGhee, vcl/gtr. with ten; Harry Van Walls, pno; bs; dms.

New York City, February 28, 1950

A 390	Tee Nah-Nah	Atlantic 904
A 391	Ain't Gonna Scold You	–
No details		1952
A 919	After Midnight	Atlantic 980
A 920		
A 921	Solid Sender	Atlantic 980

COOT VENSON

Born Belzoni, Mississippi in 1914
Vcl/hca. with Big Joe Williams, gtr

Crawford, Miss. 1965

Sugar Mama	Storyville SLP 180

W

J. W. WALKER

Vcl/gtr. with saxes; pno; bs; dms.

? November 17, 1955

Untitled Blues	Modern unissued
Sitting Here Wondering	–
Can't See You Baby	–

JIMMY WALKER

Vcl/pno. with Erwin Helfer, pno(-1)   Chicago, 1964
   Rough And Ready -1   Testament T-202
   Give Me 10 Cents Worth Of Love -1   –
   Mam Told Me -1   –
   Makin' The Changes -1   –
   Sweet Patootie -1   –
   On Your Way -1   –
   Going Back To Texas   –
   Walkin' With Walker   –
   Ella Mae   –
   Mr. Freddie   –

LEE WALKER

Ten (-1); hca (-2); org (-1); pno; gtrs; dms. Los Angeles, c. 1965
A   Slipping In -2   Clara 110
B   Cold Sand -1   –

T-BONE WALKER

Real name Aaron Walker. Born Linden, Texas On May 28, 1910
Vcl/gtr. with Freddie Slack, pno; Jud DeNaut, bs; Dave Coleman, dms.
            Hollywood, July 20, 1942
54   I Got A Break Baby   Capitol 10033, 15033
55A   Mean Old World   –

Vcl/gtr. with Marl Young & His Orch; Brass; Saxes; Marl Youn, pno; gtr; bs; dms.
            Chicago, poss. May 1945
3305-1 Sail On Boogie   Rhumboogie 4000, 33
3306-1 I'm Still In Love With You   –
3307
3308-2 You Don't Love Me Blues   Rhumboogie 4003
3309-1, 2 T-Bone Boogie   Rhumboogie 4002
3310-1 Mean Old World Blues   Rhumboogie 4003
3311-2 Evenin'   Rhumboogie 4002

Vcl/gtr. with brass; saxes; pno; bs; dms   Chicago, 1945
409-2, 1036-
SW   My Baby Left Me   Mercury 8016, Old Swingmaster 11
410-2 Come Back To Me Baby (Blues) Mercury 8016, Constellation CS-6
311, 1040
SW   She Is Going To Ruin Me (Blues) Old Swingmaster 11,
            Constellation CS-6
   I Can't Stand Being Away From You –

  Note: Above 4 titles probably Marl Young recordings.
Vcl/gtr. with Jack McVea's All Stars: Joe "Red" Kelly, tpt; Jack McVea, ten; Tommy "Crow"
Kahn, pno; Frank Clarke, bs; Rabon Tarrant, dms. Hollywood, 1946
BW 410-2 No Worry Blues   Black & White 111
BW 411-2 Don't Leave Me Baby   –
BW 412-2 I'm Gonna Find My Baby   Black & White 110
BW 413-4 Bobby Sox Blues

Vcl/gtr. with Al Killian Quartet; Al Killian, tpt; Jack McVea, ten; Tommy "Crow" Kahn, pno;
Frank Clarke, bs; Rabon Tarrant, dms.   Hollywood, 1947
BW-504-2 I'm In An Awful Mood   Black & White 121
BW-505-4 It's A Lowdown Dirty Deal   Black & White 115
BW-506-1 Don't Give Me The Runaround
BW-507-1 Hard Pain Blues   Black & White 121

Vcl/gtr. with Teddy Buckner, tpt; Bump Meyers, ten; Lloyd Glenn, pno; Arthur Edwards,
bs; Oscar Lee Bradley, dms.   Hollywood, mid 1947
BW-635-3 I Know Your Wig Is Gone   Black & White 122, Capitol
(4378-3D-1)   57-70014, H-370, EP 20370
BW-636-1 T-Bone Jumps Again   Black & White 125, Capitol T1958
BW-637-3 Call It Stormy Monday   Black & White 122, Capitol
(4379-3D-1)   57-70014, H-370, EP 1-370, T1958

Vcl/gtr. with Teddy Buckner, tpt; Bumps Meyers, ten; Willard McDaniel, pno; Billy
Hadnott; bs; Oscar Lee Bradley, dms.   Los Angeles, November 6, 1947
BW-645-3   Midnight Blues   Black & White 127
BW-646
BW-647
BW-648-3   Long Skirt Baby Blues   Black & White 123
BW-649-1   Good Bye Blues   –
BW-650
BW-651-4   I'm Waiting For Your Call   Black & White 126

Vcl/gtr. with George Orendorff, tpt; Bumps Meyers, ten; Willard McDaniel, pno; Billy Hadnott, bs;
Oscar Lee Bradley, dms.   Los Angeles, November 1947
BW-656-1   That's Better For Me   Black & White 126
BW-657   First Love Blues   Comet T-53, Capitol 57-70042,
(4394-2D-2)   H-370, EP 2-370
BW-658-5   Lonesome Women Blues   Comet T-50

John Davis, bs. replaces Hadnott: Los Angeles, November 1947
BW-660-2   Inspiration Blues   Comet T-51
BW-661-2   Description Blues   Comet T-52
BW-662   T-Bone Shuffle   Comet T-53, Capitol 57-70042
(4395)-2D-1)   H-370, EP 1-370, T1958

Jack Trainor, tpt. replaces Orendorff; Hadnott, bs. replaces Davis:
                                                     Hollywood, 1947
BW-657-2   That Old Feeling Is Gone   Comet T-52
BW-684-2   Plain Old Down Home Blues   Black & White 127

Same:
BW-695-2   I Want A Little Girl   Black & White 125, Capitol T 1958
BW-696-1   I'm Still In Love With You   Comet T-51, Capitol T 1958
BW-697
BW-698-3   West Side Baby   Comet T-50, Capitol T1958

Vcl/gtr. with same instrumentation:
4397-2D-1   She's My Old Time Uesed To Be   Capitol 944, H-370
4398
4399-4D-2   Long Lost Love Blues   Capitol 57-70023
4400
4401-3D-1   Too Much Trouble Blues   Capitol 944
4402-2D-1   Hypin' Women Blues   Capitol 57-70025, H-370
4403
4404-1D-1   On Your Way Blues   Capitol 799
4405
4406-3D-3   Vacation Blues   Capitol 57-70012
4407
4408-3D-2   Prison Blues (Hometown Blues)   Capitol 57-70012
4415-2S-2   Born To Be No Good   Capitol 57-70025, H-370, T1958
4416-3D-1   Go BackTo The One You Love   Capitol 799, H-370, T1958
4417, 2D-1 You're My Best Poker Hand (no tpt)   Capitol 57-70023, T1958

Vcl/gtr. with similar to last:
            I Wish You Were Mine   Black & White unissued
            Wise Man Blues   Black & White unissued

T-BONE WALKER & HIS BAND
Vcl/gtr. with Eddie Hutcherson, tpt; Eddie Davis, ten/bari; Edward Hale, alt; Zell Kindred,
pno; Buddy Woodson, bs; Robert "Snake" Simms, dms.   Los Angeles, April 5, 1950
IM 174-5   Glamour Girl   Imperial 5071, LP 9116
IM 175-3   Strollin' With Bones   –   , LP 9098
IM 176   The Sun Went Down   Imperial 5086,   – , 9210
IM 177   You Don't Love Me   –   –
IM 178   Travelin' Blues   Imperial 5094, LP 9210
IM 179   The Hustle Is On   Imperial 5081, LP 9116
IM 180   Baby Broke My Heart   –
IM 181   Evil Hearted Woman   Imperial 5094, LP 9098

Vcl/gtr. with Marl Young, pno; Billy Hadnott, bs + others.   Los Angeles, 1950

IM 221	I Walked Away	Imperial 5103
IM 222	No Reason	Imperial 5116
IM 223	Look Me In The Eye	–
IM 224	Too Lazy	Imperial 5103

Vcl/gtr. with tpt; alt; Maxwell Davis, ten; Willared McDaniel, pno; Billy Hadnott, bs; Oscar
Lee Bradley, dms.   Los Angeles, 1951

IM 329	Alimony Blues	Imperial 5153, LP 9116
IM 330	Life Is Too Short	– , LP 9146
IM 331	You Don't Understand (Alibi)	Imperial 5147, LP 9098, 5384
IM 332	Welcome Blues (Say Pretty Baby)	– , LP 9146, 9098, 5384
IM 333	I Get So Weary	Imperial 5161, Post 2002, LP 9146, 9210
IM 334	You Just Wanted To Use Me	Imperial 5161, LP 9146
IM 335	Tell Me What's The Reason	Imperial 5247, LP 9098, Post 2002
IM 336	I'm About To Lose My Mind	Imperial 5261, LP 9116

Vcl/gtr. with   Hollywood, 1951

IM 383	Cold, Cold Feeling	Imperial 5171, LP 9098, 9210
IM 384	News For You Baby	– , LP 9116
IM 385	Get These Blues Off Me	Imperial 5181
IM 386	I Got The Blues Again	– LP 9098
IM 387	Through With Women	Imperial LP 9146
IM 388	Street Walkin' Woman	Imperial 5202, LP 9146
IM 389	Blues Is A Woman	– , LP 9098
IM 390	I Got The Blues	Imperial 5193, LP 9116

Vcl/gtr. with T. J. Fowler's Band; John Lawton, tpt; Lee Gross, alt; Walter Cox, ten; T. J. Fowler,
pno; Henry Ivory, bs; Clarance Stamps, dms.
or
Vcl/gtr. with Jim Wynn & His Orch; ? Smith, tpt; 2nd tpt; Pete ?, Maxwell Davis, tens; Edward
Hale, alt; Jim Wynn, bari; Willard McDaniel or Zell Kindred, pno; R. S. "T-Bone Jr." Rankin,
gtr; Buddy Woods, bs; Oscar Lee Bradley or Robert "Snake" Sims, dms.

Hollywood, 1952

IM 403	Here In The Dark	Imperial 5239, LP 9146
IM 404	Blue Mood	Imperial 5216, LP 9098
IM 405	Everytime	Imperial 5247, LP 9116
IM 406	I Miss You Baby	Imperial 5261, LP 9146

Hollywood, March 10, 1952

IM 409	Lollie Lou	Imperial 5193, LP 9146
IM 410	Party Line	Imperial 5239,
IM 411	Love Is A Gamble	Imperial 5311, LP 9116
IM 412	High Society	– , LP 9146
IM 519	I'm Still In Love With You	Imperial LP 9116
IM 520	Got No Use For You	Imperial 5216, LP 9146
IM 521	Railroad Station Blues	Imperial 5228
IM 522	Long Distance Blues	–
IM 493	My Baby Left Me Blues	unissued
IM 494	Come Back To Me Baby	–
IM 495	Fast Woman	–
IM 496	I Can't Stand Being Away From You	–

Hollywood, late 1953

IM 644	Vida Lee	Imperial 5274
IM 645	My Baby Is Now On My Mind	–
IM 646	Doin't Time	Imperial 5962
IM 647	Bye Bye Baby	Imperial 5284, LP 9116
IM 651	When The Sun Goes Down	Imperial 5264
IM 652	Pony Tail	→
IM 653	Wanderin' Heart	Imperial 5284
IM 654	I'll Always Be In Love With You	unissued

Hollywood, early 1954

IM 738	I'll Understand	Imperial 5330
IM 739	Hard Way	–
IM 740	Teen-Age Baby	Imperial 5299, LP 9116
IM 741	Strugglin' Blues	–

Vcl/gtr. with Andrew "Goon" Gardner, alt; Eddie Chamblee, ten; McKinley Easton, bari;
Junior Wells, hca(-1); Johnny Young, pno; Ransom Knowling, bs; Leroy Jackson, dms.

		Chicago, April 21, 1955
A 1517	Papa Ain't Salty	Atlantic 1065, LP 8020
A 1518		
A 1519	Why Not	Atlantic 1074, LP 8020
A 1520	T-Bone Shuffle	Atlantic 1065, –
A 1521	Play On Little Girl -1	Atlantic 1074, –
	Shufflin' The Blues	Atlantic LP 8020

Vcl/gtr. with Lloyd Glenn, pno; Billy Hadnott, bs; Oscar Lee Bradley, dms.

		Los Angeles, December 14, 1956
	Mean Old World	Atlantic LP 8020
	Stormy Monday	–
	Blues For Marili	–
	T-Bone Blues	–

Vcl/gtr. with Plas Johnson, ten; Ray Johnson, pno; R. S. Rankin, gtr; Barney Kessel, gtr;
Joe Comfort, bs; Earl Palmer, dms.

		Los Angeles, December 27, 1959
	Two Bones And A Pick	Atlantic LP 8020
	Evenin'	–
	Blues Rock	–

Vcl/gtr. with 2 tens: bari; org; gtr; bs-gtr; dms.

		Chicago, October 1964
	Jealous Woman	unissued
	Hey, Hey Baby	Modern 1004,
	Should I Let You Go	–

Vcl/gtr. with tpt; ten; org; bs-gtr; dms

		Pasadena, Texas 1966
TBW 1,		
40002	Reconsider Baby	Jet Stream 730
TBW 2,		
40003	I'm Not Your Fool No More	–
TBW 3	She's A Hit	Jet Stream 738
TBW 4	T-Bone's Back	–

No details;		
119, 101	Treat Your Daddy Well	Decca unissued
119, 102	You Ought To Know Better	–
119, 103	Let Your Hair Down Baby	–
119, 104	Old Time Used To Be	–
119, 105	You Don't Love Me And I Don't Care	–
119, 106	It Ain't No Right In You	–
119, 107	I Ain't Your Fool No More	–
119, 108	Don't Let Your Heartache Catch You Crying	–
119, 109	I Don't Be Jiving	–
119, 110	Hate To See You Go	–.
119, 111	It Takes A Lot Of Know-How	–

Note: Above purchased by Decca Records, New York from Jet Stream.

T-BONE WALKER JR.

Real name R. S. Rankin
Vcl/gtr. with the Untouchables Orch; tpt; saxes; pno; bs; dms.

		Los Angeles, 1962
MN-101-A	Midnight Bells Are Ringing	Midnite 101
MN-101-B	Empty Feeling	–

SIPPIE WALLACE

Born
Vcl. with Artie Starks, clt; Albert Ammons, pno; Lonnie Johnson, gtr; John Lindsey, bs;
Tommy Taylor, dms

		Chicago, September 25, 1945
117	Bedroom Blues	Mercury 2010
118		
119		
121	Buzz Me	Mercury 2010

FINE ARTS TRIO

Vcl/pno. with gtr;   Detroit, 1959

A	Mother Nature Is The Cause	Fine Art 201
B	Junior My Little Parakeet	–
A	Caught In The Web Of Sin	Fine Art 203
B	Loving You As I Loved You	–
B	Here I Go Where The Morning Glories Grow	Fine Art 204
	(rev. by Bill Thomas)	

WITH JAMES COHEN TRIO

Vcl. with pno; gtr; dm.   Detroit Mid 1962

B	Loving You As I Loved You	Bango 506
	(rev. by James Cohen)	
	I'm A Might Tight Woman	unissued
	Let It End Like That	

Vcl/pno.   Copenhagen, October 23, 1966

Up The Country Blues	Storyville 198

Vcl. with Roosevelt Sykes, pno;

Trouble Everywhere I Roam	Storyville 198
Lonesome Hours Blues	–
Gambler's Dream	–
Shorty George Blues	–
Bedroom Blues	–

Vcl. with Little Brother Montgomery, pno.

Woman Be Wise	Storyville 198
Special Delivery Blues	–
Murder Gonna Be My Crime	–
Caldonia Blues	–
You Got To Know How	–
I'm A Mighty Tight Woman	–

Note: Also recorded with Albert Ammons.

MUDDY WALTERS

Vcl. with tpt; alt; ten; pno; gtr; bs; dms,   Detroit, 1948

K 5619	Dissatisfied	Federal 12409, King LP 725
K 5620	Baby Look At You	
K 5621	There Goes My Heart	unissued
K 5622	Good Morning Baby	unissued

Note: This artist also recorded with Paul Williams.

JAMES WALTON

JAMES WALTON & HIS BLUES KINGS

Vcl/hca. with pno; gtr; dms.   Detroit, 1963

H 75	Leaving Blues	Hi-Q 5029
H 76	Miss Jessie James	–

J. WALTON

Vcl/hca. with saxes; org; Clarence Walton, gtr; bs-gtr; dms.   Detroit, c. 1964

RITE 1296/		
13833 003A	Tell Me What You Got	Big Star 003
RITE 1296/		
13834 003B	Shade Grove	–

MERCY DEE WALTON

See under Mercy Dee.

SQUARE WALTON

Vcl/gtr. with Sonny Terry, hca; pno; gtr; dms.   New York City? 1953

E3VB-1911	Bad Hangover	Victor 20-5584
E3VB-1912	Gimme Your Bank Roll	Victor 20-5493

| E3VB-1913 | Fish Tail Blues | Victor 20-5584 |
| E3VB-1914 | Pepper Head Woman | Victor 20-5493 |

WADE WALTON

Born in Lombardy, Mississippi on October 10, 1923
Vcl/gtr. or razor-stropping with R. C. Smith, gtr(-1)   Clarksdale, July 24, 1960

| | Barbershop Rhythm -1 | Arhoolie F 1005 |
| | Rooster Blues | – |

Vcl/hca./gtr. with Memphis Mango, gtr(-1)   Clarksdale, summer 1962

	Big Fat Mama	Bluesville BVLP 1060
	Choo Choo De Shoo Shoo -1	–
	Short-Hair Woman	–
	Forty-Four	–
	Kansas City Blues	–
	Rock Me Mama	–
	Blues Stay Away From Me	–
	Parchman Farm	–
	Big Six	–
	Shake 'Em Down	–

HAROLD "THUNDERHEAD" WARD

No details: Chicago, 1959

| | I Want You To Come Back Home | Allan 108 |
| | How Wild Can A Woman Be | – |

EDDIE WARE & HIS BAND (see also in APPENDIX)

Vcl/pno. with Eddie Chamblee, vcl(-1)/ten; Little Walter, gtr; Ransom Knowling, bs; dms.

		Chicago, 1951
U 7311	Jealous Woman	Chess 1507
U 7312	Wandering Lover	Chess 1461
U 7313		
U 7314	Lima Beans -1	Chess 1461, LP 2973
No details:		Chicago, 1952
U 7425	Give Love Another Chance	Chess 1507
No details:		Chicago , 1953
U 1296	That's The Stuff I Like	States 130
U 1297	Lonely Broken Heart	

PETER WARFIELD

Vcl/pno.   Houston, 1947

| Hu 141 | Morning Train Blues | Miltone 5249, Blues Classics BC-14 |
| Hu 142 | Ragtime Boogie | – |

BABY BOY WARREN

Real name Robert Warren
Vcl/gtr. with Charley Mills, pno.   Detroit, 1949

PR706A	My Special Friend Blues	Staff 706, Gotham 507
PR706B	Nervy Woman Blues	
RW707A	Lonesome Cabin Blues	Staff 707
RW707B	Don't Want No Skinny Woman	–
BW 709A-1,		
F 1016	Forgive Me Darling	Staff 709, Federal 12008
BW 709B-1,		
F 1017	Please Don't Think I'm Nosey	– –

Note: Staff 707 credited to Baby Boy Warren & His Buddy.

JOHNNY WILLIAMS

Vcl/gtr. with Boogie Woogie Red, pno; Curtis Foster, dms. Detroit, 1950
717A 255A I Got Lucky   Staff 717, Swing Time 225
717B, 255B Let's Renew Our Love   –   –

BABY BOY WARREN

Vcl/gtr. with Sonny Boy Williamson, hca; Boogie Woogie Red, pno; Calvin Frazier, gtr;
Washboard Willie, wbd.   Detroit, 1953/54
26A, 2211A Sanafee (Not Welcome Anymore)   JVB 26, Excello 2211, Blues
                                                            Classics 12
26B   Hello Stranger   JVB 26
59A   Chicken   Drummond 3002, Blues Classics 12
59B   Baby Boy Blues   –   –
 2211B   Chuck-A-Luck -1   Excello 2211

          Note: -1 This is an alternate take of "Chicken".

Omit hca;
54-113   Mattie Mae   Blue Lake 106
54-114   Santa Fe   –   , Blues Classics 12

Vcl/gtr. with Johnny Hooks, ten(-1); Boogie Woogie Red, pno; Little George Jackson, lead gtr;
Jimmy Tarrant, dms.
310   Somebody Put Bad Luck On Me -1   Drummond 3003
311   Stop Breakin' Down -1   –
633A   Taxi Driver   Sampson 633
633B   Bad Lover Blues   –

WASHBOARD PETE

See under Ralph Willis.

WASHBOARD SAM

Real name Robert Brown. Born Memphis, Tennessee in 1910, Died Chicago, Illinois in 1966.
Vcl/wbd, withJ. T. Brown, ten; Roosevelt Sykes, pno; Big Bill Broonzy, gtr; Willie Dixon, bs.
                                                            Chicago, February 18, 1947
D7-VB-316   You Can't Make The Grade   Victor 20-2440
D7-VB-317   You Can't Have None Of That   Victor 20-2297
D7-VB-318   I Just Couldn't Help It   –
D7-VB-319   Soap And Water Blues   Victor 20-2440

Vcl/wbd. with Oett "Sax" Mallard, alt/clt; Bob Call, pno; Big Bill Broonzy gtr; Ernest "Big"
Crawofrd, bs   Chicago, October 16, 1947
D7-VB-1078 Facing Life   Victor 20-3024
D7-VB-1079 No Special Rider   Victor 20-2606
D7-VB-1080 Ramblin' With That Woman   –
D7-VB-1081 Love Me Or Let Me Be   Victor 20-3024

Ransom Knowling, bs; replaces Crawofrd, add Judge Riley, dms.
                                                            Chicago, November 4, 1947
D7-VB-1132 She's Just My Size   Victor 20-2856
D7-VB-1133 You Know How I Feel   Victor 20-3201
D7-VB-1134 Fool About That Woman   Victor 20-2856
D7-VB-1135 Dollar Is Your Best Friend   Victor 20-3201

Vcl/wbd. withEddie "Sugarman" Penigar, ten; Bob Call, pno; Willie Lacey, gtr; Ransom
Knowling, bs.   Chicago, February 25, 1949
D9-VB-388   No. 1 Drunkard   Victor 22-0017
D9-VB-389   I'm Just Tired   Victor 22-0039, 50-0023
D9-VB-390   Maybe You Love Me   –
D9-VB-391   Nothing In Rambling   Victor 22-0017

Same: Chicago, October 27, 1949
D9-VB-1999 You Said You Loved Me   Victor 22-0063, 50-0048
            Market Street Swing   –
            Motherless Child Blues   Victor 22/50-0090
            Gamblin' Man   –

338

Vcl/wbd. with Lee Cooper, gtr; Ernest "Big" Crawofrd, bs.		Chicago, 1953
U 7512	Bright Eyes	Chess 1545, LP 1468
U 7513	Diggin' My Potatoes	– – , 1446, Argo LP 4034, Checker 1071
U 7514	Never, Never	Chess LP 1468
U 7515	By Myself	–
U 7516	Shirt Tail	–

Vcl/wbd. with Memphis Slim, pno; Big Bill Broonzy, gtr; Ernest "Big" Crawford, bs.		Chicago, 1953
U 7518	Mindin' My Own Business	Chess LP 1468
U 7519	Horseshoe Over My Door	–
U 7520	I'm A Lonely Man	–
U 7517	untitled	unissued

Note: Checker 1071 issued as by Little Walter.

WASHBOARD WILLIE

Real name William Emsley
WASHBOARD WILLIE & HIS SUPER SUDS OF RHYTHM

Vcl/wbd/dm. with Calvin Frazier, gtr;		Palmer House, Detroit, 1956
A	Cherry Red Blues	JVB 59
B	Washboard Shuffle	–
A	Washboard Blues Pt. 1	JVB 70
B	Washboard Blues Pt. 2	–

Vcl/percussion.		Detroit, c. 1964
A	A Fool On A Mule In The Middle Of The Road	Von 702
B	Hambone	–

Vcl/wbd. with prob. Evans McLendon, gtr; Angelo Willis, bs-gtr;		Detroit, 1966
ZTSC 121014	Natural Born Lover	Herculon (no number)
ZTSC 121015	Wee Baby Blues	–

Note: See also Calvin Frazier.

ALBERT WASHINGTON & THE KINGS

Vcl. with org; 2 gtrs; dms.		Boston, 1965
M 5036	You're Gonna Miss Me	Bluestown 703
M 5037	Ramble	–
No details		
	So Tired	VLM 1100
	I Haven't Got A Friend	–

D. C. WASHINGTON'

Real name D. C. Bendy. Born Arbana, Texas on June 19, 1919.

Vcl/gtr.		Houston, 1949
A	Rebob Boogie	Gold Star 661
B	Happy Home Blues	–

Note: See also Big Son Tillis & D. C. Bender.

CROWN PRINCE WATERFORD

Real name Charles Waterford,

Vcl. with Gerald Wilson's Band; tpt; saxes; pno; gtr; bs; dms.		Los Angeles, March 13, 1947
129-1 (AL 189A)	The Prince Strikes Back	Aladdin 534
131-1 (AL 189B)	Whistler's Blues	–
130	Washboard Blues	Aladdin 535, 3009
132	Undercover Blues	– –

Vcl. with   Chicago, 1946
    Girl Friend   Hytone 20
    Satisfied Blues   —

Vcl. with ten; Pete Johnson, pno; Shifty Henry, bs; Jesse Price, dms.
               Los Angeles, November, 1947

2562	Move Your Hand Baby	Capitol 40074
2563	L. A. Blues	Capitol 40132
2564	Coal Black Blues	Capitol 40103
2565	Weeping Willow Blues	Capitol 40074
2566	Strange Woman's Boogie	Capitol 40132
2567	P. J. Blues	Capitol 40137
2568	Crown Prince Blues	Capitol 40103
2569	Leaping Boogie (no ten)	Capitol 40137, T 1057

Vcl. with Harold Land, ten; Leon Pettis, dms; John Jackson, Froebel Brigham, William Doty, Stanley Joyce, unk, insts.   Los Angeles, June 3, 1949

5734	All Over Again	unissued
5735	You Turned Your Back On Me	King 4310
5736	Get Away From My Door	unissued
5737	Bow Wow Boogie	King 4310

Vcl. with Johnny Grimes, tpt; Dickie Harris, tbn; Joe Thomas, ten; Orrington Hall, bari; George Rhodes, pno; George Duvivier, bs; Alphonso Bright, dms. Cincinnati, March 15, 1950

K 5866	I'm Sweet On You	King 4393
K 5867	Kissing Bug Boogie	King 4374
K 5868	Hard Driving Woman	—
K 5869	Time To Blow	King 4393

Vcl. with brass & rhythm: Dallas, 1952

2026	Eatin' Watermelon	Torch 6911
2027		
2028	Love Awhile	Torch 6911

Vcl. with ten; bari; pno; gtr; bs; dms.   Nashville? 1956

A	Driftwood Blues	Excello 2065
B	I'm Gonna Do Right	—

Vcl. with
    Teenage Twister   Orbit 6942
    I Don't Want To Get Married —

    Note: Also recorded with Jay McShann.

KATIE WATKINS

Vcl. with Sax Kari's Orch; 2 gtrs; dms.   Detroit, 1957
A	Trying To Get You Off My Mind	Viceroy 3333, Checker 879
	(rev. by Texas Red & Jimmy q.v.)	

ALABAMA WATSON

Vcl/gtr. with dms   Boston, 1964

M 5054	Cost Time	Bluestown 704
M 5055	Mean Old Train	Bluestown 706
M 5056	I Wanna Boogie	—
M 5057		
M 5058		
M 5059		
M 5060	My Baby Left Me	Bluestown 704

K. C. "MO JO" WATSON

Vcl. with ten; pno; gtr; bs; dms.   Los Angeles, 1961

NR 1105	Love Bloodhound	Nanc 003
NR 1106	I Keep On Trying	—

    Note: Is This Mojo Watson?

MOJO WATSON

Vcl/gtr. with pno; gtr; dms.   New York City, 1952
| 1203 | You Know You Don't Want Me | Atlas 1080 |
| 1204 | All Alone | – |

JAMES WAYNE (or WAYNES)

Vcl. with tpt; Ed Wiley, ten; Willie Johnson, pno; Donald Cooks, bs; Ben Turner, dms.

Houston, 1951
2200	Gypsy Blues (I'm A Real Gypsy Fellow	SIW 573, Time LP 4
2201	Please Baby Please	SIW 622, Time LP 7006
2215	Millionaire Blues (If I Were A Millionaire)	SIW 573, Time LP 4
2274	Love Me Blues	SIW 588
2275	Tend To Your Business	–

Vcl. with saxes; pno; gtr; bs; dms.   Atlanta, 1951
2354	Which Woman Do I Love	SIW 607, Imperial LP 9210
2355	I'm Going To Tell Your Mother	SIW 622
2356	Junco Partner	SIW 607, Time LP 2, LP7006
2359	Money Blues	SIW 639, – –
2360	Bullcorn	–

Vcl/dms. with Warren Bell, alt; Lee Allen, ten; Edward Frank, pno; Justin Adams, gtr;
Frank Fields, bs.   New Orleans, September 13, 1951
IM 341	When Night Falls	Imperial 5151, LP 9144
IM 342	Crazy About You	unissued
IM 343	Home Town Blues	Imperial 5151, LP 9144
IM 344	Bad Morning Blues	Imperial LP 9144

Same: New Orleans, September 19, 1951
IM 345	Agreeable Woman	Imperial 5166, LP 9144
IM 346	Vacant Pillow Blues	– –
IM 347	A Two Faced Woman	Imperial 5160, –
IM 348	Bad Weather Blues	– –

Similar   omit saxes.   New Orleans, 1951
IM 395	Hard To Handle	Imperial LP 9144, 5696
IM 396	I'm In Love With You	Imperial 5258, LP 9144
IM 397	Let's Have A Ball	Imperial LP 9144, 5696
IM 398-RE	Sweet Little Woman	Imperial 5258, LP 9144, 5725
IM 398	Lover's Return	Imperial 5725, LP9144

Vcl. with saxes; pno; gtr; bs; dms.   Los Angeles, March 1, 1954
RR 2260	Crying In Vain	Aladdin 3234
RR 2261	All The Drinks Are Gone	unissued
RR 2262	Lonely Room	Aladdin 3234
RR 2263	My Greatest Love	unissued

Same: Los Angeles, 1954
| A | Junco's Return | Million 2009 |
| B | Gotta Good Girl | – |

WEE WILLIE WAYNE
Vcl/whistling. with pno; gtr; bs; dms.   New Orleans? 1955
IM 876	Travelin' Mood	Imperial 5355, 5725 LP 9144
IM 877	I Remember	Imperial 5355, LP 9144
IM 898	Good News	Imperial 5368
IM 899	Wee Willie Shuffle	unissued

New Orleans? October, 1956
| IM 928 | Don't Mention My Name | unissued |
| IM 929 | Kinfolks | Imperial 5368 |

JAMES WAYNE
Vcl. with pno; gtr; bs; dms.   Houston? 1956
| FR 1016 | Yes I Do | Peacock 1672 |
| FR 1017 | Please Be Mine | – |

No details.   1960
                        The Trust   Angletone 540
                        This Little Letter   –

WEE WILLIE WAYNE
Vcl. with   New Orleans? 1961
IM 2898   I Got To Be Careful   Imperial 5737
IM 2899   Tend To Your Business   Imperial LP 9210
IM 2900   All I'm Asking Of You   unissued
IM 2901   Woman I'm Tired   Imperial 5737
            Note: Imperial LP 9144 credited to Wee Willie Wayne
IM 2974   You're The Girl For Me   unissued
IM 2975   I Still Love You   unissued

WEE WILLIE WAYNE

See under James Wayne

CURLEY WEAVER

Vcl/gtr. with Blind Willie McTell, gtr;   Atlanta, early 1950
C 2042   My Baby's Gone   SIW 547
C 2043   Ticket Agent   –
Same: Atlanta, 1950
1274   Wee Midnight Hours   unissued
1275
1276
1277
1278
               She Don't Treat Me Good No More   Savoy MG 16000

CURLEY WEAVER & HIS GUITAR
Vcl/gtr.
J-481   Some Rainy Day   SIW 646
J-482   Trixie   –

BOOGIE BILL WEBB

Born ? in 1926.
Vcl/gtr. with gtr; dms.   New Orleans,1953.
IM 585   I Ain't For It   Imperial 5257
IM 586   Love Me Mama   unissued
IM 587   Bad Dog   Imperial 5257
IM 588   Bill's Boogie   unissued

ERVIN WEBB

Vcl.   Parchman Farm, Miss.,1959
               I'm Goin' Home   Prestige Int. 25010

KATIE WEBSTER

Born Houston, Texas on January 9, 1939.

KATIE WEBSTER & ASHTON CONROY
Vcl/pno. with Ashton Savoy, vcl/gtr; Little Brother Griffin, dms.
                                                               Crowley, La. 1958
K 1   Baby, Baby   Kry 100
K 2   I Want You To Love Me   –
KATIE WEBSTER
Vcl/pno. with   Crowley La, 1960/62
               Sea Of Love   Decca ?
               I Feel So Low
Vcl/pno. with Lionel Prevo, ten; Al Foreman, gtr; Bobby McBride, bs-gtr; Warren Storm, dms.
R 7004   Open Arms   Rocko 503
R 7005,

                                    342

A702	On The Sunny Side Of Love	− , Action 1000
A 701	Close To My Heart	Action 1000
LH 1925	Glory Of Love	Spot 1000
LH 1926	The Katie Lee	−
R 7024	Goodbye Baby I'm Still Leaving You Pt. 1	Rocko 513
R 7025	Goodbye Baby I'm Still Leaving You Pt. 2	−
Z 7450	Hoowee Sweet Daddy	Zynn 505
Z 7451	I Need You Baby, I Need You	−

Vcl/hca. (-1) with Donald Hankins, Jarrett "Gerry" Gibson, saxes; John Walker, pno;
Earl Hooker, gtr; Jack Meyers, bs-gtr; Fred Below, dms.

25-157	Messin' With The Kid	Chief 7021
25-158	You Sure Look Good To Me	Chief 7034
25-159	So Tired	Chief 7037
25-160	Universal Rock -1	Chief 7021

Add vibes(-2):

26-114	Love Me	Chief 7037
26-115	It Hurts Me Too	Chief 7035
26-116		
26-117	I Need Me A Car -2	Chief 7038

Vcl/hca. with Jarrett "Gerry" Gibson, ten; Lafayette Leake, pno; Billy Emerson, org;
Lacey Gibson, gtr; Jack Meyers, bs-gtr; Gill Day, dms.   Chicago, February 28, 1963

2558	I'll Get You Too	USA 736
2559	Every Goodbye Ain't Gone	−
2560, USA		
788	She's A Sweet One	USA 742
2560, USA		
787	When The Cat's Gone The Mice Play	−

Vcl/hca. with Buddy, Guy, gtr; Jack Meyers, bs-gtr; Billy Warren, dms.

		Chicago, late 1965
	Snatch It Back And Hold It	Delmark DL-612
	Ships On The Ocean	−
	Good Morning Schoolgirl	−
	Hound Dog	−
	In The Wee Wee Hours	−
	Hey Lawdy Mama	−
	Hoodoo Man Blues	−
	Early In The Morning	−
	We're Ready	−
	You Don't Love Me	−
	Chittlin Con Carne	−
	Yonder Wall	−

Fred Below, dms. replaces Warren:

	A Tribute To Sonny Boy Williamson	Vanguard VRS 9216
	It Hurts Me Too	−
	Messin' With The Kid	−
	Vietcong Blues	−
	All Night Long	−

Vcl/hca. with saxes; pno; bs-gtr; dms,   Chicago, 1966

BS-10740	Up In The Heah	Bright Star 149
BS-10741	Junior's Groove	−

Vcl/hca. with Buddy Guy, gtr; Leroy Stewart, bs-gtr; Fred Below, dms.

		Peppers Lounge, Chicago, 1966
	It's My Life Baby	Vanguard VRS 9231
	It's So Sad To Be Lonely	−
	Early In The Morning	−
	Look How Baby	−

Little Al, dms. replaces Below: add Walter Beasley, gtr;   Chicago, 1966

	Country Girl	Vanguard VRS 9231
	You Lied To Me	−
	Stormy Monday	−
	Shake It Baby	−
	Checking On My Baby	−

343

Stomach Ache   –
Slow, Slow   –
Everything's Going To Be Alright   –

Vcl/hca. with Otis Rush, gtr; Jack Meyers, bs-gtr; Fred Below, dms.

                                         Berlin, October 16, 1966
Checkin' On My Baby   Fontana 885.431TY
A Tribute To Sonny Boy Williamson   –

OTIS WEBSTER

Vcl/gtr.   Angola, La. 1960
Penitentiary Blues   Storyville SLP 125
Standing At The Greyhound Bus Station   –
Ball And Chain For Me   –

ROBERT "GUITAR" WELCH

Born Memphis, Tennessee on May 5, 1896.

Vcl/gtr.   Angola, La. 1960
Electric Chair Blues   Louisiana Folk Society LF-3
Back Water Blues   –
Lonesome Blues   Storyville SLP 125
Boll Weevil Blues   –
Bad Luck   –

JUNIOR WELLS

Born West Memphis, Arkansas on December 9, 1932

JUNIOR WELLS & HIS EAGLE ROCKERS
Vcl/hca. with Henry Gray pno(-1); Louis Miles, gtr; David Miles, bs-gtr; Fred Below, dms.
Muddy Waters, gtr; replaces Louis Miles (-2).   Chicago, 1953

1325	Cut That Out	States 122
1326		
1327	Hodo Man -1, 2	States 134, Blues Classics BC-8
	Hoodoo Man	
	Somebody Hoodooed The Hoodoo Man	
1328	So All Alone -1	States 143
1329	Eagle Rock	States 122
1330	Junior's Wail -1	States 134

Note: 1327 issued under all three titles at various times.

Same:
1441	'bout The Break Of Day	States 139
1442	Lawdy! Lawdy!	–
1443	Tomorrow Night	States 143

Note: Muddy Waters reputed to play 2nd harmonica on 1443. Aural evidence suggests that 122 and 134 were cut at different sessions despite matrix numbers.

Vcl/hca(-1). with Syl Johnson, gtr; David Miles, bs-gtr; Willie Dixon, bs; Eugene Lounge, dms.
                                        Chicago, 1957
25-111	Two-Headed Woman	Chief 7005,
25-112	Lovey Dovey Lovely One	– , 7034, USA 790
25-113	I Could Cry	Profile 4005
25-114	Cha Cha Cha In Blues (Cut My Toenail) -1	Chief 7035, Profile 4005 Bright Star 146

Note: Matrix number for Bright Star 146 is 1005. Vocal comments by Willie Dixon have been overdubbed.

Earl Hooker, gtr; replaces Johnson: add Lafayette Leake, pno;
25-119	Little By Little (I'm Losing You)	Profile 4011, Bright Star 146
25-120	Come On In This House -1	– USA 790

Note: Matrix number for Bright Star 146 is 1006.

Vcl. with Memphis Slim, pno; J. B. Lenoir, gtr; bs; dms.   New York City, 1959
K90-W 2916 So Tired   Shad 5010
K90-W 2917 Can't Live Without You Baby   –

Vcl. with Lafayette Leake, pno; Earl Hooker, gtr; David Miles, bs-gtr; Willie Dixon, bs;
Eugene Lounge, dms.   Chicago, 1960
S 866   You Don't Care   Profile 4013
S 867   Prison Bars All Around Me   —

Vcl. with John Walker, org; Earl Hooker, gtr; Willie Dixon, bs; dms.
                                                                Chicago, 1960/62
25-145   Galloping Horses A Lazy Mule   Chief 7016, 7039
             (rev. by Earl Hooker)

Vcl/hca. (-1) with Donald Hankins, Jarrett "Gerry" Gibson, saxes; John Walker, pno; Earl
Hooker, gtr; Jack Meyers, bs-gtr; Fred Below, dms.
25-157   Messin' With The Kid   Chief 7021
25-158   You Sure Look Good To Me   Chief 7034
25-159   So Tired   Chief 7037
25-160   Universal Rock -1   Chief 7021

Add vibes (-2);
26-114   Love Me   Chief 7037
26-115   I Hurts Me Too   Chief 7035
26-116
26-117   I Need Me A Car -2   Chief 7038

Vcl/hca. with Jarrett "Gerry' Gibson, ten; Lafayette Leake, pno; Billy Emerson, org;
Lacey Gibson, gtr; Jack Meyers, bs-gtr; Gill Day, dms.   Chicago, February 28, 1963
2558   I'll Get You Too   USA 736
2559   Every Goodbey Ain't Gone   —
2560, USA
788   She's A Sweet One   USA 742
2561, USA
787   When The Cat's Gone The Mice Play   —

Vcl/hca, with Buddy Guy, gtr; Jack Meyers, bs-gtr; Billy Warren, dms.
                                                                Chicago, late 1965
             Snatch It Back And Hold It   Delmark DL-612
             Ships On The Ocean   —
             Good Morning Schoolgirl   —
             Hound Dog   —
             In The Wee Wee Hours   —
             Hey Lawdy Mama   —
             Hoodoo Man Blues   —
             Early In The Morning   —
             We're Ready   —
             You Don't Love Me   —
             Chittlin Con Carne   —
             Yonder Wall   —

Fred Below, dms; replaces Warren:
             A Tribute To Sonny Boy Williamson   Vanguard VRS 9216
             It Hurts Me Too   —
             Messin' With The Kid   —
             Vietcong Blues   —
             All Night Long   —

WEST TEXAS SLIM

See under Ernest Lewis.

WALTER J. WESTBROOK & HIS PHANTOM FIVE

Vcl. with saxes; hca(-1); pno; gtr; bs; dms; Hubert Wings, vcl(-2).
                                                                St. Louis, 1959
13398-1   Midnight Jump -1   Bobbin 106
13398-2   Bring Your Clothes Back Baby -2   —

ARTHUR WESTON

Vcl/gtr.
East St. Louis, 1964

	Uncle Sam Called Me	Testament T-2209
	Early In The Morning	–

Add George Robertson, hca; Big Joe Williams, gtr:

	Someday Baby	Storyville SLP 180
	Roll Me Over Slow	Storyville SLP 181

LITTLE DAVID WHEATON

Vcl/gtr. with wbd.
Los Angeles, 1947

1900	It Just Ain't For Me	Capitol 40139
1901	I Just Couldn't Help It	Capitol 40009
1902	There's All Kinds Of Women	–

Vcl/gtr. with org; dms.

2114	That's What I'm Talking About	Capitol 40139
2115	Too Long Blues	Capitol 40034
2116		
2117	Just You And Me	Capitol 40034

BUKKA WHITE

Real name Booker T. Washington White. Born Houstin, Mississippi on November, 12, 1909.
Vcl/gtr/pno(-1).
1963

	Baby Please Don't Go	Takoma LP 1001
	Aberdeen, Mississippi Blues	–
	New Orleans, Streamline	–
	Parchman Farm Blues	–
	Poor Boy Long Way From Home	–
	Rememberance Of Charlie Patton	–
	Shake 'Em On Down	–
	I Am In The Heavenly Way	–
	Atlanta Special	–
	Drunk Man Blues -1	–
	Army Blues	–
4051A	World Boogie	Takoma 31364
4051B	Midnight Blues	–

Same:
Berkeley, November 8, 1963

	My Baby -1	Arhoolie F 1019
	Drifting	unissued
	Boogie Twist	unissued
	World Boogie	unissued
	Boogie	unissued
	Blues	unissued

Same, add Big Willie, wbd(-1):
Berkeley, November 25, 1963

	Sugar Hill	Arhoolie F 1019
	SingleMan Blues	Arhoolie F 1020
	Bald Eagle Train -1	–
	Alabama Blues -1	Arhoolie F 1019
	Morgan David Wine	unissued
	Hip Cat Boogie	unissued
	Blues	unissued
	Boogie	unissued
	Baby, Good Bye -1	unissued
	John Henry Boogie -1	unissued
	Boogie -1	unissued
	Midnight Blues -2	Arhoolie F 1018

Note: -2 add Jimmy Rainey, dms.

Vcl./gtr.
Berkeley, November 26, 1963

	Georgia Skin Game	Arhoolie F 1020
	Jesus Died To Save The World	Arhoolie F 1019
	Good Gin Blues	unissued
	Jitterbug Swing	unissued
	Blues	unissued

	Corrinna	unissued
	Coming Around The Mountain	unissued
	Bald Eagle Train	unissued
	Mixed Water (no gtr)	Arhoolie F 1020
Vcl/gtr.		New York City, 1966
	Black Bottom	Verve-Folkways 3010
	Aberdeen Mississippi	–
	Thunderbird Blues	–
	Poor Boy	–

ARNOLD WILEY

ARNOLD WILEY
Vcl/pno. with Skippy Williams, ten/clt; Eddie Gibbs, gtr; John Brown, bs; George Turner, dms.

New York City, 1945/46

N 542	My Best Gal	Chicago 105
N 543	Barking Dog	–

Vcl/pno.　　　　　　　　　　　　　　　　New York City, July 29, 1947

R 1251	Wiley's Boogie	Apollo 391
R 1252	Plain Food Blues	–

DOC WILEY TRIO
Vcl/pno. with ten; gtr;　　　　　　　　　Detroit, 1948

K 5487	Bewildered	unissued
K 5488	Big Four Boogie	King 4241
K 5489	Big House Blues	–
K 5490	Chain Gang Blues	unissued
K 5491	Every Day In The Week	unissued
K 5492	Hard Hearted Lover Blues	unissued
K 5493	How Long	unissued
K 5494	I Want No One But You	unissued
K 5495	I'm Longing For Your Love	unissued
K 5496	I'm In Love Again	unissued
K 5497	In My Heart You're Everything	unissued
K 5498	Sugar Lips	unissued
K 5499, V1933	Track No. 19	Sensation 24
K 5500	Prison Bound Blues	unissued
K 5501, V1934	Wild Cat Boogie	Sensation 24

DOC WILEY
No details:　　　　　　　　　　　　　　1949

	Play Your Hand	Bullet 323
	The Doctor's Jump	–

ARNOLD WILEY'S BAND
Vcl. with Johnny Letman, tpt; Buster Bailey, clt; George Kelly, ten; Sammy Price, pno; Ralph Williams, gtr; Gene Ramey, bs; "Speedy", dms.　　New York, September 1959

A 111	It'll Be A Long Time	Ace 111
A 112	Squares Ain't Walking No More	–

DOC WILEY

See under Arnold Wiley.

ED WILEY

Teddy Reynolds, King Tut or J. Robins vcl. with Ed Wiley, ten; Henry Hayes, alt; Willie Johnson, pno; Donald Cooks, bs; Ben Turner, dms.　　　Houston 1950/51

2036	Blues After Hours	SIW 545
2038	Cry, Cry Baby	
2054	My Heart Is Going Down Slow	SIW 562
2055	Drifting All Alone	SIW 577
2104	Cotton Pickin' Blues	SIW 562
2214	Where Are You Baby	SIW 577

2261	Pack Up, Move Out	SIW 585
2262	West Indian Blues	–
4000	Molasses Molasses	SIW 582
4001	Jumpin' With The Blues	–
No details:		New York, December 22, 1951
A 756	So Glad I'm Free	Atlantic 959
A 757	Deep Moanin' Blues	–

IRENE WILEY

Vcl. with Ken Billing's Trio; pno; gtr; bs.

		New York City, c. 1946
2037A	Boa Hog Blues	Diamond 2037
2037X	Irene's Boogie Blues	–
	Big Fat Joe	Diamond 2038
	?	–

Note: Related to Arnold Wiley, q.v.

SLIM WILLETT SPECIAL ISSUE

Unknown 2 pnos.

| | | Los Angeles, 1953 |
| OP 188 | Four Hand Blues | Slim Willett OP-133 |

Unknown Vcl. with pno; gtr.

| OP 187 | The Fight | Slim Willett OP-133 |

Note: Record issued by hillbilly artist Willett, but is blues.

B. WILLIAMS - His Guitar & Trio

Vcl/gtr. with pno; bs.

		Houston, c. 1950
101A	You're So Near To Me	Top Tunes 101
101B	Mortgaged Love	–

BLIND BOY WILLIAMS

See under Brownie McGhee.

BLIND CONNIE WILLIAMS

Vcl/gtr.

		Philadelphia, May 5, 1961
	One Thin Dime	Storyville SLP 181
	Key To The Highway	Milestone LP 3002

Note: Florida Artist.

DONNIE WILLIAMS

Vcl. with ten; hca(-1); org; gtr; dms.

		Memphis, 1965
PG-522	Boogie Chillun's Playhouse -1	Pure Gold 311
PG-523	Mister B	–

EDDIE WILLIAMS

EDDIE WILLIAMS & THE BROWN BUDDIES
Floyd Dixon, vcl/pno; with Mitchell "Tiny" Webb, gtr; Eddie Williams, bs; Ellis Welsh, dms.
Add maraccas (-1).

		Los Angeles, 1947
SU 190	Houston Jump	Supreme 1528, Swing Time 261
SU 191	You Need Me Now	Supreme 1546, Swing Time 287
SU 192	Johnny Katherine	Supreme 1548
SU 193	Blues In Cuba -1	Supreme 1528
SU 194	I Saw Stars	Supreme 1547
SU 216	Red Head 'n' Cadillac	Supreme 1535
	Mississippi	Supreme 1542
SU 218	Broken Hearted	Supreme 1535, Swing Time 261
	Saturday Night Fish Fry	Supreme 1542
SU 220	Worries	Supreme 1547, Swing Time 287

SU 221	Umbrella Song	Supreme 1548
SU 222	Prairie Dog Hole	Supreme 1546

Lester Myrat, vcl/pno. with Edgar Rice, gtr; Eddie Williams, bs.

		Los Angeles, 1949
SE 88	Unfaithful Woman	Selective 121
SE 91	Right Now	–

Add Roy Porter, bongos:

		Los Angeles,
D 330	Wandering	Discovery 526
D 331	Blues For Cuba	–

No details:

Tingle Kissing Daddy	Crystal 303
Your Papa Is A Soldier Again	–
Sweet Pea	Crystal 304
I'm Singing The Blues Tonight	–

Note: See also Floyd Dixon.

JIMMY RAY WILLIAMS

Born Memphis, Tennessee ?
Vcl. with Elmore Nixon, pno; Lightnin' Hopkins, gtr; Robert Ingram, dms.

	Houston, November 24, 1965
Nobody Loves Me Take 1	unissued
Nobody Loves Me Take 2	unissued
I Don't Believe Take 1	unissued
I Don't Believe Take 2	unissued
I Don't Believe Take 3	unissued
You Know I Love You	unissued
On My Way To Memphis	unissued
Things I Need To Try	unissued
Too Late	unissued

JO JO WILLIAMS

Vcl/gtr. with hca; pno; gtr; dms.

		Chicago, 1959
A-1-310	All Pretty Wimmins	Atomic H (no number)
B-2-311	Rock 'n' Roll Boogie	–

Vcl. with Stephen Hawkins, tpt; Tommy Reader, ten/flt; Abraham Smothers, Robert Lee Whitehead, gtrs; Elijah Jordan, bs; Richard Fisher, dms.

	Chicago,
If You Love Me Baby	unissued
A Woman's World	unissued
Shakin' Around	unissued
untitled instrumental	unissued

Note: Above titles recorded by Jump Jackson.

JODY WILLIAMS

Real name Joe Leon Williams.

LITTLE PAPA JOE
Vcl/gtr. with ten; pno; bs; dms.

		Chicago, 1955
55-133	Looking For My Baby	Blues Lake 116
55-134	Easy Lovin'	–

JODY WILLIAMS
Vcl/gtr. with Harold Ashby, ten; Lafayette Leake, pno; Willie Dixon, bs; Phillip Thomas, dms.

		Chicago, 1957
8400	You May	Argo 5274
8482	Lucky Lou	–

SUGAR BOY WILLIAMS
Vcl/gtr. with saxes; pno; bs; dms.

		Chicago, 1960
H 1472	Five Long Years	Herald 555
H 1473	Little Girl	–

JODY WILLIAMS
Vcl/gtr. with   Chicago, 1962
         Hideout   Nike
         Moaning For Molasses   –

SUGAR BOY WILLIAMS
Vcl/gtr. with   1965
         Little Girl Take Your Time   Raines 2906
         Someday Darling   –

JODY WILLIAMS
Vcl/gtr. with   1966
         Time For A Change   Yulando 8665

JOE (LEE) WILLIAMS

Born Crawford, Mississippi on October 16, 1903.
Vcl/gtr. with Sonny Boy Williamson, hca; Jump Jackson, dms.

		Chicago, July 12, 1945
D5-AB-354	Drop Down Blues	unissued
D5-AB-355	Somebody's Been Worryin'	Bluebird 34-0739
D5-AB-356	Wanita	unissued
D5-AB-357	Vitamin A	Bluebird 34-0739

Vcl/gtr. with Clifford Dinwaddie, wbd.   Chicago   1945
A   His Spirit Lives On   Chicago 103
         (rev. by James McCain)

Vcl/gtr. with Sonny Boy Williamson, hca; Ransom Knowling, bs; Judge Riley, dms.

		Chicago, July 22, 1947
CCO 4833	Baby Please Don't Go	Columbia 37945, 30099
CCO 4834	Stack Of Dollars	Columbia 38055, 30107
CCO 4835	Mellow Apples	– –
CCO 4836	Wild Cow Moan	Columbia 37945, 30099
Same:		Chicago, December 18, 1947
CCO 4942	P Vine Blues	Columbia 30191
CCO 4943	Bad And Weakhearted Blues	unissued
CCO 4944	King Biscuit Stomp	Columbia 30129
CCO 4945	I'm A Highway Man	Columbia 30191
CCO 4946	Banta Rooster Blues	Columbia 38190, 30119
CCO 4947	Mean Step Father Blues	unissued
CCO 4948	House Lady Blues	Columbia 38190, 30119
CCO 4949	Don't You Leave Me Here	Columbia 30129

Vcl/gtr. with Singleton Palmer, bs.   St. Louis, 1949
         Jivin' Woman   Bullet 337
         She's A Married Woman   –

BIG JOE WILLIAMS & HIS 9 STRING GUITAR
Vcl/gtr.   Jackson, Miss.,1952

DRC 58	Mama Don't Allow Me	Trumpet 151
DRC 59	Delta Blues	–
Add bs:		
DRC 94,		
ACA 2125	Overhauling Blues	Trumpet 169
DRC 95,		
ACA 2126	Whistling Pines	–
ACA 2127	Friends And Pals	Trumpet 170 (unissued)
ACA 2128	Juanita	–
DRC 98,		
ACA 2124	She Left Me A Mule	Trumpet 171
DRC 99,		
ACA 2123	Bad Heart Blues	–

PO' JOE WILLIAMS
Vcl/gtr. with Sam Fowler, hca; Al Duncan, dms.   Chicago, October 16, 1956
56-558   Going Back Home   Vee Jay 227

56-559	Baby Left Town	Vee Jay 227
56-560	King's Highway	unissued
56-561	Eula Mae	unissued

Vcl/gtr. with Erwin Helfer, pno.   St. Louis, June 6, 1957

You Can't Do Me This Way	Delmark unissued
Wild Cow Moan	unissued
44 Blues	—
You Goin' Meet King Jesus	—
Every Day Brings About A Change	—
Haunted House Blues	—
Feel Like Rocking	—
Nobody Know Chicago Like I Do	—
Going Down State Street	—
He Got Wild	—
Bottle Up And Go	—
John Henry	—
Blues For Yancey	—
Rocks And Gravel	—
Hairdressin' Blues	—
88 and 8 Stomp	—
Loping Blues	—
Out Out Blues	—
Late Hours On A Ball	—
Shake 'Em On Down	—

POOR JOE WILLIAMS

Vcl/gtr. with Erwin Helfer, pno.   Chicago, September 1/3, 1957

Joe Williams' Blues	Collector JEN 3
All I Want Is My Train Fare Home	—
I'm Talking About You	—
Don't Leave Me Here (no pno)	—
Cow Cow Blues	Collector JEN 4
Crawlin' King Snake	—
I May Be Wrong (no pno)	—
Keep A Knockin'	—

Vcl/gtr.   St. Louis, January 10/11, 1958

Peach Orchard Mama	Delmark DL-602
Tailor Made Babae	—
Mellow Peaches	—
Omaha Blues	—
Baby Please Don't Go	unissued
Highway 49	→
I Got Wild	—
Hey Lawdy Mama	—
Tired	—
Back Door Blues	—
Interview	Delmark DL-602

Vcl/gtr. with J. D. Short, vcl(-1)/gtr/hca.   St. Louis February 8, 1958

No More Whiskey	Delmark DL-602
Drop Down Mama	—
Good Morning Little Schoolgirl	—
Shetland Pony Blues	—
Nobody Knows Chicago Like I Do	Delmark DL-609
Ramblin' Mind Blues (Mean Stepfather)	—
Stavin' Chain Blues -1	—
St. Louis Trouble Blues	unissued
Roll And Tumble	unissued
You're Gonna Need King Jesus	Delmark DL-609
Sweet Old Kokomo	—
Gonna Check Up On My Baby	—
Jumpin' In The Moonlight	—
You've Got To Help Me Some -1	—
Tailor Made Babay	unissued
J. D. Talks -1	Delmark DL-609

	Rambled And Wandered	Delmark DL-609
	Going Back To Crawford, Miss.	–
Vcl/gtr.		St. Louis, February 19, 1958
	Baby Please Don't Go	Delmark DL-602
	Jaunita	–
	Delmar Hop	unissued
	Prison Bound	–
	Good Morning Schoolgirl	–
	G. M. & O. Blues	–
	Stomping The Blues	–
	Wondering Blues	–
	Nobody Knows Chicago Like I Do	–
	Desert Blues	–
	Someday Baby	Delmark DL-602
Vcl/gtr.		Oakland, late 1959
	She Left Me A Mule To Ride	Arhoolie F 1002
	V-8 Ford Blues	unissued
	Peach Tree Blues	–
	New Car Blues	–
	Baby Please Don't Go	–
	Something Wrong With My Little Machine	–
Vcl/gtr.		Los Gatos, Calif. Oct. 5, 1960
	Greystone Blues	Arhoolie F 1002
	Sloppy Drunk Blues	–
	President Roosevelt	–
	Brother James	–
	So Glad	–
	Shake Your Boogie	–
	Mean Stepfather	–
	Vitamin A Blues	–
	Yo Yo Blues	–
	Married Woman Blues	Arhoolie 101
	Trouble About To Keep Me Down	unissued
	Lonesome Call Blues	–
	Woman I'm Loving Is Sleeping In A Grave	–
	Must I Holler	–
	Something Wrong With My Little Machine (2 takes)	unissued
	Break 'Em On Down	–
	Mama Don't Allow	–
	My Heart Is Getting Weak	–
	Don't You Leave Me Here	–
	Prison Bound	–
	Mellow Peaches	–
	Hitch Up My Pony, Saddle Up My Mare	–
	Bluebird Blues	–
	Tailor Made Baby	–
	Tom Moore's Farm	–
	P-Vine Blues	–
	Highway 49	–
	Someday Baby	–
	This Ain't My House	–
	Texas Blues	–
	Stack O'Dollars	–
Vcl/gtr. with Ransom Knowling, bs(-1)		Chicago, July 13, 1961
	Highway 49 Blues -1	Delmark DL-604
	Blues Left Texas	–
	13 Highway	–
	Down In The Bottom	–
	Overhaul Your Machine	–
	That Thing's In Town -1	–
	Walk On Little Girl	–

Arkansas Woman	Delmark DL-604
Four Corners Of The World -1	—

Vcl/gtr.   Chicago, July 20, 1961

Poor Beggar	Delmark DL-604
Tiajuana Blues	—

from Last sessions:

Whistling Pines	Folkways FS-3820
Bluebird Blues	—
She'll Be Coming Round The Mountain	—
Elevate Me Baby -1	—
Mama Don't Allow Me To Fool Around All Night Long	—
Kingshighway Blues (sic)	—
Somebody's Been Fooling Take 1 -1	—
Somebody's Been Fooling Take 3 -1	—
Rooting Ground Hog	—
Don't Leave Me Here	—
T. B. Blues	—
King Biscuit Stomp Take 2 -1	—
Delta Blues Take 2 -1	—

Vcl/gtr. with hca.

Momma's Milk Cow	Xtra 1033
Stack O'Dollars	—
Some Changes Gotta Be Made	—
Something's Wrong with My '52 Ford	—
Don't Know Right From Wrong	—
Going Back To Louisiana	—
Worried Life Blues	—
Schoolgirl	—
Going To St. Louis	—
Put On Your Black Dress Baby	—
Somethin' Worryin' My Mind	—
Careless Love	—

Vcl/gtr. with Larry Johnson, hca; Willie Dixon bs.   New York City, 1962

38 Pistol Blues	Bluesville BVLP 1056
I'm A Fool About My Baby	—
Pearly Mae	—
Walking Blues	—
Highway 45	—
Meet Me In The Bottom	—
Skinny Mama	—
Jockey Ride Blues	—
Coal And Iceman Blues	—
Army Man Blues	—
Black Gal	—
Pallet On The Floor	—

no hca, except on (-1)

Levee Camp Blues	Bluesville BVLP 1080
Low Down Dirty Shame -1	—
Gambling Man	—
Ain't Gonna Rain No More -1	—
Feel So Good	—
Prowling Ground Hog	—
Back Home Again (Dixon out)	—
Sugar Babe -1	—
Tell Me Mama	—
Studio Blues	—

Vcl/gtr/kazoo   New York City, 1962

Mink Coat Blues	Bluesville BVLP 1067
Burned Child Is Scared Of Fire	—
Baby, I Ain't Gonna Let You Go	—
Trouble Gonna Take Me To My Grave	—
Bugle Blues	—

Just Want To Be Your Man	Bluesville BVLP 1067
I'm Gonna Do It This Time	–
She's Doggin' Me	–
How Do You Want Your Rollin' Done	–
I Can't Sign My Name	–
Bottle Up And Go	–
I'm Tired Woman	–

BIG JOE WILLIAMS

Vcl/gtr.   Bremen, October 13, 1963

| I Have No Friends | Fontana 681.510ZL |

Vcl/gtr.   Copenhagen, October 16, 1963

Shake 'Em Down	Storyville SLP 163
Soon I'll Be Going My Way Home	–
Saturday Night Jump	–
Jinx Blues	–
Pick A Pickle	–
Ramblin' And Wanderin' Blues	–
Old Saw Mill Blues	–
Don't The Apples Look Mellow	–
El Paso Blues	–
Back Home Blues	–
Don't You Leave Me Here	–
Shaggy Hound Blues	–
Juanita Blues	Storyville SLP 166
Wild Ox Moan	–
Vitamin A Blues	–

Vcl/gtr. with Bob Dylan, hca (-1)   New York City, late 1963

Sitting On Top Of The World -1	Spivey LP 1004
Strange Girl Blues	–
Wichita -1	–
No Partnership Woman	–

Vcl/gtr.   Chicago, 1964

| A Man Amongst Men | Testament S-01 |

Vcl(-1)/gtr. with Jimmy Brown, vcl(-2)/vln; Willie Lee Harris, vcl(-3)/hca.

Chicago, 1964

Ain't Gonna Be Your Lowdown Dog -1	Testament T-2205
You Can Stay Out -2	–
Worry You Off My Mind (no hca) -1	–
Miss Ida B -3	–
Put On Your Nightcap -1	–
I Got My Ticket -1	–
Shake Your Boogie -1	–
See See Rider -2	–
Blues Everywhere I Go (no vln) -1	–
Worried And Lonesome -3	–
The Moon Is Rising -1	–
Down The Line -2	Testament T-2205
My Baby Left Me A Mule To Ride -1	–
Desert Blues -2	–
Breakdown (no hca)	–
Annie Mae -1 (no hca)	–
Mean Backstabber (Williams solo)	–

Jimmy Brown, vcl/gtr. with Willie Lee Harris, hca (-1)

| Woody Woodpecker | Testament T-2205 |
| My Black Woman -1 | – |

Vcl/gtr. with Bill Foster, gtr(-1); Coot Venson, vcl(-3)/hca(-4)

Your Close Friend	Testament T-2209
Walkin' Ground Hog	
Hellhound On My Trail -1	Storyville SLP 181
Sugar Mama -4	Storyville SLP 180
Long Road Blues -3, 4	–

Vcl/gtr.   Chicago, July 29 or Sept. 26, 1964
    Rollin' And Tumblin'   Milestone 3001
    Hellhound On My Trail   —
    Bird's Nest Bound   —
    Crossroads Blues   —
    Special Rider   —
    Pony Blues   —
    Pea Vine Special   —
    Walking Blues   —
    Dirt Road Blues   —
    Terraplane Blues   —
    Jinx Blues   —
    Ranty Rooster Blues   —
    Rambling On My Mind   Milestone 3002
Vcl/gtr.   New York City, November 24/27, 1966
    Whiskey Headed Woman   Verve 3010
    So Soon   —
    Somebody Evil   —

Note: See also Sleepy John Estes, Lightnin' Hopkins and Mr. Shortstuff.
No connection with the Joe Williams on Nashboro and Cincinnatti.

JOE WILLIAMS RECORDINGS

(unissued)

BIG JOE WILLIAMS
Vcl/gtr.   St. Louis, September 10, 1951
    Baby Please Don't Go
    Highway 49
Add Sam Fowler, hca; Willie Ealey, pno:
    Whistling Pine Blues
    Mama Don't Allow No Boggin' (sic) All Night Long

TREE TOP SLIM (Willie Ealey)
Vcl/pno. with Sam Fowler, hca; Joe Williams gtr;
    Thousand Year Blues
    She's Been Shaking A Little Boogie

LEE WILLMANS
Vcl. with Sam Fowler, hca; Joe Williams, gtr;   St. Louis March 11, 1952
    Strange Girl Blues
    Early Morning Blues

HARP BLOWING SAM (Fowler)
Vcl/hca. with Joe Williams, gtr;
    Shake A Little Boogie
    Early In The Morning

BIG JOE WILLIAMS
Vcl/gtr. with Willie Ealey, pno.   St. Louis, April 5, 1952
    New Car Blues
    Taylor Made Stomp

Note: All above cut for Joe Williams at The Baul Recording Co. in St. Louis and
used for audition purposes.

JOHNNY WILLIAMS (Staff Records)

See under John Lee Hooker or Baby Boy Warren.

JOHNNY WILLIAMS

See under Johnny Young.

L. C. WILLIAMS

Born Millican, Texas on March 12, 1924. Died Houston, Texas on October 18, 1960.

L. C.(LIGHTNIN' JR.) WILLIAMS
Vcl. with Lightnin' Hopkins, pno(-1)/gtr(-2)   Houston, 1947
614A   Trying, Trying -1*   Gold Star 614, Dot 1052
615B   You'll Never Miss The Water -2   —
          I Wonder -2   Arhoolie R 2006
          * Also on Blues Classics 16

L. C. WILLIAMS
Vcl. with Lightnin' Hopkins, gtr.   Houston, 1948
A   Hole In The Wall   Gold Star 623, Blues Classics 16
B   Boogie All The Time   —
A   Strike Blues   Gold Star 667, Arhoolie R 2006
B   You Can't Take It With You Baby   —

LIGHTNIN' JR. WILLIAMS.
Vcl. with Leroy Carter, pno(-1); Elmore Nixon, pno(-2)
A   Black Woman -1   Gold Star 648
B   I Won't Be Here Long -2   —   , Arhoolie R 2006

L. C. WILLIAMS ORCH.
Vcl. with Sam Williams, ten; Conrad Johnson, alt; Lonnie Lyons, pno; Louis 'Nunu' Pitts,
bs; Allison Tucker, dms.   Houston 1948
A   Why Don't You Come Back   Eddie's 1203, Freedom 1501
B   I Don't Want Your Baby -1   —   —

          Note: Eddie's 1203 issued as by Connie's Combo.

CONNEY'S COMBO WITH L. C. WILLIAMS
Same: Houston, 1949
ACA 1066 That's Alright   Freedom 1510
ACA 1067 Gonna Change My Love   —

L. C. WILLIAMS WITH J. C. CONNEY's COMBO
Same:
ACA 1140 Shout Baby Shout   Freedom 1517
ACA 1141 Ethel Mae   —
SMK 1229 Jelly Roll   Freedom 1524
SMK 1230 Louisiana Boogie   —

L. C. WILLIAMS
Vcl. with Elmore Nixon, pno; Lightnin' Hopkins, gtr;
1277, IM421 All Through My Dreams (My Darkest Hour)   Freedom 1529, Imperial 5195, Bayou
1278, IM422 Mean And Evil Blues (Want My Baby Back)   Freedom 1529, Imperial 5195, Bayou

          Note: Above listed in ACA files as ACA 1773/4.

Vcl. with Lightnin' Hopkins, gtr;   Houston, 1951
J 476   So Sorry   SIW/Jax 640
J 477   Baby Child   —
J 484   The Lazy J   SIW/jax 648
J 487   Fannie Mae   —
Vcl. with tpt; Henry Hayes, alt; Ed Wiley, ten; Willie Johnson, pno; Donald Cooks, bs;
Ben turner, dms.   Houston, 1951
9009   Don't Want No Woman   Mercury 8276
9010   Louise   —

          Note: See also Connie McBooker

LEE WILLMANS

See under Joe Williams Recordings (unissued).

356

LESTER WILLIAMS

Born Groveton, Texas on June 24, 1920
Vcl/gtr. with Ike Smalley, alt; Ferdinand Banks, ten; Johnnie Mae Brown, pno; James Moseley, bs; L. D. MacKintosh, dms. Houston, 1949

ACA 1225	Winter Time Blues	Macy's 5000
ACA 1226	I'm So Glad I Could Jump And Shout	–
ACA 1227	Heart Full Of Blues	unissued

Same:

ACA 1231	Dowling Street Hop	Macy's 5006
ACA 1232	All I Need Is You	Macy's 5004
ACA 1233	I Know That Chick	–
ACA 1234	Don't Treat Me So Low Down	Macy's 5006

Vcl/gtr. with Blankey Broadie, alt; Ferdinand, Banks, ten; James Hurdle, pno; Oscar 'Yogi' Adams, bs; Luther Taylor, dms. Houston, 1950

ACA 1519-2	Texas Town	Macy's 5009
ACA 1520	Hey Jack	Macy's 5016
ACA 1521	The Folks Around The Corner	–
ACA 1522	Mary Lou	Macy's 5009

Vcl/gtr. with Frank Minn, tpt; Bill Bailey, alt; Joe Calloway or Johnny Spencer, ten; James Hurdle, pno; Oscar Adams, bs; Luther Taylor, dms. Houston, 1951/52

SP422	My Home Ain't Here	Specialty 422
XSP 422	I Can't Lose With The Stuff I Use	–
ACA 1962	Sweet Lovin' Daddy	Specialty 437
ACA 1963	Let Me Tell You A Thing Or Two	Specialty 431
ACA 1964	Lonely Heart Blues	unissued
ACA 1965	Since I Lost That Gal Of Mine	unissued
XSP 431	Tryin' To Forget	Specialty 431
XSP 437	Lost Gal	Specialty 437
XSP 450	Brand New Baby	Specialty 450
SP 450	If You Knew How Much I Love You	–

Vcl/gtr. with saxes; pno; bs; dms. Houston, 1954

ACA 2751	Let's Do It	Duke 123
ACA 2752	Crazy'bout My Baby	Duke 131
ACA 2753	Don't Ever Take Your Love From Me	–
ACA 2754	Good Loving Baby	Duke 123

Vcl/gtr. with Dave Bartholomew's Band New Orleans, 1956

IM 1064	McDonald's Daughter	Imperial 5402
IM 1065	Daddy Loves You	–
IM 1066	In The Summertime	unissued
IM 1067	Rich Man Blues	unissued

LIGHTNIN' JR. WILLIAMS

See under L. C. Williams.

LONNIE WILLIAMS

Vcl/hca. with gtr; bs. Shreveport, La.1951

2204	Tears In Mt Heart	SIW 567
2205	New Road Blues	–
2294	Wavin' Sea Blues	SIW 593
2295	I'm Tired Of Running Around	–

MARY WILLIAMS

Vcl. with Big Joe Williams, gtr; Los Gatos, October 5, 1960

| | I Want My Crown | Arhoolie F 1002 |
| | Oakland Blues | unissued |

R. G. WILLIAMS

Vcl. with group vcl. Ramsey Far, Texas, March 17, 1951

| | Hammer Ring | "77" LA 12/3 |

357

ROBERT PETE WILLIAMS

Born Zachary, Louisiana on March 14, 1914.

Vcl/gtr. with Robert "Guitar" Welch, gtr (-1).　　　　　Angola, La., 1959/61
	Levee Camp Blues	Louisiana Folk Society A3
	Prisoner's Talking Blues	–
	Motherless Children Have A Hard Time	–
	Some Got Six Months	–
	I'm Lonesome Blues	–
	Mississippi Heavy Water Blues -1	Folk Lyric FL-111

Vcl/gtr. with Hogman Maxey, gtr (-1).
	Louise	Folk Lyric FL-109
	I'll Be Glad When I'm From Behind	–
	Prison Walls	–
	Blues In Me	–
	Come Here Baby	–
	I Got The Blues So Bad	–
	Boogy Woman -1	–
	Pardon Denied Again	–
	Army Blues -1	–
	Blues In The Dark	–
	Make Me A Pallet On The Floor	–
	Angola Special	–

Vcl/gtr.
	Free Again	Bluesville SVLP 1026
	Almost Dead Blues	–
	Rolling Stone	–
	Two Wings	–
	A Thousand Miles From Nowhere	–
	Thumbing A Ride	–
	I've Grown So Ugly	–
	Death Blues	–
	Hobo Worried Blues	–
	Hay Cutting Song	–

Vcl/gtr.　　　　　　　　　　　　　　　　　　　　Newport, R.I. July 25, 1964
	Levee Camp Blues	Vanguard VRS 9180
	On My Way From Texas	–
	Midnight Boogie	–
	Bulldog Blues	Vanguard VRS 9183

Vcl/gtr.　　　　　　　　　　　　　　　　　　　　Berlin, October 16, 1966
| | Louise | Fontana 885.431TY |

SLY WILLIAMS

Vcl. with saxes; pno; gtr; bs; dms.
| | Boot Hill | Sutton LP 316 |
| | I Believe In A Woman | – |

Note: Tracks not identified on record. Sly Williams is listed as appearing and these two tracks are probably by him.

SUGAR BOY WILLIAMS

See under Jody Williams.

SUNNY WILLIAMS TRIO

Real name Enoch "Sonny Boy" Williams.

Vcl/pno. with gtr; bs.　　　　　　　　　　　　　　New York City, 1947
MF 115-02	The Boogie Man	Super Disc 1030
MF116-02	Reverse The Charges	–
	Jump It, Don't Bump It	Super Disc 1058
	You'll Never Cry Again	–

358

JAMES WILLIAMSON

Real name James Williamson. Born Somerville, Tennessee on May 3, 1914.

JAMES WILLIAMSON AND HIS TRIO
Vcl/gtr. with Lazy Bill Lucas, pno; Alfred Erskine, dms.   Chicago, 1952/53

U 2157	Lonesome Ole Train	Chance 1121
U 2158	Farmer's Blues	–
U 2232	Johnny Mae	unissued
U 2233		
U 2234	Little Women	unissued
U 2235	Bad Luck Blues	unissued
U 2333	Homesick	Chance 1131, Blues Classics BC-8
U 2334	Dirty Rat	unissued
U 2335	The Woman I Love	Chance 1131
U 2336	Wartime	unissued
C 5040	Lonesome Blues	unissued
C 5041	Late Hours At Midnight	unissued
C 5042	Williamson Shuffle	unissued
C 5043	First St. Station	unissued
C 5044	Long Lonesome Days	unissued

HOMESICK JAMES
Vcl/gtr. with Lazy Bill Lucas, pno; Joe Harris, dms.   Chicago, 1960

	Telephone Blues	Atomic H
	Johnnie Mae	–

> Note: The credit on the above is uncertain. Atomic H do not usually have issue numbers.

HOMESICK JAMES
Vcl/gtr. with Lazy Bill Lucas, pno; Hound Dog Taylor, gtr; Willie Knowling, dms.
    Chicago, 1962

632 A	Can't Afford To Do It	Colt 632
632 B	Set A Date	

Vcl/gtr. with Donald Hankins, bari; Lafayette Leake, pno; Milton Rector, bs-gtr; Clifton James, dms.   Chicago, July 23, 1962

4-18926	Crossroads	USA 746
4-18927	My Baby's Sweet	–

Vcl/gtr. with Lazy Bill Lucas, pno; Andrew McMaran, bs-gtr; Cascell Barrows, dms.

She May Be Your Woman	unissued
Can't Afford To Do It	unissued
Tell Me What You Mean	unissued
If I Get Lucky	unissued
Good Morning Little Schoolgirl	unissued

Walter Smith, bs-gtr. replaces McMaran:

She May Be Yours	unissued
Please Set A Date	unissued
If I Get Lucky	unissued
Jam The Blues	unissued
untitled instrumental	unissued

> Above two sessions recorded for Jump Jackson during 1962.

HOMESICK JAMES
Vcl/gtr. with Lafayette Leake, pno; Lee Jackson, bs-gtr; Clifton James, dms.
    Chicago, January 7, 1964

826A	The Woman I'm Lovin'	Bluesville 826, Prestige 7388
826B	Crawlin'	– –
	She May Be Your Woman	Prestige 7388
	Goin' Down Swingin'	–
	Homesick's Shuffle	–
	Johnny Mae	–
	Gotta Move	–
	Lonesome Road	–
	Working With Homesick	–
	The Cloud Is Crying	–

| | Homesick's Blues | Prestige 7388 |
| | Stones In My Passway | |

Vcl/gtr. with Evans Spencer, gtr; Washboard Sam, wbd.   Chicago, March 25, 1964

185	Can't Hold Out	Spivey LP 1003
186		
187		
188	Queen's Rock	Spivey LP 1003

Vcl/gtr. with Henry Gray, pno; Joe Young, gtr; Willie Dixon, bs; Clifton James, dms.

Chicago, 1964

| | Crutch And Cane | Decca LK 4748 |
| | Got To Move | – |

Vcl/gtr. with Willie Dixon, bs; Frank Kirkland, dms.   Chicago, late 1965

	Dust My Broom	Vanguard VRS 8217
	Somebody's Been Talking	–
	Set A Date	–
	So Mean To Me	–

SONNY BOY WILLIAMSON

Real name John Lee Williamson. Born Jackson, Tennessee in 1912.
Died Chicago, Illinois on June 1, 1948.
Vcl/hca. with Blind John Davis, pno; Ted Summitt, gtr; Armand "Jump" Jackson, dms.

Chicago, December 14, 1944

D4-AB-324	Miss Stella Brown Blues	Bluebird 34-0736
D4-AB-325	Desperado Woman Blues	–
D4-AB-326	Win The War Blues	Bluebird 34-0722
D4-AB-327	Check Up On My Baby Blues	–

Vcl/hca. with Eddie Boyd, pno; Bill Sid Cox, gtr; Ransom Knowling, bs.

Chicago, July 2, 1945

D5-AB-339	G.M. & O. Blues	Victor 20-2369
D5-AB-340	We Got To Win	unissued
D5-AB-341	Sonny Boy's Jump	Bluebird 34-0744
D5-AB-342	Elevator Woman	– , Camden
		CAL 740

Vcl/hca. with Big Maceo, pno; Tempa Red, gtr; Charles Sanders, dms.

Chicago, October 19, 1945

D5-AB-396	Early In The Morning	Victor 20-1875
D5-AB-397	The Big Boat	Victor 20-3218
D5-AB-398	Stop Breaking Down	Victor 20-3047
D5-AB-399	You're An Old Lady	Victor 20-1875

Vcl/hca. with Blind John Davis, pno; Willie Lacey, gtr; Ransom Knowling, bs.

Chicago, August 6, 1946

D6-VB-1917	Sonny Boy's Cold Chills	Victor 20-2184
D6-VB-1918	Mean Old Highway	Victor 20-2056
D6-VB-1919	Hoodoo Hoodoo	Victor 20-2184
D6-VB-1920	Shake The Boogie	Victor 20-2056

Vcl/hca. with Blind John Davis, pno; Big Bill Broonzy, gtr; Willie Dixon, bs; Charles
Sanders, dms.   Chicago, March 28, 1947

D7-VB-374	Mellow Chick Swing	Victor 20-2369
D7-VB-375	Polly Put Your Kettle On	Victor 20-2521
D7-VB-376	Lacey Belle	–
D7-VB-377	Apple Tree Swing	Victor 20-2893

Vcl/hca. with Eddie Boyd, pno; Willie Lacey gtr; Ransom Knowling, bs; Judge Riley, dms.

Chicago, September 19, 1947

D7-VB-1036	Wonderful Time	Victor 22-0001
D7-VB-1037	Sugar Gal	Victor 20-2623
D7-VB-1038	Willow Tree Gal	–
D7-VB-1039	Alcohol Blues	Victor 20-2893

Vcl/hca. with Blind John Davis, pno; Willie Lacey, gtr; Ransom Knowling, bs; Judge Riley,
dms.   Chicago, November 12, 1947

| D7-VB-1149 | Little Girl | Victor 22-0021, 50-0005 |
| D7-VB-1150 | Blues About My Baby | Victor 22-0001 |

D7-VB-1151	No Friend Blues	unissued
D7-VB-1152	I Love You For Myself	Victor 22-0046, 50-0030
D7-VB-1153	Bring Another Half Pint	Victor 22-0021, 50-0005
D7-VB-1154	Southern Dream	Victor 22-0046, 50-0030
D7-VB-1155	Rub A Dub	Victor 20-3047
D7-VB-1156	Better Cut That Out	Victor 20-3218

LITTLE SON WILLIS

See under Mac Willis.

MAC WILLIS

Born Fort Worth, Texas?
Vcl/pno. with E. McInnis, gtr.   Los Angeles, 1950
| 101A | Pretty Woman | Elko 254 |
| 101B | Howling Woman | – |

LITTLE SON WILLIS
Vcl/pno. with gtr; bs.   Los Angeles, 1952
ST304A+	Bad Luck And Trouble	Swing Time 304, Arhoolie 3001
ST304A	Operator Blues	
ST305A+	Harlem Blues	Swing Time 305, Arhoolie 3001
ST305A	I Love You Just The Same	–
ST306A+	Nothing But The Blues	Swing Time 306, Arhoolie 1018
ST306A	Skin And Bones	
Add dms.		Los Angeles, 1953
ST341A+	Roll Me Over Slow	Swing Time 341
ST341A	Baby Come Back Home	–

MILTON WILLIS COMBO

Hubert Robinson, vcl (-1); ten; pno; gtr; bs; dms.   Houston, 1949
| ACA 1399 | Little Joe's Boogie | Lucky 7 5001 |
| ACA 1416 | Three O'Clock Boogie -1 | |

Note: ACA 1399 has a live audience.

RALPH WILLIS (the late)

RALPH ('BAMA) WILLIS
Vcl/gtr.   New York City, 1944
| S 1098 | Worried Blues | Regis 118, 1018 |
| S 1099 | Comb Your Kitty Kat | – – |

RALPH WILLIS
Vcl/gtr.   New York City, 1946
SRC 817	Just A Note	Signature 32016
SRC 818	Church Bells	–
SRC 819	Trouble Don't Last	Signature 32012, Lee 105
SRC 820	Shake That Thing	– –

RALPH WILLIS & HIS ALABAMA TRIO
Vcl/gtr. with gtr; bs. Judson Coleman, vcl (-1).   New York City, c. 1946
2000	So Many Days	20th Century 20-09
2001	That Gal's No Good	
2002	New Goin' Down Slow	20th Century 20-11
2003	Goin' To Chattanooga -1	–
2004	Steel Mill Blues -1	20th Century 20-12
2005	I Will Never Love Again	

ALABAMA SLIM
Vcl/gtr.   New York City, 1947/48
| 35121 | Boar Hog Blues | Savoy 5553 |
| 35122 | Eloise | – |

361

WASHBOARD PETE -1
SLEEPY JOE'S WASHBOARD BAND -2
Vcl/gtr. with Pete Sanders, wbd.

35160	Christmas Blues -1	Savoy 5556
35161	Amen Blues -2	Savoy 753
35162		
35163	Neighbourhood Blues -1	Savoy 5556
35164	Mama, Mama Blues -2	Savoy 753

RALPH WILLIS
Vcl/gtr. with Brownie McGhee, gtr; bs.   New York City, 1949

| 673 | Cool That Thing | Abbey 3002 |
| 674 | Sportin' Life | – |

RALPH WILLIS featuring BROWNIE MAGEE
Vcl/gtr. with Brownie McGhee, gtr; Dumas Ransom bs.   New York City, 1950/51

JR 1500	Everyday I Weep And Moan	Jubilee 5034
JR 1501	Somebody's Got To Go	Jubilee 5044
JR 1502	Blues, Blues, Blues	–
JR 1503	I Got A Letter	Jubilee 5034
4462	Income Tax Blues	Jubilee 5078
4463	Bed Tick Blues	–

Same: New York City, 1951

MU 1006A	Church Bell Blues	Signature 1006, Prestige 907
MU 1006B	Tell Me Pretty Baby	
	Tell Me Pretty Baby (alt. take)	Prestige 907
MU 1007A	Goodbye Blues	Signature 1007, Prestige 906
MU 1007B	Lazy Woman Blues	– –

Vcl/gtr.   New York City, October 3, 1951

206	Seven Years Blues	unissued
207	Dan Girl Blues	unissued
208	Old Home Blues	Prestige 919
209	It's Bad	unissued
210	Salty Dog	Prestige 919
211	I've Been A Fool	unissued
212	Wishing Boogie	unissued
213	Krooked Woman Blues	unissued
214	Walkin' Guitar Blues	unissued

RALPH WILLIS COUNTRY BOYS
Vcl/gtr. with Sonny Terry, hca (-1); Brownie McGhee, gtr.   New York City? February 1952

305	It's Too Late	Par 1306
306	Put It In The Sand	unissued
307	I'll Never Love Again	Par 1306
308	Cold Chills -1	Prestige 923
309	Remember Last Night	unissued
310	Amen	Prestige 923
311	Country Jail Blues	unissued

Vcl/gtr. with Sonny Terry, hca; Brownie McGhee, gtr; Gary Mapp, bs.
       New York City, January 15, 1953

K 8350	Gonna Hop On Down The Line	King 4631
K 8351	Do Right	King 4611
K 8352	Door Bell Blues	King 4631, LP 875
K 8353	Why'd You Do It	King 4611

SLIM WILLIS

Vcl/hca. with saxes; Lafayette Leake, pno; gtr; bs; dms.   Chicago, 1961/62

A	Strange Feeling	C.J. 622
B	I Love To Play	–
A	Running Around	C.J. 627
B	No Feeling For You	–
A	You're The Sweetest Girl I Know	C.J. 635
B	From Now On	–

No details: Chicago, 1966
      Tighten Up Your Game, Baby   Biscayne 010
      Why Don't You Believe   –

TURNER WILLIS

Vcl. with pno; gtr; bs.   Oakland, 1945
1058A   Re-Enlistment Blues   Trilon 1058, Big Town 1058
      (rev. by Bob Geddins)

OSCAR WILLS

Born Near Houston Texas, February 10, 1916.

T.V. SLIM
Vcl/gtr. with   Shreveport, La., 1957
      Going To California   Speed?
      Ain't Got But 15 Cents   –

T.V. SLIM & HIS HEARTBREAKERS
Vcl/gtr. with saxes; pno; bs; dms.   Shreveport, La., 1957
3584, 8540 Flat Foot Sam   Cliff 103, Checker 870
3585, 8541 Darling Remember   –   –

Vcl/gtr. with Fats Domino's Band   New Orleans, 1957
8540   Flat Foot Sam   Argo 5277, LP 4042
      (rev. by Paul Gayten)
      Note: Argo 5277 issued as by Oscar Wills.

Vcl/gtr. with pno; gtr; dms.   Shreveport, La., 1958
A   To Prove My Love   Speed 6865
B   You Can't Buy A Woman   – , 704
      Note: The following sides on Speed were issued with a variety of artist credits, as
      listed below.

T.V. SLIM
T.V. SLIM & HIS GUITAR
T.V. SLIM & HIS BLUESMEN
T.V. SLIM & HIS HEARTBREAKERS
OSCAR WILLS & HIS GOOD ROCKING BAND
OSCAR "T.V. SLIM" WILLS & HIS HEARTBREAKERS
Vcl/gtr. with saxes (-1); pno (-2); gtr; dms.   Los Angeles, 1958/65
S-101   Flat Foot Sam Meets Jim Dandy -1, 2   Speed 704
S-102   Tired Of Your Cheatin' And Lyin' -1, 2 –
S-103, 12042 Bad Understanding Blues -2   Speed 807, Checker 1029
S-103, 34668 My Ship Is Sinking -1, 2   Speed 705
S-104   My Love Will Never Change -1, 2   Speed 705, 711
S-105, 34801 My Baby Is gone (vcl/gtr. solo)   Speed 706, 709
S-106   Don't Reach Cross My Plate   Speed 711
S-107
S-108   Every Man Needs A Woman -2   Speed 706, 709
S-109, 37417 Dancing Senorita   Speed 710
S-110
S-111   Don't Reach Cross My Plate   Speed 711
S-112   Boogie Woogie Guitar Twist   Speed 807
S-113   Bad Understanding Blues   –
S-114, 12041 The Big Fight -2   Speed 803, 807, 808, Checker
             1029
S-115   Hen Peck Joe   Speed 808
S-116
S-117   Hold Me Close To Your Heart   Speed 810, U.S.A. 739
S-118   You Can't Love Me -1, 2   Speed 810, U.S.A. 739
S-119   Dream Girl -1, 2   Speed 714
S-120   Gravy Around Your Steak   Speed 715
S-121
S-122   Mean Man (vcl. Sheila Jane Wills)   Speed 715
S-118?   Your Kisses Send Me -1, 2   Speed 714

S-6934	Don't Reach Cross My Plate	Speed 703
S-6935	Your Kisses Changed Me	–
	Flat Foot Sam Made A Bet	Speed ?
	Pearly Mae	–
	You Won't Treat Me Right	–
	My Dolly B.	–
	Down The Line, You Can't Buy My Time	–
	I'm A Real Man	–

T.V. SLIM & HIS BLUESMEN
Vcl/gtr. with ten; pno; gtr; dms. Los Angeles, 1966
| 5032, (5030) T.V. Man | Excell 104 |
| 5033, (5031) Flat Foot Sam No. 2 | – |

T.V. SLIM & THE SOUL BROTHERS
Vcl/gtr. with gtr; dms.
| 5062 | Can't Be Satisfied | Timbre 510 |
| 5063 | Juvenile Delinquent | – |

HOP WILSON

Real name Harding Wilson. Born Crockett, Texas in 1927.

HOP WILSON & HIS TWO BUDDIES
Vcl/gtr. with 'Ice Water', bs-gtr; Ivory Semien, dms. Lake Charles, 1958
| A | Chicken Stuff | Goldband 1071, Goldshot 1071 |
| B | That Wouldn't Satisfy | – |

Vcl/gtr. with Willie Jackson, hca. (-1); Elmore Nixon, pno; Clarence Green, bs; Ivory Semien, dms. Houston, 1959
| ACA 3655 | Broke And Hungry | Goldband 1078 |
| ACA 3656 | Always Be In Love With You -1 | – |

POPPA HOP
Vcl/gtr; Elmore Nixon, pno; Pete ?, gtr; Ivory Semien, dms. Houston, late 1960
| ACA 4142 | I'm A Stranger | Ivory 127 |
| ACA 4143 | My Woman Has A Black Cat Bone | – |

POPPY HOP
Same: Houston, early 1961
| A | A Good Woman Is Hard To Find | Ivory 133 |
| B | I Met A Strange Woman | – |

Same: Houston, November 7, 1961
L 134	Merry Christmas Darling	Ivory 134
L 135	Be Careful With The Blues	Ivory 135
	I Ain't Got No Woman	unissued
	untitled blues	unissued

JIMMY WILSON

Born ? Died Dallas, Texas in 1965.

JIMMY WILSON & HIS ALL STARS
Vcl. with pno; Lafayette Thomas, gtr; bs; dms. Oakland, 1951
CAV 105, SF 1659		
	Honey Bee	Cavatone ?, Aladdin 3087
CAV 106	It's A Sin To Tell A Lie	Cavatone 252, Aladdin 3140
CAV 107	Please Believe In Me	Cavatone ?, Aladdin 3087
CAV 108, SF 1660		
	Mistake In Life	Cavatone 252, Aladdin 3140

Add Que Martyn, ten: Oakland, July 11, 1952
SF 2052	Every Dog Has His Day	Aladdin 3169
SF 2053	Lemon Squeezer	–
SF 2054	It's Time To Change	Aladdin 3241
SF 2055	Any Man's A Fool	–

Vcl. with saxes; pno; gtr; bs; dms.   Los Angeles, May 14, 1953
UN 2137 Ethel Mae   7-11 2104
UN 2138 Baby Don't Want Nobody But Me 7-11 2105
UN 2139 Crying Like A Baby Child   –
UN 2140 Tell Me   7-11 2104

Vcl. with Que Martyn, ten; King Solomon, pno; Lafayette Thomas, gtr; bs; dms.
                  Oakland, 1953
6244   Tin Pan Alley   Big Town 101
6245   Big Town Jump   –
6253, BT 105Instrumental Jump   Big Town 103
6262, BT 106Call Me A Hound Dog   –
6388   A Woman Is To Blame   Big Town 107
6389   Blues At Sundown   –

Similar: Oakland, 1954/55
A   Strangest Blues   Rhythm 1765, Elko 915
B   I Used To Love A Woman –   –
6593   Teardrops On My Pillow   Big Town 113, ET 1002
6594   Mountain Climber   –   –
6703   Trouble In My House   Big Town 115
6705   Jumping From Six To Six –
       I've Found Out   Big Town 123

JIMMY WILSON & THE BLUES BLASTERS BAND:
13320   Oh Red   Big Town 123, Irma 107
13322   Blues In The Alley   Irma 107

No details: 1956
C 125   Louise   Chart 610
C 126   Send Me The Key   Chart 629
C 127   Alley Blues   Chart 610
C 128   Poor Poor Lover   Chart 629
    Note: See also under Bob Geddins. Later records not included. Elko 915 issued as
    by Jimmy Nolen.

JOHN WRENCHER

Vcl/hca. with Johnny Young, gtr; John Lee Granderson, gtr. Chicago, 1964
      I'm Going To Detroit   Testament T-2203

ARTHUR WRIGHT

No details: 1955
      Drizzling Rain   Spitfire 13
      Don't Take Your Love Away –
    Note: See also Sir Arthur.

Y

JIMMY YANCEY

Born Chicago, Illinois in 1898. Died Chicago on September 18, 1951.
Pno/org. with Mama Yancey, vcl (-1).   Chicago, December, 1943
113   Boodlin'   Session 10-001, Pax LP 6011

117	How Long Blues	Session 12-003, Pax LP 6012, Folkways FP 55, FJ 2802
	The Rocks	Pax LP 6011, Jazztone J1224
119	Jimmy's Rocks	Session 10-001
120	How Long Blues -1	Session 12-002
	Mama's Blues -1	Session 12-004
	Rough And Ready	–
131	Eternal Blues	Session 12-001, Pax LP 6012, Jazztone J1023
132		
133	Yancey Special	Session 12-001, Pax LP 6012, Jazztone J1023
134	Midnight Stomp	Session 12-002, Pax LP 6011, Jazztone J1224
135	Pallet On The Floor	Session 12-003, Pax LP 6012, Jazztone J1023
136	Shave 'Em Dry	Session 10-005, Pax LP 6012, Jazztone J1023
137	At The Window	Session 10-005, Pax LP 6011, Jazztone J1224
	White Sox Stomp	Pax LP 6012, Jazztone J1023, J1224
	Yancey's Mixture	Pax LP 6011, Jazztone J1224
	Death Letter Blues	–

Pno. solo.   Chicago, December 23, 1950
   Barber Shop Rag   Paramount CJS 101
   Assembly Call Boogie   –
   The Yancey Special   –
   Jimmy's Good Night Blues   –
   Everlasting Blues   –
   Keep A Knockin'   –

Pno. with Mama Yancey, vcl (-1); Israel Crosby, bs.   Chicago, July 18, 1951
How Long Blues -1	Atlantic LP 130, LP 1283	
Make Me A Pallet On The Floor -1	–	–
Monkey Woman Blues -1	–	–
Four O'Clock Blues -1	–	–
Santa Fe Blues -1	–	–
Yancey Special	–	–
Blues For Albert	Atlantic LP 134	
35th And Dearborn	–	, LP 1283
Salute To Pinetop	–	–
Shave 'Em Dry	–	–
How Long Blues		– ,
	EP 525	
Yancey's Bugle Call	–	–
Yancey Special (alt. take)	–	–
Mournful Blues	–	

MAMA YANCEY

Vcl. with Don Ewell, pno.   Chicago, August 21, 1952
   Mama's Blues   Windin' Ball LP 102
   Baby Won't You Please come Home   –
   Nobody Knows You When You're Down And
   Out   –
   Lonesome Road   –
   Weekly Blues   –
   Everybody Loves My Baby   –
   Sundown Blues   –

Vcl. with Little Brother Montgomery, pno; Sam Hill, gtr; Geroge "Pops" Foster, bs;
Earl Watkins, dms.   Chicago, September 8, 1961
389	How Long Blues	Riverside RLP 403
390	Four O'Clock Blues	–
391	Make Me A Pallet On The Floor	–

| 392 | Mama Yancey's Blues | Riverside RLP 403 |
| 393 | The Santa Fe Blues | Riverside RLP 389 |

Vcl. with Art Hodes, pno.

	Good Package Blues	Verve-Folkways 9015
	Cabbage Patch	–
	Good Conductor	–
	How Long	–
	Every Day In The Week	–
	Get Him Out Of Your System	–
	Sweet Lovin' Daddy	–
	Trouble In Mind	–
	Grandpa's Bells	–

YAS YAS GIRL

Real name Merline Johnson.
Vcl. with Chicago, March 14, 1947

CCO 4754	Bad Whiskey Blues	Okeh unissued
CCO 4755	Don't Think I'm Buster Brown	–
CCO 4756	Schoolboy Blues	–
CCO 4757	Rattlesnake Blues	–

THE YOUNG WOOLF

See under Gus Jenkins.

FREDDY YOUNG

Vcl. with org; gtr; bs; dms. Chicago, 1963

| 783 | Monkey Business | Friendly Five 740 |
| 784 | Someday Baby | – |

MIGHTY JOE YOUNG

Vcl/gtr. with Monroe, La., 1956

ACA 3306	Broke, Downhearted And Disgusted	Jiffy ?
ACA 3307	You Been Cheatin' On Me	–
	Note: Later records not included.	

JOHNNY YOUNG

Born Vicksburg, Mississippi on January 1, 1917.
Vcl(-1)/mdln. with Johnny Williams, vcl (-2)/gtr. Chicago, 1947

| A | Worried Man Blues -2 | Ora Nelle 712 |
| B | Money Takin' Woman -1 | – |

MAN YOUNG
Vcl/mdln. with Snooky Pryor, hca; Johnny Williams, gtr. Chicago, 1948

| PL 103 | My Baby Walked Out On Me | Planet 103, Old Swingmaster 19 |
| PL 104 | Let Me Ride Your Mule | Planet 104, – |

Vcl/gtr (-1)/mdln (-2). with Slim Willis, hca; Otis Spann, pno; Robert Whitehead, dms.
Omit dms (-3). Chicago, 1963/64

	I Tried Not To Cry -3	Testament S-01
	Mean Old Train	unissued
	My Baby Walked Out In 1954 -1	Testament T-2203
	You Make Me Feel So Good -1	–
	Money Takin' Woman -2	–
	Bad Blood -1	–
	Tired Of You Smiling -2	–
	Let Me Ride Your Mule -1	–

Vcl/gtr. with Jimmy Walker, pno (-1).

| | Pony Blues | Storyville SLP 180 |
| | Back To Chicago | Testament T-2203 |

Vcl/gtr. with John Wrencher, hca; John Lee Granderson, gtr.
                    Green Door Blues   Storyville SLP 181
Vcl/gtr/mdln (-1). with Shakey Horton, hca (-2); Wille Mabon, pno; Andrew Stephenson,
bs-gtr; Clifton James, dms.   Chicago, 1964
                    One More Time -2   Decca LK 4748
                    Little Girl -1   —
Vcl/mdln. with Otis Spann, pno.   Chicago, November 22, 1965
                    Keep Your Nose Out Of My Business   Arhoolie F 1029
                    I'm Doing All Right   —
                    Moaning And Groaning   —
                    Stealin'   —
Vcl/gtr. with Otis Spann, pno; James Cotton, hca; Jimmy Lee Morris, bs-gtr; S.P. Leary, dms.
                    Wild Wild Woman   Arhoolie F 1029
                    I'm Having A Ball   —
                    My Trainfare Out Of Town   —
                    Keep On Drinking   —
                    Hot Dog   —
                    Come Early In The Morning   —
                    Cross-Cut Saw   —
                    Slam Hammer   —
Vcl/gtr/mdln. with Walter Horton, hca; Hayes Ware, bs-gtr; Elgar Edmonds, dms.
                                                            Chicago, late 1965
                    One More Time   Vanguard VRS 9218
                    Kidman Blues   —
                    My Black Mare   —
                    Stealin' Back   —
                    I Got Mine In Time   —
                    Tighten Up On It   —
Vcl/mdln. with Little Walter, hca; Jimmy Walker, pno.
                    Hear That Whistle Blow   Milestone LP 3002

LONNIE YOUNG

Lonnie Young St., vcl/bass dm. with Ed Young, cane-fife; Lonnie Young Jr., snare dm;
hand-clapping.   Mississippi, 1959
                    Hen Duck   Atlantic LP 1346
                    Jim And John   Atlantic LP 1348
                    Jim And John (diff. take)   Prestige Int. 25010
                    Chevrolet   Atlantic LP 1348
                    Oree   —
                    Sittin' On Top Of The World   Atlantic LP 1352

MAN YOUNG

See under Johnny Young.

APPENDIX I

The details of the following Aladdin Sessions arrived too late to be included in the main discography. No release numbers are given, as these can be found under the individual artist's discography.

JOHNNY FULLER SESSION
Capitol Recording Studio, Hollywood, March, 1955.

CAP 2360	Cruel, Cruel World
CAP 2361	My Darling (I'm Crying)
CAP 2362	My Heart Beats For You
CAP 2363	My Heart's On Fire

CLARENCE GARLOW SESSION
Radio Recorders, Los Angeles. July 24, 1953. Band – Maxwell Davis.

RR 2185	I'm Beginning To Miss You
RR 2186	Jumping At The Zadacoe
RR 2187	I'm Hurt
RR 2188	No Other Love

CLARENCE GARLOW SESSION
J & M Studio, New Orleans. March 4, 1953.

NO 2093	Hey Mr. Bon Ton
NO 2094	New Bon Ton Roulay
NO 2095	You Got Me Crying

LONNIE JOHNSON SESSION
Chicago. June 2, 1947.

4005A	How Could You
4006	Love Is The Answer
4007A	Don't Blame Her
4008	Why A Man Goes Wrong
4009	Your Last Time Out
4010A	You Know I Do
4011A	I Love It
4012	Blues For Lonnie

LIGHTNIN' HOPKINS SESSION
Commercial Studios, Houston. February 25, 1948.

501	Miss Me Blues
502	Sugar Mama
503	Nightmare Blues
504	You're On My Mind
505	Come Back Baby
506	Lightnin's Boogie
507	(not allocated)
508	You're Not Going To Make A Fool Outa Me
509	Daddy Will Be Home One Day
509A	The Moon Is Rising
510A	Howling Wolf Blues
511A	Instrumental Boogie
512A	Baby Child
513A	You're Gonna Reap What You Sow
511-1, HTN 11A	
	Morning Blues
511-2, HTN 11A	
	Have To Let You Go
HTN 1	Mistreated Blues
HTN 2	My California
HTN 3	Honey
HTN 4	So Long
HTN 5	See Baby Blues (See See Rider)
HTN 6	Changing Weather Blues (Unpredictable Woman)
HTN 7	Sun To Sun (I Just Don't Care)
HTN 8A	Liquor Drinking Woman
HTN 8B	Abilene
HTN 9A	Shotgun Blues

HTN 9B	Rollin' Blues
HTN 10	Ain't Foolin' No More
HTN 12	Whiskey Blues
HTN 13	Loretta's Blues

LIGHTNIN' HOPKINS SESSION
Quinn Studio, Houston. November, 1947.

450	Can't Get That Woman Off My Mind
451	Woman, Woman (Change Your Way)
452	Picture On The Wall
453	You're Not Going To Worry My Life Anymore

AMOS MILBURN SESSION
Los Angeles. September 12, 1946.

15	After Midnite
16	My Baby's Booging
17	Darling How Long
18	Down The Road Apiece
19	Amos' Blues
20	Instrumental Boogie

AMOS MILBURN SESSION
Radio Recorders, Los Angeles. December 13, 1946.

79	Don't Beg Me
80	Operation Blues
81	The Cinch Blues
82	Everything I Do Is Wrong

AMOS MILBURN SESSION
Radio Recorders, Los Angeles. April 26, 1947.

157	My Love Is Limited
158	Blues At Sundown
159	Money Hustlin' Woman
160	Sad And Blue
161	That's My Chick
162	I've Tried To Prove My Love, Dear
163	Mean Woman
164	Aladdin Boogie
165	Nickel Plated Baby
166	Real Gone

AMOS MILBURN SESSION
Universal Studio, Los Angeles. November 19, 1947.

250	It's A Married Woman
251	My Tortured Mind
252	Don't Tell Her
253	Hold Me Baby
254	Chicken Shack Boogie
255	Rapture In Bloom
256	Hard Driving Blues
257	I'm Gonna Leave You

AMOS MILBURN SESSION
Universal Studio, Los Angeles. December 11, 1947.

258	I Love Her
259	Pool Playing Blues
260	Hen Party
261	Rocky Road Blues
262	Lonesome For The Blues
263	Slow Down Blues

AMOS MILBURN SESSION
Chicago. October 15, 1948.

| no mx. | Bewildered |
| no mx. | A & M Blues |

AMOS MILBURN SESSION
Radio Recorders, Los Angeles. October 27, 1947.

401	Rainy Weather Blues
402	Train Whistle Blues
403	Train Time Blues
404	What Can I Do
405	Bye-Bye Boogie
406	Pot Luck Boogie

AMOS MILBURN SESSION
Universal Studio, Los Angeles. December 18, 1947.

272	Anybody's Blues
273	It Took A Long, Long Time
274	Wolf On The River
275	I Still Love You
276	Frank's Blues
277	Empty Arms Blues

AMOS MILBURN SESSION
Radio Recorders, Los Angeles. February 28, 1949.

RR 660-5	In The Middle Of the Night
RR 661-1	Won't You Kinda Think It Over
RR 662-3	Jitterbug Fashion Parade
RR 663-1	Where Are You
RR 664-1	My Luck Is Bound To Change

AMOS MILBURN SESSION
Radio Recorders, Los Angeles. July 13, 1949.

RR 900	Roomin' House Boogie
RR 901	Walkin' Blues
RR 902	Blue And Lonesome

APPENDIX II – Chess Records

BLUE SMITTY & HIS STRING MEN
Rewrite session: Chicago, July 11, 1952
C 1028   Crying   Chess 1522
C 1029   Sad Story   –
C 1030   Elgin Movement   unissued
C 1031   Date Bait   unissued
     Note: Chess 1522 has numbers U-1128/29 in wax.

EDDIE BOYD
Rewrite the following session:
C 4310   Blues For Baby   unissued
C 4311   Cool Kind Treatment   Chess 1523
C 4312   untitled   unissued
C 4313   Rosalee Swing   Chess 1523
Add the following session after C 4313:
No details:
7384   I Got The Blues   unissued
7385   Got Lonesome Here   unissued
7386   Began To Sing The Blues   unissued

Rewrite the following session:
U 7486   24 Hours   Chess 1533, LP 1446
U 7487   Hard Time Getting Started   unissued
U 7488   Best I Could   unissued
U 7489   The Tickler   Chess 1533

Rewrite the following session:
8553   She's The One   Chess 1674
8554   Walk That Walk   unissued
8555   Every Day Every Night   unissued
8556   Indeed I Do   unissued
8557   Hip Hip Hooray   unissued

EDDIE BURNS
Rewrite 'Big Ed' session as follows:
U 4409   Superstition (vcl. duet)   Checker 790
U 4410   Biscuit Baking Mama   –
U 4411   untitled   unissued
U 4412   untitled   unissued

BUDDY GUY
Insert following session after Argo LP 4031:
Vcl/gtr. with 2 saxes; pno; bs-gtr; dms.   Chicago, August 14, 1963
12624   untitled instrumental   unissued
12625   Stick Around   unissued
12626   untitled instrumental   unissued
12627   Moanin'   unissued

Insert new artist:

HONEY EDDIE

No details: Chicago, 1953
U 4339   Drop Down Mama   Chess unissued
U 4340   Sweet Home Chicago   –
U 4341   Santa Fe   –
U 4342   Frisco Line   –
     Note: This is likely to be Honeyboy Edwards, q.v.

JOHN LEE HOOKER
Delete 'Down At The Landing' from 1951 session.
Rewrite 1952 sessions making the following a separate session after
U 7433   –   Sugar Mama
9544   I Don't Want Your Money   Chess LP 1454
9545   Hey Baby   –
9546   The Journey (Sentimental Journey)   –

9547	Bluebird	Chess LP 1454
9548	Love Blues	–
9549	Apologize	–
9550	Lonely Boy Boogie (New Boogie)	–
9551	Please Don't Go	–
9552	Worried Life Blues	–
9553	Down At The Landing	Chess LP 1438
	Just Me And My Telephone -1	Chess LP 1454

HOWLIN' WOLF
Insert following session after U 7566 + 'Just My Kind':
No details:

no mx.	Hi-Way My Friend	unissued
no mx.	Hold Your Money	unissued
no mx	Streamline Woman	unissued
no mx.	California Blues	unissued
no mx.	Stay Here Till My Baby Comes Back	unissued

ALBERT KING
Insert following session after Bobbin 126
Vcl/gtr. with saxes; pno; bs; dms.　　　　St. Louis, March 1, 1961

10790	Searching For A Woman	Chess unissued
10791	California Blues	–
10792	Wild Women	–
10793	Won't Be Hangin' Around No More	–
10794	Calling On My Darling	–

B. B. KING
Insert following session after 'Past Day' Crown CLP 5063:
No details:　　　　1958

8930	Don't Keep Me Waiting	Chess unissued
8931	Recession Blues	–
8932	Tickle Britches	–
8933	Don't Break Your Promise	–

J. B. LENOIR
Rewrite the following session:

P-55224	Mama Your Daughter Is Going To Miss Me	Parrot 814
P-55225	What Have I Done	–
P-55226	We've Both Got To Realise	unissued
P-55227	Give Me One More Shot	unissued

Rewrite the following session:

7900	Everybody Wants To Know	unissued
	untitled instrumental	unissued
7901	Don't Dog Your Woman	unissued
7902	Let Me Die With The One I Love	Checker 844
7903	If I Give My Love To You	–
7904	Lowdown Dirty Shame	unissued

Rewrite the following session:

8360	Don't Touch My Head	Checker 856
8361	When I Am Drinking	unissued
8362	I've Been Down So Long	Checker 856
8363	What About Your Daughter	Checker 874
	How Much, How Much Long	unissued

Rewrite the following session:

8488	You Gonna Miss Me	unissued
8489	Give Me One More Shot	unissued
8490	Five Years (What Have I Done)	Checker 874
8491	We Can't Go On This Way	unissued

Rewrite the following session:

8728	Daddy Talk To Your Son	Checker 901
8729	She Don't Know -1	–
8730	I'm Looking For A Woman	unissued
8731	Voo Doo Woman	unissued

LIGHTNIN' SLIM
Rewrite following session:

3034, 7801	Bad Feeling Blues	Ace 505, Chess unissued
3035, 7802	Lightnin' Slim Boogie	— —
7803	School Day Jump	Chess unissued
7804	Station Blues	—
7805	Good Understanding	—
7806	Shake It Baby	—

Insert new artist:

LITTLE HENRY
No details: Chicago, 1953

U 4377	Nobody Loves Me	Chess unissued
U 4378	Maybe Blues	— unissued
U 4379	Got A Little Girl	— unissued
U 4380	You Look Good To Me	— unissued
U 4381	I Declare That Ain't Right	— unissued
U 4382	Matchbox Blues	— unissued

LITTLE WALTER
Rewrite following session:

U 7437	Juke	Checker 758, LP 1428
U 7438	Can't Hold Out Much Longer	— —
U 7439	Mercy Babe	unissued

Rewrite following session:

1051	Boogie	unissued
1052	Mean Old World	Checker 764, LP 1428
1053	Sad Hours	— —

Insert following session after above:
No details:

U 4318	Fast Boogie	unissued
U 4319	untitled	unissued
U 4320	Driftin'	unissued

Rewrite following session:

U 4394	Quarter To Twelve (4398 in file)	Checker 780
U 4395	Go On Baby	unissued
U 4396	(by Morris Pejoe)	
U 4397	That's It	unissued
U 4398	Blues With A Feeling (4394 in file)	Checker 780, LP 1428, Argo LP 4026, 4027
U 4399	Last Boogie	unissued
U 4400	Too Late	Checker 825
U 4401	Fast Boogie	unissued
U 4402	Lights Out	Checker 786
U 4403	Fast Large One	unissued
U 4404	You're So Fine	Checker 786, LP 1428

Rewrite following session:

7604	Rocker	Checker 793
7605	I Love You So	unissued
7606/7	(by Eugene Fox)	
7608	Oh Baby	Checker 793

Rewrite following session:

7653	I Got To Find My Baby	Checker 1013
7654	Big Leg Mama	unissued

Rewrite following session:

7772	Bread	unissued
7773	Love	unissued
7774	Baby Want To Rock	unissued
7775	Say Love Me	unissued
7776	Thunder Bird	Checker 811

(then as existing)

WILLIE MABON

Rewrite following session:

U 4314	Worry Blues	Parrot 1050, Chess 1531
U 4315	I Don't Know	− − , LP 1439, Argo LP 4042
4315A	See Me Cry	unissued
4315B	L.A.	unissued

Rewrite following session:

U 4328	I'm Mad	Chess 1538, LP 1439
U 4329	Got To Have It	unissued
U 4330	Beggar Or Bandit	unissued
U 4331	Night Latch	Chess 1538

Rewrite following session:

U 7611	Would You Again	Chess 1564
U 7612	Late Again	−
U 7613	Mabon's Boogie	unissued

Rewrite following session:

U 7678	Come On Baby	Chess 1592
U 7679	Lonely Blues	unissued
U 7680	Willie's Blues	unissued

MEMPHIS MINNIE
Rewrite following session:

MEMPHIS MINNIE WITH LITTLE JOE AND HIS BAND
Vcl. with hca; pno (-1); gtr; dms. Chicago, July 11, 1952

C 1024	Broken Heart	Checker 771
C 1025	Conjur Man	unissued
C 1026	Lake Michigan	unissued
C 1027	Me And My Chauffeur	Checker 771

Note: Checker 771 has numbers 1124/27 in wax.

MUDDY WATERS
Rewrite following session:

U 7131-R	Train Fare Home	Aristocrat 1306, Chess LP 1511
U 7132	Down South Blues	Chess LP 1511
U 7133	Kind Hearted Woman	−
U 7134-R	Sittin' Here And Drinkin' (Whiskey Blues)	Aristocrat 1306, Chess LP 1511

Rewrite following session:

U 7413	They Call Me Muddy Water	unissued
U 7414	All Night Long	Chess 1509
U 7415	Gal You Gotta Watch	unissued
U 7416	Lonesome Day	unissued
U 7417	Overseas	unissued
U 7418	Playhouse	unissued

Rewrite following session:

U 7476	Who's Gonna Be Your Sweet Man	Chess 1542
U 7477	Standing Around Crying	Chess 1526, LP 1427
U 7478	Gone To Main Street	
U 7479	Codeine In My Coffee	unissued

Rewrite following session:

U 4332	Flood	unissued
U 4333	Land Lady	unissued
U 4334	She's All Right	Chess 1537
	She's All Right (alt. take)	Chess LP 1511
U 4335	Sad, Sad Day	Chess 1537
	My Life Is Ruined	Chess LP 1511

Rewrite following session:

U 7589	I'm Your Hoochie Coochie Man	Chess 1560, LP 1427
U 7590	She's So Pretty	−
U 7591	Blues Leave Me Alone	unissued
U 7592	Memphis Blues	unissued

Rewrite following session:

U 7697	I'm Ready	Chess 1579, LP 1427
U 7698	Smoke Stack Lightning	unissued
U 7699	I Don't Know Why	Chess 1579
U 7700	Shake It Baby	unissued

Rewrite following session:

U 7783	This Pain	unissued
U 7784	Young Fashioned Ways	Chess 1602
U 7785	I Want To Be Loved	Chess 1596
U 7786	My Eyes (Keep Me In Trouble)	–

MORRIS PEJOE
Rewrite 2nd Checker session as follows:

4390	That's It	unissued
4391	Blues With A Feeling	unissued
4392	Can't Get Along	Checker 781
4393	Call It Gone	unissued
4394/5	(by Little Walter)	
4396	I'll Plumb Get It	Checker 781

Note: 4392 listed in files as 'Make A Hit With You'.

OTIS RUSH
Rewrite following session:

9966	So Many Roads, So Many Trains	Chess 1751, Argo LP 4027
9967	I'm Satisfied	–
9968	So Close	unissued
9969	All Your Love	unissued

Rewrite following session, adding recording date:

Chicago, September 29, 1960

10447	You Know My Love	Chess 1775
10448	I Can't Stop Baby	–
10449	So Many Ways	unissued
10450	Love You Baby	unissued

(Delete note after this session)

SUNNYLAND SLIM
Rewrite following session:

U 7108	Good Lookin' Woman	unissued
U 7109	Mean Disposition	unissued
U 7110	She Ain't Nowhere	Aristocrat 1304
U 7111	My Baby, My Baby	–

EDDIE WARE
Insert following session after Chess 1507:
No details:

no mx.	Failure Is My Destiny	Chess unissued
no mx.	Lonesome And Forgotten	–
no mx.	Unlucky Gambler	–
no mx.	Crying Shame	–

Details of Modern and Chess sessions sent by Frank Scott and Gary Paulsen that arrived too late to include in the main text. No issue numbers are given as these can be found in the appropriate discography. If no issue number is available, then the title remains unissued.

CHARLIE BRADIX
Add following session:

Vcl/pno. with ten; gtr; dms.   Dallas, c. 1951

no mx	Bleeding Heart	Modern
no mx	Waiting For My Baby	–
no mx	Bad Understanding	–
no mx	You'll Regret What You've Done	–

JOHN BRIM
Rewrite session:
Personnel as for Checker 769.

| 7505 | Ice Cream Man | Chess |
| 7506 | Lifetime Baby | – |

BIG BILL BROONZY
Rewrite Chess session:

U 7507	Jacqueline	Chess
U 7508	Little City Woman	–
U 7509	Lonesome	–
U 7510	Romance Without Finance	–

CLIFTON CHENIER
Rewrite Argo session:

8330	Baby Please	Argo
8331	Where Can My Baby Be	–
8332	Dixie Special	–
8333	The Big Wheel	–

SYLVESTER COTTON
Add title:

| B 7023 | Brown Skin Woman | Modern |

LOWELL FULSON
Rewrite session:

7882	Trouble, Trouble	Chess
7883	I Still Love You Baby	–
7884	It's A Long Time	–
7885	Rollin' Blues	–
7886	The Chocker (?)	–
7887	My Baby's Gone	–

Add to 8018/21 session:

| 8020 | Smokey Room | Chess |

Add new artist:-

KITTY DE CHAVIS
Vcl. with pno.   Memphis, c. 1951

no mx	Don't Raise No Sand	Modern
no mx	My Own Way Of Loving	–
no mx	My Daddy Told Me	–
no mx	Don't Talk To Me Daddy	–

LIGHTNIN' HOPKINS
Add following titles:

MM 1270	Gimme Back That Wig	Modern
MM 1279	Everyday Blues	–
MM 1662	Drifting	–
MM 1666	Ticket Agent	–
no mx	War News Blues	–
no mx	Home Upon The Hill	–

WALTER (MUMBLES) HORTON
Rewrite session:

MM 1504	Cotton Patch Hotfoot	Modern
MM 1505	What's The Matter With You	–
MM 1506	Now Tell Me Baby	–
MM 1507	Blues In The Morning	–
MM 1508	Little Boy Blue	–
MM 1509	I'm In Love With You Baby	–

Rewrite session:

MM 1619	Black Gal	Modern
MM 1620	Hard Hearted Woman	–
MM 1621	Jumpin' Blues	–
MM 1622	So Long Woman	–

HOWLIN' WOLF
Rewrite session - Date. Memphis, February 12, 1952.

no mx	Worried About You Baby	Modern
no mx	House Rockin' Boogie (alt. take)	–
no mx	Brown Skin Woman	–
no mx	Driving This Highway	–
no mx	The Sun Is Rising	–
no mx	Stealing My Clothes	–
no mx	I'm The Wolf	–

Add date for MM 1685/, and 1748/49 -   Memphis, October 2, 1951
Rewrite Session:

7556	I've Got A Woman	Chess
7557	Just My Kind	–

Rewrite session:

U 7618	No Place To Go	Chess
U 7619	Neighbours	–
U 7620	I'm The Wolf	–
U 7621	Rockin' Daddy	–

Add to 7795/9 session:

7800	You're The One	Chess

Add to 8175/8 session:

8177	Break Of Day	Chess

Add new Artist:-

JIM LOCKHART
Vcl/gtr. with wbd(-1)   Memphis, C. 1951

no mx	Empty House Blues	Modern
no mx	Boogie Woogie -1	–

JOE HILL LOUIS
Rewrite session:

no mx	Come Back Baby	Modern
MM 1459	I Fee Like A Million	–
no mx	Great Big House	–
MM 1460	Heartache Baby	–
no mx	Train Ticket	–
MM 1540	Walkin' (And) Talkin' Blues	–
no mx	The Way You Treat Me	–
MM 1565	Going Down Slow	–
no mx	Joe Hill's Boogie (Gotta Go Baby?)	–
no mx	Boogie Woogie All Night Long	–
no mx	Highway 99	–
no mx	Early In The Morning	–
MM 1631	Big Leg Woman (Big Legged Woman)	–

Rewrite session:

no mx	Nappy Head Woman	Modern
MM 1492	Boogie In The Park	–
MM 1541	Street Walkin' Woman	–

no mx	Mistreat Me Woman	Modern
MM 1493	Cold Chills	–

ELMON (DRIFTING SLIM) MICKLE
Add following titles:

no mx	Shout	Modern
no mx	You're Getting Old Lady	–
no mx	I Feel So Good	–

ALEXANDER MOORE
Rewrite session:

MM 1614-1	If I Lose You Woman	RPM
MM 1615	Neglected Woman	–
MM 1616	Carolina	–
MM 1617	Lillie Mae Boogie	–
MM 1618	If I Lose My Woman	–

Add new artist:-

CHARLES MOSELY
Vcl. with Ike Turner, pno; Baby Face Turner, Junior Brooks, gtrs; Bill Russell, dms.

North Little Rock, 1952

no mx	Blues	Modern

PINETOP SLIM
Rewrite session:

Atlanta, February 23, 1949

MM 1035	Applejack Boogie	Colonial
no mx	Mean Old Frisco	–
no mx	John Henry	–
MM 1036	I'm Gonna Carry On	–
no mx	Poor Boy Long Ways From Home	–
no mx	Baby Please Don't Go	–
no mx	Wonder If I'm Right Or Wrong	–

JIMMY ROGERS
Rewrite session:

U 7361	Money, Marbles And Chalk	Chess
U 7362	untitles	–
U 7363	Chance To Love	–
U 7364	untitled	–
U 7365	untitled	–
U 7366	untitled	–

Rewrite session:

U 7444	Mistreated Baby	Chess
U 7445	The Last Time	–
U 7446	What's The Matter	–
U 7447	Out On The Road	–

SONNY BOY WILLIAMSON (Rice Miller)
Rewrite session:

7889	Walk With Me	Checker
7890	Don't Start Me To Talkin'	–
7891	All My Love In Vain	–
7892	Good Evening Everybody	–
7893	You Killing Me	–

Rewrite session:

7980	Let Me Explain	Checker
7981	I Know What Love Is All About	–
7982	I Wonder Why	–
7983	Your Imagination	–
7984	Don't Look Your Eye (?)	–

ARBEE STIDHAM
Add to 1952 session:

no mx	Blues	Checker
no mx	Stop The Clock	–

UNKNOWN ARTISTS
The following artists are not named in Company files or on acetates:
1) Vcl/hca/gtr. with gtr.

no mx	Sufficient Clothes	Modern
no mx	Miss Darlene	–

2) Vcl/gtr. with gtr.

no mx	13th Highway	Modern

3) Vcl/gtr. with gtr.

No mx	Keep 'Em Down	Modern

4) No details.

No mx	Under A Neon Sign	Chess
no mx	Catch Me A Freight Train	–
no mx	Looking For The Mail Now	–
no mx	Gonna Leave This Town	–
no mx	The Man Won't Go Down	–
no mx	Raining And Snowing	–
no mx	Rock Me Mama	–
no mx	Courtenay (?)	–

5) No details.

ACA 2033	Little Daddy's Boogie	Freedom
ACA 2034	Better Change Baby	–

MUDDY WATERS
Rewrite session:

8012	40 Days And 40 Nights	Chess
8013	All Aboard	–
8014	Tears Of Joy	–
8015	Three Time Loser	–
8016	Is This Goodbye	–
8017	Get Off My Wagon	–

Odd items missed in main text.

JIMMY McCRACKLIN
Rewrite Courtney session:
Vcl/pno. with tpt; tbn; 2 saxes; Shifty Henry, bs; Alray Kidd, dms.

Oakland, 1948

SA 295	Rock And Rye Pt. 1	J & M Fullbright 124
SA 296-4	Rock And Rye Pt. 2	–
SA 297-5	You Had Your Chance	J & M Fullbright 123, Courtney 123
SA 298-7	Special For You	– – –

GUITAR FRANK
Hca(-1); Vcl/gtr(-2). with ten; org; gtr; el-bs; dms.

Los Angeles, c. 1960

B 3203	Wild Track -1	Bridges Music Den (No number)
B 3204	Mo-Tatoes -2	–

MAGIC SLIM
Vcl/gtr. with Ter-Drops Band - ten; bs-gtr; dms.

Chicagom C. 1966

D 0105A	Love My Baby	Ja-Wes 105
D 0105B	Scuffling	–

NOTES

Readers may wish to use these pages to enter additional or revised information that comes to light after this discography has been published.